D1001212

Microeconomics for MBAs

This is the first textbook in microeconomics written exclusively for MBA students. McKenzie and Lee minimize attention to mathematics and maximize attention to intuitive economic thinking, examining key questions such as "How should organizations and incentives be structured to best encourage profit maximization?" The text is structured clearly and accessibly: Part A of each chapter outlines the basic theory with applications to social and economic policies and Part B applies this basic theory to management issues, with a substantial focus on the emerging subdiscipline of organizational economics. On the publisher's website for *Microeconomics for MBAs* (www.cambridge.org/micro4mbas), the authors have provided an array of additional materials that complement the theory and applications in the printed textbook. They have placed online a "perspective" for each chapter, which provides a new line of argument or different take on a business or policy issue and which we highly recommend for ten- and fifteen-week courses. To make this edition of the textbook more workable for shorter (five- and seven-week) courses, the authors have moved coverage of more than two dozen topics to the publisher's website, listing them under "Further readings online." The textbook is also accompanied by several dozen online video modules in which Professors McKenzie and Lee give a personal tutorial on the key microeconomic concepts which MBA students need to understand, as well as elucidate complex lines of argument covered in the chapters and help students to review for tests. Throughout the text, McKenzie and Lee aim to infuse students with the economic way of thinking in the context of a host of problems that MBA students, as future managers of real-world firms, will find relevant to their career goals.

Richard B. McKenzie is the Walter B. Gerken Professor of Enterprise and Society in the Paul Merage School of Business at the University of California, Irvine.

Dwight R. Lee is Professor of Economics and William J. O'Neil Chair of Global Markets and Freedom in the Edwin Cox School of Business at Southern Methodist University.

Microeconomics for MBAs

The Economic Way of Thinking for Managers

Second Edition

Richard B. McKenzie

Dwight R. Lee

CAMBRIDGE
UNIVERSITY PRESS

CAMBRIDGE UNIVERSITY PRESS
Cambridge, New York, Melbourne, Madrid, Cape Town, Singapore,
São Paulo, Delhi, Dubai, Tokyo

Cambridge University Press
The Edinburgh Building, Cambridge CB2 8RU, UK

Published in the United States of America by Cambridge University Press, New York

www.cambridge.org
Information on this title: www.cambridge.org/9780521191470

First Edition © Richard B. McKenzie and Dwight R. Lee 2006
Second edition © Richard B. McKenzie and Dwight R. Lee 2010

All rights reserved. This publication is protected by copyright and permission should be obtained
from the copyright holder prior to any prohibited reproduction, storage, in a retrieval system, or
transmission in any form or by any means, electronic, mechanical, photocopying, recording, or
likewise. For information regarding permission(s), write to: Richard B. McKenzie, Merage School
of Business, University of California, Irvine 92697 (or mckenzie@uci.edu).

This publication is in copyright. Subject to statutory exception
and to the provisions of relevant collective licensing agreements,
no reproduction of any part may take place without the written
permission of Cambridge University Press.

First published 2006
Second Edition 2010

Printed in the United States of America

A catalogue record for this publication is available from the British Library

ISBN-13 978-0-521-19147-0 Hardback

Cambridge University Press has no responsibility for the persistence or
accuracy of URLs for external or third-party internet websites referred to in
this publication, and does not guarantee that any content on such websites is,
or will remain, accurate or appropriate.

There is only one difference between a bad economist and a good one: the bad economist confines himself to the visible effect; the good economist takes into account both the effect that can be seen and those effects that must be foreseen.

Frédéric Bastiat (1801–50).
Selected Essays on Political Economy

Contents

Book II Demand and production theory

Preface

Almost all (if not all) textbooks used in MBA students' first course in micro-economics are designed with undergraduate economics majors or first-year PhD students in mind. Accordingly, MBA students are often treated to a course in intermediate microeconomic theory, full of arcane mathematical explanations. The applications in such standard textbooks deal mainly with the impact of social or government policies on markets with little discussion of how managers can make better decisions within their firms in response to market forces or how market forces can be expected to affect firms' institutional and financial structures.

Much microeconomic theory simply assumes firms into existence without explanation of why they are needed in the first place. Managers and their staff are assumed to do exactly what firms employ them to do – maximize owners' profits – with no discussion of how firms' organizational structures affect incentives and how incentives affect firms' production and profit outcomes.

That is to say, little is written in standard textbooks used in MBA courses about exactly how real-world firms pursue the goal of profit maximization. And that void in microeconomics textbooks is a real problem for MBA students, for an obvious reason: MBA students have typically come back to school to learn how to improve their management skills, which involves learning about how they can improve their ability to extract more profits from the scarce resources available to the firms where they work (or the firms where they expect to move after graduation). They do not come back to school to become economic theorists. Standard microeconomic textbooks are of little value to MBA students in helping them achieve their career objectives.

MBA students stand a quantum leap apart from undergraduate students, who typically have little idea of what they want to do with their lives, and have far less real-world business experience to which they can relate. MBA students also are sacrificing far more by attending school than undergraduates and must get value for their time spent reading textbooks and attending class because of the cost of their education, in terms of both their tuition payments and the valuable work opportunities they have to set aside.

Microeconomics for MBAs breaks dramatically from the standard textbook mold. As the title suggests, we have designed this textbook with only MBA students in mind. In Part A of every chapter, we cover standard microeconomic theory in an accessible way, and we provide an array of applications to government policies which MBA students need to understand. After all, managers everywhere face the constraints of government-imposed laws and regulations that are ever-changing, and managers must work to maximize their firms' profits within those constraints. Moreover, professors in marketing, finance, accounting, strategy, and operations research who teach first- and second-year elective courses in MBA programs will expect their students to have a firm grounding in conventional microeconomic theory.

To help students learn the material covered in these pages and lectures, we have provided a set of video modules posted on the Internet that deals with three classes of topics:

(1) basic economic concepts that all MBA students should understand at some level upon entering their programs of study
(2) concepts, principles, and modes of analysis that are often hard to comprehend the first time they are presented in text or lectures
(3) topics that have a high probability of being covered in examinations.

Of course, these videos can be stopped at any time to allow for note taking, and can be replayed repeatedly.

In Part B of every chapter, we go where other microeconomics textbooks seldom, if ever, go with such completeness. We drop the usual assumption that firms exist and that they automatically maximize owners' profits by simply following maximization rules. Instead, we bring to the forefront of our analysis a crucial problem that firms face. This problem (dubbed the "principal–agent problem" within the economics profession and in this textbook) is that both owners and workers are more interested in pursuing their own well-being than someone else's well-being.

Owners ("principals") want to maximize their income stream and wealth through the firms they create by getting the most they can out of their employees. Similarly, managers and line workers (the owners' "agents") seek to maximize some combination of income, on-the-job perks, and job security, which are often in conflict with maximizing profits for the firm's owners. Without effective firm policies that align the incentives of owners and workers (for their mutual benefit), the work in a firm can be a self-destructive tug of war, with the demise of the firm virtually assured in competitive markets.

In this textbook, we focus MBA students' attention on thinking through the complex problems of getting incentives right. This is mainly because there is as much (maybe more) profit to be made from creatively structuring incentives as there can be made from creatively developing products for sale.

Getting hourly and monthly pay systems right is obviously an important means of aligning the interests of owners and managers. However, we also explain how firms' organizational structure, in terms of both people and finances, can affect the alignment of owners' and workers' incentives. And make no mistake about it, both owners and their employees have a stake in finding the right alignment. Workers' jobs can hang in the balance. Owners' investments can hang just as precariously on a cost-effective, balanced alignment of incentives.

Accordingly, this book places a great deal of emphasis on a field within economics that has grown rapidly in professional prominence, especially as the subject relates directly to the business world – and MBA programs: *organizational economics*, which is the study of the design of firms' organizational and financial structures using the analytical tools of microeconomic analysis. The mode of thinking presented in these pages is crucial for managers – MBAs – who want to move up their corporate hierarchy or create successful companies of their own.

On the publisher's website for *Microeconomics for MBAs* (www.cambridge.org/micro4mbas), we have provided "Perspectives" for each chapter that are highly recommended short discussions of topics related to themes in the chapters. These perspectives provide a new or different take on a business or policy issue; they can be easily streamed or downloaded by students taking longer (ten- and fifteen-week) courses. For example, everyone *knows*, don't they, that the "first mover" in any market has a competitive advantage. In the Perspective for Chapter 8, we discuss a startling observation made by management scholars: there is no first-mover advantage. Indeed, second and third movers frequently have competitive advantages, not the least of which is that they don't have to incur the costs of identifying and proving the profitability of product markets.

For longer courses, we have provided online more than two dozen "Readings" assigned to the different chapters that extend the theories and array of applications covered in the chapters. These readings can also be easily streamed and downloaded for extended reading assignments. For example, for chapter 1, we have posted the classic short article on "I, pencil," in which Leonard Read cogently observes that no one in the world knows how to make pencils totally from scratch, yet millions of pencils are produced at low cost every year. In chapter 7, we take up "opportunistic behavior." Online we have posted a discussion of a particular form of opportunistic behavior known as "the last-period problem," which covers why the problem emerges and how it can be mitigated by firm policies.

Each chapter ends with two sections. The first ending section offers practical advice that emerges from the discussions of theory and studies covered in the chapter. The second ending section, which we have dubbed "the bottom line," contains listings of "key takeaways" – succinct statements of the most important lessons to be drawn from the chapter. We understand that MBA students, you included, face serious time constraints, especially when you are working full time and have family responsibilities. "The bottom line" section is designed to focus your attention when reviewing the material covered in the chapter, with the hope that your study time will be more productive.

The scholarly and policy literature in economics and management relating to most of the topics considered in this volume is massive. We have tried to give credit where credit is due, especially when "classic," path-breaking treatments by distinguished scholars are concerned, but we have tried to hold references and footnotes in check in order that the flow of the argument is not constantly disrupted. Still, our references section at the end of the book is extensive. To smooth out the flow of the core material, we have relegated topics that will be only selectively used in classes to footnotes and to online readings.

Many textbook authors and their publishers play the development of their course books "safe" by taking up only those topics that have become fixtures in the profession's "conventional wisdom." We see such an approach as sucking the life out of a discipline and its treatment in textbooks. Topics that have not yet been fully settled through decades of professional debate can give life to a discipline, demonstrating to students that disciplines have an organic quality and are constantly evolving. As a consequence, you can expect many topics in this book to spark lively, and instructive, debates among student team members and between class members and professors in class. That is how we want the book to be received.

We have appended to each chapter a series of review questions that we expect will activate discussions within your student teams. In addition, we have set up a website for the book on which we will post additional readings for extended courses, as well as interesting pointers and puzzles that have occurred to us since the book went to press. We also expect to post on the website video commentaries on management issues and related economic policies that are bound to arise while you are reading this book and taking your course.

You may be interested in knowing that we – the authors of this book – have between us more than eighty years of university teaching experience, with most of our teaching careers spent in business schools. For the last twenty or so years, we both have taught *only* MBA students. That should tell you that we have a pretty good fix on our readers and their interests, not the least of which is to have a course of study that is intellectually challenging as well as having practical application.

We fully understand that MBA students don't want to be loaded down with current business "facts," if for no other reasons than "facts" can easily become dated as modern business never stays still. What students want are some good economic and business "principles" that will help them cut through the myriad facts and events business people encounter each day and that change with passing days and weeks. In no small way, the purpose of this textbook, and our classes (or any other business course worthy of academic respect), is to explore ways to *think* creatively about how business is done and can be done better, not to actually *do* business. In this regard, we take to heart an observation made by the late economist Kenneth Boulding:

It is a very fundamental principle indeed that knowledge is always gained by the orderly loss of information; that is, by conducing and abstracting and indexing the great buzzing confusion of information that comes from the world around us into a form we can appreciate and comprehend. (1970, 2)

The way of thinking we take up in class, and that which Professor Boulding had in mind, is necessarily abstract – that is, without the clutter of many business details. We approach thinking with abstractions principally because no one's brain is sufficiently powerful to handle all the complex details of everyday business life. In no small way, productive thought requires that the complexity of business life be reduced enough to allow us to focus on the few things that are most important to the problems at hand and find meaningful relationships between those things. That is why Professor Boulding insists that knowledge can so often (if not "always") be gained only "by the orderly loss of information."

Without thinking, many business people often spurn theory on the grounds that it lacks practical value. We insist, "not so at all." The abstract way of thinking that we shall develop in this textbook has a very practical, overriding goal, which is to afford students more *understanding* of the business world than they could have if they tried some alternative approach – that is, if they tried to keep the analysis cluttered up with the "buzzing confusion" of facts MBA students leave behind in their workplaces when they set out for class.

There is another highly practical goal to be achieved by theory (or rather thinking with the use of theory). If people can *think* through business problems in some organized way, albeit abstractly, they may be able to avoid mistakes when they actually go out and do business. In economic terms, business mistakes imply a regrettable misuse and loss of firm resources – and firm profitability! *Thinking* before doing offers the prospect of reducing waste in doing business.

If this textbook, and our classes, are about *thinking* (not doing), then we – Richard McKenzie and Dwight Lee and students' other professors – have some justification for being in front of our classes. Also, if the course is about the thinking process, there must be some method for thinking through problems, business-related or otherwise. The development of that *method* is the focus of our classes and this textbook. Our goal in this volume is to develop *the economic way of thinking* in the context of a host of problems that MBA students, as current and future managers of real-world firms, will find relevant to their career goals.

We understand that some readers may worry about our emphasis on theory because they may have read theory-grounded books that seemed sterile or irrelevant, mainly because of the heavy reliance on highly technical mathematics or complicated charts. That will not be the case in this book. The first principle of economics that has guided this work is one that many readers will appreciate: *Keep the theory as simple as possible and illustrate it with real problems.* We hold to the firm belief that the first principle in any course in principles of economics should be economy in the principles that are covered. The value of a textbook or course should be judged by what can be done with the principles developed, not by how many principles are developed.

This book carries the subtitle *The Economic Way of Thinking for Managers* for a very good reason: In the following pages, we bring together a host of large and small ideas that economists have developed over the past several decades that have transformed the way we must think about the way the business world works. Readers' reactions to large and small ideas will, we expect, have changed radically by the time they have read the last words of this volume. Two of those large questions are:

- How should organizations and incentives be structured to best encourage profit maximization?
- How does the competition in the market for goods and in the market for corporate control discipline executives?

The small questions that can be addressed from studying this volume are no less important and can be just as intriguing:

- Should used cars really be expected to be "better deals" than new ones (as so many people seem to think)?

- If competitive markets are expected to "clear" (with quantity demanded equaling quantity supplied), why are so many queues observed in grocery stores and at concerts?
- If queues are not mutually beneficial to buyers and sellers, then why aren't they eliminated?

Readers who think that these questions have simple, obvious, pat answers need to read on.

We expect that readers will end this book the way our students end our courses: changed for life in the way they see the business world around them. But then that is what MBA students typically want – or should want – from every course in their MBA programs. Readers have our best wishes for the journey of a lifetime.

This book was developed over the past two decades as we taught our microeconomics courses for our MBA students at our respective universities. Our students have made innumerable and invaluable suggestions for improvement in the book, and we are indebted to them. We are also indebted to Oxford University Press for allowing us to draw freely from our previously published book with the Press, *Managing Through Incentives*. All excerpts from that book have been substantially revised and updated for inclusion in this textbook.

In redeveloping this textbook for the second edition, we continued to listen to the advice of our students and to professors who used the first edition of this textbook around the world. We note the following major changes:

- First and foremost, we have sought to update the book to account for new research findings and recent world economic events, including the recession that emerged from the meltdown of the housing mortgage-backed securities markets. Readers will find far more attention given to the "moral-hazard problem" (to be explained in the book) that is bound to emerge when business ventures are highly leveraged. In various chapters of this new edition, we explain how the moral hazard and leverage have been at the foundation of the financial and economic turbulence that began to emerge in late 2007 and continued as this new edition went to press.
- Second, with the added material, we have taken pains to economize on examples. Again, we understand that MBA students are hard pressed to find time to do the reading for their courses.
- Third, microeconomics courses in MBA programs vary in length, from five to fifteen weeks. We have sought to make the book more flexible. We have included enough material in the twelve chapters to take up more than a quarter-length course. With the addition of the available online perspectives and readings, we have provided enough material for a full semester-length course. Short

courses of five and seven weeks can be developed by covering the first four chapters, plus some combination of chapters 6, 7, 9, and 10 (which will cover competitive product and labor markets and monopoly product markets with attention to pricing strategies under markets for "normal" and "network" goods).

- Fourth, we understand that the microeconomics course is a prerequisite for second-year courses in global business and foreign residentials. In the first edition, international economics was literally at the back of the book. In this edition, we have placed international topics in chapter 5 where we note the interplay of environmental and international economic forces in an ever more integrated world economy.
- Fifth, most courses remain organized around a printed textbook. With all students having ready access to the Internet, we have made the printed textbook a component – albeit an important one – in a broader course-delivery system that relies heavily on the delivery of the full sweep of course materials through the Internet. Accordingly, professors will find a wealth of easily accessible resource materials on the publisher's website for the textbook. The materials include:

  - "Perspectives" for each chapters (see the list of perspectives that follows this preface)
  - additional "readings" (see the list of topics covered in the list of further readings online that follows this preface): the online readings will allow for continuing updating of the course materials as readings on current economic and management topics become available after the second edition of the textbook is released
  - fifty-eight video modules that students can stream or download to their computers (see the list of topics covered on the website)
  - student self-tests for each chapter
  - a testbank of over 1,500 multiple-choice questions that can be accessed by adopting instructors
  - an electronic version of the textbook that can be downloaded to laptops and electronic readers (such as the Kindle)
  - video and print commentaries on current economic and management topics that will be written and posted by the authors as the textbook is used through the years of the second edition
  - an electronic "room" in which users of the textbook from different universities around the world can interact with each other and the authors on a continuing basis.

Throughout the revision, we have kept our eye on the key distinguishing feature of the book: it is designed specifically for MBA students. We have tried to fortify that feature by making sure that discussions of organizational and incentive issues in the second half of each chapter draw on the economic principles developed in the first half.

How to use this book

Chapter structure

Each chapter is split into two parts:

Part A of every chapter covers the microeconomic theory needed for MBA programs and looks at the way theory is applied to the government policies that future managers need to understand.

> **Part A Theory and public policy applications**
>
> Rationality: a basis for exploring human behavior
>
> People's wants are expansive and ever expanding. We can never satisfy all our wants because we will always conceive of new ones. The best we can do is to maximize our satisfaction, or utility, in the face of scarcity. Economists attempt to capture in one word – utility – the many varied contributions made to our wellbeing when we buy and sell, achieve a success (small or large), earn a living, drink, eat, have sex, read a good book, have children, play – or make an A on a microeconomics exam!
>
> *Utility is the satisfaction a person receives from the consumption of a good or service or from participation in an activity. Happiness, joy, contentment or pleasure might all be substituted for satisfaction in the definition of utility.*
>
> The ultimate assumption behind this theory is that *people act with a purpose.* In the words of Ludwig von Mises, they act because they are "dissatisfied with the state of affairs as it prevails" (Mises 1962, 2–3).
>
> The acting individual
>
> If people act in order to satisfy their consciously perceived wants, their behavior [...] directed rather than [...]

> **Part B Organizational economics and management**
>
> The logic of group behavior in business and elsewhere
>
> In following chapters, we introduce the usefulness of markets as means of generating a form of cooperation, through trades, or buying or selling. However, as is evident inside firms, not all human cooperation is through "markets." People often act cooperatively in groups or, as the case may be, in "firms." In this section, we make use of the rationality principles developed in Part A, applying them to the organization of groups and firms. The focus of our attention is on the viability of groups – such as families, cliques, communes, clubs, unions, and professional associations and societies, as well as firms, in which individual participation is voluntary – to cohere and pursue the common interests of the members.
>
> We consider two dominant and conflicting theories of group behavior, both of which take a partial view of complex life and yield insight about groups. They are "the common-interest theory" and "the economic theory" of group behavior, with the economic theory the focus of the rest of the chapter because it is founded on the premise of rational behavior developed in Part A. This economic theory of groups [...] understand why firms are organ[...] way they are and why owners [...] share a com[...] being "tough [...]

Part B of every chapter applies the basic theory developed in Part A to management issues. The discussion emphasizes *organizational economics,* which is the study of the design of firms' organizational and financial structures using the analytical tools of microeconomic analysis.

Understanding organizational economics is crucial for managers – MBAs – who want to move up their corporate hierarchy or create successful companies of their own.

To help you learn and remember

Practical lessons for MBAs at the end of every chapter are new to this edition and offer useful advice to MBA students that emerges from the discussions of theory and practice covered in every chapter.

The **bottom line** is a list of "key takeaways" – short statements of the most important lessons to be drawn from the chapter.

Review questions at the end of each chapter are designed to encourage discussions of the key concepts.

This book is part of an integrated package of text and online materials which collectively deliver the information MBAs need to build a working knowledge of microeconomics.

> **Practical lessons for MBAs: profits from optimal shirking**
>
> One of the more important lessons from the analysis in this chapter is that size matters in bus[...] As firms expand, shirking can be a growing problem. Firms will have to incur growing monit[...] costs with growing firm size, which means that bosses will have to become progressively tou[...] or incentives will have to overcome workers' inclinations to shirk, which means not doing w[...] they know they are supposed to do. To keep the analysis clear in this chapter, we have discu[...] shirking as if it were all "bad," always and everywhere a net drain on corporate profits. Hence [...] task of managers is, in such a world, relatively simple: Eliminate any and all shirking by monito[...] and "cracking the corporate whip." While our approach has been useful to highlight key po[...] we need to stress [...] viewed as a work [...] this is the case, so [...] supply of [...]

> **The bottom line**
>
> The key takeaways from chapter 2 are the following:
>
> 1 The concept of rational behavior means that the individual has alternatives, [...] those alternatives on the basis of preference, and can act consistently on that b[...] rational individual will also choose those alternatives whose expected benefits [...] their expected costs.
>
> 2 Traditionally, economics has focused on the activities of business firms, and much [...] book is devoted to exploring human behavior in a market setting. However, the [...] rational behavio[...] life and leisure [...]

> **Review questions >>**
>
> 1 What are the costs and benefits of taking this course in microeconomics? Devel[...] of how much a student can be expected to study for this course. How might th[...] current employment status affect her studying time?
>
> 2 Some psychologists see people's behavior as determined largely by family hist[...] external environmental conditions. How would "cost" fit into their explanatio[...]
>
> 3 Okay, so no one is totally rational. Does that undermine the use of "rational beh[...] means of thinking about markets and management problems?
>
> 4 How could drug use and suicide be considered "rational"?
>
> 5 If [...] consistently [...] irrational beh[...] the ov[...]

Additional material online

Online
ective

Perspectives provide a new or different take on a business policy or issue related to themes in the chapters. These are listed between Parts A and B of each chapter and are referred to at relevant points in the text.

R

Readings offer more on the theory and range of applications covered in the chapters and are referred to throughout the book. A list of appropriate readings is provided at the end of each chapter.

V

Video modules feature the authors and reinforce your understanding of:

- basic economic concepts that all MBA students should understand at some level upon entering their programs of study
- concepts, principles, and modes of analysis that are often hard to comprehend the first time they are presented in text or lectures
- topics that have a high probability of being covered in examinations.

Review questions are multiple choice questions for each chapter that students can use to test whether they have understood the material covered.

Video and print commentaries about current topics in economics and management and **links** to useful newspaper and journal articles provide up-to-date exposure to how microeconomic theory is relevant in our day-to-day world. New commentaries will be posted at intervals.

For instructors we also provide:

Multiple choice questions: a testbank of 1,500 questions and answers that instructors can set for their students.

Solutions to selected review questions at the ends of chapters.

Figures and **tables** from the book that instructors can incorporate into lecture slides and presentations.

- This book is now more flexible for courses of different lengths.

Our suggested use:
For 10+ week courses
Use all twelve chapters
For 7 week courses
Use chapters 1–4/5, as well as
chapters 6, 7, 9, and 10
For 5 week courses
Use chapters 1–5 and chapter 10

RESOURCES
Perspectives
Readings
Video modules
Newspaper & journal articles
Video commentaries
Written commentaries

STUDENTS
Self-test multiple choice questions

LECTURERS
Testbank
Solutions to review questions
Figures
Tables

An introduction from the author...

Bonus Commentary #2 - The Misguided...

Microecon
problems th
simple and

- End-of-chapter review questions and self-test multiple choice questions will appeal to students with a variety of learning styles.
- Fifty-eight video modules revise key concepts covered in the text.

How to use this site...

V VIDEO MODULES
Feature the authors and reinforce your understanding of basic economic concepts that all MBA students should understand at some level upon entering their programs of study.

R READINGS
Offer more on the theory and range of applications covered in the chapters and are referred to throughout the book.

Online
Perspective **PERSPECTIVES**
Provide a new or different take on a business policy or issue related to themes in the chapters.

VIDEO AND PRINT COMMENTARIES
About current topics in economics and management and links to useful newspaper and journal articles provide up-to-date exposure to how microeconomic theory is relevant in our day to day world.

MULTIPLE CHOICE QUESTIONS
A testbank of 1,500 questions and answers that instructors can set for their students.

SOLUTIONS TO SELECTED REVIEW QUESTIONS
At the ends of chapters.

Online perspectives by chapters

(Accessible at www.cambridge.org/micro4mbas)

Further readings online

(Accessible at www.cambridge.org/micro4mbas)

Video modules by chapters

Book I
The market economy, overview and application

The first five chapters of *Microeconomics for MBAs*, which constitute Book I, develop the broad outlines of *The Economic Way of Thinking for Managers*. We explore in these chapters what economists mean by "rational behavior" and show how rationality-based thinking can illuminate public and management policies. The chapters will focus on how markets can be analyzed through the forces of supply and demand, developed with graphical analysis. We show how supply and demand curves can be used to explain how and why competitive markets work efficiently and under what conditions competitive markets can fail to work efficiently. In chapters 4 and 5, supply and demand curves are used to explore the market consequences of an array of governmental and organizational policies. Throughout the first five chapters, we will consider how management policies can affect the forces of supply and demand and how market forces can affect management policies. Our goal in this first book is to provide a broad overview of the market economy. In Book II, chapters 6 through 8, and Book III, chapters 9 through 12, we will examine many of the theoretical details underpinning supply and demand. In those chapters, we will develop a theory of firms and how they can be pressed to minimize their production costs in markets with different levels of competitiveness and in markets dominated by firms with differing levels of monopoly power.

1

Microeconomics: a way of thinking about business

In economics in particular, education seems to be largely a matter of unlearning and "disteaching" rather than constructive action. A once famous American humorist observed that "it's not ignorance that does so much damage; it's knowin' so darn much that ain't so" … It seems that the hardest things to learn and to teach are things that everyone already knows.

    Frank H. Knight

The late Frank Knight was a wise professor at the University of Chicago who realized that students beginning a study of economics, no matter the level – even those who are in advanced business programs – face a difficult task. They must learn many things in a rigorous manner that, on reflection and with experience, amount to common sense. To do that, however, they must set aside – or "unlearn" – many preconceived notions of the economy and of the course itself. The problem of "unlearning" can be especially acute for MBA students who are returning to a university after years of experience in industry. People in business rightfully focus their attention on the immediate demands of their jobs and evaluate their firms' successes and failures with reference to production schedules and accounting statements, a perspective that stands in stark contrast to the perspective developed in an economics class.

You are now one of the many students to whom Knight directed his comments. As all good teachers must do, we intend to challenge you in this course to rethink your views on the economy and the way firms operate. We shall ask you to develop new methods of analysis, maintaining all the while that there is, indeed, an "economic way of thinking" that deserves to be mastered. We shall also ask you to reconsider, in light of the new methods of thinking, old policy issues – both inside and outside the firm – about which you may have fixed views. These tasks will not always be easy for you, but we are convinced that the rewards from the study ahead are substantial. The greatest reward may be that this course of study will help you to better understand the way the business world works and how businesses may be made more efficient and profitable.

V

[See online Video Module 1.1 Introduction]

Each chapter is divided into two major parts. The first part (Part A) will always develop microeconomic concepts and theories and apply the concepts and theories to social and economic policies. Part B will always apply the theory developed in Part A directly to issues that mid-level and executive-level managers confront all the time.

On the publisher's website for this book, we provide a "perspective" that extends the discussion in the chapter, covers some policy or management topic new to economics, or provides a novel take on a topic that economists and lay people to economics have mistakenly accepted as settled. For example, in this chapter we discuss a topic traditionally considered in microeconomics textbooks, "the tragedy of the commons" (or the tendency of resources to be overused when property rights are not defined). Online, in Perspective 1, we present the opposite tragedy, "the tragedy of the anticommons" (or the tendency for resources to be underutilized when there are too many decision makers from the assignment of property rights, or just decision rights).

Online Perspective

On the publisher's website, we also provide one or more additional "readings" on topics relating to themes in the different chapters. In the chapter, we briefly review a famous article by the late economic journalist Leonard Read titled " I, pencil," which covers a paradox of sorts: no one in the world knows how to produce a pencil from scratch, but yet millions of pencils are produced each year. Online, under Reading 1.1 we provide Reed's short but very insightful and easy to read article.

R

We understand that time is a scarce commodity for most MBA students, especially those who have to balance their studies with the demands of a full-time job and a family. Accordingly, we conclude each chapter with a "box" in which we identify one or two key "practical lessons for MBAs" that emerge from the analytics of each chapter. With these "lessons" we seek to show how some aspect of the economic way of thinking can be used to understand workplace problems and to devise profit-enhancing solutions to the problems managers face on a daily basis. Then, we close with a section we call "the bottom line," which itemizes and crystallizes the most important large and small points developed in the chapter. We have deliberately kept these lists of "key takeaways" short, but at the same time we expect this section will ease student reviews of the chapters.

Throughout the volume, we have one goal: to change the way you think about the world in large and small ways. When you complete this book, your view of how markets work (and fail to work) should be greatly clarified, with an improved ability to predict market outcomes. You will see more clearly the manager's role as one of coping with and responding to the competitive market forces that are ever-present outside the doors of every business, pressing both owners and executives to pay as much attention to the way business organizations and executive and line workers' incentives are structured as to how products are created and developed. We submit that by your thinking through problems with clarity, you will be able to avoid the waste of resources in your personal and work lives that comes from making errors in judgment that are bound to arise when people make decisions from "gut feelings" or simply wrongheaded presumptions about how the world works. After all, Knight was on target when he mused, quoting Mark Twain, "It's not ignorance that does so much damage; it's knowin' so darn much that ain't so."

We began revising this book during the fall of 2008 as the United States and the world slid into the worst economic recession since the Great Depression of the 1930s, with the current downturn set off by a "financial crisis" that left many major banks and investment houses and insurance companies struggling to stay alive because of the bursting of the "housing bubble" and subsequent meltdown of the market for "mortgage-backed securities" and other exotic financial instruments. At this writing, the daily economic news was dismal. Foreclosures on homes and businesses were mounting monthly as the unemployment rate broached 10 percent. With housing and stock prices in freefall, Americans lost in 2008 over $11 trillion, or 18 percent, of their net household wealth (an amount equal to the annual output of Germany, Japan, and the United Kingdom combined) (Kalita 2009). When you complete this book, you will better understand the microeconomic foundations of the crisis (which, when you read these words, will be widely known as the Great Recession) by understanding how investments based on borrowed money can inspire risk taking, with one rule elevated to prominence: the greater the leverage on business ventures, the greater the incentive to undertake risk – and excessive risks. You will understand what is meant by "moral hazard" and how that concept was at the foundation of the housing bubble and the mortgage meltdown. You might also worry about how subsequent government bailouts of failing banks and a range of other companies can inspire incentives on risk taking that can give rise to another (perhaps larger) moral-hazard problem, which could harbor the potential for an even more severe economic crisis in the future.

When you complete this book, you will also naturally be able to make observations that might, without going through this course of study, escape your attention. For example, most people now understand the entire world, not just the developed nations, faces a growing obesity problem, which is giving rise to a growth in obesity-related health problems that, in turn, are driving up firms' health insurance costs and depriving workers of increases in money wages (Brody 2005; Girion 2005).

You might now be aware of how obesity problems have been caused by long-term reduction in the price of calories (especially those obtained from fast-food restaurants) and the long-term growth in real incomes. Having completed this book, you will be able to easily extend the cause-and-effect change. You will naturally think about how people's weight problems are founded, at least partially, on the growing openness and competitiveness of the world's food markets, which are driving down the cost of food and driving up people's real incomes, with both effects leading to more food consumption – and people's expanded girths and backsides. You will also naturally wonder how managers will change their pay offers for prospective overweight workers, since the health care costs of such workers can be expected to feed into company health insurance costs. Indeed, might not competitive market forces be expected to put downward pressures on the money wages of overweight workers and upward pressures on prospective workers who maintain a healthy weight (and lifestyle)? You also will be naturally inclined to think of how people's excess weight may increase the demand for and market price of gasoline and jet fuel. You also will wonder why airlines that charge thin passengers extra for their checked bags weighing over 50 pounds do not add extra charges on obese passengers.

On completing this book, you will no longer be able to assess the terrorists' attack on the World Trade Center towers on September 11, 2001 as having only political or military consequences. After all, the 9/11 attack immediately hiked many people's perceived risk of flying, as well as causing a substantial lengthening of security lines at airports, with both factors – risk and wait time – increasing the total cost of plane trips. You will naturally understand why economic academic researchers have looked for, and found, that the greater cost of flying from the terrorists' actions should be expected to lead to – and apparently has led to – more people driving to many destinations, the consequence of which should be more automobile accidents, injuries, and deaths (Blalock, Kadiyali, and Simon 2005a, 2005b).

Hence, you will understand with greater facility after completing this book how airport security is truly a management problem with life-and-death consequences: Tighter airport security can have two opposing effects. First, it can increase the cost of flying (by increasing the length of the security lines), which can lead to less flying and more driving – and more highway accidents, injuries, and deaths. Second, the greater security can reduce the risk of flying and, thus, can increase the demand for flying (and reduce the demand for driving). Which effect is stronger? To date, the evidence suggests that, on balance, raising the alert status at airports from, say, yellow to orange can lead to more driving and more road deaths (Blalock, Kadiyali, and Simon 2005a, 2005b). Managers of the nation's homeland security system must weigh their actions very carefully and, before they raise the alert status, feel reasonably confident that the higher alert status will avert more deaths in the air than will arise on the nation's roads. Hence, we should expect that airport homeland security managers often will not elevate the alert status when the increase in the perceived risk of terrorist attacks is small.

In casual conversations, businesspeople talk as if they *know* many things that few listeners think to challenge:

- "Houses with views sell more quickly than houses without views."
- "Buying a house is a better deal than renting a comparable size apartment because houses carry tax advantages (interest on home mortgages is deductible from taxable incomes)."

On completing this textbook and hearing any such comment, you will be inclined to ask reflectively and in earnest, "How can that be?"

The kind of economic thinking that will be central to this book, and evident in the foregoing discussions of the housing bubble and burst, obesity, airport security, and any assessment of the above statements, springs from an innocuous observation: *people have a basic drive to improve their lot in life because they don't have everything they want and need.* Much of this introductory chapter and the book (and the course), both in theory and in application, is directed at driving home this easily overlooked lesson. Oddly enough, many lessons covered in this book are crystallized in a classic story of what happened in a German prisoner-of-war (POW) camp during the Second World War, as related by a prisoner who happened to be a trained economist.

Part A Theory and public policy applications

The emergence of a market

Economic systems spring from people's drive to improve their welfare. R. A. Radford, an American soldier who was captured and imprisoned during the

> A **market** is the process by which buyers and sellers determine what they are willing to buy and sell and on what terms. It is the process by which buyers and sellers decide the prices and quantities of goods that are to be bought and sold.

Second World War, left a vivid account of the primitive **market** for goods and services that grew up in the most unlikely of places, his POW camp (Radford 1945). Because the inmates had few opportunities to produce the things they wanted, they turned to a system of exchange based on the cigarettes, toiletries, chocolate, and other rations distributed to them periodically by the Red Cross.

The Red Cross distributed the supplies equally among the prisoners, but "very soon after capture … [the prisoners] realized that it was rather undesirable and unnecessary, in view of the limited size and the quality of supplies, to give away or to accept gifts of cigarettes or food. Goodwill developed into trading as a more equitable means of maximizing individual satisfaction" (Radford 1945, 190).

As the weeks went by, trade expanded, and the prices of goods stabilized. A soldier who hoped to receive a high price for his soap found he had to compete with others who also wanted to trade soap. Soon shops emerged, and middlemen began to take advantage of discrepancies in the prices offered in different prisoner bungalows.

For example, a priest, one of the few prisoners allowed to move freely among the prisoner bungalows, found that he could exchange a pack of cigarettes for a pound of cheese in one bungalow, trade the cheese for a pack and a half of cigarettes in a second bungalow, and return home with more cigarettes than he had started with. Although he was acting in his own self-interest (not so much out of religious convictions), he had provided the people in the second bungalow with something they wanted – more cheese than they would otherwise have had. In fact, prices for cheese and cigarettes differed partly because prisoners in different bungalows had different desires and partly because they could not all interact freely. To exploit the discrepancy in prices, the priest moved the camp's store of cheese from the first bungalow, where it was worth less, to the second bungalow, where it was worth more. Everyone involved in the trade benefited from the priest's enterprise.

A few **entrepreneurs** in the camp hoarded cigarettes and used them to buy up the troops' rations shortly after issue, and then sold the rations just before the next issue,

> An **entrepreneur** is an enterprising person who discovers potentially profitable opportunities and organizes, directs, and manages productive ventures.

at higher prices. Although these entrepreneurs were pursuing their own private interest, like the priest, they were providing a service to the other prisoners. They bought the rations when people wanted to get rid of them and sold them when people were running short. The difference between the low price at which they bought and the high price at which they sold gave them the incentive they needed to make the trades, hold on to the rations, and assume the risk that the price might not rise.

Soon the troops began to use cigarettes as money, quoting prices in packs or fractions of packs. (Only the less desirable brands of cigarettes were used this way; the better brands were smoked.) Because cigarettes were generally acceptable, the soldier who wanted soap no longer had to search out those who might want his jam; he could buy the soap with cigarettes. Even nonsmokers began to accept cigarettes in trade.

This makeshift monetary system adjusted itself to allow for changes in the money supply. On the day the Red Cross distributed new supplies of cigarettes, prices rose, reflecting the influx of new money. After nights spent listening to nearby bombing, when the nervous prisoners had smoked up their holdings of cigarettes, prices fell. Radford saw a form of social order emerging in these spontaneous, voluntary, and completely undirected efforts. Even in this unlikely environment, the human tendency toward mutually advantageous interaction had asserted itself.

Today, markets for numerous new and used products spring up spontaneously in much the same way. At the end of each semester, college students can be found trading books among themselves, or standing in line at the bookstore to resell the books they bought at the beginning of the semester. Garage sales are now common in practically all communities (with eBay effectively being the largest global "garage sale"). Indeed, like the priest in the POW camp, many people go to garage sales to buy what they believe they can resell – at a higher price, of course. "Dollar Stores" have sprung up all over the country for one purpose, to buy the surplus merchandise from manufacturers and to unload it at greatly reduced prices to willing customers. There are even firms that make a market in getting refunds for other firms on late overnight deliveries. Many firms don't think it is worth their time to seek refunds for late deliveries, mainly because they individually don't have many late deliveries (because the overnight delivery firms have an economic incentive to hold the late deliveries in check). However, there are obviously economies to be had from other firms collecting the delivery notices from several firms and sorting the late ones out, with the refunds shared by all concerned.

Gift cards have become a big and profitable business for retailers, partially because many of the cards go unused. Recipients lose them or don't care to shop where the card is redeemable. Plastic Jungle has created an exchange for gift cards, offering recipients $80 (typically) for a $100 gift card from Macy's. It will then put the card up for sale on Plastic Jungle's website for more than $80. Recipients can also donate the unused balances on their cards to charity through DonorsChoose.org (Wortham 2009).

Today, we stand witness to an explosion of a totally new economy on the Internet, which many students reading this book will, like the priest in the POW camp, help to develop. The development of the new economy has obviously brought gains to many firms – most notably Microsoft, Apple, and Amazon – and their customers who have gained from higher-quality products that have fallen in price through competition. But then the new economy has wreaked havoc for other firms – most notably brick-and-mortar bookstores and a host of major city newspapers – that have lost market share or have closed. The expansion of some industries – regardless of whether they are seen as a part of the "old" or "new" economy – and the contraction of others are interrelated for a reason that lies at the heart of economics: we simply can't do everything.

The economic problem

Our world is not nearly as restrictive as Radford's POW camp, but it is no Garden of Eden either. Most of us are constantly occupied in securing the food, clothing, and shelter we need to exist, to say nothing of those things we would only like to have – a high-definition television, a trip to Tahiti, and a shopping spree. Indeed, if we think seriously about the world around us, we can make two general observations.

> **Resources** are things used in the production of goods and services. There are only so many acres of land, gallons of water, trees, rivers, wind currents, oil and mineral deposits, trained workers, and machines that can be used in any one period to produce the things we need and want.

First, the world is more or less fixed in size and limited in its **resources**. We can plant more trees, find more oil, and increase our stock of human talent, but there are limits on what we can accomplish with the resources at our disposal.

Economists have traditionally grouped resources into four broad categories: land (surface of the world and everything in nature), labor (human and mental efforts devoted to production), capital (also called investment goods), and technology (knowledge of how resources can be productively combined). To this list, some economists would add a fifth category, *entrepreneurial talent*. The entrepreneur is critical to the success of any economy, especially if it relies heavily on markets. Because entrepreneurs discover more effective and profitable ways of organizing resources to produce the goods and services people want, they are often considered a resource in themselves. Entrepreneurs not only create "better mousetraps," they often do nothing more than what the priest did in the POW camp, find novel ways of redistributing the available but scarce resources and goods, to the benefit of everyone.

Second, in contrast to the world's physical limitations, human wants abound. You yourself would probably like to have books, notebooks, pens, and a calculator, perhaps even a computer with a several gigahertz microprocessor and a 200 gigabyte hard-disk drive. A stereo system, a car, more clothes, a plane ticket home, a seat at a big concert or ballgame – you could probably go on for a long time, especially when you realize how many basics, like three good meals a day, you normally take for granted.

In fact, most people want far more than they can ever have. One of the unavoidable conditions of life is the fundamental condition of scarcity. Put simply, there isn't enough of everything to go around. Consequently, society must face unavoidable questions: (1) What will be produced? (2) How will those things be produced? (3) Who will be paid what, which converts to who will get the goods produced? (4) Perhaps most important, who will determine how the above questions shall be answered?

> Scarcity is the fact that we all cannot have everything we want all the time.

These questions have no easy answers. Most of us spend our lives attempting to come to grips with them on an individual level. In a broader sense, these questions are fundamental not just to the individual but to all the social sciences, economics in particular. Indeed, most economists see the fact of scarcity as the foundation of economics. More to the point, economics is a way of *thinking* about how people, individually and collectively in various organizations (including firms), cope with scarcity.

> Economics is a method of thinking founded on the study of how people cope with the pressing choice problems associated with scarcity, with all effort directed toward satisfying as many wants as possible.

The problem of allocating resources among competing wants is not as simple as it may first appear. You may think that economics is an examination of how one person, or a small group of people, makes fundamental social choices on resource use. That is not the case. The problem is that we have information about our wants and the resources at our disposal that may be known to no one else. This is a point the late Leonard Read made (Read 1983) in a short article concerning what it takes to produce a product as simple as a pencil, and it also is a point that F. A. Hayek stressed in many of his writings that, ultimately, gained him a Nobel Prize in Economics (Hayek 1945).

In his short article, Read makes the startling observation that no one in the world knows how to make a product as seemingly simple as a pencil, not from scratch at least, but tens of billions of pencils are made each year, all through markets that mysteriously guide the economic decisions of millions of producers and consumers through multiple layers of production. Hayek stressed that the mystery of production (of pencils and numerous other more complicated products) can be understood by viewing the pricing system as a decentralized information system that is critical to coordinating so many people's decisions to employ and redeploy the world's scarce resources to satisfy people's wants. These wants may be known in detail only by the people who have them, which means they can't be known by centralized authorities who might imagine that they can do what markets do, but can't because they can't know and can't absorb the vast information that people have access to individually. Hayek argued that market prices are especially important because they reveal the values of resources and goods and direct people's efforts in optimizing the allocation of resources across space and time.[1] (See online Reading 1.1.)

As Read and Hayek might note, you may know you want a calculator because your statistics class requires you to have one, but even your friends (much less the people at Hewlett-Packard or Samsung) do not yet know your purchase plans. You also may be the only person who knows how much labor you have, which is determined by exactly how long and intensely you are willing to work at various tasks in your MBA program and at work. At the same time, you may know little about the wants and resources that other people around the country and world may have (or even your cohorts in your MBA study groups). Before resources can be effectively allocated, the information we hold about our individual wants and resources must somehow be communicated to others. This means that economics must be concerned with systems of communications, e.g. the priest in the POW camp who used both words and prices to convey information about how the troops in the various bungalows assessed the value he had to offer. Indeed, the field is extensively concerned with how information about wants and resources is transmitted or shared through, for example, prices in the market process and votes in the political process. Indeed, the "information problem" is often acute within firms, given that the CEO often knows little about how to do the jobs at the bottom of the corporate "pyramid." The information problem is one important reason that firms must rely extensively on *incentives* to get their workers (and managers) to pursue the firm's goals.

Markets like the one in the POW camp and even the firms that operate within markets emerge in direct response to scarcity. Because people want more than is immediately available, they produce some goods and services for trade. By exchanging things they like less for things they like more, they reallocate their resources and enhance their welfare as individuals. As we will see, people organize firms, which often substitute command-and-control structures for the competitive negotiations and exchanges of markets, because the firms are more cost-effective than markets. Firms can be expected to expand only as long as things can be done more cost-effectively through firms than through competitive market trades. This means that many firms fail not only because of things they do wrong (allow costs to get out of control), but because market trades between firms become less costly (through improved telecommunications), thus causing firms to outsource their needed services and shed their employees.

---

[1] The full text of Hayek's article and a number of other articles cited in following chapters can be accessed through the publisher's website for *Microeconomics for MBAs*, under "Resources and materials," www.cambridge.org/catalogue/catalogue.asp?isbn=9780521859813.

The scope of economics

MBA students often associate economics with a rather narrow portion of the human experience: the pursuit of wealth; money and taxes; commercial and industrial life. Critics often suggest that economists are oblivious to the aesthetic and ethical dimensions of human experience. Such criticism is partly justified. Increasingly, however, economists are expanding their horizons and applying the laws of economics to the full spectrum of human activities.

The struggle to improve one's lot is not limited to the attainment of material goals. Although most economic principles have to do with the pursuit of material gain, they can be relevant to aesthetic and humanistic goals as well. The appreciation of a poem or play can be the subject of economic inquiry. Poems and plays, and the time in which to appreciate them, are also scarce.

Jacob Viner, a distinguished economist active in the first half of the twentieth century, once defined economics as "what economists do." Today, economists study an increasingly diverse array of topics. As always, they are involved in describing market processes, methods of trade, and commercial and industrial patterns. They also pay considerable attention to poverty and wealth; to racial, sexual, and religious discrimination; to politics and bureaucracy; to crime and criminal law; and to revolution. There is even an economics of group interaction, in which economic principles are applied to marital and family problems. And there is an economics of firm organization and the structure of incentives inside firms.

What is the unifying factor in these diverse inquiries? What ties them all together and distinguishes the economist's work from that of other social scientists? Economists take a distinctive approach to the study of human behavior, and they employ a mode of analysis based on certain presuppositions. For example, much economic analysis starts with the general proposition that people prefer more to fewer of those things they value and that they seek to maximize their welfare by making reasonable, consistent choices in the things they buy and sell. These propositions enable economists to derive the "law of demand" (people will buy more of any good at a lower price than at a higher price, and vice versa) and many other principles of human behavior.

One purpose of this book is to describe the economic approach in considerable detail – to develop in precise terms the commonly accepted principles of economic analysis and to demonstrate how they can be used to understand a variety of problems, including pollution, unemployment, crime, and ticket scalping – as well as firms' organizational and financial structures. In every case, economic analysis is useful only if it is based on a sound theory that can be evaluated in terms of real-world experience. This mode of analysis – sometimes dubbed the "economic way of thinking" – will appear time and again as you move through your MBA programs, most prominently in your finance, accounting, marketing, and strategy courses.

Developing and using economic theories

The real world of economics is staggeringly complex. Each day millions of people engage in innumerable transactions, only some of them involving money (about 30 percent), and many of them undertaken for conflicting reasons (McMillan 2002, 168–9). To make matters worse, people are confronted with terabytes of data coming from the five senses (hearing, sight, touch, taste, and smell), far more than they can absorb by the brain, which weighs on average slightly less than three pounds and has only 100 billion neurons with which to work. To make sense of all these activities, people must first economize on their scarce mental powers before they seek to economize on resources in the external real world, partially by ignoring or filtering out much sensory data before it has a chance to throttle thinking altogether with "sensory overload." Additionally, economists turn to **theory** to further economize on their limited brain power (and the brain power of their students).

A **theory** is a model of how the world is put together; it is an attempt to uncover some order in the seemingly random events of daily life. Theory is how we make sense of the world.

Economic theory is abstract, but not in the sense that its models lack concreteness. On the contrary, good models are laid out with great precision. Economic theories are simplified models *abstracted from* the complexity of the real world. Economists deliberately simplify their models to best concentrate attention on the problems of greatest interest. As explained in the following chapter, economists assume people are *rational*, which is to say that they weigh the costs and benefits of options available to them, consistently choosing in such a way as to maximize their well-being. We even assume that people are more rational than we know them to be, but only because such an abstraction promotes (in an economical way) understanding and offers insights that might not otherwise be achieved.

Just as a map is useful because it ignores most of the details between the various points along our route of travel, so a model is useful because it ignores the details not relevant to the questions being investigated. Although a theory is not a complete and realistic description of the real world, a good theory should incorporate enough data to simulate real life. That is, it should provide some explanation for past experiences and permit reasonably accurate predictions of the future. When you evaluate a new theory, ask yourself:

- Does this theory explain what has been observed?
- Does it provide a better basis for prediction than other theories?

Microeconomics and macroeconomics

The discipline of economics is divided into two main parts that are typically covered in two different MBA courses – microeconomics and macroeconomics.

When economists measure, explain, and predict the demand for specific products such as bicycles and PDAs, they are dealing with microeconomics. This book will deal almost exclusively with microeconomic theory, policy implications, and applications inside firms.

 Questions of interest to microeconomists include:

- What determines the price and output level of particular goods and services?
- What determines workers' wages, interest rates, and business profits?
- How do government policies – such as price controls and excise taxes – affect the price and output levels of individual markets?
- Why do incentives matter inside firms?

These questions are relevant to the performance of the entire economy, but they also are questions that concern the managers of individual firms. Decisions on what goods and services to produce, how to produce them, what prices to sell them for, and how much to pay employees are obviously important to the profitability – and, indeed, viability – of firms. The competitiveness of a firm is determined by the decisions its managers make on:

1 how best to compensate employees (commonly considered a concern of personnel management)
2 the best mix of debt versus equity financing (commonly considered a concern of financial management)
3 how best to distribute the product (commonly considered a concern of marketing management)
4 whether to purchase a productive input from an outside supplier or expand the firm through vertical integration by producing the input in-house (commonly considered a concern of purchasing and organizational management).

In many respects, the business firm faces the same problems faced in the overall economy. In both cases, success depends on somehow motivating a large number of people to take action that promotes the general interest of all when those people have:

1 widely different abilities and interests
2 little concern for the interests of others
3 limited knowledge on how to serve the interests of others, even if they were concerned with doing so.

By keeping this problem in mind when examining the structures, strategies, practices, and procedures of real business firms, and applying the insights of the economic way of thinking, we can and will take a giant step toward a better understanding of business management.

Economists also study broad **macroeconomic** subdivisions of the economy, such as the total output of all firms that produce goods and services. Instead of concentrating on how many bicycles or PDAs are sold, macroeconomists watch overall production level and overall price level. These and similar issues are of more than academic interest, as the dramatic downturn in the world economy in 2008 demonstrated once again. But we hasten to repeat that this book and course are devoted primarily to "microeconomic" theory and applications, although you will find that our study will not avoid addressing the microeconomic foundations of the *macro*economic debacle of 2008 and beyond.

We make microeconomics our focus because we are firmly convinced that an understanding of the "macroeconomy" is necessarily dependent on an understanding of the "microeconomy." Many of the microeconomic concepts developed in this book – supply and demand, adverse selection and moral hazard, risk aversion, and incentives – will speak to the world's economic problems of the early 2000s, which originated with a credit binge in the 1990s, if not 1980s, that quickly morphed into a stock-market bubble (and bust) in the late 1990s and a housing-market bubble (and bust) in the early 2000s.

Private property rights, game theory, and the Prisoner's Dilemma

Microeconomics is replete with graphical and mathematical devices for illuminating people's interactions inside firms and markets with various intensities of market competition. Supply and demand curves, which we introduce in chapter 3, are devices for discussing price and output determination under intense competition. As we will see, much microeconomic analysis is about achieving cooperation among people to produce goods and services cost-effectively when all want the goods and services. Cooperation may not always be "natural," but only in the sense that people may have personal incentives to take noncooperative strategies, as in our discussion of two people – Fred and Harry – seeking to develop a social contract to follow.

Game theory is a matrix device used to discuss people's decisions when their most preferred course of action depends on the choices of others.

To illuminate people's problems of achieving cooperative solutions, we employ another microeconomic device, game theory, which comes from applied mathematics and is often portrayed as a decision matrix, as in table 1.1. Such a matrix permits us to reveal in a variety of social settings – most notably business – the problems people face in achieving cooperation when their decisions must be made strategically, that is, with the understanding that their most preferred choices depend upon the choices of others. We start with a discussion of the emergence of property rights in a game-theoretic setting in part because property rights are necessary for trade to flourish and in part to ease students into familiarity with game theory to which we will return throughout the textbook.

Private property rights and the games economists play

In microeconomics, we start with the proposition that all actions are constrained by the fact of *scarcity*. Private "property rights" are among the institutional mechanisms people have devised to help alleviate the pressing constraints of scarcity, which is why we take them up at this early stage in the course. **Property rights** are a social phenomenon; they arise out of the necessity for individuals to "get along" within a social space in which all wish to move and interact.

> **Property rights** pertain to the permissible use of resources, goods, and services; they define the limits of social behavior – what can and cannot be done by individuals in society. They also specify whether resources, goods, and services are to be used privately or collectively by the state or some smaller group.

Where individuals are isolated from one another by natural barriers or are located where goods and resources are extremely abundant, property rights have no meaning. In the world of Robinson Crusoe, shipwrecked alone on an island, property rights were inconsequential. His behavior was restricted by the resources found on the island, the tools he was able to take from the ship, and his own ingenuity. He had a problem of efficiently allocating his time within these constraints – procuring food, building shelter, and plotting his escape; however, the notion of "property" did not restrict his behavior – it was not a barrier to what he could do. He was able to take from the shipwreck, with impunity, stores that he thought would be most useful to his purposes.

After the arrival of Friday, the native whom Robinson Crusoe saved from cannibals, a problem of restricting and ordering interpersonal behavior immediately emerged. The problem was particularly acute for Crusoe because Friday, prior to coming to Tibago, was himself a cannibal. (Each had to clearly establish property rights to his body.) The system that they worked out was a simple one, not markedly different from that between Crusoe and "Dog" (the name Crusoe gave his dog). Crusoe essentially owned everything. Their relationship was that of master and servant, Crusoe dictating to Friday how the property was to be used.

In common speech, we frequently speak of someone "owning" this land, that house, or these bonds. This conventional style is undoubtedly economical from the viewpoint of quick communications, but it masks the variety and complexity of the ownership relationship. What are owned are *rights* to *use* resources, including one's body and mind, and these rights are always circumscribed, often by prohibition of certain actions. To "own land" usually means to have the right to till (or not to till) the soil, to mine the soil, to *offer* those rights for sale, etc., but not to have the right to throw soil at a passerby, to use it to change the course of a stream, or to force someone to buy it. What are owned are *socially recognized rights of action* (Alchian and Demsetz 1973).

Property rights are not necessarily distributed equally, meaning that people do not always have the same rights to use the same resources. Students may have the right to use their voices (i.e. a resource) to speak with friends in casual conversation in the hallways of classroom buildings, but they do not, generally speaking, have the right to disrupt an organizational behavior class with a harangue on their political views. In other words, property rights can be recast in terms of the *behavioral rules,* which effectively limit and restrict our behavior. Behavioral rules determine what rights we have with regard to the use of resources, goods, and services. The rights we have may be the product of the legislative process and may be enforced by a third party, usually the government – or, more properly, the agents of government. In this case, property rights emerge from legislation.

Private property rights and the market

In the private market economy people are permitted to initiate trades with one another. Indeed, when people trade, they are actually trading "rights" to goods and services or to do certain things. For example, when a person buys a house in the market, she is actually buying the right to live in the house under certain conditions – as long as she does not disturb others, for example. This market economy is predicated upon establishing patterns of *private* property rights; those patterns have legitimacy because of government enforcement – and, perhaps just as important, because of certain social norms regarding the limits of individual behavior that are commonly accepted, observed, and self-enforced (with locks and alarm systems, for example). Without recognized property rights there would be nothing to trade – no market.

How dependent are markets on government enforcement for the protection and legitimacy of private property rights? Our answer must of necessity be somewhat speculative. We know that markets existed in the "Old West" when *formally* instituted governments were nonexistent. Further, it is highly improbable that any government can be so pervasive in the affairs of people that it can be the arbiter of all private rights. Cases in which disputes over property rights within a neighborhood are settled by association councils are relatively rare, and the disputes that end up at police headquarters are rarer still. Most conflicts over property rights are resolved at a local level, between two people, and many potential disputes do not even arise because of generally accepted behavioral limits.

Finally, the concept of property rights helps clarify the relationship between the public and private sectors of the economy – that is, between that section of the economy organized by collective action through government and that section organized through the actions of independent individuals. When government regulates aspects of the market, it redefines behavioral limits (in the sense that people can no longer do what they once could) and can be thought of as realigning the property rights between the private and public spheres. When the government imposes price ceilings on goods and services (as it does with rent controls), or price floors (as it does with minimum wage legislation and agricultural price support programs), it is redefining the rights that sellers have regarding the property they sell. One of the purposes of economics is to analyze the effect that such realignment of property rights has on the efficiency of production.

The emergence of private property rights

In an idealized world in which people are fully considerate of each other's feelings and adjust and readjust their behavior to that of others without recourse to anything resembling a dividing line between "mine" and "thine," property rights are likely no more necessary than they were for Robinson Crusoe alone on Tibago. But in the world as it now exists, there is the potential for conflict. The development of property rights, held communally by the state or held privately by individuals, can alleviate such conflict, or the potential for conflict. These rights can be established in ways that are similar but which can be conceptually distinguished: (1) *voluntary* acceptance of behavioral norms with no third-party enforcer, such as the police and courts, and (2) the specification of rights in a legally binding social contract, meaning that a third-party enforcer is established. Most of what we say for the remainder of this chapter applies to both modes of establishing rights. However, for reasons developed later in the book, the establishment of rights through voluntary acceptance of behavioral norms, although important in itself, has distinct limitations, especially in relation to size of the group (with growth in the group's size undermining the behavioral norms).

To develop the analysis in the simplest terms possible, consider a model of two people, Fred and Harry, who live alone on an island. They have, at the start, no behavioral rules or anything else that "naturally" divides their spheres of interest – that is, they have nothing that resembles property rights. Further, being rational, they are assumed to want more than they have or can produce by themselves. Their social order is essentially anarchic. Each has two fundamental options for increasing his welfare: he can use his labor and other resources to produce goods and services or he can steal from his fellow man. With no social or ethical barriers restricting their behavior, Fred and Harry should be expected to seek the allocation of their resources between these options in the most productive way. This may mean that each should steal from the other as long as more is gained that way than through the production of goods and services.

If Fred and Harry find stealing a reasonable course to take, each will have to divert resources into protecting that which he has produced (*or* stolen). Presumably, their attacks and counterattacks will lead them toward a social equilibrium in which each is applying resources to predation and defense and neither finds any further movement of resources into those lines of activity profitable (Bush 1972, 5–8). This is not an equilibrium in the sense that the state of affairs is a desirable or stable one; in fact, it may be characterized as a "Hobbesean jungle" in which "every man is Enemy to every man" (Hobbes 1968, first published in 1651).

In an economic sense, resources diverted into predatory and defensive behavior are wasted; they are taken away from productive processes. If these resources are applied to production, total production can rise, and both Fred and Harry can be better off – both can have more than if they try to steal from each other. Only through winding up in a state of anarchy, or seeing the potential for ending up there, do they question the rationality of continued plundering and unrestricted behavior; and it is because of the prospects of individual improvement that there exists a potential for a "social contract" that spells out legally defined property rights. Through a social contract they may agree to restrict their own behavior, but they will do away with the relatively more costly restraints that, through predation and required defense, each imposes on the other. The fear of being attacked on the streets at night can be far more confining than laws that restrict people from attacking one another. This is what John Locke meant when he wrote, "The end of law is not to abolish or restrain but to preserve and enlarge freedom" (Locke 1690, 23).

Once the benefits from the social contract are recognized, there *may* still be, as in the case of voluntary behavioral norms, an incentive for Fred or Harry to chisel (cheat) on the contract. Fred may find that although he is "better off" materially by agreeing to property rights than he is by remaining in a state of anarchy, he may be even "better off" by violating the agreed-upon rights of the other. Through stealing, or violating Harry's rights in other ways, Fred can redistribute the total wealth of the community toward himself.

Consider table 1.1, which illustrates the kind of "games" – involving actions and reactions of individual players – we and other economists use to draw out strategies people will (or should) use to deal with given situations. Table 1.1 contains a chart or matrix of Fred and Harry's utility (or satisfaction) levels if either respects or fails to respect the rights established for each as a part of the contract. (The actual utility levels are hypothetical, but serve the purpose of illustrating a basic point.) There are four cells in the matrix, representing the four combinations of actions that Fred and Harry can take. They can both respect the agreed-upon rights of the other (cell 1), or they can both violate each other's rights (cell 4). Alternatively, Harry can respect Fred's rights while Fred violates Harry's rights (cell 3), or vice versa (cell 2).

Table 1.1 **The games Fred and Harry can play with property rights**

	Harry respects Fred's rights		Harry violates Fred's rights	
	Cell 1		Cell 2	
Fred respects Harry's rights	Fred	Harry	Fred	Harry
	15 utils	10 utils	8 utils	16 utils
	Cell 3		Cell 4	
Fred violates Harry's rights	Fred	Harry	Fred	Harry
	18 utils	5 utils	10 utils	7 utils

The payoffs (measured in "util" terms) from Fred and/or Harry either respecting or violating the other's rights are indicated in the four cells of the matrix. Each has an incentive to violate the other's rights. If they do violate each other's rights, they will end up in cell 4, the worst of all possible states for both of them. The productivity of the "social contract" can be measured by the increase in Fred and Harry's utility resulting from their moving from cell 4, the "state of nature," to cell 1, a state in which a social contract is agreed upon.

Clearly, by the utility levels indicated in cells 1 and 4, Fred and Harry are both better off by respecting each other's rights than by violating them. However, if Harry respects Fred's rights and Fred fails to reciprocate, Fred has a utility level of 18 utils, which is greater than he will receive in cell 1 – that is, by going along with Harry and respecting his rights. Harry is similarly better off if he violates Fred's rights while Fred respects Harry's rights: Harry has a utility level of 16, whereas he will have a utility level of 10 utils if he and Fred respect each other's rights. The lesson to be learned is that inherent in an agreement over property rights is the possibility for each person to gain by violating the rights of the other. If both follow this course, they both will end up in cell 4 – that is, back in the state of anarchy.

There are two reasons why this may happen. First, as we stated above, both Fred and Harry may violate each other's rights in order to improve their own positions; the action may be strictly *offensive*. By the same token, each must consider what the other will do. Neither would want to be caught upholding the agreement while the other one violates it. If Fred thinks that Harry may violate his rights, Fred may follow suit and violate Harry's rights: he will be better off in cell 4, i.e. anarchy, than in cell 2. Thus, Fred and Harry can wind up in anarchy for purely *defensive* reasons.

Many wars and battles, at both the street and international levels, have been fought because one party was afraid that the other would attack first in order to get the upper hand. The same problem is basically involved in our analysis of the fragile nature of Fred and Harry's social contract. The problem of contract violation can grow as the community grows in number because individual persons' violations are more difficult (and more costly) to detect.

Game theory: Prisoner's Dilemmas

One of the most frequently used game-theoretic settings is called the *Prisoner's Dilemma game* in which both parties in two-person games have built-in incentives to take noncooperative solutions. Prisoner's Dilemmas are especially problematic when the parties are unable to communicate. Fred and Harry's situation is a classic example of what social scientists call a *Prisoner's Dilemma*. This dilemma represents a common problem in achieving cooperation in any number of social settings, not the least of which is business, and a topic that will come up repeatedly in this book.

[See online Video Module 1.2 Prisoner's Dilemma]

The name Prisoner's Dilemma comes from a standard technique of interrogation employed by police to obtain confessions from two or more suspected partners to a crime. If the method is used, the suspects are taken to different rooms for questioning, and each is offered a lighter sentence if he confesses. But each also will be warned that if the other suspect confesses and he does not, his sentence will be more stringent. The suspect has to try to figure out, without the benefit of communication, how the other will stand up to that kind of pressure. Worried that the other may confess, each may confess because he cannot trust his partner not to take the easy way out. The problem for the individual suspect becomes more complicated as the number of captured partners to the crime increases. There are more people on whom he must count to hold up under the pressure that he knows is being brought to bear. He must also consider the fact that the others may confess because they cannot count on all their partners to hold under the pressure.

Prisoner's Dilemma solutions: enforcement and trade

To prevent violations of both an offensive and a defensive nature, a community may agree to the establishment of a police, court, and penal system to protect the rights specified in the social contract. The system may be costly, but the drain on the community's total wealth may be smaller than if it reverts back to anarchy, in which case resources will be diverted into predatory and defensive behavior. The costs associated with making the contract and enforcing it will determine just how extensive the contract will be, a matter considered later in the book.

The social contract, which defines property rights, establishes only the limits of permissible behavior; it does not mean that Fred and Harry will be satisfied with the exact combination of property rights they have been given through the contract. To the degree that some other combination or distribution of the existing property held by Fred and Harry will give them both more satisfaction, trades are not only possible, but likely. Mutually beneficial exchanges can be expected to emerge.

For example, suppose that the only goods on Fred and Harry's island are coconuts and papayas. The social contract specifies the division of the fruits between them.

Table 1.2 Relative satisfaction from marginal units consumed

	Coconut (utils)	Papaya (utils)
Fred	10	15
Harry	90	30

Table 1.3 Specializing in production and trade

	Coconut production	Papaya production
Fred	4	8
Harry	6	24

We need not concern ourselves with the total number of the fruit each has; we need only indicate the relative satisfaction that Fred and Harry receive from the marginal units. Suppose the marginal utilities in table 1.2 represent the satisfaction they received from the last coconut and papaya in their possession.

In table 1.2, Fred receives more utility from the last papaya (15 utils) than from the last coconut (10 utils). He would be on a higher level of utility if he could trade a coconut for a papaya. He would lose 10 utils from the coconut but would more than regain that with the additional papaya. On the other hand, Harry receives more utility from the last coconut than from the last papaya. He would gladly give up a papaya for a coconut; he would be 60 utils of satisfaction better off (90 minus 30) than if he did not make the exchange. The two should continue to exchange *rights* to the coconuts and papayas until one or both of them can no longer gain via trade.

In this example, we are not concerned with production of coconuts and papayas; we are concerned merely with the benefits from trade resulting from the initial allotments of the fruits. The trades are comparable to those that took place in the POW camps as described by R. A. Radford at the start of the chapter. If the social contract allocates to Fred and Harry rights to *produce* the fruit, we can also demonstrate that both can be better off through specializing in their production and trading with each other. Consider the information in table 1.3, which indicates how many coconuts or papayas Fred and Harry can produce with, say, one hour of labor.

In one hour of labor Fred can produce either 4 coconuts or 8 papayas; Harry can produce either 6 coconuts or 24 papayas. Even though Harry is more productive in both lines of work – and thus has an *absolute advantage* in both goods – we can show that they both can gain by specializing and trading with each other. This is because each has a *comparative advantage* in one good. That is, each can produce one good at a relatively lower cost than the other person can.

If Fred produces 4 coconuts, he cannot use that hour of time to produce the 8 papayas. In other words, the cost of the 4 coconuts is 8 papayas, or, which amounts to the same thing, the cost of 1 coconut is 2 papayas. Fred would be better off if he could trade 1 coconut for *more than* 2 papayas, because that is what he has to give up in order to produce the coconut. To determine whether there is a basis for trade, we must explore the cost of coconuts and papayas to Harry. We note that the cost of 1 coconut to Harry is 4 papayas; this is because he has to give up 24 papayas to produce 6 coconuts. If Harry could give up fewer than 4 papayas for a coconut, he would be better off. He could produce the 4 papayas, and if he has to give up fewer than that for a coconut, he will have papayas left over to eat, which he would not have had without the opportunity to trade.

To summarize: Fred would be better off if he could get more than 2 papayas for a coconut; Harry would be better off if he could give up fewer than 4 papayas for a coconut. If, for example, they agree to trade at the exchange rate of 1 coconut for 3 papayas, both would be better off. Fred will produce 1 coconut, giving up 2 papayas, but he can get 3 papayas for the coconut. Hence, he is better off. Harry can produce 4 papayas, giving up 1 coconut, and trade 3 of the papayas for a coconut. He has the same number of coconuts, but has an additional papaya. Harry is better off.

Although relatively simple, the above example of *exchange* is one of economists' most important contributions to discussions of social interaction. So many people seem to think that when people trade, one person must gain at the expense of another. If people in the United States trade with people in Japan, someone must be made worse off in the process, or so the argument goes. We will deal with such arguments in more detail in chapter 5 in which we take up international trade. For now, we wish to emphasize that we have demonstrated that, through trade, both Harry and Fred can be better off. This was demonstrated even though we postulated that Harry was more efficient than Fred in the production of both fruits!

[See online Video Module 1.3 Comparative advantage]

Trades that emerge from exploitation of comparative advantages among traders can have even more profound effects than those already indicated. This is because of the efficiency benefits of specialization of labor (or any other resource). By specializing in the production of papayas, Harry can become more skilled in their production, producing more papayas in a given time period because of the greater skills and because less time will be wasted moving back and forth between the production of coconuts and papayas. The same can be said for Fred because of his specialization in coconuts. The result is that their joint production can increase for two reasons:

- First, both Harry and Fred can produce the good in which they are relatively more efficient in production and, thus, have a relatively lower cost of production.
- Second, both can achieve an even greater production because of the economies of specialization of resource use.

Restrictions on market trades (tariffs and quotas, for example) can have two adverse effects: They can reduce the ability of traders to exploit their comparative advantages in production. Second, they can narrow the scope of markets, thereby reducing the potential specialization in resource use and economies that could flow from the missed specialization (points economists as far back as the venerable Adam Smith, author of *The Wealth of Nations* [1776], have had in mind when they have opposed trade restrictions).

While this argument has been couched in terms of two independent persons' trade of coconuts and papayas, we stress that the gains to be had from exploitation of people's comparative advantages and specialized talents are fully evident within business firms. CEOs might be more talented and productive in accounting, law, and advertising than the assistants they hire. However, they hire assistants to exploit their relatively greater comparative advantage in running entire firms. Accountants hire bookkeepers not because their bookkeepers are more talented and productive in recording transactions but because they have comparative advantages in understanding what summary accounting statistics convey about the overall operation of their firms. Firms are full of people with specialized talents who are exploiting those talents at a higher level than would be possible if all sought to be "jacks of all trades." Indeed, firms' very survival depends upon their understanding the gains from trades and resource specialization.

Communal property rights and the "tragedy of the commons"

To many, the ideal state of affairs may appear to be one in which everyone has the right to use all resources, goods, and services and in which no one (not even the state) has the right to exclude anyone else from their use. We may designate such rights as "communal rights." Many rights to scarce property have been and still are allocated in this way. Rights to the use of a university's facilities are held communally by the students. No one admitted to the university has the right to keep you off campus paths or lawns or from using the library according to certain rules and regulations. (Such rules and regulations form the boundaries, much as if they were natural, within which the rights are truly communal.) The rights to city parks, sidewalks, and streets are held communally. Before the United States was settled, many Native American tribes held communal rights to hunting grounds; that is, at least within the tribe's territory, no one had the right to exclude anyone else from hunting on the land. During most of the first half of the nineteenth century, the rights to graze cattle on the prairies of the western United States were held communally; anyone who wanted to let his cattle loose on the plains could do so. Granted, the US government held by law the right to exclude cattlemen from the plains; but as long as it did not exercise that right, the land rights were communal.

The same can be said for all other resources whose "owner" does not exercise the right to exclude cattlemen.

Communal property rights can be employed with tolerably efficient results so long as one of two conditions holds:

1 there is more of the resource than can be effectively used for all intended purposes (in other words, there is no cost to its use), or
2 people within the community fully account for the effects that their own use of the resources has on others.

Without the presence of one of these conditions, the resources will tend to be "overused."

The biologist Garrett Hardin (1968) characterized the problem of overused (and abused) communal resources as "the tragedy of the commons" and considered why a pasture might be overgrazed if cattle ranchers' access to the pasture were unimpeded by property rights. In deciding on how many cattle to add, each cattleman likely will be compelled to reason that the addition of his cattle – and his cattle alone – to the pasture will make no difference to the amount of feed available to the cattle of other herdsmen. One person's cattle just don't eat that much, given the size of the pasture, but the grass eaten by one rancher's cattle is grass that can't be eaten by the cattle of other ranchers. This means that he can impose a portion of the costs of his cattle grazing on the pasture on other ranchers, which is justification enough for all ranchers to put more cattle on the pasture than they would if they individually incurred the full grazing costs of their cattle. The result is that the cattlemen can collectively face an outcome – a "tragedy" in the form of overly thin cattle – that none of them would want:

> Therein is the tragedy. Each man is locked into a system that compels him to increase his herd without limit – in a world that is limited. Ruin is the destination toward which all men rush, each pursuing his own best interest in a society that believes in the freedom of the commons. Freedom of the commons brings ruin to all. (Hardin 1968)

The prospect of the emergence of a "tragedy" under communal ownership has been a very powerful argument for conversion of communal rights to *private property rights*, which is an institutional setting under which the owners simultaneously have both usage and exclusion rights.

Under communal ownership, if the resource is not presently being used by someone else, no one can be excluded from the use of it. Consequently, once in use, the resource becomes, for that period of time, the private property of the user. The people who drive their cars onto the freeway take up space on the road that is not in use; no one else (they hope!) can then use that space at the same time. Unless the drivers violate the rules of the road, they cannot be excluded from that space; and if they are rational, they will continue to use the resource until their cost of a little additional use equals their benefits from that additional use. They may consider most of the costs involved in their use of the road, but one that they may overlook, especially as it applies to themselves personally, is that their space may have had some *alternative use*, that is, by others. Their presence also increases highway congestion and the discomfort of the other drivers (potentially nontrivial costs). As a result, they may overextend the use of their resource, meaning that they may continue to drive as long as the additional benefits *they*, themselves, get from driving additional miles is greater than the additional cost.

The state can make the driver consider the social costs of driving in an indirect way by imposing a tax on the driver's use of the road (through either a tax on gasoline or a tax on the miles driven, as determined by GSP-based monitoring devices that several states were considering deploying at the time of this revision), causing less driving, and fewer costs that drivers impose on others. This is called "internalizing the social cost." Once the state does this – and it is commonly done through gasoline taxes and/or tolls – the rights to the freeway are no longer "communal"; the rights have been effectively attenuated by the state.

There are two additional ways that social costs can be internalized.

- First, people can be considerate of others and account for the social cost in their behavior.
- Second, the right to the road can be turned into *private property*, meaning that individuals are given the right to exclude others from the use of the resource (i.e. the road). This may seem to be a totally undesirable turn of events unless we recognize that private owners can then charge for the use of the road: they can sell "use rights," in which case the marginal cost of driving will rise, resulting in an increase in the cost that individual drivers incur from traffic congestion (a form of the tragedy of the commons all too familiar to MBA students commuting to work or class).

The prime difference between this private ownership and government taxation is that, with private ownership, the revenues collected go into the coffers of individuals rather than those of the state; this is either "good" or "bad," depending upon your attitude toward government versus private uses of the funds. Furthermore, under private ownership and without viable competitors (and we have an example in which competition *may* not be practical), the owners may attempt to charge an amount that is greater than the social costs in table 1.1; they may attempt, in the jargon of economists, to acquire **monopoly** *profits*, and in so doing cause an *underuse* of the road.

> A **monopoly** (see chapter 10) is a single seller of a good or service that can charge higher prices and reap greater profits by restricting the quantity of the good it sells.

For that matter, the state-imposed taxes may be greater than the social costs. The state may also act like a monopolist. State agencies may not be permitted to make a "profit" as it is normally conceived, but this does not exclude the use of their revenues for improving salaries and the working conditions of state employees. Monopoly profits may be easy to see on the accounting statements of a firm but may be lost in bureaucratic waste or overexpenditures under state ownership. State ownership does not necessarily lead to waste, but it is a prospect, and one that only the naïve will ignore. More is said on this subject at various points in the book.

We have now considered the distinction between private and communal property. Several examples will enable us to amplify that distinction and to understand more clearly the limitations of communal property rights and the pervasive use of private property.

Pollution

Pollution of streams, rivers, air, etc. can be described as a logical consequence of communal property rights. The state and federal governments, by right of eminent domain, have always held rights to these resources; but until very recently they have inadequately asserted their right to exclude people and firms from their use. As a result, the resources have been subject to communal use and to overuse, in the same sense as that discussed above.

By dumping waste into the rivers, people, firms, and local governments have been able to acquire ownership to portions of the communal resource – they use it and pollute it. Furthermore, because of the absence of exclusion, those people doing the polluting do not have to pay to draw the resource away from its alternative uses (such as beautiful scenery) or to reimburse the people harmed by the pollution for the damage done. Under communal ownership, in which government does not exercise its control, the firm with smoke billowing from its stacks does not have to compensate the people who live around the plant for the eye irritation they experience or the extra number of times they have to paint their homes.

Pollution is often thought to be the product of antisocial behavior, as indeed it often is. Many who pollute simply do not care about what they do to others. However, much pollution results from the behavior of people who do *not* have devious motives. People may view their behavior as having an inconsequential effect on the environment. The person who throws a cigarette butt on the ground may reason that if this cigarette butt is the only one on the ground, it will not materially affect anyone's sensibilities, and in fact it may not. However, if everyone follows the same line of reasoning, the cigarette butts will accumulate and an eyesore will develop. Even then, there may be little incentive for people to stop throwing their butts on the ground. Again, a person may reason on the basis of the effects of his own individual action: "If I do not throw my butt on the ground here with all the others, will my behavior materially affect the environmental quality, *given the fact that other butts are already there*?" This type of reasoning can lead to a very powerful argument for conversion of communal rights to private or state rights, with the implied power for someone to exclude some or all of this kind of use. (More will be said on the economics of pollution in chapter 5.)

Theft

The prevalence of theft can affect people's willingness to create, invest in, and enhance property. This is because theft reduces the rewards from property. Theft can come in forms that quickly come to mind, muggings and break-ins, but it can also come in other more widespread forms, such as customer shoplifting and employee pilferage. The greater the prevalence of theft of property, the less people can be expected to willingly invest in and build up their property. That rule is transparent in the bicycles people ride in Amsterdam, the Netherlands. While bikes are every-where present, few bikes are less than thirty years old. Bikes without gears (or with no more than three gears) are common, and most show signs of wear. The reason is that bike theft is common. As residents of Amsterdam will freely admit, it simply doesn't pay to buy a modern bike. Indeed, parking a new bike on the side streets and alleys of Amsterdam is an invitation to thieves. The working rule among bike owners in Amsterdam is that the amount spent on bike locks should be greater than the amount spent on a bike.

It also very likely follows that the higher the cost of theft detection, the greater the theft problems business will have. If the cost of monitoring customer shoplifting and employee pilferage goes down, then more monitoring and less shoplifting and pilferage can be expected. Both honest customers and honest employees can have good reason to want at least some monitoring of the thieves among them. The penalties can abate a tragedy of the commons in business – added costs of doing business. The meted out penalties imposed on thieves can contain the prices of products customers buy and increase the potential pay and job security of employees.

However, in closing this section, we add a note of caution. While the assignment of property rights is important to the efficient use of resources and the smooth functioning of a market economy, there is a case to be made for the development of some balance in the assignment of property rights. If there are too many rights claimants, resources can be underutilized, giving rise to the "tragedy of the anti-commons," or so legal scholar Lawrence Lessig (2001) has argued, especially with regard to copyrights, which are a form of property right for intellectual property. You can read more about this "tragedy" in Perspective 1 on the publisher's website for this book.

Voluntary organizations and firms as solutions for "tragedies of the commons"

"Tragedies of the commons" are clearly potential problems, but they are also problems that can cause people to search earnestly for solutions that stand apart from always assigning private property rights or having the government step in with imposed regulations. Indiana University political science professor Elinor Ostrom shared the 2009 Nobel Prize in Economics for pointing out to economists steeped in Hardin's dismal view of the tragedy of the commons that people all the time form voluntary associations to restrict and direct the use of communally owned property – because communal ownership can be more cost-effective than private ownership or government control. She found voluntary associations working well all over the world when forests, fisheries, oil fields, and even grazing lands are held communally (Ostrom 1990). What the voluntary associations need, according to Ostrom, are clear, pre-established rules on how the gains from use of the communal property are to be divided and how conflicts are to be resolved. Even ranchers in the so-called "Wild West" of the nineteenth century formed cattlemen's associations that solved Hardin's potential tragedy of the commons. The associations effectively laid claim to the communal property, restricting entry of "outsiders" both in putting cattle on the common pasture and in participating in the annual roundups (Anderson and Hill 2004). The tragedy of the commons, played out in the willful poaching of elephants in Namibia, Africa, was partially solved by giving local tribes communal ownership rights to the elephant herds in their areas, insuring that they received some of the gains from tourists coming to see wild elephant herds. The tribes had incentives to control poaching (as reported by Henderson 2009).

University of California, Berkeley economics professor Oliver Williamson shared the 2009 Nobel Prize for stressing that "firms" are nothing more than voluntary associations of varying numbers of people who organize themselves to achieve economic gains that are shared. Because firms' resources are used "communally," there are ever-present prospects for tragedies of firms' commons with people misusing and abusing firm resources for their own private ends (Williamson 1967, 1990, 1998). The Part Bs of the chapters of this textbook reflect the thinking of scores of economists who have followed Williamson's lead and have explained how firms seek to abate their potential tragedies of the commons through hierarchial and financial structures and incentive systems.

Most microeconomics textbooks treat "firms" as theoretical "black boxes" that magically transform inputs into outputs all very cost-effectively, so long as their markets are competitive. Such an approach misses a major reason MBA students are in their microeconomic classes, to gain insights on how the transformations are orchestrated, which includes avoiding firm-based tragedies of the commons. This is to say, in the following chapters, we will pay due attention to how markets work, but we will also peel back the sides of the black boxes called firms to gain insights on how they can produce cost-effectively.

For a different view of the "tragedy of the commons," see online Perspective 1, The tragedy of the anticommons.

> **Online Perspective 1**
> **The tragedy of the anticommons**

[handwritten margin notes: Resource misallocation / Books printed vs. letters and words]

Part B Organizational economics and management

Managing through incentives

We noted above that much of this book and course is concerned with the problem of overcoming a basic condition of life: *scarcity*. Firms are an integral means by which the pressures of scarcity are partially relieved for all those people who either own or work for firms. How is it that tragedies of the commons developed in Part A can reveal themselves inside firms, especially large ones? Very straightforwardly. Owners and their top managers want to get as much work and production from their workers as they can for the wages paid. Many workers, on the other hand, may not want to work as hard as their bosses want. Each worker can figure that if she sloughs off, her lack of work intensity will not be noticed in terms of the firm's total production. The problem is that if all workers follow suit, then the firm's profitability, if not survivability, and workers' jobs can be jeopardized, a tragedy of the work commons that no worker may want. In order to get employees to work diligently for their firms (and to prevent a tragedy of the work commons) managers and line workers must have some reason or purpose – some *incentive* – to do that which they are supposed to do.[2]

---

[2] Those MBA students who wish to go beyond the basics of the "organizational economics" discussed in this textbook are advised to consider reading (and digesting) three important books: Rubin 1990, Milgrom and Roberts 1992, and Roberts 2004.

Incentives have been found to be important for more mundane, everyday business reasons. Tying compensation to some objective measure of firm performance can cause the affected workers' productivity to rise substantially. This is because tying pay to performance is a way of giving workers *rights* – a form of property rights – to a portion of the output they produce.

In addition, tying pay to performance can change the type of workers who are attracted to the pay-for-performance jobs. As might be expected, appropriately structured incentive pay can increase a firm's rate of return and stock price, as well as the income of the affected workers.

Productivity increases

When Safelite Auto Glass switched from paying its glass installers by the hour to paying them "piece rates," worker productivity went up by 44 percent, only half of which could be attributable to the motivational effect of the piece-rate pay system. The other half was attributable to the fact that Safelite started attracting people who were willing to work hard and began holding onto its more motivated and productive workers, even as its less motivated and productive workers were leaving the company (Lazear 2000).

One study of thousands of managers of large corporations found that adding a 10 percent bonus for good performance could be expected to add 0.3 to 0.9 percent to the companies' after-tax rate of return on stockholder investment. If managerial bonuses are tied to the market prices of the companies' stock, share prices can be expected to rise by 4 to 12 percent. The study, which covered 16,000 managers in 250 firms, also found that the greater the sensitivity of management pay to company performance, the better the performance (Abowd 1990). Another study found that firms don't have to wait around for the incentives to have an impact on the firms' bottom line to get a jump in their stock prices; all they have to do is to *announce* that executives' compensation over the long haul is going to be more closely tied (through stock options or bonuses) to performance measures and the stock will, within days, go up several percentage points, increasing shareholder wealth by tens, if not hundreds, of millions of dollars, depending on firm size (Brickley, Bhagat, and Lease 1985).

Naturally, if managers are paid just a straight salary, they have less reason to take on risky investments (Roberts 2004, chapter 4). Managers' potential gain from the higher rates of return associated with risky investments is uncertain and problematic (given that the rise in their future salaries from performance may not be clear and direct), which is why they may shy away from risky investments (more so than they would if their pay were clearly tied, in part or in whole, to some measure of firm performance). Accordingly, it should surprise no one to learn that when managers are given bonuses based on performance, they tend to undertake riskier, higher-paying investments (Holmstrom 1979; Shavell 1979; Amihud and Lev 1981; Smith and Watts 1982). But, then, if the bonuses are based on some short-term goal – say, this year's earnings instead of some longer-term goal, say, some level for the stock price – you can bet that managers will tend to sacrifice investments with higher longer-term payoffs for the smaller payoffs that are received within the performance period. The managers' time horizons can be lengthened by tying their compensation to the firm's stock value and then requiring that they hold the firm's stock until some later date – for example, retirement (Jensen and Meckling 1979).

Although incentives have always mattered, they probably have never been more important to businesses interested in competing aggressively on a global scale. Greater global competition means that producers everywhere must meet the best production standards anywhere on the globe, which requires them to have the best incentive systems anywhere. Incentives will continue to grow in importance in business as the economy becomes more complex, more global, and more competitive. Although incentives are both positive and negative, when structured properly they can ensure that managers, workers, and consumers prosper.

The growing importance of incentives

Like it or not, businesspeople will have to learn to think about incentives with the same rigor that they now contemplate their balance sheets and marketing plans. They will need to justify the incentive structures they devise, which means they will have to understand why they do what they do. High pay and so-called "golden parachutes" (or generous firing packages) for executives and stock options for workers will need to be used judiciously. They can't be employed just because they seem like a nice idea, or because everyone else is using them. Investors who find it easier and easier to move their investment funds anywhere in the world will be less inclined to allow their capital to be used for "nice ideas." Unless "nice ideas" are well designed, they can spell wasted investments. The multitude of ways that incentives can matter in business makes a study of them mandatory – if managers want to get them right.

The Lincoln Electric case

Unless policies are carefully considered, *perverse incentives* can be an inadvertent consequence, mainly because people can be very creative in responding to policies. Lincoln Electric is known for achieving high productivity levels among its production workers by tying their pay to measures of how much they produce. But the company went too far. When it tied the pay of secretaries to "production," with counters installed on typewriters to measure how much was typed, the secretaries responded by spending their lunch hours typing useless pages of manuscript to increase their pay, which resulted in that incentive being quickly abandoned (Fast and Berg 1971; Roberts 2004, 42). In seeking to reduce the number of "bugs" in its programs, a software company began paying programmers to find and fix bugs. The goal was noble but the response wasn't: Programmers began creating bugs so that they could find and fix them, with one programmer increasing his pay $1,700 through essentially fraudulent means. The company eliminated the incentive pay scheme within a week of its introduction (Adam 1995).

Lincoln Electric's experience brings us to a general rule that managers of all companies must keep in mind: incentives almost always work, but they don't always work well or in the way that is expected (a fact that has led to harsh criticisms of even the attempt to use incentives, punishments, or rewards[3]). Economic researchers in Israel sought to help ten day care centers in Haifa reduce the number of times parents picked up their children late (Gneezy and Rustichini 2000). For the first four weeks of their twenty-week research experiment, the researchers did not impose a fine for late pickups and observed that the day care centers had an average of seven late pickups per week. After the fifth week, they imposed a fee of $3 per late pickup. Contrary to their presumption, late pickups jumped to an average of twenty per week per center. The late pickups could have increased for two reasons that the researchers did not consider, according to Stephen Levitt and Stephen Dubner who report on the experiment in their best-selling economics book, *Freakonomics*. First, the parents considered the $3 fee to be an approved and cheap form of added babysitting. (Thus, a $20 late fee might have had the expected response, a curb in tardiness, because the fee would then be greater than the cost of babysitting found elsewhere.) Second, the day care centers had probably lowered, on balance, the true cost for tardiness: the monetary late fee took the place of the "psychic cost" associated with doing something considered "wrong," such as not picking up children on time (Levitt and Dubner 2005, 19–20, 23).

Mitsubishi Motors sought to increase the sales of its cars in 2003 through a promotional campaign dubbed "zero-zero-zero" – for zero down payment, zero interest, and zero payments for the first twelve months after sale. According to one automobile industry journalist, "a hefty number [of car buyers] used this promotion to drive a new car without paying anything for a year, after which they let the car get repossessed," resulting in losses of hundreds of millions of dollars for the company (Ingrassia 2005).

One source of the worldwide mortgage market meltdown is that mortgage lenders, with the encouragement of the federal government, began making mortgage loans in the 1990s to prospective homeowners with little to no down payments and at "teaser" (below-market) interest rates for two or three years, after which the interest rates, along with mortgage payments of homeowners, would increase. Many

---

[3] For criticisms of incentives, see Kohn 1993b and Pearce 1987.

prospective homebuyers (and speculators) snapped up the so-called "subprime" mortgages, figuring that they could reap an increase in their home equity if the housing price bubble continued while the teaser rates were in effect. If the housing bubble burst, then the homebuyers had little or nothing to lose. The mortgage lenders bundled their subprime mortgages and sold them off to investors around the world who assumed that the mortgages were a safe investment because of the housing bubble. Little did many securities investors recognize that the value of their securities would crash with the subsequent crash in housing prices, aggravated by many homeowners who walked away from their homes and mortgage payments when their payments escalated and the resell prices of their homes fell below their mortgage balances.

Incentives and managed earnings

Of course, incentive systems can cause managers to manage their earnings. For example, when managers are paid on the basis of *annual* performance targets, research shows that they have been induced to advance the reporting of sales when they expect to be short of the targets. When they expect to more than make their targets, managers have moved sales to the first quarter of the next year on the grounds that there is no reason for them to "waste" sales (Oyer 1998; Horngren 1999, 937–8). The fact that so many executives at the now defunct Enron and Worldcom held so much of their companies' stock can go a long way toward explaining the extensive accounting fraud at those companies. By "cooking the books," the managers were able to inflate the value of their stock holdings (Roberts 2004, 156–7), which carries a valuable lesson: beware of tying managers' pay to performance measures that are easily manipulated (Baker 2000).

In the twenty-first-century world economy, business incentives will become even more commonplace, and getting them right will be an even greater concern for managers.

Why incentives are important

But such conceptual and factual points beg two critical questions:

- Why are incentives important?
- Why do they work?

Admittedly, the answers are many. One of the more important reasons that incentives matter within firms is that firms are collections of workers whose interests are not always aligned with the interests of the people who employ them – that is, the owners. The major problem facing the owners is how to get the workers to do what the owners want them to do. The owners could just issue directives, but without some incentive to obey them, nothing may happen. Directives may have some value in themselves: people do feel a sense of obligation to do what they were hired to do, and one of the things they may have been hired to do is to obey orders (within limits). However, directives can be costly. Firms may use incentives simply as a cheaper substitute for giving out orders that can go unheeded unless the workers have some reason to heed them.

Firms may also use incentives to clarify firm goals, to spell out in concrete terms to workers what the owners want to accomplish. As every manager knows all too well, it is difficult to establish and write out the firm's strategy that will be used to achieve its stated goals, and it is an even more difficult task to get workers to appreciate, understand, and remember firm goals – and then work toward them. The communication problem typically escalates with the size of the organization.

Goals are always imperfectly communicated, especially by memoranda or through employment manuals that may be read once and tossed away. Workers do not always know how serious the owners and upper managers are: they can remember any number of times when widely circulated memos were nothing but "window dressing." Incentives are a means by which owners and upper managers can validate overall company goals and strategies. They can in effect say through incentives (reinforced regularly in paychecks and end-of-year bonuses): "This is what we think is important. This is what we will be working toward. This is what we will be trying to get everyone else to do. And this is where we will put our money." Even if workers were not sensitive to the pecuniary benefits of work, but were interested only in doing what their companies wanted them to do, incentives, because of the messages they convey, can have a valuable and direct impact on what workers do and how long and hard they work (White 1991; Robins 1996).

But there is a far more fundamental reason that incentives matter: *managers don't always know what orders or directives to give.* No matter how intelligent, hard working, and well informed managers are, they seldom know as much about particular jobs as those who are actually doing them. Knowing about the peculiarities of a machine, the difficulties a fellow worker on the production line is experiencing at home, or the personality quirks of a customer are just a few examples of the innumerable particular bits of localized knowledge that are crucial to the success of a firm. And this knowledge is spread over everyone in the firm without the possibility of its being fully communicated to, and effectively utilized by, those who are primarily responsible for managerial oversight. The only way a firm can fully benefit from such localized knowledge is to allow those who possess the knowledge – the firm's employees – the freedom to use what they know. This is what it means to *empower* workers.

But the benefits from participatory management, or employee empowerment, can be realized only if employees have not only the freedom but also the *motivation* to use their special knowledge in productive cooperation with each other. The crucial ingredient for bringing about the requisite coordination is incentives that align the otherwise conflicting interests of individual employees with the collective interests of all members of the firm. Without such incentives, there can be no real employee empowerment because there is no hope that the knowledge dispersed throughout the firm will be used in a coordinated and constructive way. The only practical alternative to a functioning system of incentives is, again, a top-down, command-and-control approach that, unfortunately, never can allow the full potential of a firm's employees to be realized.

Frederick Hayek's ageless insight about the dispersion of economically relevant information applies within the firm (Hayek 1960). With the growing complexity and sophistication of production, knowledge becomes ever more widely dispersed among a growing number of workers. Hence, the importance of incentives has grown with modern-day leaps in the technological sophistication of products and production processes. Incentives will continue to grow in importance as production and distribution processes become ever more complex.

Seen in this light, the problem of the firm is the same as the problem of the general economy. As did Hayek, economists have argued for years that no group of government planners, no matter how intelligent and dedicated, can acquire all the localized knowledge necessary to allocate resources intelligently. The long and painful experiments with socialism and its extreme variant, communism, have confirmed that this is one argument that economists got right. But the freedom for people to use the knowledge that only they individually have has to be coupled with incentives that motivate people to use that knowledge in socially cooperative ways – meaning that the best way for individuals to pursue their own objectives is by making decisions that improve the opportunities for others to pursue their objectives. In a market economy, these incentives are found primarily in the form of *prices* that emerge from the rules of private property and voluntary exchange. Market prices provide the incentive people need to productively coordinate their decisions with each other, thus making it not only possible, but desirable, for people to have a large measure of freedom to utilize the localized information and know-how they have.

A perfect incentive system would assure that everyone could be given complete freedom because it would be in the interest of each to advance the interests of all. No such perfect incentive system exists, not within any firm or within any economy. In every economy there is always some appropriate "mix" of both market incentives and government controls that achieve the best overall results. The argument over just what the right mix is will no doubt continue indefinitely, but few deny that both incentives and controls are needed. Similarly, for any firm made up of more than one person, there is some mix of incentives and direct managerial control that best promotes the objectives of the firm, i.e. the general interests of its members.

Of course, if a given firm doesn't pay attention to its incentives, it may lose more than its lunch; it may be forced out of business by those firms that do recognize the importance of incentives. Seen from this perspective, incentives can be a critical component of firm survival – perhaps just as critical as product development or technological sophistication.

The problem is in getting the incentives right and using the full range of potential incentives. Unfortunately, we can't say exactly what incentives your firm should employ. The precise incentives chosen depend on local conditions that can vary greatly across firms.

Practical lessons for MBAs: see management as a problem in solving Prisoner's Dilemmas

Management self-help books that line bookstore shelves make management out to be an extremely complex undertaking. That it can be, but the economic way of thinking about management seeks to cut through the complexity with practical pointers. Consider management problems as Prisoner's Dilemmas, which suggests that the central task of managers is to provide employees with a set of incentives so that they take the cooperative solution. Too often managers rely on directives to bring about cooperation among workers. Directives can work well, but only when managers know more about what the workers do than the workers know. In complex working environments, such is often not the case. Managers hire workers because they, managers, can't know or do all the things that workers are supposed to do. In such cases, managers should consider replacing directives with incentives that encourage workers to use their specialized and localized knowledge to use firm resources in the most cost-effective manner.

Profits can be made from product development. Profits can also be made from getting incentives right, which involves making sure that workers share in firm gains when workers do things right and in firm losses when workers do things wrong. In effect, getting incentives right can mean making workers in many (not all) job categories *residual claimants*. At the time of this writing, one of the authors' university was in the midst of a budget "crunch," desperately searching for ways to reduce its expenditures on "large ticket items" such as electricity use. The university figured that it was spending $120 a year on electricity per computer to keep each university computer running at night. Almost all of the university's 1,500 professors were leaving their computers on when they left the office for the day (or week or month!) on the chance that they might want to tap into their office computers from home through the "Desktop Remote" feature of Windows. At the time, a software program was available that would "wake up" turned-off computers, but the cost of the program was gauged at $68 per computer. Substantial cost savings even over one year were obvious, but faculty were not rushing to buy the program. Why? The university paid the electricity bill, but professors would have to pay for the wake-up program out of their discretionary budgets. One potential organizational fix should have been apparent: give each professor (or his department) an electricity budget that would more than cover the cost of the wake-up software and allow each professor to keep any residual for research purposes.

Further reading online

Reading 1.1 "I, pencil," by Leonard E. Read

R

The bottom line

The key takeaways from chapter 1 are the following:

1 Economics is a discipline best described as the study of human interaction in the context of scarcity. It is the study of how, individually and collectively, people use their scarce resources to satisfy as many of their wants as possible. The economic method is founded in a set of presuppositions about human behavior on which economists construct theoretical models.

2 Economics is a way of thinking about virtually everything, including the issues that managers confront daily.

3 Communally owned property is a common cause of resource misuse and overuse.

4 Private property rights matter because they affect people's incentives to use scarce resources. This is because they affect people's rewards from effectively utilizing scarce resources. They also affect the costs they incur from misusing and abusing scarce resources.

5 Not all potential tragedies of the commons need to be resolved through private property rights and government regulation. Voluntary associations and firms are means by which the overuse of communally owned resources has been abated.

6 For trade to recur and be systematic, it must be mutually beneficial to the trading partners, and trade can be mutually beneficial even when one party to the trades is more efficient in both goods subject to trade.

7   In general, incentives of all kinds matter in how effectively (or ineffectively) scarce resources are utilized. There is obviously profit to be made from developing better, improved goods and services. Less widely recognized is the fact that there is also profit to be made from developing better, more cost-effective incentive systems.

8   Overcoming Prisoner's Dilemmas is a pervasive problem in the development of social and management policies.

Review questions >>

1   In the prison camp described early in this chapter, rations were distributed equally. Why did trade within and among bungalows result?

2   Recall the priest who traded the cigarettes for cheese, and cheese for cigarettes, so that he ended up with more cigarettes than he had initially. Did someone else in the camp lose by the priest's activities? How was the priest able to end up better off than when he began? What did his activities do to the price of cheese in the different bungalows?

3   Theories may be defective, but economists continue to use them. Why?

4   A microeconomics book designed for MBA students could include theories more complex than those in this book. What might be the trade-offs in dealing with more complex theories?

5   Most MBA students study in "teams." Is there a potential tragedy of the commons within MBA study teams? Asked differently, what incentive problems do these teams have to overcome? How has your team sought to overcome the incentive problems? Why are teams generally small? What would be the consequence of doubling or trebling the size of study teams?

6   Some restaurants have their bartenders "tip pool" (or divide up their total tips at the end of their shifts). Servers in the rest of the restaurant often do not tip pool. What are the problems of tip pooling? Why do bartenders often tip pool while other servers in the same restaurant do not? How do restaurants overcome the potential problems with tip pooling?

2

Principles of rational behavior in society and business

We are not ready to suspect any person of being defective in selfishness.
   Adam Smith

The combined assumptions of maximizing behavior, market equilibrium, and stable preferences, used relentlessly and unflinchingly, form the heart of the economic approach.
   Gary S. Becker

Microeconomics rests on certain assumptions about individual behavior. One is that people are capable of envisioning various ways of improving their position in life. This chapter reviews and extends the discussion begun in chapter 1 of how people – businesspeople included – cope with scarcity, which means choosing among the alternatives for improvement people can envision. According to microeconomic theory, consumers and producers make choices *rationally*, so as to maximize their own welfare. This seemingly innocuous basic premise about human behavior will allow us to deduce an amazing variety of implications for business and many other areas of human endeavor. The premise undergirds our study of mutually beneficial trades considered in chapter 1 and the forces of supply and demand to be covered in chapter 3. The assumption of rationality is at the core of the economic way of thinking about everything, including managing and thinking itself.

Part A Theory and public policy applications

Rationality: a basis for exploring human behavior

People's wants are expansive and ever expanding. We can never satisfy all our wants because we will always conceive of new ones. The best we can do is to maximize our satisfaction, or **utility**, in the face of scarcity. Economists attempt to capture in one word – utility – the many varied contributions made to our well-being when we buy and sell, achieve a success (small or large), earn a living, drink, eat, have sex, read a good book, have children, play – or make an A on a microeconomics exam!

> **Utility** is the satisfaction a person receives from the consumption of a good or service or from participation in an activity. Happiness, joy, contentment, or pleasure might all be substituted for satisfaction in the definition of utility.

The ultimate assumption behind this theory is that *people act with a purpose*. In the words of Ludwig von Mises, they act because they are "dissatisfied with the state of affairs as it prevails" (Mises 1962, 2–3).

The acting individual

If people act in order to satisfy their consciously perceived wants, their behavior must be self-directed rather than externally controlled – at least to some extent. However, there is no way to prove this assertion. Economists simply presume that individuals, as opposed to groups, perform actions. It is the individual who has wants and desires, and looks for the means to fulfill them. It is the individual who attempts to render his or her state less unsatisfactory.

Group action, when it occurs, results from the actions of the individuals in the group (as we will see in Part B of this chapter). Social values, for instance, draw their meaning from the values that individuals share, while still holding the values individually. Economists would even say that group action cannot be separated from individual action, although economists do not deny that individual actions can lead to outcomes that no member of the group wants. But economists can explain such outcomes as the result of rational individuals responding to incentives that need to be improved.

Of course, individuals in a group affect one another's behavior. In fact, the size and structure of a group can have a dramatic effect on individual behavior (again, as we shall see in Part B of this chapter). When economists speak of a competitive market, they are actually talking about the influence that other competitors have on the individual consumer or firm, and the choice dynamics of the individuals involved.

Rational behavior

When individuals act to satisfy their wants, they exhibit rational behavior. The notion of rational behavior rests on three assumptions:

> **Rational behavior** is consistent behavior that maximizes an individual's satisfaction through comparisons of the costs and benefits of alternative courses of action.

- first, that the individual has a preference and can identify, within limits, what he or she wants
- second, that the individual is capable of ordering his or her wants consistently, from most preferred to least preferred
- third, that the individual will choose consistently from these ordered preferences to maximize his or her satisfaction.

Even though the individual cannot fully satisfy all her wants, when possible she will always choose more of what she wants rather than less. In short, the rational individual always stands ready to further her own interests.

Some readers will find these assertions obvious and acceptable. To others, they may seem narrow and uninspiring. Economists often talk and write *as if* people are perfectly rational; that is, they always make decisions with great care and precision and without errors in judgment (other than those that involve calculated risks and mistakes). This is not because economists truly believe that people's decisions are never prone to error – or "decision-making biases" or "irrationalities" – as critics sometimes argue people are. Rather, economists press their founding premise of rationality to the point of perfection for two reasons:

- First, an assumption of perfect rationality can ease the difficulty (cost) of thinking through the implications of decision making. If we were to assume that people are imperfectly rational, or "quasi-rational," we could find it unnecessarily difficult to model human thinking and decision making and to gain insight through the development of logical deductions and testable hypotheses, with the development of testable hypotheses a goal of all science, including the science of economics (and many economists do think of their discipline as a "science," if only a "social science"). A first and foremost requirement of economics is that it allows us (economists and people in the larger world) to economize on the scarcest of all resources, the human brain (the average weight of which is three pounds). The frailties and limitations of the brain, as documented by neuroscientists and psychologists, is all the more reason we need to simplify as much as possible our models of human decision making.

- Second, by developing theory based on a premise of perfect rationality in personal and business decision making, we can deduce a variety of principles that can lead to improved decision making for people who are not innately perfectly rational (or who are beset with decision-making biases), resulting in enhanced personal welfare and greater firm profits.

In short, our goal throughout this book is to convey the economic way of thinking. We do this on the expectation that you will gain insights about personal, business, and government behaviors with the development of supply and demand curves in the following chapter that might not otherwise have occurred to you. Leaf ahead to figure 3.5 to see the supply and demand curves. Notice that those two curves are hardly complete and fully accurate descriptions of markets. They could not be. After all, they are only two lines on a graph. Nevertheless, in chapter 3, we develop insights about how prices are determined in markets (and we do that with the assumption that markets are far more competitive than we know them to be). The economic principles that have been developed, and will be developed in this chapter and the rest of the book, can be seen as suggestions for improvements in decision making in virtually all aspects of life. Later in the chapter we examine some common objections to the concept of rational behavior, but first we must examine a few logical consequences of the rationality premise. Be prepared for a change in the way you see and think about the world of business around you.

[See online Video Module 2.1 Rational behavior]

Rational decisions in a constrained environment

Several important conclusions flow from the economist's presumption of rational behavior. First, the individual makes choices from an array of alternatives. Second, in making each choice, a person must forgo one or more things for something else. All rational behavior involves a cost, which is the value of the most preferred alternative forgone. Third, in striving to maximize his or her welfare, the individual will take those actions whose benefits exceed their costs and will continue to consume any given good until the additional value of the last unit consumed equals the additional cost incurred to obtain the last unit.

Choice

We assume that the individual can evaluate the available alternatives and select the one that maximizes her utility. Nothing in the economic definition of rational behavior suggests that the individual is completely free to do as she wishes. Whenever we talk about individual choices, we are actually talking about

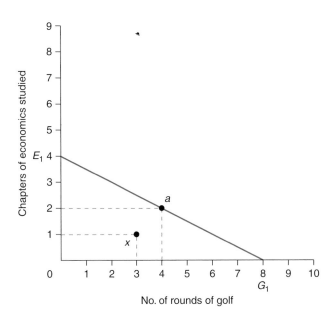

Figure 2.1 Constrained choice
With a given amount of time and other resources, you can produce any combination of study and golf along the curve E_1G_1. The particular combination you choose will depend on your personal preferences for those two goods. You will not choose point x, because it represents less than you are capable of achieving – and, as a rational person, you will strive to maximize your utility. Because of constraints on your time and resources, you cannot achieve a point above E_1G_1.

constrained choices – choices that are limited by outside forces. For example, you as a student or manager find yourself in a certain social and physical environment and have certain physical and mental abilities. These environmental and personal factors influence the options open to you. You may not have the money, the time, or the stomach to become a surgeon, and you certainly don't have the time to take all the courses listed in the schedule for your MBA program.

Although your range of choices may not be wide, choices do exist. At this moment you could be doing any number of things instead of reading this book. You could be studying some other subject, going out on a date, playing with your son or daughter, or completing a pressing company project. Or you could have chosen to go shopping, to engage in intramural sports, or to jog around the block. In fact, you not only can make choices, you must make them.

Suppose that you have an exam tomorrow in economics and that there are exactly two things you can do within the next twelve hours. You can study economics or play rounds of golf. These two options are represented in figure 2.1. Suppose you spend the entire twelve hours studying economics. In our example, the most you could study is four chapters, or E_1. At the other extreme, you could do nothing but golf – but again, there is a limit: eight rounds or G_1.

Neither extreme is likely to be acceptable. Assuming that you aim both to pass your exam and to have fun, what combination of rounds of golf and study should you choose? The available options are represented by the straight line E_1G_1, the production possibilities curve (PPC) for study and play, and the area underneath it. If

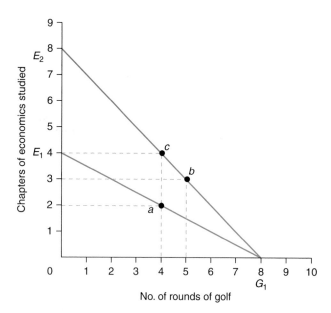

Figure 2.2 **Change in constraints**
If your study skills improve and your ability at golf remains constant, your production possibilities curve will shift from E_1G_1 to E_2G_1. Both the number of chapters you can study and the number of rounds of golf you can play will increase. On your old curve, E_1G_1, you could study two chapters and play four rounds of golf (point a). On your new curve E_2G_1, you can study three chapters and play five rounds of golf (point b).

you want to maximize your production, you will choose some point on E_1G_1, such as a: two chapters of economics and four golf rounds. You might yearn for five rounds and the same amount of study, but that point is above the curve and beyond your capabilities. If you settle for less – say one chapter and three golf rounds, or point x – you will be doing less than you are capable of doing and will not be maximizing your utility. The combination you actually choose will depend on your preference.

Changes in your environment or your physical capabilities can affect your opportunities and consequently the choices you make. For example, if you improve your study skills, your production rate for chapters studied will rise. You might then be able to study eight units of economics in twelve hours – in which case your production possibilities curve would expand outward. Even if your ability to play golf remained the same, your greater proficiency in studying would enable you to increase the number of rounds of golf played. Your new set of production possibilities would be E_2G_1 in figure 2.2.

Again, you can choose any point along this curve or in the area below it. You may decide against further golf rounds and opt instead for four chapters of economics (point c). Or you could move to point b, in which case you would still be learning more economics – three chapters instead of two – but also would be playing more golf. The important point is that you are able to choose from a range of opportunities. The option you take is not predetermined.

[See online Video Module 2.2 Productivity change and choice]

Cost

The fact that choices exist implies that some alternative must be forgone when another is taken. For example, suppose that you have decided to spend an hour watching television programs. The two programs you most want to watch are *Oprah* (a show whose guest list is dominated by celebrities) and *Jerry Springer* (a show whose guest list is dominated by weirdos). If you choose *Oprah*, the cost is the pleasure you sacrifice by not watching a (staged) brawl among the guests on *Jerry Springer*.

> **Cost** (or more precisely, opportunity cost) is the value of the most highly preferred alternative not taken at the time the choice is made.

Notice that cost does not require spending money. The cost of watching one TV show instead of another has nothing to do with money. Money can be a useful measure of costs, however, because it reduces to one common denominator. But money is not a cost itself. The shoes you are wearing may have cost you $50 (a money cost), but the real cost (the opportunity cost) is the value of what you could have purchased instead with the $50. The real cost is the actual benefits given up from the most preferred alternative not taken when a choice is made. When economists use the term "cost," they mean the real or opportunity cost – the value of the option not taken.

> **Money cost** is a monetary measure of the benefits forgone when a choice is made.

As long as you have alternative uses for your time and other resources, "there is no such thing as a free lunch," a pat phrase economists repeat often. Nothing can be free if other opportunities are available. One goal of economics courses is to help you recognize this very simple principle and to train you to search for hidden costs. There is a cost to writing a poem, to watching a sunset, to extending a common courtesy of opening a door for someone. Although money is not always involved in choices, the opportunity to do other things is. *A cost is incurred in every choice.*

Maximizing satisfaction: cost–benefit analysis

An individual who behaves rationally will choose an option only when its benefits are greater than or equal to its costs. This is equivalent to choosing the most favorable option available. That is, people will produce or consume those goods and services whose benefits exceed the benefits of the most favored opportunity not taken.

This restatement of the *maximizing principle,* as it is called, explains individual choice in terms of cost. In figure 2.1, the choices along curve E_1G_1 represent various cost–benefit trade-offs. If you choose point *a*, we must assume that you prefer *a* to any other combination because it yields the most favorable ratio of benefits to costs.

A change in cost will produce a change in behavior. Suppose you and a friend set a date to play checkers, but at the last moment he receives a lucrative job offer for the day of the match. Most likely the contest will be rescheduled. The job offer will change your friend's opportunities in such a way that what otherwise would have been a rational act (playing checkers) is no longer rational. The cost of playing checkers has risen significantly enough to exceed the benefits of the checkers game.

Economists see **cost–benefit analysis** as the basis of much (but certainly not all) of our behavior. Why do you attend classes, for example? The obvious answer is

> **Cost–benefit analysis** is the careful calculation and comparison of all costs and benefits associated with a given course of action.

that at the time you decide to attend class, you expect the benefits of attending to exceed the costs. The principle applies even to classes you dislike. A particular course may have no intrinsic value, but you may fear that by cutting class you will miss information that would be useful for the examination. Thus the benefits of attending are a higher grade than you would otherwise expect. Besides, other options open to you at 7 o'clock Tuesday evening may have so little appeal that the cost of going to class is very slight.

Take another example. Americans are known for the amount of waste they accumulate. Our gross national garbage (what Americans collectively discard annually) is estimated to be more valuable than the gross national output of many other nations. We throw away many things that people in other parts of the world would be glad to have. However morally reprehensible some people may find such "waste," it can be seen as the result of economically rational behavior. The food wrappings people throw away, for example, add convenience and freshness to the food, the value of which can exceed the costs.

So does it make sense to say that using and disposing of food wrapping is wasteful? Perhaps sometimes, but only if the person throwing away the trash is able to impose some of the waste disposal costs on others, thereby making a decision in which the personal value of the disposal is greater than the personal cost incurred – but the personal value of the disposal is less than the total cost incurred by all people (including the person who does the disposal plus others who incur a portion of the disposal cost). Indeed, much waste disposal – litter – can be an economic waste of a sort (an inefficiency) because taxpayers cover the cost of litter collection, which encourages excessive littering by all.

The behavior of businesspeople is not materially different from that of consumers or students. People in business are constantly concerned with cost–benefit calculations, except that the comparisons are often (but not always) made in dollar terms. For example, will the cost of a small improvement in the quality of a product be more than matched by the additional (marginal) revenues generated from the improvement? In other words, will consumers value the added benefits enough to pay for them? In assessing the safety of their products, for example, businesspeople must consider how much consumers are willing to pay for the additional safety and how much it costs. It doesn't pay to make products as safe as possible if providing the additional safety costs more than it is worth. Automobile manufacturers could build cars like Sherman tanks that would be safe under most driving conditions, but could not sell them at a price necessary to cover the cost of making them.

The effects of time and risk on costs and benefits

When an individual acts, all the costs and benefits are not necessarily incurred immediately. The decision to have a child is a good example. A college-educated couple's first child can easily cost more than $500,000, from birth through college, when the cost of parental time involved is considered (Craig 2003). Fortunately this high cost is incurred over a relatively long period of time (or many people would not become parents).

Benefits received in the future must also be compared with present benefits. If you had a choice between receiving $10,000 now and $10,000 one year from now, you would take $10,000 today. You could put the money in a bank, if nothing else, where it would earn interest, or you could avoid the effects of future inflation by spending the money now. In other words, future benefits must be greater than present benefits to be more attractive than present benefits.

To compare future costs and benefits on an equal footing with costs and benefits realized today, we must adjust them to their **present value** (PV). The usual procedure for calculating present value – a process called *discounting* – involves an adjustment for the interest that could be earned (or would have to be paid) if the money were received (or due) today rather than in the future. A dollar received a year from now is worth less than a dollar received today. If the rate of interest is 6 percent, then a dollar received a year from now is the same as $0.943. A dollar earned two years from now would be worth today – or has a present value – of just under $0.90 because the amount received today will rise to the value of $1 over the next two years when the interest is 6 percent. Accordingly, a dollar to be received fifty years from now will be worth a matter of a few cents.[1]

> **Present value** is the value of future costs and benefits in terms of current dollars.

---

[1] The mathematical formula for computing the present value of future costs or benefits received one year from now is $PV = [1(1 + r)] f$, where PV stands for present value, r for the rate of interest, and f for future costs or benefits.

Discounting a dollar for time may seem like a trivial exercise, and many people might not want to waste their time (incur the cost) of doing the discounting math, but the principle at stake is certainly worth contemplating when millions of dollars of a firm's costs and profits are at stake. The principle of discounting suggests a business strategy:

1 Postpone costs as long as possible and collect revenues as soon as possible.
2 The higher the interest rate, work all the more diligently to follow the first rule in the strategy.

If there is any uncertainty about whether future benefits or costs will actually be received or paid, further adjustments must be made. Without such adjustments, perfectly rational acts may appear to be quite irrational. For example, not all business ventures can be expected to succeed. Some will be less profitable than expected or may collapse altogether. The *average* fast-food franchise may earn a yearly profit of $1 million but only nine out of ten franchises may survive their first year (because the *average* profits are distorted by the considerable earnings of one franchise). Thus the estimated profits for such a franchise must be discounted, or multiplied by 0.90. If 10 percent of such ventures can be expected to fail, on average each will earn $900,000 ($1 million × 0.90).

Entrepreneurial risk taking

The entrepreneur who starts a single business venture runs the risk that it may be the one out of ten that fails. In that case, profit will be zero. To avoid putting all their eggs in one basket, many entrepreneurs prefer to initiate several new ventures, thereby spreading the risk of doing business. In the same way, investors spread their risk by investing in a wide variety of companies, and firms spread their risk by producing a number of products. The principle at stake is a simple and straightforward one: when risks and uncertainties are present, diversify! Diversify your portfolio of stocks and bond holdings, but also diversify your business ventures and product lines. By diversifying, you can play the odds and lower risk of wipeouts, which means you can take on more risks. Net gains can rise from diversifying portfolios because risky projects come with "risk premiums," as many people are risk averse.

Risk taking by banks and homeowners

Discounting for time and risk can be applied to a multitude of economic choice situations. Consider the case of prospective homeowners who seek mortgages from banks. Prospective homeowners vary in their riskiness to banks because people have different income levels, income stabilities, and credit histories. Some prospective homeowners have well-paid government jobs (professors, for example) with a very low probability of ever being laid off; other prospective homeowners have moderate-paying and unstable jobs (construction workers). When granting mortgages, banks have to consider that the loan balances will be paid off over time and that the payments will be more or less secure, which will depend on such factors as overall economic activity and the prices of houses. Banks can be expected to charge an interest rate based on four factors:

1 The mortgage payments will flow in over time. The total payments for interests and principal in nominal dollars must far exceed the dollars loaned out today. The longer the mortgage term, the greater the interest rate to accommodate the discounting of payments further into the future on longer-term mortgages.

2 Inflation can erode the real value of the mortgage payments. Thus, the higher the *expected* inflation rate, the higher the interest rate (indeed, the nominal interest rate should reflect some base interest rate, assuming zero inflation, plus the expected inflation rate).

3 The creditworthiness of the borrower can affect the interest rate charged. Prospective homeowners who have poor credit records will be considered higher risks because they are (as a group) more likely to walk away from their homes and mortgages, leaving the bank with a foreclosed home that may have to be sold at a fire-sale price. The higher the riskiness of borrowers, the greater the banks will discount the value of future payments – which is why such borrowers must suffer a greater interest rate on mortgages. The higher interest rates charged high-risk borrowers do not necessarily make such mortgages more profitable than lower interest rates charged low-risk borrowers.

4 The interest rate a bank will charge on mortgages can be expected to vary with the down payment. The lower the down payment, the smaller the loss borrowers will incur if housing prices fall and borrowers walk away from their houses. The lower the down payment, the greater the chances borrowers will take that they will not be able to make their payments and will walk away from their mortgages. The greater the down payment, on the other hand, the more assured banks can be that borrowers will be conservative in their risk taking and that borrowers will not walk from their homes when housing prices retreat.

Banks will gladly compete for creditworthy borrowers, thus lowering the interest rates of the creditworthy (and improving other terms of the mortgages). As the creditworthiness of borrowers goes down, interests can be expected to go up, which implies a "risk premium" is tacked onto some base (prime) interest rate for the most creditworthy borrowers. As the down payment goes up, the interest rate can be expected to fall because higher down payments indicate a greater means of payment and a greater commitment to making the payments.

Risk taking by banks and the mortgage crisis

Banks can deal with the risks of mortgages because they make a lot of them; that is, they diversify their mortgage portfolios across many borrowers. With risks moderated by volume and diversification, banks can then take on more risks. In fact, banks have a strong incentive to take on risks because of the risk premiums on risky loans. Banks also borrow for short terms from their checking and saving depositors to make long-term mortgage loans. They can make loans equal to, say, 90 percent of their checking and saving deposits, which means they are highly leveraged. It also means that if banks take risks on loans and the loans are paid off, the bank owners get all the gains from the risk premium. If many of the loans go bad, causing banks to go bankrupt, then the government will absorb the downside losses because checking and saving deposits are insured by the FDIC (which suggests that deposit insurance can encourage risk taking by banks).

If banks can bundle their mortgages into "mortgaged-backed securities" and sell them off to investors worldwide (who might consider such securities safe because of the past safe-loan records of banks and because the securities themselves represent a diversified portfolio), banks can use the proceeds from the security sales to originate even more mortgage loans. They can go up the risk ladder, making loans (including subprime mortgages) to less and less creditworthy prospective homeowners whose down payments can dwindle.

Banks and mortgage-backed security buyers might feel safe in their dealings when housing prices are going up, fueled by easy-money policy, the growth in the volume of investment funds going into housing, government subsidies on home purchases, and the belief that housing prices will continue upward. Higher housing prices can mean growing equity for homebuyers, suggesting to banks and mortgage-backed security buyers that mortgages have lower risks, which might be the case so long as the housing price bubble lasts, as it did until sometime in 2005 (Coleman, Lacour-Little, and Vandell 2008). Then, housing prices began to level off and turn south, causing a rise in delinquent mortgages and foreclosures. The increased supply of foreclosed housing caused housing prices to tumble farther. In turn, the safety of mortgage-backed securities was jeopardized and these securities' market prices began to fall. With the growth in home foreclosures, many (not all) banks quickly became insolvent, pushing many banks to the brink of bankruptcy, and beyond.

In brief, we have described the key risk elements of the housing and credit crisis that engulfed much of the advanced world economies in 2008 and beyond, all grounded in the rationality of risk taking when loanable funds are at stake. We will return to the tie between the leverage and risk taking at several junctures in this book.

What rational behavior does *not* mean

The concept of rational behavior often proves bothersome to some noneconomists. Most of the difficulties surrounding this concept arise from a misunderstanding of what rationality means. Common objections include the following:

1 *People do many things that do not work out to their benefit.* Many examples can be cited: A driver speeds and ends up in the hospital; a student cheats, gets caught, and is expelled from school. But saying people behave "rationally" does not mean that they never make mistakes. We can calculate our options with some probability, but we do not have perfect knowledge, nor can we fully control the future. We will make mistakes, but we base our choices on what we *expect* to happen, not on what does happen. We speed because we expect not to crash, and we cheat because we expect not to be caught. Both can be rational behaviors from a narrow cost–benefit perspective.

2 *Rational behavior implies that a person is totally self-centered, doing only things that are of direct personal benefit.* Wrong. Rational behavior need not be selfish or narrowly defined. Most of us get pleasure from seeing others happy, particularly when their happiness is the result of our actions. But whether a person's goal is to improve her own well-being or to help others, she has a motivation to act rationally – make decisions that do the most to accomplish her objectives.

3 *People's behavior is subject to psychological quirks, hang-ups, habits, and impulses.* True enough! Can such behavior be considered "rational"? Why not? Human actions are governed by the constraints of our physical and mental makeup. As is true of our intelligence, our inclination toward aberrant or impulsive behavior is one of those constraints. Such constraints make our decision making less precise and contribute to our mistakes, but they do not prevent our seeking to act as rationally as possible. Moreover, what looks to be impulsive or habitual behavior may actually be the product of some prior rational choice.

The human mind can handle only so much information and make only so many decisions in one day. Consequently, we may attempt to economize on decision making by reducing some behaviors to habit. For example, we might make slightly better decisions if we examined all the information available on the cereal selection at the grocery store every time we bought a box. But such scrutiny could cost more than the benefit of the improved choice. Instead, having found a brand of cereal that we enjoy, we tend to stick with it for a long period of time – to buy it out of habit – and use our limited time on making better decisions that yield bigger payoffs.

Moreover, if people couldn't reduce some behaviors to routines and habits and adopt heuristic techniques, their rationality would likely be impaired as their brains struggled to cope with the overload of sensory data coming from the world about them. Everyone knows the human brain is a fantastic evolutionarily devised organ, but it still has its limits and can easily be choked with too much information and too many decisions made consciously (McKenzie 2009, chapter 8). Indeed, all of economics – and the (perfect) rationality premise itself – is an attempt to enable economists and their students to work within the limits of their mental faculties. Economics as a methodology can be flawed (as behavioral psychologists and economists have stressed), but it can still be a means by which thinking can be improved. (See the Perspective 2 for this chapter on the publisher's website for this book for a longer discussion of the evolutionary origins of cooperative behavior.)

Online Perspective

4 *People do not necessarily maximize their satisfaction.* For instance, many people do not perform to the limit of their abilities. But satisfaction is a question of personal taste. To some individuals, lounging around is an economic good. By consuming leisure, people can increase their welfare. Criticizing the decisions others make is often based on the assumption that others have the same preferences and face the same constraints, including costs, that you do. Anyone who equates rational behavior with what she would do will have no trouble concluding that others are irrational.

5 *People do not always pursue their narrow self-interest. They often have the interests of others at stake.* No economist would limit rational decisions that involved only the utility of decision makers. People often get pleasure from helping others. A person might buy a basketball to practice by himself, but he also could buy the basketball to give to disadvantaged children in an adjoining neighborhood or some far-removed village in a third world country. Andrew Carnegie, the steel tycoon of the nineteenth century, worked hard (some would say ruthlessly) at maximizing profits from his investments, but one of his motivations was to build thousands of community libraries. Microsoft founder Bill Gates made tens of billions through intense efforts to dominate computer software markets, but he is now spending his days trying to find remedies for diseases that are ravaging populations in Africa and elsewhere in the world. Indeed, people today may be hardwired to share what they have, partially because the brain evolved in an age (10,000 or more years ago) when sharing made a great deal of sense, if for no other reason than kills could not be refrigerated. Sharing also can be seen as a form of diversification of risks, since individuals' livelihoods are then dependent on the work of a number of people, not just their own limited efforts (Rubin 2002; McKenzie 2009, chapter 8).

For a different view on the foundations of cooperations, see online Perspective 2, Evolutionary foundations of cooperation.

Online Perspective 2
Evolutionary foundations
of cooperation

Part B Organizational economics and management

The logic of group behavior in business and elsewhere

In following chapters, we introduce the usefulness of markets as means of generating a form of cooperation, through trades, or buying and selling. However, as is evident inside firms, not all human cooperation is through "markets." People often act cooperatively in groups or, as the case may be, in "firms." In this section, we make use of the rationality principles developed in Part A, applying them to the organization of groups and firms. The focus of our attention is on the viability of groups – such as families, cliques, communes, clubs, unions, and professional associations and societies, as well as firms, in which individual participation is voluntary – to cohere and pursue the common interests of the members.

We consider two dominant and conflicting theories of group behavior, both of which take a partial view of complex life and yield insight about groups. They are "the common-interest theory" and "the economic theory" of group behavior, with the economic theory the focus of the rest of the chapter because it is founded on the premise of rational behavior developed in Part A. This economic theory of groups helps us understand why firms are organized the way they are and why owners and workers alike can share a common interest in firms employing "tough bosses."

Common-interest logic of group behavior

All theories of group behavior begin by recognizing the multiplicity of forces which affect group members and, therefore, groups. This is especially true of what we term the *common-interest theory*. Many present-day sociologists, political scientists, and psychologists generally share this point of view, which has been prominent at least since the time of Aristotle in the fourth century BC. The determinants of group behavior most often singled out are the "leadership quality" of specific group members and the need among group members for "affiliation," "security," "recognition," "social status," or money. Groups such as clubs or unions form so that members can achieve or satisfy a want that they could not satisfy as efficiently through individual action. All these considerations are instrumental in affecting "group cohesion," which, in turn, affects the "strength" of the group and its ability to compete with other groups for the same objectives. From the perspective of this theory, when people join firms, they accept the firm's objective and pursue it because everyone else wants the same thing, leading to self-enforcing group cohesion.

The common-interest theory views the "group" as an organic whole, much like an individual, as opposed to a collection of individuals whose separate actions appear to be "group action." According to the theory, the group has a life of its own that is to a degree independent of the individuals who comprise it. Herbert Spencer, a nineteenth-century sociologist, often described the group as a "social organism" or as a "superorganic" entity (Spencer 1896). It was probably the social-organism view of groups that Karl Marx had in mind when he wrote of the "class struggle" and predicted that the proletariat class would bring down "bourgeois capitalism" and, in its place, erect a communist society. Aristotle probably had the same view of groups in mind when he wrote, "Man is by nature a political animal."

Two major reasons are given for viewing groups as social organisms. First, a group consists of a mass of *interdependencies*, which connect the individuals in the group. Without the interdependencies, there would be only isolated individuals, and the term "group" would have no meaning. Individuals in groups are like the nodes of a spider's web. The spider's web is constructed on these nodes, and the movements in one part of the web can be transmitted to all other parts. Similar to the process of synergism in biology, the actions of individuals within a group combine to form a force that is greater than the sum of the forces generated by individuals isolated from one another. The group must, so the argument goes, be thought of as more than the sum total of its individuals. This argument is often used to arouse support for labor unions, for example. Union leaders argue that unions can get higher wage increases for all workers than individual workers can obtain by acting independently. The reason is that union leaders efficiently coordinate the efforts of all. Environmental groups make essentially the same argument: with well-placed lobbyists, the environmental group can have a greater political impact than all the individuals they represent could have by writing independent letters to their representatives at different times.

Second, groups tend to emerge because they satisfy some interest shared by all the group's members. Because all share this "common interest," individuals have an intrinsic incentive to work with others to pursue that interest, sharing the costs as they work together. Aristotle wrote, "Men journey together with a view to particular advantage" (*Ethics*, 1160a) and Arthur Bentley (1870–1957), recognized as an intellectual father of contemporary political sciences and group theorist, mused, "There is no group without its interest ... The group and the interest are not separate ... If we try to take the group without the interest, we simply have nothing at all" (Bentley 1967, 211–13).

Having observed that a common interest can be shared by all of a group's members, the adherents of this theory of group behavior argue that a group can, with slight modification, be treated as an individual, meaning that the group can maximize its well-being. The implicit assumption is made that this will be true of large as well as small groups. This latter deduction prompts many economists to take issue with this approach to analysis of group behavior.

The economic logic of group behavior

Mancur Olson (1932–98), on whose (1971) work this section largely rests, agrees that the "common interest" can be influential and is very important in motivating behavior – but mainly the behavior of members of small groups. However, he, like so many other economists, insists that a group must be looked upon as a composite of rational individuals as opposed to an anthropomorphic whole, and that the common interest, which can be so effective in motivating members of small groups, can be impotent in motivating members of large groups: "Unless there is coercion in large groups ... *rational self-interested individuals will not act to achieve their common or group interest*" (Olson 1971, 2, emphasis in the original). Furthermore, he contends, "These points hold true when there is unanimous agreement in a group about the common goal and the methods of achieving it" (1971, 2). To understand this theory, we first examine the propositions upon which it is founded, and then consider some qualifications.

Basic propositions

Using economic analysis, people are assumed to be as rational in their decision to join a group (a firm or club) as they are toward doing anything else; they will join a group if the benefits of doing so are greater than the costs they must bear. These costs and benefits, like all others relevant to any other act, must be discounted by the going interest on borrowed funds to account for any time delay in the incurrence of the costs and receipt of any benefits and by the probability that the costs and benefits will be realized.

There are several direct, private benefits to belonging to groups, such as companionship, security, recognition, and social status. A person also may belong to a group for no other reason than to receive mail from it and, in that small way, to feel important. A group may serve as an outlet for our altruistic or charitable feelings. If by "common interest" we mean a collection of these types of *private benefits*, it is

A **private good** is any good – or service – the benefits of which are received exclusively by the purchaser.

easy to see how they can motivate group behavior. Entrepreneurs can emerge to "sell" these types of private benefits, as they do in the case of private golf clubs or WeightWatchers. The group action is then, basically, a market phenomenon – that is, based in straightforward exchange of **private goods**.

However, the central concern of this theory is a "common interest" that is separate and detached from the diverse private interests of members of the group. The problem arises because the public, or common, benefits that transcend the entire group cannot be provided by the market, and can be obtained only by some form of *collective action*. That is, a group of people must band together to change things from what they would otherwise be. Examples include the common interest of an environmental group in getting antipollution legislation passed; the interest of labor unions to secure higher wages and better fringe benefits than could be obtained by the independent actions of laborers; the interest of students to resist tuition increases, etc. These are examples of the common interest being a **public** (or collective) **good**, as distinguished from a private good.

A **public good** is a good – or service – the benefits of which are shared by all members of the relevant group if the good is provided or consumed by anyone.

Small groups

Small groups are not without their problems in pursuing the "common interest" of their members. They have a problem of becoming organized, holding together, and ensuring that everyone contributes her part to the group's common interest. This point is relevant to Fred and Harry's (or Crusoe and Friday's) problems of setting up a social contract considered in chapter 1, and it can be understood in terms of all those little things that we can do with friends and neighbors but that will go undone because of the problems associated with having two or three people come together for the "common good." For example, it may be in the common interest of three neighbors – Fred, Harry, and now Judy – for all to rid their yards of dandelions. If one person does it, and the other two do not, the person who removes the dandelions may find his yard full of them the next year because of seeds from the other two yards.

Even though Fred, Harry, and Judy may not ever agree to work out their common problem (or interest) cooperatively, there are several things that make it more likely that a small group will cooperate than a large group. In a small group everyone can know everyone else. What benefits or costs may arise from an individual's action are spread over just a few people and, therefore, the effect felt by any one person can be significant. (Fred knows that there is a reasonably high probability that what he does to eliminate dandelions from the border of his property affects Harry's and Judy's welfare.) If the individual providing the public good is concerned about the welfare

[handwritten margin note: fewer people to share the benefit w/ therefore more benefit per person]

of those within his group and receives personal satisfaction from knowing that he has in some way helped them, he has an incentive to contribute to the common good; and we emphasize that *before the common good can be realized, individuals must have some motivation for contributing to it.* Furthermore, so-called "free riders" are easily detected in a small group. (Harry can tell with relative ease when Fred is not working on, or has not worked on, the dandelions in his yard.) If one person tries to let the others shoulder his share, the absence of his contribution will be detected with a reasonably high probability. Others can then bring social pressure (accompanied by the sting of a cost) to bear to encourage (if not force) him to live up to his end of the bargain. The enforcement costs are low because the group is small. There are many ways to let a neighbor know you are displeased with some aspect of his behavior.

Finally, in small groups, an individual shirking her responsibilities can sometimes be excluded from the group if she does not contribute to the common good (although this would be difficult in the dandelion example) and joins the group merely to free ride on the efforts of others. In larger groups, such as nations, exclusion is usually more difficult (more costly) and, therefore, less likely.

The problem of organizing "group behavior" to serve the common interest has been a problem for almost all groups, even the utopian communities that sprang up during the nineteenth century and in the 1960s. Rosebeth Kanter, in her study of successful nineteenth-century utopian communities, concluded:

The primary issue with which a utopian community must cope in order to have the strength and solidarity to endure is its human organization: how people arrange to do the work that the community needs to survive as a group, and how the group in turn manages to satisfy and involve its members over a long period of time. The idealized version of communal life must be meshed with the reality of the work to be done in the community, involving difficult problems of social organization. In utopia, for instance, who takes out the garbage? (Kanter 1973, 64)

Kanter found that the most successful communities minimized the free-rider problems by restricting entry into the community. They restricted entry by requiring potential members to make commitments to the group. Six "commitment mechanisms" distinguished the successful from the unsuccessful utopias:

1 sacrifice of habits common to the outside world, such as the use of alcohol and tobacco or, in some cases, sex
2 assignment of all worldly goods to the community
3 adoption of rules that would minimize the disruptive effects of relationships between members and nonmembers and that would (through, for example, the wearing of uniforms) distinguish members from nonmembers

4 collective sharing of all property and all communal work

5 submission to public confession and criticism

6 expressed commitment to an identifiable power structure and tradition.

Needless to say, the cost implied in these "commitment mechanisms" would tend to discourage most potential free riders from joining the society. By identifying the boundaries to societies, these mechanisms made exclusion possible. As Kanter points out, the importance of these commitment mechanisms is illustrated by the fact that their breakdown foreshadowed the end of the community.

The cattlemen's associations formed during the nineteenth century suggest other means of bringing about collective behavior on the part of group members. At that time, cattle were allowed to run free over the ranges of the West. The cattlemen had a common interest in preventing a tragedy of the commons – i.e. ensuring that the ranges were not overstocked and overgrazed (remember the discussion of the tragedy of the commons in chapter 1) – and in securing cooperation in rounding up the cattle. To provide for these common interests, cattlemen formed associations that sent out patrols to keep out intruders and that were responsible for the roundups. Any cattleman who failed to contribute his share toward these ends could be excluded from the association, which generally meant that his cattle were excluded from the roundup or were confiscated by the association if they were rounded up (Dennen 1975).

The family is a small group, which by its very nature is designed to promote the common interest of its members. That common interest may be something called "a happy family life," which is, admittedly, difficult to define. The family obviously does not escape difficulties, given the prevalence of divorces and even more common family feuds. At present its validity as a viable institution is being challenged by many sources; however, it does have several redeeming features that we think will cause it to endure as a basic component of the social fabric. Because of the smallness of the group, contributions made toward the common interest of the family can be shared and appreciated directly. Family members are able, at least in most cases, to know personally what others in the group like and dislike; they can set up an interpersonal cost–benefit structure among themselves that can guide all members toward the common interest. Most collective decisions are also made with relative ease. However, even with all the advantages of close personal contact, the family as a small group often fails to achieve the common interest. Given the frequent failure of the family, realized in divorces or just persistent hostilities, the failure of much larger groups to achieve their expressed common objectives is not difficult to understand.

Large groups

In a large-group setting, the problems of having individual members contribute toward the development of the common interest are potentially much greater. The direct, personal interface that is present in small groups is usually lacking in larger groups; and because of the size of large groups, the public good they produce is spread over such a large number of people that no one sees his actions as having a significant effect on anyone, even themselves. As a result, no one perceives either personal benefits from his contribution, or benefits for others.

Even when an individual can detect benefits from his actions, he must weigh those benefits against the costs he has to incur to achieve them. For a large group, the costs of providing detectable benefits can be substantial. This can occur not only because there are more people to be served by the good but also because large groups are normally organized to provide public goods that are rather expensive to begin with. Police protection, national defense, and schools are examples of very costly public goods provided by large groups. If all people contribute to the public good, the cost to any one person can be slight; but the question confronting the individual is how much he will have to contribute to make his actions detectable, *given what all the others do*.

In the context of a nation (a very large group indeed) suppose there are certain common objectives to which we can all subscribe, such as a specific charitable program. It is, in other words, in our "common interest" to promote this program (by assumption, for purposes of argument). Will people be willing to voluntarily contribute to the federal treasury for the purpose of achieving this goal? Certainly some people will, but many may not. A person may reason that although he agrees with the national objective, or common interest, his contribution will have no detectable effect in achieving it. This explains why compulsory taxes are necessary, and why philanthropic contributions are an almost nonexistent source of revenues for all governments worldwide (Olson 1971, 13).

The general tenor of the argument also applies to contributions that go to organizations such as World Vision, a voluntary charitable organization interested mainly in improving the diets of impoverished people around the world. Many readers of these pages will have been disturbed by scenes of undernourished and malnourished children shown in TV commercials for World Vision. But how many people ever actually contribute so much as a dollar? Needless to say, many do give. They are like Harry, who is willing to dig, voluntarily, some of the weeds from his yard. On the other hand, a very large number of people who have been concerned never make a contribution. There are many reasons for people not giving, and we do not mean to understate the importance of these reasons; we mean only to emphasize that the large-group problem is one significant reason.

True, if all members of a large group make a small contribution toward the common interest, whatever it is, there may be sizable benefits to all within the group. But, again, the problem that must be overcome is the potential lack of *individual* incentives from which the collective behavior must emerge. In large groups, the Prisoner's Dilemma problems we highlighted in talking about a two-member group, Fred and Harry, are ever present and magnified, again because the larger the group, the less detectible are the consequences of individual behavior and the less monitoring of behavior can be done.

Through appropriate organization of group members, the common interest *may* be achieved, even if the membership is large. The organization of a large group can be construed as a public good, and making the organization workable is likely to incur costs for two reasons.

First, there are a large number of people to organize, which means that even if group members are not resistant to being organized, there will be costs associated with getting them together or having them work at the same time for the same objectives.

Second, some individuals may try to free-ride on the efforts of others, which means it will cost more to get people to become members of the group. Further, each free-rider implies a greater burden on the active members of the group. If everyone waits for "the other guy to take the initiative," the group may never be organized.

Organizational costs often prevent students who complain about the instructional quality of the faculty or some other aspect of university life from doing anything about it. The same costs block people who are disgruntled with the two major political parties from forming a party among those who share their views. The probability of getting sufficient support is frequently very low, which is another way of saying the expected costs are high.

The free-rider problem may emerge in the workplace as worker absenteeism for a variety of reasons, including sickness, real or feigned (Barham and Begum 2005, 157). The Confederation of British Industry found that, in 2006, the British economy lost 175 million days of work from absenteeism, which continued to escalate beyond what could be attributable to understandable reasons, such as illness.[2] Not surprisingly, the rate of absence for sickness was higher in the public sector than in the private sector (perhaps attributable in part to the pressure of private firms to avoid losses and make a profit). Consistent with the "logic of collective action" as developed in this chapter, another study found that the rate of absences for illness during the survey week was 29 percent higher in private firms with 500 workers than in firms with fewer than twenty-five workers (Barham and Begum 2005, 154).

Economist Stephen Levitt and journalist Stephen Dubner (2005) report on their findings from the sales data collected by Paul Feldman, who sold bagels on the "honor plan" for many years in Washington, DC. Feldman would leave bagels early in the morning at gathering places for office workers. The workers were initially

---

[2] As reported by the consulting firm of Smith & Williamson in 2008, with the report accessed on January 7, 2009 from www.mondaq.com/article.asp?articleid=52770.

asked to leave their payments in open baskets. Because the money often was taken from the baskets, Feldman made wooden boxes with slits in the top for depositing payments. Initially, in the early 1980s, when he started his bagel business, Feldman suffered a 10 percent loss of bagels (that is, he received no payment for 10 percent of the bagels he left). After 1992, his losses of bagels began a slight but steady rise. By 2001, he reached 13 percent over all companies, only to go back down to 11 percent during the two years following 9/11. (Levitt and Dubner speculate that the 15 percent decline in the nonpayment rate possibly could be attributed to the fact that many of his DC customers were connected to national security with a heightened sense for doing what was right.) Relevant to the "logic of collective action," Feldman found that honesty measured by payments received for bagels was marginally affected by firm size: "An office with a few dozen employees generally outpays by 3 to 5 percent an office with a few hundred employees" (Levitt and Dubner 2005 and 2006, 49). We have to suspect that the difference in the payment rate between small and large offices might be greater were the required payment higher than the price of a bagel.

The relevance of market prices in large-group settings

Of course, because of scarcity, people everywhere share the common interest of ensuring that the available resources are used efficiently, which means for those things people desire most and in the most cost-effective manner. If resources are used efficiently, most wants can be satisfied than otherwise. How do you get large groups of consumers to contribute to the common good of efficiently using resources through their buy decisions? One means of encouraging conservation and smart purchases in large-group settings is the pricing system. As to be discussed in chapter 3, when electricity or gasoline becomes scarce and the market supply contracts, the prices of those products rise, and consumers are induced to curb their consumption of those goods by reducing their purchases for those uses that are valued more highly than the higher prices. Restrict prices from rising when products become more scarce, and consumers will fall into the large-group trap: they will continue to buy as if nothing had happened to the scarcity of the products. Consumers can reason that their continued consumption at old levels will have no impact on the overall availability of the product, which means they will not conserve when the greater scarcity of the good indicates that they should.

In December 2003, for a variety of reasons, California suffered through a serious reduction in the supply of electricity, with threatened "brownouts." People's common interest was to conserve on electricity consumption, but government authorities held the price of electricity at its old level. The result was to be expected: very little in the way of conservation. People lit up their Christmas trees and other decorations as if nothing had happened. However, when oil supplies dropped sharply in the first half of 2008, the average price of gasoline in the country soared in the state to nearly $5 a gallon, and guess what happened? People did what was really in their common interest; they curbed their consumption of gasoline in a multitude of large ways (driving less and parking their large SUVs and RVs) and small ways (reducing the frequency with which they accelerated rapidly when stoplights turned green).

Qualifications to the economic theory

Obviously, there are many cases in which people in rather large groups appear to be trying to accomplish things that are in the common interest of the membership. Early in the civil rights struggle, the League of Women Voters pushed hard for passage of the Equal Rights Amendment to the Constitution; labor unions work for minimum wage increases; the American Medical Association lobbies for legislation that is in the common interest of a large number of doctors; and many charitable groups work fairly effectively for the "public interest." Several of the possible explanations for this observed behavior force us to step outside the standard economic arguments about public goods.

First, as Immanuel Kant, an eighteenth-century philosopher said, people can place value on the *act* itself as distinguished from the results or consequences of the act (1781). The *act* of making a charitable contribution, which can be broadly defined to include picking up trash in public areas or holding the door for someone with an armful of packages, may have a value in and of itself. This is true whether the effects of the act are detectable to the individual making the charitable contribution or not. To the extent that people behave in this way, the public good theory loses force. Notice, however, that Olson, in formulating his argument, focused on rational, *economic man* (or woman) as opposed to the *moral man* (or woman) envisioned by Kant. We expect that as the group becomes larger, a greater effort will be made to instill people with the belief that the *act* itself is important.

Second, when the *Homo sapiens* brain was forming eons ago, people lived in small to moderate-size groups, with maybe 25 to 150 members, for purposes of protection, survival, and sharing shelter and food supplies. The human brain can be hardwired to cooperate with other "tribe" members, perhaps inclined to think of the *relevant* group as small, no matter its actual size, which can lead to viable voluntary cooperative behavior in groups larger than the economic theory of groups would suggest.

Third, the contribution that a person has to make in group settings is often so slight that, even though the private benefits are small, the contribution to the common interest is also small and can be a rational policy course. This may explain, for example, student membership in groups such as a local Chamber of Commerce. All one has to do in many situations is to show up at an occasional meeting and make a small dues payment. Further, the private benefits of being with others at the meetings and finding out what the plans are for the association can be sufficient incentive to motivate limited action in the common interest.

Fourth, all group members may not share equally the benefits received from promotion of the common interest. One or more persons may receive a sizable portion of the total benefits and, accordingly, be willing to provide the public good, at least up to some limit. Many businessmen are willing to participate in local politics or to support advertising campaigns to promote their community as a recreational area. Although a restaurant owner may believe that the entire community will benefit economically from an influx of tourists, he is surely aware that a share of these benefits will accrue to him. Businessmen may also support such community efforts because of implied threats of being socially ostracized.

Fifth, large organizations can be broken down into smaller groups. Because of the personal contact with the smaller units, the common interest of the unit can be realized. In promoting the interest of the small unit to which they belong, people can promote the common interest of the large group. The League of Women Voters is broken down into small community clubs that promote interests common to other League clubs around the country. The national Chamber of Commerce has local chapters. The Lions Club collectively promotes programs to prevent blindness and to help the blind; members do this through a highly decentralized organizational structure.

Quite often, a multiplicity of small groups is actually responsible for what may appear to be the activity of a large group. Large firms almost always divide their operations into divisions and then smaller departments. The decentralization that is prevalent among voluntary and business groups tends to support the economic view of groups.

Sixth, large groups may be viable because the group organizers sell their members a service and use the profits from sales to promote projects that are in the common interest of the group. The Sierra Club, which is in the forefront of the environmental movement, is a rather large group that has members in every part of North America. The group receives voluntary contributions from members and nonmembers alike to research and lobby for environmental issues. However, it also sells a number of publications and offers a variety of environmentally related tours for its members. From these activities, it secures substantial resources to promote the common interest of its membership. The American Economic Association (AEA) has several thousand members. However, most economists do not belong to the AEA for what they can do for it; they join primarily to receive its journal and to be able to tell others that they belong – both of which are private benefits. The AEA also provides economists with information on employment opportunities.

Seventh, the basic argument for any group is that people can accomplish more through groups than they can through independent action. This means that there are potential benefits to be reaped (or, some may say, "skimmed off") by anyone who is willing to bear some of the cost of developing and maintaining the organization. A business firm is fundamentally a *group* of workers and stockholders interested in producing a good (a public good, to them). They have a common interest in seeing a good produced that will sell at a profit. The entrepreneur is essentially a person who organizes a group of people into a production unit; she overcomes all the problems associated with trying to get a large number of people to work in their common interest by providing workers with private benefits – that is, she pays them for their contribution to the production of the good. The entrepreneur-manager can be viewed as a person who is responsible for reducing any tendency of workers to avoid their responsibilities to the large-group firm.

The general point that emerges from our discussion of incentives within "small" and "large" groups is that, as a group grows in size, shared values can become progressively inconsequential in motivating people to act cooperatively. This means that as a group grows, alternative mechanisms – incentives and organizational and financial structures – must be developed to supplant the power of shared values in achieving the shared goals (with the shared goals including such matters as firm profitability, worker job security, social and environmental ends). Effective management can be construed as finding ways to overcome the large-group problems, which often reduce to Prisoner's Dilemmas.

Of course, *disincentives* that discourage people from doing anything – working or contributing to a group's welfare – can be as important for management and public policies as *incentives*. Online, we provide several additional readings that complement the analyses developed in this chapter:

- In online Reading 2.1 for this chapter, we show how disincentives can affect, and even limit, public benefits going to disadvantaged groups.
- In online Reading 2.2, we show how rational-behavior precepts can be used to conceptualize optimum management snooping on workers who may be using work time to play games and shop online.
- In online Reading 2.3, we explain how the varying "risk aversion" across people helps explain why firms tend to be owned by capital investors, not workers.
- Finally, in Reading 2.4, you will find an explanation from economists and political scientists, specializing in "public choice economics" (or the application of economic theory to politics), for why so few eligible voters vote and why many voters are ill-informed about prominent policy issues.

Overcoming Prisoner's Dilemmas through tough bosses

What does the economic theory of group behavior – including the underlying precepts of rationality – have to do with the direct interest of MBA students who seek to run businesses and direct the work of others? In a word, "plenty." Throughout the rest of this book, we demonstrate how the "logic" is central to how competitive markets (and cartels) work (or don't work), and we discuss a multitude of ways to apply the "logic" directly to management problems.

For now, we can stress a maxim that emerges from the economic view of group behavior: people often rationally spurn tough jobs, unless compensated for the personal cost and displeasure involved in them. Being a tough boss is one such job that is difficult, but a boss who isn't tough might not be worth much. And because tough bosses are valuable and lenient bosses are not, existing organizational arrangements are likely to discipline pain-avoiding bosses to ensure that they impose strict discipline on the workforce. Competition will press firms to hire tough bosses, and, as we shall show in this chapter, the owners of the firm, or their manager-agents, not workers, will tend to be the bosses. That is to say, owners or their agents will tend to boss workers, not the other way around, for the simple reason that worker-bosses are not likely to survive in competitive markets. Workers may not like tough-bossed firms but, as we explain, workers can be better off with tough bosses – and will rationally seek to work in firms that employ tough bosses.

Take this job and …

Though probably overstated, common wisdom has it that workers do not like their bosses, much less tough bosses. The sentiment expressed in Johnny Paycheck's well-known country song "Take This Job and Shove It" could be directed only at a boss. Bosses are also the butts of much humor. There is the old quip that boss spelled backward is "Double SOB."

If it were not for an element of truth contained in them, such comments would be hopelessly unfunny. Bosses are often unpopular with those they boss. But tough bosses have much in common with foul-tasting medicines for the sick: you don't like them, but you want them anyway because they are good for you. Workers may not like tough bosses, but they willingly put up with them because tough bosses mean higher productivity, more job security, and better wages.

The productivity of workers is an important factor in determining their wages. More productive workers receive higher wages than less productive workers. Firms would soon go bankrupt in competitive markets if they paid workers more than their productivity is worth, but firms would soon lose workers if they paid them less.

Many things, of course, determine how productive workers are. The amount of physical capital they work with, and the amount of experience and education

Table 2.1 **The inclination to shirk on the job**

		Other workers		
		None shirk	Some shirk	All shirk
Jane	Don't shirk	100	75	25
	Shirk	125	100	30

(human capital) they bring to their jobs are two extremely important, and commonly discussed, factors in worker productivity.

But how well the workers in a firm function together *as a team* is also important. An individual worker can have all the training, capital, and diligence needed to be highly productive, but productivity will suffer unless other workers pull their weight by properly performing their duties. The productivity of each worker is crucially dependent upon the efforts of *all* workers in the vast majority of firms.

Although each worker wants other workers to work hard to maintain the general productivity of the firm, each worker recognizes that (at least in very large firms) her contribution to the general productivity is small. By shirking some responsibilities, she receives all the benefits from the extra leisure, but suffers only a very small portion of the productivity loss, which is spread over everyone in the firm. She suffers, of course, from some of the productivity loss when other workers choose to loaf on the job, but she knows that the decisions others make are independent of whether she shirks or not. And if everyone else shirks, little good will result for her, or for the firm, from diligent effort on her part. So no matter what she believes that other workers will do, the rational thing for her to do is to capture the private benefits from shirking at practically every opportunity. With all other workers facing the same incentives, the strong tendency is for shirking on the job to reduce the productivity and the wages of all workers in the firm, and quite possibly to threaten their jobs by threatening the firm's viability. The situation just described is another example of the general problem of the logic of group behavior – or, more precisely, a form of the Prisoner's Dilemma that we considered earlier.

Game theory: Prisoner's Dilemma games in the workplace

Consider a slightly different form of the Prisoner's Dilemma that is described in the matrix in table 2.1, which shows the payoff to Jane for different combinations of shirking on her part and that of her fellow workers. No matter what Jane believes others will do, the biggest payoff to her (in terms of the value of her expected financial compensation and leisure time) comes from shirking. Clearly, she hopes that everyone else works responsibly so that general labor productivity and the

Table 2.2 **Shirking in large worker groups**

		Other workers		
		None shirk	Some shirk	All shirk
Jane	Don't shirk	100	75	25
	Shirk	95	70	0

firm's profits will be high despite her lack of effort, in which case she receives the highest possible payoff that any one individual can receive, 125. Unfortunately for Jane, all workers face payoff possibilities similar to the ones she faces (and to simplify the discussion, we assume that everyone faces the same payoffs). So, everyone will shirk, which means that everyone will end up with a payoff of 30, which is the lowest possible collective payoff for workers.

Workers are faced with self-destructive incentives when their work environment is described by the shirking version of the Prisoner's Dilemma. It is clearly desirable for workers to extricate themselves from this Prisoner's Dilemma. But how?

In an abstract sense, the only way to escape this Prisoner's Dilemma is somehow to alter the payoffs for shirking. More concretely, this requires workers to agree to subject themselves collectively to tough penalties that no one individual would unilaterally be willing to accept. Although no one likes being subjected to tough penalties, everyone can benefit from having those penalties imposed on everyone, including themselves.

The situation here is analogous to many other situations we find ourselves in. For example, consider the problem of controlling pollution that was briefly mentioned in chapter 1. Although each person would find it convenient to freely pollute the environment, when everyone is free to do so, we each lose more from the pollution of others than we gain from our own freedom to pollute. So, we accept restrictions on our own polluting behavior in return for having restrictions imposed on that of others. Polluting and shirking may not often be thought of as analogous, but they are. One harms the natural environment and the other harms the work environment.

Workers may not like bosses who carefully monitor their behavior, spot the shirkers, and ruthlessly penalize them, but they want such bosses. The penalties on shirkers must be sufficiently harsh to change the payoffs in table 2.1 and eliminate the Prisoner's Dilemma. If Jane had a boss tough enough to impose 30 units of cost on her (and everyone else) for shirking, her relevant payoff matrix would be transformed into that shown in table 2.2. Jane may not like her new boss, but she would cease to find advantages in shirking. And with a tough boss monitoring all workers, and unmercifully penalizing those who dare shirk,

Jane will find that she is more than compensated because her fellow workers also have quit shirking. Instead of being in an unproductive firm, surrounded by a bunch of other unproductive workers, each receiving a payoff of 30, she will find herself as part of a hard-working, cooperative team of workers, each receiving a payoff of 100.

The common perception is that bosses hire workers, and in most situations this is what appears to happen. Bosses see benefits that can be realized only by having workers, and so they hire them. But because it is also true that workers see benefits that can be realized only from having a boss, it is not unreasonable to think of workers hiring a boss, and preferably a tough one.

[See online Video Module 2.3 Monitoring workers]

Actual tough bosses

Even highly skilled and disciplined workers can benefit from having a "boss" who helps them overcome the shirking that can be motivated by the Prisoner's Dilemma. Consider the experience related by Gordon E. Moore, a highly regarded scientist and one of the founders of Intel, Inc. Before Intel, Moore and seven other scientists entered a business venture that failed because of what Moore described as "chaos." Because of the inability of the group of scientists to act as an effective team in this initial venture, Moore said that "The first thing we had to do was to hire our own boss – essentially hire someone to run the company" (Moore 1994).

Pointing to stories and actual cases where the workers hire their boss is instructive in emphasizing the importance of tough bosses to workers. But the typical situation finds the boss hiring the workers, not the other way around. We will explain later why this is the case, but we can lay the groundwork for such an explanation by recognizing that our discussion of the advantages of having tough bosses has left an important question unanswered. An important job of bosses is to monitor workers and impose penalties on those who shirk, but how do we make sure that the bosses don't shirk themselves? How can you organize a firm to make sure that bosses are tough?

A boss's work is not easy or pleasant. It requires serious effort to keep close tabs on a group of workers. It is not always easy to know when a worker is really shirking or just taking a justifiable break. A certain amount of what appears to be shirking at the moment has to be allowed for workers to be fully productive over the long run. There is always some tension between reasonable flexibility and credible predictability in enforcing the rules, and it is difficult to strike the best balance. Too much flexibility can lead to an undisciplined workforce, and too much rigidity can destroy worker morale. Also, quite apart from the difficulty of knowing when to impose tough penalties on a worker is the unpleasantness of doing so. Few people enjoy disciplining those they work with by giving them unsatisfactory progress reports, reducing their pay, or dismissing them. The easiest thing for a boss to do is not to be tough on shirkers. But the boss who is not tough on shirkers is also a shirker.

A boss can also be tempted to form an alliance with a group of workers who provide favors in return for letting them shirk more than other workers. Such a group improves its well-being at the expense of the firm's productivity, but most of this cost can be shifted to those outside the alliance.

Of course, a firm could always hire someone whose job it is to monitor the boss, but two problems with this solution immediately come to mind. One, the second boss will be even more removed from workers than the first boss, and so will have an even more difficult time knowing whether the workers are being properly disciplined. Second, and even more important, who is going to monitor the second boss and penalize him or her for shirking? Who is going to monitor the monitor? This approach leads to an infinite regress, which means it leads nowhere. A solution to the problem lies in the observation that workers should want their bosses to be rewarded for remaining tough in spite of all the temptations to concede in particular circumstances for particular workers.

Jack Welch, the former chief executive officer (CEO) of General Electric (GE), is an example of the central point of this "organizational economics and management" section because he surely qualifies as a tough boss. Indeed, *Fortune* once named Welch "America's Toughest Boss" (Tichy and Sherman 1993). Welch earned his reputation by cutting payrolls, closing plants, and demanding more from those that remained open. Needless to say, these decisions were not always popular with workers at GE. But today, GE is one of America's most profitable companies, creating far more wealth for the economy and opportunities for its workers than it would have if the tough and unpopular decisions had not been made. In Welch's words: "Now people come to work with a different agenda: They want to win against the competition, because they know that ... customers are their only source of job security. They don't like weak managers, because they know that the weak managers of the 1970s and 1980s cost millions of people their jobs" (Tichy and Sherman 1993, 92).

Game theory: the battle of the sexes

In the previous section we pointed out how workers could benefit from tough bosses who help them overcome the Prisoner's Dilemma that workers face. The Prisoner's Dilemma is an example of the type of situation that is analyzed by *game theory* – the study of how people make decisions when the benefit each person realizes from the decision she makes depends on the decisions others make in response. But there are "games" besides the Prisoner's Dilemma that also explain how managers can be useful as tough bosses or tough leaders. An interesting game that falls into this category is commonly called the "battle of the sexes." The name of this game comes

Table 2.3 The battle of the sexes

		Tom	
		Shakespeare in Love	*Saving Private Ryan*
Marsha	*Shakespeare in Love*	100 \ 75	60 \ 60
	Saving Private Ryan	40 \ 40	75 \ 100

from conflict between the sexes, but it illustrates a more general conflict that is best resolved by managers who can make tough decisions.

Let's consider first the conflict between the sexes. Tom and Marsha have just started dating and enjoy each other's company. Both also like going to the movies, preferably together. But they have different tastes in films – Marsha prefers romantic films while Tom prefers war films. They are planning to go out on Saturday night, but Marsha wants to see *Shakespeare in Love* and Tom wants to see *Saving Private Ryan*. The value each receives from going out on Saturday night depends on what movie he/she sees and whether he/she sees it with Marsha/Tom, or alone. The payoffs for Tom and Marsha are given in table 2.3, which shows the different possible outcomes for Saturday, with the first number in each box representing Marsha's payoff and the second number representing Tom's payoff. As shown, if both go to *Shakespeare in Love*, Marsha will receive a payoff of 100 and Tom gets a payoff of 75. If both go to *Saving Private Ryan*, Marsha receives a payoff of 75 and Tom gets the 100 payoff. If each goes to their choice of movies, but goes alone, then both receive a payoff of 60. And in the highly unlikely event that they each go alone to the other's favorite movie (but in the throes of romance, men and women do strange things) each will receive a payoff of 40.

As opposed to the Prisoner's Dilemma game, in which the best choice for each (the noncooperative choice) is the same no matter what the other is expected to do, in the battle-of-the-sexes game, the best choice for each varies, depending on what the other person is expected to do. For example, if Marsha can convince Tom that she is definitely going to see *Shakespeare in Love*, then the best choice for Tom is to see the same movie and get a payoff of 75 instead of 60. But it may be difficult for Marsha to convince Tom that she is going to her preferred movie, come what may. Tom knows that if he can convince Marsha that he is definitely going to see *Saving Private Ryan*, then that will be Marsha's best choice. So making a credible commitment may be difficult for both Marsha and Tom.

Further aggravating the problem is that both may decide that it is worth going to a movie alone (reducing their payoff by 15 this time) rather than acquiescing to the stubbornness of the other. By doing so, each can hope to establish a reputation for making credible threats that will improve the chances of getting his/her way in the future. The result can be a lot of time and emotion expended negotiating over which movie to attend when the most important thing is for both to attend the same movie – something that may not happen despite costly negotiation.

Workers routinely confront their own battle-of-the-sexes problems on the job, although these problems have nothing to do with gender-based preferences or the movies. Workplace decisions often have to be made about issues for which workers have different preferences, but that will yield the greatest payoff to all workers if they all accept the same decision. For example, some workers will prefer to start working at 6:30 a.m., have a one-hour lunch, and leave at 3:30 p.m. Others will prefer to start at 7:00 a.m., take no lunch, and leave at 3:00 p.m. Others will prefer to start at 10:00 a.m., take a two-hour lunch, and leave at 8:00 p.m. Indeed, there will probably be as many different preferences as there are workers, with these preferences changing from day to day. But typically, it is best for everyone in a firm to be in at the same time every workday.

Some may prefer to resolve such individual differences "democratically" in these situations, with everyone being able to make their case until an agreement on a decision emerges, with this consensus decision most likely to be the best one. But agreement may never emerge and even if it did, the cost would probably far exceed the benefit from a better decision. At some point fairly early in the discussion, the best approach is for a manager to assume leadership and make a decision on the starting time for work that everyone has to accept. There are a lot of characteristics that go into making a good leader, and certainly one of the first is the ability to make good decisions. And obviously it's better to have a leader who makes good decisions than one who doesn't. But keep in mind that often the most important thing in making a good decision is not the decision that is made, but getting everyone to accept it. It is hard to argue that the decision to have everyone drive on the right-hand side of the road is better than having everyone drive on the left-hand side. Either decision is a good one as long as everyone abides by it. And getting everyone to accept a decision can require a tough-minded leader who imposes his/her will on others. Ideally, leaders will get the job done through gentle persuasion rather than bull-headed arrogance. But if the former doesn't work, it's nice to have the latter in reserve.

[See online Video Module 2.4 Battle of the sexes]

The role of the residual claimant in abating Prisoner's Dilemmas in large groups

Every good boss understands that he or she has to be more than just "tough." A boss needs to be a good "leader," a good "coach," and a good "nursemaid," as well as many other things. The good boss inspires allegiance to the firm and the commonly shared corporate goals. Every good boss wants workers to seek the cooperative solutions in the various Prisoner's Dilemmas that invariably arise in the workplace. Having said that, however, a good boss will invariably be called upon to make some pretty tough decisions, mainly because the boss usually stands astride the interests of the owners above and the workers below. The lesson of this section should not be forgotten: "Woe to the boss who simply seeks to be a nice guy." But firms must structure themselves so that bosses will *want* to be tough, but appropriately tough. How can that be done?

In many firms, the boss is also the owner. The owner/boss is someone who owns the physical capital (such as the building, the land, the machinery, and the office furniture), provides the raw materials and other supplies used in the business, and hires and supervises the workers necessary to convert those factors of production into goods and services. In return for assuming the responsibility of paying for all of the productive inputs, including labor, the owner earns the right to all of the revenue generated by those inputs.

Economists refer to the owners as **residual claimants**. As the boss, the owner is responsible for monitoring the workers to see whether each one of them is properly performing her job, and for applying the appropriate penalties (or encouragement) if they aren't. By combining the roles of ownership and boss in the same individual, a boss is created who, as a residual claimant, has a powerful incentive to work hard at being a tough boss.

> **Residual claimants** are people who have legal claim to any residual (commonly referred to as profits) that remains from the sales revenue after all the expenses have been paid.

The employees who have the toughest bosses are likely to be those who work for residual claimants. But the residual claimants probably have the toughest boss of all – themselves. There is a lot of truth to the old saying that when you run your own business, you are the toughest boss you will ever have. Small business owners commonly work long and hard because there is a very direct and immediate connection between their efforts and their income. When they are able to obtain more output from their workers, they increase the residual they are able to claim for themselves. A residual claimant boss may be uncomfortable disciplining those who work for her, or dismissing someone who is not doing the job, and indeed may choose to ignore some shirking. But in this case the cost of the shirking is concentrated on the boss who allows it, rather than diffused over a large number of people who individually have little control over the shirking and little motivation to do anything about it even if they did. So with a boss who is also a residual claimant, there is little danger that shirking on the part of workers will be allowed to get out of hand.

When a residual claimant organizes productive activity, all resources – not just labor – tend to be employed more productively than when the decision makers are not residual claimants. The contrast between government agencies and private firms managed by owner/bosses, or proprietors, is instructive. Examples abound of the panic that seizes the managers of public agencies at the end of the budget year if their agencies have not spent all of the year's appropriations. The managers of public agencies are not claimants to the difference between the value their agency creates and the cost of creating the value. This does not mean that public agencies have no incentive to economize on resources, only that their incentives to do so are impaired by the absence of direct, close-at-hand residual claimants. The problem is that taxpayers gain little to nothing by incurring the personal costs associated with closely monitoring the public agencies (Tullock 1972, chapter 7).

To make the point differently, assume that as a result of your management training you become an expert on maximizing the efficiency of trash collection services. In one nearby town the trash is picked up by the municipal sanitation department, financed out of tax revenue and headed by a government official on a fixed salary. In another nearby town the trash is picked up by a private firm, financed by direct consumer charges and owned by a local businessperson who is proud of her loyal workers and impressive fleet of trash trucks. By applying linear programming techniques to the routing pattern, you discover that each trash service can continue to provide the same pickup with half the number of trucks and personnel currently being used.

Who is going to be most receptive to your consulting proposal to streamline their trash collection – the bureaucratic manager who never misses an opportunity to tell of his devotion to the taxpaying public, or the proprietor who is devoted to her workers and treasures her trash trucks?

On the other hand, the proprietor will hire you as a consultant as soon as she becomes convinced that your ideas will allow her to lay off half of her workers and sell half of her trucks. The manager who is also a residual claimant can be depended on to economize on resources despite her other concerns. The manager who is not a residual claimant can be depended on to waste resources despite her statements to the contrary.

No matter how cheaply a service is produced, resources have to be employed that could have otherwise been used to produce other things of value. The value of the sacrificed alternative has to be known and taken into account to make sure that the right amount of the service is produced. As a residual claimant, a proprietor not only has a strong motivation to produce a service as cheaply as possible but also has the information and motivation to increase the output of the service only as long as the *additional value generated is greater than the value forgone elsewhere in the economy.*

Having the residual claimant direct resources is, understandably, an organizational arrangement that workers should applaud. The residual claimant can be expected to press all workers to work diligently so that wages, fringes, and job security can be enhanced. Indeed, the workers would be willing to pay the residual claimants to force all workers to apply themselves diligently (which is what workers effectively do); both workers and residual claimants can share in the added productivity from added diligence.

But we have sidestepped in this discussion the issue of why workers aren't typically residual claimants, or owners, of their firms. Why do owners tend to be the capitalists (or providers of investment funds to be used to buy firms' capital, or plant, equipment, and other assets)? Because of space limitations, as noted earlier, we have decided to provide answers to those questions online in Reading 2.3 for this chapter.

Practical lessons for MBAs: profits from optimal shirking

One of the more important lessons from the analysis in this chapter is that size matters in business: as firms expand, shirking can be a growing problem. Firms will have to incur growing monitoring costs with growing firm size, which means that bosses will have to become progressively tougher or incentives will have to overcome workers' inclinations to shirk, which means not doing what they know they are supposed to do. To keep the analysis clear in this chapter, we have discussed shirking as if it were all "bad," always and everywhere a net drain on corporate profits. Hence, the task of managers is, in such a world, relatively simple: eliminate any and all shirking by monitoring and "cracking the corporate whip."

While our approach has been useful to highlight key points, we need to stress before closing the chapter that shirking on the job, at least up to a point, can be viewed as a worker fringe benefit, something that has intrinsic value to workers. To the extent that this is the case, some shirking can actually increase company profits because it leads to a greater supply of good workers willing to work for the firm that allows some shirking and that permits a reduction in the firm's wage rates. The company's lower productivity can (up to a point) be more than offset by its lower total wage bill. Indeed, the workers can also be "better off" with some shirking. This is because the intrinsic value of some shirking on the job can afford them more utility than the additional money wages they could receive if some shirking were not allowed. Shirking up to a point, that is, can be a win–win for both workers and firm owners. The win–win nature of some shirking is obvious in most offices and plants as workers – even highly respected workers – can be seen relaxing around vending machines, gossiping in hallways, and taking unscheduled breaks.

Of course, so long as on-the-job shirking has value to workers, firms would not want to eliminate all shirking even if doing so required them to incur zero monitoring costs. The elimination of shirking could raise the company's wage bill by more than it raises the workers' productivity. In short, as in all things, managers face a complicated problem, one of seeking an *optimum* amount of shirking. That is, they should allow shirking to mount so long as the reduction in the wage bill exceeds the lost productivity. But then, shirking that is mutually beneficial to workers and owners alike is not really "shirking." Accordingly, for the rest of the book, we will relegate "shirking" to those things workers don't do that are not mutually beneficial and, hence, not mutually agreed upon by workers and owners.

Further readings online

Reading 2.1 Disincentives in poverty relief (along with the accompanying online video module)

Reading 2.2 Management snooping

Reading 2.3 Risk taking, risk aversion, and firm ownership

Reading 2.4 "The mathematics of voting and political ignorance," by Gordon Tullock

The bottom line

The key takeaways from chapter 2 are the following:

1 The concept of rational behavior means that the individual has alternatives, can order those alternatives on the basis of preference, and can act consistently on that basis. The rational individual will also choose those alternatives whose expected benefits exceed their expected costs.

2 Traditionally, economics has focused on the activities of business firms, and much of this book is devoted to exploring human behavior in a market setting. However, the concept of rational behavior can be applied to other activities, from politics and government to family life and leisure pursuits. Any differences in our behavior can be ascribed to differences in our preferences and in the institutional settings, or constraints, within which we operate.

3 Rational behavior implies that people have choices, and choices imply that there is a cost to anything.

4 All choices involve cost–benefit calculations.

5 The timing and riskiness of options will affect their present value. The more distant into the future benefits will be received or costs incurred, the lower their present values. The more risky options are, the greater their cost (or the lower their net value).

6 The importance of the "cause" or the groups' "common interest" can significantly affect the willingness of group members to cohere and pursue the common interest of the membership. However, a "cause" or "common interest" can more effectively motivate a "small" group than a "large" group. This suggests that, given other considerations, an increase in group size beyond some point can have an adverse effect on the motivation that group members have to pursue their group's common interest.

7   The logic of collective action can explain the growth in employee shirking and the misuse of resources as firms grow. The logic can also explain why firms divide their operations into small groups, including departments and teams.

8   The basic problem of managers can be construed as one of overcoming the large-group problem that, at its heart, is one of overcoming Prisoner's Dilemmas.

9   A boss who is tough on employees can have supporters among employees as well as owners. There is, however, both an optimal amount of toughness on the part of bosses and an optimal amount of shirking on the part of workers.

10 A boss who is not tough on shirkers is also a shirker.

11 Leadership in the form of setting a course for all to follow can be productive since it can reduce the haggling over what course of action all should take.

12 Residual claimants have powerful incentives to encourage firms to minimize costs and maximize profits since such claimants have claims to any firm resources after all other claims have been fulfilled.

13 Companies are typically controlled by the owners of capital because they would otherwise have to fear that their capital, once deployed in companies, would be subject to appropriation by workers.

Review questions >>

1   What are the costs and benefits of taking this course in microeconomics? Develop a theory of how much a student can be expected to study for this course. How might the student's current employment status affect her studying time?

2   Some psychologists see people's behavior as determined largely by family history and external environmental conditions. How would "cost" fit into their explanations?

3   Okay, so no one is totally rational. Does that undermine the use of "rational behavior" as a means of thinking about markets and management problems?

4   How could drug use and suicide be considered "rational"?

5   If your firm were consistently dealing with "irrational behavior" among the owners and workers, what would happen to correct the problem? More to the point, what might you do to correct the problem?

6   Develop an economic explanation for why professors give examinations at the end of their courses. Would you expect final examinations to be more necessary in undergraduate courses or MBA courses? In which classes – undergraduate or MBA – would you expect more cheating?

7 Explain why the "free-rider" problem is likely to be greater in a large group than in a small group.

8 The common interest of people who are in a burning theater is to walk out in an orderly fashion and avoid a panic. If that is the case, why do people so frequently panic in such situations? Use rational behavior and the logic of collective action in your answer.

9 Discuss the costs of making collective decisions in large and small groups. What do these costs have to do with the viability of large and small groups?

10 In what ways do firms overcome the free-rider problems discussed in this chapter relating to large groups? How do market pressures affect firm incentives to overcome these problems?

11 You may have a class in which the professor grades according to a curve, whereby the professor adjusts the grading scale to fit the test results. Assume the class is one in which all the students would prefer *not* to learn as much as they can. If you are in such a situation (or can imagine one like it), the "common interest" of the class members can be for everyone to study less. The same grading distribution can be obtained, and everyone can receive the same relative grade for less effort. Why do class members not collude and restrict the amount of studying they do? Would you expect collusion against studying to be more likely in undergraduate general education courses, core classes in your MBA program, or elective classes in your MBA program?

12 All MBA programs have courses that are considered "bad" (in terms of lack of content and rigor and in terms of delivery) by students and/or faculty and administrators. Should MBA programs offer a "money-back guarantee" on "bad" courses? A "money-back guarantee" would mean that business schools would offer to repay students some pre-set dollar amount (all or a portion) of the tuition students have paid for the identified "bad" courses (with "bad" also carefully predefined and determined by the dean or some panel of faculty members and/or students). What would be the economic consequences of instituting such a money-back guarantee? Would students be expected to be better or worse off with such a guarantee? Or when would they be better off and worse off? If a money-back guarantee is deemed mutually beneficial for the students and school, how generous should it be?

13 Many bars have begun to serve glasses of wine to customers by first pouring the wine into a small carafe and then pouring the wine from the carafe into a larger wine glass? Given the extra dishwashing involved and added time in pouring, why do bars use carafes? Why do some bars use the carafes while others don't?

3

Competitive product markets and firm decisions

Competition, if not prevented, tends to bring about a state of affairs in which: first, everything will be produced which somebody knows how to produce and which he can sell profitably at a price at which buyers will prefer it to the available alternatives; second, everything that is produced is produced by persons who can do so at least as cheaply as anybody else who in fact is not producing it; and third, that everything will be sold at prices lower than, or at least as low as, those at which it could be sold by anybody who in fact does not do so.

    Friedrich A. Hayek

In the heart of New York City, Fred Lieberman's small grocery is dwarfed by the tall buildings that surround it. Yet it is remarkable for what it accomplishes. Lieberman's carries thousands of items, most of which are not produced locally, and some of which come from other parts of this country or the world, thousands of miles away. A man of modest means, with little knowledge of production processes, Fred Lieberman has nevertheless been able to stock his store with many if not most of the foods and toiletries his customers need and want. Occasionally Lieberman's runs out of certain items, but most of the time the stock is ample. Its supply is so dependable that customers tend to take it for granted, forgetting that Lieberman's is one small strand in an extremely complex economic network.

How does Fred Lieberman get the goods he sells, and how does he know which ones to sell and at what price? The simplest answer is that the goods he offers and the prices at which they sell are determined through the *market process* – the interaction of many buyers and sellers trading what they have (their labor or other resources) for what they want. Lieberman stocks his store by appealing to the private interests of suppliers – by paying them competitive prices. His customers pay him extra for the convenience of purchasing goods in their neighborhood grocery – appealing to his private interests in the process. To determine what he should buy, Fred Lieberman considers his suppliers' prices. To determine what and how much they should buy, his customers consider the prices he charges. The economist Friedrich Hayek (1945) has suggested that the market process is manageable for people such as Fred Lieberman, his suppliers, and his customers, precisely because prices condense a great deal of information into a useful form, signaling quickly what people want, what goods cost, and what resources are readily available. Prices guide and coordinate the sellers' production decisions and consumers' purchases.

How are prices determined? That is an important question for people in business, simply because an understanding of how prices are determined can help business-people understand the forces that will cause prices to change in the future and, therefore, the forces that affect their businesses' bottom lines. There's money to be made in being able to understand the dynamics of prices. Our most general answer to the question of how prices are determined is deceptively simple: in competitive markets, the forces of supply and demand establish prices. However, there is much to be learned through the concepts of supply and demand. Indeed, we suspect that most MBA students will find supply and demand the most useful business concepts and tools of analysis developed in this book (and perhaps their entire MBA program). To understand supply and demand, you must first understand that the market process is inherently competitive.

Part A Theory and public policy applications

The competitive market process

So far, our discussion of markets and their consequences has been rather casual. In this section, we shall define precisely such terms as "market" and "competition." In later sections, we shall examine the way competitive markets work and learn why, in a limited sense, markets can be considered efficient systems for determining what and how much to produce. Markets, along with the prices that emerge in them, make the problem of scarcity less pressing than it otherwise would be.

The market setting

Most people tend to think of a market as a geographical location – a shopping center, an auction hall, a business district. From an economic perspective, however, it is more useful to think of a market as a process. You may recall from chapter 1 that a market is defined as the process by which buyers and sellers determine what they are willing to buy and sell and on what terms. That is, a market is the process by which buyers and sellers decide the prices and quantities of goods to be bought and sold. The market process can work within the confines of a building, but also through the Internet that extends to all points on the globe.

In this process, individual market participants search for information relevant to their own interests. Buyers ask about the models, sizes, colors, and quantities available and the prices they must pay for them. Sellers inquire about the types of goods and services buyers want and the prices they are willing to pay.

This market process is *self-correcting*. Buyers and sellers routinely revise their plans on the basis of experience. As economist Israel Kirzner has written:

The overly ambitious plans of one period will be replaced by more realistic ones; market opportunities overlooked in one period will be exploited in the next. In other words, even without changes in the basic data of the market, the decision made in one period one time generates systematic alterations in corresponding decisions for the succeeding period. (Kirzner 1973, 10)

But then overly ambitious plans do affect the "basic data" people receive through resulting changes in prices, which affect the quantities and qualities of goods produced.

The market consists of people – consumers and entrepreneurs – attempting to buy and sell on the best terms possible. Through the groping process of give and take, they move from relative ignorance about others' wants and needs to a reasonably accurate understanding of how much can be bought and sold and at what price. The market functions as an ongoing *information and exchange system*.

Competition among buyers and among sellers

> **Competition** is the process by which market participants, in pursuing their own interests, attempt to outdo, outprice, outproduce, and outmaneuver each other. By extension, competition is also the process by which market participants attempt to avoid being outdone, outpriced, outproduced, or outmaneuvered by others.

Part and parcel of the market process is the concept of **competition**. Competition does not occur *between* buyer and seller, but *among* buyers or *among* sellers. Buyers compete with other buyers for the limited number of goods on the market. To compete, they must discover what other buyers are bidding and offer the seller better terms – a higher price or the same price for a lower-quality product. Sellers compete with other sellers for the consumer's dollar. They must learn what their rivals are doing and attempt to do it better or differently – to lower the price or enhance the product's appeal.

This kind of competition stimulates the exchange of information, forcing competitors to reveal their plans to prospective buyers or sellers. The exchange of information can be seen clearly at auctions. Before the bidding begins, buyers look over the merchandise and the other buyers, attempting to determine how high others might be willing to bid for a particular piece. During the auction, this specific information is revealed as buyers call out their bids and others try to top them. Information exchange is less apparent in department stores, where competition is not as transparent. Even there, however, comparison-shopping by buyers across stores will often reveal some sellers who are offering lower prices in an attempt to attract consumers.

In competing with each other, sellers reveal information that is ultimately of use to buyers. Buyers likewise inform sellers. From the consumer's point of view, the function of competition is precisely to teach us who will serve us well: which grocer or travel agent, which department store or hotel, which doctor or solicitor, we can expect to provide the most satisfactory solution for whatever particular personal problem we may have to face. (Hayek 1948, 97)

From the seller's point of view – say, the auctioneer's – competition among buyers brings the highest prices possible.

Competition among sellers takes many forms, including the price, quality, weight, volume, color, texture, durability, and smell of products, as well as the credit terms offered to buyers. Sellers also compete for consumers' attention by appealing to their hunger and sex drives or their fear of death, pain, and loud noises. All these forms of competition can be divided into two basic categories – *price* and *nonprice* competition. Price competition is of particular interest to economists, who see it as an important source of information for market participants and a coordinating force that brings the quantity produced into line with the quantity consumers are willing and able to buy. In the following sections, we shall construct a model of the competitive market and use it to explore the process of *price* competition under intense competitive market conditions called **perfect competition**. Nonprice competition will be covered in a later section.

> **Perfect competition (in extreme form)** is a market composed of numerous independent sellers and buyers of an identical product, such that no one individual seller or buyer has the ability to affect the market price by changing the production level. Entry into and exit from a perfectly competitive market is unrestricted. Producers can start up or shut down production at will. Anyone can enter the market, duplicate the good, and compete for consumers' dollars. Since each competitor produces only a small share of the total output, the individual competitor cannot significantly influence the degree of competition or the market price by entering or leaving the market.

Supply and demand: a market model

A fully competitive market is made up of many buyers and sellers searching for opportunities or ready to enter the market when opportunities arise. To be described as "competitive," therefore, a market must include a significant number of actual or potential competitors. A fully competitive market offers freedom of entry: there are no legal or artificial barriers to producing and selling goods in the market.

Our market model assumes perfect competition – an idealized situation that is seldom, if ever, achieved in real life but that will simplify our calculations. This kind of market is well suited to graphic analysis and helps us clarify the pricing forces afoot in all competitive markets. Our discussion concentrates on how buyers and sellers interact to determine the price of tomatoes, a product Fred Lieberman almost always carries. It will employ two curves. The first represents buyers' behavior, which is called their demand for the product.

The elements of demand

> **Demand** is the assumed inverse relationship between the price of a good or service and the quantity consumers are willing and able to buy during a given period, all other things held constant.

To the general public, **demand** is simply what people want, but to economists, demand has much more technical meaning. The concept of demand is important because it is so widely applicable to human behavior, not just in business, but in everyday life.

Demand as a relationship

The relationship between price and quantity is normally assumed to be *inverse*. That is, when the price of a good rises, the quantity sold, *ceteris paribus* (Latin for "everything else held constant"), will go down. Conversely, when the price of a good falls, the quantity sold goes up. Demand is not a quantity but a relationship. A given quantity sold at a particular price is properly called the *quantity demanded*.

Both tables and graphs can be used to describe the assumed inverse relationship between price and quantity.

Demand as a table or a graph

Demand may be thought of as a *schedule* of the various quantities of a particular good consumers will buy at various prices. As the price goes down, the quantity purchased goes up and vice versa. Table 3.1 contains a hypothetical schedule of the demand for tomatoes in the New York area during a typical week. Column (2) shows prices that might be charged. Column (3) shows the number of bushels consumers will buy at those prices. Note that as the price rises from zero to $11 a bushel, the number of bushels purchased drops from 110,000 to zero.

Table 3.1 **Market demand for tomatoes**

Price–quantity combinations (1)	Price per bushel ($) (2)	No. (000) of bushels (3)
A	0	110
B	1	100
C	2	90
D	3	80
E	4	70
F	5	60
G	6	50
H	7	40
I	8	30
J	9	20
K	10	10
L	11	0

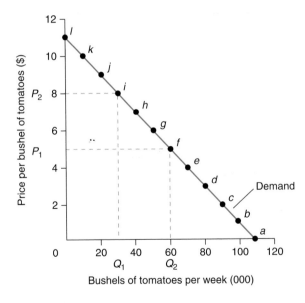

Figure 3.1 Market demand for tomatoes
Demand, the assumed inverse relationship between price and quantity purchased, can be represented by a curve that slopes down toward the right. Here, as the price falls from $11 to zero, the number of bushels of tomatoes purchased per week rises from zero to 110,000.

Demand may also be thought of as a *curve*. If price is scaled on a graph's vertical axis and quantity on the horizontal axis, the demand curve has a negative slope (downward and to the right), reflecting the assumed inverse relationship between price and quantity. The shape of the market demand curve is shown in figure 3.1, which is based on the data from table 3.1. Points *a* through *l* on the graph correspond to the price–quantity combinations *A* through *L* in the table. Note that as the price falls from P_2 ($8) to P_1 ($5), consumers move down their demand curve from a quantity of Q_1 (30,000) to the larger quantity Q_2 (60,000).

[See online Video Module 3.1 Demand]

The slope and determinants of demand

Price and quantity are assumed to be inversely related, for two elemental reasons. (See chapter 6 for more detailed explanations of the downward sloping demand curve.) First, as the price of a good decreases (and the prices of all other goods remain the same), the good becomes relatively cheaper, and consumers will substitute that good for others. This response is called the "substitution effect." The substitution can come from within product categories, say, "fruit." If the price of oranges falls (the price of apples remains constant), people can be expected to buy more oranges and fewer apples. But then a price reduction for oranges can cause some people to move from "nonconsumption" of fruit to the consumption of oranges. That is, consumers can move from consuming cookies to oranges to satisfy their desire for something with sugar content.

In addition, as the price of a good decreases (and the prices of all other goods stay the same – remember *ceteris paribus*), the purchasing power of consumer incomes rises. That is, their *real* incomes increase. More consumers are able to buy the good, and many will buy more of most (but not all) goods. This response is called the "income effect."

In sum, when the price of tomatoes (or razor blades, or any other good) falls, more tomatoes will be purchased because more people will be buying them for more purposes. Moreover, embedded in the downward sloping demand curves for many goods can be large and small behavioral changes among consumers. When the price of gasoline goes up, drivers can be expected to economize on their uses of gasoline in a variety of ways. For example, drivers can be expected to reduce the number of times they stomp down on the cars' accelerators when leaving stoplights and, if they have more than one car, to use their more fuel-efficient cars more frequently, behavioral changes that can enable them to buy fewer gallons of gasoline.

Although price is an important part of the definition of demand, it is not the only determinant of how much of a good people will want. It may not even be the most important. The major factors that affect market demand are called the *determinants of demand*. They are:

- consumer tastes or preferences
- the prices of other goods
- consumer incomes
- the number of consumers
- expectations concerning future prices and incomes.

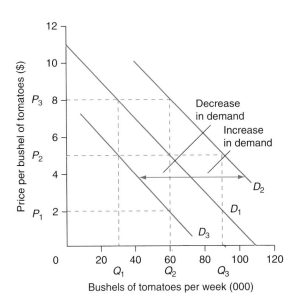

Figure 3.2 Shifts in the demand curve
An increase in demand is represented by a rightward, or outward, shift in the demand curve, from D_1 to D_2. A decrease in demand is represented by a leftward, or inward, shift in the demand curve, from D_1 to D_3.

A host of other factors, such as weather, may also influence the demand for particular goods – ice cream, for instance. A change in any of these determinants of demand will cause either an increase or a decrease in demand:

 An *increase in demand* is an increase in the quantity demanded at each and every price. It is represented graphically by a rightward, or outward, shift in the demand curve.

 A *decrease in demand* is a decrease in the quantity demanded at each and every price. It is represented graphically by a leftward, or inward, shift of the demand curve.

Figure 3.2 illustrates the shifts in the demand curve that result from a change in one of the determinants of demand. The outward shift from D_1 to D_2 indicates an increase in demand: consumers now want more of a good at each and every price. For example, they want Q_3 instead of Q_2 tomatoes at price P_2. Consumers are also now willing to pay a higher price for any quantity. For example, they will pay P_3 instead of P_2 for Q_2 tomatoes. The inward shift from D_1 to D_3 indicates a decrease in demand: consumers want less of a good at each and every price – Q_1 instead of Q_2 tomatoes at price P_2. And they are willing to pay less than before for any quantity – P_1 instead of P_2 for Q_2 tomatoes.

A change in a determinant of demand may be translated into an increase or decrease in current market demand in numerous ways. An increase in market demand can be caused by:

- *An increase in consumers' desire or taste for the good.* If people truly want the good more, they will buy more of the good at any given price or pay a higher price for any given quantity.
- *An increase in the number of buyers.* If, because more people consume the good, more of the good will be purchased at any given price, then the price will be higher at any given quantity.
- *An increase in the price of substitute goods* (which can be used in place of the good in question). If the price of oranges increases, the demand for grapefruit will increase.
- *A decrease in the price of complementary goods* (which are used in conjunction with the good in question). If the price of MP3 players falls, the demand for downloadable songs will rise. If the price of gasoline falls, the overall demand for automobiles can increase. (But the demand for various models can rise or fall, depending on their gas consumption: the demand for SUVs can fall while the demand for hybrids can rise.)
- *Generally speaking (but not always), an increase in consumer incomes.* An increase in people's incomes may increase the demand for luxury goods, such as new cars. It may also decrease demand for low-quality goods (such as hamburger) because people can now afford better-quality products (such as steak).
- *An expected increase in the future price of the good in question.* If people expect the price of cars to rise faster than the prices of other goods, then (depending on exactly when they expect the increase) they may buy more cars now, thus avoiding the expected additional cost in the future.
- *An expected increase in future incomes of buyers.* College seniors' demand for cars tends to increase as graduation approaches and they anticipate a rise in income.

The determinants of a decrease in market demand are just the opposite:

- a decrease in consumers' desire or taste for the good
- a decrease in the number of buyers
- a decrease in the price of substitute goods
- an increase in the price of complementary goods
- generally speaking (but not always), a decrease in consumer incomes
- an expected decrease in the future price of the good in question
- an expected decrease in the future incomes of buyers.

As will be noticeable throughout this book, much attention will be placed on how changes in price affect the quantity demanded, while little attention will be given to how changes in "tastes" affect the quantity demanded. The differential treatment of price and tastes does not presume that price is more important than tastes in determining the consumption level of any good. Rather, economists concentrate on price because they seek a theory of price determination (not a theory of taste determination, which is a major interest of psychology). In addition, the effect of price changes on quantity demanded is viewed as being highly predictable, given extensive consumer theory and empirical observation. The inverse relationship between price and quantity consumed is viewed as a "law," or the "law of demand." "Tastes," on the other hand, are an amorphous, subjective concept. Hence, predicting the impact of changes in "tastes" on quantity demanded is, for economists (but perhaps not for psychologists), problematic.

Similarly, as will be discussed in chapter 6, the impact of a change in buyer's real income on quantity bought has an element of uncertainty. Granted, for most normal goods, the relationship between income and quantity of a good bought can be positive, as indicated above, in which case the substitution and income effects have the same direction impact on quantity consumed. However, the relationship can be inverse for some goods (so-called "inferior goods"). When low-income people experience an increase in real income, they may switch between low-quality sources of, say, protein – beans – to high-quality sources – meat. In this case, the negative effect of an increase in real income works against the substitution effect on the quantity demanded of beans. However, economists have found that for most goods the substitution and income effects compound one another or the positive substitution effect dominates any negative income effect, which means demand curves of most – if not almost all – goods slope downward.

The elements of supply

On the other side of the market are the producers of goods. The average person thinks of supply as the quantity of a good producers are willing to sell. To economists, however, **supply** means something quite different. As with demand, supply is not a "given quantity" – that is called the "quantity supplied." Supply is a *relationship between price and quantity*. As the price of a good rises, producers are generally willing to offer a larger quantity. The reverse is equally true: as price decreases, so does quantity supplied. Like demand, supply can be described in a table or a graph.

> **Supply** is the assumed relationship between the quantity of a good producers are willing to offer during a given period and the price, everything else held constant. Generally, because additional costs tend to rise with expanded production, this relationship is presumed to be positive (a point that is developed with care in chapters 7 and 8).

Supply as a table or a graph

Supply may be described as a *schedule of the quantity that producers will offer* at various prices during a given period of time. Table 3.2 shows such a supply schedule. As the price of tomatoes goes up from zero to $11 a bushel, the quantity offered rises

Table 3.2 **Market supply of tomatoes**		
Price–quantity combinations (1)	Price per bushel ($) (2)	No. (000) of bushels (3)
A	0	0
B	1	10
C	2	20
D	3	30
E	4	40
F	5	50
G	6	60
H	7	70
I	8	80
J	9	90
K	10	100
L	11	110

from zero to 110,000, reflecting the assumed positive relationship between price and quantity.

Supply may also be thought of as a *curve*. If the quantity producers will offer is scaled on the horizontal axis of a graph and the price of the good is scaled on the vertical axis, the supply curve will slope upward to the right, reflecting the assumed positive relationship between price and quantity. In figure 3.3, which was plotted from the data in table 3.2, points *a* through *l* represent the price–quantity combinations A through L. Note how a change in the price causes a movement along the supply curve.

 [See online Video Module 3.2 Supply]

The slope and determinants of supply

The quantity producers will offer on the market depends on their *production costs*. Obviously the total cost of production will rise when more is produced because more

> **Marginal cost** is the additional cost of producing an additional unit of output.

resources will be required to expand output. The additional or **marginal cost** of each additional bushel produced also tends to rise as total output expands (beyond some point, which will be explained in chapter 7). In other words, when it costs more to produce the second bushel of tomatoes than the first, and more to produce the third than the second, firms will not expand their output unless they can cover their progressively higher marginal costs with a progressively higher price. This is the reason the supply curve is thought to slope upward.

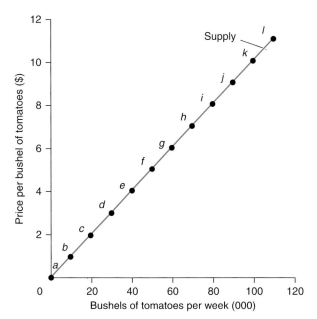

Figure 3.3 **Supply of tomatoes**
Supply, the assumed relationship between price and quantity produced, can be represented by a curve that slopes up toward the right. Here, as the price rises from zero to $11, the number of bushels of tomatoes offered for sale during the course of a week rises from zero to 110,000.

Anything that affects production costs will influence supply and the position of the supply curve. Such factors, which are called *determinants of supply*, include:

- change in productivity due to a change in technology
- change in the profitability of producing other goods
- change in the scarcity (and prices) of various productive resources.

Many other factors, such as the weather, can also affect production costs and therefore supply. A change in any of these determinants of supply can either increase or decrease supply:

- An *increase in supply* is an increase in the quantity producers are willing and able to offer at each and every price. It is represented graphically by a rightward, or outward, shift in the supply curve.
- A *decrease in supply* is a decrease in the quantity producers are willing and able to offer at each and every price. It is represented graphically by a leftward, or inward, shift in the supply curve.

In figure 3.4, an increase in supply is represented by the shift from S_1 to S_2. Producers are willing to produce a larger quantity at each price – Q_3 instead of Q_2 at price P_2, for example. They will also accept a lower price for each quantity – P_1

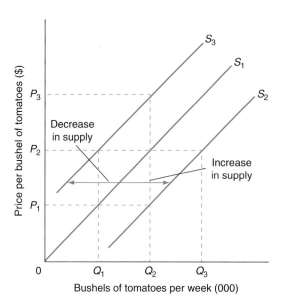

Figure 3.4 Shifts in the supply curve
A rightward, or outward, shift in the supply curve, from S_1 to S_2, represents an increase in supply. A leftward, or inward, shift in the supply curve, from S_1 to S_3, represents a decrease in supply.

instead of P_2 for quantity Q_2. Conversely, the decrease in supply represented by the shift from S_1 to S_3 means that producers will offer less at each price – Q_1 instead of Q_2 at price P_2. They must also have a higher price for each quantity – P_3 instead of P_2 for quantity Q_2.

A few examples will illustrate the impact of changes in the determinants of supply. If firms learn how to produce more goods with the same or fewer resources, the cost of producing any given quantity will fall. Because of the technological improvement, firms will be able to offer a larger quantity at any given price or the same quantity at a lower price. The supply will increase, shifting the supply curve outward to the right.

Similarly, if the profitability of producing oranges increases relative to grapefruit, grapefruit producers will shift their resources to oranges. The supply of oranges will increase, shifting the supply curve to the right. Finally, if lumber (or labor or equipment) becomes scarcer, its price will rise, increasing the cost of new housing and reducing the supply of new houses coming onto the market. The supply curve of new houses will shift inward to the left.

Market equilibrium

Supply and demand represent the two sides of the market – sellers and buyers. By plotting the supply and demand curves together, as in figure 3.5, we can explore the conditions under which the decisions of buyers and sellers will be inconsistent with

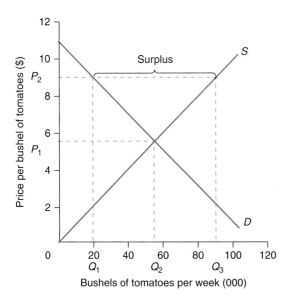

Figure 3.5 Market surplus
If a price is higher than the intersection of the supply and demand curves, a market surplus – a greater quantity supplied, Q_3, than demanded, Q_1 – results. Competitive pressure will push the price down to the equilibrium price, P_1, the price at which the quantity supplied equals the quantity demanded, Q_2.

each other, and why a market surplus or shortage of tomatoes will result. We can also illuminate the competitive market forces at work to push the market price toward the market-clearing price – or the price at which the market is said to be in equilibrium, at which the forces of supply and demand balance one another with no net pressure for the price and output to move up or down.

> **Market equilibrium** occurs when the forces of supply and demand are in balance with no net pressure for the price and output level to change.

Market surpluses

Suppose that the price of a bushel of tomatoes is $9, or P_2 in figure 3.5. At this price, the quantity demanded by consumers is 20,000 bushels, much less than the quantity offered by producers – 90,000. There is a market surplus, or excess supply, of 70,000 bushels. Graphically, an excess quantity supplied occurs at any price above the intersection of the supply and demand curves.

> A **market surplus** is the amount by which the quantity supplied exceeds the quantity demanded at any given price.

What will happen in this situation? Producers who cannot sell their tomatoes will have to compete by offering to sell at a lower price, forcing other producers to follow suit. All producers might agree that holding the price above equilibrium can be in their "common interest," since an above-equilibrium price can generate extra profits for all (even though sales might be undercut). However, in competitive markets producers are in a large-group setting in which their individual curbs on production to pursue their common interest will have an inconsequential impact on total market supply. They each can reason that they can possibly gain market share by individually lowering their price, if all others hold to the higher price. And each can reason that all others are thinking the same way, which means they can expect other producers to lower their prices. The logic leads the producers to do what is not in their common interest and to act competitively, which is cut their prices.

As the competitive process forces the price down, the quantity that consumers are willing to buy will expand, while the quantity that producers are willing to sell will decrease. The result will be a contraction of the surplus, until it is finally eliminated at a price of $5.50 or P_1 (at the intersection of the two curves). At that price, producers will be selling all they want; they will see no reason to lower prices further. Similarly, consumers will see no reason to pay more; they will be buying all they want. This point at which the wants of buyers and sellers intersect is called the *equilibrium*, with the price and quantity at that point called *equilibrium price* and *equilibrium quantity*:

- The *equilibrium price* is the price toward which a competitive market will move, and at which it will remain once there, everything else held constant. It is the price at which the market "clears" – that is, at which the quantity demanded by consumers is matched exactly by the quantity offered by producers. At the equilibrium price, the quantity sellers are willing to supply and the quantity buyers want to consume are equal. This is the equilibrium quantity.
- The *equilibrium quantity* is the output (or sales) level toward which the market will move, and at which it will remain once there, everything else held constant.

In sum, a surplus emerges when the price asked is above the equilibrium price. It will be eliminated, through competition among sellers, when the price drops to the equilibrium price.

Market shortages

Suppose that the price asked is below the equilibrium price, as in figure 3.6. At the relatively low price of $1, or P_1, buyers want to purchase 100,000 bushels – substantially more than the 10,000 bushels producers are willing to offer. The result is a **market shortage**. Graphically, a market shortage is the shortfall that occurs at any price below the intersection of the supply and demand curves.

A **market shortage** is the amount by which the quantity demanded exceeds the quantity supplied at any given price.

As with a market surplus, competition will correct the discrepancy between buyers' and sellers' plans. Buyers who want tomatoes but are unable to get them at a price of $1 will bid higher prices, as at an auction. Many buyers might have a

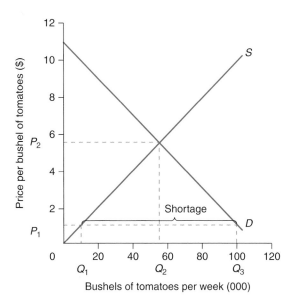

Figure 3.6 Market shortages
A price that is below the intersection of the supply and demand curves will create a shortage – a greater quantity demanded, Q_3, than supplied, Q_1. Competitive pressure will push the price up to the equilibrium price P_2, the price at which the quantity supplied equals the quantity demanded (Q_2).

"common interest" to hold the price below the equilibrium price (even with fewer units of the good they can buy). However, as with producers when there was a market surplus, buyers are in a large-group setting, with each individual buyer reasoning that not offering a higher price will not affect the market outcomes, because other buyers will offer a higher price. Each buyer can reason that they might as well offer a higher price just to get the units they want.

As the price rises, a larger quantity will be supplied because suppliers will be better able to cover their increasing production costs. Simultaneously, the quantity demanded will contract as buyers seek substitutes that are now relatively less expensive compared with tomatoes. At the equilibrium price of $5.50, or P_2, the market shortage will be eliminated. Buyers will have no reason to bid prices up further; they will be getting all the tomatoes they want at that price. Sellers will have no reason to expand production further; they will be selling all they want at that price. The equilibrium price will remain the same until some force shifts the position of either the supply or the demand curve. If such a shift occurs, the price will move toward a new equilibrium at the new intersection of the supply and demand curves.

In our graphical treatment of supply and demand, movement toward equilibrium can be thought of as instantaneous. Real-world movements in price will necessarily take some time, which means that the equilibrium price and quantity toward which the market will ultimately settle can shift with changes in supply and demand.

The effect of changes in demand and supply

Figure 3.7 shows the effects of shifts in demand and supply on the equilibrium price and quantity. In figure 3.7(a), an increase in demand from D_1 to D_2 raises the

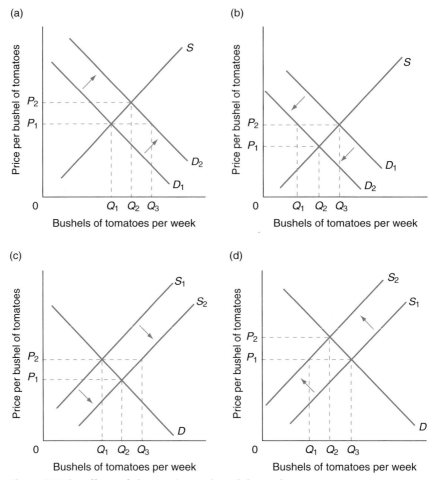

Figure 3.7 The effects of changes in supply and demand
An increase in demand – panel (a) – raises both the equilibrium price and the equilibrium quantity. A decrease in demand – panel (b) – has the opposite effect: a decrease in the equilibrium price and quantity. An increase in supply – panel (c) – causes the equilibrium quantity to rise but the equilibrium price to fall. A decrease in supply – panel (d) – has the opposite effect: a rise in the equilibrium price and a fall in the equilibrium quantity.

equilibrium price from P_1 to P_2 and quantity from Q_1 to Q_2. The equilibrium price rises because at the moment the demand curve shifts out to the right, a market shortage develops at the initial price P_1. The quantity demanded at that initial price is Q_3; the quantity supplied is less, Q_1. Those buyers who want the good but are unable to get it will bid the price up. As the price goes up, producers can justify incurring the higher marginal costs of producing more, but some buyers will retreat on their purchases. The market will clear – or quantity supplied and demand will be equal – at the higher price of P_2.

Figure 3.7(b) shows the reverse effects of a decrease in demand. When the demand initially falls, a market surplus develops at price P_2. At P_2, the quantity demanded is Q_1 while the quantity supplied is Q_3. Producers who want to sell their output will put downward pressure on the price. As the price falls, buyers increase their purchases while producers curb their output. Equilibrium is reestablished at a price of P_1 and quantity Q_2.

An increase in supply from S_1 to S_2 – figure 3.7(c) – has a different effect. The equilibrium quantity rises from Q_1 to Q_2, but the equilibrium price falls from P_2 to P_1. When supply initially expands, a market surplus emerges at price P_2. The quantity demanded is Q_1 while the quantity supplied is Q_3, which makes for a market surplus. As producers try to sell what they produce, they put downward pressure on the price. As the price falls toward P_1, the quantity produced contracts from Q_3 to Q_2. The quantity demanded rises from Q_1 to Q_2.

A decrease in supply from S_1 to S_2 – figure 3.7(d) – causes the opposite effect: the equilibrium quantity falls from Q_3 to Q_2, and the equilibrium price rises from P_1 to P_2. At the time supply decreases, a shortage develops, with the quantity supplied at Q_1 and the quantity demanded at Q_3. Buyers who want more units of the good than are available at P_1 will bid the price up. As the price rises from P_1 toward P_2, the quantity demanded decreases from Q_3 to Q_2; the quantity supplied rises from Q_1 to Q_2.

[See online Video Modules 3.3 Changes in supply and demand and 3.4 Applications of supply and demand]

The efficiency of the competitive market model

Early in this chapter we asked how Fred Lieberman knows what prices to charge for the goods he sells. The answer is now apparent: he adjusts his prices until his customers buy the quantities that he wants to sell. If he cannot sell all the fruits and vegetables he has, he lowers his price to attract customers and cuts back on his orders for those goods. If he runs short, he knows that he can raise his prices and increase his orders. His customers then adjust their purchases accordingly. Similar actions by other producers and customers all over the city move the market for produce toward equilibrium. The information provided by the orders, reorders, and cancellations from stores such as Lieberman's eventually reaches the suppliers of goods and then the suppliers of resources. Similarly, wholesale prices give Fred Lieberman information on suppliers' costs of production and the relative scarcity and productivity of resources.

The use of the competitive market system to determine what and how much to produce has two advantages. First, it coordinates the decisions of consumers and producers very effectively. Most of the time the amount produced in a competitive market system is very close to the amount consumers want at the prevailing price – no more, no less. Second, the market system maximizes the amount of output that is acceptable to both buyer and seller. In figure 3.8(a), note that all the price–quantity

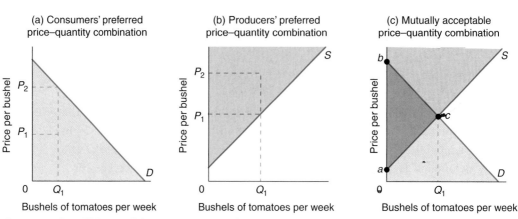

Figure 3.8 The efficiency of the competitive market
Only those price–quantity combinations on or below the demand curve – panel (a) – are acceptable to buyers. Only those price–quantity combinations on or above the supply curve – panel (b) – are acceptable to producers. Those price–quantity combinations that are acceptable to both buyers and producers are shown in the darkest shaded area of panel (c). The competitive market is "efficient" in the sense that it results in output Q_1, the maximum output level acceptable to both buyers and producers.

combinations acceptable to consumers lie either on or below the market demand curve, in the shaded area. (If consumers are willing to pay P_2 for Q_1, then they should also be willing to pay less for that quantity – for example, P_1.) Furthermore, all the price–quantity combinations acceptable to producers lie either on or above the supply curve, in the shaded area shown in figure 3.8(b). (If producers are willing to accept P_1 for quantity Q_1, then they should also be willing to accept a higher price – for example, P_2.) When supply and demand curves are combined in figure 3.8 (c), we see that all the price–quantity combinations acceptable to both consumers and producers lie in the darkest shaded triangular area. From all those acceptable output levels, the competitive market produces Q_1, the maximum output level that can be produced given what producers and consum-ers are willing and able to do. In this respect, the competitive market can be said to be *efficient*, or to allocate resources with efficiency. The achievement of efficiency means that an expansion or contrac-tion of output will reduce consumers' and/or producers' welfare.

> **Efficiency** is the maximization of output through careful allocation of resources, given the constraints of supply (producers' costs) and demand (consumers' preferences).

The competitive market exploits all the possible trades between buyers and sell-ers. Up to the equilibrium quantity, buyers will pay more than suppliers require (those points on the demand curve that lie above the supply curve). Beyond Q_1, buyers will not pay as much as suppliers need to produce more (those points on the supply curve that lie above the demand curve). Again, in this regard the market can be called efficient.

The market that produces at the intersection of supply and demand in figure 3.8(c) is said to be efficient in another regard. The demand curve shows consumers' marginal value of each unit. The total value of all Q_1 units is the area under the demand curve bounded by $0abQ_1$. The supply curve shows the marginal cost of every unit produced. The producers' total production cost for Q_1 units is the area under the supply curve bounded by $0cbQ_1$. The potential net gain from production is the differences between consumers' total value of Q_1 ($0abQ_1$) minus the producers' total cost ($0cbQ_1$), or the triangle area bounded by abc. In a competitive market, with production at Q_1, all of those net gains are generated and split between producers and consumers by way of the price charged, P_1. If production fell short of Q_1, then some of those potential net gains would not be generated. If production were greater than Q_1, then the cost of the added units to producers would exceed their added value to consumers. The net gains would again fall short of the potential net gains of the triangle abc. If more or less is produced than Q_1, the market is said to be inefficient.

> **Market inefficiency** is the extent to which potential net gains from trades are not generated.

In the foregoing section, the focus has been on the efficiency of markets, or how well they operate. However, problems abound in markets, with the most notable being pollution in product markets and discrimination in labor markets. We will take up these and other problems in Part B of this chapter and at various other points in the book.

[See online Video Module 3.5 Competitive market efficiency]

Nonprice competition

Markets in which suppliers compete solely in terms of price are relatively rare (with salt being one of those rare products). In fact, price competition is not always the best method of competition, not only because price reductions mean lower average revenues, but also because the reductions can be costly to communicate to consumers. Advertising is expensive, and consumers may not notice price reductions as readily as they do improvements in quality. Quality changes, furthermore, are not as readily duplicated as are price changes. Consumers' preferences for quality over price should be reflected in the profitability of making such improvements. If consumers prefer a top-of-the-line MP4 player (iPod) to a cheaper basic model, then producing the more sophisticated model could, depending on the cost of the extra features, be more profitable than producing the basic model and communicating its lower price to consumers.

Changes in one feature, product size
If all consumers had exactly the same preferences – size, color, and so on – producers would presumably make uniform products and compete through price

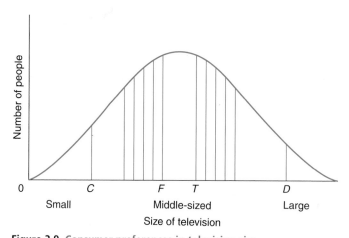

Figure 3.9 Consumer preferences in television size
Consumers differ in their wants, but most desire a medium-sized television. Only a few want a very small or a large television.

alone. For most products, however, people's preferences differ. To keep the analysis manageable, we will explore nonprice competition in terms of just one feature – product size. Suppose that in the market for plasma television sets consumer preferences are distributed along the continuum shown in figure 3.9. The curve is bell shaped, indicating that most consumers are clustered in the middle of the distribution and want a medium-sized television. Fewer consumers want a giant screen or a mini-television.

Everything else being equal, the first producer to enter the market, Alpha TV, will probably offer a product that falls somewhere in the middle of the distribution – for example, at the "hump" in figure 3.9. In this way, Alpha TV offers a product that reflects the preferences of the largest number of people. Furthermore, as long as there are no competitors, the firm can expect to pick up customers to the left and right of center. (Alpha TV's product may not come very close to satisfying the wants of consumers who prefer a very large or very small television, but it is the only one available.) The more that Alpha TV can meet the preferences of the greatest number of consumers, everything else being equal, the higher the price it can charge and the greater the profit it can make. (Because consumers value the product more highly, they will pay a higher price for it.)

The first few competitors that enter the market may also locate close to the center – in fact, several may virtually duplicate Alpha TV's product. These firms may conclude that they will enjoy a larger market by sharing the center with several competitors than by moving out into the "wings" of the distribution. They are probably right. Although they may be able to charge more (relative to production cost) for a giant screen or a mini-television that closely reflects some consumers' preferences, there are fewer potential customers for those products.

To illustrate, assume that competitor Zeta TV locates at *F*, close to *T*. It can then appeal to consumers on the left side of the curve because its product will reflect those consumers' preferences more closely than does Alpha TV's. Alpha TV can still appeal to consumers on the right half of the curve. If Zeta TV had located at *C*, however, it would have direct appeal only to consumers to the left of *C*, as well as those between *C* and *T* who are closer to *C*. Alpha TV would have appealed to more of the consumers on the left, between *C* and *T*, than in the first case. In short, Zeta TV has a larger potential market at *F* than at *C*.

However, as more competitors move into the market, the center will become so crowded that new competitors will find it advantageous to move away from the center, to *C* or *D*. At those points, the market will not be as large as it is in the center, but competition will be less intense. If producers do not have to compete directly with as many competitors, they can charge higher prices. How far out into the "wings" they move will depend on the trade-offs they must make between the number of customers they can attract and the price they can charge.

As with price reductions, the movement of competitors into the "wings" of the distribution benefits consumers whose tastes differ from those of the people in the middle. These atypical consumers now have a product that comes closer to, or even directly reflects, their preferences.

Our discussion has assumed free entry into the market. If monopoly of a strategic resource or government regulation restricts entry, the variety of products offered will not be as great as in an open, competitive market. If there are only two or three competitors in a market, everything else being equal, we would expect them to cluster in the middle of a bell-shaped distribution. That tendency has been seen in the past in the broadcasting industry, when the Federal Communications Commission (FCC) strictly regulated the number of television stations permitted in a given geographical area. Not surprisingly, stations carried programs that appealed predominantly to a mass audience – that is, to the middle of the distribution of television viewers. The government organized the Public Broadcasting System (PBS) partly to provide programs with less than mass appeal to satisfy viewers on the outer sections of the curve. When cable television emerged and programs became more varied, the prior justification for PBS subsidies became more debatable (with the future survival of PBS in serious jeopardy at the time of this writing).

Even with free market entry, product variety depends on the cost of production and the prices people will pay for variations. Magazine and newsstand operators would behave very much like past television managers if they could carry only two or three magazines. They would choose *Newsweek* or some other magazine that appealed to the largest number of people. Most motel operators, for instance, have room for only a very small newsstand, and so they tend to carry the mass-circulation weeklies and monthlies.

For their own reasons, consumers may prefer such a compromise. Although they may desire a product that perfectly reflects their tastes, they may buy a product that is not perfectly suitable if they can get it at a lower price. Producers can offer such a product at a lower price because of the economies (of cost savings) gained from selling to a large market (a topic to be taken up in greater detail in chapter 9). For example, instead of private tutorials, most MBA students take predesigned classes in sizable lecture halls. They do so largely because the mass lecture, although perhaps less suitable for their particular preferences, is substantially cheaper than tutorials. In a market that is open to entry, producers will take advantage of such opportunities.

If producers in one part of a distribution attempt to charge a higher price than necessary, other producers can move into that segment of the market and push the price down; or consumers can switch to other products. In this way, competition in markets can press buyers and sellers to move toward an optimal mix of products. Without freedom of entry, we cannot tell whether it is possible to improve on the existing combination of products. A free, competitive market gives rival firms a chance to better that combination. The case for the free market becomes even stronger when we recognize that market conditions – and therefore the *optimal product mix* – are constantly changing.

Changes in combination of features

To this point we have assumed that products bought and sold in competitive markets are given in the sense that they are of a certain quality and have a set of fixed features. We all have observed products constantly being upgraded with additional features added as new models are introduced at what seems to be a progressively rapid pace. Laptop computers have been introduced with limited processor speeds and hard drives, only for manufacturers to introduce in succession one new model after the other with faster processors and larger hard drives, along with an ever-growing array of features – built-in DVR players, WiFi connections, cameras, microphones – as well as bigger and brighter screens, etc. Cell phones have followed much the same upgrade paths, and continue on that path. Indeed, it might be said that many firms find competition over product quality and features to be far more intense than competition over price. Firms often add features to avoid price cuts. MBA students need to know the basic economics of product upgrades in competitive markets.

When product improvements pay

When should firms upgrade their products' quality and add features? In highly competitive markets (monopoly markets will be considered later in the book), the straightforward answer is that firms should and must improve their products only when the added or marginal cost of the improvement is less than the added or marginal value of the improvement to consumers. Under such a condition, producers can increase their profits because they can increase their prices by more than their costs increase. Consumers can be better off with the higher prices because the added values of the improvements will be higher than the added prices for the improved products. That is, the product improvement is mutually beneficial, or pays for both producers and consumers.

Producers will not consider improvements for which the additional values realized by consumers are less than the additional costs of the improvements to producers. If the added costs were greater than the added values, there would be no way the improvement could be mutually beneficial. The improvement would require the producers to increase their prices by more than the added value to consumers, which means customers would reject the improved products. Alternatively, the producers could raise the prices by less than the added values to consumers, but the higher prices would not then cover the added costs of the producers who made the improvements.

Product improvement and supply and demand

To see our central point relating to when product improvements can be mutually beneficial to buyers and producers, consider figure 3.10 that contains the initial supply and demand curves for a hypothetical product, S_1 and D_1, before the product is upgraded in some way (exactly how the product is upgraded is immaterial, since our points are generally applicable to any upgrade in a competitive market, just so long as the change doesn't result in a truly different product intended for a new and different

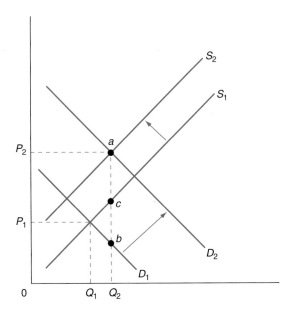

Figure 3.10 Product improvements
When a product is improved, demand will rise from D_1 to D_2 while supply will decrease from S_1 to S_2. Equilibrium price and quantity will both rise, to P_2 and Q_2. The price increase, P_2 minus P_1, is less than the added value to buyers, *ab*, but greater than the added costs incurred by producers, *ac*.

market). Competitive equilibrium price and quantity are P_1 and Q_1. Suppose that an upgrade becomes available for the product (due to, say, some technological break-through), which all producers can adopt. The added value of the improvement is greater than the added costs, making it potentially mutually beneficial to producers and consumers. The demand curve will shift up and to the right from D_1 to D_2, reflecting the added value to consumers (as measured by the added price consumers are willing to pay for the improved product, indicated by the distance *ab*). The supply curve shifts up and to the left from S_1 to S_2, reflecting the added production cost (as indicated by the higher price producers must incur to make the improvement, indicated by the distance *ac*). The new equilibrium price and quantity will be at the intersection of D_2 and S_2, or P_2 and Q_2. The price will be competed upward because at P_1, there will be a market shortage.

Are consumers and producers better off because of the product improvement? The answer is clearly "yes," as can be seen in the graph. Consumers have to pay a higher price, P_2, but the increase in the price, P_2-P_1, is less than the increase in value added from the improvement, *ab*. Producers are also better off because the increase in their price, again, P_2-P_1, is greater than the increase in their costs, *ac*. Again, both sides of the market gain.

Will the improvement in the product be made in a competitive market? You bet, for good offensive and defensive reasons. Producers will offer the improvement because they can make a profit on it and can gain a competitive advantage if other producers don't follow suit with improvements in their products. But other producers must follow suit for a defensive reason; producers who don't improve their products can expect to lose sales to the producers who do.

But improvement need not stop in figure 3.10, given the added value, if not profitability, of the one improvement. Why not add other improvements for which the added value to consumers is greater than the added production costs? The question answers itself. However, producers can expect that as improvements to products are made (as gigabytes are added to a laptop's hard drive), the value of additional improvements to buyers can be expected to decline (beyond some point at least). The marginal costs of any sequence of additional improvements will increase (at least beyond some point). Under such conditions, producers should continue to upgrade their products until the added or marginal cost of the last improvement equals the marginal value of the last improvement. With producers' marginal costs rising and consumers' marginal value falling with added improve-ments, marginal costs and marginal value will equate. Producers can be expected to (and perhaps should) follow a rule that will come back to you time and again in this textbook: *producers should equate at the margin to achieve optimum product improvement!* If producers pull up short of equality between the marginal cost and marginal value of improvements, they will have missed out on additional net profits for themselves and additional net value to buyers, and they will suffer when other producers extend mutually beneficial improvements and equate at the margin. Producers who extend their improvements beyond equality of the marginal cost and benefits of improvments will have added costs that cannot be recovered from higher prices. They also will suffer a competitive disadvantage because of their unnecessary, unrecoverable costs.

[See online Video Module 3.6 Adding features to products]

Extended discussions of competitive product markets

Even though lengthy, our discussion of competitive product markets is hardly exhaustive. To keep the chapter coverage contained, we have provided two additional readings online that develop two extensions of supply-and-demand-curve analysis to competitive product markets. The analysis to this point has been limited to equilibrium in the "short run," or when production occurs within the constraints of a firm's plant size and equipment. Reading 3.1 extends the market adjustments to the "long run," or when firms can expand their use of plant and equipment and when totally new producers can enter the market. In that reading, we use the short-run and long-run adjustments in equilibrium price and quantity in the ballpoint pen industy after ballpoint pens emerged in the late 1940s.

In Perspective 3 for this chapter, we ponder issues that might have occurred to alert readers: in response to all of the changes in market conditions taken up in this section, the market clears with appropriate adjustments in price and quantity toward equilibrium. If that is the case, then why are there so many queues – in grocery stores and at concerts, to name just two highly competitive markets? Put another way, do queues indicate that markets are not in equilibrium or fail the test of economic efficiency? We've talked about how markets are based on mutually beneficial trades. Can queues be seen in any sense as mutually beneficial?

> **Short-run equilibrium** is the price–quantity combination that will exist as long as producers do not have time to change their production facilities (or some resource that is fixed in the short run).
> **Long-run equilibrium** is the price–quantity combination that will exist after firms have had time to change their production facilities (or some other resource that is fixed in the short run).

For now, we can show how supply-and-demand-curve analysis is as applicable to competitive labor markets as to competitive product markets.

Competitive labor markets

We undertake a detailed study of the workings of labor markets in chapter 12. Here, we can note that competitive labor markets can be analyzed with supply and demand curves in much the same way products have been considered. An elemental difference between a "product" and "labor" is that the "price of labor" on the vertical axis of any supply and demand graph has a special name, the *wage rate* (per hour or

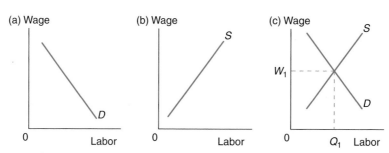

Figure 3.11 Supply and demand of labor
The demand for labor is the assumed inverse relationship between the wage rate paid and the number of workers demanded by employers (panel (a)). The supply of labor is the assumed positive relationship between the wage rate and the number of workers willing to work (panel (b)). In competitive markets, the wage rate and number of workers hired will be pressed toward the intersection of supply and demand (panel (c)).

per day or per week). The quantity of labor on the horizontal axis is the count of workers in a given skill category who want to work and who are demanded by employers during a given time period. (The quantity of labor on the horizontal axis can also be so many hours or days or weeks of work.)

The demand for labor comes from employers who hire workers. Employers' demand for labor is founded on two major considerations:

1 how productive the workers are, and
2 how much employers can charge for their workers' output.

The demand for labor (like the demand for a product) will be downward sloping, as is the demand for labor in figure 3.11(a). That is, the price of labor – the wage rate – and the quantity of workers employers will hire are inversely related: The lower the wage rate, *ceteris paribus*, the greater the quantity of labor demanded by employers, and vice versa.

Such a proposition is intuitively plausible, but it also has a firm theoretical underpinning. As more workers are hired, the additional or marginal value of each additional worker can be expected to decline for one or both of two reasons: The additional or marginal contribution of additional workers can be expected to decline (because of the *law of diminishing marginal returns*, a principle of production economics that will be considered in detail in chapters 7 and 8). Also, as more workers are hired in an industry to produce a product, the market supply of the product can be expected to increase, causing the price of the product to fall. Hence, as the marginal market value of the additional production of additional workers declines, the wage rate must fall to induce employers to extend their hiring.

The labor demand, accordingly, can be expected to rise and fall with worker productivity and the price of the product workers produce. An increase in worker productivity and/or an increase in the price of the product the workers produce can give rise to an increase in the demand for labor, and vice versa. Labor regulations also can affect the demand for labor. For example, if employers are required by law to provide health insurance, then their demand for labor can be expected to fall, since some of the wages employers are willing to pay workers can be soaked up in health insurance costs. (Of course, health insurance might increase worker productivity by more than insurance costs go up, which can increase the demand for labor on balance. However, if such were the case, government need not mandate health insurance, since employers would gladly provide such a benefit that more than pays for itself in terms of greater worker productivity, a point we cover with more precision in chapter 4.)

The supply of labor comes from workers. They make available their hours of labor. The relationship between the wage rate and the count of workers (or count of hours worked) can be expected to be positive, with the supply curve upward sloping (just as is the supply of a product upward sloping), as shown in figure 3.11(b). If the wage rate goes up, *ceteris paribus*, more workers will be willing to work (and to work more hours). This positive relationship is also intuitively plausible, mainly because workers can be expected to offer themselves for work depending on their opportunity costs (or the value of what else they have to do). When the wage rate is low, only those workers with opportunity costs lower than the wage rate can be expected to offer themselves for work. To bring more workers with higher opportunity costs into the labor market, the wage rate will have to be raised.

Changes in workers' opportunity costs can affect the supply of labor. The higher workers' opportunity costs, the lower the supply of labor, and vice versa. The supply curve can also be affected by the nonmonetary benefits of employment, including fringe benefits of various kinds and the attributes of the workplace environment. Employers providing health insurance can expect to see the supply of labor increase (so long as workers value health insurance). Hostilities in the workplace (caused by sexual harassment, back-biting, or water-cooler politics) can curb the supply of labor.

The two sides of the labor market – the supply and demand for labor – can now be put together in figure 3.11(c). Competitive market forces determine the price of labor – the wage rate – in the same manner as they determine the price of any product. The market wage rate will be pressed toward the wage at the intersection of the supply and demand for labor, W_1, which is the equilibrium wage rate. The quantity of labor demanded and supplied at that wage rate will be equal to Q_1.

As in the case of our product–market discussion, if the wage rate is below the equilibrium wage, there will be a market shortage of labor. Employers will be forced to offer a higher wage to hire more workers. As the wage rate rises toward W_1, employers will curb their hires, as more workers come onto the market, with the workers giving up progressively higher-value opportunities. If the wage rate is above the equilibrium wage, a market surplus of labor will emerge, putting downward pressure on the wage rate. As the wage rate falls from above the equilibrium wage toward the equilibrium wage, some workers will withdraw from the market (to take advantage of their then higher-valued alternative opportunities) and employers will expand their hires.

Again, changes in supply of and demand for labor can have much the same market effects as changes in the supply of and demand for products. An increase in demand for labor, due to an increase in the productivity of labor, can be expected to cause the wage rate to rise, which will lead to a higher employment level. An increase in the supply of labor, due to a reduction in workers' opportunity costs or to an improvement in the workplace environment, can cause the equilibrium wage rate to fall and the equilibrium quantity of labor hired to increase. (We encourage students to work through the graphs for these and other stipulated changes in supply and demand.)

For an explanation for why markets don't appear to clear as suggested by supply-and-demand-curve analysis, see online Perspective 3, Why queues?

Online Perspective 3
Why queues?

Part B Organizational economics and management

Making worker wages profitable in competitive markets

This chapter has been about how "markets" do things such as set product prices and production levels through the forces of competition. However, while supply and demand curves are very useful, there is much about the way markets operate that doesn't seem fully amenable to supply-and-demand-curve analysis. Real, live people are involved who sometimes seem to do things that defy conventional market explanation, but which can actually be explained by competitive labor market forces. The creative things managers do to motivate their employees are powerful forces underneath supply and demand curves. When someone or some firm develops a more powerful payment scheme, then others are pressed to follow for fear of losing sales and profits.

Henry Ford's "overpayment"

Take, for example, Henry Ford, who is remembered for his organizational inventiveness (the assembly line) and for his presumption that he could ignore the wishes of his customers, as in his claim that he was willing to give buyers any color car they wanted as long as it was black. However, he outdid himself when it came to workers: he *seemed* to want to deny the control of the market when it came to setting his workers' wages. But did he?

In 1914, he stunned his board of directors by proposing to raise his workers' wages to $3 a day, a third higher than the going wage ($2.20 a day) in the Detroit automobile industry at the time. When one of his board members wondered aloud why he was not considering giving workers even more, a wage of $4 or $5 a day, Ford quickly agreed to go to $5, more than twice the prevailing market wage. Why?

In the competitive framework illustrated with supply and demand curves, the "market wage" will settle where the market clears, or where the number of workers who are demanded by employers exactly equals the number of workers who are willing to work. And, once more, no profit-hungry employer (at least in the textbook discussions) would ever pay above (or below) the market wage. For that matter, in standard textbooks, employers in competitive markets are *unable* to pay anything other than the market wage, given competition. If employers ever tried to pay more, they could be underpriced and competed out of business by other producers who paid the lower market wage for their labor. If employers paid below the market wage, they would not be able to hire employees and would be left without products to sell.

An answer to why Ford paid more than the prevailing wage won't be found on the pages of standard economics textbooks (Meyer 1981). In those texts, wages are determined by *market conditions* – namely, the forces of supply and demand, as just discussed. The supply of labor is determined by what workers are willing to do, whereas the demand for labor is determined by the combined forces of worker productivity and the prices that can be charged for what the workers produce. The curves are more or less stationary (at least, in the way they are presented), and are certainly not subject to manipulation by employers and their policies.

There are two problems with that perspective from the point of view of this book. First, we don't wish to assume away the problem of business strategy and policy choices. On the contrary, we want to discuss how policies might affect worker productivity, or how employers might achieve maximum productivity from workers. We seek a rationale for Ford's dramatic wage move, if there is one to be found. In doing so, we don't deny that productivity affects worker wages, which is a well-established theoretical proposition in economics. What we insist on is that the reverse is also true – worker wages affect productivity – for very good economic reasons.

Second, a problem with standard market theory is that there is a lot of real-world experience that does not seem to fit the simple supply and demand model. Granted, the standard model is highly useful for discussing how wages might change with movements in the forces of supply and demand. From that framework, we can appreciate, for example, why wages move up when the labor demand increases (which can be attributable to productivity and/or price increases). At the same time, many employers have followed Ford's lead and have paid more than so-called "market wages." All one has to do to check out that claim is to watch how many workers put in applications when a plant announces that it is hiring. Sometimes, the lines stretch for blocks from the plant door. When the departments of history or English in our universities have an open professorship, the departments can expect a hundred or more qualified applicants. The US Postal Service regularly receives far more applications for its carrier jobs than it has jobs available. When Dell computers announced its intention to hire workers at a new computer assembly plant in Winston-Salem, North Carolina in the early 2000s, the queue at the work fair stretched for blocks down the street; the end, in fact, could not be seen from the door. These examples cannot be explained by market-clearing wages.

Consider the persistence of unemployment. The traditional view of labor markets would predict that the wage should be expected to fall until the market clears and the only evident unemployment should be transitory, encompassing people who are not working because they are between jobs or are looking for jobs. But "involuntary unemployment" abounds and persists, which must be attributable, albeit partially, to employers paying workers "too much" (or above the market-clearing wage rate).

We don't pretend to provide a complete explanation for "overpaying" workers here. It may be that employers overpay their workers for some psychological reasons. Overpaying workers might make the employers feel good about themselves and their employees, which can show up in greater loyalty, longer job tenure, and harder and more dedicated work. The above-market wages may also remove workers' financial strains, leaving them with fewer problems at home and more energy to devote themselves to their jobs. Although we think that these can be relevant considerations, we prefer to look for other reasons, mainly as a means of improving incentives for workers to do as the employer wants.

As it turns out, Henry Ford was not offering his workers something extra for nothing in return (Halberstam 1986). He "overpaid" his workers primarily because he could then demand more of them. He could work them harder and longer, and he did. He also could expect to lower his training costs and could be more selective in the people he hired, which could be a boon to all Ford workers. Workers could reason that they would be working with more highly qualified cohorts, all of whom would be forced to devote themselves to their jobs more energetically and productively, creating a more viable firm and greater job security. But there were other benefits for Ford as well.

When workers are paid exactly their market wage, there is little cost to quitting. A worker making his market (or opportunity) wage can simply drop his job and move on to the next job with little loss in income. And, as was the case, Ford's workers were quitting with great frequency. In 1913, Ford had an employee turnover rate of 370 percent! That year, the company had to hire 52,000 workers to maintain a workforce of 13,600 workers.

The company estimated that hiring a worker cost from $35 to $70, and even then workers were hard to control (and the costs of hiring workers today, even in the pizza business, is far higher than in Ford's time[1]). For example, before the pay raise, the absentee rate at Ford was 10 percent. Workers could stay home from work, more or less when they wanted, with virtually no threat of penalty. Given that they were being paid the market wage, the cost of their absenteeism was low to the workers. In effect, workers were buying a lot of absent days from work. It was a bargain. They could reason that if they were only receiving the "market wage rate," then they could easily replace that wage rate elsewhere should Ford fire them for absenteeism or other misbehavior.

At any one time, most workers were new at their jobs. Shirking was rampant. Ford complained that "the undirected worker spends more time walking about for tools and material than he does working; he gets small pay because pedestrianism is not a highly paid line" (Halberstam 1986, 94). In order to control workers, the company figured that the firm had to create some buffer between itself and the fluidity of a "perfectly" functioning labor market.

The nearly $3 Ford paid above the market was, in effect, a premium paid to enforce the strict rules for employment eligibility that he imposed. Ford's so-called Sociology Department was staffed by investigators who, after the pay hike, made frequent home visits and checked into workers' savings plans, marital happiness, alcohol use, and moral conduct, as well as their work habits on the job. Ford was effectively paying for the right to make those checks, which he thought would lead to more productive workers.

Ford was also paying for obedience. He is quoted as saying after the pay hike, "I have a thousand men who if I say 'Be at the northeast corner of the building at 4 a.m.' will be there at 4 a.m. That's what we want – obedience" (Halberstam 1986, 94). How much obedience or allegiance he got may be disputed. What is not disputable is that he got dramatic results. In 1915, the turnover rate was 16 percent – down from 370 percent – and productivity increased about 50 percent.

It should be pointed out that control over workers is only part of the problem. Even if a boss has total control, there must be some way of knowing what employees should be doing to maximize their contribution to the firm. That wasn't a difficult

---

[1] In 2005, Domino's Pizza incurred a hiring cost of $2,500 for every hourly worker and $20,000 for every store manager (White 2005).

problem for Ford. On the assembly line, it was obvious what Ford wanted his workers to do, and it was relatively easy to spot shirkers. According to David Halberstam, there was small chance for the shirker to prosper in the Ford plant. After the plant was mechanized and the $5-a-day policy was implemented, foremen were chosen largely for physical strength. According to Halberstam, "If a worker seemed to be loitering, the foreman simply knocked him down" (1986, 94). Given that the high wage attracted many applicants, Ford's workers simply put up with the abuse and threat of abuse because they didn't want to be replaced. The lines outside the employment office were a strong signal to workers.

Of course, this type of heavy-handed control wasn't prevalent in the Ford plants because workers quickly shaped up and responded to the new incentives. And it should be emphasized that the threat of physical punishment doesn't work in every work environment, particularly not today. When productivity requires that workers possess a lot of specialized knowledge that they must exercise creatively or in response to changing situations, heavy-handed enforcement tactics can undermine creativity and productivity. How is a manager to know whether a research chemist, a software developer, or a manager is behaving in ways that make the best use of his or her talents in promoting the objectives of the firm? Do you knock workers down if they gaze out the window? Of course not. Managers typically provide more subtle incentive programs than a high daily salary and a tough foreman. The big problem is controlling employees who have expertise you lack. One way to inspire effort from those who can't be monitored directly on a daily basis is to "overpay" workers, and ensure that they suffer a cost in the event that their performance, as measured over time, is not adequate. The "overpayment" gives workers a reason to avoid being fired or demoted for such reasons as lack of performance and excessive shirking. Even when shirking is hard to detect, the threat of losing a well-paying job can be sufficient to motivate diligent effort (Lawler 1968; Shapiro and Stiglitz 1984; Bulow and Summers 1986; Roberts 2004).

Overpayments to prevent misuse of firm resources

Many workers are in positions of responsibility, meaning that they have control over firm resources (real and financial) that they typically use with discretion but could misuse or appropriate for their own uses. Their actions are also difficult to monitor. Misuse of funds may only infrequently be discovered. How should such employees be paid? More than likely, they should be "overpaid." That is, they should be paid more than their market wage as a way of imposing a cost on them if their misuse of funds – especially, their dishonesty – is ever uncovered. The expected loss of "excess wages" must exceed the potential (discounted) value of the misused funds. The less likely it is that the employees will be found out, the greater the overpayment must be in order for the cost to be controlling.

Why do managers of branch banks make more than bank tellers? One reason is that the managers' talents are scarcer than tellers' are. That is a point frequently drawn from standard labor market theorizing, but it can't be the whole story because the pay difference between manager and teller can be greater than the skill gap. We add here two additional factors that can help explain the pay gap: First, the manager is very likely in a position to misuse, or just steal, more firm resources than is each individual teller. Second, the manager's actions are less likely to be discovered than the teller's. The manager usually has more discretion than each teller does, and the manager has one less level of supervision.

Why does pay escalate with rank within organizations? There are myriad reasons, several of which we cover later. We suggest here that as managers move up the corporate ladder, they typically acquire more and more responsibility, gain more discretion over more firm resources, and have more opportunities to misuse firm resources. In order to deter the misuse of firm resources, the firm needs to increase the threat of penalty for any misuse, which implies a higher and higher wage premium for each step on the corporate ladder.

Workers in the bowels of their corporations often feel that the people in the executive suite are drastically "overpaid," given that their pay appears to be out of line with what they do. To a degree, the workers are right. People in the executive suite are often paid a premium simply to deter them from misusing their powers. The workers should not necessarily resent the overpayments. The overpayments may be the most efficient way available for making sure that firm resources are used efficiently. To the extent that the overpayments work, the jobs of people at the bottom of the corporate ladder can be more productive, better paying, and more secure.

The under- and overpayment of workers

Should workers accept "overpayment"? Better yet, is a greater overpayment always better for workers? The natural tendency is to answer with a strong "Yes!" Well, we think a more cautious answer is in order, as in "Maybe" or, again, "It depends." Workers would be well advised to carefully assess what is expected of them, immediately and down the road. High pay means that employers can make greater demands – in terms of the scope and intensity of work assignments – on their employees. This is because of the cost they will bear if they do not consent to the demands.

Clearly, workers should expect that their employers will demand value equal to, if not above, the wage payments, and workers should consider whether they contribute as much to their firms' coffers as they take. Otherwise, their job tenure may be tenuous. The value of a job is ultimately equal to how much the workers can expect to earn over time, appropriately adjusted for the fact that future payments are not worth as much to workers as current ones are and for the fact that uncertain payments are not worth as much as certain payments. A high-paying job that is lost almost immediately for inadequate performance may be a poor deal for an employee.

The overpayment/underpayment connection

Firms might also "overpay" their workers because they have "underpaid" their workers early in their careers. The "overpayments" are not so much "excess payments" as they are "repayments" of wages forgone early in the workers' careers. Of course, the workers would not likely forgo wages unless they expected their delayed overpayments to include interest on the wages forgone. So, the delayed overpayments must exceed underpayments by the applicable market interest rate. In such cases, the firms are effectively using their workers as sources of capital. The workers themselves become "venture capitalists" of an important kind.

Why would firms do that? Some new firms must do it just to get started. They don't have access to all of the capital they need in their early years, given that their product or service has not been proven. They must ask their workers to invest "sweat equity," which is equal to the difference between what the workers could make in their respective labor markets and what they are paid by their firms. The underpayments not only extend the sources of capital to the firm but also give the workers a strong stake in the future of the firm, which can make the workers work all the harder to make the firm's future a prosperous one. The up-front underpayments can make the firm more profitable and increase its odds of survival, which can be a benefit to workers as well as owners. Of course, this is one reason that many young workers are willing to accept employment in firms that are just starting out. Young workers often have a limited financial base from which to make investments; they do, however, have their time and energy to invest.

Underpayments to workers that are coupled with later overpayments can also be seen as a means by which managers can enhance the incentives workers have to become more productive. If workers are underpaid when they start, their rewards can be hiked later by more than otherwise to account for productivity improvements. These hikes can continue – and must continue – until the workers are effectively overpaid later in their careers (or else the workers would not have accepted the underpayments earlier in their careers). However, managers must understand that they must be able to *commit* themselves to the overpayments and that there must be some end to them.

Mandatory retirement

Not too many years ago, firms regularly required their workers to retire at age sixty-five. Retirement was ritualistic for managers. Shortly after a manager had his or her sixty-fifth birthday, someone would organize a dinner at which the manager would be given a gold watch and a plaque for venerable service and then be shown to the door with one last pleasant goodbye.

Why would a firm impose a mandatory retirement age on its workers? Such a policy seems truly bizarre, given that most companies are intent on making as much money as they can. Often the workers forced to retire are some of the more productive in the firm, simply because they have more experience with the firm and its customer and supplier networks.

Although we acknowledge that mandatory retirement may appear to be a mistake, particularly in the case of highly productive employees, we think that for many companies a mandatory retirement policy makes good business sense – when they have been "overpaying" their workers for some time. (Otherwise, we would be hard pressed to explain why such policies would survive and would need to be outlawed.) To lay out that logic, we must take a detour into an analysis of the way that workers who come under mandatory retirement policies are paid throughout their careers.

Paying market wages, or exactly what workers are worth at every stage in their career, does not always maximize worker incomes. That was a central point of the discussion to this point. We extend that discussion here by showing how the manipulation of a worker's *career* wage structure, or earnings path over time, can actually raise worker productivity and lifetime income. However, as also will be shown, when worker wages diverge from their value over the course of their careers, mandatory retirement is a necessary component of the labor contract (Lazear 1979).

Suppose that a worker goes to work for Apex, Inc. and is paid exactly what she is worth at every point in time. Assume that she can expect to have a modest productivity improvement over the course of a thirty-year career, described by the slightly upward sloping line A in figure 3.12. If her income follows her productivity, her salary will rise in line with the slope of line A. In year Y_1, the worker's annual income will be I_1; in year Y_2, it will be I_2, and so forth.

Is there a way by which management can restructure the worker's income path and simultaneously enable both the workers and the firm to gain? No matter what else is done, management must clearly pay the worker an amount equal at least to what she is worth *over the course of her career*. Otherwise, the worker would not stay with the company. The worker would exit the firm, moving to secure the available higher career income. However, management need not pay, each year, an amount equal to the income points represented on line A. Management could pay the worker less than she is worth for a while, as long as management is willing to compensate by overpaying her later.

For example, suppose that management charts a career pay path given by line B, which implies that up until year Y_3, the workers are paid less than they are worth, with the extent of the underpayment equaling the shaded area between the origin and Y_3. However, the workers would be compensated for what amounts to an

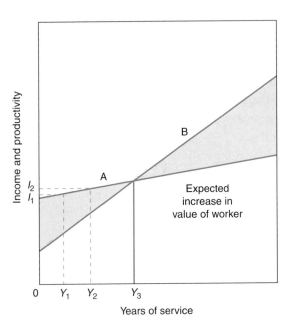

Figure 3.12 Twisted pay scale
The worker expects her productivity to rise along line *A* with years of service. If she starts work with less pay than she could earn elsewhere, then her career pay path could follow line *B*, representing greater increases in pay with time and greater productivity.

investment in the firm by an overpayment after year Y_3, with the extent of the overpayment equal to the shaded area above line *A* after Y_3.

Are the firm and worker likely to be better off? Notice that the actual proposed pay line *B* is much steeper than line *A* which, again, represents the worker's income path in the absence of management's intentional twisting of the pay structure. The greater angle of line *B* means that the worker is less likely to leave the company after she has been with the firm for a while. This increases the expected payoff the firm realizes from investing in the worker with varied assignments and training, investments that would not make sense if the firm thought that the worker was going to take the training and then take her improved skills to another firm. The additional training obviously improves the worker's productivity which shifts up her productive curve in figure 3.12 and her compensation line. This can mean not only more compensation over a worker's entire career, but more compensation at every point in time, even early on when she is being "undercompensated" if her productivity curve shifts up enough.

There is another advantage workers receive from the deferred compensation illustrated in figure 3.12, especially good workers. When interviewing prospective employees, a firm would like to know how dedicated and hard working a worker will be, and how confident the worker is that he will do what it takes to become highly productive, the type of person they want to hire. Of course, anyone can claim to be a great employee, but the interviewers are likely to discount such claims since they know that they are self-serving, and difficult to verify. If the prospective employee really is an ambitious, hard-working person who does have confidence that he will be a great employee, it would be to his advantage to be able to convince the firm of those attributes. And one of the most credible ways of doing so is to accept a pay arrangement in which he works for something less than he might be worth initially, proving his worth before receiving a really significant salary. That is exactly what he is able to do by accepting a job with a steep earning profile (deferred compensation).

There is another reason why good workers may want to work for a firm that intentionally underpays them when they are young or just starting out with the company. The workers can reason that everyone in the firm will have a greater incentive to work harder and smarter. Hence, they can all enjoy higher prospective incomes over the course of their careers.

Normally, commentaries on worker pay implicitly assume that the pay structure is what management imposes on workers. Seen from the perspective of the economic realities of what is available for distribution to all workers in a firm, we could just as easily reason that the kind of pay structure represented by line *B* in figure 3.12 is what the workers would encourage management to adopt. Actually, the twisting of the pay structure is nothing more than an innovative way for managers to increase the money they make off their workers while also increasing the money that workers are able to make off their firms. In short, it is a mutually beneficial deal, something of a "free good," in the sense that more is available for everyone.

The role of employers' "credible commitments"

If twisting the pay structure is such a good idea, why isn't it observed more often than it is in industry? Perhaps some variant of twisted pay schedules is more widely used than it is thought to be, primarily because such pay schedules are not identified as such. Public and private universities are notorious for making their assistant professors work harder than full professors who have tenure and far more pay. Large private firms, such as General Motors and IBM, appear to have pay structures that are more like line *B* than line *A* in figure 3.12. However, millions of firms appear to be unwilling or unable to move away from a pay structure such as line *A*.

One of the problems with line *B* is that young workers must accept a cut in pay for a promise of greater pay in the future – and the pay later on must exceed what the workers can get elsewhere *and*, what is crucial to workers, more than what their firm would have to pay if they simply hired replacement workers at the going market wage. Obviously, the workers take the considerable risk that their firm will not live up to its promise and fail to raise their pay later to points above their market wage or, even worse, fire them.

Needless to say, the firm must be able to make a *credible commitment* to its workers that it will live up to its part of the bargain, the *quo* in the *quid pro quo*.

Truly credible commitments require that the firm must be able to demonstrate a capacity and inclination to do what it says it will do. Many firms are not going to be able to twist their pay structures, and thereby gain the productivity improvements, because they are new, maybe small, with a shaky financial base and an uncertain future. New firms have little history by which workers can assess the value of their firms' commitments. Small firms are often short-lived firms. Financially shaky firms, especially those that suffer from problems of insolvency or illiquidity, are not likely to be able to garner their workers' trust. Firms that are in highly fluid, ever-changing, and competitive markets are also unlikely candidates for having the ability to twist their pay structures. They all will tend to have to pay workers their market worth, or even a premium, to accommodate the risks that workers must accept when the company's existence is in doubt. We have to qualify these comments when considering a new firm with the prospects of a very profitable future (some high-tech firms, for example) even though there is a good chance that it will fail, as will be discussed in a moment.

Which firms are most likely to twist their pay structures? Ones that have been established for some time, have a degree of financial and market stability, have some monopoly power – and have proven by their actions that their word is their bond. To prove the latter, firms cannot simply go willy-nilly about dismissing workers or cutting their pay when they find cheaper replacements. To do so would be to undermine their credibility with their workers.

We can't be too precise in identifying the types of firms that can twist their pay structures, for the simple reason that there can be extenuating circumstances. For example, we can imagine that some unproved upstart companies would be able to pay their workers below-market wages. As noted, they may have to do so, simply because they do not have the requisite cash flow early in their development. New firms often ask, or demand, that their workers provide "sweat equity" in their firms through the acceptance of below-market wages, but always with the expectation that their investment will pay off. Which new firms are likely to be able to do this?

We suspect that firms with new products that represent a substantial improvement over established products would be good candidates. The likely success of the new product gives a form of baseline credibility to firm owner commitments that they intend to – and can – repay the "sweat equity" later. Indeed, the greater the improvement the new product represents, the more likely it is that the firm can make the repayment, and do so in an expeditious manner, and the more likely the workers will accept below-market wages to start with. The very fact that the product is a substantial improvement increases the likelihood of the firm's eventual success, for two reasons. The first reason is widely recognized: a product that represents a substantial improvement will likely attract considerable consumer attention. The

B

second reason is less obvious: the firm can delay its wage payments, using its scarce cash flow in its initial stages of production for other things, such as quality control, distribution, and promotion. The firm gets capital – sweat equity – from an unheralded source, workers. The workers' investment of their sweat equity can enhance the firm's survival chances and, thereby, even lower the interest rate that the firm must pay on their debt (because the debt is more secure).

[See online Video Module 3.7 Twisting salary]

Breaking commitments

Of course, there are times when firms must break with their past commitments. For example, if a firm that was once insulated from foreign competition suddenly must confront more cost-effective foreign competitors in domestic markets (because, say, transportation costs have been lowered), then the firm may have to break with its commitments to overpay workers late in their careers. A firm facing such a situation does not revise its wage commitments; the competition will simply pay people the going market wage and erode the markets of those firms who continue to overpay their older workers. Without question, many older American workers – for example, middle managers in the automobile industry – have hard feelings about the advent of the "global marketplace." They may have suffered through years of hard work at below-market wages in the belief that they would be able, later in their careers, to slack off and still see their wages rise further and further above the market rate. The advent of global competition, however, has undercut the capacity of many American firms to fulfill their part of an implied bargain with their workers.

Even though they may have hard feelings, it does not follow that the workers would want their firms to try to hold to their prior agreements. Many workers understand that their wages can be higher *than they otherwise would be* if their firms have kept their prior agreement. Without the reneging, the firm might fold. In a sense, the workers made an investment in the firm through their lower wages, and the investment didn't pay off as much as expected. However, we hasten to add that some American workers have probably been burned by firms that have used changing market conditions as an *excuse* to break with their commitments or that have sold their firms to buyers who felt no compulsion to hold to the original owners' prior commitments.

The answer to the question central to this discussion – "Why does mandatory retirement exist?" – can now be provided, at least partially. Mandatory retirement at, say, sixty-five or seventy may be instituted for any number of plausible reasons. It might be introduced simply to move out workers who have become mentally or physically impaired. Perhaps, in some ideal world, the policy should not, for this reason, be applied to everyone. After all, many older workers are in the midst of their more productive years, because of their accumulated experience and wisdom, when they are in their sixties and seventies. However, it may still be a reasonable *rule* because its application to *all* workers may mean that *on average*, by applying the policy without exception, the firm is more efficient and profitable than it would be had it incurred the costs of individually scrutinizing workers at retirement time.

However, the *expected* fitness of workers at the time of retirement is simply not the only likely issue at stake. We see mandatory retirement as we see all employment rules, as a part of what is presumed to be a mutually beneficial employment contract, replete with many other rules. It is a contract provision that helps both the firms that adopt it and their workers who must abide by it. Parts of the contract can make the mandatory retirement rule economically sound.

We have spent much of this section exploring the logic of twisting workers' career income paths. If such a twist is productive and profitable, and if workers must be overpaid late in their careers to make the twist possible, then it follows that firms will want, at some point, to cut the overpayments off. What is mandatory retirement? It is – at least at the margin – a means of cutting off at some definite point the stream of overpayments. It is a means of making it possible, and economically practical, for a firm to engage a twisted pay scale and to improve incentives to add to the firm's productivity and profitability. To continue overpayments until workers – even the most productive ones – collapse on the job is nothing short of a policy that courts financial disaster.

Having said that, suppose Congress decides that mandatory retirement is simply an inane employment policy (as it has done). After all, members of Congress might reason, many of the workers who are forced to retire are still quite productive. What are the consequences?

Clearly, the older workers who are approaching the prior retirement age, who suffered through years of underpayment early in their careers, but who are, at the time of the abolition of mandatory retirement policy, being overpaid, will gain from the passage of the law. They can continue to collect their overpayments until they drop dead or decide that work is something they would prefer not to do. They gain more in overpayments than they could have anticipated (and they get more back from their firms than they paid for in terms of their early underpayments). These employees will, because of the actions of Congress, experience an unexpected wealth gain.

There are, however, clear losers. The owners will suffer a wealth loss; they will have to continue with the overpayments. Knowing that, the owners will likely try to minimize their losses. Assuming that the owners can't lower their older workers' wages to market levels and eliminate the overpayment (because of laws against age discrimination), they will simply seek to capitalize the expected stream of losses from keeping the older workers on and buy them out – that is, pay them some lump-sum amount to induce them to retire.

To buy the workers out, the owners would not have to pay their workers an amount equal to the current value of their expected future wages. The reason is that the worker should be able to collect some lower wage in some other job if he or she is bought out. Presumably, the buyout payments would be no less than the value of the expected stream of *overpayments* (the pay received from the company minus the pay the worker could get elsewhere, appropriately discounted).

In order for the buyout to work, of course, both the owners and the workers must be no worse off and, preferably, each group should gain by any deal that is struck. How can that be? The owners simply pay the workers the current value of the overpayments (adjusted for the timing and uncertainty of the future payments).

But, can both sides *gain* by a buyout deal? That may not always be so easy a result to bring about. The owners would have to be willing to pay workers more than they, the workers, are willing to accept as a minimum. There are several reasons such a deal may be possible in many, but not necessarily all, cases. First, the workers could have a higher discount rate than the owners, and this may often be the case because the owners are more diversified than their workers in their investments. Workers tend to concentrate their capital, a main component of which is *human capital*, in their jobs. By agreeing to a buyout and receiving some form of lump-sum payment in cash (or even in a stream of future cash payments), the workers can diversify their portfolios by scattering the cash among a variety of real and financial assets. Hence, workers might accept less than the current (discounted) value of their overpayments just to gain the greater security of a more diversified investment portfolio. Naturally (and we use that word advisedly), the workers cannot be sure how long they will be around to collect the overpayments. By taking the payments in lump-sum form, they reduce the risk of collection and increase the security of their heirs.

Second, sometimes retirement systems are overfunded – that is, they have greater expected income streams from their investments than are needed to meet the expected future outflow of retirement payments. This was the case, for example, of the University of California Employee Retirement System. Therefore, if the company can tap the retirement funds, it can pay workers more in the buyout than they would receive in overpayments by continuing to work. In so doing, it can move those salaries "off budget," which is what California did in the mid-1990s in order to match its budgeted expenditures with declining state funding levels for higher education. With the nation's financial and economic crisis that emerged full blown in 2008, the market value of California's retirement portfolio had deteriorated so much that the state could no longer tap the retirement fund to cover the state's ballooning budget deficit.

Third, some workers may take the buyout because they expect that their companies will meet with financial difficulty from competition down the road. The higher the probability that the company will fail in the future (especially the near future), the more likely workers would be willing to accept a monetary buyout that is less than the current value of the stream of overpayments.

Fourth, some workers might take the buyout simply because they are tired of working for the company or want to walk away from built-up hostilities. To that extent, the buyout can be less than the (discounted) value of the overpayments.

Fifth, of course, older workers have to fear that the employer will not continue to pay workers more than they are worth indefinitely. The owners can, if they choose to do so, lower the amount of the buyout payment simply by making life more difficult for older workers in ways that are not necessarily subject to legal challenge (for example, by changing work and office assignments, secretarial assistance, discretionary budgeted items, flexibility in scheduling, etc.). The owners may never actually have to take such actions to lower the buyout payments. All that is necessary is for the *threat* to be a real consideration. Workers might rightfully expect that the greater their projected overpayments, the more they must fear their owners will use their remaining discretion to make a buyout possible.

The abolition of mandatory retirement

We should also expect that workers' fears will vary across firms and will be related to a host of factors, not the least of which will be the size of the firm. Workers who work for large firms may not be as fearful as workers for small firms, mainly because large firms are more likely to be sued for any retaliatory use of their discretionary employment practices (and efforts to adjust the work of older workers in response to any law that abolishes mandatory retirement rules). Large firms simply have more to take as a penalty for what are judged to be illegal acts. Moreover, it appears that juries are far more likely to impose much larger penalties on large firms, with lots of equity, than on their smaller counterparts. This unequal treatment before the courts, however, suggests that laws that abolish mandatory retirement rules will give small firms a competitive advantage over their larger market rivals.

However, we hasten to stress that all we have done is to discuss the transitory adjustments firms will make with their older workers, who are near the previous retirement age. We should expect other adjustments for younger workers, not the least of which will be a change in their wage structures. Not being able to overpay their older workers in their later years will probably mean that the owners will have to raise the pay of their younger workers. After all, the only reason the younger workers would accept underpayment for years is the prospect of overpayments later on.

There are three general observations from this line of inquiry that are interesting:

1 The abolition of mandatory retirement will tend to help those who are about to retire. Such workers may have been overpaid because the companies anticipated being able to terminate the overpayment at the set retirement age; but abolition of

mandatory retirement can mean that the workers can continue to receive the overpayment, perhaps indefinitely, at owners' expense, of course.

2 Abolition might help some older workers who are years from retirement, who work for large firms, and who can hang on to their overpayments. It can hurt other older workers who are fired, demoted, not given raises, or have their pay actually cut.

3 It can increase the wages of younger workers by lowering the amount by which they will be underpaid. However, their increase in wages while they are young will come at the expense of smaller overpayments later in their careers. Many, if not all, of these younger workers will not be any better off because of the abolition of mandatory retirement than they would have been with a retirement rule in place.

Overall, productivity might be expected to suffer, given that owners can no longer twist their career pay structures for their workers. As a consequence, workers will not have as strong an incentive to improve their productivity; they simply cannot gain as much by doing so. This means that the abolition of mandatory retirement rules can lower worker wages from what they otherwise would have been.

The simple point that emerges from this line of discussion is that the level and structure of pay count for reasons that are not always obvious. But our point about "overpayment" is fairly general, applying to the purchase of any number of resources other than labor. You may simply want to "overpay" suppliers at times just to ensure that they will provide the agreed-upon level of quality and will not take opportunities to shirk because they can lose, on balance, if they do so (Klein and Leffler 1981).

Practical lesson for MBAs: recognize that management credibility can be a source of profits in business

MBA students are usually fully aware that firm profits can be made from producing the proverbial "better mousetrap." In highly competitive markets, product improvement can be a business necessity for offensive and defensive reasons. The offensive reason comes from firms with improved products being able to charge higher prices and gain market share and profits. The defensive reason for improving products is that firms that resist product improvements can lose market share and can be forced to charge lower prices, or can be forced to close. In highly competitive environments, cost-effective product improvement is not an open choice. To assess the competitiveness of their markets, managers must assess the ease with which new firms can enter their markets and the ease with which buyers can shift among existing and new producers.

MBA students often fail to fully appreciate that manager (and firm) credibility can be no less of a profit source than product improvements. Managers whose word is their bond can reduce the risk that cost-relevant others (workers, suppliers, and buyers) incur in their dealings with the managers. Such managers (and their firms) will not have to pay a "risk premium" in the wages they pay their workers or in the prices they pay their suppliers and will obtain price advantages in dealing with buyers. Although ephemeral and never captured on accounting statements, "risk cost" is no less a real cost of doing business than the cost of materials.

Managers who can make credible commitments can achieve a competitive advantage in lieu of developing their products and/or selling their products at lower prices. One of the best ways managers can make credible commitments is to find ways to convey to others how they, the managers, will suffer if they break their commitments. Managers who have established reputations for making credible commitments can be expected to earn a salary premium because of the cost saving they can bring to the firms that hire them.

Further reading online

R

Reading 3.1 Price competition in the short run and the long run

The bottom line

The key takeaways from chapter 3 are the following:

1 The market is a system that provides producers with incentives to deliver goods and services to others. To respond to those incentives, producers must meet the needs of

society. They must compete with other producers to deliver their goods and services in the most cost-effective manner.

2   A market implies that sellers and buyers can freely respond to incentives and that they have options and can choose among them. It does not mean, however, that behavior is totally unconstrained or that producers can choose from unlimited options. What a competitor can do may be severely limited by what rival firms are willing to do.

3   Demand curves for products and labor (or any other input) slope downward (and represent inverse relationships between price and quantity demanded). Supply curves for products and labor slope upwards (and represent positive relationships between price and quantity produced). The positions of these curves are determined by a number of market forces.

4   Price and quantity in competitive markets will tend to move toward the intersection of supply and demand, which is the point of maximum efficiency.

5   Market shortages will lead to price increases. Market surpluses will lead to price decreases.

6   Equilibrium price and quantity in competitive markets can be expected to change in predictable ways relative to increases and decreases in supply and demand.

7   Obstructions to price movement upward to equilibrium give rise to market shortages. Obstructions to price movement down toward equilibrium give rise to market surpluses.

8   Wage rates are determined by the interaction of essentially the same market forces that determine the prices of products. The demand for labor is a function of workers' productivity and the prices secured for the products that workers help produce. The supply of labor is determined by workers' opportunity costs and by working conditions.

9   An increase in the price of the product workers produce can lead to an increase in workers' wage rate in competitive labor markets. An increase in worker non-wage benefits can be expected to lead to a reduction in workers' wage rate in competitive labor markets.

10 The market system is not perfect. Producers may have difficulty acquiring enough information to make reliable production decisions. People take time to respond to incentives, and producers can make high profits while others are gathering their resources to respond to an opportunity.

11 An uncontrolled market system also carries with it the possibility that one firm will acquire at least some monopoly power, restricting the ability of others to enter into competition, produce more, and push prices and profits down (a topic to which we shall return in chapter 10).

12 Under certain conditions, firms would be well advised not to match up worker pay with worker "worth" at every moment in time. Current and prospective pay can be used as a means of increasing worker productivity and rewards over time.

13 Mandatory retirement can also have unheralded benefits for workers as well as their employers. Mandatory retirement can allow for "overpayments" for workers, which can increase workers' incentives to improve their productivity over the course of their careers.

Review questions >>

1 Why does the demand curve have a negative slope and the supply curve a positive slope?

2 Why will the competitive market tend to move toward the price–quantity combination at the intersection of the supply and demand curves?

3 What might keep the market from moving all the way to that equilibrium point?

4 Suppose that a price ceiling is imposed on the product. What will be the effects on producers' welfare? On consumers' welfare? How does the ceiling affect overall market efficiency?

5 Suppose that a price floor is imposed on the product. What will be the effects on producers' welfare? On consumers' welfare? How does the price floor affect overall market efficiency?

6 Consider the analysis of product improvements in the chapter. Suppose you work for Levi-Strauss and the demand for blue jeans suddenly increases. Discuss possible short-run and long-run movements of the market and the consequences for your company. What will tend to happen to worker wage rates?

7 Henry Ford more than doubled his workers' wages. Did workers' real income double by Ford's pay policy? Reflecting on the general principles behind Ford's pay action, when should any firm – your firm – stop raising the pay of workers (not in terms of actual dollar amount but in terms of some economic/management principle that you can devise)?

8 Workers and their employers often talk about how workers "earn" their wages but firms "give" their workers health insurance (or any other fringe benefit). Should these different methods of pay be discussed in different terms?

9 Suppose the government requires employers to provide health (or dental) insurance. How might the requirement affect the supply of and demand for labor in competitive markets?

4

Applications of the economic way of thinking: domestic government and management policies

Without bandying jargon or exhibiting formulae, without being superficial or condescending, the scientist should be able to communicate to the public the nature and variety of consequences that can reasonably be expected to flow from a given action or sequence of actions. In the case of the economist, he can often reveal in an informal way, if not the detailed chain of reasoning by which he reaches his conclusions, at least the broad contours of the argument.

E. J. Mishan

Chapters 1–3 showed how the models of competitive markets are fundamental to the economic way of thinking. With such models we can illuminate the economic effects of market changes, such as an increase in the price of oil. This chapter examines how domestic government policies and management practices can affect the operations of markets, product prices, and output levels, as well as worker wages and employment levels. In Part A, we apply supply-and-demand-curve analysis developed in the first three chapters to five types of government control: excise taxes, gasoline price controls, rent controls, minimum-wage laws, and mandated fringe benefits. As you will see, government controls imposed in competitive markets can inspire (if not force) management reactions that negate some of the expected effects of the controls. Along the way, we consider how management policies toward work demands, fringe benefits, and honest dealing affect wage rates and firms' efficient operations in competitive markets. Our goal is to demonstrate how the application of just a few economic principles, and twists and turns of argument, can generate interesting and useful insights and testable predictions that policy makers and managers should consider before finalizing various policies.

In Part B, we examine how the economic way of thinking, founded on rational behavior and market analysis, can be used to understand the role of trust in business, or how trust can affect firms' profitability and market competition. This is to say, trust is an unheralded force influencing market supply and demand and competitive-market outcomes. We use the game-theoretic models employed in the first three chapters to understand how trust can overcome Prisoner's Dilemma games. We also use game-theoretic models to develop mechanisms that business can use, and does use, to inspire greater trust with their workers, buyers, and suppliers.

The approach economists take to analyzing human satisfaction stands in contrast to the approach taken in psychology and other social sciences. MBA students will, at some point in their programs, confront the "Maslow's Hierarchy of Needs," which psychologists (and business school professors in organizational behavior and marketing, for example) use to explain the way people go about satisfying their various wants. In online Perspective 4 and Video Module 4.7 for this chapter, we lay out the Maslow's Hierarchy of Needs with two goals in mind. First, we want to use Maslow's hierarchy to clarify the distinguishing characteristics in the economic approach to human want satisfaction. Second, we want to use demand-curve analysis to better understand why Maslow developed the exact structure of his hierarchy the way he did, and why the structure might have been different had prices of various "levels" of goods been different at the time he did his scholarly work.

Online Perspective

Part A Theory and public policy applications

Who pays the tax?

Most people are convinced that consumers bear the burden of excise (or sales) taxes. They believe that producers simply pass the tax on to consumers in higher prices. Yet every time a new (or increased) excise tax is proposed, producers lobby against it. If excise taxes could be passed on to consumers, firms would have little reason to spend hundreds of thousands of dollars opposing them. In fact, excise taxes do hurt producers.

Figure 4.1 shows the margarine industry's supply and demand curves, S_1 and D. In a competitive market, the price will tend toward P_2 and the quantity sold toward Q_1. If the state imposes a $0.25 tax on each pound of margarine sold and collects the tax from producers, it effectively raises the cost of production. The producer must now pay a price not just for the right to use resources, such as

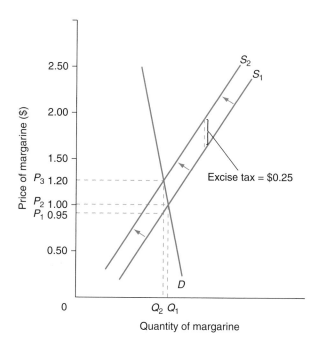

Figure 4.1 The economic effect of an excise tax
An excise tax of $0.25 will shift the supply curve for margarine to the left, from S_1 to S_2. The quantity produced will fall from Q_1 to Q_2; the price will rise from P_2 to P_3. The increase, $0.20, however, will not cover the added cost to the producer, $0.25.

equipment and raw materials, but for the right to continue production legally. The supply curve, reflecting this cost increase, shifts to S_2. The vertical difference between the two curves, P_1 and P_3, represents the extra $0.25 cost added by the tax.

Given the shift in supply, the quantity of margarine produced falls to Q_2 and the price rises to P_3. Note, however, that the equilibrium price increase (P_2 to P_3) is less than the vertical distance between the two supply curves (P_1 to P_3). That is, the price increases by less than the amount of the tax that caused the shift in supply. Clearly, the producer's net, after-tax price has fallen. If the tax is $0.25, but the price paid by consumers rises only $0.20 ($1.20 – $1.00), the producer loses $0.05 per unit sold. It now nets only $0.20 per unit on a product that had brought $0.25. In other words, the tax not only reduces the quantity of margarine producers can sell but also lowers the after-tax price to the margarine producers, which is reason enough for them to oppose such excise taxes.

Incidentally, butter producers have a clear incentive to support a tax on margarine. When the price of margarine increases, consumers will seek substitutes. The demand for butter will rise, and producers will be able to sell more butter and charge more for each pound.

The $0.25 tax in our example is divided between consumers and producers, although most of it ($0.20) is paid by consumers because they are relatively unresponsive to the price change. The result, as depicted in figure 4.1, is that

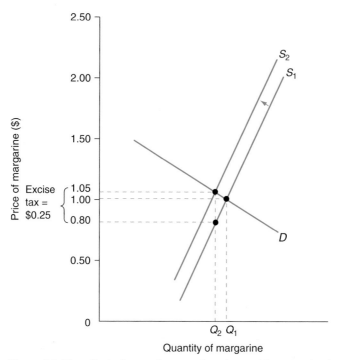

Figure 4.2 The effect of an excise tax when demand is more elastic than supply
If demand is much more elastic than supply, the quantity purchased declines significantly
when supply decreases from S_1 to S_2 in response to the added cost of the excise tax. Producers
will lose $0.20; consumers will pay only $0.05 more.

consumers bear most of the tax burden while producers pay only a small part
(20 percent) of the tax. If consumers were more responsive to the price change,
then a greater share of the tax burden would fall on producers, who would then have
more incentive to oppose the tax politically.

As can be seen in figure 4.2, when consumers are more responsive to a price
change, the price consumers pay rises from $1 to $1.05. The after-tax price received
by producers falls from $1 to $0.80, meaning that the producers pay 80 percent of
the tax in this case. This suggests that the more responsive consumers are to price
changes, the more producers should be willing to spend to oppose an excise tax on
their products.

Consumer responsiveness to a price change also can affect the level of the tax
imposed by a legislature interested in maximizing excise tax revenues. Suppose a
state government imposes an excise tax on sugar content of sodas to raise revenues
that can be used to reduce the state's budget deficit as well as sugar consumption
and the prevalence of obesity (which is precisely what the governor of New York
proposed to do in early 2009).

Suppose that with a tax of $1, soda prices rise and consumption falls to 100 million cans. State revenues from the tax will be $100 million ($1 × 100 million cans of sodas). If the tax is raised by 50 percent to $1.50, the consumption level falls to 80 million cans, leading to total tax revenues of $120 million ($1.50 × 80 million cans), or an increase of $20 million in state revenues. However, suppose that the tax is raised to $2, which causes consumption to fall to 45 million cans and total tax revenues to fall to $90 million ($2 × 45 million cans). With the higher tax the state might lower the obesity rate, but not its budget deficit by as much as it would have at a tax of $1 or $1.50. We should not be surprised that some of the heavier excise taxes are imposed on products (alcohol, gasoline, and tobacco) bought by consumers who are relatively price insensitive. On such products state legislators do not have to worry as much about a tax hike undercutting tax revenues.

The perceptive reader might worry that in the above calculations we have chosen our sales levels to get the desired revenue results. But clearly, an excise tax can be so high that tax revenues will fall simply because a progressive increase in the tax will progressively raise the product's price and progressively lower consumption. Hence, at some point a high tax rate will result in zero sales and, consequently, zero tax revenues. This means that tax revenues must fall beyond some high tax rate, before sales reach zero. Similarly, all governments must choose their taxes applied to labor (in the form of, say, an income tax) with the view that, beyond some high tax rate, tax revenues can fall, which can cause a curb in government services.

All government decision makers – federal, state, and local – have a real management problem (not unlike the kinds of pricing problems managers face in private firms): they must choose their excise tax rates carefully when their goal is maximum revenue collections. The general rule that follows from this illustration is important to remember: the more responsive consumers (or workers or owners of capital) are to a price increase, the lower the tax must be to maximize tax revenues. (The discussion of "elasticity of demand" in chapter 6 further clarifies these points.)

[See online Video Module 4.1 Excise taxes]

Price controls

Price controls are by no means a modern invention. The first recorded legal code, the 4,000-year-old Code of Hammurabi, included regulations governing the maximum wage, housing prices, and rents on property such as boats, animals, and tools. In AD 301, the Roman Emperor Diocletian issued an edict specifying maximum prices for everything from poultry to gold, and maximum wages for everyone from lawyers to the cleaners of sewer systems. The penalty for violating the edict was death. More recently in the United States, wage and price controls have been used both in wartime (during the Second World War and the Korean War) and in peacetime.

President Richard Nixon imposed an across-the-board wage–price freeze in 1971. President Jimmy Carter controlled energy prices in 1977 and later proposed the control of natural gas. As is true of attempts to control expenditures, wage and price controls often create more problems than they solve, as they did in the 1970s. When gasoline prices were controlled, long lines at gas pumps resulted everywhere, an outcome completely consistent with economic theory.

Gasoline price controls

In a competitive market, any restriction on the upward movement of prices will lead to shortages. Consider figure 4.3, which shows supply and demand curves for gasoline. Initially, the supply and demand curves are S_1 and D, and the equilibrium price is P_1.

Now suppose that the supply of gasoline shifts to S_2, and government officials, believing that the new equilibrium price is unjust, freeze the price at P_1. What will happen to the market for gasoline if the government imposes a **price ceiling**?

A **price ceiling** is a government-determined price above which a specified good cannot be sold.

At price P_1, which is now below the equilibrium, the number of gallons demanded by consumers is Q_2, but the number of gallons supplied is much lower, Q_1. A shortage of $Q_2 - Q_1$ gallons has developed. As a result, some consumers will not get all the gasoline they want. Some may be unable to get any.

Because of the shortage, consumers will have to wait in line to get whatever gasoline they can. To avoid a long line, they may try to get to the service station

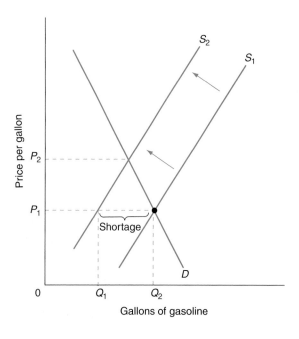

Figure 4.3 The effect of price controls on supply
If the supply of gasoline is reduced from S_1 to S_2, but the price is controlled at P_1, a shortage equal to the difference between Q_1 and Q_2 will emerge.

early – but others may do the same. To assure themselves a prime position, consumers may have to sit at the pumps before the station opens. In winter, waiting in line may mean wasting gas to keep warm. The moral of the story: although the pump price of gasoline may be held constant at P_1, the effective price – the sum of the pump price and the values of time lost waiting in line – will rise.

Shortages can raise the effective price of a product in other ways. With a long line of customers waiting to buy, a service station owner can afford to lower the quality of services provided and allow stations to become less clean. As a result, the effective price of gasoline rises still higher. Again, during the energy crises of the 1970s, the last time controls were used, the country learned a valuable economic lesson. Some service station owners started closing on weekends and at night. A few required customers to sign long-term contracts and pay in advance for their gasoline. The added interest cost of advance payment raised the price of gasoline even higher.

In addition to such legal maneuvers to evade price controls, some businesses may engage in fraud or black marketeering. They can tie the sale of the controlled good with the sale of an uncontrolled good; then, they can raise the price of the controlled good by increasing the price of the uncontrolled good. Indeed, the ways of circumventing price controls are limited only by firms' creativity.

During the 1970s, many gasoline station owners filled their premium tanks with regular gasoline and sold it at premium prices. At the same time, a greater-than-expected shortage of heating oil developed. Truckers, unable to get all the diesel fuel they wanted at the controlled price, found they could use home heating oil in their trucks. They paid home heating oil dealers a black market price for fuel oil, thus reducing the supply available to homeowners. As always, government controls bring enforcement problems.

To assure fair and equitable distribution of goods in short supply, some means of *rationing* is needed. If no formal system is adopted, supplies will be distributed on a first-come, first-served basis – in effect, rationing by congestion. A more efficient method is to issue coupons that entitle people to buy specific quantities of the rationed good at the prevailing price. By limiting the number of coupons, the government reduces the demand for the product to match the available supply, thereby eliminating the shortage and relieving the congestion in the marketplace. In figure 4.4, for example, demand is reduced from D_1 to D_2.

The coupon system may appear to be fair and simple, but how are the coupons to be distributed? Clearly the government will not want to auction off the coupons, for that would amount to letting consumers bid up the price. Should coupons be distributed equally among all consumers? Should the distribution of coupons be based on the distance traveled? (And if such a system is adopted, will people lie about their needs?) Not everyone lives the same distance from work or school. Some,

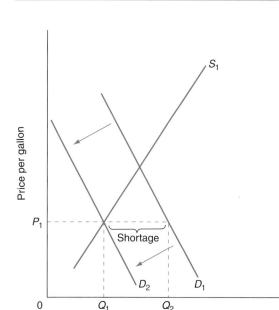

Figure 4.4 The effect of rationing on demand

Price controls can create a shortage. For instance, at the controlled price P_1, a shortage of $Q_2 - Q_1$ gallons will develop. By issuing a limited number of coupons that must be used to purchase a product, the government can reduce demand and eliminate the shortage. Here, rationing reduces demand from D_1 to D_2, where demand intersects the supply curve at the controlled price.

such as salespeople, must travel much more than others. Should a commuter receive more gas than a retired person? If so, how much more? These are formidable questions that must be answered if a coupon system is to be truly equitable. By comparison, the pricing system inherently allows people to reflect the intensity of their needs in their purchases.

After the coupons have been distributed, should the recipients be allowed to sell them to others? That is, should legal markets for coupons be permitted to spring up? If the deals made in such a market are voluntary, both parties to the exchange will benefit. The person who buys coupons values gasoline more than money. The person who sells coupons may have to cut back on driving but values the additional money more than enough to compensate for the inconvenience. The positive (and often high) market value of coupons that will inevitably occur shows that price controls have not really eliminated the shortage.

Furthermore, if the coupons have a value, the price of a gallon of gasoline has not really been held constant. If the price of an extra coupon for one gallon of gasoline is $0.50 and the pump price of that gallon is $2.00, the total price to the consumer is $2.50. The existence of a coupon market means that the price of gasoline has risen. In fact, the price to the consumer will be greater under a rationing system than under a pricing system. This added price increase will occur because the quantity supplied by refineries will be reduced.

Perhaps the most damaging aspect of a rationing system is that the benefits of such a price increase are received not by producers – oil companies, refineries, and service stations – but rather by those fortunate enough to get coupons. Thus the price increase does not provide producers with an incentive to supply more gasoline.

Rent controls

Controls on apartment rents have been tried in the name of fairness to low-income tenants. The effect of rent controls is similar to gasoline price controls (Tucker 1997). As long as the rent is controlled below the equilibrium price, the result should be a market shortage as the quantity of available apartments is reduced and the number of people wanting to rent the available units increases. Faced with this greater demand and a shortage of apartments available at the controlled rent, landlords can be expected to respond in any number of ways:

- If the rent controls apply to "low-income housing," some landlords can be expected to upgrade their apartments and escape the controls. Otherwise, they can sell their apartments as condominiums.
- Landlords can rent to higher-income tenants who are more likely to pay their rent and pay it on time, thus shifting the benefits of the rent controls away from the targeted low-income tenant group.
- Landlords can reduce their costs by lowering maintenance and improvements to their units.

In the absence of rent controls, landlords can be expected to upgrade the quality and amenities (for example, appliances and maintenance) in their rental units when tenants value the improvements by more than the cost of the improvements to the landlords, as shown in detail in chapter 3 (review the discussion surrounding figure 3.10). Hence, tenants are willing to pay an increase in rent that more than covers the landlords' costs of the improvements. The tenants gain by the difference between their assessed value of the improvements minus their higher rental pay-ments. The landlords gain because the increase in rental payments can exceed their added costs. But if rents are controlled, landlords are likely to reduce their costs by lowering the quality of their units, possibly shifting the maintenance costs to the tenants or in other ways undercutting the value of the units to the tenants. In this case, the tenants' demand will fall (from D_2 to D_1 in figure 3.10, indicating a reduction in the rent tenants are willing to pay for lower-quality units), but the reduced demand is of no consequence to the landlords since they still have more prospective tenants than they can accommodate. The point is that the landlords can offset some (but not all) of the effect of the suppressed rent with lower costs. Hence, when the quality of the apartments is reduced, both the tenants and the landlords can be worse off.

[See online Video Module 4.2 Rent control]

Fringe benefits, incentives, and profits

Varying the form of pay is one important way in which firms seek to motivate workers – and overcome the Prisoner's Dilemma problems described earlier. And workers' pay can take many forms, from simple cash to an assortment of fringe benefits. However, it needs to be noted that workers tend to think and talk about their fringe benefits in remarkably different terms than they do about their wages. Workers who recognize that they "earn" their wages will describe their fringe benefits (or "fringes") with reference to what their employers "give" them. "Gee, our bosses *give* us three weeks of vacation, thirty minutes of coffee breaks a day, the right to flexible schedules, and discounts on purchases of company goods. They also give us medical and dental insurance. Would you believe we have to pay only 20 percent of our medical and dental costs!"

Wages are the result of hard work, but fringe benefits, it seems, are a matter of employer generosity, or so people seem to think. Fringe benefits are assumed to come from a substantially different source, such as the pockets of the stockholders, than do wages, which come out of the revenues that workers add to the bottom line.

Employers use some of the same language, and their answers for why fringe benefits are provided are typically equally misleading, though probably more gratuitous. The main difference is that employers inevitably talk in terms of the cost of their fringe benefits. "Would you believe that the annual cost of health insurance to our firm is $12,486 *per employee*? That means that we give away millions, if not tens of millions, each year on all of our employees' health insurance. Our total fringe benefit package costs us an amount equal to 36.4 percent of our total wage bill!" The point that is intended, though often left unstated, is: "Aren't we nice?"

Our argument here will be a challenge to many readers because it will develop a radically different way of thinking about fringe benefits, requiring readers to set aside any preconceived view that fringe benefits are a gift. We employ *marginal* analysis, or the evaluation of fringe benefits in terms of their *marginal (or added) cost* and the *marginal (or added) value* of successive units of the benefit provided. This analysis is grounded in the principle that profits can be increased as long as the marginal value of doing something in business is greater than the marginal cost.

This principle implies that a firm should extend its output for as long as the marginal value of doing so (in terms of additional revenue) exceeds the marginal cost of each successive extension. Firms should do the same with a fringe benefit: provide it as long as it "pays," meaning as long as the marginal cost of the fringe benefit is less than its marginal value to workers (that is, in terms of the wages that workers are willing to forgo). This way of looking at firm decision making means that changes in the cost of fringe benefits can have predictable consequences. An increase in the cost of any fringe benefit can give rise to a cut in the amount of the benefit that is provided. An increase in the value of the benefit to workers can lead to more of it being provided.

Workers as profit centers

We don't want to be overly crass in our view of business (although that may appear to be our intention from the words we have to use within the limited space we have to develop our arguments). We only want to be realistic when we surmise that the overwhelming majority of firms that provide their workers with fringe benefits do so for the very same reason that they hire their workers in the first place: *to add more to their profits than they could if they didn't hire the workers or didn't provide the fringe benefit*. Like it or not, most firms are in the business of making money off their employees – in all kinds of ways.

The reason many firms don't provide their workers with fringe benefits – with health insurance being the most common missing benefit, in small businesses especially – is that they can't add to profits by doing so. The critical difference between employers who do provide benefits and those who don't is not likely to have anything to do with how nice each group of employers wants to be to its employees. There is no reason to suspect that one group is nicer, or more crass, than the other.

When making decisions on fringe benefits, employers face two unavoidable *economic* realities: First, fringe benefits are costly, and some, such as health insurance, are extraordinarily costly. Second, there are limits to the value that workers place on such benefits. The reason is simply that workers value a lot of things, and what they *buy*, whether directly from vendors or indirectly via their employers, is largely dependent on cost.

Workers *buy* fringe benefits from employers when the value they place on the benefits exceeds their cost to the firms. When that condition holds, firms can make money by, effectively, "selling" benefits – for example, health insurance – to their workers. Of course, most firms don't send sales people around their offices and plants selling health insurance or weeks of vacation to their employees the way they sell fruit in the company cafeteria, but they nevertheless make the sales. How? If workers truly value a particular benefit, then the firms that provide it will see an increase in the supply of labor available to them. They will be able to hire more workers at a lower wage and/or be able to increase the "quality" (productivity) of the workers that they do hire.

Firms are paid for the cost of providing fringe benefits primarily in two ways: One, their real wage bill goes down with the increased competition for the available jobs that results from the greater number of job seekers (who are attracted by the benefit). This reflects the willingness of workers to *pay* employers for the benefits. Two, employers gain by being more discriminatory in terms of whom they hire, employing more productive workers for the wages paid.

The supply of and demand for fringe benefits

A simple graph using familiar supply and demand curves displays the labor market effects of fringe benefits with greater clarity. Figure 4.5 shows normal labor supply and demand curves. The downward sloping labor demand curve, D_1, shows that more workers will be demanded by firms at lower wage rates than will be at higher wage rates, and it reflects the circumstance in which no fringe benefit is provided. The upward sloping curve, S_1, shows that more workers will come on the markets at higher wage rates than at lower ones and reflects an initial circumstance in which a given fringe benefit (such as health insurance) is not provided. These embedded assumptions regarding the slopes of the curves are totally reasonable and widely accepted as reflecting market conditions. At any rate, without the fringe benefit, the workers will receive a wage rate of W_1, where the market clears.

Consider the simplest of cases, the one in which the firm's cost in providing a fringe benefit is a uniform amount for each worker and in which the provision of the benefit has no impact on worker productivity, but increases the value of work and increases the supply of workers. The demand curve in figure 4.5 drops down vertically by the per-worker cost of the benefit, from D_1 to D_2, which means that the vertical drop ab equals the added cost of the fringe. This happens because the firms are simply not willing to pay as high a wage to their workers as they would be if they didn't have to cover the cost of the benefit. On the other hand, the supply of workers shifts outward, from S_1 to S_2, because the firm is now more attractive to workers because of the benefit, leading to more workers applying for jobs. Workers

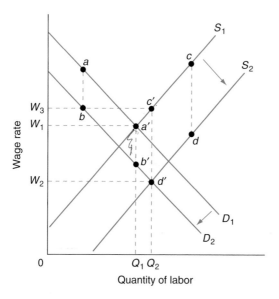

Figure 4.5 Fringe benefits and the labor market
If fringe benefits are more valuable to workers and impose a cost on the employers, the supply of labor will increase from S_1 to S_2 while the demand curve falls from D_1 to D_2. The wage rate falls from W_1 to W_2, but the workers get fringe benefits that have a value of $c'd'$, which means that their overall payment goes up from W_1 to W_3.

are willing to work for a lower money wage *when the fringe benefit is provided* (and, again, for simplicity we assume that each worker values the benefit by the same amount). The vertical difference between S_1 and S_2, *cd*, represents how much each worker values the benefit and is willing to give up in her wage rate to obtain it; this vertical difference is a money measure of the value of the benefit to workers.

What happens, given these shifts in supply and demand? First, understand that if providing a fringe benefit is advantageous to one firm in a competitive market, it will be advantageous to all firms. All firms in the market can be expected to provide the benefit for offensive and defensive reasons. Firms will offer the benefit for offensive reasons because they can add to their profits by doing so. They will offer the benefit for defensive reasons because if other firms offer the benefit and they don't, they can be at a competitive disadvantage in attracting workers and containing their labor costs.

These points can be seen in figure 4.5. With the provision of the benefit to all workers, the supply of labor will increase (due to the fact that the workers *want* the benefit) by more than demand falls (due to the fact that the benefit is costly to employers who must compensate by lowering the wages). With these changes in supply and demand the wage falls from W_1 to W_2. Are workers and firms better off? A close examination of figure 4.5 shows that more workers are employed (Q_2 instead of Q_1), which suggests that something good must have happened. Otherwise, we must wonder why firms would want to hire more workers and why more workers would be willing to be employed. It just doesn't make much sense to argue that firms and/or workers are not better off when both sides agree to more work (and when the benefit is provided voluntarily).

Notice that the total cost of the benefit, the vertical distance between the two demand curves, or $a'b'$, is less than the reductions in the wage, $W_1 - W_2$, from which we can draw two implications: First, the firm is clearly making money off its original employees ($W_2 + a'b'$ is less than W_1). Second, the firm's total cost per worker ($W_2 + a'b'$) falls, which explains why the firm is willing to expand its hires.

Notice also that while the workers accept a lower wage rate, W_2 instead of W_1, they gain the value of the benefit, which in figure 4.5 is the vertical distance *cd*. The sum of the new lower wage, W_2, plus the value of the benefit, $c'd'$, is W_3, which is higher than the wage without the benefit ($W_2 + c'd' = W_3 > W_1$). Both sides gain.

How much of the fringe benefit should be provided? It would be silly to try to tell each person reading this book what to do, given the variation of business and market circumstances. But generally applicable rules provide guidance. The rule that firms should follow is no different from the rule they should follow in any other productive market circumstance: firms should continue to expand the benefit as long as the *added (marginal) cost from the benefit is less than the marginal reduction in their wage bills, which can be no greater than the workers' evaluation of the marginal increase in the benefit.*

For example, the number of days of paid vacation should be extended as long as the value that workers place on additional vacation days is greater than the marginal cost to the employer of providing the additional days. As additional vacation days are added, workers' evaluation of each additional day off will fall (at least after a certain number of days) and the cost of the additional days off will rise. A point will be reached beyond which equality between the additional cost of the next vacation day will exceed its marginal value (or the possible reduction in the wage bill). At that point, employers have maximized their profit from "selling" the benefit to their workers.

Of course, tax rules will affect the exact amount of the benefit, as well as the combination of benefits offered. Certainly, if the value of fringe benefits – for example, health insurance – is not subject to taxation, then employers should, naturally, provide more of them than otherwise, simply because a reduction in worker taxes will partially cover the cost of the benefit. The result might be that workers actually get more of the benefit than they would buy, *if they were covering all of the cost themselves.* Employers must provide such benefits; otherwise, they will not keep their compensation costs competitive with those of rival employers.

Optimum fringe benefits

We expect employers and workers to treat such benefits the way they do everything else, seeking some *optimum* combination of benefits and money wages. Again, this means that employers and workers should be expected to weigh their additional (or marginal) value against their additional (or marginal) cost. An employer will add to a benefit such as health insurance as long as the marginal value (measured in money wage concessions or increased production from workers) is greater than the marginal cost of the added benefit. Similarly, workers will "buy" more of any benefit from their employer as long as its marginal value (in terms of improved health or reduction in the cost of private purchase) is greater than its marginal cost (wage concessions).

Although we can't give specifics, we do know that managers are well advised to search earnestly for the "optimum" combination (which means that some experimentation would likely be in order), even though the process of finding the optimum is never precise. The firms that come closest to the optimum will make the most money from their employees and also provide their employees the greatest compensation for the money spent – and so will have the lowest cost structure and be the most competitive. By trying to make as much money as possible from their employees, firms not only stay more competitive, but also benefit their workers.

So far, we have considered only fringe benefits in which the added cost of the benefit to the firm is less than the value of the benefit to the workers. What if that is not the case? Looking at figure 4.5, suppose that the cost of the benefit to firms were greater than its value to workers (in the graph, the vertical distance *ab* would be greater than the vertical distance *cd*, which means that the increase in demand would have to be greater than the increase in supply). What would happen? The straight answer is: nothing. The benefit would not be provided. The reason is obvious: both sides, workers and owners, would lose. The resulting drop in the wage would be less than the cost of the benefit to the employers and greater than the value of the benefit to the workers. (To see this point, try drawing a graph with the vertical drop in the demand greater than the outward shift of the supply.) *Such a benefit would not – and should not – be provided, simply because it is a loser for both workers and employers.*

Firms that persisted in providing such a benefit would have difficulty competing because their cost structure would be higher than other producers'. Such firms would be subject to takeovers. The takeover would very likely be friendly because those bidding for the firm would be able to pay a higher price for the stock than the going market price, which would be depressed by the fact that one or more benefits provided to workers were not profitable. Those involved in the takeover could, after acquiring control, eliminate the excessively costly benefit(s), or reduce it (them) to profitable levels, enhance the firm's profitability and competitive position, and then sell the firm's stock at a price higher than the purchase price.[1]

The workers would support such a takeover – and might be the ones managing it – because they could see two advantages: They could have a benefit eliminated that is not worth the cost that they would have to pay in terms of lower wages. They could also gain some employment security, given the improved competitive position of their firm. The workers might even take the firm over for the same reason anyone else might do so: they could improve the firm's profitability and stock price.

[See online Video Module 4.3 Fringe benefits]

Fringe benefits provided by large and small firms

We can now understand why many large firms provide their employees with health insurance and many small firms do not. At the most general level, it pays for large firms to provide the insurance, whereas it does not pay for small firms to do so.

---

[1] A firm is not likely to be taken over because of the failure of the firm to provide one efficiency-enhancing fringe benefit. But when enough of these types of mistakes are made, the inefficiency mounts, increasing the chance that the firm will be a takeover target.

Large firms can sell a large number of health insurance policies, achieving economies associated with scale and spreading the risk. That is a widely recognized answer.

At another level, the answer is more complicated and obscure. "Small" and "large" firms do not generally hire from the same labor markets. Small firms tend to provide lower-paying jobs. The workers in lower-paying jobs within small firms simply don't have the means to buy a lot of things that workers in larger firms have, and one of the things workers in small firms don't seem to buy in great quantities is insurance. Given their limited income, workers simply don't think that insurance is a good deal, and they would prefer to buy other things with higher monetary compensation. One of the reasons that low-income workers may gravitate to small firms is that if they worked for large firms they would have to give up wages to buy the insurance because of company policies that apply to all workers.

Of course, the analysis gets even trickier considering that lower-income workers, many of whom work for small firms, tend to be younger workers – who also tend to be healthier and prefer a different combination of fringe benefits than older workers. The young can appreciate that the price they would have to pay for health insurance through their firms is inflated by a number of factors related to supply and demand. These may include the increased liability doctors face when things go wrong and the added cost of expensive medical technologies to care for older, dying patients.

Second, older workers, many of whom are in large firms and tend to have a strong demand for health insurance, have increased the demand for insurance (and health care). The exemption of health insurance from taxable income (which helps higher-income workers in higher tax brackets more than lower-income workers) also has artificially inflated the demand for health insurance (and health care). The net result of the cost and demand effects has been to increase health insurance costs, making the insurance an unattractive deal for many young and low-income workers.

If the analysis of this section has led to any clear conclusion, it is that the workers pay for what they get. They may not hand over a check for the benefits, but they give up the money nonetheless, through a reduction in their pay. If workers didn't give up anything for the fringe benefit, we would have to conclude that it was not worth anything to the workers, the supply curve would not move out, and the wage rate would not fall. That would mean that the employers would have to cover the full cost of the fringe benefit, which would put them in the rather irrational position of adding to their costs without getting anything for it. Workers should not want that to happen, if for no other reason than that their job security would be threatened.

But critics might argue that managers don't know that certain fringe benefits are "good" for business and their workers. That is often the case, and the history of business is strewn with the corpses of firms that failed to serve the interests of their workers and customers and who were forced into bankruptcy by other firms who were better at finding the best way to increase value at lower cost, including providing the right combination of fringe benefits. However, we see the market as a powerful, though imperfect, educational system. If the critics know better than existing firms, they could make lots of money by pointing out to firms why they are wrong and how they could make money from their employees by providing (selling) fringe benefits not now being provided, or adjusting the combination of existing fringe benefits in marginal ways.

We think that workers and owners should talk as frankly about fringe benefits as they do about their wages. Workers earn their wages. The same is true for fringe benefits. No gift is involved. Both wages and fringe benefits represent mutually beneficial exchanges between workers and their firms, at least in the absence of workplace mandates, such as required minimum wages.

Minimum wages

Minimum wages imposed at the federal or state governmental level are classic examples of **price floors**. As with price ceilings, price floors disable the market's ability to clear and have consequences for employees and employers.

> A **price floor** is a government-determined price (or wage) below which a specified good (labor) cannot be sold.

The minimum wage has been raised in a series of nineteen steps from 25 cents an hour when the first federal minimum wage took effect in October 1938 to $7.25 an hour in 2009 (at this writing). However, in constant 2009 dollars, the minimum wage rose irregularly from $3.77 an hour in 1938 to just above $10 an hour in 1968, only to fall irregularly from the 1968 peak to its 2009 level of $7.25, which is more than 25 percent below the 1968 peak. This means that the 2009 minimum wage was significantly below the real minimum wage when it was raised to $1 in 1956 at which time it was worth about $8.00 an hour in 2009 dollars. Proponents use this fact to justify a higher minimum wage, but a higher real minimum wage can be expected to have profound economic consequences.

In this section, we offer two lines of analysis, the standard and extended, on the effect of the minimum wage on covered labor markets. Under the conventional perspective, employers don't alter the way in which workers are paid and how much workers are asked to work. Under the extended line of analysis perspective, employers alter both the form of compensation and work demands.

The standard view
Economists traditionally have argued that increases in the minimum wage reduce employment in competitive markets, thereby increasing the welfare of those low-skilled workers who remain employed but decreasing the welfare of others who

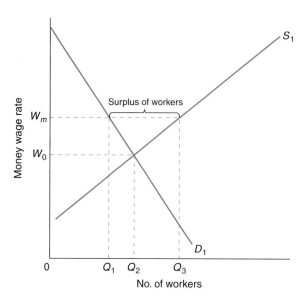

Figure 4.6 The standard view of the impact of the minimum wage When the minimum wage is set at W_m (and the market clearing wage is W_0), employment will fall from Q_2 to Q_1; simultaneously, the number of workers who are willing to work in this labor market will expand from Q_2 to Q_3. The market surplus is then $Q_3 - Q_1$.

lose their jobs. The latter may remain unemployed or accept less gainful employment in areas of the economy in which minimum wage regulations are not applied. Also, economists point out that the minimum wage can increase the crime rate. The following discussion examines how economists reach such conclusions.

Labor-market effects

Consider figure 4.6, which depicts a demand and supply curve for low-skilled labor in which demand slopes downward and supply upward. The downward sloping demand curve implies that employers will hire more workers (everything else remaining constant) at a lower rather than a higher wage. There are several reasons for this:

- First, profit-maximizing employers will tend to expand production until the marginal contribution of additional workers begins to diminish, which implies that within the relevant range of production, additional workers will be worth (in terms of the market value of the product they can produce) progressively less as more are hired. When the wage rate falls, employers can hire workers who are worth less at the margin.
- Second, lower wages can inspire a substitution of low-skilled workers for other resources used in production, such as higher-skilled workers and expensive equipment.
- Third, a decline in the wage rate implies lower costs and prices for the product produced by the firms, which can inspire more sales and lead, in turn, to a greater need for workers to satisfy the additional quantity demanded of the product.

The upward sloping curve that represents the supply of labor implies that the wage must be raised in order to attract additional workers. The main reason for this upward slope is that some workers have higher-valued opportunities than others. Any given wage will attract workers into the market whose alternative opportunities are lower than that wage rate. The wage offered in a low-skilled (or any other) labor market must be progressively raised to offset the progressively higher-valued opportunities the additional workers must forgo.

If the market is competitive and free of government intervention, the wage rate will settle, as shown in figure 4.6, at the intersection of the supply and demand curves, or at W_0. A wage above W_0 would indicate that more workers are seeking jobs than there are jobs available and that competitive pressure would push the wage down. A wage below W_0 would imply that more workers are demanded than there are workers willing to work at the going wage, which causes upward competitive pressure on the wage.

Suppose, however, that politicians who consider market wage, W_0, too low to provide a decent living pass a law requiring employers to pay no less than W_m. The law reduces employment because, in the face of worker productivity and reduced sales, employers cannot afford to employ as many people and the quantity of labor demanded falls from Q_2 to Q_1.

As economists normally develop the argument, those who manage to keep their jobs at the minimum wage will be better off (their take-home pay will increase from W_0 to W_m). Others, however, will no longer have jobs. These workers will either become permanently unemployed or settle for work in different, lower-paying, and/or less desirable labor markets. If the minimum wage displaces them from their preferred employment, their full-wage rate – that is, their money wage plus the nonmonetary benefits of their jobs – is reduced. Of course, for those who become permanently unemployed, their money wage will drop to zero.

To make matters worse, when a minimum wage is introduced, greater numbers of workers are willing to work. Workers with jobs paying W_0, and who have fewer opportunities at W_m, must now compete with an influx of other workers. Almost all of the empirical studies done since the 1970s support the gloomy predictions of the model.[2]

Economists have probably understated the adverse consequences of the minimum wage for the targeted worker groups by making the common presumption that low-skilled workers who retain their jobs are "better off." Economists also

---

[2] For review of the economic literature on the economic effects of the minimum wage, see Peterson and Stewart 1969, 151–5; Kosters and Welch 1972; Ragan 1977; Brown, Gilroy, and Kohen 1982; Neumark and Wascher 2008.

commonly presume that the workers who have the Q_1 jobs, after the minimum wage is imposed, represent a subgroup of the workers who had the Q_2 jobs when the wage was determined strictly by the forces of supply and demand. But this is unlikely, because the minimum wage will attract additional workers, $Q_3 - Q_2$, into the market. In comparison to the workers who were in the market when the wage was W_0, some of these additional workers will likely be more productive because they have been positioned further up the supply curve and have had higher-valued opportunities elsewhere. In short, many if not all of the workers who have jobs at W_0 can be expected either to withdraw from the market or to be supplanted by new arrivals who have been induced by the higher wage to enter the market.

Social effects

Economists maintain that minimum-wage laws also have several social effects that often are overlooked. By increasing unemployment, minimum-wage laws increase the number of people receiving public assistance and unemployment compensation. (Proponents of the minimum wage argue the opposite – that is, that the minimum wage reduces the need for welfare by raising the income of low-skilled workers above the poverty level.) The laws may also account for increases in some criminal activity, because the unemployed who lack opportunities in the legitimate labor market may see crime as an alternative to employment (indeed, crime is a form of employment). With the larger labor pool that develops when the minimum wage increases, competition for jobs is likely to harbor potential for increased discrimination on the basis of sex, race, religion, and so on (Williams 2005).

Political support

Why do minimum-wage laws attract so much political support? Part of the reason may be that the general public is largely unaware of their negative effects. Many forces operate on the labor market, making it almost impossible for the average person to single out the effects of one law. Few give enough thought to the idea of a minimum wage adversely affecting employment opportunities. Those who bear the burden of these laws – that is, young, relatively unproductive workers – are least likely to understand the negative effects, and many cannot vote. The people who retain their jobs at the higher wage are also visible members of the workforce; those who lose their jobs are often far less visible, many of whom are concentrated in urban ghettos.

Following the standard minimum-wage argument, another reason that minimum-wage laws attract political support is that many people may benefit from the laws – mainly, those who retain their jobs and receive higher paychecks. Many college students may favor the minimum wage, perhaps because they are generally more productive than less-educated members of their generation and are less likely to lose their entry-level jobs because of the minimum wage. Labor unions, too, have an incentive to support minimum-wage laws: unions are in a better bargaining position when the government raises wages in nonunion sectors of the economy. Under such circumstances, union wage demands are not as likely to prompt employers to move into nonunionized sectors of the economy.[3]

The extended view

The extended line of analysis and policy proposals relating to the market consequences of the minimum wage misses several important but relatively simple points. The most important of these is that the minimum wage does not necessarily make a significant share of the targeted workers better off. Moreover, the analysis leads to the conclusion that minimum-wage increases should not be expected to have substantial adverse employment effects in most low-skilled labor markets, primarily because employers can be expected to adjust to the added labor costs of the minimum wage by lowering the nonwage benefits of employment or increasing the work demands imposed on covered workers. The analysis that follows helps to explain why studies have generally found that a 10 percent increase in the minimum wage can be expected to reduce employment among teenagers (the group of workers most likely to be affected by the minimum wage) by as little as 0.5 to 3 percent (Brown, Gilroy, and Kohen 1982). Economists David Card and Alan Krueger have found, in their study of the impact of a minimum-wage hike in the fast-food restaurant industry, that employment actually increases with the hike. Although these researchers do not appear to believe the positive relationship between the wage increase and employment, they do deduce that the wage increase probably has had a close to zero, if not zero, employment effect (Card and Krueger 1995). However, a new line of analysis, which lends theoretical support to such findings, fortifies the case against the minimum wage.

Payment effects

Minimum-wage laws establish a legal floor for *money wages*; they do not, however, suppress competitive pressures. These restrictions cap the pressures in only one of the multitude of competitive outlets, namely money wages. More to the point, they do not set a legal minimum for the *effective wage* (including the money and non-money benefits of employment) that is paid to workers.

The impact of mandating minimum wages depends on the ability of the employer to adjust the nonmoney conditions of work, or fringe benefits, in response to a

---

[3] In fact, as was argued by the editors of the *New York Times* in 1937 when the federal minimum wage was originally proposed, the first minimum wage retarded the exodus of firms and jobs to the nonunionized South from the unionized North. The introduction of the minimum wage reduced the net benefit of moving south, slowing the exodus (McKenzie 1994).

required pay change. Basic analysis of minimum-wage laws, embedded in many economics textbooks, implicitly assumes that money wages are the only form of labor compensation. Hence, when the money wage is set at a legal minimum, employment falls by some amount given by the demand for labor.

The standard line of analysis already presented may still be fully applicable to those few labor markets in which money is the only form of compensation and in which employers can do little or nothing to change the skill and production demands imposed on workers. In such cases, minimum-wage laws may still have the predicted effect, a labor-market surplus of unemployed menial workers caused by an above-market level of compensation.

However, the standard line of analysis does not consider the possibility that profit-maximizing competitive employers are quite capable of adjusting other conditions of work in response to the labor market surplus that follows the minimum wage law. Indeed, to remain cost competitive, employers may cut their labor costs in nonwage ways – for example, eliminating workplace outings, reducing fringe benefits, or increasing production demands.[4] Employers can be expected to reduce their labor costs in these ways until the worker surplus diminishes – that is, until their labor markets clear once again.[5] That being said, employers' nonmoney adjustments made in response to a wage minimum also have their effects on the labor market equilibrium.

Employers can be expected to respond to a minimum-wage law by cutting or eliminating those fringe benefits and conditions of work, such as workplace outings, that increase the supply of labor but do not materially affect labor productivity. By reducing such nonmoney benefits of employment, the labor costs are reduced from what they would otherwise have been and nothing is lost in the way of reduced labor productivity.

Continuation of such nonmoney benefits is made uneconomical by the money-wage minimum; they no longer pay for themselves in terms of lower wage rates.

---

[4] Clearly, many minimum-wage jobs do not carry standard fringe benefits, such as life and medical insurance and retirement plans. However, most do offer fringe benefits in the form of conditions in the work environment, attitudes of the bosses, breaks, frequency and promptness of pay, variety of work, uniforms, use of company tools and supplies, meals and drinks, flexible hours, and precautions against accidents. These fringe benefits are subject to withdrawal when minimum wages are mandated.

[5] More precisely, the labor markets should, after adjustments, clear more or less to the same extent as they did before the minimum-wage law was imposed. Of course, employers are not directly concerned with ensuring that their labor market clears. They are, however, interested in minimizing their labor costs, a motivation that drives them to adjust the conditions of work until the market clears. The point is that, if confronted with a surplus of workers, an employer can offer less compensation, broadly defined, until the surplus is eliminated.

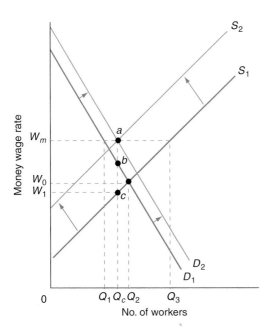

Figure 4.7 An extended view of the impact of the minimum wage
When the minimum wage is raised to W_m, a surplus is created equal to $Q_3 - Q_1$. As a consequence, employers can be expected to respond to the surplus by reducing fringe benefits or increasing work demands on workers. The supply curve of labor contracts, reflecting the greater wage the workers will demand to compensate for the reduction in fringe benefits or increase in work demands. The employers' demand for labor increases, reflecting the higher wage they are *willing to* pay workers in terms of money wages who get fewer fringe benefits or work harder and produce more.

Furthermore, employers in highly competitive final-products markets must adjust such work conditions to remain competitive and to survive. Otherwise, other firms will lower their labor costs (by contracting or by eliminating fringe benefits) and force out of business the employers who retain their fringe benefits and continue to pay the higher minimum-wage rate.

Because of the changes in work conditions, the supply curve of labor (the position of which is partially determined by working conditions and fringe benefits) can be expected to shift upward. The effects of such a supply shift are shown in figure 4.7, which incorporates the supply and demand curves of figure 4.6. The vertical shift in the supply curve will be equal to labor's dollar valuation, on the margin, of what they lost because of the decline in employment conditions. The demand curve for labor will shift upward to the right, reflecting the reduced expenditure per unit of labor on fringe benefits.

As before, fringe benefits are provided as long as their cost to the firm per unit of labor is less than the reduced wage rate – and as long as labor's evaluation of the fringe benefits lost because of the minimum wage is greater than the firm's costs. Therefore, when the fringe benefits are taken away, the vertical, upward shift in the supply curve will be greater than the vertical, upward shift in the demand curve. In figure 4.7, the vertical shift in the supply curve is *ac*, and the vertical shift in the demand curve is less, *ab*. It is important to note that the market clears, however, at the minimum wage because of secondary market adjustments in fringe benefits. But it is equally important to see that the market clears at an employment level, Q_c, which is lower than the employment level before the minimum wage is imposed, Q_2. In other words, the surplus of labor that the standard analysis suggests exists in face of a minimum-wage law is eliminated by the shifts in the curves. However, labor is worse off because of the wage floor and adjustments in fringe benefits. After the vertical distance between the two supply curves, ac (which, again, is labor's dollar evaluation of the fringe benefits lost because of the minimum wage), is subtracted from the minimum wage W_m, the effective wage paid to labor is reduced to W_1, or by $W_m - W_1$. In short, when labor is paid in many forms, a minimum wage $reduces$, not increases, the effective payment going to affected workers, even those who keep their jobs.

The standard line of analysis suggests that a minimum wage of W_m will cause employment opportunities for labor to fall to Q_1. The adjustments that employers make to nonmoney conditions of work cause employment opportunities to fall by less, to only Q_c in figure 4.7.

If employers increase work demands without (or even with) fringe benefit reductions, the analysis is much the same. The demand for labor will rise, given that workers' productivity per hour worked goes up, making employers willing to pay workers more per hour. Nevertheless, the vertical shift in the supply curve will be greater than the vertical shift in the demand curve. Again, this is because employers would initially have relaxed work demands in the absence of the minimum wage only if workers would then have been willing to give up more in pay than employers lost in productivity.

Differences in perspective

This analysis conflicts with the standard textbook treatment of minimum wages in several important respects. The standard analysis holds that the effective wage rate increases for some workers and declines for others. As noted, this is because of the implicit assumption that an increase in the minimum wage rate is equivalent to an increase in the effective wage rate. Our analysis, however, leads to the conclusion that the effective wage rate of all workers, including those who retain their jobs in spite of minimum wages, decreases; they are worse off to the extent that employers have the opportunity to adjust working conditions and fringe benefits. For that reason, minimum wages appear patently unfair to those who are covered by them, even by the standards of many of those who promote legislated minimum wages. Although still not a mainstream view, this new perspective on the adverse effects of minimum-wage laws is supported by a growing body of research. Key econometric studies of the minimum wage are briefly reviewed in the online Reading 4.1.

[See online Video Module 4.4 Minimum wage]

The draft versus the all-volunteer military service

For many economists, the late University of Chicago economist Milton Friedman settled the issue of the relative efficiency of the draft versus all-volunteer military service: the all-volunteer army was more efficienct (cost-effective) than the draft, period (no qualifications). Milton Friedman and his wife Rose Friedman recalled in their joint memoir:

In the course of his [General Westmoreland's] testimony, he made the statement that he did not want to command an army of mercenaries. I [Milton Friedman] stopped him and said, "General, would you rather command an army of slaves?" He drew himself up and said, "I don't like to hear our patriotic draftees referred to as slaves." I replied, "I don't like to hear our patriotic volunteers referred to as mercenaries." But I went on to say, "If they are mercenaries, then I, sir, am a mercenary professor, and you, sir, are a mercenary general; we are served by mercenary physicians, we use a mercenary lawyer, and we get our meat from a mercenary butcher." That was the last that we heard from the general about mercenaries. (Friedman and Friedman 1998, 380)

Friedman's argument in support of the higher economic efficiency of the all-volunteer service over the draft (developed in his widely read *Capitalism and Freedom*, 1962) went something like this. Suppose there are five potential military recruits (A, B, C, D, and E) in the population that have the following annual opportunity costs for their serving in the military (or could earn these annual wages in the non-military sector of the economy if they do not serve in the military):

A $10,000
B $20,000
C $30,000
D $40,000
E $50,000

Suppose the military needs three recruits (a small number intended to simplify the analytics; you can raise the number to three million without doing damage to the standard argument). Under a draft system, in which there is a true lottery (every one of the five potential recruits has an equal chance of being drafted), the three chosen to serve can be A, C, and E, which means that the total opportunity cost of the three recruits serving in the military would be $90,000 ($10,000 + $30,000 + $50,000). Of course, A, B, and C could be drawn from the lottery, making the opportunity cost total $60,000, but over a series of lottery draws of three people, the expected or mean value of the recruits' opportunity cost should be $30,000 each, or $90,000 for the three recruits.

If an all-volunteer service is instituted, the wage can be raised until three recruits volunteer. The required wage would have to be something greater (to account for any added military duty risks) than the opportunity annual wage of recruit C, $30,000, which means that A, B, and C would volunteer, making the total opportunity cost of the three recruits equal to $60,000 ($10,000 for A, $20,000 for B, and $30,000 for C). Hence, as measured by recruits' opportunity costs (which is a measure of the value of private goods not produced), the all-volunteer service is more cost-effective than the draft ($60,000 versus $90,000). This line of analysis, as simple and straightforward as it is, formed one of the major economic (not political) arguments for the United States jettisoning the draft system in the 1970s for the all-volunteer service, which continues to this day.

But then why does Israel have a mandatory service (draft) system for virtually everyone? Our argument is straightforward (McKenzie and Lee 1992): Friedman's basic argument for the all-volunteer service doesn't account for the distorting effects of taxes needed to pay military personnel. Whether the draft or all-volunteer military is more cost-effective (when all costs are tallied, opportunity costs plus the distortion costs of taxation) depends on what proportion of the available recruits are needed in the military to deal with national threats. As the proportion of the available recruits needed for military duty increases, the cost advantage of the all-volunteer service can erode. If all five recruits in the example above are needed, both the draft and the all-volunteer service systems will have the exact same total opportunity costs of $150,000 ($10,000 + $20,000 + $30,000 + $40,000 + $50,000).

In addition, the all-volunteer system will require higher military pay than would be required under the draft, and the taxes needed to generate the greater military pay for the all-volunteer service can impose an inefficiency or distortion in economic activity (due to the fact that, for example, higher income tax rates can discourage work, saving, and investment). The greater the size of the military, the greater the pay rate must be, and in turn, the greater the tax rates and the economic distortions. Beyond some point as the number of recruits needed increases, the all-volunteer system loses its relatively lower cost-effectiveness.

Understandably, Israel uses the draft today because it requires almost universal service to defend itself against hostile neighbors. The United States needs (in peacetime) only a tiny fraction of available recruits to defend against aggressors (at least so far) and continues to use the all-volunteer service. From the perspective of the argument developed here, it is altogether understandable why the United States used the draft system during World War II (McKenzie and Lee 1992).[6]

---

[6] The answer we (the authors) developed is one that Milton Friedman accepted, which we know to be the case because he was on our side in a debate on the topic with other market-oriented economists.

Moreover, the conventional economic cost argument in favor of the all-volunteer system fails to consider another potential effect: the volunteer nature of the all-volunteer service can reduce the potential economic cost a country faces when choosing to go to war, which means the all-volunteer system might increase the likelihood a country might choose to go to war. Without having to face the threat of being drafted, many citizens might be more eager than otherwise to support military aggression or defensive measures (or less inclined to oppose such measures) when they individually do not have to face the probability of actually having to serve in the military, an argument that has been posited by geopolitical commentators (for example, see Bacevich 2008). One of the unheralded advantages of the draft is that such a military service system can discourage aggression (but could also discourage defensive measures) because it puts all potential recruits at risk of serving. We do not, of course, consider such arguments conclusive, but they are the type of argument that economists would not want to preclude from discussion.

For a discussion of how the economic way of thinking differs from the psychology way of thinking, see online Perspective 4, Maslow's Hierarchy of Needs and economists' supply and demand curves (along with the accompanying online video module).

> **Online Perspective 4**
> Maslow's Hierarchy of Needs and economists' supply and demand curves

Part B Organizational economics and management

In Part A of this chapter, we used supply and demand curves to draw insights about various government policies. In this part, we apply insights from our study of "organizational economics" to show how markets are contained and directed by incentives, which can promote values – a prime example of which is honesty – that are normally considered to be matters of ethics and philosophy, if not theology. As we will see, such matters as "honesty" and "trust," often thought to be outside of economists' purview, can affect firms' costs and market share, which means they can affect supply and demand, the intensity of competition, and the efficiency of markets just as government policies can.

How honesty can pay in business

A popular perception states that markets fail because business is full of dishonest scoundrels – especially high-ranking executives – who cheat, lie, steal, and worse to increase their profits. This perception is reflected in and reinforced by the way businesspeople are depicted in the media. No one can deny that people in business have done all kinds of nasty things for a buck. But the impression of pervasively dishonest businesspeople is surely greatly exaggerated. Businesspeople are no more likely to behave dishonestly than are other people. In fact, businesspeople might behave more honestly than the typical American on the street because they find it advantageous to commit themselves to incentive arrangements that motivate honest behavior.

We can make no claim to keen insights into the virtue of businesspeople or anyone else. But we do claim to know one simple fact about human behavior: people respond to incentives in predictable ways. In particular, the lower the personal cost of dishonesty, the more dishonesty we shall observe. If businesspeople act honestly to an unusual degree, it must be in part because they expect to pay a high price for behaving dishonestly. This is, in fact, the case because businesspeople have found, somewhat paradoxically, that they can increase profits by accepting institutional and contractual arrangements that impose large losses on them if they are dishonest.

A businessperson who attempts to profit from dishonest dealing faces the fact that few people are naïvely trusting, certainly not of those who have taken advantage of that trust. Perhaps it is possible to profit from dishonesty in the short run, but those who do so find it increasingly difficult to get people to deal with them in the long run. Businesspeople, therefore, have a strong motivation to put themselves in situations in which their own dishonest behavior would be penalized. Only by doing so can they provide potential customers, workers, and investors with the assurance of the honest dealing required for those people to become *actual* customers, workers, and investors.

Consider this illustration: Mary has a well-maintained older-model Honda Accord that she is willing to sell for as little as $4,000. If interested buyers know how well maintained the car is, they will be willing to pay as much as $5,000 for it. Therefore, a wealth-increasing exchange appears to be possible because any price between $4,000 and $5,000 will result in the car being transferred to someone who values it more than the existing owner. But there is a problem. Many owners of same-year Honda Accords who are selling their cars are doing so because their cars have not been well maintained and are about to experience serious mechanical problems. More precisely, assume that 75 percent of the used Honda Accords being sold are in such poor condition that the most a fully informed buyer would be willing to pay for one of them is $3,000. The remaining 25 percent of these cars on the market are worth $5,000. This means that a buyer with no information on the condition of a car for sale would expect a same-year Honda Accord to be worth, on average, only $3,500. But if buyers are willing to pay only $3,500 for an Accord as old as Mary's, many of the sellers whose cars are in good condition will refuse to sell, as is the case with Mary, who is unwilling to sell for less than $4,000.

So, the mix of such Accords for sale will tilt more in the direction of poorly maintained cars, their expected value will decline, and even fewer well-maintained Accords will be sold. This situation is often described as a market for "lemons," and illustrates the value of sellers being able to commit themselves to honesty (Akerlof 1970). If Mary could somehow convince potential buyers of her honesty when she claims that her Accord is in good condition, she would be better off, and so would those who are looking for a good used car. The advantage of being able to commit to honesty in business extends to any situation in which it is difficult for buyers to determine the quality of products they are buying.

Game theory: games of trust

The advantages of honesty in business and the problem of trying to provide credible assurances of that honesty can also be illustrated as a game. In table 4.1, we present a payoff matrix for a buyer and a seller, giving the consequences from different choice combinations. The first number in the brackets gives the payoff to the seller; the second number gives the payoff to the buyer. If the seller is honest (the quality of the product is as high as he claims) and the buyer trusts the seller (she pays the high-quality price), then both realize a payoff of 100. On the other hand, if the seller is honest but the buyer does not trust him, then no exchange takes place and both receive a payoff of zero. If the seller is dishonest while the buyer is trusting, then the seller captures a payoff of 150, while the buyer gets the sucker's payoff of 50. Finally, if the seller is dishonest and the buyer does not trust him, then an exchange takes place with the buyer paying a price that reflects the presumed low quality of the product and getting a lower-quality product than she would be willing to pay for. Both the seller and the buyer receive a payoff of 25. From a joint perspective, honesty and trust are the best choices because this combination results in more wealth for the two to share.

But this will not likely be the outcome, given the incentives created by the payoffs in table 4.1. The buyer will not trust the seller. The buyer knows that if her trust of the seller is taken for granted by the seller, he will attempt to capture the largest possible payoff from acting dishonestly. On the other hand, if the seller believes that the buyer does not trust him, his highest payoff is still realized by acting dishonestly. So the buyer will reasonably expect the seller to act dishonestly. This is a *self-fulfilling expectation* because when the seller doesn't expect to be trusted, his best response is to act dishonestly.

Table 4.1 The problem of trust in business

		BUYER	
		Trust	Doesn't trust
SELLER	Honest	(100, 100)	(0, 0)
	Dishonest	(150, –50)	(25, 25)

Table 4.2 The problem of trust in business, again

		BUYER	
		Trust	Doesn't trust
SELLER	Honest	(100, 100)	(0, 0)
	Dishonest	(50, –50)	(25, 25)

The seller would clearly be better off in this situation (and so would the buyer) if he somehow created an arrangement that reduced the payoff he could realize from acting dishonestly. If, for example, the seller arranged it so that he received a payoff of only 50 from acting dishonestly when the buyer trusted him, as is shown in table 4.2, then the buyer (assuming that she knows of the arrangement) can trust the seller to respond honestly to her commitment to buy. The seller's commitment to honesty allows both seller and buyer each to realize a payoff of 100 rather than the 25 they each receive without the commitment.

But how can a seller commit himself or herself to honesty in a way that is convincing to buyers? What kinds of arrangements can sellers establish that penalize them if they attempt to profit through dishonesty at the expense of customers?

Business arrangements and practices that can cause sellers to commit to honest dealing are varied, as one would expect, because the ways a seller can profit from dishonest activity are also varied. Notice that our discussion of the situation described in table 4.1 implicitly assumes that the buyer and seller deal with each other only once. This is clearly a situation in which the temptation for the seller to cheat the buyer is the strongest, because the immediate gain from dishonesty will not be offset by a loss of future business from a mistreated buyer. If a significant amount of repeat business is possible, then the temptation to cheat decreases, and may disappear altogether. So, one way for sellers to attempt to move from the situation described in table 4.1 to the one described in table 4.2 is by demonstrating that they are in business for the long run. For example, selling out of a permanent building with the seller's name or logo on it, rather than on a street corner, informs potential customers that the seller has been (or plans on being) around for a long time. Sellers commonly advertise how long they have been in business (for example, "Since 1982" is added under the business name), to inform people that they have a history of honest dealing (or otherwise they would have been out of business long ago) and plan on remaining in business.

However, the advantages motivated by repeated encounters tend to break down if it is known that the encounters will come to an end at a specified date. For this reason firms will attempt to maintain continuity beyond what would seem to be a natural end-period. Single proprietorships, for example, would seem to be less trustworthy when the owner is about to retire or sell. But, as discussed earlier, a common way of reducing this problem is for the owner's offspring to join the business ("Samson and Sons" or "Delilah and Daughters") and ensure continuity after their parent's retirement. Indeed, even though large corporations have lives that extend far beyond that of any of their managers, they often depend on single proprietorships to represent and sell their products. Caterpillar, the heavy equipment company, has a program to encourage the sons and daughters of these single proprietors to follow in their parents' footsteps.

Another way that businesses may create trust is to provide their customers with a "hostage" – something of value to the seller that customers can destroy by taking their business elsewhere if the seller does not keep her promises. The online Reading 4.2 for this chapter describes the role of "hostages" in business.

[See online Video Module 4.5 Trust]

Moral hazards and adverse selection

Although guarantees and warranties reduce the incentive of sellers to act dishonestly, they create opportunities for buyers to benefit from less than totally honest behavior. These opportunities, which are present to one degree or another in all forms of insurance, come as two separate problems: moral hazard and adverse selection. Consider first the problem of moral hazard.

> A **moral hazard** is the tendency of behavior to change after contracts are signed, resulting in unfavorable outcomes from the use of a good or service.
>
> **Adverse selection** is the tendency of people with characteristics undesirable to sellers to buy a good or service from those sellers.

Knowing that a product is under guarantee or warranty can tempt buyers to use the product improperly and carelessly and then blame the seller for the consequences. With this moral hazard in mind, sellers put restrictions on guarantees and warranties that leave buyers responsible for problems that they are in the best position to prevent. For example, refrigerator manufacturers insure against defects in the motor but not against damage to the shelves or finish. Similarly, automobile manufacturers insure against problems in the engine and drivetrain (if the car has been properly serviced) but not against damage to the body and the seat covers. Although such restrictions obviously serve the sellers' interests, they also serve the buyers. When a buyer takes advantage of a guarantee through misrepresentation of the cause, all consumers pay because of higher costs to the seller. Buyers are in a Prisoner's Dilemma in which they are better off collectively using the product with care and not exploiting a guarantee for problems they could have avoided. But without restrictions on the guarantee, each individual is tempted to shift the cost of her careless behavior to others.

Moral hazard was in several ways likely at the root of the world financial and economic crisis that emerged in full bloom in 2008 (if not earlier) and was still under way as this chapter was being finalized in early 2010. We can briefly mention two ways moral hazard played a significant role. Up until the 1970s, banks would originate long-term mortgages and then hold on to them until the balances were fully paid off, in fifteen or thirty years. Under such circumstances, bank loan officers had a strong incentive to scrutinize their borrowers for creditworthiness. The banks originating the mortgages would be the ones holding difficult-to-sell houses if borrowers became delinquent in their payments and foreclosures were required. But in recent decades, when banks began bundling large numbers of mortgages into securities that they then sold to investors on Wall Street, the incentive to scrutinize borrowers' creditworthiness was impaired. Banks had more funds to lend and they could originate risky mortgages that could be slipped into the mortgage-backed securities where they would be more difficult to scrutinize.

When bank deposits are not insured, depositors have strong reasons to monitor the financial health of their banks. Before the advent of deposit insurance, banks had stronger incentive to maintain a strong financial position through conservative lending practices, just to ward off runs on banks by depositors. When the government insures depositors, depositors have less incentive to monitor their banks' financial positions, which can give banks greater leeway in making risky investments. Banks no longer have to worry as much about runs; and they can make riskier loans with confidence that most of their depositors will not lose much in the event the bank fails.

The second problem, adverse selection, is one associated with distortions arising from the fact that buyers and sellers often have different information that is relevant to a transaction. In the case of warranties, the buyer has crucial information that is difficult for the seller to obtain. Some buyers are harder on the product than others. For example, some people drive in ways that greatly increase the probability that their cars will need expensive repair work. If a car manufacturer offers a warranty at a price equal to the average cost of repairs, only those who know that their driving causes greater-than-average repair costs will purchase the warranty, which is therefore being sold at a loss. If the car manufacturer attempts to increase the price of the warranty to cover the higher-than-expected repair costs, then more people will drop out of the market, leaving only the worst drivers buying the warranty.

Even though people would like to be able to reduce their risks by purchasing warranties at prices that accurately reflect their expected repair bills, the market for these warranties can obviously collapse unless sellers can somehow obtain information on the driving behavior of different drivers. If all buyers were honest in revealing this information, they would be better off collectively. But because individual buyers have a strong motivation to claim that they are easier on their cars than they actually are, sellers of warranties try to find indirect ways of securing honest information on the driving behavior of customers. For example, warranties on "muscle" cars that appeal to young males are either more expensive or provide less coverage than warranties on station wagons.

Adverse selection and moral hazard can also play a role in rental rates on apartments. Apartment complex owners who advertise apartments for rent with utilities (for example, water and electricity) included in the fixed rental payments can expect to attract disproportionately renters who plan to make heavy use of the included utilities. Once such renters move in they can be expected to increase their use of the utilities because the cost of their increased use will be spread over other renters through higher rental payments. Because of the high rental payments when utilities are included in apartment rents, renters who expect to use little of the included utilities will select apartment complexes that don't include utilities in rental payments.

[See online Video Module 4.6 Leverage, moral hazard, and risk taking]

Practical lesson for MBAs: seek mutually beneficial deals with workers

Employers pay their workers' wages in competitive labor markets for two reasons. First, they have to make payments in line with offers workers can get from others, and second, they can make a profit from paying workers, at least up to a point.

We are confident that many employers would very much like to "overpay" just so their workers can better support their families and friends. Such warm-hearted employers have a problem, however. Worker wages feed into their products' costs and prices. Any overpayment can undermine firms' competitive positions in their final product markets, causing the firms who insist on overpaying workers to lose market share, if not to close down. Consequently, even workers have an economic interest in not being overpaid.

In addition to money wages, workers typically want their firms to provide fringe benefits of various kinds (health insurance, vacation days, workplace ambience, respect, and recognition), and are often willing to forgo wages for these nonmonetary benefits (especially when there are tax advantages to workers' taking their earnings in fringe benefits). That is, workers are willing to pay for benefits through wage reductions. Employers would be well advised to treat workers as buyers of fringe benefits and to search out that "payment bundle" (money wages and nonmonetary benefits) that minimizes their firms' labor costs. The rules for minimizing labor cost are straightforward:

1 Extend employment (number of workers or hours worked) so long as the additional value of the workers' contribution to firm output exceeds the value of workers' payment bundles.
2 Extend the provision of each fringe benefit so long as the workers are willing to give up more in money wages than each fringe benefit costs the firm.

Most MBA students understand that firms should seek competitive advantage in their final product markets through product development. We suggest here that firms should also seek competitive advantage in their final product markets through cost savings that can come with the development of improved payment bundles that are mutually beneficial to firms and their workers. If government policy dictates that workers be paid a higher money wage (as in "minimum wage" or a "living wage"), then firms would be well advised to reconstruct their payment bundles to mitigate the higher costs associated with the mandated higher money wage – all for the goal of remaining competitive, given that other firms will be reconstructing their payment bundles to remain competitive.

Further readings online

Reading 4.1 Key econometric findings on the effects of the minimum wage

Reading 4.2 The role of "hostages" in business

The bottom line

The key takeaways from chapter 4 are the following:

1 The market system can perform the very valuable service of rationing scarce resources among those who want them; however, markets are not always permitted to operate unobstructed. Government has objectives of its own, objectives that are determined collectively rather than individually. This fact has important implications for the types and the efficiency of policies that are selected (a topic to which we return again and again in this book).

2 Excise taxes, under normal market conditions, tend to be passed on only partially to consumers, meaning producers often pay a portion of the tax in the form of a lower after-tax price. How the tax is shared between buyers and sellers depends upon the elasticity of supply and demand.

3 Price and rent controls – "price ceilings" – tend to result in shortages. They also tend to result in costs being passed along to buyers in various ways and tend to result in a reduction in the quality of whatever good's price is subject to control.

4 Firms offer fringe benefits because they pay. They can increase costs, but they can also increase productivity and increase the market supply of labor wanting to work where fringe benefits are offered, which can result in a lower market wage rate.

5 With a fringe benefit provided, workers can be better off in spite of the lower wage rate because the value of the benefit to workers exceeds the value of the lost money wages. The employers can be better off because the wage reduction caused by the increase in the worker supply can be greater than the cost of the benefit to employers.

6 Fringe benefits will tend not to be offered unless they are mutually beneficial to workers and employers.

7 The provision of fringe benefits will be extended until the additional value to employees of the last unit equals the additional cost of the fringe benefit to employers.

8 Minimum-wage laws – and other "price floors" – tend to result in market surpluses. However, such surpluses enable employers to offset at least partially the employment effects of minimum wages by reducing fringe benefits or increasing work demands.

9 When a minimum wage is imposed, both workers and employers can be worse off. Employers can be worse off because the higher wage exceeds the possible cost reductions from fringe benefits being taken away and/or the productivity gains from the imposition of greater work demands on employees. Workers can be worse off because the value of the loss of fringe benefits and the greater work demands imposed can exceed the higher wage rate.

10 Honesty in business has both a moral and an economic dimension. Honesty is an economic force because it can pay.

Review questions >>

1   Is a tax on margarine "efficient" in the economic sense of the term? Why would margarine producers prefer to have an excise tax imposed on both butter and margarine? Would such a tax be more or less efficient than a tax on margarine alone?

2   If, in a competitive market, prices are held below market equilibrium by government controls, what will be the effect on output? How might managers be expected to react to the laws?

3   Why might some managers want price controls? Why wouldn't they get together and control prices themselves (if it were legal)?

4   How could price controls affect a firm's incentive to innovate? Explain.

5   "If a price ceiling is imposed in only one competitive industry, the resulting shortage in that industry will be greater than if price ceilings were imposed in all industries." Do you agree? Explain.

6   "Price controls can be more effective in the short run than in the long run." Explain.

7   "The existence of external costs is not in itself a sufficient reason for government intervention in the market." Why not?

8   Explain how a reputation for "honest dealing" on the part of executives can elevate a company's stock.

9   Why do many consumers pay extra for goods with "brand names"?

5

Applications of the economic way of thinking: international and environmental economics

Money moves over, around and through them [national borders] with the speed of light. The flows of capital are now in the range of 30 to 50 times greater than world trade. The world's capital market that moves along this electronic highway goes where it is wanted and it stays where it is well-treated … As long as our free-market system permits and delivers an acceptable rate of return on investment in an environment of political stability that is competitive with other areas of investment, the capital will keep coming.

Walter Wriston (long-time CEO of Citicorp)

I n this chapter we extend our applications of the economic way of thinking to international trade and finance and environmental economics, relying again extensively on supply and demand graphs. We cover international economics early in the book for a straightforward reason: international trade and finance have become progressively more important issues for business. Moveover, national economies have become integrated and interdependent to a degree not imagined just a few decades back. The business of much business has become global in scope because of technological gains in transportation and telecommunications. The extent of the integration of national economies has been dramatized in recent years through the rapid spread of the financial crisis, attributable to the bursting of the housing price bubble and the collapse of the market for mortgage-backed securities, that became evident in the United States's banking system in late 2007, only to cause a growing list of major banks around the world to hover on the brink of bankruptcy in 2008 and 2009. In effect, the United States metaphorically sneezed, and the rest of the world caught pneumonia.

Many CEOs and lower-ranking managers can no longer see their role as one of allocating resources within the walls of their firms, or even within their local, geographically bound markets. They must think across national boundaries with the intent of minimizing costs and maximizing sales and profits globally. Managers at all levels also must consider the costs of various government policies, treating them in much the same way as labor-cost considerations that affect where goods are produced and sold. At one time, managers had to be mindful of competitive pressures only from local or national sources. Now, they must worry about competitive pressures that are truly global in scope. The ever decreasing cost of transportation and telecommunications within and across national borders has made global competition possible. Managers in company headquarters are able to stay in touch and monitor far-flung offices and plants and to develop project teams without regard to geography or ethnicity. Telecommunications allow firms to draw on specialized talents of people around the world who can design products that have the potential for global sales.

To think globally, managers must first understand the basics of international trade and finance. They need to know that being the most cost-effective producer of a good will not necessarily guarantee success in world trade. How can that be? Read on. We unravel the paradox in our review of the law of comparative advantage introduced in chapter 1. The basic international economic principles developed in this chapter will prepare students for later courses in global business and foreign residentials.

In this chapter we combine our discussion of international economics with a discussion of environmental economics for the simple reason: both market and environmental forces are now global in scope. And each set of forces affects the other. The way business is done around the world obviously affects the global environment. Pollutants emitted from factory chimneys in one country can rain down on people a world away. Environmental quality (or lack thereof) can affect business costs and profitability through, for example, workers' health care and health insurance costs. Although environmental regulations can directly impact people's health and welfare around the globe, they also can impact business production costs and, in turn, firms' location decisions and international trade patterns.

Managers need to know how environmental degradation affects human welfare, but also, perhaps as important for MBA students, business costs. Managers also need to understand how different environmental remedies can achieve environmental goals at different costs. Surely, governments, consumers, and managers share a common goal, selecting environmental remedies that make the most economic sense and also contribute to human welfare around the globe.

In Part A of this chapter, international and environmental economics are discussed separately to streamline and ease the development of the theory in each

A

subdiscipline. For longer courses, we provide several online readings that review or expand on basic international and environmental theory; these topics are indicated in Part A where appropriate.

In Part B, we show how international trade and finance affect the environment, and how environmental quality and policies can affect firms' location decisions and, therefore, the international flow of goods. We also explore how the growing mobility of financial capital and physical capital (plant and equipment) on a global scale is tightening economic pressures on firms. In online Perspective 5, "The travels of a T-shirt in a global economy," we discuss the mobility of resources globally by providing a short history of the cotton and textile industries during the past two centuries as they moved from England to New England, to the American South, and now to China and Southeast Asia.

Online Perspective

Environmental decay may be an increasing concern for the future of the planet, but capital mobility also can be checking (partially at least) governments' ability to freely regulate business within their jurisdictions. Regulations can translate into business costs, which can cause mobile businesses to migrate to more hospitable locations. This means that the growing globalization of business can have feedback effects on the environment.

More than ever, policy makers need to choose environmental and other regulatory policies with an eye toward the regulations' cost-effectiveness. And more than ever, managers need to understand the interplay between economics and political dynamics. This chapter is designed to give you a solid economic foundation for a course in global business, which is often followed by a foreign residential.

Part A Theory and public policy applications

A discussion of global economics has two major divisions: (1) the actual movement of real goods and services across national boundaries that comes with trade, and (2) the financial considerations involved in multinational trade.

Global economics: international trade

The term "international trade" can be misleading in capturing the nature of the growing volume of exchanges across national boundaries. Nations never really trade; people do. Although we might discuss trade in terms of nations as a matter of convenience, we are talking about trades that are negotiated by real people (or their firms), and certainly not by countries as some sort of amorphous whole. This simple point – that people are at the heart of cross-country exchanges – is important because it allows us to approach international trade as an extension of supply-and-demand and other trading models – indeed, the economic way of thinking in general.

Understanding that trade is between people, not nations, is important for another reason. If we focus solely on aggregate gains from trade to nations taken as unified political entities, we may overlook the *distributional effects* of international commerce – the gains and losses to individuals (whether they act as independent contractors or as managers and owners of multinational firms). As we shall show, even though international trade increases a *nation's* total income, it can reduce some individuals' incomes while increasing others'. These individual gains and losses contain valuable lessons for MBA students and are important to any discussion of free trade among nations and to objections to protectionist policies. To get to those lessons, we must review the concepts of absolute and comparative advantage considered in chapter 1. (If you are confident you understand these concepts, you can skip to the section below on "The distributional effects of trade.")

Aggregate gains from trade

Most of the gains from trade result from producing goods at a minimum cost in terms of sacrificed alternatives and the distribution of what is produced to those who value it most. Joint output is maximized and consumption opportunities are enhanced as nations produce and sell those things which they can produce at the lowest opportunity costs. Adam Smith told us in the 1770s about the nature of gains from trade: "It is a maxim of every prudent master, never to attempt to make at home what it will cost him more to make than to buy" (Smith 1937, 422). Cost savings in individual countries on producing any given output level necessarily imply that more can be produced with any given resource base cross-nationally.

Trade also allows a greater variety and wider choice of available products. The gains from it are clearest when no domestic substitute exists for an imported good. For example, the United States does not have any known reserves of chromium, manganese, or tin. For those basic resources, which are widely used in manufacturing, American firms must rely on foreign suppliers. The gains from trade are also clear for goods that are very costly or difficult to produce in the United States. For example, cocoa and coffee can be grown in the United States, but only in greenhouses. Obviously it is less costly to import coffee in exchange for some other good, such as wheat, for which the US climate is better suited.

Foreign competition also offers benefits to the American consumer. By challenging the market power of domestic firms, foreign producers who market their goods in the United States expand market supplies, reduce product prices, and expand domestic consumption (which means that consumer surplus value from consuming imported goods can rise), not to mention the fact that foreign competition also increases the variety of goods available. Without competition from the thirty or more foreign automobile producers who sell in the American market, US domestic automakers would each get a much larger percentage of the market. They would be less hesitant to raise their prices if consumers had fewer alternative sources of supply. Collusion among major manufacturers also would be much more likely without foreign competitors. And domestic producers would feel less competitive pressure to improve their organization design and management policies as well as their products.

International trade also promotes specialization, the benefits of which should now be fairly clear. By concentrating on producing a small number of goods and selling to the world market, a nation can reap the benefits of greater worker and firm proficiency in production. The resulting cost savings can result in *greater aggregate production* in both trading nations – even when production in all goods in one trading nation is more efficient than elsewhere in the world. To see these points with clarity, return to chapter 1 and review the discussion on the law of comparative advantage developed there in terms of trade between Fred and Harry. You can redevelop the discussion for international trade by substituting China and the United States for Fred and Harry. You can make the discussion more directly related to modern trade flows between those two countries by substituting textiles and beef for coconuts and papayas. You may also want to consult online Reading 5.1, The law of comparative advantage and trade between China and the United States.

Below we extend our treatment of trade between people in different countries by considering the distributional effects of international trade within countries.

[See online Video Module 5.1 Gains from international trade]

The distributional effects of trade
Despite the insights that the law of comparative advantage provides, international trade remains a controversial subject because not all firms – their owners and workers – within nations may gain from trade. Individual gains tend to go to domestic firms that produce goods and services for export; losses tend to go to domestic firms that produce goods and services that are imported. This is true of any trade, domestic as well as foreign. If more American consumers decide that they prefer to buy Dell computers assembled in the United States to Lenovo computers assembled in China, then Dell's assembly workers and stockholders will benefit, and Lenovo's will be harmed, although the harm may be temporary.

Gains to exporters
Exporters of domestic goods gain from international trade because the market for their goods expands, increasing demand for their products, thus raising their output and the prices they can charge. The increase in their revenue can be seen in figure 5.1. When the demand curve shifts from D_1 to D_2 because of the added foreign

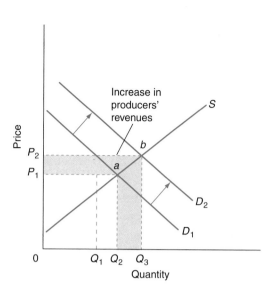

Figure 5.1 Gains from the export trade
Opening up foreign markets to US producers increases the demand for their products, from D_1 to D_2. As a result, domestic producers can raise their price from P_1 to P_2 and sell a larger quantity, Q_3 instead of Q_2. Revenues increase by the shaded area $P_2bQ_3Q_2aP_1$. The more price-elastic or the flatter the supply function (S), the larger the change in quantity and the smaller the change in price.

demand, producers' revenues rise from $P_1 \times Q_2$ (point a) to $P_2 \times Q_3$ (point b). (The more price-elastic or the flatter the supply function [S], the larger the change in quantity and the smaller the change in price.) The increase in revenues is equal to the shaded L-shaped area bounded by $P_2bQ_3Q_2aP_1$. Producers benefit because they receive greater profits, equal to the shaded area above the supply curve, P_2baP_1 (that portion of the increased revenues that is not additional cost). Workers and suppliers of raw materials benefit because their services are in greater demand, and therefore more costly. The cost of producing additional units for export is equal to the shaded area below the supply curve between Q_2 and Q_3, Q_2abQ_3.

Losses to firms competing with imports

Most domestic buyers welcome the importation of cheaper and higher-quality products, but domestic producers who face competition from foreign suppliers have an incentive to object to importation. If imports are allowed, the domestic supply of a good increases. Domestic competitors will sell less, and they may have to sell at a lower price. In short, the business opportunities and the employment opportunities of their workers and suppliers decline as a result of foreign competition, with a potential reduction in their real incomes.

Figure 5.2 shows the effects of importing foreign textiles. Without imports, demand is D and supply is S_1. In a competitive market, producers will sell Q_2 units at a price of P_2. Total receipts will be $P_2 \times Q_2$. The importation of foreign textiles increases the supply to S_2, dropping the price from P_2 to P_1. Because prices are lower, consumers increase their consumption from Q_2 to Q_3 and get more for their money. (The more price-elastic or the flatter the demand curve [D], the greater the change in quantity and the smaller the change in price.)

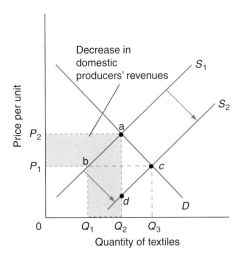

Figure 5.2 Losses from competition with imported products Opening up the market to foreign trade increases the supply of textiles from S_1 to S_2. As a result, the price of textiles falls from P_2 to P_1, and domestic producers sell a lower quantity, Q_1 instead of Q_2. Consumers benefit from the lower price and the higher quantity of textiles they are able to buy, but domestic producers, workers, and suppliers lose. Producers' revenues drop by an amount equal to the shaded area $P_2aQ_2Q_1bP_1$. Workers' and suppliers' payments drop by an amount equal to the shaded area Q_2abQ_1. Starting at point c, a tariff or tax equal to ad is levied, shifting the supply curve from S_2 to S_1. In an industry whose costs are increasing, the increase in price from P_1 to P_2 in the importing country is less than the increase in the tariff (ad), because a price fall in the exporting country absorbs some of the burden of the duty.

Domestic firms, their employees, and their suppliers lose. Because the price is lower, domestic producers must move down their supply curve (S_1) to the lower quantity Q_1. Their revenues fall from $P_2 \times Q_2$ to $P_1 \times Q_1$. In other words, the revenues in the shaded L-shaped area bounded by $P_2aQ_2Q_1bP_1$ are lost. Of this total loss in revenues, owners of domestic firms lose, on balance, the area above the supply curve, P_2abP_1, representing profits. Workers and suppliers of raw materials lose the area below the supply curve, Q_2abQ_1. This is the cost domestic firms do not have to incur when they reduce domestic production from Q_2 to Q_1, the payments that would be made to domestic workers and suppliers in the absence of foreign competition. If workers and other resources are employed in textiles because it is their best possible employment, the introduction of foreign products can be seen as a restriction on some workers' employment opportunities. In summary, although international trade lowers import prices and raises export prices in the domestic nation, the net impact is expanded total available output and consumption opportunities for people in the trading countries.

[See online Video Module 5.2 Distribution of gains and losses]

The effects of trade restrictions
Domestic restrictions on international trade undercut economic gains that result when countries, and the people in them, exploit the benefits of trading according to the law of comparative advantage. Restrictions also narrow markets. Thus, they can undercut economies of specialization and scale in both resources and production.

A **tariff** is a special tax or duty on imported goods that can be a percentage of the price (*ad valorem* duty) or a specific amount per unit of the product (specific duty).

An examination of the impact of **tariffs** can illustrate the distributional impact of various forms of trade protection. If tariffs are imposed on a foreign good such as textiles, the supply of textiles will decrease – say, from S_2 to S_1 in figure 5.2 – and the price of imports will rise. As domestic demand shifts from the higher-priced imported textiles to domestic sources, domestic producers will be able to raise their prices too, and domestic production will go up. If the tariff is high and all foreign textiles are excluded, the supply will shift all the way back to S_1. A lower tariff will have a more modest effect, shifting the supply curve only part way toward S_1. The price of textiles will rise and domestic producers will expand their production, but imports will continue to come into the country. How much the price rises and the quantity falls after the imposition of the tariff depends not only on how high the tariff is, but also on how responsive consumers are to a price increase. The more price-responsive consumers are, the greater the fall in the total quantity of textiles consumed domestically and the less the rise in price for any given tariff.[1]

In summary, tariffs reduce the market supply in the country where they are imposed, raise domestic market prices, and encourage domestic production, thereby helping domestic producers and harming domestic consumers. Tariffs also narrow the scope of markets, which means they can narrow the scope of specialization of labor (and other resources) and reduce the benefits that come with specialization. From the days of Adam Smith, many economists have favored the reduction, if not elimination, of tariffs (and other forms of trade restrictions such as quotas) because the benefits of specialization can expand with an expansion in the scope of markets. The cases for and against protectionism have been extended in online Reading 5.2. Also, in Reading 5.3 you will find a famous satire on protectionism written by Frédéric Bastiat, a nineteenth-century French economist.

Special interests politics and trade restrictions

Tariffs promote a less efficient allocation of the world's scarce resources, but because domestic producers stand to gain private benefits from them we should expect those producers to seek tariffs as long as their market benefits exceed the political cost of acquiring protection. Politicians are likely to expect votes and campaign contributions in return for tariff legislation that generates highly visible

---

[1] An import quota has the same general effect as a tariff, although its price–cost effect can be much more drastic. Both tariffs and quotas reduce the market supply, raise the domestic market price, and encourage domestic production, thereby helping domestic producers and harming domestic consumers. A quota is a physical or dollar-value limit on the amount of a good that can be imported or exported during some specified period of time.

benefits to special interests. Producers (and labor) usually will make the necessary contributions because the elimination of foreign competition promises increased revenues in the protected industries. The difference between the increase in profits caused by import restrictions and the amount spent on political activity can be seen as a kind of profit in itself. That is, the potential for the imposition of tariffs can be expected to lead to lobbying efforts (or what economists call "rent seeking"). Because lobbying for protection can soak up real resources, the aggregate economic costs from protectionist policies can be greater than the loss from restricted imports.

In contrast to producers, consumers have reason to oppose tariffs or quotas on imported products. Such legislation inevitably causes prices to rise, because a tariff amounts to a subsidy to the domestic producer of the dutiable product, the cost of which consumers of the product pay in higher prices. Consumers typically do not offer very much resistance, as the financial burden that any one consumer bears may be very slight, particularly if the tariff in question is small, as most tariffs are. The benefits of a tariff accrue principally to a relatively small group of firms, whose lobbyists may already be well entrenched in Washington. These firms have a strong incentive to be fully informed on the issue and to make campaign contributions. The political influence of the producers can, at times, be offset partially by the political activism of large retailers who bear some of the burden of protectionist policies through higher prices of imported goods and through lower sales to American buyers. Walmart, Sears, J. C. Penney, and Target have been active in opposing US textile and apparel tariffs and quotas (Rivoli 2006).

Protection retaliation and trade wars

Tariffs (or quotas or other forms of protection) can lead to more economic harm than indicated above. This is because tariffs will cut production in the exporting countries, which then have reason to retaliate with protective tariffs of their own (1) to increase employment in their own protected industries, and (2) to impose economic costs on the foreign countries with the hope that these countries will reduce tariffs. When the United States economy turned downward after the 1929 stock-market crash, prices (especially in agriculture goods) began to fall and unemployment began to rise. To reverse the price and unemployment trends, the US Congress passed the Smoot-Hawley Tariff Act, which imposed higher tariffs, averaging 62 percent, on some 60,000 agricultural and industrial goods. Countries around the world began retaliating with their own higher tariffs on American goods for the two reasons given above. The resulting worldwide decay in international trade was a major (but not only) contributor to the development of the Great Depression that became global in scope (Eichengreen 1989; Crucini and Kahn 1996).

Trade protectionism poses a global Prisoner's Dilemma. Every nation may have strong domestic political incentives to impose protectionist measures for both employment and retaliatory purposes, but if all (or just a number of) nations impose tariffs, then everyone can be worse off. The World Trade Organization was established in 1995 to push for freer international trade and to mitigate, if not prevent, "trade (protection) wars." That is, the WTO was set up to discourage countries from taking the noncooperative strategies in their ever-present Prisoner's Dilemmas.

Nevertheless, destructive trade wars continue to break out, with the so-called "banana wars" being a recent illustration. Europe peels back about 2.5 billion tons of bananas a year. Since 1975, Europe has permitted the virtually unobstructed importation of bananas from former colonies in Africa, the Pacific, and the Caribbean, but has imposed heavy tariffs on bananas from Latin American countries where bananas are grown on large, mechanized, and cost-effective farms. Major Latin American farms are owned by US multinational companies whose CEOs have been heavy contributors to the presidential campaigns in the 1990s, which helps explain why in 1995 the United States filed a petition with the WTO, arguing that European countries' tariffs on bananas were violating WTO trade rules. The United States won its case in 1996, causing the European Union to adjust trade policies, but not to US satisfaction.

The United States responded by imposing a retaliatory tariff of up to 100 percent on European products, ranging from Scottish cashmere to French cheese (Barkham 1999). The economies of former European colonies in the Caribbean – Martinique, Dominica, Grenada, St. Lucia and St. Vincent, and the Grenadines – are heavily dependent on bananas, and the European Union was reluctant to move rapidly toward free trade despite the US retaliation. The United States filed another complaint in 2001, arguing that the EU was not holding to the spirit of the WTO rules, which caused the EU to relent and all but eliminate the trade protections on bananas by 2006. In 2008, the EU finally negotiated a deal that would reduce its tariff on Latin American bananas by close to 50 percent (€222 per ton to €114 per ton in 2016) (Fresh Plaza 2008).

As a consequence of such a deal, banana production for the European market can be expected to shift gradually from Africa, the Caribbean, and the Pacific to Latin American countries. The freer trade can be expected to lead to aggregate gains for the world, but the distributional effects should be noted. The most notable negative effect is that the beneficiaries of EU banana protection will have to lower their prices as they lose market share (with many high-cost producers going out of business and unemployed workers having to find other jobs). Prices of bananas can be expected to fall in Europe; however, with the increase in demand for Latin American bananas, the price of bananas in the United States and elsewhere is likely to go up as banana sales move toward Europe.

In early 2009, the European Union threatened to ban the importation of beef treated with hormones on the grounds that the hormones could impair consumer health. Seeing the proposed ban on beef imports into Europe as nothing more than protectionism for EU cattlemen, the United States threatened to impose retaliatory tariffs (as high as 100 percent) on a range of gourmet foods imported from European countries, from mineral waters to high-end chocolates (Chung 2009).

In late 2009, another trade war was brewing between China and the United States over the importation of Chinese tires into the United States. In September, the Obama administration raised the US tariff on Chinese tires from 4 percent to 35 percent (with the encouragement of the Steelworkers union) on the grounds that the Chinese government was heavily subsidizing tire production. The Chinese government responded by threatening to impose duties of its own on Chinese imports of chickens and cars from the United States and to file a complaint with the World Trade Organization (Dyer and Braithwaite 2009). Such continuing and erupting trade disputes, of course, can end up making citizens in the affected countries worse off.

Interconnections of comparative advantage

The discussion of comparative advantage to this point might leave the impression that a country's comparative advantage in the production of a good (or an array of goods) is solely a function of production costs and efficiencies within that country. China's comparative advantage in, say, toys may be a function only of its cheap labor (and other cheap resources). That is hardly the case in today's global economies. Given how many computers are produced in China, China obviously has a comparative cost advantage in computers – but that may be the case partly because it buys (and imports) microprocessors from US-based Intel and AMD (and other components from other companies in other countries) at lower costs than it can develop and produce them.

China's comparative advantage in the production of many goods leads to its ever-expanding exports to the United States. But then, because the United States buys so many goods from China, the United States produces a lot of garbage, which gives it a comparative advantage in recyclable waste paper, plastics, and aluminum cans. Indeed, by volume (weight, not dollar value), garbage has for years been the United States' number one export category (McCormack 2008), and a lot of the United States' garbage is exported back to China for reprocessing into many of China's toys and household goods that are returned to the United States. This is to say, if the United States didn't have such a strong comparative advantage in garbage, China might not have such a strong comparative advantage in so many of the products it produces with imported garbage as a cheap input.

For a discussion of how international trade has evolved over the centuries, see online Perspective 5, The travels of a T-shirt in a global economy.

Online
Perspective

Global economics: international finance

People rarely barter to consummate trades, particularly long-distance trades. Exchanging one toy for two pens or three pots for the rear end of a steer simply is not practical. Because the bartering seller must also be a buyer, buyers and sellers may have to incur very substantial costs to find one another, even in the domestic market. When people are separated by hundreds or thousands of miles, national boundaries, and foreign cultures and languages, barter is all the more complicated. We rarely see exporters acting as importers, exchanging specific exports for specific imports, although barter is not absent in international trade, mainly as a means of avoiding trade restrictions and taxes. (If you are someone who does a lot of international business and travel, you probably understand exchange rates and currency conversion well; you might skip to the section on the "Determination of the exchange rate" on p. 177.)

The process of international monetary exchange

Imagine you own a small gourmet shop that carries special cheeses. You may buy your cheese either domestically – cheddar from New York, Monterey Jack from California – or abroad. If you buy from a domestic firm, it is easy to negotiate the deal and make payment. Because the price of cheese is quoted in dollars and the domestic firm expects payment in dollars, you can pay the same way you pay other bills – by writing a personal check. Only one national currency is involved.

Purchasing cheese from a French cheese maker is a little more complicated, for two reasons. First, the price of the cheese will be quoted in euros. Second, you will want to pay in dollars, but the French cheese maker must be paid in euros. Either you must exchange your dollars for euros, or the cheese maker must convert them to euros. At some point, currencies must be exchanged at some recognized *foreign exchange rate*. Before you buy, you will want to compare the prices of French and domestic cheeses. To do so, you must convert the euro price of cheese into its dollar equivalent. To do that, you need to know the **international exchange rate** between dollars and euros. Once you know the current exchange rate, conversion of currencies is not difficult.

> The **international exchange rate** is the price of one national currency (such as the euro) stated in terms of another national currency (such as the dollar). In other words, the international exchange rate is the dollar price you must pay for each euro you buy.

Assume that you want to buy €5,000 worth of cheese, and that the international exchange rate between dollars and euros is $1.25 (that is, $1.25 buys €1), roughly the exchange rate as this chapter was being finalized. This means that €5,000 will cost you $6,250.

The international exchange rate determines the dollar price of the foreign goods you want to buy. A different exchange rate would have changed the dollar price of cheese. For instance, suppose the exchange rate rose from $1.25 = €1 to $2.00 = €1.

Table 5.1 Likely long-run effects of depreciation and appreciation of the dollar on US exports and imports

	Depreciation of dollar	Appreciation of dollar
Price of exports	Decrease	Increase
Total dollar value of exports	Increase	Decrease
Price of imports	Increase	Decrease
Total dollar value of imports	Decrease	Increase

In the jargon of international finance, such a change represents a **depreciation** of the dollar. The dollar has depreciated relative to the euro because it now takes more dollars to buy one euro, or a single dollar now buys fewer euros. This necessarily means that the euro has *appreciated* relative to the dollar because it now takes fewer euros to buy a dollar (0.5 euros now buys a dollar as opposed to 0.8 before).

> A **depreciation** of a national currency, such as the dollar, is a reduction in its exchange value or purchasing power, brought about by market forces, in relation to other national currencies.

As an American, your willingness to buy French cheese obviously depends on the euro price of cheese and the exchange rate between dollars and euros. If the euro price of cheese increases or decreases, your dollar price increases or decreases at any given exchange rate. If the dollar depreciates relative to euros, the dollar price of French cheese rises. It is very likely you (and other Americans) will be inclined to import less because American cheese consumers will buy less at the higher price. On the other hand, if the dollar appreciates (that is, if a dollar buys more euros), the dollar price of French cheese falls. Very likely, you will import more because you can lower your own price and sell more.

In general, depreciation of the dollar discourages imports and encourages exports, which reduces a merchandise balance of trade deficit (when imports exceed exports), or increases a merchandise balance of trade surplus (when exports exceed imports) in the long run. These long-run consequences of changes in the international rate of exchange are summarized in table 5.1.[2]

---

[2] In the (very) short run, however, a depreciation in the dollar can increase the dollars we spend on imports and reduce the dollars we receive from our exports because we will have to spend more dollars on each imported item and we will receive fewer dollars on each exported item. This short-run reduction in revenue from exports after a depreciation in the dollar, followed by a long-run increase in revenue from exports, is often referred to as the "J-curve phenomenon" (Dornbush and Krugman 1976). Thus, although a depreciation in the exchange rate will eventually achieve a balance of trade equilibrium as shown in table 5.1, it may take some time.

The exchange of national currencies

Assume that as a cheese importer you have figured the dollar price of French cheese using the exchange rate, and you find it satisfactory. Because your American customers pay for their groceries in dollars, that is the currency you receive when you sell the cheese. Yet cheese makers in France want euros since that is what they need to pay for their mortgages and groceries. How do you convert your dollars into euros?

Again, if you want to buy French cheese and need euros, a bank will exchange your dollars for you. Banks deal in different currencies for the same reason that businesspeople trade in commodities – to make money. An automobile dealer buys cars at a low price with the hope of selling them at a higher price. Banks do the same thing, except that their commodities are currencies. They buy dollars and pay for them in euros, pounds, and yen, with the idea of selling them at a profit. So you can use dollars to buy the euros you need from an American bank, and have those euros transferred to the account of the French cheese maker. Or you can pay for your French cheese by writing a check against your dollar checking account in the United States and send the check to the French firm.[3] The French cheese maker will accept the check knowing that your dollars can be traded for euros (that is, sold to a French bank) at the rate of exchange. Of course, if you expect the French cheese maker to accept a check in dollars, you will have to pay more to compensate him for the cost of converting the dollars into euros. Either way, you will have to pay a premium for the euros since, as indicated, banks are in the business of selling currencies for a profit.

This hypothetical purchase of French cheese leads to an important observation. Be it cheese, or watches, or anything else, a US import will increase the dollar holdings of foreign banks. So will American expenditures abroad, whether for tours or for foreign stocks and bonds. Americans must have euros to buy goods and services in most European countries; therefore, they must offer American dollars in exchange. Foreign banks end up holding some of the dollars that Americans have used to buy euros, and other foreign currencies. And as these purchases increase the dollars they are holding relative to other currencies, the value of dollars declines relative to the value of other currencies on the foreign exchange market.

In the same way, US exports reduce the dollar holdings of foreign banks. Exports are typically paid for out of the dollar accounts of foreign banks. Foreign expenditures on trips to the United States or on the stocks and bonds of US corporations have the same effect. They reduce the dollar holdings of foreign banks and increase

---

[3] Instruments of exchange other than checks are often used in international transactions. The process, however, is essentially the same.

the foreign currency holdings of US banks. In this case, the value of dollars increases relative to the value of other currencies on the foreign exchange market.

As the dollar depreciates or appreciates, market forces come into play that counteract the move in the dollar's value. For example, depreciation of the US dollar in the exchange rate will have several effects, all tending to reduce the number of dollars coming onto the international money market. As explained earlier, the exchange will make French goods more expensive for Americans to buy. Thus it will tend to reduce US imports and, accordingly, the number of dollars that must be exchanged for foreign currencies. Depreciation will also tend to reduce the price of American goods to foreigners. For instance, at an exchange rate of $1.25 for €1, the euro price of a $1 million American computer is €800,000. At an exchange rate of $1.50 for €1, the euro price of the same computer is €666,667 – a substantial reduction in price. To buy American goods at the new lower euro price, the French will increase their demand for dollars. Again, the quantity of dollars being offered on the money market will fall, and the growth in foreign dollar holdings will be checked.

Determination of the exchange rate

As with the prices of most things, exchange rates are determined by the forces of demand and supply, although governments often interfere to alter the rate from what market forces alone would have produced. When there is no government interference, the rates are dubbed "free" or "floating." When government intervenes by having the central bank or some other government agency buy or sell currency in the foreign exchange markets, the exchange rates are dubbed "fixed" (also "pegged"), or kept within specified limits. From 1945 to 1971, the dollar exchange rates for all currencies were basically fixed by the US government. Since 1971, however, rates have been set flexibly, with some government intervention in a "dirty," or *managed*, floating exchange rate system, in which the prices of currencies are partly determined by competitive market forces and partly determined by official government intervention. That is, governments may not prevent minor movements in exchange rates, but will try to keep the exchange rate from changing substantially during any short period of time.

> A **free exchange rate system** is one in which the prices of all national currencies in terms of other national currencies are determined by the unfettered forces of the supply of and demand for national currencies.
>
> A **fixed exchange rate system** is one in which the prices of currencies are established and maintained by government intervention. Under such systems, governments become active traders in their currencies.

National currencies have a *market value* – that is, a price – because individuals, firms, and governments use them to buy foreign goods, services, and securities. There is a market demand for a national currency such as the euro. Furthermore, the demand for the euro (or any other currency) slopes downward, like curve *D* in figure 5.3. To see why, look at the market for euros from the point of view of US

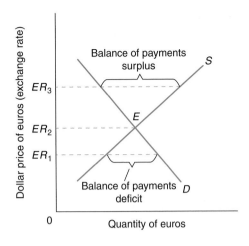

Figure 5.3 Supply and demand for euros on the international currency market
The international exchange rate between the dollar and the euro is determined by the forces of supply and demand, with the equilibrium at *E*. If the exchange rate is below equilibrium, say at ER_1, the quantity of euros demanded, shown by the demand curve, will exceed the quantity supplied, shown by the supply curve. Competitive pressure will push the exchange rate up. If the exchange rate is above equilibrium, say, at ER_3, the quantity supplied will exceed the quantity demanded and competitive pressure will push the exchange rate down. Thus the price of a foreign currency is determined in much the same way as the price of any other commodity.

residents. As the dollar price of the euro falls (it takes fewer dollars to buy €1, or more euros can be bought for $1), the price Americans must pay for European goods also falls. As a result, Americans will want to buy more European goods. They will require a larger quantity of euros to complete their transactions. As the price of euros goes down, the quantity demanded of euros goes up – and correspondingly, as the price of euros goes up, the quantity demanded of euros goes down.

The supply of euros coming onto the market reflects the European demand for American goods, services, and securities. To get American goods, Europeans need dollars. They must pay for those dollars with euros, and in doing so they supply euros to the international money market. As the dollar price of the euro increases, the price of American goods to the Europeans falls. To take advantage of the increased dollar price of euros, Europeans buy a larger quantity of American goods, which means that they need more dollars and must offer more euros to get them. Therefore, the quantity of euros supplied on the market rises as the dollar price of euros rises. Thus, the supply curve for euros slopes upward to the right, like curve *S* in figure 5.3.

The buyers and sellers of euros make up what is loosely called the *international money market* in euros. Banks are very much involved in such markets. They buy euros from the sellers (suppliers) and sell them to the buyers (demanders). As in other markets, the interaction of suppliers and demanders determines the market price. That is, given the supply and demand curves in figure 5.3, in a competitive market the dollar price of the euro will move toward the equilibrium point at *E* involving the intersection of the supply and demand curves. The equilibrium price, or exchange rate, will be ER_2, the price at which the quantity of euros supplied exactly equals the quantity of euros demanded.

At the market equilibrium point, no build-up of dollars or euros occurs in the accounts of foreign banks. European and US banks have no reason to modify the exchange rate to encourage or discourage the purchase or sale of either currency. In the language of international finance, the net balance of payments coming into and going out of each country is zero.

If the exchange rate is below equilibrium level – say, ER_1 – the quantity of euros demanded will exceed the quantity supplied. An *imbalance of payments* will develop. Again in the jargon of international finance, the United States will develop a *balance of payments deficit* – a shortfall in the quantity of a foreign currency supplied. (This is a conceptual definition. When it comes to defining the balance of payments deficit in a way that can be measured by the Department of Commerce, economists are in considerable disagreement.)

As in other markets, this imbalance will eventually right itself. Because of the excess demand for euros, European banks will accumulate excess dollar balances – they will want to buy more euros than they can at the prevailing dollar price for euros, which is the same as wanting to sell more dollars than they can at the prevailing euro price for dollars. Competitive pressure will then push the exchange rate back up to ER_2. People who cannot buy euros at ER_1 will offer a higher price. As the price of euros rises, French goods will become less attractive to Americans, and the quantity of euros demanded will fall. Conversely, American goods will become more attractive to the French, and the quantity of euros supplied will rise.

Similarly, at an exchange rate higher than ER_2 – say, ER_3 – the quantity of euros supplied will exceed the quantity demanded. The surplus of euros will not last forever, however. Eventually the exchange rate will fall back toward ER_2, causing an increase in the quantity of euros demanded and a decrease in the quantity supplied. In short, in a free foreign currency market, the price of a currency is determined in the same way as the prices of other commodities.

The two major advantages of a floating system of monetary exchange are (1) that free market forces exclusively and automatically determine exchange rates without government intervention, controls, or regulations; and (2) external adjustment, under favorable conditions, is attained without requiring major domestic or internal price, income, or employment changes. A floating system's one major disadvantage is that instability in the form of possible frequent, hard-to-predict, and large fluctuations could discourage international trade, transactions, and investment.[4]

---

[4] However, it needs to be noted that since flexible exchange rates were reintroduced in 1971, the volume of world trade has significantly increased, despite considerable volatility in exchange rates. At the same time, the realized volume of trade could be lower than what would have occurred without the shift from fixed to flexible exchange rates.

Exchange rates and changes in domestic market conditions

By modifying exchange rates to correct for imbalances in payments, the international money market can accommodate vast changes in the economic conditions of nations engaged in trade. A good example is the way the market handles a change in consumption patterns. These changes in consumption, and hence in foreign exchange rates, can be caused by changes in a nation's tastes and preferences, real income, level of prices (including interest rates), costs, and expectations as to future exchange rates.

A change in preferences

Suppose that American preferences for French goods – say, wines and perfumes – increase for some reason. The demand for euros will increase because Americans will need more of them at every dollar price to buy the additional French goods they desire. If, as in figure 5.4, the US demand for euros shifts from D_1 to D_2, the quantity of euros demanded at the old equilibrium exchange rate of ER_1 will exceed the quantity supplied by $Q_3 - Q_1$. Those who cannot buy more euros at ER_1 will offer to pay a higher price. The exchange rate will rise toward the new equilibrium level of ER_2 as the equilibrium point shifts from E_1 to E_2. As the dollar depreciates in value, which is the same as an increase in the dollar price for euros, the imbalance in payments is eliminated.

A change in real income

Now suppose that Americans' real incomes rise. Americans will be likely to demand more foreign imports, both directly and in the form of domestic goods that incorporate foreign parts or materials. Either way, an increase in real incomes leads to an

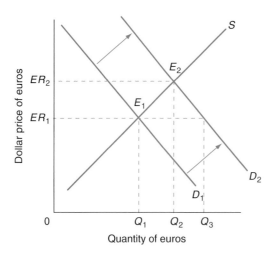

Figure 5.4 Change in the demand for euros

An increase in the demand for euros from D_1 to D_2 will give rise to a shortage of euros at the exchange rate ER_1. The exchange rate will rise from ER_1 to ER_2, eliminating the shortage.

increase in the demand for foreign currencies. Again the demand for euros will rise, as in figure 5.4. The dollar price of euros will rise with it to bring the quantity supplied into line with the quantity demanded.

A change in the rate of inflation

A change in the rate of inflation can have a similar effect on the exchange rate. If the inflation rates are about the same in two nations that trade with each other, the exchange rate between their currencies will remain stable, everything held constant. Because the relative prices of goods in the two nations stay the same, people will have no incentive to switch from domestic to imported goods, or vice versa. If one nation's inflation rate exceeds another's, however, the relative prices of foreign and domestic goods change. If prices increase faster in the United States, for example, Americans will want to buy more foreign goods and fewer domestic goods. Foreigners, on the other hand, will have an incentive to buy more goods from their own countries, where prices are not rising as fast as in the United States. In sum, a higher US inflation rate spells a rise in the demand for foreign currencies, a fall in their supply, and a depreciation of the dollar. This increases the dollar price of foreign currencies and, therefore, increases the dollar price of foreign goods. Similar flows occur when interest rate differentials exist between nations.

Monetary and fiscal policies

A host of government policies, most notably monetary and fiscal policies, can affect international exchange rates, as we will see below. We also will see how managed exchange rates can affect domestic fiscal policies.

Monetary policy

Monetary policy conducted by the Federal Reserve in the United States can affect international exchange rates through interest rates and inflation. When monetary policy is "eased" (which means the Fed steps up the growth in dollars) while monetary policy abroad is held constant, short-term interest rates in the United States can fall relative to interest rates that can be secured abroad. Many people and businesses with dollar balances can be expected to seek the higher interest rates abroad, which will give rise to a higher demand for euros (and other currencies). The higher euro demand can translate into a higher price of euros, which spells a depreciation of the dollar, a force that can curb imports and expand exports.

The long-run effects of an easy money policy can be the exact opposite, because the higher growth rate in the money supply can feed domestic inflation that can increase the domestic demand for relatively lower priced imports and decrease the foreign demand for relatively more expensive US exports in foreign markets.

Fiscal policy

Federal government fiscal (or tax and expenditure) policies can also have exchange rate effects through interest rates. Suppose the US government increases its budget deficit due to increased social or military spending (or the government bailout and stimulus expenditures following the recent world financial crisis). The government will have to issue bonds to cover the deficit. The greater supply of government bonds can mean that the government will have to pay higher interest rates. Attracted by the higher interest rates, foreign investors can be expected to demand more dollars and, in the process, supply more, say, euros. The greater supply of euros on international money markets can be expected to cause a fall in the exchange rate, which translates into an appreciation of the dollar. The appreciation of the dollar will give rise to a reduction in the dollar prices of foreign goods, which means more imports. The dollar's appreciation will also mean that US exports become more expensive in foreign countries, which means fewer US exports.

The impact of exchange rates on exports and imports can cause countries to manage their exchange rates. To spur its exports, and domestic growth, China has for a number of years followed a policy course of holding down the international value of its currency, the yuan, by 15 to 40 percent (Navarro 2008). By deliberately depreciating the value of the yuan (which means the Chinese government has raised the yuan price of dollars), China has lowered the price of its exports to the United States (and elsewhere) and increased the price of imports. A principal way the Chinese government can hold the yuan price of dollars above its equilibrium level is through buying up the resulting market surplus of dollars.

Because of its abundant supply of cheap labor (made all the cheaper by the decades of Communist Party rule that suppressed productivity growth in all phases of the economy), China would today have a significant comparative advantage in many manufactured goods. However, China's policy toward the yuan has distorted the country's comparative advantage. Lax environmental and workplace regulations have further distorted China's comparative advantage (Navarro 2008). Through such distortions, China has made many manufactured goods cheap for Americans, thus making life all the easier for US importers but more difficult for US manufacturers and exporters.

Accordingly, China's efforts to hold down the value of its yuan has been a source of the United States' substantial and growing balance of trade deficit with China (which surpassed $250 billion during 2008, up from $200 billion in 2006 [Reuters 2009]). China's corrresponding trade surpluses have meant that China has perennially piled up dollar balances. To get something in return for the country's exports to the United States, the Chinese government has used its dollar balances to buy interest-earning US government securities. China's demand for government securities, in turn, has held down the interest rate on the securities, which has made US government deficit spending all the cheaper and more politically attractive. China's exchange rate policy very well could have been an international economic force that contributed to the credit upsurge in the United States, fueling the housing bubble and burst in the 1990s and early 2000s. The growing volume of cheap goods from China could have held down inflation in the United States, enabling the Federal Reserve to lower interest rates and expand the money supply in the 2000–3 period with the hope of combating a potential recession after 9/11 (Norberg 2009, chapter 2). It also could have marginally added to US budget deficits, reflected in greater federal government (military and social) expenditures and lower taxes than the United States could have afforded had China allowed the yuan to seek its free-market value.

Green economics: external costs and benefits

During the past half century, environmental economics has grown in prominence within the economics discipline and public policy arenas because of the growth in the world population and production that increases demands on environmental resources worldwide that, for many, are becoming increasingly scarce. Environmental scientists and activists have reached a growing consensus that humans have been doing irreparable damage to the planet and that continued global warming is very likely during the next century. The United States, as the largest energy-consuming country in the world, of course, has the largest economy and largest carbon footprint. The total annual energy (measured in thousands of tons of oil equivalent across all energy sources) consumed in the United States in 2005 (the latest year of available data) was a third higher than the total energy consumed in the next closest energy-using country, China, and over four times the total energy consumed by the fifth-largest energy-using country, Japan (Buurma 2009, citing the International Energy Agency). And global warming can have an array of economic effects, not the least of which are the destruction of arable farmlands and the damage to major cities along all of the world's coastlines as sea levels rise (if the science of global warming proves accurate). Former Vice President and presidential candidate Al Gore elevated public political interest in environmental issues through the release of his book and film, *An Inconvenient Truth*, and through public awareness lectures around the world for which he was awarded the 2007 Nobel Peace Prize.

Nevertheless, as there are almost always two sides to any scientific debate, many of the policy issues surrounding global warming remain highly contentious. We will not seek to settle the scientific debate on the impact of human economic activity on global warming or any other environmental issue. Key facts in the debate are that carbon dioxide emissions from energy consumption in the United States grew by close to a fifth between 1990 and 2006 (from 5.0 billion metric tons in 1980 to 5.9 billion metric tons in 2006) (Energy Information Administration 2007). Still, CO_2 emissions per dollar of gross domestic product declined by about an eighth during the last decade of the twentieth century (US Department of State 2002). However, it needs to be noted that China's CO_2 emissions, coming primarily from coal-burning electricity plants (which it planned to continue to expand over the next decade or more), more than doubled from 1986 and 2006 (Krugman 2009).

Rather than debate the statistics and effects of pollutants here, we seek a more modest objective: to describe how economists think about environmental problems (assuming that human activity exacerbates environmental decay independent of natural forces) and solutions to them. The first goal of economic thinking is to ensure that environmental damage is not made worse by policy solutions. A second, but just as important, goal is that environmental decay is remedied by the least costly policy courses. In Part B, we will address how environmental controls in some countries (the United States and Western Europe) can be linked to environmental degradation in other countries (China and India).

Competitive markets and environmental failures

In a competitive market, producers must minimize their production costs at each level of production and quality in order to lower their prices, increase their production levels, and improve the quality of their products. The *supply curve* marks the success of their efforts. Consumers demonstrate how much they value another unit of the product by their willingness to pay for it, a willingness shown by the *demand curve*. In a competitive market, production will move toward the intersection of the market supply and demand curves – Q_1 in figure 5.5. At that point, the

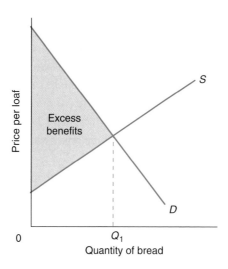

Figure 5.5 Marginal benefit versus marginal cost
The demand curve reflects the marginal benefits of each loaf of bread produced. The supply curve reflects the marginal cost of producing each loaf. For each loaf of bread up to Q_1, the marginal benefits exceed the marginal cost. The shaded area shows the maximum welfare that can be gained from the production of bread. When the market is at equilibrium (when supply equals demand), all those benefits will be realized.

marginal cost of the last unit produced will equal its marginal benefit to consumers. (For a review of why Q_1 is the efficient, welfare-maximizing output level, see the discussion on market efficiency in figure 3.8 in chapter 3.)

The output results cannot be achieved unless competition is intense, buyers receive all the product's benefits, and producers pay all the costs of production. If such optimum conditions are not achieved, the market fails, or there is a so-called market failure.

One potential for such failure occurs when exchanges between buyers and sellers affect people who are not directly involved in the trades; they are said to have external effects, or to generate externalities. When such effects are pleasurable they are called *external benefits*. When they are unpleasant, or impose a cost on people other than the buyers or sellers, they are called *external costs*. The effects of external costs and benefits on production and market efficiency can be seen with the aid of supply and demand curves.

> A market failure occurs when maximum efficiency is not achieved by trades (which means that part of the excess benefits shown by the shaded area in figure 5.5 are not realized by either buyers or sellers). Externalities are the positive or negative effects that exchanges may have on people who are not in the market. They are sometimes called third-party effects.

External costs

Figure 5.6 represents the market for a paper product. The market demand curve, D, indicates the benefits consumers receive from the product. To make paper, the producers must pay the costs of labor, chemicals, and pulpwood. The industry supply curve, S_1, shows the cost on which paper manufacturers must base their production decisions. In a highly competitive market, the quantity of the paper product that is bought will be Q_2, and the price paid by consumers will be P_1.

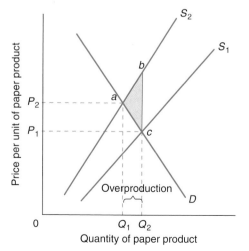

Figure 5.6 External costs
Ignoring the external costs associated with the manufacture of paper products, firms will base their production and pricing decisions on the supply curve S_1. If they consider external costs, such as the cost of pollution, they will operate on the basis of the supply curve S_2, producing Q_1 instead of Q_2 units. The shaded area abc shows the amount by which the marginal cost of production of $Q_2 - Q_1$ units exceeds the marginal benefits to consumers. It indicates the inefficiency of the private market when external costs are not borne by producers.

Producers may not bear all the costs associated with production, however. A by-product of the production process may be waste dumped into rivers or emitted into the atmosphere. The stench of production may pervade the surrounding community. Towns located downstream may have to clean up the water. People may have to paint their houses more frequently or seek medical attention for eye irritation. Homeowners may have to accept lower prices than usual for their property. All these costs are imposed on people not directly involved in the production, consumption, or exchange of the paper product. Nonetheless, these external costs are part of the *total cost of production to society* (or just to all affected parties). When the external costs in the form, say, of CO_2 emissions give rise to a depletion of the ozone layer in the atmosphere and contribute to global warming, then costs of production (or consumption) are spread globally and all of the world's current and future inhabitants can bear a part of the costs.

In a highly competitive market, in which all participants act independently, survival may require that a producer impose external costs on others. An individual producer who voluntarily installs equipment to clean up pollution will incur costs higher than those of its competitors and will not be able to match price cuts. In the long run, it may be out of business. Other producers may not care whether they cause harm to others by polluting the environment. Even socially concerned producers may not be able to abate the pollution because of the competitive consequences. Producers who care about the environment are in a classic Prisoner's Dilemma, with the result of the extant incentives inducing them to forgo the cooperative solution and endure a level of environmental degradation that they do not want, but have to suffer.

The supply curve S_2 incorporates both the external production costs of pollution and the private costs borne by producers. If producers have to bear all those costs, the price of the product will be higher (P_2 rather than P_1), and consumers will buy a smaller quantity (Q_1 rather than Q_2). Thus the true marginal cost of each unit of paper between Q_1 and Q_2 is greater than the marginal benefit to consumers. The marginal cost of those units exceeds their marginal benefit by the shaded triangular area bounded by *abc* in figure 5.6, which is a measure of market inefficiency (or the extent of the market failure).[5]

---

[5] Inefficiency is the amount by which the costs of doing anything exceeds the benefits. In figure 5.6, the total benefits from Q_2–Q_1 units equals the area under the demand curve between those two quantities, or Q_1acQ_2. (The points on the demand curve are the marginal values of each and every unit, which means the total value of all units is the sum of their marginal values.) The total costs of producing those units is greater, the area under the supply curve bounded by Q_1abQ_2. (The points on the supply curve reflect the marginal costs of each and every unit. The total costs between Q_1 and Q_2 are the sum of the marginal costs for each of those units, or the area bounded by Q_1abQ_2.) The inefficiency from producing Q_2–Q_1 units is the difference between the total costs (Q_1abQ_2) and total benefits (Q_1acQ_2), which equals the triangular area *abc*.

If consumers have to pay for external costs, the price of the good will rise to P_2. Consumers will value other goods more highly than those units. In a sense, then, the paper manufacturers are *overproducing* by $Q_2 - Q_1$ units. Pollution that gives rise to the overproduction of paper also gives rise to an underproduction of other goods, as well as an underproduction of a higher-quality environment. It's easy to think that the culprits in the pollution problem are the producers, but their competitive market prediction can trap them in a Prisoner's Dilemma. Even when they care about the environment, they cannot organize themselves to curb production and pollution. But then consumers could also be seen as culprits, since they are buying "too much" at "too low" prices. They also could solve the pollution problem, but they are in a competitive Prisoner's Dilemma and can't organize themselves to curb their excessive purchases.

Other examples of external costs that encourage overproduction are highway congestion and the noise in and around airports. The argument also can be extended to include such examples as the death and destruction caused by speeding and reckless driving. If government does not penalize such behaviors, people will overproduce them, at a potentially high external costs to others. In the same way, adult bookstores, street drugs, and brothels can impose costs on neighboring businesses. Their often sordid appearance may drive away many people who might otherwise patronize more reputable businesses in the area. Cell phones have been found to be a significant distraction to drivers, causing more accidents and deaths on highways. Cell phone users in effect impose external costs on drivers around them in the form of a greater risk of being in an accident with the cell phone users. Cell phone users might prefer that the externalized risks be reduced, but simply because much of their risk cost is externalized, the vast majority of cell phone users continue to use their phones unless penalized for doing so. The logic of external costs and the Prisoner's Dilemma has caused California and other states to ban drivers from using cell phones while on the road.

The problem computer users in and out of business experience with spam can also be understood as a pollution problem, both for spammers and spammees. We discuss spam as a pollution and Prisoner's Dilemma problem in online Reading 5.4 for this chapter.

External benefits

Sometimes market inefficiencies are created by external benefits. Market demand does not always reflect all the benefits received from a good. Instead, people not directly involved in the production, consumption, or exchange of the good receive some of its benefits.

To see the effects of external benefits on the allocation of resources, consider the market for flu shots. The cost of producing a vaccine includes labor, research and

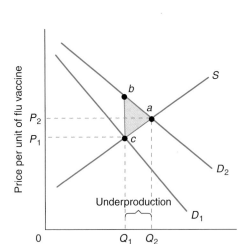

Figure 5.7 External benefits
Ignoring the external benefits of getting flu shots, consumers will base their purchases on the demand curve D_1 instead of D_2. Fewer shots will be purchased than could be justified economically – Q_1 instead of Q_2. Because the marginal benefit of each shot between Q_1 and Q_2 (as shown by demand curve D_2) exceeds its marginal cost of production, external benefits are not being realized. The shaded area abc indicates market inefficiency.

production equipment, materials, and transportation. Assuming that producers bear all those costs, the market supply curve will be S in figure 5.7.

The fact that many millions of people pay for flu shots every year shows that there is a demand, illustrated by curve D_1. In getting shots, people receive important personal benefits and also provide external benefits for others. By protecting themselves, they reduce the probability that the flu will spread. When others escape the medical expenses and lost work time associated with the flu, those benefits are not captured in the market demand curve, D_1. Only in the higher societal demand curve, labeled D_2, are those benefits realized. Left to itself, a highly competitive market will produce at the intersection of the market supply and market demand curves (S and D_1), or at point c. At that point, the equilibrium price will be P_1 and the quantity produced will be Q_1. If external benefits are considered in the production decision, however, the marginal benefit of flu shots between Q_1 and Q_2 (shown by the demand curve D_2) will exceed their marginal cost of production (shown by the supply curve).

In other words, if all benefits, both private and external, were considered, Q_2 shots would be produced and purchased at a price of P_2. At Q_2, the marginal cost of the last shot would equal its marginal benefit. Social welfare would rise by an amount equal to the triangular shaded area abc in figure 5.7. The problem of this external benefit is even worse when production problems reduce the quantity of flu shots available below the quantity people want at prices that normally cover the marginal cost of production, as was the case in the fall of 2004 in the United States. Long lines for the shots formed all across the country.

Because a free market can fail to capture such external benefits, government action to subsidize flu shots may be justified. On such grounds governments all over the world have mounted programs to inoculate people against diseases such as smallpox. The external benefits argument has been used to justify (up to a point) government support of medical research and also can be extended to other public services. For example, city buses provide direct benefits to the general population, and education that leads to an informed and articulate citizenry raises both the level of public discourse and the general standard of living.[6]

The analysis of external benefits in this section is widely applicable to a range of activities, for example beautification of communities through planting trees and flowers and disposing of litter. Because the benefits are externalized for such activities, or are provided to everyone once the activities are undertaken, no one can charge for them, which means they can be underproduced, if they are produced at all, in market settings (although there are market solutions for some such externality problems, as we will see later in the chapter).

[See online Video Module 5.3 External costs and benefits]

The pros and cons of government action

Perhaps more often than not, exchanges between buyers and sellers affect others. People buy clothes for comfort and protection, but most people value the appearance of clothing at least as much as its comfort. We choose clothing because we want others to be pleased or impressed (or perhaps irritated). The same can be said about the cars we purchase, the places we go to eat, the DVDs we buy, the haircuts and styling we get, and even the MBA programs we select. We impose the external effects of our actions deliberately as well as accidentally.

The presence of externalities in economic transactions does not necessarily mean that government should intervene. First, the economic distortions created by some externalities are often quite small, if not inconsequential. So far, our main examples of external costs and benefits have involved possibly significant distortions of market forces. In figure 5.8, however, the supply curve S_2, which incorporates both private and external costs, lies only slightly to the left of the market supply curve, S_1. The difference between the market output level, Q_2, and the optimum output level, Q_1, is small, as is the market inefficiency, shown by the shaded triangular area. Little can be gained, therefore, by government intervention.

This limited benefit must be weighed against the cost of government action. Whenever government intervenes in any situation, agencies are set up, employees

---

[6] The ratio of public to private benefits varies by educational level. Elementary school education develops crucial social and communication skills; its private benefits (or those benefits received by the people who are educated) are largely side effects. At the college level, however, the private benefits to students may dominate the public benefits. Thus elementary education is supported almost entirely by public sources, whereas college education is only partially subsidized.

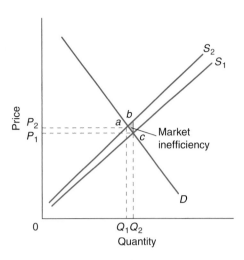

Figure 5.8 Is government action justified?
Because of external costs, the market illustrated produces more than the efficient output. Market inefficiency, represented by the shaded triangular area *abc*, is quite small – so small that government intervention may not be justified on economic grounds alone.

are hired, papers are shuffled, and reports are filed. Almost invariably, suits are brought against firms and individuals who have violated government rules, often obscure and sometimes silly. In short, significant costs can be incurred in trying to correct small market inefficiencies. If the cost of government intervention exceeds the cost of the market's inefficiencies, government action will actually increase inefficiency, even if the government action corrects the market inefficiencies.

A second reason for limiting government action is that it generates external costs of its own. When government dictates the construction methods to be used in building homes, the way firms should reduce pollution, and who has the qualifications to cut hair, regulation costs are created. Those whose services are regulated bear these costs, as do their customers. We may agree with some government rules but strenuously object to others.

In certain markets, government action may not be necessary. Over the long run, some of the external costs and benefits that cause market distortions may be *internalized*. That is, they may become private costs and benefits. Suppose the development of a park would generate external benefits for all businesses in a shopping district. More customers would be attracted to the district, and more sales would be made. An alert entrepreneur could internalize those benefits by building a shopping mall with a park in the middle. Because the mall may attract more customers than other shopping areas, the owner could benefit from higher rents. When shopping centers can internalize such externalities, economic efficiency will be enhanced – without government intervention.

When Walt Disney built Disneyland on a small plot of land in Orange County, California, he conferred benefits on merchants in the surrounding Anaheim area. Other businesses quickly moved in to take advantage of the external benefits – the crowds of visitors – spilling over from the amusement park. Disney did not make the same mistake twice. When he built Disney World in Orlando, Florida, he bought enough land so that most of the benefits of the amusement park would stay within the Disney domain. Inside the more than 6,000 acres of Disney-owned land in Florida, development has been controlled and profits captured by the Disney Corporation. Although other businesses have established themselves on the perimeters of Disney World, their distance from its center makes it more difficult for them to capture the benefits spilling over from the Disney amusement park.

Methods of reducing externalities

Government action can undoubtedly guarantee that certain goods and services will be produced more efficiently. The benefits of such action may be substantial, even when compared with the costs. In such cases, only the form of government intervention remains to be determined. Government action can take several forms: persuasion; assignment of communal property rights to individuals; government production of goods and services; regulation of production through published standards; and control of product prices through taxes, fines, and subsidies. Economists generally argue that if government is going to intervene, it should choose the least costly means sufficient for the task at hand.

Persuasion

External costs arise partly because we do not consider the welfare of others in our decisions. Indeed, if we fully recognized the adverse effects of our actions on others, external cost would not exist. Our production decisions would be based as much as possible on the total costs of production to society.

Government can thus alleviate market distortions by persuading citizens to consider how their behavior affects others. Forest Service advertisements urge people not to drop litter or risk forest fires when camping. Other government campaigns encourage people not to drive if they drink, to cultivate their land so as to minimize erosion, and to conserve water and gas. Although such efforts are limited in their effect, they may be more acceptable than other approaches, given political constraints.

Persuasion can take the form of publicity. The government can publish studies demonstrating that particular products or activities have external costs or benefits. The resultant publicity may in turn encourage those activities with external benefits and discourage those activities with external costs. The government has, for example, used this method in the case of cigarettes, publishing studies showing the external costs of smoking.

We should anticipate that persuasion will have some but limited effect on overall environmental quality. The reason is that the "environment" that spans a nation covers a large number of people, which can mean (as discussed in chapter 3) that many individuals in such a large group might share concern for the environment but can remain largely unmotivated to do anything about it. People can reason that the impact of their individual efforts are inconsequential, while their personal costs are consequential. Hence, they can find themselves in Prisoner's Dilemmas in which free riding is often the welfare-maximizing or profit-maximizing course of action (or nonaction).

This isn't to say that no one will do the "right thing" in response to environmental pleas. After all, some people do buy hybrid vehicles strictly for environmental reasons (apart from saving money on gasoline or from the opportunity to use car-pool lanes with only one person in the car). People walking in public parks do carry their own trash until they reach trash cans. Many people will show up when asked to pick up trash on beaches or lakeshores. The point is that many will not do any of these good things, which explains why there are so many environmental problems all around us that beg for institutional and policy solutions.

Assignment of property rights

As discussed in chapter 1, when property rights are held communally or left unassigned, property tends to be overused. As long as no one else is already using the property, anyone can use it without paying for its use. Costs that are not borne by users are, of course, passed on to others as external costs. When public land was open to grazing in the American West in the 1850s, for instance, ranchers allowed their herds to overgraze. The external cost of their indiscriminate use of the land has been borne by later generations, who have inherited a barren, wasted environment.

The assignment of property rights can thus eliminate some externalities. If land rights are assigned to individuals, they will bear the cost of their own neglect. If owners allow their cattle to strip a range of its grass, they will no longer be able to raise their cattle there – and the price of the land will decline with its productivity.

Some resources, such as air and water, cannot always be divided into parcels. In those cases, the property rights solution will work poorly, if at all. Consider the whales. For hundreds of years, whales have been hunted as more or less communal property. However, because people in former centuries did not have the technology we now have to kill and slaughter whales far out at sea, the sheer cost of hunting them prevented men from exceeding the whales' reproductive capacity. Today, the whales are at risk of extinction. Theoretically, the problem could be solved by applying the same solution to the whale overkill as the Native Americans applied in their hunting grounds: establish private property rights. However, the annual migrations of whales can take them through 6,000 miles of ocean. Establishing and enforcing private property rights to such an expanse of ocean is an onerous task, even without the complications of securing agreement among several governments. These costs complicate possible solutions.

Overhunting of whales – or overfishing in general – represents a tragedy of the commons noted in chapter 1, which is another way of saying that the world's fishermen are in a Prisoner's Dilemma *la grande* (all in a large-group setting). They might all want everyone to fish less, but each is faced with a noncooperative incentive to continue fishing as if overfishing is not a problem. Each fisherman can reason that if he or she stops fishing there will be no detectible reduction in overfishing, given what others do. Indeed, when one fisherman cuts back, others can step up their fishing.

Government production

Through nationalization of some industries, government can attempt to internalize external costs. The argument is that because government is concerned with social consequences, it will consider the total costs of production, both internal and external. On the basis of that argument, governments in the United States operate schools, public health services, national and state parks, transportation systems, harbors, and electric power plants. In other nations, governments also operate major industries, such as the steel and automobile industries.

Government production can be a mixed blessing. When other producers remain in the market, government participation may increase competition. Sometimes, however, it means the elimination of competition. Consider the US Postal Service, which has exclusive rights to the delivery of first-class mail. As a government agency, the Post Office is not permitted to make a profit that can be turned over to shareholders. Because of its market position with little competition for home delivery of mail, however, it may tolerate higher costs and lower work standards than competitive firms could.

Some government production, such as the provision of public goods, for example national defense, is unavoidable. In most cases, however, direct ownership and production may not be necessary. Instead of producing goods with which external-ities are associated, government could simply contract with private firms for the business. That is precisely how most states handle road construction, how several states handle the penal system, and how a few city governments provide ambulance, police, and firefighting services.

Taxes and subsidies

Government can deal with some external costs by taxing producers. Pollution can be discouraged by a tax on either the pollution itself or the final product. Imposing a tax on firms' emitted pollution (in, say, the form of the widely recommended and hotly debated "carbon tax") internalizes external costs, increasing the total costs to the producer. Imposing such taxes should have a twofold effect in reducing pollution:

- First, many producers would find the cost of pollution control cheaper than the pollution tax.
- Second, the tax would raise the prices of final products, reducing the number of units consumed – and hence reducing the level of pollution.

The size of the tax can be adjusted to achieve whatever level of pollution is judged acceptable. If a tax of $1 per unit produced does not reduce pollution sufficiently, the tax can be raised to $2. In figure 5.6, the ideal tax would be just enough to encourage producers to view their supply curve as S_2 instead of S_1, which would be equal to the distance bc. The resulting cutback in production from Q_1 to Q_2 would eliminate market inefficiency, represented by the shaded area abc.

In spite of the efficiency gains, such taxes can be expected to face political opposition. The gains from the pollution tax will be thinly spread over the population, while the pains from the tax will be concentrated on far fewer producers and consumers. Producers who bear a portion of the tax can be expected to grumble because the tax undermines profits. Consumers of the taxed products will also be unhappy because they will then have to pay for the cost of resources – environmental resources – that are of value to others.

Theoretically, the government could subsidize firms to achieve the same result in their efforts to eliminate pollution. Government could give tax credits for the installation of pollution controls or pay firms outright to install the equipment. In fact, until 1985, the federal government used tax credits to encourage the installation of fuel-saving devices, which indirectly reduced pollution. To encourage the purchases of hybrid automobiles in 2006 and 2007, the federal government provided a tax credit of as much as $3,400 to car buyers who bought hybrids (which, at the time, meant only two, the Toyota Prius and the Honda Civic Hybrid). California gave out stickers to owners of hybrids permitting them to drive in the state's carpool lanes without passengers. Both policies propped up the demand for hybrids, which means more hybrid purchases and higher prices on hybrids (with the hybrid price premium as much as $4,000 over comparably equipped non-hybrid cars).

Production standards

Alternatively, the government could simply impose pollution standards on all producers. It could rule, for example, that polluters may not emit more than a certain amount of pollutants during a given period. Offenders would either have to pay for a cleanup or risk a fine. A firm that flagrantly violated the standard might be forced to shut down.

Choosing the most efficient remedy for externalities

Selecting the most efficient method of minimizing externalities can be a complicated process. To illustrate, we compare the costs of two approaches to controlling
pollution – government standards versus property rights.

Suppose five firms are emitting sulfur dioxide, a pollutant that causes acid rain. The
reduction of the unwanted emissions can be thought of as an *economic good* whose
production involves a cost. We can assume that the marginal cost of reducing sulfur
dioxide emissions will rise as more and more units are eliminated. We can also assume
that such costs will differ from firm to firm. Table 5.2 incorporates these assumptions.
Firm *A*, for example, must pay $100 to eliminate the first unit of sulfur dioxide and
$200 to eliminate the second. Firm *B* must pay $200 for the first unit and $600 for the
second. Although the information in table 5.2 is hypothetical, it reflects the structure
of real-world pollution cleanup costs. Firms face increasing marginal costs when they
clean up the air as well as when they produce goods and services.

Suppose the Environmental Protection Agency (EPA) decides that the maximum
acceptable level of sulfur dioxide is ten units. To achieve that level, the EPA
prohibits firms from emitting more than two units of sulfur dioxide each. If each
firm were emitting five units, each would have to reduce its emissions by three units.

Table 5.2 **Costs of reducing sulfur dioxide emissions**

	Firms				
	A	B	C	D	E
Marginal cost of eliminating each unit of pollution:	($)	($)	($)	($)	($)
First unit	100	200	200	600	1,000
Second unit	200	600	400	1,000	2,000
Third unit	400	1,800	600	1,400	3,000
Fourth unit	800	5,400	800	1,800	4,000
Fifth unit	1,600	16,200	1,000	2,200	5,000

Cost of reducing pollution by establishment of government standards		Cost of reducing pollution by sale of pollution rights	
Cost to A of eliminating 3 units	700	Cost to A of eliminating 4 units	1,500
Cost to B of eliminating 3 units	2,600	Cost to B of eliminating 2 units	800
Cost to C of eliminating 3 units	1,200	Cost to C of eliminating 5 units	3,000
Cost to D of eliminating 3 units	3,000	Cost to D of eliminating 3 units	3,000
Cost to E of eliminating 3 units	6,000	Cost to E of eliminating 1 unit	1,000
Total cost for all five firms' units	13,500	Total cost for all five firms' units	9,300

The total cost of meeting the limit of two units is shown in the lower half of table 5.2. Firm *A* incurs the relatively modest cost of $700 ($100 + $200 + $400). But firm *B* must pay $2,600 ($200 + $600 + $1,800). The total cost to all firms is $13,500.

What if the EPA adopts a different strategy and sells the rights to pollute? Such rights can be thought of as tickets that authorize firms to dump a unit of waste into the atmosphere. The more tickets a firm purchases, the more waste it can dump, and the more cleanup costs it can avoid.

Remember that the EPA can control the number of tickets it sells. To limit pollution to the maximum acceptable level of ten units, all it needs to do is sell no more than ten tickets. Either way, whether by pollution standards or by rights, the level of pollution is kept down to ten units, but the pollution rights method allows firms that want to avoid the cost of a cleanup to bid for tickets.

Conventional supply and demand curves, as in figure 5.9, illustrate the potential market for such rights. The supply curve is determined by EPA policy makers, who limit the number of tickets to ten. Because in this example the supply is fixed, the supply curve must be vertical (perfectly inelastic). Whatever the price, the number of pollution rights remains the same. The demand curve is derived from the costs firms must bear to clean up their emissions. The higher the cost of the cleanup, the more attractive pollution rights will be. As with all demand curves, price and quantity are inversely related. The lower the price of pollution rights, the higher the quantity demanded.

Table 5.3 shows the total quantity demanded by the firms at various prices. At a price of zero, the firms want twenty-five rights (five each). At a price of $201, they demand only twenty-one. Firm *A* wants only three, because the cost to clean up its first two units (at costs of $100 and $200) is less than to buy rights to emit them at a price of $201. Firm *B* wants four rights, as its cleanup costs are higher.

Given the information in table 5.3, the market clearing price (the price at which the quantity of property rights demanded exactly equals the number of rights for

Table 5.3 **Demand for pollution rights**

Price ($)	Quantity	Price ($)	Quantity
0	25	1,601	9
101	24	1,801	7
201	21	2,001	6
401	19	2,201	5
601	16	3,001	4
801	14	4,001	3
1,001	11	5,001	2
1,401	10	5,601	0

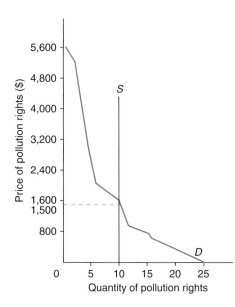

Figure 5.9 Market for pollution rights
Reducing pollution is costly (see table 5.2). It adds to the costs of production, increasing product prices and reducing the quantities of products demanded. Therefore, firms have a demand for the right to avoid pollution abatement costs. The lower the price of such rights, the greater the quantity of rights that firms will demand. If the government fixes the supply of pollution rights at ten and sells those ten rights to the highest bidder, the price of the rights will settle at the intersection of the supply and demand curves – here, about $1,500.

sale) will be something over $1,400 (say $1,500, as shown in figure 5.9). Who will buy those rights, and what will the cost of the program be?

At a price of $1,500 per ticket, firm A will buy one and only one ticket. At that price, it is cheaper for the firm to clean up its first four units (the cost of the cleanup is $100 + $200 + $400 + $800). Only the fifth unit, which would cost $1,600 to clean up, makes the purchase of a $1,500 ticket worthwhile. Similarly, firm B will buy three tickets, firm C none, firm D two, and firm E four. The cost of any cleanup must be measured by the value of the resources that go into it. The value of the resources is approximated by the firms' expenditures on the cleanup – not by their expenditures on pollution tickets. (The tickets do not represent real resources, but a transfer of purchasing power from the firms to the government.) Accordingly, the economic cost of reducing pollution to ten units is $9,300: $1,500 for firm A; $800 for B; $3,000 each for C and D; and $1,000 for E. This figure is significantly less than the $13,500 cost of the cleanup when each firm is required to eliminate three units of pollution. Yet in each case, fifteen units are eliminated. In short, the pricing system is more economical – more cost-effective or efficient – than setting standards. Because it is more efficient, it is also the more economical way of producing goods and services. More resources go into production and fewer into cleanup.

The idea of selling rights to pollute may not sound attractive, but it makes sense economically. When the government sets standards, it is giving away rights to pollute. In our example, telling each firm that it must reduce its sulfur dioxide emissions by three units is effectively giving each one permission to dump two units into the atmosphere. One might ask whether the government should be giving away rights to the atmosphere, which has many other uses besides the absorption of pollution. Though some pollution may be necessary to continued production, that is no argument for giving away pollution rights. Land is needed in many production processes, but the Forest Service does not give away the rights to public lands. When pollution rights are sold, on the other hand, potential users can express the relative values they place on the right to pollute.[7] In that way, rights can be assigned to their most valuable and productive uses.

The problem with the government selling rights to pollute to the five firms in our tabular example is that all five have a reason politically to oppose the sales of rights. They incur higher out-of-pocket expenditures under the pollution rights sales than they incur under the standards, partially because they have to buy all rights for the pollution units they want to continue to emit under the sales system. They get two pollution rights free under the standard system. The government can break the business political opposition by simply giving polluters the rights to pollute, which they can then turn around and sell. When they do sell them, the equilibrium price of the rights will be the same as it was when the government sold them (because the supply of pollution rights, ten, and the demand for them are unchanged). This is exactly what the US Congress proposed to do in its environmental laws passed by the House and Senate in 2009 (Talley and Bartley 2009).

[See online Video Module 5.4 Selling rights to pollute]

Part B Organizational economics and management

The consequences of "quicksilver capital" for business and government

In Part A, we developed the theory of international trade and environmental economics. In this Part B, we explore the ways in which international trade and trade policies can affect the environment and how environmental policies can affect international trade. Critical links between the two include resource and capital mobility on a global scale.

Economists and policy makers alike widely acknowledge the growing competition that springs from goods and services moving with greater ease across national borders. Cars made in Korea, Germany, and Japan compete for market share in the United States, and elsewhere. Wines from Australia and Chile sell around the world.

---

[7] Note that the system allows environmental groups as well as producers to express the value they place on pollution rights. If environmental groups think that ten units of sulfur dioxide is too much pollution, they can buy some of the tickets themselves and then not exercise their right to pollute.

The growing global competition has been spawned by companies tapping their comparative cost advantages and by the falling price of transportation. Economists have paid less attention to the global competition that springs from the increased mobility of capital (meaning real capital in the form of plant and equipment, as well as financial capital). Capital mobility could very well be as powerful a competitive force, as the mobility of goods within and across countries has escalated. Real capital doesn't actually have to move. Financial capital can move through electronic shifts in bank balances. The result can be the shut down of a plant in one country and the construction of a plant in another. In this way, much of the US textile and furniture industry concentrated in North and South Carolina has "moved" to China and Southeast Asian countries.

How has capital become more mobile? Consider that the mobility of much capital is inversely related to its size, and then consider the continuing effect technology is having on the size of capital. We cannot possibly recount here all of the details of recent technological and restructuring trends, but a few observations may be helpful in describing the trends we have in mind.[8]

The most dramatic example of the downsizing of capital is found in the computer field. When universities bought their first mainframe computers in the early 1960s, computers filled suites of offices and had a meager 8K of internal memory. Today, a high-end laptop (if not netbook) computer has more memory and computing power than university mainframes had in the mid-1990s.

With the miniaturization of computers has come the downsizing of other types of capital. Factories made of steel and concrete still dot the landscape, but their economic dominance seems to be a feature more of the underdeveloped and still developing economies of China, India, and Southeast Asia than of the western world. Capital in the form of steel and concrete plants, much like caterpillars, is hardly fleet of foot. Much capital in advanced economies has turned into something of a butterfly. The critical assets of companies are no longer just, or even primarily, steel and concrete buildings. They are increasingly the information and the brainpower at the companies' disposal for creating the quintessential company asset – good ideas for doing things better, faster, more cheaply, and more profitably at the most favorable location (a point captured by the late Walter Wriston in the epigraph to this chapter).

Knowledge is not only the major productive input in many firms, it is often the primary output as well. As economic pundit George Gilder recognized before many other technology watchers, "The displacement of materials with ideas is the essence of all real economic progress" (Gilder 1989, 63). With information, knowledge, and ideas now representing some of the most productive capital and resources, consumers of business obviously benefit. Productive capacity can be moved around the

---

[8] See McKenzie and Lee 1991; McKenzie 1997.

globe literally with a few keystrokes on a computer and at the speed of electrical impulses, allowing those firms who can produce the best products at the lowest price to attract productive capital and resources from all over the world and sell their products to consumers all over the world.

Trade and mobility of capital make businesses more competitive and increase our standard of living. With the emergence of a global economy, consumers are no longer as dependent as they once were on local suppliers. Producers can move their capital to locations where the resources they need for production are relatively more abundant than in their national markets. Then with modern telecommunications technology, managers can stay in touch with their home offices at much lower cost than at any time in human history. By the same token, executives in home offices can readily monitor the operations of their companies' far-flung production facilities with modern wireless telecommunications and Internet technology. Of course, with the same technology, consumers can buy what they want from producers abroad who have relatively lower costs and can, again, do so with a few computer keystrokes. Moreover, the expanded competition from international sources can undermine the market power of firms that once may have conducted business comforted by the fact that it was too costly for foreign firms to move into the domestic markets.

As we will see later in this section, the growing mobility of goods and services and of capital on a global scale can have profound effects on environmental quality and policies in two principal ways. First, more intense competition can induce firms to seek ways of externalizing their production costs where they are. Second, firms can be induced to move from countries with more constraining environmental laws to those with fewer constraints, the result of which can be increased environmental degradation and pressure on governments to enact environmental regulations with greater concern for costs to capital.

To read about the mobility of whole industries – cotton and textiles – across the globe and through the last two centuries, consult online Perspective 5, The travels of a T-shirt in a global economy.

Online Perspective

Capital mobility and business competitiveness

The very technology lauded for expanding investment and market opportunities has a downside for firms, their workers, and governments: workers in different nations are pitted against one another for wages and fringe benefits. If they seek payment bundles (wages and fringe benefits) that are out of line with their productivity and drive up the relative costs of their firms vis-à-vis firms in other countries, imports can be expected to flow into their countries from abroad, undermining their job security. Such heightened competitiveness in goods markets can translate into managers seeking to shift their own production facilities to the sources of their competition from imports. Businesses can be expected to move their capital to countries where production costs are contained by the relative abundance of workers or to countries that have a comparative advantage in labor-intensive goods.

Capital mobility literally can force managers to trim the "fat" out of their organizations and seek worker incentive systems that can drive up the demands managers impose on their workers. If firms in the domestic economy can outsource a portion or all of their production to foreign countries, then the more mobile capital becomes and the greater the pressure to outsource. If firms can outsource but don't outsource to lower-cost foreign venues, then their market positions are subject to being undermined by firms that do take opportunities to outsource. Accordingly, firms can be forced to curb their enthusiasm for "green" production policies, since such policies can add to their cost structures and hand their domestic and foreign competition a pricing advantage. Greater capital mobility, in other words, intensifies the Prisoner's Dilemmas faced by businesses and their workers, making them global in scope.

Capital mobility and government competitiveness

Less obvious, but just as true, the growth in capital mobility also can affect taxpayers as governments around the globe are subject to more competitive pressures. We are all consumers of not just the output of businesses, but also the output of governments. We pay for government services through taxes, and hope to get good value for the money we spend. Unfortunately, we have far less control, as consumers, over the cost and quality of government services we receive because we cannot easily shift our patronage to another government. Governments have not faced nearly as much competition for their taxpayers' dollars as businesses have faced in getting consumers' dollars. But the technological improvements that put more competitive pressures on businesses to serve consumer interests also can be pressuring governments, albeit with less force and lower effect.

What does the growing mobility of capital on a global scale mean for governments and the policies they choose? First and foremost, governments must face up to the fact that governments do business within a *given* parcel of land. On the other hand, with growing capital mobility on a global scale, a growing number of firms can and must do business on practically *any* parcel of land. All the while businesses must treat governmentally imposed taxes and regulations like any other cost of doing business and must respond accordingly – that is, move elsewhere if government-imposed cost conditions warrant it. In general, all levels of government must realize that their public policies should hamper the business competitiveness within their jurisdiction as little as possible. To do otherwise can mean that capital and jobs go elsewhere.

In bygone eras, politicians and policy makers could sit around glibly chatting about what they *wanted* to do, or what their constituents would allow them to do, with little regard for what governments elsewhere in the nation or world were doing. They could tax and regulate in the knowledge that capital could not move, except at a snail's pace and at great cost. If an interest group wanted an added tax or a subsidy, the only relevant issue was typically whether the politicians had the votes. And political leaders didn't have to worry much about how efficient they were compared with other governments. As a result, few governments were very efficient (especially since they often were monopoly suppliers and were not subject to the pressures of corporate takeover markets, topics covered in later chapters).

But in a global economy, governments at all levels have to think more *competitively*, which is something many governments around the world are not yet fully experienced at doing. But now, more than ever, political authorities must begin to look around the world to determine who has the very highest standards for government performance and seek to meet those standards with enhanced diligence. When the Obama Administration proposed higher taxation of American corporations' profits earned outside the country in early 2009, the editors of the *Wall Street Journal* had "quicksilver capital" in mind when they warned that the United States already has a relatively high corporate tax rate (39.25 percent) relative to other major countries, as measured by the Organization for Economic Cooperation and Development (Editors, *Wall Street Journal* 2009). Japan has a slightly higher corporate tax rate at 39.54 percent, but other countries have lower rates:

France	34.43 percent
Germany	30.18 percent
United Kingdom	28.00 percent
Korea	27.50 percent
Netherlands	25.50 percent
Czech Republic	21.00 percent
Ireland	12.50 percent

When the US economy tumbled into the "Great Depression" in late 2007, the California economy fell into an even "Greater Depression," partially because its housing market had become more inflated than in almost all other states and partially because its personal and corporate income tax rates were higher than other states. In 2009, California had the third-highest unemployment rate and the largest state budget deficit because of the fall-off in income tax receipts due to businesses moving to other states (Nevada, Texas, and Idaho). A tax study commission recommended the elimination of the 8.84 percent corporate income tax (to be replaced by a "value-added tax," akin to a sales tax) and a reduction in the top personal income tax rate from 10.55 percent to 7.5 percent – all founded on the argument that such tax moves could abate, if not reverse, the capital outflow from the state (Parsky 2009; *Wall Street Journal* 2009).

Obviously, large states and major countries can still impose significant tax rates on business (and people), but the point is that governments must be mindful in selecting their tax rates that they, like businesses, are in competition with "the very best" in the world for the capital they need (although the competitiveness of governments may be less intense than the competitiveness in business). Governments must realize, at the very least, that the growing mobility of capital necessarily makes tax cuts more attractive and tax increases more questionable than when capital could move only at a crawl. Why? Because the greater responsiveness of capital means governments can have more capital in their jurisdictions with tax cuts, and with that potentially expanded base will be able to more than offset the impact of tax cuts. The converse also applies. Of course, tax increases also can attract business so long as the revenues are used for purposes that increase business (and worker) productivity by more than they deduct from businesses' after-tax bottom lines. The point is that growing capital mobility can impose fiscal discipline on governments in the same way that it can impose competitive discipline on businesses.

For that matter, everyone associated with government – all those who draw from government in various forms (professors included!) – must accept the tightening grip of the *economic*, as distinct from *political*, limits to what governments can do. Hence, every proposed program must be evaluated to a greater extent in terms of the other programs that will have to be given up. Many commentators have suggested that the ongoing long-term decline in national tariff barriers around the world, less regulation, lower marginal tax rates, and more privatization is evidence of political leaders' adoption of a free-trade ideology. Perhaps that is the case, but we suspect that the growing mobility of capital (and production and jobs) has contributed to political leaders seeing the necessity of freeing up markets and international trade in order to contain the production costs businesses face within their jurisdictions.

Proponents of privatization of various government services – from garbage collection to the distribution of public housing units to the provision of education – make an important point: just because the public treasury funds a service does not mean that public agencies must deliver it. Privatization proponents' goal is to make government more efficient by choosing from an array of alternative delivery systems (government included) that can make governmental jurisdictions more efficient and competitive among themselves and increase the likelihood of sustaining the existing capital base and additional capital flow. Needless to say, governments, especially large ones such as the United States and China, retain considerable political discretion. Our point here is that global economic and technological forces have at least marginally undercut governments' political discretion.

Capital mobility has significant economic downsides and upsides for degradation of the global environment and for environmental policies; these are discussed in online Reading 5.5 for this chapter.

Practical lesson for MBAs: protectionist strategies

The cases for and against free – or more accurately, freer – trade are extended in a reading on the publisher's website for this book. Here, we note that the debate over trade protection generally concerns what "nations" want, should want, or can expect to occur from the imposition of tariffs and quotas. Many MBA students will likely have been reading the preceding pages from a different perspective, how the analysis can be used to promote their own and their firms' interests – or just their firms' profitability. And there are major lessons to be taken from the analysis from such a perspective.

If your firm faces foreign competition, it can increase its profits by producing a better product, cutting costs, or developing an effective marketing campaign. But your firm also may seek to influence politicians to impose tariffs on imports that compete with your firm's products, which will allow your firm to increase both its prices and sales because the firm's market demand will rise. Your firm may also seek the elimination of tariffs imposed on parts and materials you use in your production processes. You can then reduce your production costs and increase sales as you lower your prices.

If you can't secure tariff protection, your best bet can be to join the importers. Either increase your purchases of foreign imports or shift production to the countries that have a comparative cost advantage in your product. You can shift production for offensive and defensive reasons. The offensive reason is that the production-location shift can increase your firm's profitability. The defensive reason is that, if you don't make the shift, firms that are willing to move their capital can outcompete you in your product markets.

On the other hand, if your firm exports products to foreign countries, you should consider seeking the elimination of import restrictions on products you do not produce. Such import restrictions can reduce the sales of firms in foreign countries. The reduction of sales by foreign firms in other countries can crimp the ability of people in those countries to buy imports, including goods your firm exports. Your firm should consider being an "anti-protectionist" for a good old-fashioned reason: to improve your firm's profitability by increasing foreign sales. Because of the inexorable tie between imports and exports, soybean farmers in South Carolina and Boeing Aircraft, both of whom export a substantial share of their production to foreign countries, have opposed the lobbying efforts of, say, textile firms to acquire tariffs and quotas on imported textiles.

Further readings online

Reading 5.1 The law of comparative advantage and trade between China and the United States

Reading 5.2 The cases for and against free trade

The bottom line

The key takeaways from chapter 5 are the following:

1 Trade can be mutually beneficial so long as the traders specialize in the production of the good(s) in which they have a comparative advantage. That is to say, even a trader who is less productive than everyone else in everything can find trade beneficial.

2 Generally speaking, tariffs and quotas reduce the aggregate real incomes of the countries that impose them, as well as countries that are subject to them, because they deny mutually beneficial trades.

3 Those industries protected by tariffs and quotas can gain from them, but only at the expense of consumers who must pay higher prices for the protected goods and at the expense of exporters who are not able to export as much as they would without the trade protections.

4 A market economy will overproduce goods and services that impose external costs on society. It will underproduce goods and services that confer external benefits.

5 Sometimes, but not always, government intervention can be justified to correct for externalities. To be worthwhile, the benefits of action must outweigh the costs.

6 Some ways of dealing with external costs and benefits are more efficient than others.

7 Some critics of markets suggest that markets are bound to fail because of the gains to business from being dishonest, which implies a form of "externality." Nevertheless, markets have built-in incentives for people to be more honest than they might otherwise be.

Review questions >>

1 Using supply and demand curves, show how a US tariff on a foreign-made good will affect the price and quantity sold in the country that imports the good and in the country that exports the good.

2 How will an import quota on sugar affect (a) the price of sugar produced and sold domestically, (b) sugar produced domestically and sold abroad?

3   If a tariff is imposed on imported autos and the domestic demand for autos rises, what will happen to auto imports? If a quota is imposed on imported autos and the demand for autos increases, what will happen to auto imports?

4   If the major domestic auto producers are given a bailout for their financial troubles (as they were in 2009 in the United States), what will be the market effects on domestic and foreign auto producers?

5   Consider the following production capabilities of France and Italy for cheese and bread for a given use of inputs. Which nation will export cheese to the other? What might be a mutually beneficial exchange rate for cheese and bread?

	Cheese units		Bread units
France	40	or	60
Italy	10	or	5

6   "Tariffs on imported textiles increase the employment opportunities and incomes of domestic textiles workers. They therefore increase aggregate employment and income." Evaluate this statement.

7   Because the balance of payments must always balance, how can a disequilibrium situation occur?

8   How much would a business spend to get a tariff? What economic considerations will have an impact on the amount spent?

9   Developers frequently buy land and hold it on speculation; in effect, they "bank" land. Should firms be permitted to buy and bank pollution rights in the same way? Would such a practice contribute to overall economic efficiency?

10   "If allowing firms to trade pollution rights lowers the cost of meeting pollution standards, it should also allow government to tighten standards without increasing costs." Do you agree or disagree? Why?

11   If businesses are permitted to sell pollution rights, should brokers in pollution rights be expected to emerge? Why or why not? Would such agents increase the efficiency with which pollution is cleaned up?

12   If pollution rights are traded, should the government impose a price ceiling on them? Would such a system contribute to the efficient allocation of resources? If you were a producer, which method of pollution control would you favor, the setting of government standards or the auction of pollution rights by government? Why?

13 Reconsider the pollution abatement costs of the five firms in table 5.2. Which firms can be expected to vote for the standard method of pollution control? For the sale-of-pollution-rights method?

14 Suppose the five firms in table 5.2 were each given two rights to pollute that they can sell. Which firms would buy additional pollution rights? Which firms would sell? What would be the cost of pollution control before and after the firms buy and sell rights?

15 How can greater capital mobility across national boundaries affect governments' tax policies? Why must businesses pay attention to the tax rates in different countries?

16 How might greater capital mobility affect countries' environmental policies? Will businesses necessarily be pleased with the consequences of capital mobility on countries' environmental policies?

17 Consider the case in which tighter environmental controls have consequential positive effects on the environment within the next generation. Then consider the case in which the consequential positive environmental effects are not realized for a thousand years. Under which case would you expect greater environmental controls? Why?

Book II
Demand and production theory

In the first five chapters we provided a broad overview of the forces of supply and demand. In Book II, we develop with greater care and depth the theoretical underpinnings of demand (chapter 6) and supply (chapters 7 and 8). We will use these theories in Book III to explore firms' production and organizational strategies under different competitive and monopolistic market conditions.

6

Consumer choice and demand in traditional and network markets

It is not the province of economics to determine the value of life in "hedonic units" or any other units, but to work out, on the basis of the general principles of conduct and the fundamental facts of social situations, the laws which determine prices of commodities and the direction of the social economic process. It is therefore not quantities, not even intensities, of satisfaction with which we are concerned ... or any other absolute magnitude whatever, but the purely relative judgment of comparative significance of alternatives open to choice.

Frank H. Knight

People adjust to changes in some economic conditions with a reasonable degree of predictability. When department stores announce lower prices, customers will pour through the doors. The lower the prices go, the larger the crowd will be. When the price of gasoline goes up, drivers will make fewer and shorter trips. If the price stays up, drivers will buy smaller, more economical cars. Even the Defense Department will reduce its planned purchases of tanks and bombers when their prices rise.

Behavior that is not measured in dollars and cents is also predictable in some respects. Students who stray from the sidewalks to dirt paths on sunny days stick to concrete when the weather is damp. Professors who raise their course requirements and grading standards find their classes shrinking in size. Small children shy away from doing things for which they recently have been punished. When lines for movie tickets become long, some people go elsewhere for entertainment.

On an intuitive level, you very likely find these examples of behavior reasonable. Going one step beyond intuition, the economist would say that such responses are governed by the *law of demand*, a concept we first introduced in chapter 3 and now take up in greater detail, with greater precision, and with more varied applications. In this chapter, we show how our understanding of a firm's strategy can be enhanced by simply classifying various goods into such categories as "normal" and "inferior" goods, "substitute" and "complementary" goods, and "network" and "lagged-demand" goods, with the nature of the goods affecting their demands. We will also introduce formally the concepts of "elastic" and "inelastic" demands, all of which suggests that the development of profit-maximizing pricing strategies requires that MBAs know more about goods than merely that their demands slope downward.

Part A   Theory and public policy applications

Predicting consumer demand

The assumptions about rational behavior described in chapter 2 provide a useful basis for explaining behavior. People will do things for which the expected benefits exceed the expected costs. They will avoid doing things for which the opposite is true. The law of demand, which is a logical consequence of the assumption of rational behavior, allows us to make such general predictions of consumer behavior.

Our ability to predict is always limited. We cannot specify with precision every choice the individual will make. For instance, we cannot say at the conceptual level anything about what a particular person wants or how sensitive her desire for what she values is to changes in prices. But we can predict the general direction of her behavior, given her wants, with the aid of the *law of demand* which we now derive.

 [See online Video Module 6.1 Law of demand.]

Rational consumption: the concept of marginal utility

The essence of the economist's notion of rational consumer behavior is that consumers will allocate their incomes over goods and services so as to maximize their satisfaction, or utility. This implies that consumers compare the value of consuming an additional unit of various goods.

Generally speaking, the value the individual places on any one unit of a good depends on the number of units already consumed. For example, you may be planning to consume two hot dogs and two Cokes for your next meal. Although you may pay the same price for each unit of both goods, the value you place on the second unit of each good will generally be less than the value realized from the first unit (at least beyond some point as consumption proceeds).[1] For example, the value of the second hot dog – its marginal utility – depends on the fact that you have already eaten one. We represent marginal utility as *MU*, which equals the change in total utility from consuming one more unit.

Achieving consumer equilibrium

Marginal utility determines the variety and the quantity of goods and services you consume. The rule is simple. If the two goods, Cokes and hot dogs, both have the same price (a temporary assumption), you will fully allocate your income so that the marginal utility of the last unit consumed of each will be equal. This rule can be stated as

$$MU_c = MU_h$$

where MU_c equals the marginal utility of a Coke and MU_h equals the marginal utility of a hot dog. This is to say, if the price of a Coke is the same as the price of a hot dog, the last Coke you drink should give you the same amount of enjoyment as the last hot dog you eat. If this is not the case, you could increase your utility with the same amount of money by reducing your consumption of the good with the lowest marginal utility by one unit and buying another unit of the one with the highest marginal utility. When the marginal utilities of goods purchased by the consumer are equal, the resulting state is called consumer equilibrium. Unless conditions – income, taste, prices, etc. – change, the consumer equilibrium remains the same.

> **Consumer equilibrium** is a state of stability in consumer purchasing patterns in which the individual has maximized her utility.

An example can illustrate how equilibrium is reached. Suppose for the sake of simplicity that you can buy only two goods, Cokes and hot dogs. Suppose further that each costs the same, $1, and you intend to spend your whole income. For purposes of illustrating the point, assume that utility (joy, satisfaction) can be measured. Finally, suppose that the marginal utility of the last Coke you consume

---

[1] We focus on *diminishing* marginal utility because that is the relevant range of consumption for most people consuming most goods. If people experience *increasing* marginal utility for goods, then they will continue to consume them and will face choice problems only when diminishing marginal utility sets in.

is equal to 20 utils (a util being a unit of satisfaction, or utility) and the marginal utility of the hot dog is 12 utils. Obviously you have not maximized your utility, for the marginal utility of your last Coke is greater than (>) the marginal utility of your last hot dog:

$$MU_c > MU_h$$

You could have purchased one fewer hot dog and used the dollar saved to buy an additional Coke. In doing so, you would have given up 12 utils of satisfaction (the marginal utility of the last hot dog purchased), but you would have acquired an additional 20 utils from the new Coke. On balance, your total utility would have risen by 8 utils (20 − 12). You can continue to increase your utility without spending any more by adjusting your purchases of Cokes and hot dogs until their marginal utilities are equal. We make the reasonable assumption here that the marginal utility of both Cokes and hot dogs decreases as more are consumed (at least beyond some point). This is known as the *law of diminishing marginal utility*.

According to the law of diminishing marginal utility, as more of a good is consumed, its marginal utility (or value relative to the marginal value of the good or goods given up) eventually diminishes. Thus, if $MU_h > MU_c$, and MU_h falls relative to MU_c as more hot dogs and fewer Cokes are consumed, sooner or later the result will be $MU_h = MU_c$. The law of diminishing marginal utility applies to all goods.[2]

Adjusting for differences in price and unit size

Different goods, including Cokes and hot dogs, are seldom sold at exactly the same price, so we drop the assumption of equal prices. Now the condition for choosing the combination of Cokes and hot dogs that maximizes utility becomes:

$$\frac{MU_c}{P_c} = \frac{MU_h}{P_h}$$

where MU_c equals the marginal utility of a Coke, MU_h the marginal utility of a hot dog, P_c the price of a Coke, and P_h the price of a hot dog. The consumer must allocate her money so that the last penny spent on each commodity yields the same amount of satisfaction. We leave it to the reader to consider how the consumer can increase

---

[2] For some goods, as noted, it may very well be the case that as one starts consuming units of a given good (beer, for example), the marginal utility of successive units initially rises. If marginal utility always rose, then we might expect a person to end up devoting her entire income to the consumption of the one good. Since people typically consume combinations of many goods (and illustrations involving only two goods are meant to represent typical behavior), we must assume that diminishing marginal utility applies within the income constraint of the representative consumers.

her utility without spending more money if the above equality is not satisfied, and how doing so will eventually result in the equality being satisfied.

So far, we have been talking in terms of buying whole units of Cokes and hot dogs, but the same principles apply to other kinds of choices as well. Marginal utility is involved when a consumer chooses a 12-ounce rather than a 16-ounce can of Coke, or a regular-size hot dog rather than a foot-long hot dog. The concept could also be applied to the decision of whether to add cole slaw and chili to the hot dog. The pivotal question the consumer faces in all these situations is whether the marginal utility of the additional quantity consumed is greater or less than the marginal utility of other goods that can be purchased for the same price.

Most consumers do not think in terms of utils when they are buying their lunch, but this does not mean that they are not weighing the alternatives (*as if* they were thinking in terms of the utils obtained from each additional unit). Suppose you walk into a snack bar with only three dollars to spend for lunch. Your first reaction may be to look at the menu and weigh the marginal values of the various things you can eat. If you have twenty cents to spare, do you not find yourself mentally asking whether the difference between a large Coke and a small one is worth more to you than lettuce and tomato on your hamburger? (If not, why do you choose a small Coke instead of a large one?) You are probably so accustomed to making decisions of this sort that you are almost unaware of the act of weighing the marginal values of the alternatives.

Consumers do not usually make choices with conscious precision. Nor can they achieve a perfect equilibrium – the prices, unit sizes, and values of the various products available may not permit it. They are trying to come as close to equality as possible. The economist's assumption is that the individual will move toward equilibrium, not that he or she will always achieve it.

To illustrate, suppose your marginal utility for Cokes and hot dogs is as shown in table 6.1.

If a Coke is priced at $0.50 and a hot dog at $1, $3 will buy you two hot dogs and two Cokes – the best you can do with $3 at those prices. Now suppose the price of

Table 6.1 Marginal utility for Cokes and hot dogs

Unit consumed	Marginal utility of Cokes at $0.50 (utils)	Marginal utility of hot dogs at $1 (utils)
First	10	30
Second	9	15
Third	3	12

Coke rises to $0.75 and the price of hot dogs falls to $0.75. With a budget of $3 you can still buy two hot dogs and two Cokes, but you will no longer be maximizing your utility. Instead you will be inclined to reduce your consumption of Coke and increase your consumption of hot dogs.

At the old prices, the original combination (two Cokes and two hot dogs) gave you a total utility of only 64 utils (45 from hot dogs and 19 from Cokes). If you cut back to one Coke and three hot dogs now, your total utility will rise to 67 utils (57 from hot dogs and 10 from Coke). Your new utility maximizing combination – the one that best satisfies your preferences – will therefore be one Coke and three hot dogs. No other combination of Coke and hot dogs will give you greater satisfaction. (Try to find one.)

Changes in price and the law of demand

If the price of hot dogs goes down relative to the price of Coke, the rational person will buy more hot dogs. If the price of Coke rises relative to the price of hot dogs, the rational person will buy less Coke.[3] If the consumer is in equilibrium to begin with, then

$$\frac{MU_c}{P_c} = \frac{MU_h}{P_h}$$

When the price of Coke rises and the price of hot dogs falls, then there is a disequilibrium, meaning that

$$\frac{MU_c}{P_c} < \frac{MU_h}{P_h}$$

The **law of demand** states the assumed inverse relationship between product price and quantity demanded, everything else held constant.

To reestablish equilibrium, the consumer must shift expenditures from Cokes to hot dogs. This principle will hold true for any good or service, and is commonly known as the **law of demand** (first introduced in chapter 2). If the relative price of a good falls, the individual will buy more of the good. If the relative price rises, the individual will buy less.

Figure 6.1 shows the demand curve for Coke – that is, the quantity of Coke purchased at different prices. The inverse relationship between price and quantity is reflected in the curve's downward slope. If the price falls from $1 to $0.75, the quantity the consumer will buy increases from two Cokes to three. The opposite will occur if the price goes up. (The law of demand can also be derived using what

---

[3] In our example, this equality is not always satisfied when the consumer is doing the best he can do because we aren't considering fractional amounts of Cokes and hot dogs. In our example, a price change creates a situation where a change in the consumption bundles allows the consumer to move closer to the above equality, if not actually to an equality.

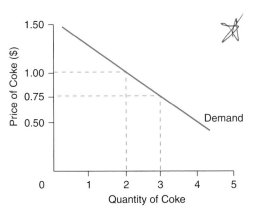

Figure 6.1 The law of demand ✓
Price varies inversely with the quantity consumed, producing a downward sloping curve such as this one. If the price of Coke falls from $1 to $0.75, the consumer will buy three Cokes instead of two.

Individual Curve Demand Curve

economists call "indifference curves," which are graphical devices for structuring consumer preferences based on the simple proposition that consumers prefer more to less of any good. For an analysis of indifference curves see online Reading 6.1 and Video Modules 6.5 and 6.6. (We apply indifference-curve thinking to the issue of how much workers need to be paid when they are relocated to an area of the country with higher housing costs in online Reading 6.2 and Video Module 6.7.)

Thus the assumption of rational behavior, coupled with the consumer's willingness and ability to substitute less costly goods when prices go up, leads to the law of demand. We cannot say how many Cokes and hot dogs a particular person will buy to maximize his satisfaction. That depends on the individual's income and preferences, which depend in turn on other factors (how much he likes hot dogs, whether he is on a diet, and how much he worries about the nutritional deficiencies of such a lunch). But we can predict the general response, whether positive or negative, to a change in prices.

Price is the value of whatever a person must give up in exchange for a unit of a good or service. It is a rate of exchange and is typically expressed in dollars per unit. Note that price is not necessarily the same as cost. In an exchange between two people – a buyer and a seller – the price at which a good sells can be above or below the cost of producing the good. What the buyer gives up to obtain the good does not have to match what the seller–producer gives up in order to provide the good.

Nor is price always stated in dollars and cents. Some people have a desire to watch sunsets – a desire characterized by the same downward sloping demand curve as the one for Coke. The price of the sunset experience is not necessarily denominated in money. Instead, it may be the lost opportunity to do something else or the added cost and trouble of finding a home that will offer a view of the sunset. (In that case, price and cost are the same because the buyer and the producer are one and the same.) The law of demand will apply nevertheless. The individual will spend some optimum number of minutes per day watching the sunset and will vary that number of minutes inversely with the price of watching. And the price of pleasant views often takes the form of money when, for example, people pay more for a house that offers a nice view of the ocean than for one that doesn't.

[See online Video Module 6.2 Optimizing behavior]

From individual demand to market demand

Thus far, we have discussed demand solely in terms of the individual's behavior. The concept is most useful, however, when applied to whole markets or segments of the population for goods consumed separately by individuals, with market demand interacting with market supply to determine price. To obtain the market demand for a product, we need to find some way of *adding up* the wants of the individuals who collectively make up the market.

Market demand is the summation of the quantities demanded by all consumers of a good or service at each and every price during some specified time period.

The market demand can be shown graphically as the horizontal summation of the quantity of a product each individual will buy at each price. Assume that the market for Coke is composed of two individuals, Anna and Betty, who differ in their demand for Coke, as shown in figure 6.2. The demand of Anna is D_A and the demand of Betty is D_B. Then to determine the number of Cokes both of them will demand at any price, we simply add together the quantities each will purchase, at each price (see table 6.2). At a price of $11, neither person is willing to buy any Coke; consequently, the market demand must begin below $11. At $9, Anna is still unwilling to buy any Coke, but Betty will buy two units per unit of time, say a week. The market quantity demanded is therefore two. If the price falls to $5, Anna wants two Cokes and Betty, given her greater demand, wants much more, six. The two quantities combined equal eight. If we continue to drop the price and add the quantities bought at each

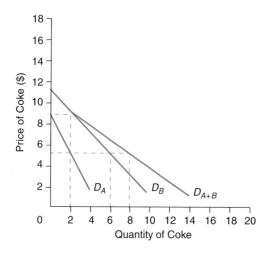

Figure 6.2 Market demand curve
The market demand curve for Coke, D_{A+B}, is obtained by summing the quantities that individuals A and B are willing to buy at each and every price (shown by the individual demand curves D_A and D_B).

Table 6.2 Market demand for Coke

Price of Coke ($) (1)	Quantity demanded by Anna (D_A) (2)	Quantity demanded by Betty (D_B) (3)	Quantity demanded by both Anna and Betty (D_{A+B}) (4)
11	0	0	0
10	0	1	1.0
9	0	2	2.0
8	0.5	3	3.5
7	1.0	4	5.0
6	1.5	5	6.5
5	2.0	6	8.0
4	2.5	7	9.5
3	3.0	8	11.0
2	3.5	9	12.5
1	4.0	10	14.0

Note: The market demand curve, D_{A+B}, in figure 6.2 is obtained by plotting the quantities in column (4) against their respective prices in column (1).

new price, we will obtain a series of market quantities demanded. When plotted on a graph, they will yield curve D_{A+B}, the market demand for Coke (see figure 6.2). This is, of course, an extremely simple example, because only two individuals are involved. The market demand curves for much larger groups of people, however, are derived in essentially the same way. The demands of Fred, Marsha, Roberta, and others would be added to those of Anna and Betty. As more people demand more Coke, the market demand extends further to the right.

Elasticity: consumers' responsiveness to price changes

In the media and in general conversation, we often hear claims that a price change will have no effect on purchases. Someone may predict that an increase in the price of prescription drugs will not affect people's use of them. The same remark is heard in connection with many other goods and services, from gasoline and public parks to medical services and salt. What people usually mean by such statements is that a price change will have only a *slight* effect on consumption. The law of demand states only that a price change will have an inverse effect on the quantity of a good purchased. It does not specify how much of an effect the price change will have.

> **Price elasticity of demand** is a measure of the responsiveness of consumers, in terms of the quantity purchased, to a change in price, everything else held constant.
> **Inelastic demand** is a relatively insensitive consumer response to price changes. If the price goes up or down, consumers will respond with a small decrease or increase in the quantity demanded.

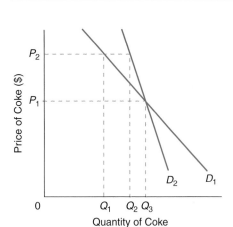

Figure 6.3 Elastic and inelastic demand
Demand curves differ in their relative elasticity. Curve D_1 is more elastic than curve D_2, in the sense that consumers on curve D_1 are more responsive to a given price change (P_2 to P_1) than are consumers on curve D_2.

In other words, we have established only that the market demand curve for a good will slope downward. The actual demand curve for a product may be relatively flat, like curve D_1 in figure 6.3, or relatively steep, like curve D_2. Notice that at a price of P_1, the quantity of the good or service consumed is the same in both markets. If the price is raised to P_2, however, the response is substantially greater in market D_1 than in D_2. In D_1, consumers will reduce their purchases all the way to Q_1. In D_2, consumption will drop only to Q_2.

Economists refer to this relative responsiveness of demand curves as the **price elasticity of demand**. Demand is relatively **elastic** or **inelastic**, depending on the degree of responsiveness to price change.

Elastic demand is a relatively sensitive consumer response to price changes. If the price goes up or down, consumers will respond with a large decrease or increase in the quantity demanded.

Demand curve D_1 in figure 6.3 may be characterized as relatively elastic. Demand curve D_2 in figure 6.3 is relatively inelastic.

The elasticity of demand is a useful concept, but our definitions of elastic and inelastic demands are imprecise. What do we mean by "relatively sensitive" or "relatively insensitive"? Under what circumstances is consumer response sensitive or insensitive? There are two ways to add precision to our definition. One is to calculate the effect of a change in price on total consumer expenditures (which must equal producer revenues). The other is to develop a mathematical formula that will yield different values for various levels of elasticity. We next deal with each in turn.

Analyzing total consumer expenditures

An increase in the price of a particular product can cause consumers to buy less. Whether total consumer expenditures (which necessarily equal total business revenues) rise, fall, or stay the same, however, depends on the extent of the consumer response. Many people assume that businesses will maximize profits by charging the highest price possible. But high prices are not always the best policy. For example, if a firm sells 50 units of a product for $1, its total revenue (consumers' total expenditures) for the product will be $50 (50 × $1). If it raises the price to $1.50 and consumers cut back to 40 units, its total revenue could rise to $60 (40 × $1.50). If consumers are highly sensitive to price changes for this particular good, however, the 50 cent increase may lower the quantity sold to 30 units. In that case, total consumer expenditures would fall to $45 ($1.50 × 30).

Similarly, lowering price doesn't always lower revenues. If a firm establishes a price of $1.50 and then lowers it to $1, the quantity sold may rise enough to increase total revenues. Whether this happens, however, depends on the degree of consumer response. In other words, consumer responsiveness determines whether a firm should raise or lower its price. (Although we shall see later that generally the firm is not interested in maximizing revenues.)

We can define a simple rule of thumb for using total consumer expenditures to analyze the elasticity of demand. Demand is *elastic* if:

- total consumer expenditures rise when the price falls, or
- total consumer expenditures fall when the price rises.

Demand is *inelastic* if:

- total consumer expenditures rise when the price rises, or
- total consumer expenditures fall when the price falls.

Demand is *unitary elastic* when total revenues remain unchanged with an increase or decrease in the price.

Determining elasticity coefficients

Although we have refined our definition of elasticity, it still does not allow us to distinguish degrees of elasticity or inelasticity. **Elasticity coefficients** do just that. Expressed as a formula,[4] the elasticity coefficient is

> The **elasticity coefficient of demand** (E_d) is the ratio of the percentage change in the quantity demanded to the percentage change in price.

$$E_d = \frac{\text{Percentage change in quantity}}{\text{Percentage change in price}} \div \frac{\text{Change in price}}{\text{Initial price}}$$

---

[4] There are actually two formulas for elasticity recognized by economists, one for use at specific points on the curve, called *point elasticity*, and one for measuring average elasticity between two points, called *arc elasticity*. The formula for point elasticity, which is used for very small changes in price and quantity, is:

$$E_d = \frac{\text{Change in quantity demanded}}{\text{Initial quantity demanded}} \div \frac{\text{Change in price}}{\text{Initial price}}$$

Elasticity coefficients can tell us much at a glance. When the percentage change in quantity is greater than the percentage change in price, the elasticity coefficient is greater than 1.0. In these cases, demand is said to be elastic. When the percentage change in quantity is less than the percentage change in price, the elasticity coefficient is less than 1.0 and demand is said to be inelastic. When the percentage change in the price is equal to the percentage change in quantity, the elasticity coefficient is 1.0, and demand is unitary elastic.[5]

Elastic demand	$E_d > 1$
Inelastic demand	$E_d < 1$
Unitary elastic demand	$E_d = 1$

Elasticity coefficients provide useful information on the relationship between price changes and revenue changes, as discussed earlier. For reasons that will

---

or

$$E_d = \frac{Q_1 - Q_2}{Q_1} \div \frac{P_1 - P_2}{P_1}$$

The formula for arc elasticity is:

$$E_d = \frac{1}{2} \frac{Q_1 - Q_2}{(Q_1 + Q_2)} \div \frac{1}{2} \frac{P_1 - P_2}{(P_1 + P_2)}$$

where the subscripts 1 and 2 represent two distinct points, or prices, on the demand curve. (Note that although the calculated elasticity is always negative, economists, by convention, speak of it as a positive number. Economists, in effect, use the absolute value of elasticity.)

[5] To prove this result, let's look at marginal revenue MR, or the change in total revenue in response to a change in quantity Q. Taking the derivative of $P(Q) \bullet Q$ with respect to Q, we obtain

$$MR = \frac{d[P(Q) \bullet Q]}{dQ} = P(Q) + \frac{dP}{dQ} \bullet Q$$

Factoring price out of the right-hand side of this equation gives us

$$MR = P\left[1 + \frac{dP}{dQ} \bullet \frac{Q}{P}\right]$$

which, because

$$E = -\left(\frac{dQ}{dP}\right)Q/P, \text{ is the same as}$$

$$MR = P\left[1 - \frac{1}{E}\right] \quad \begin{array}{l} >0 \text{ if } E>1 \\ =0 \text{ if } E=1 \\ <0 \text{ if } E<1 \end{array}$$

From this it follows immediately that an increase in Q (a decrease in P) increases total revenue if $E > 1$, has no effect on total revenue if $E = 1$, and reduces total revenue if $E < 1$.

become clear, pricing a product to maximize profits almost always requires placing the price on the elastic portion of the demand curve.

Elasticity and slope of the demand curve

Students often confuse the concept of elasticity of demand with the slope of the demand curve. A comparison of their mathematical formulas, however, shows that they are quite different:

$$\text{Slope} = \frac{\text{Rise}}{\text{Run}} = \frac{\text{Change in price}}{\text{Change in quantity}}$$

$$\text{Elasticity} = \frac{\text{Percentage change in quantity}}{\text{Percentage change in price}}$$

The confusion is understandable. The slope of a demand curve does say something about consumers' responsiveness: it shows how much the quantity consumed goes up when the price goes down by a given amount. But slope is an unreliable indicator of consumer responsiveness because it varies with the units of measurement for price and quantity. For example, suppose that when the price rises from $10 to $20, quantity demanded decreases from 100 pounds to 60 pounds The slope is −1/4:

$$\text{Slope} = \frac{-10}{40} = \frac{-1}{4}$$

If a price is measured in cents instead of dollars (with quantity still measured in pounds), however, the slope comes out at –25:

$$\text{Slope} = \frac{-1,000}{40} = \frac{-25}{1}$$

No matter what units are used to measure price and quantity, however, the percentage changes in price and quantity remain the same and the elasticity of demand is not affected by changes from one set of units to another.

Elasticity along a straight-line demand curve

Since slope and elasticity are different concepts, it should not surprise anyone that the elasticity coefficient will generally be different at different points on the demand curve. Consider the linear demand curve in figure 6.4. At every point on the curve, a price reduction of $1 causes quantity demanded to rise by ten units, but a $1 decrease in price at the top of the curve is a much smaller percentage change than a $1 decrease at the bottom of the curve. Similarly, an increase of ten units in the quantity demanded is a much larger percentage change when the quantity is low than when it is high. Therefore, the elasticity coefficient falls as consumers move down their demand curve. Generally, a straight-line demand

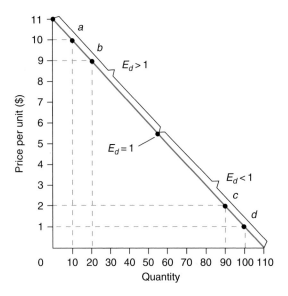

Figure 6.4 Changes in the elasticity coefficient

The elasticity coefficient decreases as a firm moves down the demand curve. The upper half of a linear demand curve is elastic, meaning that the elasticity coefficient is greater than one. The lower half is inelastic, meaning that the elasticity coefficient is less than one. This means that the middle of the linear demand curve has an elasticity coefficient equal to one.

curve has an inelastic range at the bottom, a unitary elastic point in the center, and an elastic range at the top.[6]

 [See online Video Module 6.3 Elasticity.]

---

[6] To prove this, we recognize that the equation for a linear domain curve can be expressed mathematically as

$$P = A - BQ$$

where P represents price, Q is quantity demanded, and A and B are positive constants. The total revenue associated with this demand curve is given by

$$PQ = AQ - BQ^2$$

The marginal revenue is obtained by taking the derivative of total revenue with respect to Q, or

$$MR = A - 2BQ$$

We know that when marginal revenue is equal to 0, elasticity is equal to 1. This implies that $E = 1$ when

$$A - 2BQ = 0$$

or when

$$Q = \frac{1}{2} \cdot \frac{A}{B}$$

We know that when the demand curve intersects the Q axis, $P = 0$ and

$$Q = \frac{A}{B}$$

Thus, with a linear demand curve, $E = 1$ when Q is one-half the distance between $Q = 0$ and the Q that drives price down to 0.

Applications of the concept of elasticity

Elasticity of demand is particularly important to producers. Together with the cost of production, it determines the prices firms can charge for their products. We have shown that an increase or decrease in price can cause total consumer expenditures to rise, fall, or remain the same, depending on the elasticity of demand. Thus if a firm lowers its price and incurs greater production costs (because it is producing and selling more units), it may still increase its profits. As long as the demand curve is elastic, revenues can (but will not necessarily) go up more than costs. Cell phone companies have lowered their rates in response to intense competition, but also partly in response to their highly elastic demand.

Producers of concerts and dances estimate the elasticity of demand when they establish the price of admission. If tickets are left unsold at an admission price of $10, a lower price, say $7, may increase profits. Even if costs rise (for extra workers and more programs), revenues may still rise more.

We noted in passing in chapter 4 that government, too, must consider elasticity of demand, for the consumer's demand for taxable items is not inexhaustible. If a government raises excise taxes on cars or jewelry too much, it may end up with lower tax revenues. The higher tax, added to the final price of the product, may cause a negative consumer response. It is no accident that the heaviest excise taxes are usually imposed on goods for which the demand tends to be inelastic, such as cigarettes and liquor.[7]

We also mentioned earlier how a "fat tax" on fatty and sugary foods and drinks can be used for two purposes: (1) to raise revenues for governments and (2) to curb the country's growing obesity and related health care problems.[8] However, while most researchers agree that obesity is a growing problem around the world, especially in

---

[7] The same reasoning applies to property taxes. Many large cities have tended to underestimate the elasticity of demand for living space. Indeed, a major reason for the recent migration from city to suburbs in many metropolitan areas has been the desire of residents to escape rising tax rates. By moving just outside a city's boundaries, people can retain many of the benefits a city provides without actually paying for them. This movement of city dwellers to the suburbs lowers the demand for property within the city, undermining property values, and destroying the city's tax base. Thus, even governments need to pay attention to the elasticity of demand for the services they provide if they want to maintain their tax revenues. We can predict that the elasticity of demand for the services of local governments is greater than the elasticity of demand for services of the national government because people can more easily move from one local government to another (vote with their feet) than they can from one national government to another.

[8] According to one study, calorie intake per capita in the United States from beverages increased by nearly threefold in the last quarter of the twentieth century. At the start of the twenty-first century beverages accounted for 10–15 percent of the calorie intake of children and adolescents, with each extra can of soda drunk per day increasing children's chances of becoming obese by 60 percent (Ludwig, Peterson, and Gortmaker 2001).

the United States, the exact effect of price increases from a proposed fat tax on the consumption of fatty and sugary foods and drinks varies considerably across studies.[9]

- One study by academic nutritionists found that a 10 percent increase in the price of soft drinks leads to a 7.8 percent decrease in sales, making demand inelastic (Brownell and Frieden 2009).
- A beverage industry study showed that a 6.8 percent increase in the price of sodas leads to a 7.8 percent drop in consumption; a 12 percent increase in the price of Coca-Cola taken by itself causes sales to fall by 14.6 percent, making for elastic demands in both cases (*Beverage Digest* 2008).
- Economists have found that a 10 percent tax on sodas will reduce consumption by 8 to 11 percent, making the elasticity of demand close to unitary elastic and leaving government tax revenues more or less constant, and soda tax would likely have little effect on people's excess weight (Brownell and Frieden 2009).

The effects of "fat taxes" on weight gain also vary from study to study.

- One set of researchers have found that, for more than 800 people studied, reducing people's intake of 100 calories a day from sodas leads to a weight reduction of only half a pound over eighteen months (reported by Kaplan 2009).
- Other researchers found that a "fat tax" on all fatty and sugary foods would reduce the obesity rate by only 1 percent (Gelbach, Klick, and Stratmann 2007).
- The academic nutritionists cited above have concluded that a 1-cent-per-ounce tax on sodas could reduce the average weight of Americans by 2 pounds a year (Brownell and Frieden 2009).

The important point in the emerging debate over "fat taxes" is that the political and public acceptance of fat taxes will likely depend critically on the computed elasticity of demand for fatty and sugary foods.

Determinants of the price elasticity of demand

So far, our analysis of elasticity has presumed that consumers are able to respond to a price change. However, various factors can affect consumers' ability to respond, such as the number of substitutes and the amount of time consumers have to respond to a change in price by shifting to other products or producers.

---

[9] In 1960–2, the average obesity rate for adults was 13.3 percent. By 2003–6, the average obesity rate for adults had more than doubled to 34.1 percent, as measured by the National Center for Health Statistics (2009). Thirty-five diseases – including hypertension; heart disease; cancers of the breast, colon, and prostate; type 2 diabetes; osteoarthritis; gallbladder disease; and incontinence – have been linked to obesity, according to the National Heart, Lung, and Blood Institute (1998).

Substitutes

Substitutes allow consumers to respond to a price increase by switching to another good. If the price of orange juice goes up, you can substitute a variety of other drinks, including water, wine, or soda.

The elasticity of demand for any good depends very much on what substitutes are available. The existence of a large number and variety of substitutes means that demand is likely to be elastic. That is, if people can switch easily to another product that will yield approximately the same value, many will do so when prices increase. The similarity of substitutes – how well they can satisfy the same basic want – also affects elasticity. The closer substitutes are to a product, the more elastic the demand for the product will be. If there are no close substitutes, demand will tend to be inelastic. What we call "necessities" are often things that lack close substitutes.

Few goods have *no substitutes* at all. Because there are many substitutes for orange juice – soda, wine, prune juice, and so on – we would expect the demand for orange juice to be more elastic than the demand for salt, which has fewer viable alternatives. Yet even salt has synthetic substitutes. Furthermore, although human beings need a certain amount of salt to survive, most of us consume much more than the minimum and can easily cut back if the price of salt rises. The extra flavor that salt adds is a benefit that can be partially recouped by buying other things.

At the other extreme from goods with no substitutes are goods with *perfect substitutes*. Perfect substitutes exist for goods produced by an individual firm engaged in perfect competition. An individual wheat farmer, for example, is only one among thousands of producers of essentially the same product. The wheat produced by others is a perfect substitute for the wheat produced by the single farmer. Perfect substitutability can lead to perfect elasticity of demand.

The demand curve facing the perfect competitor is horizontal, like the one in figure 6.5. If the individual competitor raises her price even a minute percentage

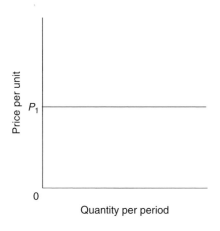

Figure 6.5 Perfectly elastic demand
A firm that has many competitors may lose all its sales if it increases its price even slightly. Its customers can simply move to another producer. In that case, its demand curve is horizontal, with an elasticity coefficient of infinity.

A **perfectly elastic demand** is a demand that has an elasticity coefficient of infinity. It is expressed graphically as a curve horizontal to the *X*-axis.

above the going market price, consumers will switch to other sellers. The elasticity coefficient of such a horizontal demand curve is infinite. Thus this demand curve is described as **perfectly elastic**.

Time

Consumption requires time. Accordingly, a demand curve must describe some particular time period. Over a very short period of time – say, a day – the demand for a good may not react immediately. It takes time to find substitutes. With enough time, however, consumers will respond to a price increase. Thus a demand curve that covers a long period will be more elastic than one for a short period.[10]

Changes in demand

The determinants of the elasticity of demand are fewer and easier to identify than the determinants of demand itself. As discussed in chapter 3, the demand for almost all goods is affected in one way or another by:

- consumer incomes
- prices of other goods
- number of consumers
- expectations concerning future prices and incomes
- consumer tastes and preferences.

Additional variables apply in differing degrees to different goods. The amount of ice cream and the number of golf balls bought both depend on the weather (in Montana fewer golf balls are sold in the winter than the summer). The number of cribs demanded depends on the birthrate. Together, all these variables determine the

---

[10] Oil provides a good example of how the elasticity of demand can change over time. When the price of oil, and therefore gasoline, increased sharply in the first half of 2008, consumers were limited in their ability to reduce consumption because of their gas-guzzling SUVs and suburban homes located far from their workplaces. If those high gas prices remain high for a long time, however, consumers will begin buying smaller cars and some will relocate closer to work, and the consumer response to the higher gas prices will become greater. The long-term demand curve for gasoline is much more elastic than the short-term demand curve. The short-run demand for large SUVs plunged, along with their prices, which is another reason for lower elasticity of demand for gasoline in the short run. With the lower resell prices of SUVs (and the hikes in the prices of smaller cars), the prices of operating SUVs did not rise as much as the price in gasoline.

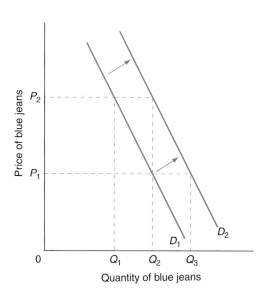

Figure 6.6 Increase in demand
When consumer demand for low-rise pants increases, the demand curve shifts from D_1 to D_2. Consumers are now willing to buy a larger quantity of low-rise pants at the same price, or the same quantity at a higher price. At price P_1, for instance, they will buy Q_3 instead of Q_2. And they are now willing to pay P_2 for Q_2 low-rise pants, whereas before they would pay only P_1.

position of the demand curve. If any variable changes, so will the position of the demand curve.

We showed in chapter 3 that if consumer preference for a product – say, low-rise pants – increases, the change will be reflected in an outward movement of the demand curve (as we show here in figure 6.6). That is what happened during the early 2000s, when people's (mainly women's) tastes changed and wearing pants (at times, at half-moon!) became chic. By definition, such a change in taste means that consumers are willing to buy more of the good at the going market price. If the price is P_1, the quantity demanded will increase from Q_2 to Q_3. A change in tastes can also mean that people are willing to buy more low-rise pants at each and every price. At P_2 they are now willing to buy Q_2 instead of Q_1 low-rise pants. We can infer from this pattern that consumers are willing to pay a higher price for any given quantity. In figure 6.6, the increase in demand means that consumers are willing to pay as much as P_2 for Q_2 pairs of low-rise pants, whereas formerly they would pay only P_1. (If consumers' tastes change in the opposite direction, the demand curve moves downward to the left as a quantity demanded at a given price decreases, see figure 6.7.)

Whether demand increases or decreases, the demand curve will still slope downward. Everything else held constant, people will buy more of the good at a lower price than a higher one. To assume that other variables will remain constant is, of course, unrealistic because markets are generally in a state of flux. In the real world, all variables do not stay put just to allow the price of a good to change by itself. Even if conditions change at the same time that price changes, the law of demand tells us that a decrease in price will lead people to buy more than they would otherwise, and an increase in price will lead them to buy less.

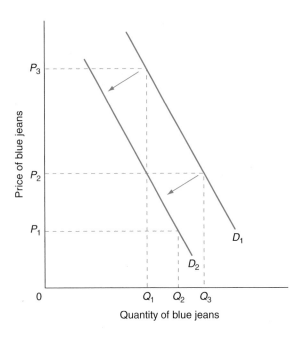

Figure 6.7 Decrease in demand
A downward shift in demand, from D_1 to D_2, represents a decrease in the quantity of low-rise pants consumers are willing to buy at each and every price. It also indicates a decrease in the price they are willing to pay for each and every quantity of low-rise pants. At price P_2, for instance, consumers will now buy only Q_1 low-rise pants (not Q_3, as before); and they will now pay only P_2 for Q_1 low-rise pants – not P_3, as before.

For example, figure 6.7 shows a situation where the demand for low-rise pants has decreased because consumers are less willing to buy the product as another style becomes fashionable. A price reduction can partially offset the decline in demand. If producers lower their price from P_2 to P_1, quantity demanded will fall only to Q_2 instead of Q_1. Although consumers are buying fewer low-rise pants than they once did (Q_2 as opposed to Q_3) because of changing tastes, the law of demand still holds. Because of the price change, consumers have increased their consumption over what it would otherwise have been.

Normal and inferior goods

A change in consumer incomes will affect demand in more complicated ways. The demand for most goods, called **normal goods**, increases with income. Golf lessons are very likely a good example of a normal good (since so many higher-income people can be seen taking them, relatively speaking). Beans are an example of what a good many people would consider **inferior**. People who rely on beans as a staple or filler food when their incomes are low may substitute meat and other higher-priced foods when their incomes rise.

> A **normal good or service** is any good or service for which demand rises with an increase in income and falls with a decrease in income. An **inferior good or service** is any good or service for which demand falls with an increase in income and rises with a decrease in income.

Thus, whereas economists can confidently predict the directional movement of consumption when prices change, they cannot say what will happen to the demand for a particular good when income changes, because each individual determines whether a particular good is a normal or inferior good. Different people will tend to answer this question differently in different markets. Beans may be an inferior good to most low-income consumers but a normal good to many others.

For example, how do you think a change in income will affect the demand for low-, medium-, and high-quality liquor? You may have some intuitive notion about the effect, but you are probably not as confident about it as you are about the effect of a price decrease. In fact, during past recessions, the demand for both low- and high-quality liquor has increased. Some consumers may have switched to high-quality liquor to impress their friends, and to suggest that they have been unaffected by the economic malaise. Others may have tried to maintain their old level of consumption by switching to a low-quality brand.

When the recession began in late 2007, most retailers started reporting declines in sales of their goods, especially stores catering to higher-end customers. However, Walmart and Costco began reporting increases in sales throughout 2008 and 2009, as buyers moved to down-market products.

Substitutes and complementary goods

The effect of a change in the price of other goods is similarly complicated. Here the important factor is the relationship of one good – say, ice cream – to other commodities. Are the goods in question substitutes for ice cream, such as frozen yogurt? Are they complements, such as cones? Are they used independently of ice cream? Demand for ice cream is unlikely to be affected by a drop in the price of baby rattles, but it may well decline if the price of frozen yogurt drops.

Substitute goods

Two products are generally considered *substitutes* if the demand for one goes up when the price of the other rises. Zippers are substitutes for buttons in clothing construction. If the price of zippers goes down, the demand for buttons can be expected to fall as consumers and clothing companies shift from buttons to zippers.

The price of a product does not have to rise above the price of its substitute before the demand for the substitute is affected. Assume that the price of sirloin steak is $6 per pound and the price of hamburger is $2 per pound. The price difference reflects the consumer belief that the two meats differ in quality. If the price of hamburgers rises to $4 per pound while the price of sirloin remains constant at $6, many buyers will increase their demand for steak. The perceived difference in quality now out-weighs the difference in price.

Complementary goods

Because *complementary* products – razors and razor blades, oil and oil filters, Blu-Ray DVDs and Blu-Ray DVD players – are consumed *jointly*, a change in the price of one will cause an increase or decrease in the demand for both products simultaneously. An increase in the price of razor blades, for instance, will induce some people to switch to electric razors, causing a decrease in the quantity of razor blades demanded and a decrease in the demand for safety razors. Again, economists cannot predict how many people will decide that the switch is worthwhile; they can merely predict from theory the direction in which demand for the product will move. (Many students often worry about the law of demand on the grounds that people are not always as rational as economists assume and that some goods may have upward sloping demand curves because prices carry messages about goods' relative value and about the relative economic standing of the buyers of the goods.)

Objections to demand theory

From years of teaching the theory of demand, we have learned that MBA students often question aspects of demand theory, pointing out that:

- Consumers are not as rational as the law of demand presumes.
- Consumers exhibit some randomness in their buying decisions.
- Consumers often buy goods even as prices rise because higher prices convey a message to others whom the consumers want to impress.

These objections are also discussed in online Perspective 6, which reinforces the basic conclusion: Demand curves slope downward.[11]

Online Perspective 6
Common concerns relating
to the law of demand

---

[11] In the new subdiscipline *behavioral economics*, psychologists and economists have documented a variety of "irrational" behaviors (Ariely 2008; Thaler and Sunstein 2008).

Part B Organizational economics and management

Pricing strategies based on lagged demands, network effects, and rational addiction

Almost all microeconomics textbooks provide a lengthy discussion of the demand for "standard" goods, as we have done in Part A of this chapter. They (and we) explain that the quantity of the good purchased will be related to the price of the good in question and a number of other considerations (such as weather, income, and the prices of other goods), as we have stressed. The lower the price of a candy bar, for example, the greater the quantity purchased, and vice versa. This inverse relationship between price and quantity is so revered in economics that it has a special label, the "law of demand." The general rule deduced is that the more scarce the good, the greater the (marginal) value and price.

Little is said in most textbooks, however, about how the consumption level of a good (candy bars) today might affect the demand in the future. Also, little or nothing is written about how the benefits (and demand) can depend upon how many other people have bought candy bars. This lack of coverage is understandable. The benefit that one person gets from eating a candy bar in one time period does not materially affect the benefits received from eating another bar later, and is also not materially affected by how many other people are buying and consuming candy bars. People just buy and consume candy bars independently of one another, and couldn't care less about how much other people are enjoying candy bars.

This is not true for two special classes of goods called lagged-demand goods and network goods. A lagged-demand good has one defining feature: the greater the quantity purchased today, the greater the demand tomorrow. Good examples of lagged-demand goods include cigarettes, alcohol, and street drugs, given that they tend to be addictive. As we shall show, the theory of lagged demand is similar to the theory of "rational addiction," or the view that before consumption begins, people can rationally weigh the

> A **lagged-demand good** is one in which consumption today affects consumption tomorrow (or in future time periods).
> A **network good** is a product or service whose value to consumers depends intrinsically on how many other people buy the good.

long-term costs and benefits, or pros and cons, of consuming goods that can be physically compelling in consumption. In the emerging demand theory relating to lagged, network, and addictive goods are pricing strategies that do not surface in discussions of the demand for standard goods.

A **network good** has one defining feature: The greater the number of buyers, the greater the benefits to most, if not all, buyers. These goods are said to exhibit a "network effect" (or are sometimes called "network externalities"), which means that the attractiveness or value of a product to buyers increases with others' use of that product. Good examples of network goods include telephones, fax machines, and computer software. One person's telephone is useless unless someone else owns a phone, and the more people there are who are buying phones, the greater the value of the phone is to everyone, because more people can be called.

As you can see, lagged-demand goods and network goods have much in common – the interconnectedness of consumption. This commonality has important implications for pricing strategy.

[See online Video Module 6.4 Demand for network goods]

Lagged demands

One of the authors of this book (Lee) was involved in the development of the theory of lagged demands (Lee and Kreutzer 1982). He and economist David Kreutzer have argued that the future demands for some goods can be, and often are, dependent on the current demand. From this perspective, a lagged-demand good is one in which the future good is a complement to the current good; they go together. According to Lee and Kreutzer,

The crucial assumption behind our analysis is that lags exist in the demand for the resource; future demands are influenced by current availability. The demand for petroleum is clearly an example of such a lagged demand structure, with future demand for petroleum significantly influenced by investment decisions made in response to current availability. (1982, 580)

As with all complements, the future demand for a product depends upon the current price for the good. Behind such an obvious point lie important insights that might otherwise go unrecognized when seen from the usual view of demand.

As a consequence of the complementarity in consumption over time, firms faced with lagged demand have an incentive to lower their current price in order to stimulate future sales. They might even charge a price in the inelastic range of their current demand curves (or approach that range), despite losing current revenues (and profits) from doing so, just so that they can stimulate a greater future demand, which will permit them to raise future prices and generate greater profits in the future. This is only true, of course, as long as the producers' rights to exploit future profits are not threatened.

What makes this perspective interesting is that, under conditions of lagged demand, a cartel of firms (considered in detail in chapter 11) may form, not with the intent of raising the group's current price but rather with the intent of lowering the current price (below) and expanding current output (above) levels that would exist under competition. The standard view is that firms form cartels to increase their prices above the level that would be possible under competition, and that cartels tend to break down because individual firms will cheat on the cartel agreement by lowering price to gain customers at the expense of the other cartel firms.[12]

Also, the conventional treatment of demand, under which tomorrow's demand is unrelated to today's consumption, predicts that threats to the future stability of property rights will lead to "overproduction" during the current time period. This is the case because if a firm – for example, an oil company – fears losing its property rights to its reserves, then it has an incentive to increase production and expand sales today. Never mind that the added supply of oil might depress the current price. The oil firm can reason that if it doesn't pump the oil out of the ground in the short term, it will not have rights to the oil in the future.

For goods subject to the lagged-demand phenomenon, any looming threat to property rights can cause some firms to do the opposite: reduce the production of oil (or the exploitation of any other resource), hike the current price, and extract whatever profits remain. When its property rights are threatened, the firm no longer has an incentive to artificially suppress its current price in order to cultivate future demand.

Similarly, standard excise tax theory suggests that producers' opposition to excise taxes should be tempered by the fact that the tax can be extensively passed on to the consumers in the form of a price increase (that must always be less than the tax itself). The theory of lagged demand suggests otherwise: producers of such goods have a substantial incentive to oppose the tax because of the elastic nature of their long-run demands. Although they may be able to pass along a major share of the tax in the short run, they will not be able to do so in the long run.

Rational addiction

Gary Becker and Kevin Murphy (1988) have developed a similar argument but with the purpose of developing an economic theory of "addiction," a general concept that suggests a connection between current and future consumption of a good or activity. The connection is, however, physical, or maybe chemical, as in the case of cigarettes. People's future demand for smokes can be tied to their current consumption simply because of the body's chemical dependency on nicotine. As in the case of lagged-demand goods, producers of addictive goods have an incentive to suppress the current price of their good – cigarettes – in order to stimulate the future demand for it. The lower the current price, the greater the future demand and the greater the future consumption.

---

[12] Such a cartel may also dissolve because of rampant cheating involving price increases, with all firms seeking to benefit from the greater demand stimulated by lower prices charged by other cartel members.

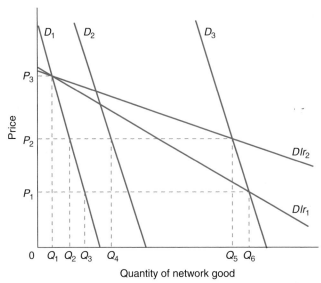

Figure 6.8 Rational addiction and network effects and demand
As the price falls from P_3 to P_2, the quantity demanded in the short run rises from Q_1 to Q_2. However, sales build on sales, causing the demand in the future to expand outward to, say, D_2. The lower the price in the current time period, the greater the expansion of demand in the future. The more the demand expands over time in response to greater sales in the current time period, the more elastic is the long-run demand.

This complementarity in consumption for an addictive (and lagged demand) good is illustrated in figure 6.8. At price P_3 in the current time period, the consumption will be Q_1 in the current time period. However, because of that current consumption level, the demand in the future rises to D_2. At a price of P_2, current consumption rises to Q_2, but the future demand rises to D_3. You can imagine that at even lower prices, P_1, some even higher demand curve, D_3, will occur in the future. Figure 6.8 shows why firms have an incentive to lower the current price: The future demand rises. With other complementary goods, if the price of one complement goes down and more of it is sold, then the demand for the other complement goes up, with its price rising. The same thing happens in this case, but the complements are the same good that are consumed in different time periods.

The current demand for one addictive good, cigarettes, might be highly inelastic, as is commonly presumed in microeconomics, but this does not mean that the long-run demand is necessarily inelastic. As illustrated in figure 6.8, the short-term demand curves D_1–D_3 are each very inelastic, but the long-term demand curve (Dlr_1, Dlr_2) is rather elastic.

Indeed, Becker and Murphy (1988, 695) maintain that the more addictive the good, the more elastic will be the long-term demand. This is the case because a reduction in the *current* time period might not stimulate *current* sales very much. However, for highly addictive goods, current consumption can give an even greater increase in the future demand because the buyers "have to have more of it," thus resulting in even more future consumption than would be the case for less addictive goods. Hence, it is altogether understandable why in the 1960s cigarette firms would often have "cigarette girls" in short skirts giving away small packs of cigarettes, and why many drug dealers to this day eagerly give away the first "hits" to their potential customers. Indeed, it seems reasonable to conclude from the Becker–Murphy line of argument that the more addictive the good, the lower the current price for first-time users. We might not even be surprised that, for some highly addictive goods, the producers would "sell" their goods at below-zero prices (or would pay their customers to take the good).

In contrast to the theory of lagged demand, this theory of rational addiction suggests explanations for a variety of behaviors, most notably the observed differences in the consumption behavior of young and old, the tendency of overweight people to go on "crash diets" even when they may want to lose only a modest amount of weight, or alcoholics who become "teetotalers" when they decide to curtail their drinking. Old people may be less concerned about addictive behavior, everything else held constant, than the young. Old people simply have less to lose over time from addictions than do younger people (given older people's shorter remaining life expectancies). People who are addicted to food may rationally choose to drastically reduce their intake of food even though they may need to lose only a few pounds because their intake of food compels them to "overconsume." Similarly, alcoholics may "get on the wagon" in order to temper their future demands for booze because even a modest consumption level can have a snowballing effect, with a little consumption leading to more drinks, which can lead to even more.

Network effects

The theory of "network effects" shares one key construct with the theory of lagged demand: the interconnectedness of demands (Arthur 1996; Farrell and Klemperer 2007). In the theory of lagged demand, interconnectedness is formed through time; in the theory of network effects, it is formed across people and markets. The theory of network effects is analogous to telephone systems that form "networks" tied together with telephone lines (as well as microwave disks and satellites). No one would want to own a phone or buy a telephone service if he or she were the only phone owner. There would be no one to call. However, if two people – A and B – buy phones, then each person has someone to call, and there are two pair-wise calls that can be made: A can call B, and B can also call A. As more and more people buy phones, the benefits of phone ownership escalate geometrically – there are progressively more people to call and even more possible pair-wise calls.[13] The benefits that buyers garner from others who join the network can rise simply from the *potential* to call others; they need not ever call all the additional joiners.

Accordingly, the demand for phones can be expected to rise with phone ownership. That is to say, the benefits from ownership go up as more people join the network. Hence, people should be willing to pay more for phones as phone ownership increases. Some of the benefits of phone ownership are said to be "external" to the buyers of phones because people other than those who buy phones gain by the purchases (as was true in our study of public goods and external benefits in chapter 6). In more concrete terms, when one of the authors, Lee, buys a phone, then the other author, McKenzie, gains from Lee's purchase – and McKenzie pays nothing for Lee's phone. For that matter, everyone who has a phone gains more opportunities to call as other people buy phones, or as the network expands (at least up to some point). The gains that others receive from Lee's or anyone else's purchase are "external" to Lee, hence are dubbed "external benefits" or, more to the point of this discussion, "network externalities."

Accordingly, network effects can be discussed with the same figure that was developed for rational addiction, figure 6.8. Under both market conditions – rational addiction and network effects – short-term prices of zero and even below zero are potential market-development strategies. Such low prices can encourage current consumption, which can elevate future demand and future prices. Indeed, the prospects of higher prices (and profits) in the future are a key motivation for short-price reductions, even to zero and beyond.

Scarcity, abundance, and economic value

Networks and network goods tend to turn one basic economic proposition on its head: as any good becomes scarcer, it becomes more valuable. But in the case of network goods, just the opposite is true: as a good becomes more abundant, its value goes up (Kelly 1998, chapter 3). This does not mean, however, that the demand curve for a network good slopes upward. Given the number of phones that others have, people can be expected to buy more phones at a low price than a high price.

A phone company faces two basic problems in building its network. First, the company has the initial problem of getting people to buy phones, as the benefits will be low at the start. Second, if some of the benefits of buying a phone are "external"

---

[13] If there are three phone owners – *A*, *B*, and *C* – then calls can be made in six pair-wise ways: *A* can call *B* or *C*, *B* can call *A* or *C*, and *C* can call *A* or *B*. If there are four phone owners, then there are twelve potential pair-wise calls; five phone owners, twenty potential pair-wise calls; twenty phone owners, 380; and so forth. If the network allows for conference calls, the count of the ways in which calls can be made will quickly go through the roof with the rise in the number of phone owners.

to the buyer, then each buyer's willingness to buy a phone can be impaired. How does the phone company build the network? One obvious solution is for the phone company to do what the producers in the theory of lagged demand do: "underprice" (or subsidize) their products – phones – or, at the extreme, give them away or even pay people to install phones in their homes and offices.

Software networks

The network effects in the software industry – for example, operating systems – are similar but, of course, differ in detail from the network effects in the telephone industry. Indeed, the software developer may face more difficult problems, given that the software development must somehow get the computer users on one side of the market and application developers on the other side to join the network more or less together.

Few people, other than "geeks," are likely to buy an operating system without applications (for example, word processing programs or games) being available. If a producer of an operating system is able to get only a few consumers to buy and use its product, the demand for the operating system can be highly restricted. A major problem is that few software firms will write applications for an operating system with very limited users because the software firms will have few opportunities to sell their products, which in turn keeps demand for the operating system low. However, if the firm producing the operating system can motivate more consumers to purchase it, a cycle of increased demand can result as the number of applications written for the operating system grows, stimulating yet more demand for the system, and more applications written for it, and so on.

As in the case of telephones, some of the benefits of purchasing the operating system (and applications) are "external" to the people who buy them. People who join the operating system network increase the benefits to all previous joiners because they have more people with whom they can share computers or files. All joiners have the additional benefit of knowing that, as the network increases, they are likely to have a greater number of applications from which to choose. However, as in phone purchases, when the benefits are "external," potential users have an impaired demand for buying into the network. The greater the "external benefits," the greater the buying resistance (or willingness to cover the operating system cost).

The network may grow slowly at the start because people (both computer users and programmers) may be initially skeptical that any given operating system will be able to become a sizable network (and provide the "external benefits" that a large network can provide). But if the network for a given operating system continues to grow, more and more people will begin to believe that the operating system will become sizable, if not "dominant," which means that the network can grow at an escalating pace.

In short, such network growth can reach a "tipping point," beyond which the growth in the market for the operating system will take on a life of its own – grow at an ever-faster pace *because* it has grown at an ever-faster pace (Gladwell 2000). People will buy the operating system because everyone else is using it (which can mean that the accelerating growth of one operating system causes a contraction in the market share for other operating systems). After the "tipping point" has been reached, the firm's eventual market dominance and monopoly power (according to the US Department of Justice, Klein *et al.* 1998) is practically assured.

This discussion is relevant to the history of the Apple and Microsoft operating systems. Before the introduction of the IBM personal computer, Apple was the dominant personal computer (PC), running the ProDOS operating system; however, IBM and Microsoft jointly developed their respective operating systems, PC-DOS and MS-DOS, in 1981. At that time, 90 percent of programs ran under some version of the CP/M operating system. Two important factors likely undermined CP/M's market dominance. First, CP/M was selling at the time for $240 a copy; DOS was introduced at $40. Second, IBM's dominance of the mainframe computer market no doubt convinced many buyers that some version of DOS would eventually be the dominant operating system. In addition, Apple refused to "unbundle" its computer system: it insisted on selling its own operating system with the Macintosh (and later-generation models), and at a price inflated by the restricted availability of Apple machines and operating systems (Evans, Nichols, and Reddy 1999, 4).

Microsoft took a radically different approach: It got IBM to agree to allow it to license MS-DOS to other computer manufacturers, and then did just that to all comers, in the expectation that competition among non-Apple computer manufacturers would spread the use of their computers – and, not incidentally, Microsoft's operating system. This expectation was realized and the "abundance" of MS-DOS systems led to an even greater demand for such systems, and to a lower demand for Apple systems. Many people started joining the Microsoft network, not necessarily because they thought that MS-DOS or Windows was a superior operating system to Apple's but because of the benefits of the larger network. There was a "tipping point" for Microsoft sometime in the late 1980s or early 1990s (possibly with the release of Windows 3.1) that caused Windows to take off, sending Apple into a market-share tailspin.

In 1998, the Justice Department took Microsoft to court for violation of antitrust laws. Among other charges, the government maintained that Microsoft was a monopolist because it held more than 90 percent of the market share in operating systems, and that the company was engaging in "predatory" pricing of its browser, Internet Explorer. Microsoft had been giving away Internet Explorer with Windows 95 and had integrated it into Windows 98. The Justice Department claimed that the only possible reason Microsoft could have to offer Internet Explorer was to eliminate Netscape Navigator from the market. We can't settle these issues here (see McKenzie 2000), but we can point out that the Justice Department starts its case against Microsoft with the admission that the operating system and software markets are full of "network effects."

Although it may be true that Microsoft engaged in pricing designed to eliminate competition, it may also be true that Microsoft was responding to the dictates of "network effects," underpricing its product to build future demand. The company had another reason for its actions: If Microsoft lowered its price on Internet Explorer (or lowered its *effective* price for Windows by including Internet Explorer), then more computers could be sold, which means that more copies of Windows would be sold *and* more copies of Microsoft's applications – Word, Excel, etc. – would be sold. This means that a lower price for Internet Explorer or Windows could give rise to higher sales, prices, and profits on the other applications. (More details on the Microsoft antitrust case of 1998 will be provided in chapter 10, which is on monopoly theory.)

Practical lessons for MBAs: treat the law of demand for what it is, a *relatively absolute absolute*

The late University of Chicago economics professor Frank Knight, whose words form the epigraph for this chapter, often told his students that there are no absolutes in this world – other than that statement. However, some principles come so close to being absolutes that they can be characterized as *relatively absolute absolutes,* by which Knight meant that we can treat the principles more or less as absolutes until strong evidence proves otherwise. For economists the *law of demand* is treated not as an absolute absolute, but as a relatively absolute absolute. The law of demand is a principle that has been tested and validated so often in so many varied ways by so many economists that the overwhelming majority of economists have come to think of it as true, bordering on a law of nature.

Granted, the law of demand may not always hold in every conceivable circumstance, but it holds with such frequency and durability that MBA students would be well advised to presume the law of demand holds for whatever pricing problem they are considering until strong evidence proves otherwise. Unless their firms operate in a perfectly competitive market producing a "commodity," which means their firms are price takers, all managers should develop their pricing policy on the presumption that price and quantity are inversely related.

Having adopted the law of demand as a guiding pricing principle, managers assess the elasticity of their market demand. If their demands are found to be inelastic (or unitary elastic) within the relevant range of market sales, then they should definitely consider raising their prices to improve their profitability. If demand is inelastic, a higher price will lead to greater revenues. The resulting lower sales will lead to lower production costs. If the demand is unitary elastic, then revenues will remain the same when the price is raised, but costs will fall with lower sales. Accordingly, in both cases a higher price will improve firm profitability.

Even when demand is elastic, a price hike can be a profitable move, in spite of lower resulting revenues. Profits can go up when the reduction in costs from lower sales is greater than the reduction in revenues. As we will explain with greater clarity in chapter 10, a firm producing a non-network good intent on maximizing profits should raise its price until its price is in the elastic range of the demand curve.

As indicated in this chapter, a firm producing a good that has network effects should consider a radically different pricing strategy. The firm should consider pricing its product at a low (below-cost), zero, or even negative level with an eye toward boosting current sales. The increase in current sales in and of itself can add to consumer value and can boost future demand and sales even at elevated future prices. Pricing among initial producers of a network good can be expected to be aggressive because more than current sales will be at stake. The prospects of future market dominance can drive initial prices below production costs because of the potential for elevated profits from future market dominance.

Further readings online

Reading 6.1 Indifference curves and budget lines (with accompanying video modules)

Reading 6.2 Covering relocation costs of new hires (along with an accompanying video module)

The bottom line

The key takeaways from chapter 6 are the following:

1 Rational consumers will equate at the margins. That is to say, they will so allocate their expenditures that the marginal utility of the last unit of every good is equal to every other.

2 The law of demand is a natural consequence of rational behavior.

3 Demand does not consist of what people would like to have or are willing to buy at a given price; rather, it represents the inverse relationship between price and quantity, a relationship described by a downward sloping curve.

4 Although economists do not have complete confidence in all applications of the law of demand, they consider the relationship between price and quantity to be so firmly established, both theoretically and empirically, that they call it a law.

5 In the real world, when the price of a good goes down, the quantity purchased may fall rather than rise. In such cases, economists normally assume (until strong evidence is

presented to the contrary) that some other variable has changed, offsetting the positive effects of the reduction in price.

6 The market demand curve for a private good is obtained by horizontally summing individuals' demand curves for the good.

7 Total revenue will rise when demand is elastic and the price is reduced, and vice versa. Total revenue will fall when demand is inelastic and the price is reduced, and vice versa.

8 The slope and elasticity of a demand curve are not the same. The slope of a straight-line demand curve is the same at all points along the demand curve. The elasticity of demand, as measured by the elasticity coefficient, increases with movements up a straight-lined demand curve.

9 When the price of a network good is lowered, the demand for the good can (eventually) rise as the value of the good rises with the increase in the number of consumers. Producers of the network good can (depending on the extent of the network effects) have an incentive to charge zero and negative prices.

10 Not all downward sloping demand curves are alike. They differ radically in terms of the elasticity of demand, or the responsiveness of consumers to a price change. The elasticity of demand can heavily influence business pricing strategies.

Review questions >>

1 What role does the law of demand play in economic analysis?

2 If the price of jeans rises and the quantity sold goes up, does this mean that the demand curve slopes upward? Why or why not?

3 If the prices of most goods are rising by an average of 15 percent per year, but the price of gasoline rises just 10 percent per year, what is happening to the real, or relative, price of gasoline? How do you expect consumers to react?

4 Suppose that a producer raises the price of a good from $4 to $7, and the quantity sold drops from 250 to 200 units. Is demand for the good elastic or inelastic?

5 If the campus police force is expanded and officers are instructed to increase the number of parking tickets they give out, why might the initial effect of this policy increase revenues from fines more than the long-run effect? What does your answer have to do with the elasticity of demand for illegal parking?

6   If the government subsidizes flood insurance, what will happen to the price of that insurance? What will happen to the value of the property that is lost during floods? Why?

7   Many computer programs – for example, operating systems and word processors – are said to be "network goods." Software piracy is often relatively easy because of the digital nature of software. Should software developers oppose all piracy?

8   Consider two markets, one in which the market "tips" and another in which it does not. Compare the incentives of firms in the two markets to lower their prices initially before the market tips.

9   Assume network effects in two markets. In one market, there are no "switching costs." In the other, there are substantial switching costs. How will the switching costs (or the absence thereof) affect the initial price competition in the two markets?

10 Why would any firm ever pay consumers to take their products? Can you think of examples of such a pricing strategy?

7

Production costs and the theory of the firm

The economist's stock in trade – his tools – lies in his ability to and proclivity to think about all questions in terms of alternatives. The truth judgment of the moralist, which says that something is either wholly right or wholly wrong, is foreign to him. The win–lose, yes–no discussion of politics is not within his purview. He does not recognize the either–or, the all-or-nothing situation as his own. His is not the world of the mutually exclusive. Instead, his is the world of adjustment, of coordinated conflict, of mutual gain.

    James M. Buchanan

Amazing things happen when people take responsibility for everything themselves. The results are quite different, and at times people are unrecognizable. Work changes and attitudes to it, too.

    Mikhail Gorbachev, former Premier of the Soviet Union

Cost is pervasive in human action. Managers (as well as everyone else) are constantly forced to make choices, to do one thing and not another. Cost – or more precisely, opportunity cost – is the most highly valued opportunity not chosen. Although money is the most frequently used measure of cost, it is not cost itself.

Although we may not recognize it as such, cost also pervades our everyday thought and conversation. When we say "that course is difficult" or "the sermon seemed endless" or "changes to the product design at this stage can't be made," we are really indicating something about the cost involved. If the preacher's extended commentary delayed the church picnic, the sermon was costly. Although complaints about excessive costs sometimes indicate an absolute limitation, more often they merely mean that the benefits of the activity are too small to justify the cost. Many people who "can't afford" a vacation actually have the money but do not wish to spend it on travel, and most students who find writing research papers "impossible" are simply not willing to put forth the necessary effort.

This chapter explores the meaning of cost in business, specifically, and in human behavior, generally. We begin by showing how the hidden costs of a choice often can explain seemingly irrational behavior. We then develop further the concept of marginal cost which, together with the related concepts of demand and supply, defines the limits of rational behavior, from personal activities such as painting and fishing to business decisions such as how much to produce.

In this and the following chapters, we use the cost analysis to make points that seem to defy common sense in business. For example, we show that a firm should not necessarily seek to produce at the level at which the average cost of production is minimized or the average revenue is maximized.

In conventional economic discussions of production costs, incentives are nowhere considered. This is the case because the "firm" is little more than a theoretical "black box" in which things happen somewhat mysteriously. MBA students who have taken an undergraduate course in microeconomics might remember that economics textbooks typically acknowledge that the "firm" is the basic production unit, but little or nothing is said of why the firm ever came into existence or, for that matter, what the firm *is*. As a consequence, we are told little about why firms do what they do (and don't do). There is nothing in conventional discussions that tells us about the role of real people in a firm.

How are firms to be distinguished from the markets they inhabit, especially in terms of the incentives people in firms and markets face? That question is seldom addressed (other than, perhaps, specifying that firms can be one of several legal forms, for example, proprietorships, partnerships, professional associations, or corporations). In conventional discussions of the "theory of the firm," firms maximize their profits, which is their only noted *raison d'être*. But students of conventional theory are never told how firms do what they are supposed to do, or why they do what they do.

The owners, presumably, devise ways to ensure that everyone in the organization follows instructions, all of which exist to squeeze every ounce of profit from every opportunity. Students are never told what the instructions are or what is done to ensure that workers follow them. The structure of incentives inside the firm never comes up because their purpose is effectively assumed away: people do what they are supposed to do, naturally or by some unspecified mysterious process.

For people in business (and MBA students), the conventional economist's approach to the "firm" must appear strange indeed, given that businesspeople spend much of their working day trying to coax people to do what they are supposed to do. Nothing is more problematic in business than getting employees to consistently devote their efforts to increasing their firms' profits (as opposed to devoting themselves to more personal concerns).

In Part A of this chapter, we start the development of a firm's cost structure by focusing on the critical issue of how much a firm should produce, *marginal cost.* Our development of a firm's cost structure will continue in chapter 8. We will use this cost structure in chapters 9 and 10 to determine how much firms in different markets facing different competitive pressures will produce to maximize profits.

In Part B of this chapter, we address the issue of *why firms exist.* This is not just an interesting academic question. Rather, the answer to this question can help us understand why the existence of firms and incentives go hand in hand. It can also help us understand production costs and the size and organization of firms, and why firms' cost structures are as they are drawn in Part A of this and the following chapter. Just how low a firm's costs are, and how profitable a firm is, will depend critically upon how well production is coordinated both inside and outside the firm. As we will see, firm size will affect its overall coordinating costs, as well as its organizational structure and features. This is to say that Part B of this and the following chapters provides practical guidance on how firms can minimize their cost structures, which is treated theoretically in Part A. We offer more practical guidance on cost control of a big-ticket item in many firms' cost structure – health insurance.

Part A Theory and public policy applications

Various cost conceptions

In this section, we begin the development of the cost *structures* of firms. We are not simply concerned with what a firm's costs are for a given output level and time period; a firm's accounting statements provide that information. Accounting statements are historical by construction, not conceptual. In this book we seek to develop the likely *structure* for a firm's costs over a wide range of output levels, which can help managers think about what output level they should choose.

Any MBA class includes students from a variety of industries that, of course, have different production costs. Our goal here is to devise a cost structure that is generally applicable to this wide range of industries, providing students with an analytical device that can be helpful in considering production decisions for any firm. We spotlight production decision rules that arise from merging our development of a firm's cost structure with the structure for demand in chapter 6. For purposes of effective communication, if nothing else, economists have identified a number of key cost concepts that will play important roles in the following analytics associated with the development of a firm's cost structure.

Explicit and implicit costs

Some costs are obvious: an out-of-pocket expenditure – the monthly price you pay for a product or service. This is called an **explicit cost**. For example, the price of your book is an explicit cost of taking a course in economics. Other costs are less immediately apparent. Such costs of the course might include the time spent going to class and studying, the risk of receiving a failing grade, and the discomfort of being confronted with material that may challenge some of your beliefs. These are **implicit costs**; together they add up to the value of what you could have done instead. Although implicit costs may not be recognized, they are often much larger than the more obvious explicit costs of an action.

> **Explicit cost** is the money expenditure required to obtain a resource, product or service.
> An **implicit cost** is the forgone opportunity to do or acquire something else or to put one's resources to another use that doesn't require a monetary payment.

"Sunk costs": why they don't matter

Then, there are some "costs" that are recognized on accounting statements that should not be considered in making business decisions. These costs are called "**sunk costs**." Accordingly, sunk costs should be ignored in decision making. This is because current decisions cannot alter costs that have already been incurred. Such costs are beyond the realm of choice.

> A **sunk cost** is a past cost. It is a cost that already has been incurred, which means it cannot be changed and, hence, is irrelevant to current decisions.

An example can help illustrate the irrelevance of sunk, or fixed, costs. Suppose an oil exploration firm purchases the mineral rights to a particular piece of property for $1 million which, for purposes of clarity in argument, we assume initially has no resale market. After several months of drilling, the firm concludes that the land contains no oil (or other valuable mineral resources). Will the firm reason that, having spent $1 million for the mineral rights, it should continue to look for oil on the land? If the chances of finding oil are nonexistent, the rational firm will cease drilling on the land and try somewhere else. The $1 million is a sunk cost that should not influence the decision to continue or cease exploration. Indeed, the firm may begin drilling on land for which it paid far less for the mineral rights, if management believes that the chances of finding oil are higher there than on the $1 million property.

The underlying reason that sunk costs do not matter to current production decisions is that the term "sunk costs" itself is misleading and something of a misnomer, since "sunk costs" are not really "costs" at all. The opportunity cost of an activity is the value of the best alternative not chosen. In the case of a historical cost, however, there are no longer any alternatives. Although the oil exploration firm at one time could have chosen an alternative way to spend the $1 million, after the money was spent the alternative ceased to be available. Nor can the firm resell the mineral rights for $1 million; those rights are now worth far less because of accumulated evidence that the land contains little or no valuable minerals. Sunk costs, however painful the memory of them might be, are gone and best forgotten. Profits are made by looking forward, not backward.

If the land can be sold, then there is a cost of using or just holding onto it. However, the cost that should be considered is not the $1 million purchase price, but rather its resale price, which could be far lower than the purchase price.

The cost of an education

A good illustration of the magnitude of implicit costs is the cost of an education. Suppose an executive or fully employed MBA student takes a course and pays $2,000 for tuition and $300 for books and other class materials. The money cost of the course is $2,300, but that figure does not include the implicit costs to the student. To take a course, the student must attend class for about thirty hours (on the quarter system) and may have to spend three times that much time traveling to and from class, completing class assignments, and studying for examinations. The total number of hours spent on any one course, then, might be 120.

The MBA student could have spent that time doing other things, including working for a money wage. If the student's time is valued at $40 per hour (the wage she might have received if working), the time cost of the course is $4,800 (120 hours × $40/hour). Moreover, if she experiences some anxiety because of taking the course, that psychic or risk cost must be added to the total as well. If she would be willing to pay $500 to avoid the anxiety, the total implicit cost of taking the course climbs to $5,300.

The implicit cost of the student's time represents the largest component of the total cost of the course, $7,600. The value of one's time varies from person to person.[1] The time cost also explains the popularity of executive MBA programs,

---

[1] For students who are unable to find work or have few productive skills, the time costs of taking a course may be quite small. That is why most college students are young. Their time cost is generally lower than that of experienced workers who must give up the opportunity to earn a good wage in order to attend classes full time.

which allow the students to do more of their work online and on weekends. By the same token, few CEOs of major corporations can be found in MBA programs of any type. Their explicit costs of the programs are much the same as everyone else's, but their implicit (time) costs are far higher, so much so that they have no hope of recovering their MBA investments. This is especially true since many CEOs are in their fifties and sixties and have only a few years left in their careers.

From a recognition of the opportunity cost involved in MBA education, it should not surprise anyone if applications to MBA programs run somewhat counter-cyclical. That is, applications to MBA programs tend to increase when the economy goes into a recession and decrease in recovery phases of the business cycles. During an economic downturn, people's opportunity costs go down with a decrease in business opportunities or, worse, unemployment. People's opportunity costs go up with a recovery.[2]

The cost of bargains

Every week, most supermarkets run large newspaper ads listing their weekly specials. Generally only a few items are offered at especially low prices, for store managers know that most bargain seekers can be attracted to the store with just a few carefully selected specials. After the customer has gone to the store that is offering a special on, say, steak, he would have to incur a travel cost to buy other items in a different store. Even though peanut butter may be on sale elsewhere, the sum of the sale price and the travel cost exceed the regular price in the first store. Through attractive displays and packaging, customers can be persuaded to buy many other goods not on sale, particularly toiletries, which tend to bear high markups. So stores manage to recoup some of the revenues lost on sale items by charging higher prices on other goods. In other words, the cost of a bargain on sirloin steak may be a high price for toothpaste.

Some shoppers make the rounds of the grocery stores when sales are announced. For such people, time and transportation are cheap. A person who values his or her time at $40 an hour is not going to spend an hour trying to save a dollar or two. The cost of gas alone can make it prohibitively expensive to visit several stores. Because of the costs of acquiring information, many shoppers do not even bother to look for sales. The expected benefits are simply not great enough to justify the information cost. These shoppers enter the market "rationally ignorant."

---

[2] The analysis must be qualified because people's incomes tend to fall and rise with an economic downturn and upturn, which means that an income effect can mute the opportunity-cost effect of the business cycle.

Normal profit as a cost

In accounting, profit is what is on the "bottom line" on profit and loss (P&L) or income statements, or the difference between recorded revenues and recorded expenses. However, some costs of doing business are never reported on a company's books. Three such frequently unrecorded costs are:

1 the opportunity cost of the firm's owner/manager (equal to the salary the owner/manager could have received elsewhere)
2 the opportunity cost of capital (the earnings that could have been received had the firm's owner invested his finance in some risk-free investment, say, a government bond)
3 the risk cost of doing business (or the expected losses from firm failure).

Even though these costs may not be recognized on a firm's books, they must be recovered in order for the firm to continue in business. These costs are called **normal profits** by economists. The "profit" reported by a firm on its P&L statement is called **book profits** by economists. Book profits can be more or less than normal profits.

> **Book profits** are the profits reported on firms' "bottom lines" of their P&L statements.
> **Normal profits** are the opportunity and risk costs of doing business not reported on firms' P&L statements that must be covered in order that the owners will not redeploy firm resources.

If book profits are less than normal profits, the firm is said to have incurred an **economic loss**. If book profits are greater than normal profits, the firm is said to make **economic profits**. The amount by which book profits exceed normal profits is economic profit. Economic profit is a return that is more than necessary to keep resources employed where they are.

> **Economic profits** are realized when firms' *total costs, including their unrecorded opportunity and risk costs*, are less than their total revenues.
> An **economic loss** occurs when firms' *total costs*, including their unrecorded opportunity and risk costs, exceed their total revenues.

Peter Drucker, a widely cited and respected management professor, once quipped that, "Few U.S. businesses have been profitable since World War II" (Drucker 2001, 117). Most readers may find such a statement hard to accept, and those who do believe it may interpret Drucker as talking about business failure. But Drucker was commenting about *economic profits* and, once that is understood, his statement can be seen as a comment on the success of the US economy. As Drucker wrote, "Until a business returns a profit that is greater than its cost of capital [opportunity cost], it operates at a loss ... The enterprise ... returns less to the economy than it uses up in resources" (2001, 117). On the other hand, if a lot of firms made large economic profits, it would also be a sign of failure of the economy – failure to reallocate resources to the profitable endeavors where the resources add more to the economy than they are adding where currently employed.

The special significance of marginal cost

So far, we have been considering cost as the determining factor in the decision to undertake a particular course of action. Obviously benefits are important as well. The rational person weighs the cost of an action against its benefits and comes to a decision: whether to invest in an education, to shop around for a bargain, or to learn how to fly. The question is, how much of a given good or service will an individual choose to produce or consume? How does cost limit a behavior after a person has decided to engage in it? The answer relies partially on the concepts of **marginal cost**.

Marginal cost is the additional cost incurred by producing one additional unit of a good, activity, or service.

We emphasize marginal cost in this chapter, but *marginal benefits* are just as critical to our production and consumption decisions, as will be discussed more fully in chapter 10.

Rational behavior and marginal cost

Marginal cost is the cost incurred by reading one additional page, making one additional friend, giving one additional gift, or going one additional mile. Depending on the good, activity, or service in question, marginal cost may stay the same or vary as additional units are produced. For example, imagine that Jan Smith wants to give Halloween candy to ten of her friends. In a sense, Jan is producing gifts by procuring bags of candy. If she can buy as many bags as she wants at a unit price of 50 cents, the marginal cost of each additional unit she buys is the same, 50 cents. The marginal cost is constant over the range of production.

However, marginal cost can vary with the level of output, for two reasons. First, the opportunity cost of time must be considered. Suppose Jan wants to give each friend a miniature watercolor, which she will paint herself over the course of the day. To make time for painting, Jan can forgo any of the various activities that usually make up her day. She may choose to give up recreational activities, gardening chores, or time spent at work or study.

If she behaves rationally, she will give up the activities she values least. To do the first painting, she may forgo laying soil on a bare spot in her lawn. The marginal cost of her first watercolor is therefore a lawn eyesore. To paint the second watercolor, Jan will give up the next more valuable item on her list of activities. As she produces more and more paintings, Jan will forgo more and more valuable alternatives. Hence, the marginal cost of her paintings will rise with her output.

If the marginal cost of each new painting is plotted against the quantity of paintings produced, a curve like that in figure 7.1 will result. Because the marginal cost of each additional painting is higher than the marginal cost of the last one, the curve slopes upward to the right. Although the marginal cost curve is generally assumed to slope upward, that need not be the case, as in the gifts of candy. In

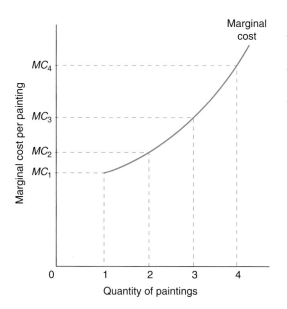

Figure 7.1 Rising marginal cost
To produce each new watercolor, Jan must give up an opportunity more valuable than the last. Thus the marginal cost of her paintings rises with each new work.

that example, Jan's marginal cost was constant and the marginal cost curve is horizontal.

The law of diminishing marginal returns

The second reason that marginal cost may vary with output involves a technological relationship known as the law of diminishing marginal returns. Under this "law," beyond some point, less output is received for each added unit of a resource used. Alternatively stated, more of the resource will be required to produce the same amount of output as before. Beyond some point, the marginal cost of additional units of output rises.

> The **law of diminishing marginal returns** states that as more and more units of one resource – labor, fertilizer, or any other resource – are applied to a fixed quantity of another resource – land, for instance – the increase in total added output gained from each additional unit of the variable resource will eventually begin to diminish.

Although the law of diminishing marginal returns applies to any production process, its meaning can be easily grasped in the context of agricultural production. Assume that you are producing tomatoes. You have a fixed amount of land (an acre) but can vary the quantity of labor you apply to it. If you try to do planting all by yourself – dig the holes, pour the water, insert the plants, and cover up the roots – you will waste time changing tools. If a friend helps you, you can divide the tasks and specialize. Less time will be wasted in changing tools.

The time you would have spent changing tools can be spent planting more tomatoes, thus increasing the harvest. At first, output may expand faster than the labor force. That is, one laborer may be able to plant one hundred tomatoes an hour; two working together may be able to plant two hundred and fifty an hour. Thus the marginal cost of planting the additional one hundred and fifty plants is lower than the cost of the first hundred. Up to a point, the more workers, the greater their efficiency and the lower the marginal cost – all because of the economies of specialization. At some point, however, the addition of another laborer will not contribute as much to production as did adding the previous one, if only because workers begin bumping into one another. The point of diminishing marginal returns has been reached and the marginal cost of putting plants into the ground will begin to rise.

Diminishing marginal returns are an inescapable fact of life. If marginal returns did not diminish at some point, and eventually become negative (adding another laborer actually reduces output), output would expand indefinitely and the world's food supply could be grown on just one acre of land. (For that matter, it could be grown in a flower box.) If more labor can be added to a fixed quantity of land, then the labor/land ratio goes up, giving rise to an increase in total output. The thinking can be reversed: the output can be increased by increasing the labor/land ratio, which can be accomplished with a reduction in land.

Since we know that the world's food supply can't be grown on an acre of land (or in a flower box), diminishing marginal returns must be observed eventually as more labor is added to the fixed resource, in this case land. However, we need to note that the point at which output begins to diminish varies from one production process to the next, but eventually all marginal cost curves will slope upward to the right, as in figure 7.1.

Table 7.1 shows the marginal cost of producing tomatoes with various numbers of workers, assuming that each worker is paid $5 and that production is limited to one acre. Working alone, one worker can produce a quarter of a bushel; two can produce a full bushel, and so on (columns [1] and [2]). Column (3) shows the amount that each additional worker adds to total production, called the marginal product. The first worker contributed 0.25 (one quarter) of a bushel; the second worker, an additional 0.75 of a bushel, and so on. These are the marginal products of successive units of labor.

> Marginal product is the increase in total output that results when one additional unit of a resource – for example, labor, fertilizer, and land – is added to the production process, everything else held constant.

The important information is shown in columns (4) and (5) of table 7.1. Although two workers are needed to produce the first bushel (column [4]), the efficiencies of specialization require only one additional worker to produce the second bushel. Beyond that point, however, marginal returns diminish. Each additional worker contributes less, so two more workers are needed to produce the third bushel and five more to produce the fourth. If table 7.1 were extended, each bushel beyond the fourth would require a progressively larger number of workers and eventually additional workers would begin reducing output.

Table 7.1 Marginal costs of producing tomatoes

No. of workers employed	Total no. of bushels	Contribution of each worker to production (marginal product)	No. of workers required to produce each additional bushel	Marginal cost of each bushel, at $5 per worker
(1)	(2)	(3)	(4)	(5)
1	0.25	0.25 } (1st bushel)		
2	1.00	0.75 }	2	$10
3	2.00	1.00 (2nd bushel)	1	$5
Point at which diminishing marginal returns emerge				
4	2.60	0.60 } (3rd bushel)		
5	3.00	0.40 }	2	$10
6	3.30	0.30		
7	3.55	0.25		
8	3.75	0.20 (4th bushel)		
9	3.90	0.15		
10	4.00	0.10	5	$25

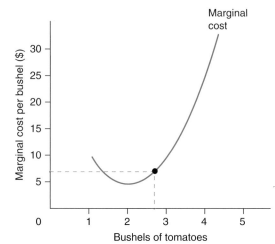

Figure 7.2 The law of diminishing marginal returns
As production expands with the addition of new workers, efficiencies of specialization initially cause marginal cost to fall. At some point, however – here, just beyond two bushels – marginal cost will begin to rise again. At that point, marginal returns will begin to diminish and marginal costs will begin to rise.

Column (5) shows that if all workers are paid the same wage, $5, the marginal cost of a bushel of tomatoes will decline from $10 for the first bushel to $5 for the second before rising to $10 again for the third bushel. That is, increasing marginal costs (or diminishing returns) emerge with the addition of the third worker, and continue to increase, going to $25 for the fourth bushel.

If the marginal cost of each bushel (column [5]) is plotted against the number of bushels harvested, a curve such as that in figure 7.2 will result. Although the curve slopes downward at first, for most purposes the relevant segment of the curve is a major part of the upward sloping portion of what will be, for most industries, a U-shaped marginal cost curve (as is explained in detail later).

In following chapters, we will make the point that while firms may not experience diminishing returns as output is initially expanded, profit-maximizing firms will tend to produce in the output range where diminishing returns are experienced with increases in output levels. This means that they will tend to produce in an output range where marginal cost of production is on the increase, which explains why market supply curves in competitive markets tend to be upward sloping, as drawn in all previously used supply-and-demand-curve graphs. It also means that if firms are not experiencing increasing marginal costs in their current output range, then they should expand output until at least increasing marginal costs set in. Before such points can be seen with clarity, we need to advance the analytics in significant ways. We introduce these points here to emphasize that the analytics have a purpose in the workplace, although they can get tedious at times.

 [See online Video Module 7.1 Marginal cost.]

The cost–benefit trade-off

Just as a producer's marginal cost schedule shows the increasing marginal cost of supplying more goods, so does the demand curve (as explained earlier) show the decreasing marginal value or marginal benefit of those goods to the consumers. Together, marginal costs and benefits determine the amount of production and consumption that creates the greatest net value. Producers and consumers gain from both producing and consuming more of a good as long as the marginal cost of producing it is less than the marginal value of consuming it. That is, there are additional gains to be had from increasing production and consumption until the marginal cost curve intersects the marginal benefit curve for the good. The intersection of the two curves represents the point where welfare is maximized. To demonstrate this point, we consider the costs and benefits of an activity such as fishing.

The costs and benefits of fishing

Assume that Gary likes to fish. What he does with the fish he catches is of no consequence to our discussion; he can make them into trophies, give them away, or store them in the freezer. Even if Gary places no money value on the fish, we can use dollars to illustrate the marginal costs and benefits of fishing to Gary. (Money figures are not values but rather a means of indicating relative value.)

What is important is that Gary wants to fish. How many fish will he catch? From our earlier analysis of Jan's desire to paint, we know that the cost of catching each additional fish will be higher than the cost of the one before. Gary will confront an

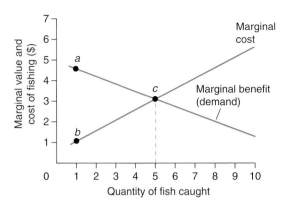

Figure 7.3 Costs and benefits of fishing
For each fish up to the fifth one, Gary receives more in benefits than he pays in costs. The first fish gives him $4.67 in benefits (point a) and costs him only $1 (point b). The fifth yields equal costs and benefits (point c), but the sixth costs more than it is worth. Therefore, Gary will catch no more than five fish.

upward sloping marginal cost curve like that in figure 7.2. Gary's demand curve for fishing will slope downward (see figure 7.3) because as he catches more fish over some period of time (say, a day) the marginal value he receives from catching fish will eventually start declining.

From the positions of the two curves, we can see that Gary will catch up to five fish before he packs up his rod and heads for home. He places a relatively high value of $4.67 on the first fish (point a in figure 7.3) and figures that the first fish caught has a relatively low marginal cost of $1 (point b) – the value of the forgone opportunities. In other words, he gets $3.67 more value from using his time, energy, and other resources to catch the first fish than he would receive from his next best alternative. The marginal benefit of the second fish also exceeds its marginal cost, although by a small amount ($4.25 – $2.75=$1.50). Gary continues to gain with the third and fourth fishes, but the fifth fish is a matter of indifference to him. Its marginal value equals its marginal cost (point c). Although we cannot say that Gary will actually bother to catch a fifth fish, we do know that five is the limit toward which he will aim. He will not catch a sixth – at least during the period of time offered by the graph – because it would cost him more than he would receive in benefits.

The costs and benefits of preventing accidents

All of us would prefer to avoid accidents. In that sense, we have a demand for accident prevention, whose curve should slope downward as do all other demand curves. We benefit more from trying to prevent the most likely and harmful accidents before trying to prevent those that are less likely and harmful. Preventing accidents also entails costs, however, whether in time, forgone opportunities, or money. Should we attempt to prevent all accidents? No. Eventually the cost of preventing an accident is greater than the expected benefit from doing so. Would you spend $10,000 to prevent an occasional paper cut from opening the mail?

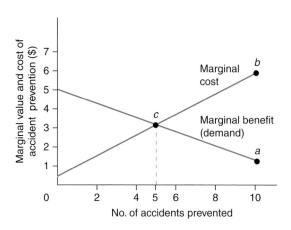

Figure 7.4 Accident prevention
Given the increasing marginal cost of preventing accidents and the decreasing marginal value of preventing the accidents, *c* or five accidents will be prevented.

As with the question of how long to fish, marginal cost and benefit curves can help illustrate the point at which preventing accidents ceases to be cost-effective. Suppose that Al Rosa's experience indicates that he can expect to have ten accidents over the course of the year. If he tries to prevent all of them, the value of preventing the last one, as indicated by the demand curve in figure 7.4, will be only $1 (point *a*). The marginal cost of preventing it will be much greater: approximately $6 (point *b*). If Al is rational, he will not try to prevent the last accident. As a matter of fact, he will try to prevent only five accidents (point *c*). As with the tenth accident, it will cost more than it is worth to Al to prevent the sixth through ninth accidents. He would try to prevent all ten accidents only if his demand for accident prevention were so great that his demand curve intersected, or passed over, the marginal cost curve at point *b*.

Some accidents may be unavoidable. In that case, the marginal cost curve will eventually become vertical. Other accidents may be "avoidable" in the sense that it is physically possible to take measures to prevent them – although the rational course may be to allow them to happen.

Price and marginal cost: producing to maximize profits

Production is not generally an end in itself in business. Most firms seek to make a profit. We can usefully consider how firms go about the task of trying to maximize profits by converting the total and marginal product curves into *cost curves*. By doing so we can engage in familiar marginal cost/marginal benefit analyses.

Granted, many businesspeople derive intrinsic reward from their work. They may value the satisfaction of producing a product that meets a human need just as much as they value the profits that they earn. Some businesspeople may even accept lower profits so that their products can sell at lower prices and serve more people. For

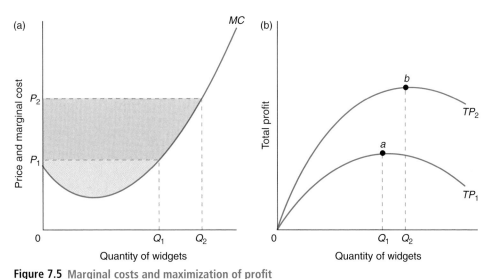

Figure 7.5 Marginal costs and maximization of profit

At price P_1 (panel [a]), this firm's marginal revenue, represented by the area under P_1 up to Q_1, exceeds its marginal cost up to the output level of Q_1. At that point total profit, shown in panel (b), peaks (point a). At price P_2, marginal revenue exceeds marginal cost up to an output level of Q_2. The increase in price shifts the profit curve in panel (b) upward, from TP_1 to TP_2, and profits peak at b.

most, however, the profit generated by sales is the major motivation for doing business. So it is useful as a first approximation to assume that firms maximize profits. In fact, firms that do not maximize profits will be subject to takeover by entrepreneurs seeking to buy firms at depressed prices, institute profit-making policies, and then sell the firms at a higher price.

How much will a profit-maximizing firm produce? Assume that its marginal cost curve is like that in figure 7.5(a), and that the owners can sell as many units as they want at a price of P_1. The price of its product, P_1, can be thought of as the marginal benefit the firm receives for each unit sold, or P_1 is the firm's marginal revenue. Each time the firm sells one additional unit, its revenues rise by P_1.

> **Marginal revenue** is the additional revenue that a firm acquires by selling another unit of output.

Clearly, a profit-maximizing firm will produce and sell any unit for which the marginal revenue (MR) exceeds the marginal cost (MC). (Profits are the difference between total costs and total revenues; therefore, a firm's profits rise whenever an increase in revenues exceeds the increase in its costs.) At a price of P_1, then, this firm will produce up to, and no more than, Q_1 units of its product. For every unit up to Q_1, price (or marginal revenue) is greater than marginal cost, and for every unit beyond Q_1, the marginal revenue is less than marginal cost.

The vertical distance between P_1 and the marginal cost of each unit, as shown by the marginal cost curve, is the additional profit obtained from each additional unit produced. By taking the difference between the vertical distance P_1 and vertical distance on the marginal cost curve for all units up to Q_1, we can obtain the firm's total profits from producing Q_1; see the dark shaded area in figure 7.5(a). Total profits can also be represented as a curve, as in the line TP_1 in figure 7.5(b). Notice that the curve peaks at Q_1, the point at which the firm chooses to stop producing. Since, beyond Q_1, marginal cost is greater than marginal revenue, total profits fall, as shown by the downward slope of the total profits curve.

What will the firm do if the price of its product rises from P_1 to P_2? For the firm that can sell all it wants at a constant price, a rise in price means a rise in marginal revenue. After the price rises to P_2, the marginal revenue of an additional $Q_2 - Q_1$ units exceeds their marginal cost. At the higher price, a larger number of units can be profitably produced and sold. The firm will seek to produce up to the point at which marginal cost equals the new, higher marginal revenue, P_2, or output, Q_2, in figure 7.5(a). As before, profit is equal to the vertical distance between the price line, P_2, and the marginal cost curve, or the dark-shaded area plus the light-shaded area in figure 7.5(a). The total profit curve shifts to the position of the line TP_2 in figure 7.5(b).

From individual supply to market supply

The upward sloping portion of the firm's marginal cost curve is its supply curve – for each price, the amount the firm will supply is given by the firm's marginal cost at that price. (More will be said about this in chapter 7.) If the market supply is the amount all producers are willing to produce at various prices, we can obtain the market supply curve by adding together the upward sloping portions of the individual firms' marginal cost curves. (This procedure resembles the one followed in determining the market demand curve in chapter 6.)

Figure 7.6 shows the supply curves S_A and S_B, derived from the marginal cost curves of two producers, A and B. At a price of P_1, only producer B is willing to produce anything, and it is willing to offer only Q_1. The total quantity supplied to the market at P_1 is therefore Q_1. At the higher prices of P_2, however, both producers are willing to compete. Producer A offers Q_1, whereas producer B offers more, Q_2. The total quantity supplied is therefore Q_3, the sum of Q_1 and Q_2.

The market supply curve, S_{A+B}, is obtained by adding the amounts that A and B are willing to sell at each price and splitting the totals. Note that the market supply curve lies further from the origin and is flatter than the individual producers' supply curves. The entry of more producers will shift the market supply curve further out and lower its slope even more. (More will be said about cost and supply in later chapters.)

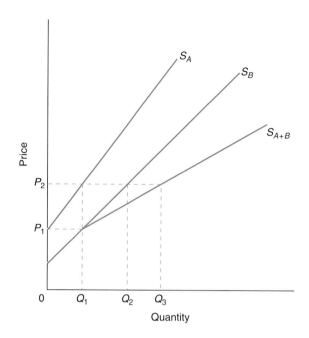

Figure 7.6 Market supply curve
The market supply curve (S_{A+B}) is obtained by adding together the amount producers A and B are willing to offer at each and every price, as shown by the individual supply curves S_A and S_B. (The individual supply curves are obtained from the upward sloping portions of the firms' marginal cost curve.)

For an explanation for the existence of the corporate form of business organization, see online Perspective 7, A reason for corporations: cost savings.

> **Online Perspective 7**
> A reason for corporations:
> cost savings

Part B Organizational economics and management

Production costs and firms' size and organizational structure

In Part A of the chapter, we assumed the "firm" exists with the intent to economize on resources, which leads the firm to equate marginal cost with marginal benefit (or marginal revenue). Given the alternative ways of organizing production, there must be some efficiency advantage to production through firms, or else firms would not arise and survive in a market economy. This is to say that firms enable owners to press their cost curves down as far as they can go.

Management of firms to contain costs is not as simple as it might seem. As we will see, there are ever-present problems associated with "principal–agent conflicts" and "opportunistic behaviors" (terms that will be defined carefully) that managers must control. To contain costs, firms face decisions to make products inside or to out-source. Firms must also consider how their organization structures will affect production costs, and firms must figure out how best to contain an ever-present, nontrivial source of excessive costs, "opportunistic behavior" of workers, suppliers, and buyers (to be explained). In online Perspective 7, we consider the question of why so many medium- and large-size firms are organized as corporations (not as partnerships and proprietorships). In the online Readings for this chapter, we take up additional issues:

Online Perspective

R

- Reading 7.1 The last-period problem
- Reading 7.2 The franchise decision
- Reading 7.3 Cutting health care costs through medical savings accounts.

First, however, we must address the seemingly innocuous, but important question of why "firms" exist in the first place.

Firms and market efficiency

Why is it that firms add to the efficiency of markets? That is an intriguing question, especially given how much of standard economic theory trumpets the superior efficiency of markets. Students of conventional theory might rightfully wonder: if markets are so efficient, why do so many entrepreneurs go to the trouble of organizing firms? Why not just have everything done by way of markets, with little or nothing actually done (in the sense that things are "made") inside firms? All of the firm's inputs could be bought instead by individuals, with each individual adding value to the inputs she purchases and then selling this result to another individual, who adds more value, and so on until a final product is produced and a final market is reached, at which point the completed product is sold to consumers.

Individuals, as producers relying exclusively on markets, could always take the least costly bid. They could also keep their options open, including the option of immediately switching to new suppliers who propose better deals. No one would be tied down to internal sources of supply for their production needs. They would not have to incur the considerable costs of organizing themselves into production teams and departments and various levels of management. They would not have to incur the costs of internal management and having to deal with the Prisoner's Dilemma of shirking workers. They could, so to speak, maintain a great deal of freedom!

So why do firms exist? More to the point, if markets are so efficient in getting things done, why do less than 30 percent of all transactions in the United States occur through markets, which means that more than 70 percent of transactions are made through firms (McMillan 2002, 168–9)? Some economists have speculated that firms exist because of the *economies of specialization* of resources, a key one being labor. Clearly, Adam Smith and many of his followers were correct when they observed that when tasks are divided among a number of workers, the workers become more proficient at what they do and can produce more during work hours. Smith began his economics classic *The Wealth of Nations* by writing about how specialization of labor increased "pin" (really, nail) production (Smith 1937, 4–12). By specializing, workers also don't have to waste time changing tasks, leaving more time to be spent directly on production.

Although efficiency improvements can certainly result from specialization of any resource, especially labor, Smith was wrong to conclude that firms were *necessary* to coordinate the workers' separate tasks. This error is clear because, as economists have long recognized, the pricing system within markets could coordinate workers' separate tasks. Conceivably, markets could exist even within the stages of production that are held together by, say, assembly lines. The person who produces soles in a shoe factory could buy the leather and then sell the completed soles to the shoe assemblers. The bookkeeping services provided to a shoe factory by its accounting department could easily be bought on the market (and many firms do buy their accounting services from accounting firms). Similarly, all the intermediate goods involved in Smith's pin production could be bought and sold until the completed pins were sold to those who want them.

What is the incentive – the driving force – behind firms? For that matter, what is a *firm* in the first place? Law and economics professor Ronald Coase, on whose classic work, "The nature of the firm," much of this chapter is based and from which many of the particular arguments are drawn, proposed a substantially new but deceptively simple explanation (see also Coase 1988, chapter 2). Coase reasoned that the *firm* is any organization that supersedes the pricing system, in which hierarchy and methods of command and control are substituted for exchanges. To use his exact words: "A firm, therefore, consists of the system of relationships which comes into existence when the direction of resources is dependent on an entrepreneur" (1988, 41–2).[3]

---

[3] Similarly, Herbert Simon (1951) argued that a firm replaces market bargaining with command and control hierarchies but stressed that the inability of anyone to foresee the ever-changing array of tasks that need to be done and the high cost of renegotiating contracts under changing market conditions necessitated management control over subordinates.

Through the years, economists have tendered various reasons for the existence of firms,[4] and there are probably many reasons people might think firms exist, several of which Coase dismisses for being wrongheaded or unimportant (1988, 41–2).[5] What Coase was interested in, however, was not a catalog of "small" explanations for this or that firm, but an explanation for the existence of virtually all firms. And in his 1937 article, he struck upon an unbelievably simple explanation, but one so insightful that it earned him the Nobel Prize in Economics, more than a half-century later!

Reasons for firms

How did Coase explain the existence of firms? Simply put, he observed that there are costs of dealing in markets. He dubbed these *marketing costs*, but most economists now call them *transaction costs*. Whatever they are called, these costs include the time and resources that must be devoted to organizing economic activity through markets. Transaction costs include the real economic costs of discovering the best deals as evaluated in terms of prices and attributes of products, negotiating contracts, and enforcing the terms of the contract. One could imagine the terribly time-consuming process of organizing shoe production through markets, especially if the suppliers and producers at the various stages were constantly looking for new people to deal with, constantly negotiating new agreements, and constantly subject to replacement by competitors.

---

[4] According to Frank Knight (1921), if business were conducted in a totally certain world, there would be no need for firms. Workers would know their pattern of rewards, and no need would exist for anyone to specialize in the acceptance of the costs of dealing with the risks and uncertainties that abound in the real world of business. As it is, according to Knight, some workers are willing to work for firms because of the type of deal that is struck: the workers accept a reduction in their expected pay in order to reduce the variability and outright uncertainty of that pay. Entrepreneurs are willing to make such a bargain with their workers because their workers effectively pay them to do so (through accepting a reduction in pay) and because, by making similar bargains with a host of workers, the employers can reduce their exposure to the risk and uncertainties individual workers face.

[5] For example, Coase concedes that some people might prefer to be directed in their work. As a consequence, they might accept lower pay just to be told what to do. However, Coase dismisses this explanation as unlikely to be important because "it would rather seem that the opposite tendency is operating if one judges from the stress normally laid on the advantage of 'being one's own master'" (1988, 38). Of course, it might be that some people like to control others, meaning that they would give up a portion of their pay to have other people follow their direction. However, again Coase finds such an explanation lacking, mainly because it could not possibly be true "in the majority of the cases" (1988, 38). People who direct the work of others are frequently paid a premium for their efforts.

Once the costs of market activity are recognized, the reason for the emergence of the firm is transparent: firms, which substitute internal direction for markets, arise because they *reduce the need for making market transactions*. Firms lower the costs that accompany market transactions. If internal direction were not, at times and up to some point, more cost-effective than markets, then no one would have an incentive to create a firm. Although firms will never eliminate the need for markets, neither will markets ever eliminate the need for the internal direction of firms.

Entrepreneurs and their hired workers essentially substitute one long-term contract for a series of short-term contracts: The workers agree to accept directions from the entrepreneurs (or their agents or managers) within certain broad limits (with the exact limits varying from firm to firm) in exchange for security and a level of welfare (including pay) that is higher than the workers would be able to receive in the market without firms. Similarly, the entrepreneurs (or their agents) agree to share with the workers some of the efficiency gains obtained from reducing transaction costs.[6]

The firm is a viable economic institution because *both sides to the contract –* owners and workers – gain. Firms can be expected to proliferate in markets simply because of the mutually beneficial deals that can be made. Those entrepreneurs who refuse to operate within firms and stick solely to market-based contracts, when in fact a firm's hierarchical organization is more cost-effective than are market-based organizations, will simply be outcompeted for resources by the firms that do form and achieve the efficiency-improving deals with workers (and owners of other resources).

If firms reduce transaction costs, does it follow that one giant firm should span the entire economy, as, say, Lenin and his followers thought was possible for the Soviet Union? Our intuition says, "No!" But aside from mere intuition, sound reasons exist for limiting the size of firms.

Cost limits to firm size

Clearly, by organizing activities under the "umbrella" of firms, entrepreneurs give up some of the benefits of markets, which provide competitively delivered goods and services. Managers suffer from their own limited organizational skills, and

---

[6] Coase recognizes that entrepreneurs could overcome some of the costs of repeatedly negotiating and enforcing short-term contracts by devising one long-term contract; however, as the time period over which a contract is in force is extended, more and more unknowns are covered, which implies that the contract must allow for progressively greater flexibility for the parties to the contract. The firm is, in essence, a substitute for such a long-term contract in that it covers an indefinite future and provides for flexibility. That is to say, the firm as a legal institution permits workers to exit more or less at will and gives managers the authority, within bounds, to change the directives given to workers.

skilled managers are scarce, as evidenced by the relatively high salaries they command. Communication problems within firms expand as firms grow, encompassing more activities, more levels of production, and more diverse products. Because many people may not like to take direction, the firm, as it expands to include more people, may have to pay progressively higher prices to workers and other resource owners in order to draw them into the firm and then direct them.

There are, in short, limits to what can be done through organizations. These limits cannot always be overcome, except at costs that exceed the benefits of doing so. Even with the application of the best organizational techniques, whether through the establishment of teams, through the empowerment of employees, or through the creation of new business and departmental structures (for example, relying on top-down, bottom-up, or participatory decision making), firms are limited in their ability to reduce organizational costs.

The agency problem

Firms are restricted in their size because they suffer from what is called the **agency problem** (or, alternatively, the **principal–agent problem**), considered and reconsidered often in this book. This problem is easily understood as a conflict of interests between identifiable individuals and groups within firms. The entrepreneurs or owners of firms (the *principals*) organize firms to pursue their (the principals') own interest, which is often (but, admittedly, not always) seeking greater profits. To pursue profits, however, the entrepreneurs (or shareholders)

> The **agency (or principal–agent) problem** inside firms is the conflict of interest between owners (principals) of firms and their hired employees (agents) that emerges because both want to maximize their own gain from the use of firm resources.

must hire managers who then hire workers (all of whom are *agents*). However, the interests of the worker/agents are not always compatible with the interests of the owner/principals. Indeed, they are often in direct conflict.

Principals face the problem of getting the agents to work diligently to serve the principals' interests (which is the business problem that Adam Smith recognized in the 1770s [1937, 700]). Needless to say, agents often resist doing the principals' bidding, a fact that makes it difficult – costly – for the principals to achieve their goals.

Many of these conflicts can be resolved through contracts; however, as with all business arrangements, contracts have serious limitations, not the least of which is that they cannot be all-inclusive, covering all aspects of even "simple" business relationships. Contracts simply cannot anticipate and cover all possible ways that the parties to the contract can get around specific provisions, if they are so inclined. Enforcing contracts can be problematic, and represents an added cost, even when both parties know that provisions have been violated. Each party will recognize these enforcement costs and may be tempted to exploit them, assuming that the other is equally tempted. Ideally, contracts will be *self-enforcing* – that is, the provisions of the contracts encourage each party to live up to the letter and spirit of the contract because it is in each party's interest to do so. This is where incentives will come in, helping to make contracts as self-enforcing as possible, though they can seldom be perfectly self-enforcing. Incentives can encourage the parties to follow more faithfully the intent and letter of contracts.

Competition serves as a powerful force in minimizing agency costs. Firms in competitive markets that are not able to control agency costs are not likely to survive for long, mainly because of the "market for corporate control" (Manne 1963). Firms that allow agency costs to get out of hand risk either failure or takeover (by way of proxy fights, tender offers, or mergers). In chapters 7, 8, 9, and 11, we discuss at length how managers can solve their own agency problems, including controlling their own behavior as agents for shareholders. At the same time, market pressures compel managers to solve such problems, even if they are not naturally inclined to do so. If corporations are not able to adequately solve their agency problems, we can imagine that the corporate form of doing business will be "eclipsed" as new forms of business emerge (according to Jensen 1989). Of course, this means that obstruction in the market for corporate control (for example, legal impediments to takeovers) can translate into greater agency costs and less efficient corporate governance. This also suggests why both firms and markets are needed if we are to fully benefit from either one.

Why are firms the sizes they are? When economists in or out of business address that question, the usual answer relates to **economies of scale**. In some industries, it is indeed true that as more and more of all resources are added to production within a given firm, output expands in percentage terms by more than the use of resources. That is to say, if resource use expands by 10 percent and output expands by 15 percent, then the firm experiences economies of scale, that is, its (long-run) average cost of production declines. Why does that happen? The answer that is almost always given is "technology," which is another way of saying that it "just happens," given what is known about combining inputs and getting output. This is not the most satisfying explanation, but it is nonetheless true that economies of scale are available in some industries (steel and automobile) but not so much in others (beauty shops and music composition).

> **Economies of scale** are the cost savings that emerge when all resource inputs – labor, land, and capital – are increased together.

We agree that the standard approach toward explaining firm size is instructive. We have spent long hours at our classroom overhead projectors with markers in hand developing and describing scale economies in the typical fashion of professors, using (long-run) average cost curves and pointing out when firms should contemplate starting a new plant. We think the standard approach (which we take up in some detail in chapter 9) is useful, but we also believe it leaves out a lot of interesting forces at work on managers within firms. This is understandable, given that standard economic theory assumes away the roles of managers, which we intend to discuss at length.

Coase and his followers have taken a dramatically different tack in explaining why firms are the sizes they are in terms of scale of operations and scope of products delivered to market. The new breed of theorists pays special attention to the difficulties managers face as they seek to expand the scale and scope of the firm. They posit that as a firm expands, *agency costs* increase. This happens primarily because workers (including managers) have more and more opportunities to engage in *opportunistic behavior* – or taking advantage of their position for personal gain at the expense of the firm's profits (and therefore at the expense of the firm's owners). *Shirking*, or not working with due diligence, is one form of opportunistic behavior that is known to all employees. Theft of firm resources is another form. Employees politicking their bosses for advancement or choice assignments and their selectively using firm and market information to make the case for their advancement or reassignment are other common forms of opportunistic behavior that can drive up agency costs and the need for more monitoring costs.[7] ("Opportunistic behavior" is further developed in the online Reading 7.1 for this chapter under the so-called "last-period problem" that emerges when firms are about to close down. Briefly, just before a supplier closes due to an unannounced but pending bankruptcy filing, that supplier might be tempted to act opportunistically by taking payment for an order but then close before the order is filled. We outline the various ways firms seek to solve the last-period problems they face, a discussion that advances a major theme of this book: "problems" beg for solutions if for no other reason than that problems often mean that profits can be had from solving them.)

As the firm grows, the contributions of the individual worker become less detectable, which means that workers have progressively fewer incentives to work diligently on behalf of firm objectives or to do what they are told by their superiors. They can more easily hide.

The tendency for larger size to undercut the incentives of participants in any group is not just theoretical speculation. It has been observed in closely monitored experiments. In a still relevant experiment conducted more than a half-century ago,

Check this out for test

R

---

[7] One way firms have attempted to control employee politicking (or internal "rent seeking") has been to develop well-defined rules and procedures for salary increases and promotions, relying on measures – say, seniority – that may have little connection to workers' relative productivity. Having seniority determining outcome may impair workers' incentive to work harder and smarter for the firm, but seniority can also reduce the incentive for workers to waste resources in internal politicking (Roberts 2004, chapter 3).

a German scientist asked workers to pull on a rope connected to a meter that would measure the effort expended. Total effort for *all* workers *combined* increased as workers were added to the group doing the pulling. Simultaneously, the *individual* efforts of the workers declined. When three workers pulled on the rope, the individual effort averaged 84 percent of the effort expended by one worker. With eight workers pulling, the average individual effort was half the effort of the one worker (Furnham 1993). Hence, group size and individual effort were – as they are in most group circumstances – inversely related.

The problem is that each worker's incentive to expend effort deteriorates as the group expands. Each person's effort counts for less in the context of the larger group, a point that Mancur Olson (1971) elaborated upon in the 1970s (see chapter 2). The "common objectives" of the group become less and less compelling in directing individual efforts. Such a finding means that if each worker added to the group must be paid the same as all others, the cost of additional production obviously rises with the size of the working group. The finding also implies that to get a constant increase in effort with the additional workers, all workers must be given greater incentive to hold to their previous level of effort.[8]

Optimum-size firms

The optimum size of a firm depends on more than technology-based economies of scale. Technology determines what *might* be done, but not what *is* done. And what is done depends on policies that minimize shirking and maximize workers' use of the technology. This means that scale economies depend as much or more on what happens within any given firm as they do on what is technologically possible. The size of the firm obviously depends on the extent to which owners must incur greater monitoring costs and additional layers of hierarchy as the firm's size increases (a point well developed by Williamson [1967] in a classic article in organizational economics).

Management information system theorists Vijay Gurbaxani and Seungjin Whang (1991) have devised a graphical means of illustrating the "optimal firm size" as the consequence of two opposing cost forces: "internal coordinating costs" and "external coordinating costs." As a firm expands, its internal coordinating costs are likely to increase. This is because the firm's hierarchical pyramid will likely become larger with more and more decisions made at the top by managers who are further and further removed from the local information available to workers at the bottom of the

---

[8] Workers can also reason that if the residual from their added effort goes to the firm owners, they can possibly garner some of the residual by collusively (by explicit or tacit means) restricting their effort and hiking their rate of pay, which means that the incentive system must seek to undermine such collusive agreements (FitzRoy and Kraft 1987).

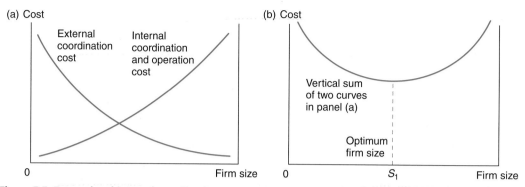

Figure 7.7 External and internal coordinating costs

As the firm expands, the internal coordinating costs increase as the external coordinating costs fall. The optimum firm size is determined by summing these two cost structures, which is done in panel (b) of the figure.

pyramid. There is a need to process information up and down the pyramid. When the information goes up, there are unavoidable problems and, hence, costs – costs of communication, costs of miscommunication, and opportunity costs associated with delays in communication – all of which can lead to suboptimal decisions. These "decision information costs" become progressively greater as the decision rights are moved up the pyramid.

Attempts to rectify the decision costs by delegating decision making to the lower ranks may help, but this can – and *will* – also introduce another form of costs, those that we previously referred to as *agency costs*. These include the cost of monitoring (managers actually watching employees as they work or checking their production) and bonding (workers providing assurance that the tasks or services will be done as the agreement requires), and the loss of the residual gains (or profits) through worker shirking, which we covered in chapter 2.

Managers must balance the decision information costs with agency costs and find a location for decision rights that minimizes the two forms of costs. From this perspective, where the decision rights are located will depend heavily on the amount of information flow per unit of time. When upward flow of information is high, the decision rights will tend to be located toward the floor of the firm, mainly because the costs of suboptimal decisions by having the decision making done high up the hierarchy can be considerable. The firm, in other words, can afford to tolerate agency costs because the costs of avoiding them, via centralized decisions, can be higher.

Nevertheless, as the firm expands, we should expect the internal coordinating costs (both the decision information cost and the agency cost) along with the cost of operations to increase. The upward sloping line in figure 7.7 depicts this relationship.

But internal costs are not all that matter to a firm contemplating an expansion. It must also consider the cost of the market, or what Gurbaxani and Whang (1991) call "external coordination costs." If the firm remains "small" and buys many of its parts, supplies, and services (such as accounting, legal, and advertising services) from outside vendors, then it must consider the resulting "transaction costs." These include the costs of transportation, inventory holding, communication and contract writing, monitoring, and enforcing. However, as the firm expands in size, these transaction costs should be expected to diminish. After all, as a firm becomes larger it will have eliminated those market transactions with the highest transaction costs. The downward sloping line in figure 7.7(a) depicts this inverse relationship between firm size and transaction costs.

Again, how large should a firm be? If a firm vertically integrates, it will engage in fewer market transactions, lowering its transaction costs. It can also benefit from technical economies of scale (or increases in productivity that lead to costs rising less rapidly than production as all factors of production are increased). However, in the process of expanding, it will confront growing internal coordination costs, or all the problems of trying to move information up the decision-making chain, getting the "right" decisions, and then preventing people from exploiting their decision-making authority to their own advantage.

The firm should stop expanding in scale and scope when the total of the two types of costs – external and internal coordinating costs – are minimized. This minimum can be shown graphically by summing the two curves in figure 7.7(a) to obtain the U-shaped curve in figure 7.7(b). The *optimal* (or most efficient/cost-effective) firm size is at the bottom of the U.

This way of thinking about firm size would have only limited interest if it did not lend itself to additional observations about the location, shape, and changes in the curve. First, the exact location of the bottom will, of course, vary for different firms in different industries. Different firms have different capacities to coordinate activities through markets and hierarchies. Second, firm size will also vary according to the changing abilities of firms to coordinate activities internally and externally.

Of course, knowing that the owners recognize that their manager/agents can exploit their positions to their own benefit, managers will see advantages in "bonding" themselves against that possibility. (The term "bonding" is not used in the modern pop-psychology sense of developing warm and fuzzy relationships; rather, it is used in the same way as when accused criminals post a bond, or give some assurance that they will appear in court if released from jail.) That is to say, managers have an interest in letting the owners know that they, the managers, will suffer some loss when exploitation occurs. Devices such as audits of the company are clearly in the interest of stockholders. But they are also in the interest of managers because reducing the scope for managerial misdeeds increases the market value of the company – and the market value of its managers. By buying their companies' stock, manager/agents can also bond themselves, assuring stock-holders that they will incur at least some losses from agency costs. To the extent that manager/agents can bond themselves convincingly, the firm can grow from expanded sources of external investment funds. By bonding themselves, manager/agents can demand higher compensation. Firms can be expected to expand and contract with reductions and increases in the costs of developing effective managerial bonds (Jensen and Meckling 1976).

Changes in organizational costs

The size of the firm can be expected to change with fluctuations in the relative costs of organizing a given set of activities by way of markets and hierarchies. For example, suppose that the costs of engaging in market transactions are lowered, meaning markets become relatively more economical vis-à-vis firms. Entrepreneurs should be expected to organize more of their activities through markets, fewer through firms. Then, those firms that more fully exploit markets and rely less on internal directions should be able to reduce their costs without sacrificing output by becoming smaller – or by *downsizing*, to use a popular expression.

An old, well-worn, and widely appreciated explanation for downsizing is that modern technology has enabled firms to produce more with less. Personal computers, with their ever-escalating power, have enabled firms to lay off workers (or hire fewer workers). Banks no longer need as many tellers, given the advent of the ATM.

One less widely appreciated explanation is that markets have become cheaper, which means that firms have less incentive to use hierarchical structures and more incentive to use markets. One good reason that firms have found markets relatively more attractive is the rapidly developing computer and communication technology, which has reduced the costs of entrepreneurs operating in markets. The new technology has lowered the costs of locating suitable trading partners and suppliers, as well as negotiating, consummating, and monitoring market-based deals (and the contracts that go with them). In figure 7.7, the downward sloping transaction costs curve has dropped down and to the left, causing the bottom of the U to move leftward.

"Outsourcing" became a management buzzword as far back as the 1980s because the growing efficiency of markets, through technology, made it more economical to use markets, often on a global scale. Outsourcing continued apace in the 1990s (Byrne 1996), contributing significantly to the relatively faster pace of manufacturing productivity growth in the 1990s and the first few years of the twenty-first century (Bureau of Labor Statistics 2004).

But modern technology has also improved the monitoring of employees – reducing the costs of providing employee incentives and encouraging cooperation among workers – thereby reducing agency costs and enabling the expansion of firms (Roberts 2004, chapter 3). This is because firms have been able to use technology to garner more of the gains from economies of scale and scope.

The optical scanners at grocery store checkout counters are valuable because they can speed up the flow of customers through the checkout counters, but they also can be used for other purposes, such as inventory control and restocking. Each sale is immediately transmitted to warehouse computers that determine the daily shipments to stores. The scanners also can be used to monitor the work of the clerks, a factor that can diminish agency costs and increase the size of the firm. (Even "Employee of the Month Awards" at large retail stores are often apparently made based on reports from scanners.) In figure 7.7, the upward sloping curve moves down and to the right, while the U-shaped curve in the lower panel moves to the right.

Companies as diverse as FedEx and Frito-Lay have issued their salespeople hand scanners that are connected by satellite to their offices, in part to increase the reliability of the flow of information to company distribution centers, but also to track employees' work. The company can obtain data on each employee's start and stop time, the time spent on trips between stores, and the number of returns. Accordingly, the salespeople can be asked to account for more of their time and activities while they are on the job.

Obviously, we have not covered the full spectrum of explanations for the many various sizes of firms in the "real world" of business. We also have left the net impact of technology somewhat up in the air, given that it is pressing some firms to expand and others to downsize. The reason is simple: technology is having a multitude of impacts that firms in different situations can exploit in different ways.

[See online Video Module 7.2 Firm size]

Overcoming the large-numbers Prisoner's Dilemma problems

The discussion to this point reduces to a relatively simple message: *firms exist to bring about cost savings, and they generate the cost savings through cooperation.* Firms enable owners to optimize their marginal cost of production (and other cost curves to be covered in chapter 8), which means pushing the marginal cost curve down as far as it can go, which is needed to meet the competition. However, cooperation within firms is not always and everywhere "natural" (at least, not beyond some point as the group of cooperators expands, although, as explained, some cooperation in small groups can have evolutionary roots [see Rubin 2002]).

The problem is that people often realize personal gains by "cheating," or not doing what they are supposed to do or have agreed to do. This may be the case because of the powerful incentives toward noncooperation that are built into many business environments.

An illustration of the tendency toward noncooperative behavior, despite the general advantage from cooperation, is a classic so-called "conditional-sum game," also known as the Prisoner's Dilemma (which we have already introduced without using the proper game-theoretic name), discussed in earlier chapters. Motivating cooperative behavior to overcome a large-number Prisoner's Dilemma is obviously difficult, but not impossible. The best hope for those who are in a Prisoner's Dilemma situation *is to agree ahead of time to certain rules, restrictions, or arrangements that will punish those who choose the noncooperative option.* For example, those who are jointly engaging in criminal activity will see advantages in forming gangs whose members are committed to punishing noncooperative behavior. The gang members who are confronted with the Prisoner's Dilemma orchestrated by the police will seriously consider the possibility that the shorter sentence received for confessing will hasten the time when the gang will impose a far more harsh punishment for "squealing" on a fellow gang member.

> **Conditional-sum games** are games in which the value available to the participants is dependent on how the game is played.

Many areas of business are fertile grounds for the conditional-sum game situations represented by the Prisoner's Dilemma. A number of examples of business-related dilemmas are discussed in some detail in subsequent chapters because an important task of managers is to identify and resolve these dilemmas as they arise both within the firm and with suppliers and customers. Indeed, we see the task of "management" as being largely concerned with finding resolutions of Prisoners' Dilemmas. Good managers constantly seek to remind members of the firm of the benefits of cooperation and of the costs that can be imposed on people who insist on taking the noncooperative course.

Consider, for example, the issue of corporate travel, which is a major business expense that can run into the hundreds of billions of dollars each year. If a business were able to economize on travel costs, it would realize significant gains. And many of these gains would be captured by the firms' traveling employees who, if they were able to travel at less cost, would earn higher incomes as their net value to the firm increased. But the employees are often in a Prisoner's Dilemma because each recognizes that she is personally better off by flying first class, staying at hotels with multiple stars, and dining at elegant restaurants (behaving noncooperatively) than by making the least expensive travel plans (behaving cooperatively) regardless of what the other employees do. Each individual employee would be best off if all other employees economized, but if others make the more expensive travel arrangements, an individual would be foolish not to do so as well because the sacrifice would not noticeably increase her salary. Management of travel is a problem of making cooperative solutions pay for individual workers.

However, airlines, which have an interest in excessive business travel, have recognized the "games" people play with their bosses and other workers, and have played along by making the travel game more rewarding to business travelers, more costly to the travelers' firms, and more profitable to the airlines – all through their "frequent-flier" programs. Of course, you can bet that managers are more than incidentally concerned about employees' use of frequent-flier programs.

When American Airlines initiated its AAdvantage frequent-flier program in 1981, the company was intent on staving off the fierce price competition that had broken out among established and new airlines after fares and routes were deregulated in 1978. As other writers have noted, the airline was seeking to enhance "customer loyalty" by offering its best, most regular customers free or reduced-price flights after they had built up their mileage accounts. Greater customer loyalty can mean that customers are less responsive to price increases, which could translate into actual higher prices than could otherwise be charged.[9]

At the same time, there is more to the issue than "customer loyalty." No doubt, American Airlines figured that it could benefit from the obvious Prisoner's Dilemma its business travelers were in. By setting up the frequent-flier program, American Airlines (and all others that followed suit) increased the individual payoff to business travelers for noncooperative behavior. American Airlines frequent-flyer program allowed travelers to benefit from more free flights and first-class upgrades when they chose more expensive and sometimes less direct flights. They encouraged businesspeople to act opportunistically, to use their discretion for their own benefit at the expense of everyone else in their firms.

The Prisoner's Dilemma problem for workers and their companies has, of course, prompted a host of other firms – rental car companies, hotels, and restaurants – to begin granting frequent-buyer points, if not frequent-flier miles, in conjunction with selected airlines for the travel services people buy with them, encouraging once again higher than necessary travel costs. The company incurs the cost of the added miles plus the lost time.

Now, use of frequent-flier miles might actually lower worker wages (because of the added cost to their firms, which can reduce the demand for workers and the benefit of the miles to workers, and can increase worker supply and lower wages).

---

[9] For a discussion of frequent-flier programs as a means of enhancing customer loyalty, see Brandenburger and Nalebuff (1996, 132–58).

Still, workers have an incentive to exploit the program. Again, they are in a Prisoner's Dilemma under which the cooperative strategy might be best for all, but the noncooperative strategy dominates the choice each individual faces. These problems created by frequent-flier programs are significant for many businesses, and we expect that the bigger the firm, the greater the problem (given the greater opportunity for opportunistic behavior in large firms) (Stephenson and Fox 1992; Dahl 1994). In the effort to cut these costs, managers are also in a game with the airlines, which respond to cost-cutting measures with new wrinkles designed to intensify the Prisoner's Dilemma business travelers face (Stephenson and Fox 1992). The resulting costly airfares, particularly for business travelers, are being countered by the low-cost airlines such as Southwest, AirTran, and Jet Blue, whose low-fare, no-frills service is capturing an increasing share of the market.

Make-or-buy decisions

Exactly what should firms make inside their organizations, and what should they buy from some outside vendor? Business commentators have a habit of coming up with rules that don't add very much to the answer. For example, one CEO deduced, "You should only do in-house what gives you a competitive advantage" (Dunlap and Andelman 1996, 55). Okay, but how can anyone get a competitive advantage from in-house production when such a move reduces, to one degree or another, the advantage of buying from the cheapest outside competitor? Answers have varied over time, although the one we intend to stress relates to incentives.

At one time, the answer to the make-or-buy problem would have focused on technological considerations: firms often produce more than one product because of what economists call **economies of scope**. But even firms with diverse product lines are actually quite specialized in that they purchase most of the inputs they use in the market rather than produce them in-house.

> **Economies of scope** emerge because the skills developed in the production, distribution, and sale of one product lower the cost of producing other products.

General Motors, for example, does not produce its own steel, tires, plastic, or carpeting. Instead, it is cheaper for General Motors and other automobile manufacturers to purchase these products from firms that specialize in them and to concentrate on the assembly of automobiles. Neither do many restaurants grow their own vegetables, raise their own beef, catch their own fish, and none that we know of produces its own toothpicks.

Given the advantages of specialization in productive activities and buying most of the necessary inputs in the marketplace, a reasonable question is: why do firms do as much as they do internally? Why don't firms buy almost all the inputs they need, as they need them, from others and use them to add value in very specialized ways? Instead of having employees in the typical sense, for example, a firm could hire workers on an hourly or daily basis at a market-determined wage reflecting their alternative value at the time. Instead of owning and maintaining a fleet of trucks, a transport company could rent trucks, paying only for the time they were in use. Loading and unloading the trucks could be contracted out to firms that specialized in that work and the transport firm would specialize in actually transporting products. Similarly, the paperwork required for such things as internal control, payroll, and taxes could be contracted out to those who specialized in providing these services. Indeed, taking this concept to the limit would eliminate firms as we typically think of them.

The problem with total reliance on the market should now be familiar: significant costs – transaction costs – are associated with making market exchanges. In general, the higher the cost of transacting through markets, the more a firm will make for itself with its own employees rather than buying from other firms. The reason that restaurants don't make their own toothpicks is that the cost of transactions is extremely low. It is hard to imagine the transaction costs of acquiring toothpicks ever getting so high that restaurants would make their own.

Pipelines

Negotiating an agreement between two parties can be costly, but the most costly part of a transaction often involves attempts to avoid opportunistic behavior by the parties after the agreement has been reached. Agreements commonly call for one or both parties to make investments in expensive plants and equipment that are highly specific to a particular productive activity. After the investment is made, plants and equipment have little, if any value in alternative activities. Investments in highly specific capital are often very risky, and therefore unattractive, even though the cost of the capital is less than it is worth. The problem is that once someone commits to an investment in specific capital to provide a service to another party, the other party can take advantage of the investor's inflexibility by paying less than the original agreement called for. There are so-called "quasi-rents" that are appropriable, or that can be taken by another party through unscrupulous, opportunistic dealing.[10] The desire to avoid this risk of opportunistic behavior can be a major factor in a firm's decision to make rather than buy what it needs.

---

[10] Appropriable quasi-rents are the differences between the purchase and subsequent selling price of an asset, when the selling price is lower than the purchase price simply because of the limited resale market for the asset (Klein, Crawford, and Alchian, 1978).

Consider an example of a pipeline to transport natural gas to an electric generating plant. Such a pipeline is very expensive to construct, but assume that it lowers the cost of producing electricity by more than enough to provide an attractive return on the investment. To be more specific, assume that the cost of constructing the pipeline is $1 billion. Assuming an interest rate of 10 percent (which we select only for clarity of calculations), the annual capital cost of the pipeline is $100 million. Further assume that the annual cost of maintaining and operating the pipeline is $25 million. Obviously it would not pay investors to build the pipeline for less than a $125 million annual payment, but it would be attractive to build it for any annual payment greater than that. Finally, assume that if the pipeline is constructed, it will lower the cost of producing electricity by $150 million dollars a year. The pipeline costs less than it saves and is clearly a good investment for the economy. But would you invest your money to build it?

Any price between $125 million and $150 million a year would be attractive both to investors in the pipeline and to the electric generating plant that would use it. If, for example, the generating plant agrees to pay investors $137.5 million each year to build and operate the pipeline, both parties would realize annual profits of $12.5 million from the project. But the investors would be taking a serious risk because of the lack of flexibility after the pipeline is built. The main problem is that a pipeline is a *dedicated* investment, meaning that there is a big difference in the return needed to make the pipeline worth building and the return needed to make it worth operating after it is built. Although it takes at least $125 million per year to motivate the building of the pipeline, the firm will find that, after building the pipeline, any payment over $25 million will be a paying proposition. Why? Because that is all it takes to operate the line. The pipeline investment itself is a sunk cost, literally and figuratively, not to be recaptured once it has been made. So after investors have made the commitment to construct the pipeline, the generating plant would be in a position to capture almost the entire value of initial pipeline investment by repudiating the original agreement and offering to pay only slightly more than $25 million per year.[11]

---

[11] Economists refer to this as "capturing all the quasi-rents from the investment." To elaborate on what we have already said about quasi-rents, rent is any amount in excess of what it takes to motivate the supply of a good or service before any investment has been made. In the case of the pipeline, anything in addition to $125 million a year is rent. On the other hand, a quasi-rent is any amount in excess of what it takes to motivate the supply of a good or service after the required investment is made. In the pipeline example, anything in excess of $25 million a year is quasi-rent. So once the investor has committed to the pipeline, any offer over $25 million a year will motivate the supply of a pipeline service and allow the generating plant to capture almost all of the quasi-rent.

Of course, our example is much too extreme. The generating plant is not likely to risk its reputation by blatantly repudiating a contract. And even if it did, the pipeline investors would have legal recourse, with a good chance of recovering much, if not all, of their loss. Furthermore, as the example is constructed, the generating plant has more to lose from opportunistic behavior by the pipeline owners than vice versa. If the pipeline refuses service to the plant, the cost of producing electricity increases by $150 million per year. So the pipeline owners could act opportunistically by threatening to cut off the supply of natural gas unless they receive an annual payment of almost $150 million per year.

But cost-minimizing and profit-maximizing businesspeople dare not overlook our main point: any time a transaction requires a large investment in dedicated capital (limited in use to a particular project), there is *the potential for costly problems in negotiating and enforcing agreements.*

True, opportunistic behavior (actions taken as a consequence of an investment that has been made and cannot be recaptured) will seldom be as blatant as in the above example, in which it is clear that a lower price is a violation of the contract. But in actual contracts involving long-term capital commitments, unforeseen changes in circumstances (higher costs, interrupted supplies, stricter government regulations, etc.) can justify changes in prices or other terms of the contract. Typically, contracts will attempt to anticipate some of these changes and incorporate them into the agreed-upon terms, but it is impossible to anticipate and specify appropriate responses to all possible changes in relevant conditions. Ambiguities in long-term contractual arrangements, therefore, can open the door for opportunistic behavior, which can be resolved only through protracted and expensive legal action.

So, committing to investments in dedicated capital carries great risk without some assurance that such opportunistic behavior will not pay. One way to obtain this assurance is for the investment to be made by the same firm that will be using the output it produces. Alternatively, the firm that makes the investment in the specific capital can merge with the firm that depends on the output from that investment.

[See online Video Modules 7.3 Quasi-rent and 7.4 Make-or-buy decisions]

Hold-ups and equipment rentals

When buying a crucial input, a firm can reduce the risks of being "held-up" by a supplier who uses specialized equipment to produce the input. For example, the firm can buy the specialized equipment and then rent it to the supplier. If the supplier attempts to take advantage of the crucial nature of the input, the firm can move the specialized equipment to another supplier rather than be forced to pay a higher than expected price for the input. This is exactly the arrangement that automobile companies have with some of their suppliers. Ford, for example, buys components from many small and specialized companies, but commonly owns the specialized equipment needed and rents it to the contracting firms (Cooter and Ulen 1988, 245–6).

Firms also are aware that those who supply them with services are reluctant to commit themselves to costly capital investments that, once made, leave them vulnerable to *hold-up* (demands that the terms and conditions of the relationship be changed after an investment that cannot be recaptured has been made). In such a case, the firm that provides the capital equipment and rents it to the supplier can benefit from the fact that less threatened suppliers will charge lower prices. This consideration may also be a motivation for auto manufacturers to own the equipment that some of their suppliers use and provides a very good explanation for a business arrangement that has been widely criticized.

Company towns

An arrangement that reduced the threat of firms' opportunistic behavior against their workers has been the much-criticized "company town." In the past, it was common for companies (typically mining companies) to set up operations in what were at the time very remote locations. In the company towns, the company owned the stores in which employees shopped and the houses in which they lived. The popular view of these company towns is that they allowed the companies to exploit their workers with outrageous prices and rents, often charging them more for basic necessities than they earned from backbreaking work in the mines. The late Tennessee Ernie Ford captured this popular view in his famous song "Sixteen Tons."

Without denying that the lives of nineteenth-century miners were tough, company stores and houses can be seen as a way for the companies to reduce (but not totally eliminate) their ability to exploit their workers through opportunistic behavior. Certainly workers would be reluctant to purchase a house in a remote location with only one employer. The worker who committed to such an investment would be far more vulnerable to the employer's opportunistic wage reductions than would the worker who rented company housing. Similarly, few merchants would be willing to establish a store in such a location, knowing that once the investment was made they would be vulnerable to opportunistic demands for price reductions that just covered their variable costs, leaving no return on their capital cost.

Again, in an ideal world without transaction costs – and without opportunistic behavior – mining companies would have specialized in extracting ore and would have let suppliers of labor buy their housing and other provisions through other specialists. But in the real world of transaction costs (including the temptations of opportunistic behavior), it was better for mining companies also to provide basic services for their employees. This is not to deny that there was exploitation. But the exploitation was surely less under the company town arrangement than if, for example, workers had bought their own houses (Fishback 1992, chapters 8, 9). Exploitation of workers on rent and company store prices could restrict the supply of workers and increase the wages company would have to pay.

The value of reputation, again

A theme that runs through this chapter is that when firms make investments to serve very specific purposes, they open themselves to opportunistic behavior – or more to the point, to hold-ups. The threat of hold-ups invariably converts to risk costs, which have to be covered one way or another and can undermine firms' competitive positions in their product markets.

As noted, American automakers have generally solved the hold-up problem for their suppliers by buying the specialized equipment their suppliers need to provide the automakers with parts (Roberts 2004, 204–6). Toyota has solved its suppliers' hold-up threat by developing a reputation among its suppliers for not acting opportunistically. To increase its suppliers' confidence in its pledge, Toyota encourages its suppliers to talk with one another through an association of suppliers. Each supplier can reason that such ongoing interactions among them can increase the cost that Toyota will incur from taking advantage of any one supplier, thus reducing the probability that Toyota will engage in forms of opportunistic behavior, especially hold-ups. Toyota's formal and informal contracts with suppliers are thus made *self-enforcing* (to a greater degree than they otherwise would be).

As a consequence, Toyota's suppliers have no problem with investing in equipment – for example, dies for Toyota parts – that can be used only for meeting Toyota's orders. Toyota's reputation for fair dealing translates into lower risk costs throughout its supply chain which, in turn, translates into lower production costs for suppliers and lower prices for Toyota's parts. The economies of reputation can reveal themselves to consumers in the relatively lower prices of the company's cars.

In online Readings 7.2 and 7.3, we extend our discussion of ways firms can grow through a consideration of the questions, "The franchise decision" and "Cutting health care costs through medical savings accounts."

Practical lessons for MBAs: recognize potential decision-making biases and think more rationally

This chapter is full of practical advice for MBA students in developing production and organizational strategies. In this practical lesson, we recommend two widely read books in an emerging subdiscipline in economics, "behavioral economics." The recommended books are Richard Thaler and Cass Sunstein's *Nudge: Improving Decisions about Health, Wealth, and Happiness* (2008) and Dan Ariely's *Predictably Irrational: The Hidden Forces that Shape Our Decisions* (2008). These authors report an array of findings from laboratory and classroom research that shows people are subject to a variety of "decision-making biases" and outright "irrationalities." People, even businesspeople, do not always discount costs and benefits appropriately, treat opportunity costs and out-of-pocket expenditures differently (supposedly favoring the former), value the things they have higher than the things they don't have, don't consider marginal costs and benefits, and often fail to ignore sunk costs.

While we have serious concerns with many of the conclusions drawn from behavioral research conducted by economists and psychologists (which one of the authors, McKenzie, has taken up in some detail in another book [2010]), we still think MBA students should recognize that not all people behave at all times with the level of rationality (perfect rationality) assumed in microeconomic theory. We suggest that recognition of human rational limitations and failures make, paradoxically, the analytics in this chapter all the more important for MBA students. This chapter explains how MBA students can make decisions more rationally and, hence, give them a potential competitive advantage in the markets in which they operate. How? Very simply. Even though they might not be naturally predisposed to do so, they should think carefully and rationally, which means they should

- discount costs and benefits for time and risk
- ferret out as best they can marginal cost and marginal value with an eye toward equating at the margin
- treat all costs – whether opportunity costs or out-of-pocket expenditures – the same
- ignore sunk costs.

And they should follow many of the other production and organizational strategies developed in this chapter (as well as all others in this book), for offensive and defensive reasons. The offensive reason for managers to follow such rational production and organizational rules is that the guiding rules can (at least potentially) make firms more profitable – precisely because people in firms may fall prey to decision-making biases and irrationalities if they are not guided by the production and organizational rules we have deduced.

The defensive reason for following the production and organizational rules deduced from a premise of rational behavior should by now be transparent to readers: if some managers don't follow the rules while other do follow them, there is a good chance that firms that fail to follow the rules will have higher cost structures and will be at a competitive disadvantage in the pricing of their products and in securing financial resources to continue and expand their operations. Making irrational decisions consistently without correction seems to us to be the foundation of a business strategy that has failure written all over it.

Further readings online

Reading 7.1 The last-period problem

Reading 7.2 The franchise decision (along with the accompanying online Video Module 7.5 Franchising agreements)

Reading 7.3 Cutting health care costs through medical savings accounts

The bottom line

The key takeaways from chapter 7 are the following:

1   Cost plays a pivotal role in a producer's choices. Costs change with the quantity produced. The pattern of those changes determines the limit of a producer's activity – from the production of saleable goods and services to the employment of leisure time.

2   The maximizing individual will produce a good or service, or engage in an activity, until marginal cost equals marginal benefit (marginal revenue). Graphically, this is the point at which the supply and demand curves for the individual's behavior intersect. At this point, although additional benefits might be obtained by producing additional units of the good, service, or activity, the additional costs that would be incurred discourage further production.

3   Costs will not affect an individual's behavior unless she perceives them as costs. For this reason, managers can often improve incentives – increasing firm profits and employees' benefits – by looking for hidden or implicit costs in the choices being made, and making the changes necessary to ensure that they and their workers confront those choices.

4   All costs – explicit and implicit – must be considered when deciding whether to produce anything and when deciding how much of anything should be produced if profits are to be maximized.

5   Sunk costs, which are costs that cannot be recouped, don't matter in production decisions.

6   Normal profit is a cost of doing business.

7   Marginal cost is a key cost concept.

8   The market supply curve in a competitive goods market is the horizontal summation of individual firms' supply curves (or their marginal cost curves above the minimum of the average variable cost curve).

9   Firms exist because they tend to reduce the overall cost of doing business, most prominently external coordinating (or transaction) costs.

10 Firm size is limited not only by economies of scale but also by agency costs.

11 Firm size, profitability, and survival is crucially dependent on balancing internal and external coordinating costs. Firms can be expected to contract in size if market transactions costs are lowered, everything else equal.

12 Firms are advised to buy as many of their inputs as they can from competitive sources of supply. They often make their inputs because of the potential for opportunistic behavior – or hold-up – in dealing with outside suppliers when investments in firm-specific resources must be made before payments for the produced good are made.

13 In their effort to get incentives right, it is understandable why firms provide fringe benefits: such benefits can reduce firms' compensation costs while increasing the incentive for better workers to seek employment with firms that provide them.

14 People will behave opportunistically. However, it is wrong to conclude that *all* people are *always* willing to behave opportunistically, which is also contradicted by everyday experience. The business world is full of both saints and sinners, and most people are some combination of both. Opportunistic behavior has been emphasized because that is the threat managers want to protect themselves against. Businesspeople don't have to worry about the Mother Teresas of the world. They do have to worry about less than saintly people. (And they do have to worry about people who pretend to be like Mother Teresa before any deal is consummated.) They need to understand the consequences of opportunistic behavior in order that they can appropriately structure their contracts and embedded incentives.

Review questions >>

1   Evaluate the old adages "haste makes waste" and "a stitch in time saves nine" from an economic point of view.

2   If executives' time is as valuable as they claim, why are they frequently found reading the advertisements in airline magazines en route to a business meeting?

3   When cell phones were first introduced, the price of a one-minute long-distance call on a cell phone was several times the cost of a call on a landline phone. Does that mean that at the time of their introduction, cell phones increased the cost of long-distance calling?

4   In discussing accident prevention, we assumed an increasing marginal cost. Suppose, instead, that the marginal cost of preventing accidents remains constant. How will that assumption affect the analysis?

5   Using the analysis of accident prevention, develop an analysis of pollution control. Using demand and supply curves for clean air, determine the efficient level of pollution control.

6   People take some measures to avoid becoming victims of crime. Can the probability of becoming a victim be reduced to (virtually) zero? If so, why don't people eliminate that probability? What does the underlying logic of your answer suggest about the cost of committing crimes and the crime rate?

7   If the money price of a good rises from $5 to $10, the economist can confidently predict that less will be purchased. One cannot be equally confident that denying a child a dessert for bad behavior will improve his behavior, however. Explain why.

8   Consider the information in the production schedule that follows. (a) At what output level do diminishing returns set in? (b) Assume that each worker receives $8. Fill in the marginal product column, and develop a marginal cost schedule and a marginal cost curve for the production process.

No. of workers	Total product of all workers per day	Marginal product of each worker
1	0.10	
2	0.30	
3	0.60	
4	1.00	
5	1.45	
6	2.00	
7	2.50	
8	2.80	
9	3.00	
10	3.19	
11	3.37	
12	3.54	
13	3.70	
14	3.85	
15	4.00	
16	3.90	
17	3.70	

9   Why are some firms "large" and other firms "small"? Use the concept of "coordinating costs" in your answer.

10   Suppose firms get smaller. Why might that happen?

11   If worker monitoring costs go down, what will happen to the size of the firm?

12   What have been the various effects of the computer/telecommunication revolution on the sizes of firms?

13   Why would a firm hire its own accountants to keep the books but, at the same time, use outside lawyers to do its legal work?

14   If your firm fears being "held-up" by an outside supplier of a critical part to your production process, what can your firm do to reduce the chance of such a hold-up?

15   Authors typically get a royalty, stated as a percentage of the revenues publishers receive on their books. Why is it that authors typically get only a minor fraction (say, 15 percent) of the revenue stream? What are the economic advantages of large "advances" (payments by publishers to authors before books are published)?

8

Production costs in the short run and long run

In economics, the cost of an event is the highest-valued opportunity necessarily forsaken. The usefulness of the concept of cost is a logical implication of choice among available options. Only if no alternatives were possible or if amounts of all resources were available beyond everyone's desires, so that all goods were free, would the concepts of cost and of choice be irrelevant.

Armen Alchian

The individual firm plays a critical role both in theory and in the real world. It straddles two basic economic institutions: the markets for resources (labor, capital, and land) and the markets for goods and services (everything from trucks to truffles). The firm must be able to identify what people want to buy, at what price, and to organize the great variety of available resources into an efficient production process. It must sell its product at a price that covers the cost of its resources, yet allows it to compete with other firms. Moreover, it must accomplish those objectives while competing firms are seeking to meet the same goals.

How does the firm do all this? Clearly, firms do not all operate in exactly the same way. They differ in organizational structure and in management style, in the resources they use and in the products they sell. This chapter cannot possibly cover the great diversity of business management techniques. Rather, our purpose is to develop the broad principles that guide most firms' production decisions. In the process we develop an alternative explanation for why firms are the sizes they are that complements the theory of firm size in chapter 7.

As with individuals, firms are beset by the necessity of choice which, as Armen Alchian reminds us in the chapter epigraph, implies a cost. Costs are both the result of having to make choices and obstacles to those choices; they restrict us in what we do. Thus a firm's cost structure (the way cost varies with production) reflects how firms deal with the obstacles of making a profitable production decision in both the short and the long run. MBA students should understand a firm's *cost structure* because firms don't do anything on their own. Managers are the forces behind the firm's activities and the decisions that ultimately determine profitability.

As noted in chapter 7, our analysis of a firm's "cost structure" is different from the costs on accounting statements. Accounting statements provide only a snap-shot of costs incurred in a given time period and for a given output level. In this chapter, we devise a cost structure that relates production costs to many different output levels. The reason is simple: we want to use this structure to determine which among many possible output levels will enable the firm to maximize profits. As we did in the previous chapter, we explain in Part B ways by which firms can actually contain their costs – which is to say, lower their cost structures as much as is economical – to remain competitive. Accordingly, we develop the ways in which the firm's financial structure – its combination of debt and equity – can affect managers' incentives to economize on firm resources and, thus, to contain its cost structure. This line of explanation will help you understand the Savings and Loan debacle some years ago and the more recent "mortgage meltdown," which was, to a nontrivial extent, founded on risk taking encouraged by mortgages that required little to no down payment from new home buyers.

Online Perspective

Many business commentators glibly tout the supposed advantages of being a "first mover" in a market. In online Perspective 8 for this chapter, we discuss "The myth of the first-mover advantage." As you will see, being a "first mover" can be a decided disadvantage. Second, third, and subsequent movers for given products often come to dominate their markets because of cost advantages that go with not having to develop products and the markets for them. Imitation does have its cost rewards, which can add to firm competitiveness.

First, we need to finalize the development of a firm's cost structure in broad terms.

Part A Theory and public policy applications

Fixed, variable, and total costs in the short run

Time is required to produce any good or service; therefore, any output level must be founded on some recognized time period. Even more important, the costs a firm incurs vary over time. To think about costs clearly, we must identify the time period during which they apply. For reasons that will become apparent, economists speak of costs in terms of the extent to which they can be varied, rather than the number of months or years required to pay them off. Although in the long run all costs can be varied, in the short run firms face some costs that cannot be varied. Short-run costs can be either fixed or variable. Total fixed costs (TFC) remain the same whether the firm's factories are standing idle or producing at capacity. As long as the firm faces even one fixed cost, it is operating in the short run. Variable costs include wages (workers can be hired or laid off on relatively short notice), material, utilities, and office supplies. Total variable costs (TVC) increase with the level of output.

> The **short run** is the period during which one or more resources (and thus one or more costs of production) cannot be changed – either increased or decreased.

> A **fixed cost** is any cost that does not vary with the level of output. Fixed costs include overhead expenditures that extend over a period of months or years: insurance premiums, leasing and rental payments, land and equipment purchases, and interest on loans.

> A **variable cost** is any cost that changes with the level of output.

Together, total fixed and total variable costs equal total cost. Total cost (TC) is the sum of fixed costs and variable costs at each output level:

$$TC = TFC + TVC$$

Columns (1) through (4) of table 8.1 show fixed, variable, and total costs at various production levels. Total fixed costs are constant at $100 for all output levels (see column [2]). Total variable costs increase gradually, from $30 to $395, as output expands from one to twelve widgets. Total cost, the sum of all fixed and variable costs at each output level (obtained by adding columns [2] and [3] horizontally), increases gradually as well.

Graphically, total fixed cost can be represented by a horizontal line, as in figure 8.1 The total cost curve starts at the same point as the total fixed cost curve (because total cost must at least equal fixed cost) and rises from that point. The vertical distance between the total cost and the total fixed cost curves shows the total variable cost at each level of production.

Marginal and average costs in the short run

The central issue of this chapter, and chapters 9 and 10, is how to determine the profit-maximizing level of production. In other words, we want to know what

Table 8.1 Total, marginal, and average cost of production

(1) Production level (no. of widgets)	(2) Total fixed costs ($)	(3) Total variable costs ($)	(4) Total costs (2) + (3) ($)	(5) Marginal cost (change in [3] or [4]) ($)	(6) Average fixed cost ([2]/[1]) ($)	(7) Average variable cost ([3]/[1]) ($)	(8) Average total cost ([4]/[1]) or ([6] + [7]) ($)
1	100	30	130	30	100.00	30.00	130.00
2	100	50	150	20	50.00	25.00	75.00
3	100	60	160	10	33.33	20.00	53.33
4	100	65	165	5	25.00	16.25	41.25
5	100	75	175	10	20.00	15.00	35.00
6	100	90	190	15	16.67	15.00	31.67
7	100	110	210	20	14.29	15.71	30.00
8	100	140	240	30	12.50	17.50	30.00
9	100	180	280	40	11.11	20.00	31.11
10	100	230	330	50	10.00	23.00	33.00
11	100	300	400	70	9.09	27.27	36.36
12	100	395	495	95	8.33	32.92	41.25

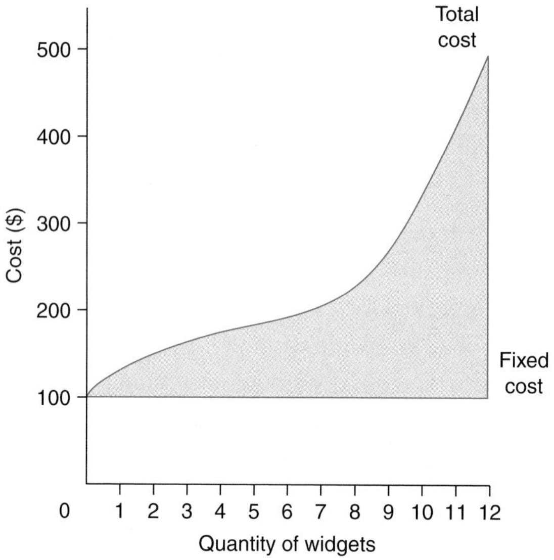

Figure 8.1 Total fixed costs, total variable costs, and total costs in the short run
Total fixed cost does not vary with production; therefore, it is drawn as a horizontal line. Total variable cost does rise with production. Here, it is represented by the shaded area between the total cost and total fixed cost curves.

output the firm that is interested in maximizing profits will choose to produce. Although fixed, variable, and total costs are important measures, they are not very useful in determining the firm's profit-maximizing (or loss-minimizing) output. To arrive at that figure, as well as to estimate profits or losses, we need four additional measures of cost: (1) marginal, (2) average fixed, (3) average variable, and (4) average total. When graphed, those four measures represent the firm's cost structure, which covers all costs associated with production, including risk cost and opportunity cost. A cost structure is the way in which various measures of cost (total cost, total variable cost, and so forth) vary with the production level.

Marginal cost

We have defined marginal cost (MC) as the additional cost of producing one additional unit. By extension, marginal cost can also be defined as the change in total cost. Because the change in total cost is due solely to the change in variable cost, marginal cost can also be defined as the change in total variable cost per unit:

$$MC = \frac{\text{Change in TC}}{\text{Change in quality}} = \frac{\text{Change in TVC}}{\text{Change in quantity}}$$

As you can see from table 8.1, marginal cost declines as output expands from one to four widgets and then rises, as predicted by the law of diminishing marginal returns. This increasing marginal cost reflects the diminishing marginal productivity of extra workers and other variable resources that the firm must employ in order to expand output beyond four widgets.

The marginal cost curve is shown in figure 8.2. The bottom of the curve (four units) is the point at which marginal returns begin to diminish.

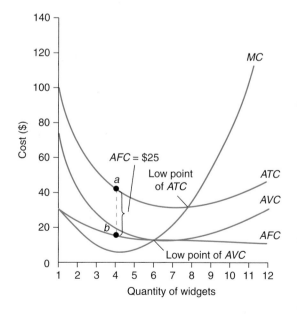

Figure 8.2 Marginal and average costs in the short run
The average fixed cost curve (*AFC*) slopes downward and approaches, but never touches, the horizontal axis. The average variable cost curve (*AVC*) and the average total cost curve (*ATC*) are mathematically related to the marginal cost curve and both intersect with the marginal cost curve (*MC*) at their lowest point. The vertical distance between the average total cost curve (*ATC*) and the average variable cost curve (*AVC*) equals the average fixed cost at any given output level. There is no relationship between the *MC* and *AFC* curves.

Average fixed cost

Average fixed cost (AFC) is total fixed cost divided by the number of units produced (Q):

$$AFC = \frac{TFC}{Q}$$

In table 8.1, total fixed costs are constant at $100. As output expands, therefore, the average fixed cost per unit must decline. (That is what businesspeople mean when they talk about "spreading the overhead." As production expands, the average fixed cost declines.)

In figure 8.2, the average fixed cost curve slopes downward to the right, approaching, but never touching, the horizontal axis. That is because average fixed cost is a ratio, TFC/Q, and a ratio can never be reduced to zero, no matter how large the denominator (Q). (Note that this is a principle of arithmetic, not economics.)

Average variable cost

Average variable cost (AVC) is total variable cost divided by the number of units produced, or

$$AVC = \frac{TVC}{Q}$$

At an output level of one unit, average variable cost necessarily equals marginal cost. Beyond the first unit, marginal and average variable costs diverge, although they are mathematically related. Whenever marginal cost declines, as it does initially in figure 8.2, average variable cost must also decline: the lower marginal value pulls the average value down. A basketball player who scores progressively fewer points in each successive game, for instance, will find her average score falling, although not as rapidly as her marginal score.

Beyond the point of diminishing marginal returns, marginal cost rises, but average variable cost continues to fall for a time (see figure 8.2). As long as marginal cost is below the average variable cost, average variable cost must continue to decline. (The two curves meet at an output level of six widgets.) Beyond that point, the average variable cost curve must rise because the average value will be pulled up by the greater marginal value. (After a game in which she scores more points than her previous average, for instance, the basketball player's average score must rise.) The point at which the marginal cost and average variable cost curves intersect is, therefore, the low point of the average variable cost curve. Before that intersection, average variable cost must fall. After it, average variable cost must rise. For the same reason, the intersection of the marginal cost curve and the average total cost curve must be the low point of the average total cost curve.

Average total cost

Average total cost (ATC) is the total of all fixed and variable costs divided by the number of units produced (Q), or

$$\text{ATC} = \frac{\text{TFC} + \text{TVC}}{Q} = \frac{\text{TC}}{Q}$$

Average total cost can also be found by summing the average fixed and average variable costs, if they are known (ATC = AFC + AVC). Graphically, the average total cost curve is the vertical summation of the average fixed and average variable cost curves (see figure 8.2).

Because average total cost is the sum of average fixed and variable costs, the average fixed cost can be obtained by subtracting average variable from average total cost: AFC = ATC – AVC. On a graph, average fixed cost is the vertical distance between the average total cost curve and the average variable cost curve. For instance, in figure 8.2 at an output level of four widgets, the average fixed cost is the vertical distance *ab*, or $25 ($41.25 – $16.25, or column [8] minus column [7] in table 8.1).

From this point on, we do not show the average fixed cost curve on a graph because doing so complicates the presentation without adding new information. Average fixed cost is hereafter indicated by the vertical distance between the average total and average variable cost curves at any given output.

[See online Video Module 8.1 Firm cost structure]

Marginal and average costs in the long run

So far, our discussion has been restricted to time periods during which at least one resource is fixed. That assumption underlies the concept of fixed cost. Fortunately, all resources that are used in production can be changed over the long run. By definition, there are no fixed costs in the long run; all long-run costs are variable.

> The **long run** is the period during which all resources (and thus all costs of production) can be changed – either increased or decreased.

The foregoing short-run analysis is still useful in analyzing a firm's long-run cost structure. In the long run, the average total cost curve (*ATC* in figure 8.2) represents one possible scale of operation, with one given quantity of plant and equipment (in table 8.1, $100 worth). A change in plant and equipment will change the firm's cost structure, increasing or decreasing its productive capacity.

Economies of scale

Figure 8.3 illustrates the long-run production choices facing a typical firm. The curve labeled ATC_1 is the average total cost curve developed in figure 8.2.

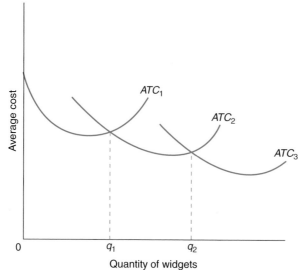

Figure 8.3 Economies of scale
Economies of scale are cost savings associated with the expanded use of resources. To realize such savings, however, a firm must expand its output. Here the firm can lower its costs by expanding production from q_1 to q_2 – a scale of operation that places it on a lower short-run average total cost curve (ATC_2 instead of ATC_1).

Additional plant and equipment will add to total fixed costs, resulting in an average total cost curve such as ATC_2 in figure 8.3. Because of the additional fixed cost, at low output levels (up to q_1) the average total costs will be higher – curve ATC_2 will lie above ATC_1. But the additional plant and equipment allow **economies of scale** to be realized beyond output q_1, resulting in lower average total costs than is possible with the plant and equipment associated with ATC_1.

> **Economies of scale** are cost savings that technology allows when all resource inputs are increased together.

Economies of scale can occur for several reasons. Expanded operation generally permits greater specialization of resources. Technologically advanced equipment, such as super computers and management information systems (MIS) combined with telecommunication systems, can be used and more highly skilled workers can be employed. Expansion may also permit improvements in organization, such as with assembly-line production. Also, by expanding production the firm can spread the higher cost of additional plant and equipment over a larger output level, reducing its average cost of production.

> **Diseconomies of scale** are added costs that, beyond some point, accompany the expansion of production through the use of more of all inputs.

The advantages of economies of scale are always limited, with average costs eventually going up as output increases with more plant and equipment added. When this occurs, we have the point where **diseconomies of scale** become operative. For example, as more people are hired to work with the additional plant and equipment, the problem of free-riders becomes increasingly troublesome and this can lead to diseconomies of scale.[1]

And in some lines of production, diseconomies of scale are encountered at very small output levels independently of free-rider problems. For example, such things as the production of original works of art, cutting hair, repairing shoes, and writing books are typically done by individuals working alone or by firms with very little capital and very few workers.

However, as long as economies of scale remain in force, the average cost curve can be reduced over larger output levels by increasing plant and equipment. Just as curve ATC_2 in figure 8.3 cuts curve ATC_1 and then dips down to a lower minimum average total cost at a higher output level, so does curve ATC_3 with respect to the curve ATC_2, indicating that economies of scale haven't been exhausted with the plant and equipment associated with curve ATC_2. But at some point, diseconomies of scale will be encountered.

It is possible, of course, that economies of scale will still be operating when a firm is producing more than it can sell at a profit. In this case, the firm will set its output below the point where diseconomies of scale are limiting it (a topic that will be reconsidered with the addition of the market demand curve in chapter 10).

Long-run average and marginal cost curves

When a firm has enough time to change the amount of all the inputs it is using – to change its scale of operation – it is interested in its long-run cost curves. Therefore, the firm can minimize its overall cost of operation by expanding along the envelope portion of the curve ATC_2, and it can push its average costs down to the lowest point by expanding its scale to ATC_4 and output to q_1.

Assuming that there is a very large number of possible scales of operation, the firm's expansion path can be seen as a single overall curve that envelops all of its short-run average cost curves. Such a curve is shown in figure 8.4 and reproduced in figure 8.5 as the long-run average cost curve ($LRAC$). As do short-run average cost curves, the long-run average cost curve has an accompanying long-run marginal cost curve. If long-run average cost is falling, as it does initially in figure 8.5, it must be because long-run marginal cost is pulling it down. If long-run cost is rising, as it does eventually in figure 8.5, then long-run marginal cost must be pulling it up.

---

[1] For a while, a firm may be able to avoid diseconomies of scale by increasing the number of its plants. Management's ability to supervise a growing number of plants is limited, however, and eventually diseconomies of scale will emerge at the level of the firm, if not the plant. If diseconomies of scale did not exist, in the long run each industry would have only one firm.

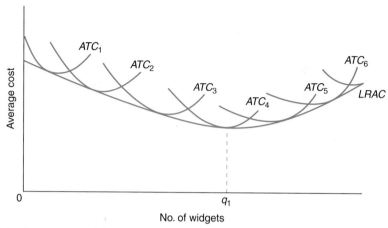

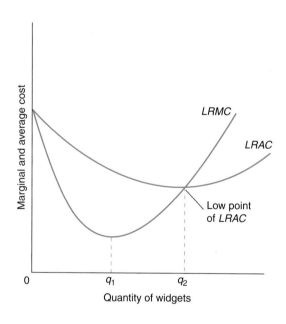

Figure 8.4 Diseconomies of scale

Diseconomies of scale may occur because of the communication problems of larger firms. Here the firm realizes economies of scale through its first short-run average total cost curves. The long-run average cost curve begins to turn up at an output level of q_1, beyond which diseconomies of scale set in.

Figure 8.5 Marginal and average cost in the long run

The long-run marginal and average cost curves are mathematically related. The long-run average cost curve slopes downward as long as it is above the long-run marginal cost curve. The two curves intersect at the low point of the long-run average cost curve.

Hence at some point, long-run marginal cost must turn upward, intersecting the long-run average cost curve at its lowest point, q_2.

In our development of a firm's cost-curve structure, for reasons of space we have sidestepped the issue of how a firm actually goes about choosing the most efficient combination of resources. We have chosen to cover such technical details in online Reading 8.1.

[See online Video Modules 8.2 Long-run cost structure and 8.3 Long-run production]

Industry differences in average cost

Not all firms experience economies and diseconomies of scale to the same degree or at the same levels of production. Their long-run average cost curves, in other words, look very different. Figure 8.6 shows several possible shapes for long-run average cost curves. The curve in figure 8.6(a) belongs to a firm in an industry with few

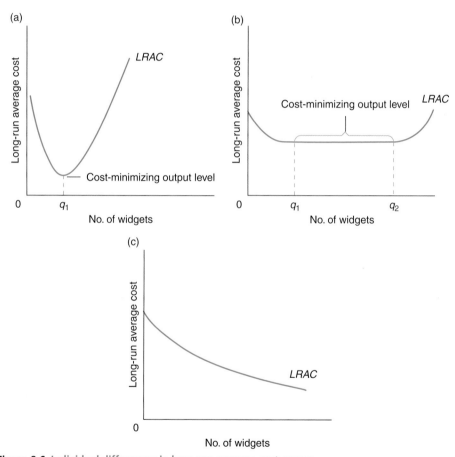

Figure 8.6 Individual differences in long-run average cost curves
The shape of the long-run average cost curve varies according to the extent and persistence of economies and diseconomies of scale. Firms in industries with few economies of scale will have a long-run average cost curve like the one in panel (a). Firms in industries with persistent economies of scale will have a long-run average cost curve like the one in panel (b), and firms in industries with extensive economies of scale may find that their long-run average cost curve slopes continually downward, as in panel (c).

economies of scale and significant diseconomies at relatively low output levels. (This curve might belong to a firm in a service industry, such as a shoe repair business.) We would not expect firms in this industry to be very large because firms with an output level beyond q_1 can easily be underpriced by smaller, lower-cost firms.

Figure 8.6(b) shows the long-run average cost curve for a firm in an industry with modest economies of scale at low output levels and no diseconomies of scale until the firm reaches a fairly high output level. In such an industry – perhaps apparel manufacturing – we would expect to find firms of various sizes, some small and some large. As long as firms are producing between q_1 and q_2, larger firms do not have a cost advantage over smaller firms.

Figure 8.6(c) illustrates the average costs for a firm in an industry that enjoys extensive economies of scale – for example, an electric power company. No matter how far this firm extends its scale, the long-run average cost curve continues to fall. Diseconomies of scale may exist but, if so, they occur at output levels beyond the effective market for the firm's product. This type of industry tends toward a single seller – a **natural monopoly**. Given the industry's cost structure, that is, one firm can expand its scale, lower its cost of operation, and underprice other firms that attempt to produce on a smaller, higher-cost scale. Electric utilities have been thought for a long time to be natural monopolies (which has supposedly justified their regulation, a subject to which we return in chapter 11).

> A **natural monopoly** is an industry in which long-run marginal and average costs generally decline with increases in production within the relevant range of the market demand for a good or service.

Shifts in the average and marginal cost curves

The average cost curves we have just described all assume that the prices for resources remain constant. This is a critical assumption. If those prices change, so will the average cost curves. The marginal cost curve may shift as well, depending on the type of average cost – variable or fixed – that changes.

Thus if the price of a variable input – such as the wage rate of labor – rises, the firm's average total cost will rise along with its average variable cost ($AFC + AVC = ATC$), shifting the average total cost curve upward. The firm's marginal cost curve also will shift because the additional cost of producing an additional unit must rise with the higher labor cost (see figure 8.7[a]). If a fixed cost, such as insurance premiums, rises then average total cost also will rise, shifting the average total cost curve upward, as in figure 8.7(b). The short-run marginal cost curve will not shift, however, because marginal cost is unaffected by fixed cost. The marginal cost curve is derived only from variable costs.

Because changes in variable cost affect a firm's marginal cost, they influence its production decisions. As first noted in chapter 7, the profit-maximizing firm selling

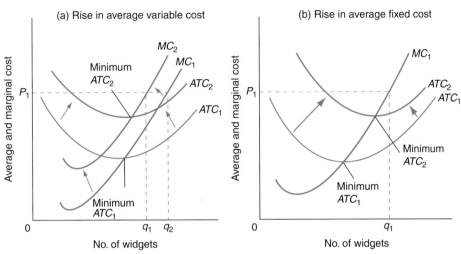

Figure 8.7 Shifts in average and marginal cost curves
An increase in a firm's variable cost (panel [a]) will shift the firm's average total cost curve up, from ATC_1 to ATC_2. It will also shift the marginal cost curve, from MC_1 to MC_2. Production will fall because of the increase in marginal cost. By contrast, an increase in a firm's fixed cost (panel [b]) will shift the average total cost curve upward from ATC_1 to ATC_2, but will not affect the marginal cost curve. (Marginal cost is unaffected by fixed cost.) Thus the firm's level of production will not change.

at a constant price will produce up to the point at which marginal cost equals price ($MC = P$). At a price of P_1 in figure 8.7(a), the firm will produce q_2 widgets. After an increase in variable costs and an upward shift in the marginal cost curve, however, the firm will cut back to q_1 widgets. At q_1 widgets, price again equals marginal cost. The cutback in output has occurred because the marginal cost of producing widgets from q_1 to q_2 now exceeds the price. In other words, an increase in variable cost results in a reduction in a firm's output.

Because a shift in average fixed cost leaves marginal cost unaffected, the firm's profit-maximizing output level in figure 8.7(b) remains at q_1. The firm may make lower profits because of its higher fixed cost, but it cannot increase profits by either expanding or reducing output.

This analysis applies to the short run only. In the long run, all costs are variable, and changes in the price of any resource will affect a firm's production decisions. Long-run changes in the output levels of firms, of course, change the market price of the final product as well as consumer purchases. More will be said on all these points later.

The very long run

Economic analysis tends to be restricted to either the short or the long run for one major reason: for both periods, costs are known with reasonable precision. In the short run, firms know that, beyond some point, increases in the use of a resource (for example, fertilizer) will bring diminishing marginal returns and rising marginal costs. They also know that with increased use of all resources, certain economies and diseconomies of scale can be expected over the long run. Given what is known about the technology of production and the availability of resources, economists can draw certain conclusions about a firm's behavior and the consequences of its actions.

As economists look further and further into the future, however, they can predict less about a firm's behavior and its consequences in the marketplace. Less is known about the technology and resources of the distant future. In the **very long run**, everything is subject to change – resources themselves, their availability, and the technology for using them.

The **very long run** is the time period during which the technology of production and the availability of resources can change because of invention, innovation, and discovery of new technologies and resources.

By definition, the very long run is, to a significant degree, unpredictable. Firms cannot know today how to make use of unspecified future advances in technology. A hundred years ago firms had little idea how important lasers, satellites, airplanes, and computers would be to today's economy. Indeed, many products taken for granted today were invented or discovered quite by accident. Edison developed the phonograph while attempting to invent the light bulb. John Rock developed the birth control pill while studying penicillin. Charles Goodyear's development of vulcanization and Wilhelm Roentgen's invention of the X-ray were both accidents. And even if these inventions could have been predicted, they all had economic consequences that could not have been predicted.

Not all inventions or innovations are accidental, and we can know something about the very long run. Firms have some idea of the value of investments in research and development (R&D). Research on substitute resources can yield improvements in productivity that translate into cost reductions. Research on new product designs will yield more attractive and useful products. There will be failures as well – research projects that accomplish little or nothing – but, over time, the rewards of research and development can exceed the costs.

Because of the risks involved in research and development, some firms may be expected to fail. In the very long run, they will not be able to keep up with the competition in product design and productivity. They will not adjust sufficiently to changes in the market and will suffer losses. The computer industry provides many examples of firms that have tried to build a better machine but could not keep pace with the rapid technological advances of competitors.

Proponents of a planned economy see the uncertainty of the very long run as an argument for government direction of the nation's development. They stress that competitors often do not know what other firms are doing and, therefore, need guidance in the form of government subsidies and tax penalties to ensure that the nation's long-term goals are achieved.

Proponents of the market system agree that it is difficult to look ahead to the very long run, but they see the uncertainties as an argument for keeping production decisions in the hands of firms. Private firms have the economic incentive of profit to stay alert to changes in market conditions and to respond quickly to changes in technology and resources. Government control might slow the adjustment process.

For an explanation why being a "first mover" in a market is rarely an advantage, see online Perspective 8, The myth of the first-mover advantage.

> **Online Perspective 8**
> **The myth of the first-mover advantage**

[handwritten: ✦ Understand Part B]

Part B Organizational economics and management

Firms' debt/equity structures and executive incentives

The cost structure developed in Part A helps us conceptualize the problem a firm faces in deciding how much to produce, but such production decisions could be the least of a firm's problems. The exact placement of the cost structure that a firm faces is not *given* to the firm by some divine being. It emerges from managers' decisions, and these decisions depend critically upon the incentives managers face, along with a number of other factors. Here, we stress the importance of a firm's financial structure – the combination of equity and debt – in shaping managers' incentives and their firm's cost structure. A firm's financial structure can affect managers' risk taking, which can, of course, affects firms' overall cost structure and, hence, competitive market position.

The ideal firm is one with a single owner who produces a lot of stuff with no resources, including labor. Such a firm would be infinitely productive. It would totally avoid agency costs, or those costs that are associated with shirking of duties and the misuse, abuse, and overuse of firm resources for the personal benefit of the managers and workers who have control of firm resources. However, such an ideal firm cannot possibly exist. Resources are always required in the productive process, and whenever more than a very few people are involved, agency costs will result in lost output and a smaller bottom line for the firm.

The world of business is one in which firms often need more funds for investment than one person can generate from his or her own savings or would want to commit to a single enterprise. Any single owner, if the business is even moderately success-ful, typically must find ways of encouraging others to join the firm as owners or lenders (including bondholders, banks, and trade creditors).

Therein lies the source of many firms' problems, not the least of which is that a firm's expansion can give rise to the *agency costs* that a single-person firm would avoid. Managers and workers can use the expanding size of the firm as a screen for their shirking. The addition of equity owners (partners or stockholders) can dilute the incentive of any one owner to monitor what the agents do. Hence, as the firm expands, the agency costs of doing business can erode, if not totally negate, any economies of scale achieved through firm expansion (Jensen and Meckling 1976).

One of the more important questions any single owner of a growing firm must face is: "How will the method of financing growth – debt or equity – affect the extent of the agency cost?" Given that agency costs will always occur with expand-ing firms, how can the combination of debt and equity be varied to minimize the amount of costs from shirking and opportunism? That question is really one dimension of a more fundamental question: "How can the financial structure affect the firm's costs and competitiveness? That is, how can a firm's financial structure affect its short-run and long-run cost structure?"

In this chapter, our focus is on debt, but that is only a matter of convenience of exposition, given that any discussion of debt must be juxtaposed with some dis-cussion of equity as a matter of comparison, if nothing else. We could just as easily draw initial attention to equity as a means of financing growth. In fact, debt and equity are simply two alternative categories of finance (subject to much greater variation in form than we are able to consider here) available to owners. Owners need to search for an "optimum combination," given the advantages and disadvan-tages of both in reducing production costs.

Debt and equity as alternative investment vehicles

By debt, of course, we mean the borrowed funds that must be repaid fully at some agreed-upon time and on which regular interest payments must be made in the interim. The interest rate is simply the annual interest payment divided by the principal. Also, we must note that in the event the firm gets into financial problems, the lenders have first claim on the firm's remaining assets (after due worker claims have been paid).

By equity, or stock, we mean the funds that people provide in return for ultimate control over the disposition of firm resources and who accept the status of residual claimants, which means that a return on investment (which is subject to variation) will be paid only after all other claims on the firm have been satisfied. That is to say, the owners (stockholders) will not receive dividends until all required interest payments have been met; the owners are guaranteed nothing in the form of repayment of their initial investments. Obviously, owners (stockholders) accept more risk on their investment than do lenders (or bondholders).[2]

Does it matter whether a firm finances its investments by debt or equity? You bet it does (otherwise, we must wonder why the two broad categories of finance would ever exist). With debt, the payments – both the payoff sum and the interest payments – are fixed, which is important for two reasons. First, fixed payments enable firms to attract funds from people who want security and certainty in their investments. The modern aphorism, "Different strokes for different folks," if followed in the structuring of financial instruments, can mean lower costs of investment funds, and therefore production cost, which means more growth and greater competitiveness. Debt attracts funds from people who get their "strokes" from added security. Second, if the firm earns more than the required interest payments on any given investment project, the residual goes to the equity owners. If the company fails because of investments gone sour, and it has to be liquidated for less than the amount owed to lenders, then stockholders (those who bought equity in the firm) will get nothing. Stockholders can claim only what is left after all expenses and the lenders have been paid. That's it.

Clearly, the nature of debt biases, to a degree, the decision making of the owners, or their agent/managers, toward seeking risky investments, ones that will likely carry high rates of return. But these high rates can tempt equity owners to take unduly high risks, given that they get what is left after the fixed interest payments are deducted from high returns and the lenders will suffer most of the cost if the investment fails. If a firm borrows funds at a 10 percent interest rate, for example, and invests those funds in projects that have an expected rate of return of 12 percent, the residual left for the equity owners will be the difference, 2 percent. If, on the other hand, the funds are invested in a much riskier project that has a rate of return of 18 percent, then the residual that can be claimed by the equity owners is 8 percent, four times as great as that of the first case.

Granted, the project with the higher rate has a risk premium built into it (or else everyone investing in the 12 percent projects would direct their funds to the 18 percent projects, causing the rate of returns in the latter to fall and in the former to rise). However, notice that much of that additional risk is imposed on the lenders.

---

[2] We recognize that debt and equity come in a variety of forms. Common and preferred stock are the two major divisions of equity. Debt can take a form that has the "look and feel" of equity. For example, the much-maligned "junk bonds" often carry with them rights of control over firm decisions and may also be about as risky as common stock.

They are the ones who must fear that the risk incurred will translate into failed investments (which is what risk implies). But they are not the ones who are compensated for the assumed risk they bear. Indeed, after a lender has made a loan for a specified rate of interest, the managers can increase the risk imposed on the original lenders by pursuing much riskier projects than those lenders anticipated, or by increasing the firm's indebtedness by more borrowing.

As a general rule, the greater the indebtedness, the greater incentive that managers have to engage in risky investments. Again, this is because much of the risk is imposed on the lenders, and the benefits, if they materialize, are garnered by the equity owners. When a firm has no debt, then the equity owners incur all downside risks of risky investment projects. If projects fail, then owners lose whatever was invested. If the firm is 100 percent leveraged, then lenders will suffer the losses from risky investments, but owners will garner all of the risk premium embodied in their investment successes.

Not surprisingly, as a firm takes on more debt, lenders will become progressively more concerned about losing some or all of their investments. As a consequence, lenders will demand compensation in the form of higher interest payments, which reflect a risk premium. Those lenders who fear that the firm will continue to expand its indebtedness after they make the initial loans will also seek compensation prior to the rise in indebtedness by way of a higher interest rate. To keep interest costs under control, firm managers will want to make commitments as to how much indebtedness the firm will incur, and they must make the commitments believable. Again, we return to a recurring theme: managers' reputations for credibility have an economic value. In this case, the value emerges in lower interest payments.

Lenders, of course, will seek to protect themselves from risky managerial decisions in other ways. They may, as they often do, seek to obtain rights to monitor and even constrain the indebtedness of the firms to whom they make loans. Managers also have an interest in making such concessions because, although their freedom of action is restricted in one sense, they can be compensated for the accepted restrictions in the form of lower interest rates. Firm managers are granted greater freedom of action in another respect; they are given a greater residual with which they can work (to add to their salary and perks, if they have the discretion to do so; to extend the investments of the firm; or to increase the dividends for stockholders).

Lenders may also specify the collateral the firm must commit, and will be most interested in having the firm pledge "general capital," or assets that are resaleable, which means that the lenders can potentially recover their invested funds. Lenders will not be interested in having "firm-specific capital," or assets that are designed only for their given use inside a particular firm as collateral, since they have little, if any, resale market.

Of course, firm assets are often more or less "general" or "firm-specific," which means they can be better or worse forms of collateral. A firm can pledge assets with "firm-specific capital" attributes. However, managers must understand that the more firm-specific the asset (the narrower the resale market), the greater the risk premium that will be tacked onto the firm's interest rate, and the lower the potential residual for the equity owners.

Lenders will also have a preference for lending to those firms that have a stable future income stream and that can be easily monitored. The more stable the future income, the lower the risk of nonpayments of interest. The more easily the firm can be monitored, the less likely managers will be able to leave creditors with uncompensated risks. The more willing lenders are to lend to firms, the greater the likely indebtedness.

Electric utility companies have been good candidates for heavy indebtedness, because their markets have been protected from entry by government controls and regulations, what they do is relatively easily measured, and their future income stream can be assumed to be relatively stable. Accordingly, their interest rates should be relatively low, which should encourage managers to take on additional debt just so that equity owners can claim the residual for themselves. (At the time of writing, the deregulation of electric power production was under way in a few US states, allowing open entry into the generation of electricity. We should expect deregulation to lead to a higher-risk premium in interest rates, although the price of electricity can be expected to fall for consumers with increased competition for power sales.)

Past failed incentives in the S&L industry

The incentives of indebtedness are dramatically illustrated by one of the biggest financial debacles of modern times, the dramatic rise in savings and loan (S&L) bank failures of the 1980s. The S&L industry was established in the 1930s to ensure that the savings of individuals, who effectively loaned their funds to the S&Ls, could be channeled to the housing industry (a concentrated focus of S&L investment portfolios that in itself added an element of risk, especially because housing starts vary radically with the business cycle). S&Ls were in a position to loan money for housing, deriving up to 97 percent of the funding from their depositors and only 3 percent from the S&L owners (given reserve and equity requirements). Such a division, of course, made the owners eager to go after high-risk but high-return projects. They could claim the residuals from what was then interest payment on deposits that were kept low by a federal ceiling on the interest rates S&Ls could pay depositors. Of course, depositors might be concerned about the risks S&L owners could take with their funds. But because in the 1970s the federal government insured the deposits up to $10,000, depositors' incentives to be concerned about and to monitor S&L risk taking were muted.

The emergence of the crisis

When interest rates began to rise radically with the rising inflation in the late 1970s, alternative market-based forms of saving became available – not the least of which were money market and mutual funds, which were unrestricted in the rates of return they could offer savers. As a consequence, savings started flowing out of S&Ls, which greatly increased the pressure on them to hike the interest rates paid on their deposits (which they were free to do in the early 1980s), and to offset the higher interest rates with investments that were riskier but carried higher rates of return. To compensate, the federal government closely monitored and regulated investments of S&Ls and controlled the competition S&Ls faced.

But in 1982, the S&Ls' incentive for risky investment was heightened when the federal deposit insurance on S&L accounts was increased to $100,000, effectively assuring the overwhelming majority of all depositors that they would lose nothing if their S&L companies lost all their deposits on risky loans. In the same year, the federal government gave S&Ls greater freedom to pursue high-risk investments. The hope was that the S&Ls' greater investment freedom would stave off the looming S&L financial crisis (which amounted to hoping that the S&Ls would win a national financial lottery!).

The result should have been predictable, based on the simple idea that people respond to incentives. S&Ls went after the high-risk/high-return – and high-residual – investments. The S&Ls that made the risky investments were in a position to pay high interest rates, drawing funds from other more conservative S&Ls. The incentives that had been created for them was "heads they won, tails the taxpayer lost." To protect their deposit base, conservative S&Ls had to raise their interest rates, which meant that they also had to seek riskier investments, all of which led to a shock wave of risky investments spreading through the S&L/development industry.

Unfortunately, many of those investments did what should have been expected given their risky nature: they failed. The government (taxpayers) had to absorb the losses and then return to doing what it had done before 1982 – closely monitoring the industry and severely restricting the riskiness of the investments. (The government was unwilling to lower the size of deposits that were subject to federal deposit insurance, which would have given depositors greater incentives to monitor their S&Ls.)

Clearly, fraud was a part of the S&L debacle. Crooks were attracted to the industry (Black, Calavita, and Pontell 1995; Wauzzinski 2003). However, the debacle is a grand illustration of how debt can, and did, affect management decisions. It also enables us to draw out a financial/management principle: if owners want to control the riskiness of their firms' investments, they had better look to how much debt their firms accumulate. Debt can encourage risk taking, which can be "good" or "bad," depending on whether the costs are considered and evaluated against the expected return.

Why then would the original equity owners ever be willing to issue more shares of stock and attract more equity owners with whom the original owners would have to share the residual? Sometimes, of course, the original owners are unable to provide the additional funds that a firm may need to pursue what are known (in an expectation sense) to be profitable investment projects. The original owners can figure that although their *share* of firm profits will go down, the *absolute level* of the residual they claim will go up. A 60 percent share of $100,000 in profits beats 100 percent of $50,000 in profits any day.

Also, in situations where the firm is involved in new ventures in which the risks are high, and bondholders (lenders) have no protection against losses as S&L depositors did, the firm will have to pay very high interest rates to borrow money. This doesn't mean that firms in high-risk businesses will not borrow any money, but most of their financing will come from equity holders. Only when most of the financing comes from equity will lenders see their risks low enough (even if the firm fails, bondholders can be fully paid from the sale of assets) to loan money at reasonable rates. So additional equity investment means that the equity owners can claim a greater residual (if the firm is successful) because the firm's interest payments decrease with the reduction in the risk premium to bondholders.

Investment projects often require a combination of firm-specific and general capital to be used. Consider, for example, the predicament of a remodeling firm that uses specially designed pieces of floor equipment (which may have little or no market value outside the firm) as well as trucks that can easily be sold in well-established used-truck markets. The investment projects can be divided according to the interests of the two types of investors. The equity owners can be called upon to take the risk associated with the floor equipment while the lenders are called upon to provide the funds for the trucks. Of course, it is better for the lenders if the firm profitably uses the trucks and other general equipment rather than selling its assets. So lenders might not even make the loan for the general part of the investment without equity owners taking the firm-specific part precisely because the general investment is less valuable to the firm without the firm-specific capital investment. (The trucks will not be useful to the firm without the output produced by the floor equipment.)

Spreading risks

The original owners can also have an interest in selling a portion of their ownership share because, by doing so, they can reinvest among a number of firms and reduce the overall risk of their full portfolio of investments. If the original owners held their full investments in the firm and refused to sell off a portion, then they might be "too cautious" in the choice of investments – not making risky investments that yield a higher expected profit than more conservative investments. Once the original owners have spread their ownership over a number of firms, they will find the riskier investments more attractive, since diversification has made them collectively less risky. Again, the financial structure of the firm is important – and it can matter to both management policies and the bottom line.

Free cash flow problem

Former Harvard finance professor Michael Jensen argues for another reason for some firms to stay in debt: debt avoids the problems executives may have in dealing with the so-called "free cash flow problem." The interest payments on the debt can tie the hands – or reduce the discretionary authority – of managers who might otherwise engage in opportunism with their firms' residual (Jensen 1989). If a firm has little debt, then the managers can have a great deal of funds, or residual, to do with as they please. They can use the residual to provide themselves with higher salaries and more perks. They can also use the funds to contribute to local charities that may have little impact on their firm's business (they may have a warm heart for the cause they support or they may want simply to take credit for being charitable with their firm's funds). They may also use the funds to expand (without the usual degree of scrutiny) the scope and scale of their firms, thereby justifying their higher salaries and greater perks (because firm size and executive compensation tend to go together).

Even if the investment projects that the managers choose are profitable, if the funds were distributed to the stockholders, they might find even more profitable investments (and even more worthy charitable causes).

Industry maturity and funds misuse

As industries mature (or reach the limits of profitable expansion), the risk of managers "misusing" firm funds increases. Few opportunities may be available for managers to reinvest the earnings in their own industry. They may then be tempted to use the "excess residual" to fulfill some of their own personal flights of managerial fancy (more expensive perks and greater "generosity"), or reinvest the funds in other industries that may or may not have a solid connection to the original firm's core activities.

How can the firm be made to disgorge the residual? Jensen suggests that indebtedness is a good way to accomplish this: the greater the indebtedness, the smaller the residual and the less waste that can go up in the smoke of managerial opportunism. Jensen argues that one of the reasons for firm takeovers by way of "leveraged buyouts," which means heavy indebtedness, is that the firm that is taken over is forced to give up the residual through higher interest payments. Again, the hands of the agent/managers are tied; their ability to misuse firm funds is curbed. Indebtedness can enhance the firm's value mainly because it reduces the discretion of managers who have been misusing the funds. And managers can misuse their discretion in counterproductive ways, not the least of which is by diversifying the array of products and services provided on the grounds that diversity can smooth out the company's cash flows over the various cycles that go with the products and services. But shareholders are able to do that for themselves very easily with the large number of mutual funds now available.

Experience teaches that indebtedness is not necessarily the only or easiest way that firms can disgorge such cash: they can pay dividends. Moreover, experience also teaches that what a firm should do with "free cash flow" is not always obvious and can prompt strong disagreements among board members and top executives, mainly because of the limitations of available information on the riskiness and rates of returns on alternative corporate strategies.

The thorny issue of what to do with free cash emerged in 2005 when Karl Icahn, renowned for "raiding" (or taking over) faltering corporations, became the biggest stockholder in Blockbuster, the largest bricks-and-mortar video rental retailer in the United States. According to reports, Icahn believed that Blockbuster's management had gone on a "spending spree" and, in the process, had begun to "gamble" away "shareholders' money" on risky investments (Peers 2005). As a new board member, Icahn began insisting that management disgorge its accumulating cash with large dividend payments to stockholders, a strategy that would restrict the ability of top management to engage in investment misadventures, including the company's then ongoing efforts to "reinvent" the company by moving away from rentals at retail stores and toward rentals over the Internet. Seeing that the retail rental business was dying, Icahn wanted management to use its retail outlets as "cash cows," continuing to operate them for as long as the growing competition from mail-order video rental companies would allow. On the other hand, John Antico, chairman of Blockbuster, believed that the company had to reinvent itself, and use its cash flow to undertake a "corporate makeover" to fend off erosion of Blockbuster's market from Internet-based movie rental companies such as Netflix and Walmart (Peers 2005).

Who is right? At the time of writing the answer remains unclear, dependent upon information on rates of return and risk on alternative investment strategies that can be known only to corporate insiders. However, there is at least one strong argument to think that Icahn's strategy of paying dividends could be most persuasive. At least having disgorged its free cash flow, Blockbuster's top executives would be required to convince outside investors and Blockbuster's own shareholders that Antico's proposed strategy of reinventing the company could provide them with a greater rate of return than they could achieve by sticking with its bricks-and-mortar rental model, but could also offer investors a greater return than they could achieve in other companies.

Blockbuster's very act of paying out the dividends could be a sign of considerable confidence on the part of management that they had a solid case for reinventing the company, and hence could easily fund their new investment plans. Of course, critics could argue that dividend payouts, along with the issue of new investment instruments, could impose crippling time delays on management's efforts to reposition the company in a highly competitive market. In some matters (this one included) only time will tell who – Icahn and the other board members or Antico and the other top executives – will control the future of the company and the movie-rental industry. At this writing, Blockbuster rental revenues at its brick-and-mortar stores was in full retreat from Internet rental companies such as Netflix, cable companies offering movie rentals on demand, and growing competition from downloads over the Internet from, for example, Apple via its iTunes store.

Firm maturity and indebtedness

This all leads us to an interesting proposition. We should expect firm indebtedness to increase with the maturity of its industry. Firms in a mature industry have more stable future income streams than do those in fledgling industries and can be monitored more easily. People gain experience working with established firms and learn how the firms operate and when they may be inclined to misappropriate funds. Also, by taking on more debt, firms in mature industries can alert the market to their intentions to rid themselves of their residual, conveying the message to the market that managers' discretion to use and misuse firm financial resources will be constricted, all of which can increase the price of the firm's stock.

Of course, if firms in mature industries don't take on relatively more debt and managers continue to misuse the funds by reinvesting the residual in the mature industry or other industries, then the firm can be ripe for a takeover. An outside "raider" may see an opportunity to buy the stock at a depressed price, paying for the stock with debt. The increase in indebtedness can, by itself, raise the price of the stock, making the takeover a profitable venture. However, if the takeover target is a disparate collection of production units that do not fit well together because of past management indiscretions in investment, the profit potential for the raiders is even greater. The firm should be worth more in pieces than as a single firm. The raiders can buy the stock at a depressed price, take charge, and break the company apart, selling off the parts for more than the purchase price. In the process, the market value of the "core business" can be enhanced.

The bottom-line consequences of firms' financial structures

*Read +
Understand
For test*

The moral of this section should now be self-evident: *The financial structure of firms matters, and it matters a great deal.* By choosing the best combination of debt and equity in financing the firm's productive activities, managers can do a lot to keep the cost curves discussed earlier in this chapter as low as possible. Keeping those cost curves low is a crucial factor determining how effective a firm is at producing wealth and remaining viable in a competitive market. This also means that choice on debt and equity financing can determine whether the firm will be subject to a takeover. The one great antidote for a takeover should be obvious to managers, but it is not always (as evidenced by the fact that takeovers are not uncommon): firms should be structured, in terms of both their financial *and* other policies, *to create incentives to use their resources to produce as much wealth as possible, which will maximize the stock price.* In that case, potential raiders will have nothing to gain by trying to take the firm over. One of the primary functions of a board of directors is to monitor the executives and the policies that are implemented with an eye toward maximizing stockholder value. As we will show in a later chapter, those executives and their boards that do not maximize the price of their stocks do have something to fear from corporate raiders.

[See online Video Module 8.4 CEO compensation]

The emergence of the housing bubble and burst of the early 2000s

How did the country get into the mortgage meltdown and economic crisis that emerged full-blown as a serious recession in 2008, perhaps the deepest and longest recession since the Great Depression? Since the housing and more general economic crisis continues apace at this writing, any explanation is risky history and has to be suggestive and tentative. No doubt, a part of the problem can be laid at the doorstep of modern loan sharks (inside and outside the commercial banking industry) who snared unsuspecting and unqualified home buyers with mortgage deals dubbed "subprime mortgages" that really were too good to be true. Many home buyers saw the newfangled mortgages as an opportunity to buy houses they could not afford on the cheap, or so they were led to believe (or wanted to believe).

But, as so often is the case, the history of the modern mortgage mess has been neglected as politicians point the finger of guilt solely at "greedy" lenders and borrowers and declare a need for more federal bailouts in one form or another. "Greed" is a facile answer for any major economic problem, although often containing more than an ounce of truth. But greed is a perennial human problem that doesn't illuminate the contemporary economic crisis. Without understanding the history of the mortgage mess, the easy solutions may prompt another financial meltdown in the country's future. We will need to learn from our recent history.

Possible origin of the housing bubble

One possible origin of the housing crisis of 2008 and beyond can be traced to the 1970s and before, when savings and loan banks were practically the only mortgage game in most American towns. They made the overwhelming majority of their mortgages in their communities, and they loaned almost all of their funds for purchases of homes and other real estate. S&Ls were not, in other words, highly diversified in their investments. They could not diversify their portfolios by buying stock in other companies or even by making consumer loans. They were, in short, highly exposed to the ups and downs of their local housing markets, with their narrowly focused investment exposure translating into a lot of risk that perhaps could have been abated somewhat had they been allowed to diversify their loan assets. The government offset some of their investment risk by limiting S&Ls' competition through strict limits on entry into the savings and mortgage business. As a consequence, S&Ls paid low interest rates on deposits (partially because of restrictions on the interest rates deposit banks could make on checking account deposits), which enabled S&Ls to charge low, fixed interest rates on their mortgages. S&Ls did not have to worry very much about the risk of losing market share to innovative new entrants into their markets.

Under such market and regulatory conditions, S&Ls understandably sought to mitigate their exposure to loan risks by carefully scrutinizing mortgage borrowers, taking great care to ensure borrowers could make a substantial down payment and had the wherewithal to make thirty years of monthly payments. (In the 1920s and before, S&Ls sought to contain their risks further by making mortgage loans for fifteen years or even as few as five years.) Of course, the regulated system, with careful scrutiny of borrowers' creditworthiness, meant that a lot of Americans were left out of the housing market. However, careful regulation of the mortgage business could be justified on the grounds that S&Ls were highly leveraged, getting up to 97 percent of their loanable funds from savings depositors and only 3 percent from owners. If left unregulated, the S&L owners would have been greatly tempted to go after the premiums embedded in risky investment projects outside of housing.

Government deposit insurance heightened the temptation to undertake risky projects. The S&Ls and other banks were secure knowing that even if borrowers defaulted en masse, their depositors, with whom they may have built up personal, community-based relationships, would not be losers (taxpayers would!). As noted, because of the inflationary spiral of the 1970s, S&Ls began bleeding money. To save many S&Ls from going belly up, Congress relaxed regulations, allowing them to diversify their portfolios, with the disastrous effects of considerable risk taking.

Then, to provide for constraining market competition, the government relaxed the regulations on mortgage-market entry.

The securitization of mortgages

In the 1970s, someone got the idea of grouping mortgages into securities, which could be sold to investors on Wall Street and, for that matter, around the world. Banks of all kinds and other institutions, which began to emerge to serve the housing market just outside of the still regulated banking industry, began to serve the role of mortgage "retailers," finding borrowers and then selling their paper in "bundles" to far-removed investors. Many investors in so-called "mortgage-backed securities" might have understandably believed that they were buying securities backed with mortgages of high quality, as mortgages in the 1970s and before were largely made to high creditworthy borrowers and foreclosure rates were low.

The "securitization" of mortgages infused more investment funds into mortgages and, thus, the housing industry. The infusion of funds into the mortgage market elicited an increase in the proportion of American families who became homeowners from 64 percent in the early 1990s to 69 percent by 2005, a thought-to-be notable political accomplishment of the Bill Clinton and George W. Bush administrations.

The system was built to a degree on the presumption that mortgage lenders would continue to be fairly conservative (or risk averse) in developing mortgage contracts and selecting borrowers. Many Wall Street investors in mortgage-backed securities probably did not realize that retail mortgage lenders could, under pressure of competition, be pressed to view the mortgage-backed securities as "black boxes" into which lenders could obscure some risky loans. The infusion of funds from investors around the world into mortgages required lenders to go downstream in the creditworthiness of borrowers and to become creative in their mortgage contracts, offering subprime loans to questionable borrowers. For example, borrowers could be enticed into mortgages with delayed "balloon payments" (or jumps in monthly payments) after several years. Investors in mortgage-backed securities may not have been fully aware of how the securitization process could fuel the bubble in housing prices and construction, which could justify more loans on houses whose prices were in free flight.

"Irrational exuberance"

Yale University financial economist Robert Shiller argues that a major source of the housing (and stock-market) bubble was "irrational exuberance" or "bubble thinking" that, in turn, was founded on some "new era story" that "*is not warranted by rational analysis of economic fundamentals*" (2005, 18; emphasis in the original). The stock-market bubble of the late 1990s was rationalized, according to Shiller, by reference to the emergence of the Internet economy that everyone thought in the mid-1990s would revolutionize the way business would be conducted and that would allow advanced countries to tap the hordes of low-wage workers in China and India. The economic revolution that the Internet inspired, in turn, could justify historically high price–earnings ratios for dot.com stocks. In the case of the housing bubble of the early 2000s, Shiller argues that people came to widely believe that the rising housing prices of the late 1990s and early 2000s could be justified on the belief that the land available for development (especially in key cities such as Los Angeles, Miami, and New York) was becoming ever scarcer and that the cost of building houses would continue to rise, with the growing scarcities feeding the demand for housing (Shiller 2008, chapter 4).

Indeed, the housing price bubble that emerged after 2003 and that gave rise to housing prices outpacing borrowers' ability to pay could have led to greater profitability of banks and other lenders because the overinflated housing prices made their loans look more secured (Coleman, Lacour-Little, and Vandell 2008). After all, with the bubble under way, home buyers saw their equity quickly rise. The expected emergence of equity in houses meant that lenders could go even further downstream in the creditworthiness of borrowers. With the housing price bubble, the assessed creditworthiness of many borrowers could have risen, or might have appeared to have risen. With lower down payments for mortgages, which were guaranteed by the Federal Housing Administration (down payments for FHA mortgages averaged 3 percent in 2004 [Berlau 2007]), many prospective homeowners could have fallen prey to the temptation to undertake risky housing ventures of their own when they were highly leveraged. And a mortgage for which the homeowners make only a 5 or 10 percent down payment is a highly leveraged investment – that is, the borrowers/homeowners can garner potential gains while the lenders shoulder any losses from a downturn in housing prices. (In the 1990s and 2000s, these lenders increasingly became far-removed investors in mortgage-backed securities, often princes in Middle East oil-rich principalities.)

Along the way, the government began subsidizing low-income (and credit-unworthy) prospective home buyers, in some cases making sure that the buyers had to make no down payment from their own funds, which means buyers were 100 percent leveraged. A sequence of administrations and Congresses induced Freddie Mac and Fannie Mae to encourage homeownership through Freddie's and Fannie's purchases of mortgage-backed securities that were collections of mortgages based on lower credit standards. Indeed, according to Hoover Institution economist Thomas Sowell, a variety of federal regulatory agencies, at the behest of members of Congress, began to press banks and other financial institutions to lower their lending standards and to increase the granting of mortgages to lower-income and identified ethnic groups. Indeed, Sowell argues that the political pressure effectively instituted quotas for financial institutions to make loans to groups that had not been able to meet former credit standards, all under the banner of promoting "affordable housing" for disadvantaged Americans who had previously faced lending discrimination, or so Sowell argues (Sowell 2009, chapter 2). If there was "herding" in the housing market, the problem was not irrationality on the part of lenders and borrowers, but a problem of market participants actually being herded by errant public policies.

Of course, all efforts to increase the "affordability" of housing fueled the speculative housing price bubble and people's temptation to take risks with borrowed funds. In 2001, subprime and all other nonprime mortgages accounted for 10 percent of all mortgage originations. By 2006, subprime mortgages accounted for 34 percent of all mortgage originations, and Freddie and Fannie held, with federal guarantees, half of the $12 trillion in mortgages (White 2008, 1 and 4, citing the Federal Reserve Bank of St. Louis).

The Federal Reserve further inflated the housing price bubble with its easy money policy; the Fed lowered the federal funds rate (the interest rate banks charge each other for short-term, often overnight, loans) from 6.25 percent to 1.74 percent in only one year, 2001 (perhaps in anticipation of an economic slump as a result of the bursting of the stock-market bubble in 2000 and the 9/11 terrorist acts). The Fed further lowered the federal funds rate to a then historic low of 1 percent in mid-2003. Ben Bernanke, a member of the Fed's governing board at the time and now (at this writing) chairman of the Fed's board, saw no problem with the easy money policy and warned in a statement before the Federal Open Market Committee against tightening the growth in the money supply on the grounds that economic "growth not be choked off unnecessarily." Bernanke pointed to the "considerable slack" that at the time remained in the economy, as evident by the continuing gap between actual national output and the potential output (Bernanke 2009).

The continuation of the easy money policy following Bernanke's remarks set off what one monetary economist called "the mother of all liquidity cycles and yet another massive bubble" (as quoted by White 2008, 4). During the 2003–7 period, sales of goods and services in the United States expanded by an annual rate of 7 percent, while real estate loans expanded by an annual rate of 10–17 percent (White 2008, 1 and 4, citing the Federal Reserve Bank of St. Louis). The stock-market and housing bubbles were probably aggravated by a boom in Asian saving in the 1990s and 2000s, which gave rise to an increase in the cross-national capital flows from just above 1 percent in 1990 to 3 percent in 2008, with much of the capital flowing into the United States through purchases of stocks and mortgage-backed securities (Whitehouse 2009).

But so much of the bubble economics was more or less illusory, dependent upon people continuing to expect a rise in housing prices (if not an increase in the rate of housing price increases).

"A failure of capitalism"

Federal Judge Richard Posner, a founder of the University of Chicago's program in law and economics, maintains that the United States' and the world's financial mess was nothing less than a "failure of capitalism," with capitalism being a system that is "inherently unstable" (Posner 2009b): "At its [capitalism's] heart is a banking system that enables large-scale borrowing and lending, without which most businesses cannot bridge the gap between incurring costs and receiving revenues and most consumers cannot achieve their desired level of consumption" (Posner 2009a). Since lending opportunities vary in risk, many lending opportunities are necessarily highly risky. Posner suggests that we got into the financial mess for many of the same reasons that Shiller articulated, one of the more important of which has been the gradual deregulation of the financial industry that enabled banks and non-banks to undertake ever more highly leveraged ventures. The Federal Reserve's policy of "easy money" or low interest rates encouraged greater leverage in the 1990s and the early 2000s. When the Glass Steagall Act (which kept deposit banking and investment banking separate) was repealed in 1999, deposit banks, which had access to readily available liquidity through the Federal Reserve's discount window, could acquire or build investment banking operations and extend their leverage on loans through their investment banking operations. New financial intermediaries – most notably, hedge funds – were allowed to arise without regulatory oversight: "Deregulation increased competition in banking by allowing other financial firms to offer close substitutes for banking services. Increased competition in turn compressed the margin between the interest rates that banks paid to borrow capital for lending and the interests they charged their borrowers. The narrower the margin, the more leverage banks need in order to obtain enough revenue net of their borrowing costs" (Posner 2009b, 130).

The increased leverage increased the riskiness of banks' lending and, at the same time, increased threat to the stability of their deposit banking operations, if the economy suddenly turned sour or interest rates turned upward and caused a downturn in asset (housing) prices and undermined the market value of mortgage-backed securities. The banks' narrower margins from more intense competition in financial intermediation markets encouraged banks to increase their margins by seeking the risk premiums that go with lending to borrowers with shakier credit records.

Why so much deregulation? Posner argues that a major culprit was the growing grip of "free-market ideology" adopted from the Reagan Administration through the Clinton Administration to the second Bush Administration, with the adopted ideology teaching that "competitive markets are on the whole self-correcting" and failing to recognize the "economy as a kind of epileptic, subject to unpredictable and strange seizures," especially when in the application of free-market, deregulatory principles no distinction is made between banking and financial intermediation industry and other industries (for example, airline and trucking industries) (Posner 2009b, 134–5).

Even the long-past elimination of controls on interest rates financial institutions can charge ("usury laws") contributed to risk taking and, ultimately, the epileptic seizure the US and world economies experienced in 2008. In chapter 4, we stressed the potential negative consequences of price ceilings in labor and apartment rental markets. Usury laws are a form of price ceiling on interest rates for loans. Posner argues that interest-rate ceilings can have an unheralded benefit for financial institutions that make highly leveraged investments: with upper legal limits on the interest rates that could be charged with usury laws in force, financial institutions rationally contained the risks they took (Posner 2009b, 21). When interest rates were deregulated, it follows that banks became more willing to make risky loans. This could very well be the case because of the risk premiums built into the interest rates they could charge less creditworthy customers.

Moreover, the crisis emerged because mortgage-backed securities were relatively new financial instruments in the 1990s, created during a prolonged recovery, which means that assessments of the probability of failure of mortgage-backed securities could be only guesses. Banks lacked historical experience on which to estimate risks.

When banks bought mortgage-backed securities, they may have thought they were containing their risks. Mortgage-backed securities were collections of large numbers of loans with different levels of risk and credit ratings. Banks could further diversify away risk, or so they thought, by buying a number of mortgages from different parts of the country and world. Even if they made some loans to formerly credit-unworthy borrowers, their overall risk could go down.

Whereas Shiller emphasizes the role of "irrationality" at the foundation of the financial crisis, Posner is "skeptical that readily avoidable mistakes, failures of rationality, or intellectual deficiencies of financial managers" are at the heart of the crisis. He argues that so much of the crisis can be explained by rational decision making that concocting an array of "irrationalities" is unnecessary. Instead, Posner posits that people were, in the main, acting rationally throughout the expansion of the housing bubble. Even "herding" behavior in asset markets, which is thought to be founded on irrational or non-rational decision making, can have a rational foundation. Often, it makes sense for individual decision making to follow what others are doing because others are often right, especially in the midst of an expanding bubble. Moreover, while it can be risky to follow the "herd," "it is also risky to abandon the safety of the herd – ask any wildebeest" (Posner 2009b, 84).

Borrowers and lenders rationally responded to the lower interest rates the Federal Reserve orchestrated. Buyers of the mortgage-backed securities assumed such securities (especially the AAA-rated tranches) were reasonably safe investments, especially since housing prices were mounting and homeowners' home equity was on the rise. Posner asks his readers:

Suppose the best guess was that there was a 10 percent probability that the price rise [in housing] was a bubble and the same probability that [housing prices] would fall by at least 20 percent. Then the probability that house prices would fall by at least 20 percent was only 1 percent (0.1×0.1), and so disaster would be unlikely to occur for many years, and the risk of disaster would have seemed worth taking. A 1 percent risk of bankruptcy is not like a 1 percent risk of a nuclear war. Bankruptcy is common enough, in fact is an indispensable institution of the capitalist system. Because risk and return are positively correlated, a firm that plays it safe is, paradoxically, courting failure because investors will turn elsewhere. (Posner 2009b, 79)

However, what is rational from the perspective of individual borrowers, lenders, and investors can give rise to a true house price bubble and to the systemic risk that the bubble will burst either with a reversal of easy money policy (which happened in 2005) or with curbs in the growth of government encouragements for low-income and credit-unworthy people to buy homes with little to no "skin in the game" (which means buying highly, if not totally, leveraged homes). What can be rational for individuals in financial markets, however, can be collectively irrational in the same way polluting can be rational for individuals but can have collective consequences that no one wants. Individuals can reason that their little bit of pollution will do no damage to the environment, which can be true, but everyone's pollution taken together can result in environmental devastation, a line of argument we have made in various contexts in this textbook (see chapters 3 and 5) (Posner 2009b, 107).

Granted, we now know with hindsight that a housing price bubble was under way from at least 2003 onward through 2005 to 2007, but no one *knew* that to be the case *during* the bubble. During the bubble's expansion, "a bubble could only be suspected, not confirmed," and even current Federal Reserve Chairman Bernanke assured everyone in the fall of 2005 (when he was chairman of President George W. Bush's Council of Economic Advisors) that the then escalation in housing prices did not constitute a bubble because prices reflected the growing scarcity of land and the inelasticity of the supply of housing (Posner 2009b, 90). Even as late as spring 2007 and after the housing bubble had burst, Bernanke observed, "Importantly, we see no serious broader spillover to banks or thrift institutions from the problems in the subprime market" (as reported by Posner 2009b, 132). Assessments of economic conditions can be wrongheaded, but they are not necessarily irrational, given that information needed for better assessments is costly or often unavailable. People can be rationally ignorant.

Posner goes on to argue that it is quite rational for people and banks to continue making risky loans during a suspected bubble. This is because rising interest rates on loans can compensate lenders for the assumed risks, or so it can be thought so long as asset prices are rising. Besides, bankers can have a tough time convincing their boards of directors that they should sell off mortgage-backed securities, taking a short-term discount on them and giving up the prospective future interest income stream with the built-in risk premiums, especially when everyone else in the industry is building their portfolios of mortgage-backed securities. In addition, when executives' pay is based on short-term profits and when executives have negotiated handsome severance packages (so-called "golden parachutes" on dismissal for firms' losses), they have incentives to make risky loans because such loans, with built-in risk premiums, can boost short-term profits and executives' pay and bonuses. The lending decisions can increase the threat of bankruptcy in the future, but executives can live comfortably when they are dismissed. In Posner's words, "The more generous an executive's compensation and the more insulated his compensation package is from adversity that may befall his company, the greater will be his incentive to maximize profits in the short run – especially in a bubble, where the short run is highly profitable but the long run a looming disaster" (Posner 2009b, 94–5).

One of the failures of capitalism is that many firms have not figured out how to provide appropriate incentives to executives because of pervasive conflicts of interest between executives and their boards that determine executives' pay (Posner 2009b, chapter 3). Posner repeatedly insists that the financial crisis needs to be assessed through the conventional microeconomic lens of rational decision making. This is because such a way of thinking can lead people to see that financial industries are in special need of governmental oversight (for much the same reason that the environment is in special need of regulatory oversight), given the damage that can be done to people's lives from excessive risk taking from highly leveraged investments. If economists and policy makers assume that an array of irrationalities, which are intrinsic to all human decision making, are at the heart of the financial crisis, then the analysis can lead to excessive regulations of many industries, which can carry long-term economic costs.

The bursting of the bubble

After 2005, the introductory "teaser" interest rates made on mortgages that had attracted many otherwise unqualified buyers began to end, and foreclosures began to mount. Housing prices first began to level off in 2005 and then began to fall in 2006, undermining the creditworthiness of many home buyers and destroying the only foundation for many home purchases, expected higher resale prices.

In early 2009, the country's financial and economic troubles had been mounting for more than a year. In 2008, the Standard & Poor's Index of five hundred stocks declined by 38 percent, the median home price declined 22 percent, 2.6 million jobs were lost, and the market value of the Dow Jones Wilshire Index of five thousand declined by nearly $7 trillion. At the start of 2009 the unemployment rate stood at 7.2 percent, up from 5.9 percent a year earlier, with more than 40 percent of the job losses for 2008 coming in the last two months of that year. The unemployment rate for African-Americans topped 11 percent at the start of 2009. Few economists expected anything other than a rising unemployment rate through at least the end of 2009, and maybe through the first half of 2010. About the only major economic bright spot for 2008 was that the price of a barrel of oil had declined from $145 in July 2008 to $45 by the end of the year. By mid-2009, the economic activity in the United States and other major economies was sliding downward at rates not seen for half a century (Uchitelle and Andrews 2009). During the first quarter of 2009, French gross domestic product fell at an annualized rate of 1.2 percent; the US economy declined by 6.3 percent; the Spanish economy by 1.8 percent; the Italian economy by 2.4 percent; the German economy by 14.4 percent; the Mexican economy by 21.5 percent; the Japanese economy by 15.2 percent (Davis 2009; Walker 2009).

By the start of 2009, the federal government had spent the first $350 billion installment of the so-called Troubled Asset Relief Program (with $25 billion allocated to Citigroup, $19 billion to the domestic automobile industry, and $270 billion to other financial institutions). Congress approved disbursement of the remaining $350 billion of TARP bailout fund (Soloman and Paletta 2009 and Herszenhorn 2009). The bailouts to date meant that the federal government already owned stock in 206 banks, and the federal deficit was predicted to reach $1.2 trillion, or 8.3 percent of national production – even *without the additional bailouts and stimulus packages that were being considered in Congress.*

The bailout and stimulus policy debate, for and against

As we were writing this, it appeared that the country (and world) stood witness to what was in part a "mortgage crisis" of confidence. Understandably, many Wall Street investors saw themselves as having been duped by errant mortgage lenders and by their own herd mentality. Many became more cautious about buying more securitized mortgages until they could once again trust mortgage lenders. Few believed at the start of 2009 that the economic crisis would abate quickly because the crisis was founded on broken trust, and trust is one of the most unheralded, yet exceptionally important, cornerstones of any modern financial system.

Policy makers suggested two fixes. First, government subsidies, loan guarantees, and stock purchases could, in one way or another, bail out lenders and borrowers. Second, the Federal Reserve could simply crank up the growth in the money stock and inflate away the real value of borrowers' debt.

The major arguments for a massive bailout of banks and other financial institutions (American International Group [AIG] and Wachovia, for example) and other large firms (General Motors and Chrysler) are the following:

- Without the bailouts of financial institutions on Wall Street, credit markets would otherwise remain "frozen," and credit is a necessary lubricant for all business throughout the country.
- The failure of large firms like General Motors and Chrysler could have devastating ripple effects throughout the economy, adding to the country's recession woes.
- The consequences of not bailing out anyone could ensure the development of another Great Depression.

The case for a massive "stimulus" package of federal expenditures is founded on macroeconomic arguments that date to the 1930s:

- In a major economic downturn, monetary policy can be ineffective (which it seemed to have been through the end of 2008).
- The federal expenditures can replace the downturn in consumer and investment spending and the expenditures could have a "multiplier effect" in line with the macroeconomic theorizing of British economist John Maynard Keynes (1936). This means that $1 trillion in federal deficit spending can have a potential impact of, say, $1.5 trillion on overall national production, as federal "stimulus" expenditures lead to greater incomes for workers and business owners who then add to the aggregate expenditure flow through their consumption and investments.
- A major economic crisis requires a major governmental response. Thus, President Barack Obama, with both Democratic and Republican support in Congress, pressed for an additional stimulus package of close to $1 trillion, two-thirds of which would be new federal or state spending and a third of which would be in various forms of tax relief (Bendavid, Williamson, and Reddy 2009; Herszenhorn 2009).
- The country was in a classic "liquidity trap," which means that monetary policy will be largely ineffective since people will leave idle any increase in their money balances for fear that their investments in financial assets will depreciate. When monetary policy is impotent, fiscal stimulus is the only remaining major policy option.

The case against both the bailout and stimulus packages is organized around the view that such policy courses can be snares and delusions:

- When the government spends deficit dollars, it must borrow the funds. On the one hand, the federal expenditures inject funds into the economy. On the other hand, the government borrowing withdraws funds from the credit market and economy, with the injections and withdrawals largely canceling one another out in terms of relieving the country's aggregate expenditure troubles.

- Bailout and stimulus packages can simply aggravate moral-hazard problems in the financial system because they take away the pain of risky credit and other bad management decisions of the past and encourage people to continue to be careless in their business decision making, both immediately when private investors buy the "toxic" mortgage-backed securities at the encouragement of government policy makers and far into the future as investors imagine that their losses on risky and uncertain investments will be covered by additional bailout schemes.[3]

- Bailout and stimulus packages may have the public interest in mind, but are likely to be heavily weighed down with log-rolled political compromises and pork-barrel projects necessary to garner the requisite count of congressional votes. The US Conference of Mayors has, at this writing, proposed including more than 11,000 essential and "ready-to-go" public works projects totaling more than $73 billion that included a Waterfront Duck Pond Park for Hercules, California; a Midway Park Family Life Center for Euless, Texas; and a community center for Miami, Florida (Poole 2008).

- The resulting federal deficit that, at this writing, was rapidly approaching $2 trillion, could lead people to expect higher future tax rates to cover the higher interest payments on the debt and the pay-downs of the debt over time.

- Anticipating the encouragement for misbehavior and higher tax rates, investment spending in the near term could be curtailed, impairing economic growth.

- Investors might be expected to demand higher rates of returns on the securities they buy in anticipation of future misbehaviors, higher tax rates, and slowed growth.

The proponents of an expansionary monetary policy argue that, between 1929 and 1933, the Federal Reserve allowed the money supply to contract by a third, helping to turn a recession into the Great Depression. Depositors panicked and withdrew their funds, and banks collapsed. Proponents of easy money also have argued that

---

[3] Nobel laureate in economics and former Democratic economic advisor Joseph Stiglitz has argued that the Obama Administration's proposal for the federal government to loan financial entities that bought the "toxic" mortgage-backed securities as much as 85 percent of the purchase prices and then fork over another 7.5 percent of the purchase prices would mean that the investments of financial entities would once again be highly leveraged (private investors' equity in the investments would be 7.5 percent). Such a policy course would create a form of "ersatz capitalism," under which any gains from the investments in the "toxic" and highly risky securities would be "privatized" and any losses would be largely "socialized," aggravating the moral-hazard problem that got the country into a mess in the first place (Stiglitz 2009).

an expansion in the money supply can loosen credit terms, encouraging borrowers to expand their expenditures. But a monetary expansion may be as ill-guided as that of the 1970s and early 2000s, and could lead to an inflationary spiral and higher interest rates demanded by lenders in anticipation of a depreciation in the future value of the dollars used to pay off loans.

We will have to wait and see how the policy debate evolves and the economy changes. In the meantime, readers might consult Robert Shiller's two books for a far more complete discussion of the background of the stock-market bubble of the 1990s and the housing bubble of the early 2000s (Shiller 2005; 2008). More than any other economist, Shiller warned the public and policy makers about the coming bursts in the stock-market and housing bubbles. In contrast to Shiller's decidedly pro-government view of the remedies for the crisis, University of Missouri-St. Louis economist Lawrence White offers a decided pro-market assessment of the foundations of the crisis and solutions (White 2008).

Practical lessons for MBAs: cost structures, indebtedness, and risk taking

MBA students are familiar with accounting documents such as balance sheets and income statements, but such documents are of little help in conceptualizing the larger issue at the heart of the cost curves developed in this chapter: how much should a firm produce if it wants to maximize profits? To answer that question properly, all costs must be considered in a firm's cost structure, including two key numbers that accounting statements do not capture – risk cost and normal profits. Even though such costs are elusive, they are no less real and important than payments to workers and suppliers. Managers must make rough estimates of such costs. Otherwise, the firm can underestimate its costs and overextend production.

The extent that a firm's ventures are leveraged can affect risk costs. Generally, the higher the leverage, the greater the risk costs a firm will incur. This is because when a firm's business ventures are 100 percent leveraged, the firm stands to collect the extra gains that come with successful ventures while creditors will suffer all of the losses from failed ventures. Accordingly, managers can be expected to undertake more risky ventures when they know the projects are highly leveraged, especially since risky ventures usually carry a risk premium that can lead to above-normal profits when ventures are successful.

Understandably, creditors will demand progressively higher interest rates from firms as their indebtedness escalates, and those progressively higher interest rates affect a firm's cost structure. This suggests that minimizing the cost curves that have been drawn in this chapter is a far more complicated task than might be thought, requiring a delicate balancing of a firm's debt and equity. By adding equity, firm owners can push down the interest rates they pay on borrowed funds, but they also incur greater risk costs as more of their own capital can evaporate with failed projects. Clearly, a firm's financial structure and cost structures are inextricably intertwined and interdependent. Managers do indeed need to understand high finance to contain their costs and obtain competitive advantages in the pricing of their products.

Further reading online

Reading 8.1 Choosing the most efficient resource combination, isoquant and isocost curves

R

The bottom line

The key takeaways for chapter 8 are the following:

1 Cost structures for firms (made up of average fixed, average variable, average total, and marginal cost curves) are a graphical device designed to yield insights on how much a firm should produce in order to maximize profits over a range of output levels. Such structures help managers go beyond the limitations on thinking presented by a firm's accounting statements, which report the costs incurred for a given output level.

2 The law of diminishing marginal returns is a fact of nature that shapes a firm's short-run marginal cost curve and ultimately imposes a constraint on how much a firm can produce in the short run if it intends to maximize profits.

3 A firm in the short run (or long run) should not seek to produce where its average cost is at a minimum. It should produce where marginal costs and marginal revenue (price in the case of a perfect competitor) are equal.

4 Fixed costs should be ignored in short-run production decisions.

5 Economies of scale and diseconomies of scale will shape a firm's long-run cost structure.

6 Research has not substantiated the so-called "first-mover advantage." Indeed, researchers have found market advantages for second movers and their followers.

7 The build-up of equity in a firm can lower the firm's interest rates on borrowed funds, for two reasons. First, firm's lenders stand to lose less in the case of default on interest payments. Second, firms with a lot of equity and few borrowed funds will be inclined to restrain the riskiness of their business ventures.

8 Indebtedness can inhibit executives' inclination to waste firm resources by reducing the available cash that can be misused.

9   The maturing of a firm can lead to more indebtedness because mature firms have proven records and tend to have more stable earnings prospects.

10 The sources of financial and economic crisis of 2008 and forward can be traced to the housing price bubble that took off in 2003, fueled by easy money policies of the Federal Reserve from 2001 to 2005 and to federal government encouragement in the 1990s and early 2000s for lending institutions to extend mortgages to less-qualified borrowers. Mortgage-backed securities also could have introduced a moral-hazard problem into the housing market and added funds for an expansion of the housing demand. This in turn could have fueled the housing price bubble and expectations of even higher future housing prices, and encouraged subprime and other mortgages that increased the leverage of homeowners.

11 Leverage can increase the riskiness of investments undertaken because equity owners gain from the risk premium on risky investment projects while the losses that go with failures can be imposed on lenders.

In chapters 9 and 10, we extend our analysis of firms' production decisions by combining the average and marginal cost curves described in this chapter with the demand curves described in previous chapters. Within that theoretical framework, we can compare the relative efficiency of competitive and monopolistic markets, as well as the role of profits in directing the production decisions of private firms.

Review questions >>

1   Complete the cost schedule shown below and develop a graph that shows marginal, average fixed, average variable, and average total cost curves.

Output level	Total fixed costs ($)	Total variable costs ($)	Total cost ($)	Marginal cost ($)	Average fixed cost ($)	Average variable cost ($)	Average total cost ($)
1	200	60	260				
2	200	110	310				
3	200	150	350				
4	200	180	380				
5	200	200	400				
6	200	230	430				
7	200	280	480				
8	200	350	550				
9	200	440	640				
10	200	550	750				

2   Explain why the intersection of the average variable cost curve and the marginal cost curve is the point of minimum average variable cost.

3   Suppose that no economies or diseconomies of scale exist in a given industry. What will the firm's long-run average and marginal cost curves look like? Would you expect firms of different sizes to be able to compete successfully in such an industry?

4   Why would you expect that all firms would eventually encounter diseconomies of scale? Why might it be irrelevant that some firms will eventually encounter diseconomies of scale?

5   Suppose that the government imposes a $100 tax on all businesses, regardless of how much they produce. How will the tax affect a firm's short-run cost curves? Its short-run production?

6   Suppose that the government imposes a $1 tax on every unit of a good sold. How will the tax affect a firm's short-run cost curves? Its short-run output?

7   Suppose that interest rates fall. How will managers' incentives be affected, and how will the firm's cost structure be affected?

8   Since this book was published, there no doubt have been major developments in the bailout and stimulus packages enacted by Congress and signed into law by the Obama Administration. What have been the major developments? What has the total dollar value of the bailout and stimulus packages been? What has been the consequence of those packages and the downturn on the economy on the overall federal budget deficits for the fiscal years since fiscal year 2008 (which ended October 31, 2008)? What have been the arguments for and against the bailout and stimulus packages, beyond those developed in this chapter? What has been the estimated impact of the deficit spending on annual gross domestic product and unemployment to date? What are the likely positive and negative economic consequences for years to come? What has happened to the inflation rate? Does moral hazard have anything to do with your analysis?

Book III
Competitive and monopoly market structures

In chapters 9, 10, and 11 of this final book, we use the demand theory and cost structures developed in chapter 6 through 8 to examine the organizational and production decisions under four market structures:

- perfect competition
- pure monopoly
- monopolistic competition
- oligopoly.

In chapter 12, we revisit the market for a critical resource input, labor. We review and extend our analysis of how wage rates are determined in competitive labor markets, first briefly considered in chapter 3. We then explain how a sole employer in a given market, called a "monopsony," will determine the wage rate it will pay its workers.

9

Firm production under idealized competitive conditions

Economists understand by the term market, not any particular market place in which things are bought and sold, but the whole of any region in which buyers and sellers are in such free intercourse with one another that the prices of the same goods tend to equality, easily and quickly.

Augustin Cournot

Chapters 6 through 8 largely dealt separately with the two sides of markets – consumers and producers. We devised graphic means of representing consumer preferences (the demand curve) and producer costs (the average and marginal cost curves). This chapter brings demand and cost analysis together in a way that allows us to examine how individual firms react to consumer demand in competitive markets. Our focus is on a highly competitive market structure. We investigate an intriguing question: at the maximum, how much can competitive markets contribute to consumer welfare?

We do not attempt to give a full description of a real-world competitive market setting. Markets are too diverse for such a description to be very useful. Rather, our aim is to devise a theoretical framework that can enable us to *think* about how competitive markets work in general, as a constructive behavioral force. Although our model cannot tell much that is specific about real-world markets, it provides a basis for predicting the general direction of changes in market prices and output.

Through the analysis in Part A of this chapter, we should gain a deeper understanding of the meaning and competitive foundations of the market forces of supply and demand and of market efficiency. We can see how the absence of restrictions on entry can impose intensive pressures on existing producers to contain their costs or be replaced. In Part B, we explain how getting the sizes of teams and their pay incentives right can be crucial to firms' survivability when they face intense competitive pressures.

Online
Perspective

In the online Perspective 9 for the chapter, we take up a widely unrecognized business problem, "the Innovator's Dilemma," which helps explain why many established producers are inclined to stay with their tried and true products, only to sign, often deliberately, their market "death warrants" and to be replaced by innovative new entrants.

The competitive market structure considered in this chapter is only one of four basic market structures. The other three and the detrimental effects of their restrictions on competition are the subjects of following chapters.

Part A Theory and public policy applications

How a firm decides to price its product and how much it decides to produce are functions of many considerations (labor and material costs, weather, etc.), but one of the more important factors is the nature of its market, or what economists call its "market structure," which really is about the extent of the competition (or lack thereof) that any given firm faces. In this and the following chapter, we will see how a firm's pricing and production strategies will vary with the competitiveness of their markets.

Pricing and production strategies under four market structures

Markets can be divided into four basic categories, based on the degree of competition that prevails within them – that is, on how strenuously participants attempt to outdo their rivals and avoid being outdone. The four categories are described below and their characteristics are summarized in table 9.1. The most competitive of the four market structures is perfect competition.

Table 9.1 Characteristics of the four market structures

	No. of firms	Freedom of entry	Type of product	Example
Perfect competition	Many	Very easy (or costless)	Homogeneous	Wheat, computers, gold
Pure monopoly	One	Barred (or prohibitively costly)	Single-product	Public utilities, postal service
Monopolistic competition	Many	Relatively easy	Differentiated	Pens, books, paper, clothing
Oligopoly	Few	Difficult	Either standardized or differentiated	Steel, light bulbs, cereals, autos

Perfect competition

As discussed earlier, **perfect competition** represents an ideal degree of competition, recognized by the following characteristics:

> **Perfect competition** is a market structure in which price competition is so intense that maximum efficiency in the allocation of resources is obtained.

1 There are *many producers* in the market, no one of which is large enough to affect the going market price for the product. All producers are price takers, as opposed to price searchers or price makers.
2 All producers sell a *homogeneous product*, meaning that the goods of one producer are indistinguishable from those of all others. Consumers are fully knowledgeable about the different producers' prices and are totally indifferent as to which producer they buy from.
3 Producers enjoy complete *freedom of entry into and exit from* the market – that is, entry and exit costs are minimal, although not completely absent.
4 There are *many consumers* in the market, no one of whom is powerful enough to affect the market price of the product. As with producers, consumers are price takers.

As we have shown previously in chapter 6, the demand curve facing the individual perfect competitor is not the same as the demand curve faced by all producers. The *market* demand curve slopes downward, as shown in figure 9.1(a). The demand curve facing an *individual* producer – price taker – is horizontal, as in figure 9.1(b). This horizontal demand curve is *perfectly elastic*. That is, the individual firm cannot raise its price even slightly above the going market price without losing all its customers to the numerous other producers in the market or to other producers waiting for an opportunity to enter the market. On the other hand, the individual

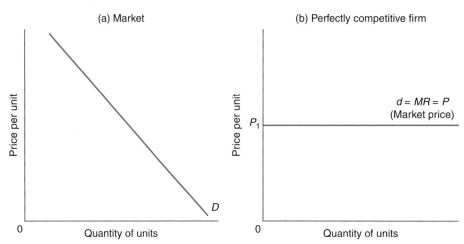

Figure 9.1 Demand curve faced by perfect competitors
The market demand for a product (panel [a]) is always downward sloping. The perfect competitor is on a horizontal, or perfectly elastic, demand curve (panel [b]). It cannot raise its price above the market price even slightly without losing its customers to other producers.

firm can sell all it wishes at the going market price. Hence it has no reason to offer its output at a lower price. The markets for wheat and for integrated computer circuits, or computer chips, are both good (but hardly perfect) examples of real-world markets that come close to perfect competition.

The extreme conditions of competition in perfect competition ensure that economists can make very precise predictions when key variables change under such market conditions. We will develop the principles below that, under perfect competition, price will equal the marginal cost of producing the last unit and that firms will earn only normal profits, not economic profits. This does not mean that such conclusions are not applicable in less than perfectly competitive markets; such can happen and likely does. All that is required is that individual producers (no matter how few producers there are) see themselves as being price takers (or assess their demands curves to be perfectly elastic at the going market-determined price). Even in so-called "contestable markets" in which entry is fairly open, producers can, in key ways, act as if they must be price takers (above some price) because of the fear of entry. (Contestable markets are considered in online Reading 9.1 for this chapter.) Experimental research has shown that subjects in laboratory settings can perceive themselves as price takers even when there are as few as a dozen other producers (Smith 1962). Hence, the model of perfect competition can have broader application to real-world markets than might be surmised from the specified extreme competitive conditions.

Moreover, one of the predictions of the perfectly competitive market is that, because of open entry into markets and the resulting intense price competition, consumers will receive much of the surplus value (consumer evaluation of units of the good minus the producer's costs of producing those units) available from goods, even though consumers may have nothing to do with the creation and production of the good. Such an outcome is self-evident in many markets, not the least of which are technology markets. Personal computers have grown ever more powerful during the last four decades as their prices have collapsed, enabling consumers to buy laptops (or even netbooks) as powerful as mainframe computers a couple decades ago and at a price of only several hundred dollars. Similarly, the prices of ever more feature-rich cell phones and MP3 players have become affordable even to low-income workers. Quality all-cotton or silk shirts that were once expensive can be bought at discount stores (Walmart and Costco included) for a few dollars (and rarely for more than $20).

Pure monopoly

Pure monopoly is a market structure that is the polar opposite of perfect competition. Under a **pure monopoly** there is no price competition because the only producer in the market is protected by prohibitively costly market entry barriers. (The barriers to entry into the monopolist's market are described in chapter 10.) Without competitors to undercut its price, the monopolistic firm can raise prices without fear that customers will move to other producers of the same product or similar products. All the pure monopolist has to worry about is losing some customers to producers of distantly related products.

> A **pure monopoly** consists of a single seller of a product for which there are no close substitutes and which is protected from competition by barriers to entry into the market.

Because the monopolist is the only producer of a particular good, the downward sloping market demand curve (figure 9.1[a]) is its individual demand curve. In contrast to the perfect competitor, the monopolist can raise its price and sell less, or lower its price and sell more.

As will be discussed in chapter 10, the critical task of the pure monopolist is to determine the one price–quantity combination of all price–quantity combinations on its demand curve that maximizes its economic profits. In this sense, the pure monopolist is a price searcher. The best (but not perfect) real-world examples of a pure monopoly are regulated electric power companies, which dominate in given geographical areas, and the government's first-class postal service (which is losing more of its monopoly power every year as technology reduces the costs of alternative ways for people to communicate, for example, e-mail).

While our discussion of pure monopoly is couched in terms of a *sole* producer, the model actually has broad application beyond markets with only a single producer. The key consideration in the monopoly model is that the producer (no matter how many producers there are) perceives itself as a price maker, or price searcher. The count of producers in a market often will affect only the elasticity of demand of individual producers. Seeking to raise its price and profits, a firm with monopoly power will restrict output below the output level chosen in a market where producers view themselves as price takers. This general conclusion applies when a firm has monopoly power, that is, faces a downward sloping demand curve.

Apple is hardly a pure monopolist in the MP3 player and cell phone markets (other producers abound), but Apple has resurrected itself (from the depths of its financial troubles in the early 1990s) through "cool" designs for those devices, enabling it to charge premium prices over other producers. Despite the critics' talk about the economic inefficiency of monopoly power, the above-normal profits that Apple and other firms with monopoly power have been able to earn could have been a necessary motivation for taking the risks to create, develop, and produce their products in the first place. And at this moment, the prospect of earning above-normal profits could be motivating other firms to create and develop an array of new products that will give them a measure of monopoly power, but also give consumers value that they might not otherwise have.[1]

Monopolistic competition

> **Monopolistic competition** is a market composed of a number of producers whose products are differentiated and who face highly elastic, but not perfectly elastic, demand curves.

Monopolistic competition is a market structure that is more descriptive of most real-world markets than perfect competition and pure monopoly, and can be recognized by the following characteristics:

1 It has a number of competitors that are producing slightly different products.
2 Advertising and other forms of nonprice competition are prevalent.
3 Entry into the market is not barred but is restricted by modest entry costs, mainly overhead.
4 Because of the existence of close substitutes, customers can turn to other producers if a monopolistically competitive firm raises its price. Because of brand loyalty, the monopolistic competitor's demand curve still slopes downward but is fairly elastic (see figure 9.2).

The market for textbooks is a good example of monopolistic competition. Most subjects are covered by two or three dozen textbooks, differing from one another in content, style of presentation, and design. (See chapter 11 for more indepth discussion.)

---

[1] For an extended discussion of the positive sides of monopoly power, see a recent book by the authors of this textbook (McKenzie and Lee 2008).

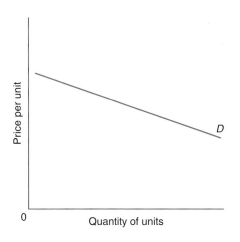

Figure 9.2 Demand curve faced by a monopolistic competitor
Because the product sold by the monopolistically competitive firm is slightly different from the products sold by competing producers, the firm faces a highly elastic, but not perfectly elastic, demand curve.

Oligopoly

Oligopoly, in which competitors are few, is a real-world market structure that has monopoly and competitive characteristics. Oligopolists may produce either an identical product (such as steel) or highly differentiated products (such as automobiles). Generally the barriers to entry into the market are significant enough to restrict new producers, but the critical characteristic of oligopolistic firms is that their pricing decisions are *interdependent*: that is, the pricing decisions of any one firm can substantially affect the sales of the others. Therefore, each firm must monitor and respond to the pricing and production decisions of the other firms in the industry. The importance of this characteristic will become clear in chapter 11.

> An **oligopoly** is a market composed of only a handful of dominant producers – as few as two and generally no more than a dozen – whose pricing decisions are interdependent.

The perfect competitor's production decision

As discussed in chapter 3, the intersection of the supply and demand curves determines the market price in a perfectly competitive market. If the price is above the equilibrium price level, a *surplus* will develop, forcing competitors to lower their prices. If the price is below equilibrium, a *shortage* will emerge, pushing the price upward (see figure 9.3[a]). How much will the individual perfect competitor produce when it has no control over the market price?

The production rule: $MC = MR$

Suppose the price in the perfectly competitive market for computer chips is $5 ($P_1$ in figure 9.3). For each individual competitor, the market price is given – that is, cannot be changed. It must be either accepted or rejected. If the firm rejects the price,

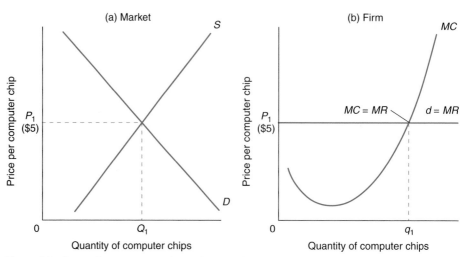

Figure 9.3 The perfect competitor's production decision
The perfect competitor's price is determined by market supply and demand (panel [a]). As long as marginal revenue (*MR*), which equals market price, exceeds marginal cost (*MC*), the perfect competitor will expand production (panel [b]). The profit-maximizing production level is the point at which marginal cost equals marginal revenue (price).

however, it must shut down. If it raises its price even slightly above the market level, its customers will move to other competitors. Demand, then, is horizontal at $5.

The firm's perfectly elastic horizontal demand curve is illustrated in figure 9.3(b). This horizontal demand curve is also the firm's marginal revenue curve. As noted, marginal revenue is defined as the additional revenue acquired from selling one additional unit. Because each computer chip can be sold at a constant price of $5, the additional, or marginal, revenue acquired from selling an additional unit must be constant at $5.

The profit-maximizing firm will produce any unit for which marginal revenue exceeds marginal cost. Thus the profit-maximizing firm in figure 9.3(b) will produce and sell q_1 units, *the quantity at which marginal revenue equals marginal cost* ($MR = MC$). Up to q_1, marginal revenue is greater than marginal cost. Beyond q_1, all additional computer chips are unprofitable. The additional cost of producing them is greater than the additional revenue acquired (with the small "*q*" being used to remind you that the output of the individual producer in figure 9.3[b] is a small fraction of the output for the market, designated by a capital "*Q*" in figure 9.3[a]).

Changes in market price

The perfectly competitive firm produces $MC = MR$, where *MR* is equal to the price at which the firm can sell its product. Thus the amount the firm produces depends on market price. As long as market demand and supply remain constant, the individual firm's demand, and its price, will also remain constant – assuming, of course, that the costs of production remain constant and the cost curves don't shift. For example, if market demand and price increase, the individual firm's demand and price also will increase.

Figure 9.4 shows how the shift occurs. The original market demand of D_1 leads to a market price of P_1 (panel [a]), which is translated into the individual firm's demand, d_1 (panel [b]). Again, the firm maximizes profit by equating marginal cost with marginal revenue, which is equal to d_1, at an output level of q_1.[2]

An increase in market demand to D_2 leads to the higher price P_2 and a higher individual firm demand curve, d_2. At this higher price, which again equals marginal revenue, the perfect competitor can support a higher marginal cost. The firm will expand production from q_1 to q_2. In the same way, an even greater market demand, D_3, will lead to even higher output, q_3, by the individual competitor.

Why does the market supply curve slope upward and to the right? The answer lies in the upward sloping marginal cost curves on which each individual firm operates. The firm will never operate where the marginal cost curve is sloping downward. If MC = price and the marginal cost is getting smaller, the firm could increase profits by increasing output which would reduce MC below price, and would continue increasing output until MC started increasing and eventually equaled price again.

---

[2] To prove this statement, first we note that

$$TR = \bar{P}Q$$

Then we define short-run total cost to be a function of output:

$$SRTC = C(Q)$$

Next, we define profits π to be

$$\pi = TR - SRTC = \bar{P}Q - C(Q)$$

Differentiating with respect to Q and equating with 0, we then obtain

$$\frac{d\pi}{dQ} = \bar{P} - \frac{dC(Q)}{dQ} = 0$$

$$\bar{P} = \frac{dC(Q)}{dQ}$$

because

$$\frac{dC(Q)}{dQ} = SRMC$$

Profits are maximized when

$$SRMC = \bar{P}$$

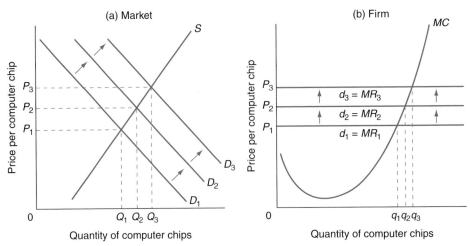

Figure 9.4 Change in the perfect competitor's market price
If the market demand rises from D_1 to D_3 (panel [a]), the price will rise with it, from P_1 to P_3. As a result, the perfectly competitive firm's demand curve will rise, from d_1 to d_3 (panel [b]).

Since the upward sloping portion of the MC curve shows us how much output each firm will produce at every price, the market supply curve is obtained by horizontally adding the firms' upward sloping marginal cost curves (as done in chapter 7).

Maximizing short-run profits

Can perfect competitors make an economic profit? One might think the answer is obviously "Yes," but it is only "Yes" in the (very) short run. To see this, we must incorporate the average and marginal cost curves developed in chapters 7 and 8 into our graph of the perfect competitor's demand curve, as in figure 9.5(b). (Figure 9.5[a] shows the market supply and demand curves.)

As before, the producer maximizes profits by equating marginal cost with price, rather than by looking at average cost. That is exactly what the perfect competitor does. The firm produces q_2 computer chips because that is the point at which the marginal revenue curve (which equals the firm's demand curve) crosses the marginal cost curve. At that intersection, the marginal revenue of the last unit sold equals its marginal cost. If less were produced than q_1, the marginal cost would be less than the marginal revenue, and profits would be lost. Similarly, by producing anything more than q_2 the firm incurs more additional costs (as indicated by the marginal cost curve) than it receives in additional revenue (as indicated by the demand curve, which beyond q_2 is below the MC curve).

At q_2, the firm's profit equals total revenue minus total cost ($TR - TC$). To find total revenue at q_2, we multiply the price, P_1 (which also equals average revenue) by the

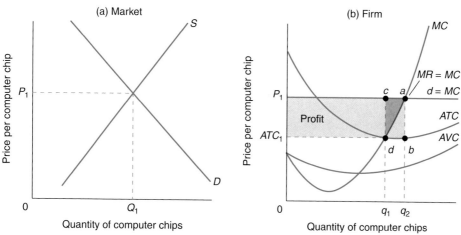

Figure 9.5 The profit-maximizing perfect competitor
The perfect competitor's demand curve is established by the market clearing price (panel [a]). The profit-maximizing perfect competitor will extend production up to the point at which marginal cost equals marginal revenue (price), or point a in panel (b). At that output level – q_2 – the firm will earn a short-run economic profit equal to the shaded area ATC_1P_1ab. If the perfect competitor were to minimize average total cost, it would produce only q_1, losing profits equal to the darker shaded area, dca, in the process.

quantity produced, q_2 ($TR = P_1q_2$). Graphically, total revenue is therefore equal to the area of the rectangle bounded by the price and quantity, or $0P_1aq_2$.[3]

Similarly, total cost can be found by multiplying the average total cost of production (ATC) by the quantity produced. The ATC curve shows that the average total cost of producing q_2 computer chips is ATC_1. Therefore total cost is ATC_1q_2, or the rectangular area bounded by $0ATC_1bq_2$. The profits of the company are therefore $P_1q_2 - ATC_1q_2$, which is the same, mathematically, as $q_2(P_1 - ATC_1)$. This quantity corresponds to the area representing total revenue, $0P_1aq_2$, minus the area representing total cost, $0ATC_1bq_2$. Profit is the shaded rectangle bounded by ATC_1P_1ab. This profit is *economic profit*, since all costs of production (including opportunity and risk costs) are captured in the ATC cost curve. This means that the firm is earning more off its deployment of resources in the production of this good than could be earned on any other good.

The perfect competitor does not seek to produce the quantity that results in the lowest average total cost. That quantity, q_1, is defined by the intersection of the marginal cost curve and the average total cost curve. If it produced only q_1, the firm would lose out on

---

[3] The area of any rectangle is one side times the other side. In this graphical illustration, one side is the price (P_1), and the other side is the quantity (q_2), which means that the area of the rectangle ($P_1 \times q_2$) represents total revenue at q_2.

some of its profits, shown by the darker triangular shaded area *dca*. This area is the summation of the profit that can be generated by producing units between q_1 and q_2.

Naturally, profit-maximizing firms will attempt to minimize their costs of production. That does not mean they will produce at the point of the minimum average total cost curve. Instead, they will try to employ the most efficient technology available and to minimize their payments for resources. That is, they will attempt to keep their cost curves as low as possible. But given those curves, the firm will produce where $MC = MR$, not where the *ATC* curve is at its lowest level. Managers who cannot distinguish between those two objectives will probably operate their businesses on a less profitable basis than they could – and will risk being run out of business.

Minimizing short-run losses

In the foregoing analysis the market-determined price was higher than the firm's average total cost, allowing it to make a profit. Perfect competitors are not guaranteed profits, however. The market price may not be high enough for the firm to make a profit. Suppose, for example, that the market price is P_1, below the firm's average total cost curve (see figure 9.6(b)). Should the firm still produce where marginal cost equals marginal revenue (price)? The answer, for the short run, is "Yes." As long as the firm can cover its variable cost, it should produce q_1 computer chips.

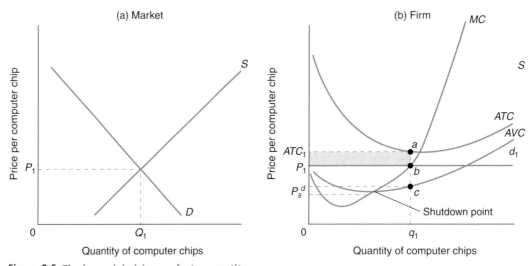

Figure 9.6 The loss-minimizing perfect competitor
The market clearing price (panel [a]) establishes the perfect competitor's demand curve (panel [b]). Because the price is below the average total cost curve, this firm is losing money. As long as the price is above the low point of the average variable cost curve, however, the firm should minimize its short-run losses by continuing to produce where marginal cost equals marginal revenue (price or point *b* in panel [b]). This perfect competitor should produce q_1 units, incurring losses equal to the shaded area P_1ATC_1ab. (The alternative would be to shut down, in which case the firm would lose all its fixed costs.)

It is true that the firm will lose money. Its total revenues are only P_1q_1, or the area bounded by $0P_1bq_1$, whereas its total costs are ATC_1q_1, or the area $0ATC_1aq_1$. On the graph, its total (economic) losses equal the difference between those two rectangular areas, or the shaded area bounded by P_1ATC_1ab. Whether the firm incurs losses is not the relevant question, however. The real issue is whether the firm loses more money by shutting down or by operating and producing q_1 chips.

In the short run, the firm will continue to incur fixed costs even if it shuts down. If it is not earning any revenues, its losses will equal its total fixed costs. In chapter 8, we showed that the average fixed cost of production is the vertical distance between the average variable cost and average total cost, and that the vertical distance, ac, is greater than the average loss, ab. Hence, the firm's total fixed cost, or loss on shutdown, is greater than the loss from operating.

In short, as long as the price is higher than average variable cost – if the price more than covers the cost associated directly with production – the firm minimizes its short-run losses by producing where marginal cost equals marginal revenue. By earning revenue in excess of its variable costs, the firm loses less than its fixed cost. Hence, we have a production rule that profit-maximizing firms should always keep in mind: ignore fixed costs in the short run.

Only if the price dips below the low point of the average variable cost curve – where the marginal and average variable cost curves intersect – will the firm add to its losses by operating. The firm will shut down when price is at or below that point, P_s in figure 9.6. At prices above that point, the firm simply follows its marginal cost curve to determine its production level. Above the average variable cost curve, then, the marginal cost curve is in effect the firm's supply curve. Therefore, if a perfect competitor produces in the short run at all, it produces in a range of increasing marginal cost – and diminishing marginal returns.

Our analysis has shown why, in the short run, fixed costs should be ignored. The relevant question is whether a given productive activity will add more to the firm's revenues than to its relevant costs – those that are affected by its current decisions. Understanding this principle, businesses may undertake activities that superficially appear to be quite unprofitable. Some grocery stores stay open all night, even though the owners know they will attract few customers. If all costs, including fixed costs, are considered, the decision to operate in the early hours may seem misguided. The only relevant question facing the store manager is, however, whether the additional sales generated are greater than the additional cost of light, goods sold, and labor. Similarly, many businesses that are obviously failing continue to operate, for by operating they can at least cover a portion of their fixed costs – such as rent – that would still be due if they shut down. They stay open until their leases expire or until they can sell out.

[See online Video Module 9.1 Production in perfect competition]

Producing over the long run

In the long run, businesses have an opportunity to change their total fixed costs. If the market price remains too low to permit profitable operation, a firm can eliminate its fixed costs, sell its plant and equipment, or terminate its contracts for insurance and office space. If the market price is above average total cost, new firms can enter the market, and existing firms can expand their scale of operation. Such long-run adjustments in turn affect market supply, which affects price and short-run production decisions. To facilitate the discussion, we will examine long-run adjustments in two stages. First, we discuss the effects of market entry and exit, assuming a constant scale of operation. Second, we add adjustments made in response to scale economies.

The long-run effect of short-run profits and losses

When profits encourage new firms to enter an industry and existing firms to expand, the result is an increase in market supply (the supply curve shifts out to the right), a decrease in market price, and a decrease in the profitability of individual firms. For example, in figure 9.7(a), the existence of economic profits (which equal revenues minus *opportunity* costs) in the computer chip market means that investors can earn

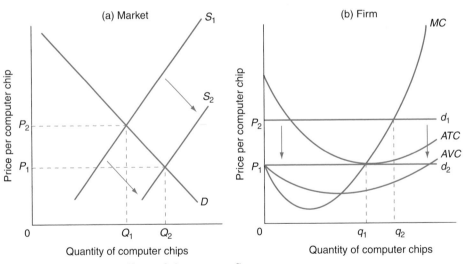

Figure 9.7 The long-run effects of short-run profits

If perfect competitors are making short-run profits, other producers will enter the market, increasing the market supply from S_1 to S_2 and lowering the market price from P_2 to P_1 (panel [a]). The individual firm's demand curve, which is determined by market price, will shift down, from d_1 to d_2 (panel [b]). The firm will reduce its output from q_2 to q_1, the new intersection of marginal revenue (price) and marginal cost. Long-run equilibrium will be achieved when the price falls to the low point of the firm's average total cost curve, eliminating economic profit (price P_1 in panel [b]).

more in that industry than in the most profitable alternative industry. Some investors will move their resources to the computer chip industry. Because the number of
producers increases, the market supply curve shifts outward, expanding total production from Q_1 to Q_2 and depressing the market price from P_2 to P_1.

The expansion of industry supply and the resulting reduction in market price
make the computer chip business less profitable for individual firms. The lower
market price is reflected in a downward shift of the firm's horizontal demand curve,
from d_1 to d_2 (see figure 9.7[b]). The individual firm reduces its output from q_2 to q_1,
the intersection of the new marginal revenue (price/demand) curve with the marginal cost curve. Note that q_1 is also the low point of the average total cost curve.
Here price equals average total cost, meaning that the economic profit is zero. The
firm is making just enough to cover its opportunity and risk costs, but no more. If
there were still profits being made in the computer chip industry, firms would
continue to move into this industry until the price is equal to the low point on the
average cost curve and economic profits are zero.

Losses have the opposite effect on long-run industry supply. In the long run, firms
that are losing money will move out of the industry, because their resources can be
employed more profitably elsewhere. When firms drop out of the industry, supply
contracts and total production falls, from Q_2 to Q_1 in figure 9.8(a). As a result, the price
of the product rises, permitting some firms to break even and stay in the business. Long-
run equilibrium occurs when the price reaches P_2, where the individual firm's demand

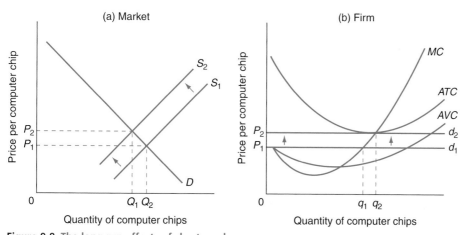

Figure 9.8 The long-run effects of short-run losses
If perfect competitors are suffering short-run losses, some firms will leave the industry,
causing the market supply to shift back from S_1 to S_2 and the price to rise, from P_1 to P_2
(panel [a]). The individual firm's demand curve will shift up with price, from d_1 to d_2
(panel [b]). The firm will expand from q_1 to q_2, and equilibrium will be reached when price
equals the low point of average total cost P_2, eliminating the firm's short-run losses.

curve is tangent to the low point of the average total cost curve (figure 9.8[b]). The output of each remaining individual firm expands (from q_1 to q_2) to take up some of the slack left by the firms that have withdrawn, but the expansion of the remaining firms is not enough to completely offset the reduction in output caused by the firms that leave the industry. Again price and average total cost are equal, and economic profit is zero.

The effect of economies of scale

In the long run, competition forces firms to take advantage of economies of scale, *if they exist*, and to do so as quickly as possible.

If expanding the use of resources reduces costs, the perfect competitor has two reasons for taking advantage of scale economies. First, if the firm expands before other firms, its lower average total cost will allow it to make greater economic profits (for a short period of time). Second, the firm *must* expand its scale for self-preservation. Otherwise, other firms will expand their scales of operation, lowering their cost structures, increasing market supply, and forcing the market price down below the minimum average cost of any firm that doesn't expand its scale.

Consider figure 9.9, for instance. Initially the market is in short-run equilibrium at a price of P_2 (figure 9.9[a]). The individual firm is on cost scale ATC_1, producing q_1 chips and breaking even (figure 9.9[b]). If the firm expands its scale of operation and

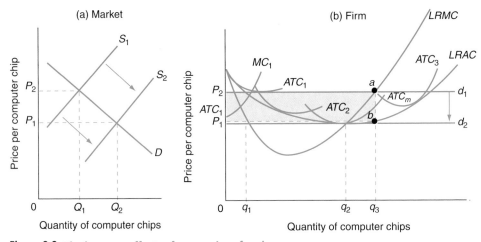

Figure 9.9 The long-run effects of economies of scale

If the market is in equilibrium at price P_1 in panel (a) and the individual firm is producing q_1 units on short-run average total cost curve ATC_1 in panel (b), firms will be just breaking even. Because of the profit potential represented by the shaded area ATC_1P_2ab, firms can be expected to expand production to q_3, where the long-run marginal cost curve intersects the demand curve (d_1). As they expand production to take advantage of economies of scale, however, supply will expand from S_1 to S_2 in panel (a), pushing the market price down toward P_1, the low point of the long-run average total cost curve, $LRAC$ in panel (b). Economic profit will fall to zero. Because of rising diseconomies of scale, firms will not expand further.

produces where its demand curve d_1 intersects the long-run marginal cost curve, it will make a profit equal graphically to the shaded area ATC_1P_2ab. That is the firm's incentive for expansion.

If the firm does not expand and take advantage of these economies, some other firm surely will. Then, any firm still producing on scale ATC_1 will lose money. That's because, when the market supply expands, the price will tumble toward P_1, the point at which the long-run average total cost curve (and the short-run curve ATC_m) are at a minimum, and both industry and firm economic profits are zero. Because of rising diseconomies of scale, firms will not be able to expand further. Any firm that tries to produce on a smaller or larger scale – for example, ATC_2 or ATC_3 – will incur average total costs higher than the market price and will lose money. Ultimately it will be driven out of the market or be forced to expand or contract its scale. Hence, each individual firm will look to the long-run average and marginal costs curves and expand as quickly as it can (and each firm must respond immediately under the idealized conditions of perfect competition).

Marginal benefit versus marginal cost

Time lags, surpluses, and shortages notwithstanding, the competitive market can produce efficient results in one important sense – the marginal benefit of the last unit produced equals its marginal cost ($MB = MC$). In figure 9.10(a), for every computer chip up to Q_1, consumers are willing to pay a price (as indicated by the demand curve, D) greater than its marginal cost (as indicated by the industry supply curve, S). The difference between the price that consumers are willing to pay – an objective indication of the product's marginal bene-fits – and the marginal cost of production is a kind of surplus, or net gain, received from the production of each unit. The net gain is composed of two surpluses, consumer surplus and producer surplus. In figure 9.10(a), consumer surplus is the triangular area below the demand curve and above the dotted price line, P_1. In figure 9.10(a), producer surplus is the triangular area

Consumer surplus is the difference between the total willingness of consumers to pay for a good and the total amount actually spent. **Producer surplus** is the difference between the minimum total revenue necessary to induce producers to supply any given quantity of output and the actual total revenue received from selling that quantity.

above the supply curve and below the dotted price line, P_1. By producing Q_1 units, the industry exploits all potential gains from production, shown graphically by the shaded triangular area in figure 9.10(a). That net gain is brought about by the price that is charged, P_1, a price that induces individual firms to produce where the marginal cost of production equals the price, which is also equal to consumers' marginal benefit.

The marginal cost of production for each individual firm is also P_1, a fact that results in the production of Q_1 units at the minimum total cost. Figure 9.10(b) and (c)

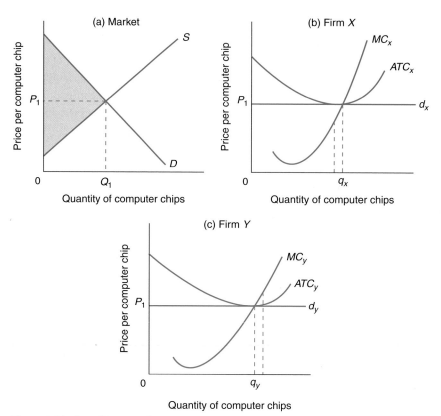

Figure 9.10 The efficiency of the competitive market

Perfectly competitive markets are efficient in the sense that they equate marginal benefit (shown by the demand curve in panel [a]) with marginal cost (shown by the supply curve in panel [a]). At the market output level, Q_1, the marginal benefit of the last unit produced equals the marginal cost of production. The gains generated by the production of Q_1 units – that is, the difference between cost and benefits – are shown by the shaded area in panel (a). The perfectly competitive market is also efficient in the sense that the marginal cost of production, P_1, is the same for all firms (panels [b] and [c]). If firm X were to produce fewer than its efficient number of units, q_x, firm Y would have to produce more than its efficient number, q_y, to meet market demand. Firm Y would be pushed up its marginal cost curve, to the point at which the cost of the last unit would exceed its benefits. But competition forces the two firms to produce to exactly the point at which marginal cost equals marginal benefit, thus minimizing the cost of production.

show the cost curves of two firms, X and Y. In competitive equilibrium, firm X produces q_x units.

Suppose that the market output were distributed between the firms differently. Suppose, for example, that firm X produced one computer chip fewer than q_x. To maintain a constant market output of Q_1, firm Y (or some other firm) would then have to expand production by one unit. The additional chip would force firm Y up its marginal cost curve. To Y, the marginal cost of the additional chip is greater than P_1, greater than X's marginal cost to produce it. Competition forces firms to produce at a cost-effective output level and therefore minimizes the cost of producing at any given level of output.

Perfectly competitive markets are attractive for another reason. In the long run, competition forces each firm to produce at the low point of its average total cost curve. Firms must either produce at that point, achieving whatever economies of scale are available, or get out of the market, leaving production to some other firm that will minimize average total cost.

The efficiency of perfect competition: a critique

Our discussion of perfect competition has been highly theoretical. In real life, the competitive market system is not as efficient as the analysis may suggest. From this perspective, several aspects of the competitive market deserve further comment.

The tendency toward equilibrium

Market forces are stabilizing: they tend to push the market toward one central point of equilibrium. To that extent, the market is predictable, and it contributes to economic and social stability. But in the real world, price does not always move as smoothly toward equilibrium as it appears to do in supply and demand models. The smooth, direct move to equilibrium may happen in markets in which all participants, both buyers and sellers, know exactly what everyone else is doing. Often, however, market participants have only imperfect knowledge of what others intend to do. Indeed, an important function of the market is to generate the pricing and output information that people need to coordinate their actions with one another.

In a world of imperfect information, then, prices may not, and probably will not, move directly toward equilibrium. Those who compete in the market will continually grope for the "best" price from their own individual perspectives. At times, sellers will produce too little and reap unusually high profits, and at other times they will produce too much and suffer losses. But the advantage of markets is that, when mistakes are made, market prices (and profits and losses) provide information on those mistakes and on what has to happen to correct them.

This process of groping toward equilibrium can be represented graphically by a supply and demand "cobweb" (see figure 9.11). Most producers must plan their production at least several months ahead on the basis of prices received today or during the past production period. Farmers, for instance, may plant for summer harvest on the basis of the previous summer's prices. Suppose farmers received price P_1 for a bushel of wheat last year. Their planning supply curve, S, will encourage them to work for a harvest of only Q_1 bushels this year. Given that limited output and the rather high demand at price P_1, however, the price farmers actually receive

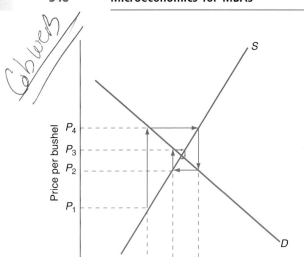

Figure 9.11 Supply and demand cobweb
Markets do not always move smoothly toward equilibrium. If current production decisions are based on past prices, price may adjust to supply in the "cobweb pattern" shown here. Having received price P_1 in the past, farmers will plan to supply only Q_1 bushels of wheat. That amount will not meet market demand, so the price will rise to P_4 – inducing farmers to plan for a harvest of Q_3 bushels. At price P_4, however, Q_3 bushels will not clear the market. The price will fall to P_2, encouraging farmers to cut production back to Q_2. Only after several tries do many farmers find the equilibrium price–quantity combination.

is P_4. The price of P_4 in turn induces farmers to plan for a much larger production level, Q_3, the following year. But the market will not clear for Q_3 bushels until the price falls to P_2. The next year, farmers plan for a price of P_2 and reduce their production to Q_2, which causes the price to rise to P_3. As you can see from the graph, instead of moving in a straight line, the market moves toward the intersection of supply and demand in a web-like pattern.

We hasten to add that while the "cobweb" is helpful in explaining gyrations in price, actual gyrations likely will be dampened over time with *learning* on the part of market participants. Farmers will learn that high prices one year can lead to "oversupply" the following year and can, accordingly, temper their planting response to high prices in any given year, thereby dampening the drop in prices the following year.

Surpluses and shortages

Some critics complain that the market system creates wasteful surpluses and short-ages. Although all resources are limited in quantity, a true market shortage can exist only if the going price is below equilibrium. Thus shortages can be eliminated by a price increase. How much of an increase, theory alone cannot say; we do know, however, that market forces, if allowed free play, will work to boost the price and eliminate the shortage. That means, of course, that people of limited financial resources will be more adversely affected than those with larger incomes – a concern that some use to justify government-imposed market restrictions (not all of which actually help the poor, as we saw in our discussion of rent controls and minimum wages in chapter 4).

Similarly, all surpluses exist because the going price is above equilibrium. Competition will reduce the price, eliminating the surplus. In the process, of course, some firms will be driven out of the market and into other activities where they can now produce more value. In the transition, of course, this can result in unemployed workers. A frequent criticism of the market system is that, when this happens, workers have difficulty finding new employment. Part of the problem, however, is that labor contracts, community custom, or minimum-wage laws prevent wages from adjusting downward. If government controls prices – that is, if prices are not permitted to respond to market conditions – surpluses and shortages will persist.

Externalities, again ~ Don't need to know

Critics stress that supply is based only on the costs that firms bear privately. As discussed in chapter 5, external costs such as air, noise, and water pollution are not counted as part of the cost of production. If the external costs of pollution were counted, the firm's supply curve would be lower (S_2 instead of S_1 in figure 5.6). If producers and consumers had to pay all the costs of production, fewer units would be bought. In this sense, competition leads to an overproduction and a market inefficiency, or *welfare loss* (equal to the shaded triangular area abc in figure 5.6). Indeed, perfect competition will maximize the externalization of costs because firms that don't externalize all costs that can be externalized will be driven from business by those that do and thereby have lower cost structures.

Wealth differences ~ Don't need to know

Critics of the market system also stress that its cost efficiencies are achieved within a specific distribution of wealth, one that depends on the existing distribution of property rights. The distribution of economic power inherent in these property rights, they argue, has no particular ethical or moral significance. But then, markets have a way of creating wealth over time, which means many people today, even those with little wealth, could have more wealth and more higher-quality goods and services than would have been possible had redistributive policies constrained markets through time.

The unreal nature of perfect competition

Finally, critics of the market system argue that most real-world markets are not perfectly competitive. Actual markets are not inhabited by numerous firms producing standard commodities that can be easily duplicated by anyone who would like to enter the market. Indeed, many markets are inhabited by a few large, powerful firms that do not take price as a given. Many firms either are monopolies or possess a high degree of monopoly power. Demanders and suppliers are rarely as well informed as the model suggests. But the model of perfect competition was never meant to represent all, or even most, markets. It is merely one of several means economists use to think about markets and the consequences of changes in market conditions and government policy.

We know from the perfectly competitive model that the predicted outcomes of the model hold if there are numerous producers and consumers. However, as noted earlier, it does not follow that if there are fewer – even far fewer – than "numerous" producers and consumers, the predicted outcomes of the perfectly competitive model do not hold. So long as the number of producers and consumers is sufficiently large that no one believes they have control over the price and acts accordingly, the perfectly competitive model can be useful in analyzing and predicting market behavior. Hence, the perfectly competitive outcomes could hold with no more than a couple of dozen producers and consumers in the market (Smith 1962). (Still, we take up more real-world markets, called "contestable markets," in online Reading 9.1.)

Finally, the perfectly competitive market can help us gain insight about production decisions precisely because its required conditions are "unreal." The model of market competition simplifies the analysis, helping us see with clarity the essential features of competitive markets and showing us exactly how managers can improve their thinking as they consider the complex tasks of achieving maximum profitability and survivability. Behavioral economists have argued that people in general and managers in particular have an array of "decision-making biases," which we fully acknowledge: people might not be naturally inclined to ignore sunk costs, and they might harbor a bias toward projects with opportunity costs rather than projects with out-of-pocket expenditures (see Ariely 2008; Thaler and Sunstein 2008). The unreal model of perfect competition helps us drive home the point that managers must consider thinking in terms of equating at the margin (producing where marginal cost and marginal revenue are equal), ignoring in short-run production decisions many (fixed) costs that they see daily on their firms' income statements. Moreover, the analysis can remind managers to treat all costs the same (the explicit costs that are recorded on income statements and the opportunity costs that never see the light of accounting statements). Firms in highly competitive markets who ignore such heuristics might very well see themselves replaced by managers who take "principles of economics" seriously.

Price takers and price searchers

Perfect competition is an extreme degree of competition, so much so that many students are understandably concerned about its relevance. They often ask: "If there are few market structures that even closely approximate perfect competition, why bother to study it?"

The question is a good one, and not altogether easy to answer. Few markets come close to having numerous producers of an identical product with complete freedom of entry and exit. Markets for gold, for some computer chips and agricultural commodities, and for stocks and bonds are probably the closest markets we have to perfect competition, but still the products are not always *completely* identical, and entry and exit costs abound in most markets. Even wheat sold by a Kansas farmer is not always viewed the same as wheat sold by a Texas farmer.

How can sense be made of perfect competition? We know that under the conditions of competition specified, certain results follow. We can logically (with the use of graphs and mathematics) derive these results, as we have in this chapter. One conclusion drawn is that in perfect competition each firm will extend production until the marginal cost of producing the last unit equals the price paid by the consumer. That conclusion *necessarily* follows from the assumptions made. Granted, the demanding conditions for perfect competition are rarely met. We nevertheless cannot conclude *that under less demanding conditions, competitive results would not be observed.* For example, it may be that the number of producers is not "numerous," that the products sold by all producers are not "identical," and that there are costs to moving in and out of markets. Nonetheless, individual producers may act *as if* the conditions of perfect competition are met. Individual producers may still act as if they have no control over market price or that there are so many other actual or potential producers that it is best to think in terms of the other producers being "numerous" – in which case many of the predicted results of perfect competition may still be observed in the less than perfect markets.

For these reasons, many economists often talk not about *perfect competitors* but about **price takers** (who may or may not fit exactly the description of perfect competitors). They simply observe the market price and either accept it (and accordingly produce to the point at which marginal cost and price are equal) or reject it (and go into some other business). Hence, the price taker is someone who acts *as if* her demand curve

> **Price takers** are sellers who do not believe they can influence the market price significantly by varying their own production levels.

is horizontal (perfectly elastic, more or less). She is therefore someone who assumes that the marginal revenue on each unit sold is constant (and equal to the price) – and that the marginal revenue curve is horizontal and the same as the firm's demand curve.

In contrast, *price searchers* are sellers who have some control over the market price. Price searchers have monopoly power because they can alter production and thereby market supply sufficiently to change the price. The individual price searcher's task is not simply to accept or reject the current market price, but (like the monopolist) to "search" through the various price–quantity combinations on her downward sloping demand curve with the intent of maximizing profits. As we

> **Price searchers** are sellers who cannot control the market price by individually varying their production levels.

demonstrate in chapter 10, the marginal revenue and demand curves of the price searcher are no longer the same. (Exactly where the monopolist's marginal revenue curve lies in relation to the demand curve is discussed in detail in chapter 10.)

For an explanation for why firms may not always be "innovative," see online Perspective 9, The Innovator's Dilemma.

Online Perspective 9
The Innovator's
Dilemma

Part B Organizational economics and management

Competing cost-effectively through efficient teams

Perfectly competitive, or even just highly competitive, market conditions put intense pressure on producers to produce cost-effectively. Those producers who don't find the most cost-effective means of production are doomed under perfectly competitive market conditions and will surely suffer in terms of market share and profitability even under intense, less extreme competitive market conditions. This means that producers in highly competitive markets must form firms when such organizational structures are more efficient than market exchanges and that they must break down their organization into cohesive and effective working groups. Otherwise, competitive pressures on prices (via the lower-cost curves employed in Part A of this chapter) in the product markets will cause the demise of firms that are not organized to identify and implement lower-cost means of production. A central message of Part B of this chapter is to remind you once again that producing cost-effectively is easier said than done.

In the first part of the chapter, we drew in a perfect competitor's cost curves, assuming the firm would organize itself in a way that minimizes its costs. In Part B, we suggest that accomplishing the goal of cost-effectiveness in production is highly complex, requiring that managers understand how the sizes of teams and the system of payments to team members can have profound effects on the firm's cost structure. Moreover, a perfectly competitive firm (or one facing market conditions approximating perfect competition) must not only produce cost-effectively, it must match the cost-effectiveness of the most cost-effective producer who is in the market or who can enter the market. The cost curves drawn in the graphs in the first part of this chapter will represent those curves of the most cost-effective producers because those producers who do not match such a standard will not long last in a perfectly competitive market (or even a market that vaguely resembles perfect competition).

As noted in chapter 7, the central reason firms exist is that people are often more productive when they work together – in "teams" – than when they work in isolation from one another but are tied together by markets. Teams are no passing and facile management fad; firms have always utilized them. Indeed, in a broad sense, a firm is a team or can be viewed as a collection of teams. What seems to be new is the emphasis within management circles on the economies that can be garnered from assigning complex sets of tasks to relatively small teams of workers – those within departments and, for larger projects, across departments – that when used can result in substantial productivity improvements.[4] However, teams also present opportunities for shirking (which should be self-evident to many MBA students who form their own study and project groups to complete class assignments). A central problem that managers face is constructing teams so that they minimize the amount of shirking and maximize production, which is made all the more urgent when competition in product markets is intense.

Team production

What do we mean by "team production"? If Mary and Jim could each produce 100 widgets independently of one another and could together produce only 200 widgets, there would be no basis for team production, and no basis for the two to form a firm with all of the trappings of a hierarchy. The added cost of their organization would, no doubt, make them uncompetitive vis-à-vis other producers such as themselves who worked independently of one another. However, if Mary and Jim could produce 250 widgets when working together, then team production might be profitable (depending on the exact costs associated with operating their two-person organization).

Hence, we would define "team production" as those forms of work in which results are highly interactive: the output of any one member of the group is dependent on what the other group members do. The simplest and clearest form of teamwork is that which occurs when Mary and Jim (and any number of other people) move objects that neither can handle alone from one place to another. The work of people on an assembly line or on a television advertising project is a more complicated form of teamwork.

---

[4] Dell computers is convinced that its team-based production has improved quality in its made-to-order mail-order sales. And Electrosource found that its output per worker doubled within twelve months of switching to teams in its battery production. Accordingly, the company was able to reduce its workforce (Thomas 1996).

Granted, finding business endeavors that have the *potential* for expanding output by more than the growth in the number of employees is a major problem businesses face. But finding such potential opportunities leads to another significant problem, which is making sure that the synergetic potential of the workers who are brought together into a team is actually realized.

We often think of firms failing for purely financial reasons – they incur financial losses. Firms are said to be illiquid and insolvent when they fail. That view of failure is instructive, but the matter can also be seen in a different light, as an organizational problem *and* a failure in organizational incentives. A poorly run organization can mean that all of the 50 "extra" widgets that Mary and Jim can produce together are lost in unnecessary expenditures and impaired productivity because of problems inherent in team production. If the organizational costs exceed the equivalent of 50 widgets, then we can say that Mary and Jim have incurred a loss which would force them to adjust their practices as a firm or to go their own ways.

Many firms do fail and break apart, not because the *potential* for expanded output does not exist, but because their collective potential is not realized. Why can't people in a team always realize their collective potential? There is a multitude of answers to that question. Firms may not have the requisite product design or a well-thought-out business strategy to promote the products. Some people just can't get along; they rub each other up the wrong way when they try to cooperate. Personal conflicts, which deflect people's energies at work into interpersonal defensive and predatory actions, can be so frequent that the production potentials are missed.

While recognizing many noneconomic explanations for organizational problems, we would reiterate our theme: managers are unable to find ways to properly align the interests of the workers with those of other workers and the owners. People in firms don't cooperate as cost-effectively as they can and should. This is a problem that exists only in teams. For obvious reasons, it doesn't exist in a one-person firm.

In our simple example, involving only two people (Mary and Jim), each party has a strong *personal* incentive (quite apart from an altruistic motivation) to work with the other. After all, each can readily tell when the other person is not contributing what is expected (or agreed upon). Accordingly, when Mary shirks, Jim can "punish" Mary by shirking also, and vice versa, ensuring that they both will be worse off than they would have been had they never sought to cooperate at all. The agreement Mary and Jim have to work together productively can be, in this way, *self-enforcing*, with each checking the other – and each effectively threatening the other with reprisal in kind. The threat of added cost is especially powerful when Mary and Jim are also the owners of the firm. The two of them fully bear the cost of the shirking and any "tit-for-tat" consequences. There is no prospect for cost-shifting to a third party.

Two-person firms are, conceptually, the easiest business ventures to organize and manage (with the exception of one-person firms) because the incentives are so obvious and strong and well aligned. Organizational and management problems can begin to mount, however, as the number of people in the firm or "team" increases. As discussed under the "logic of group behavior" in chapter 2, incentives begin to change with the growth in the size of groups. Each individual's contribution to the totality of firm output becomes less and less obvious as the number of people grows. This is especially true when the firm is organized to take advantage of people's specialties. Employees often don't know what their colleagues do and, therefore, are not able to assess their work.

When Mary is one of two people in a firm, then she is responsible for half of the output (assuming equal contributions, of course), but when she is one of a thousand people, her contribution is only one-tenth of 1 percent of firm output. If she is a clerk in the advertising department assigned to mailing checks for ads, she might not even be able to tell that she is responsible for one-tenth of a percent of output, income, and profits.

Admittedly, if no one else contributes anything to production (there are no other drops in the bucket), the contribution of any one person is material – in fact, everything. The point is that in large groups, and as output expands, each worker has an *impaired* incentive to do that which is in all of their interests to do – that is, to make their small contribution to the sum total of what the firm does. A central lesson of this discussion is not that workers never cooperate but rather that the countervailing incentive forces embedded in the way that groups of people work can undercut the power of people's natural tendencies to cooperate and achieve their synergetic potential. Consequently, managers must pay attention to the details of firm organization to counteract these forces.

If all people were angels, always inclined to do as they are told or as they said they would do, then the manager's role would be much less important. Even if almost everyone were inclined to do as he or she were told or committed to doing, managers would still want to implement policies and an organizational structure that create incentives for people to behave in the firm's best interest. Without such incentives rewarding cooperative behavior and punishing uncooperative behavior, a few "bad" people can seriously damage the firm. Even employees who forgo opportunities to shirk their responsibilities may soon cease to do so if they see others undermining their efforts and shirking their duties. As more employees shift from responsible to irresponsible behavior, the greater the incentive for the remaining employees to shift as well, and the culture of cooperation can unravel.

Why are large firms divided into departments? Although the administrative overhead of department structures may seem unnecessary (requiring that each department have a manager and an office with all the trappings of departmental power), departments are a means to reduce the size of the relevant group within the firm. The purpose is not only to ensure that bosses can more closely monitor individuals' actions, but also to allow individuals within the department to more easily recognize their own and others' contributions to output.

One good reason for the current interest in teams is that departments are often too large, meaning that people's individual contributions within departments are too small to detect and monitor. Teams can be ways of reducing the size of the relevant group of workers. Managers have now begun to realize that reducing the size of the relevant group can increase worker productivity as well as ensure that workers who know most about what needs to be done in their specialty can monitor each other. This reduces the need of managers to "micromanage" employees' work, leaving them more latitude to make the best use of their knowledge for themselves and for the firm.

Team size

The questions that are bound to puzzle business managers interested in maximizing firm output is: How large should teams be? How many members should they have? We obviously can't say exactly, given the many factors that explain the great variety of firms in the country. (If we could formulate a pat answer, this book would surely sell zillions!) However, we can make several general observations, the most important of which is that managers must acknowledge that shirking (or "social loafing") will *tend to rise along with the size of the group*, everything else held constant.

In addition, we suggest that the more alike the members, the larger the team can be, because people who have more knowledge of what their teammates are doing tend to cooperate. Also, the more training team members are given in cooperation, the larger the teams can be. Training, in other words, can pay not only because it makes workers more productive by increasing the value of their direct contribution, but also because it can reduce the added overhead of a larger number of smaller departments.[5]

---

[5] However, a lot depends on the type of training given to workers. Apparently economists, using their maximizing models (and the firmly held belief that everyone will shirk when they can), are inclined to play whatever margins are available to their own personal advantage, or to shirk when feasible, to a degree not true of other professionals. Researchers have found that in single-play experimental games designed to test the tendency of people to free ride on the group's efforts, not everyone contributed to the group's output. However, they also found that the average group produced 40–60 percent of the "optimal output" of the public good, with the exception of groups made up of graduate students in economics. These graduate students provided only 20 percent of the optimal output (Marwell and Ames 1981). Perhaps that is to be expected, given that economics students are more aware than are most people of how to capture private benefits in such games. But other researchers found that the explanation is less in what economics students learn, and more in the tendency for students who are less prone to cooperate (more "corrupt" in the terminology of the experimenters) to be more likely to major in economics (Frank, Gilgorich, and Regan 1996). As a consequence, it probably follows that teams of economists (and other people with similar conceptual leanings) should be smaller than teams of people from other disciplines. Although we may never have intended it, we must fear that the people who read this book may be less disposed to cooperate than they were before they picked it up.

The more that workers are imbued with a corporate culture and accept the firm's goals, the larger the team can be. Expenditures on efforts to define the firm's purpose can be self-financing, given that the resulting larger departments can release financial and real resources.

The more that team members can detect or measure the outputs of fellow team members, the larger the team can be. Firms, therefore, have an economic interest in developing ways to make work – or what is produced – objective. Finally, the greater the importance of quality, the more important team production should be, and the smaller teams will tend to be.

No matter how it is done, the size of the teams within a firm can affect the overall size of the firm. Firms with teams that are "too large" or "too small" can have unnecessarily high cost structures that can restrict the firms' market shares and overall size, as well as the incomes of the workers and owners.

Paying teams

Recognizing that teams can add to firm output is only half the struggle to get workers to perform as they should and to achieve greater output. A question that all too often undercuts the value of teams is: how are the workers on the team to be motivated and paid? If workers are rewarded only for the output of the team, then individual workers again have incentives to free ride on the work of others (to the extent that they can get away with it), which can be realized not only in slack work but also in absenteeism. But if team members are rewarded exclusively for their own individual contributions, then the incentive for actual teamwork is reduced.

Generally, managers effectively "punt" on compensation issues, not knowing exactly how to structure rewards, and offer compensation that is based partly on team output and partly on individual contributions to the team. Team output is generally the easier of the two compensation variables to measure, as teams are organized along functional lines with some measurable objective in mind. Peer evaluation may play a partial role in how individual contributions are often determined because team members are the ones who have localized knowledge of how much their coworkers are contributing to team output. But, here again, the compensation problem is not completely solved. Team members can reason that how they work and how they and their coworkers are evaluated can affect their slice of the "compensation pie." Each can figure that the more highly other members of the team are evaluated, the lower their own relative evaluation, a consideration that can lead team members to underrate the work of other members. Team discord can result, as has been experienced at jeans maker Levi-Strauss where supervisors reportedly spend a nontrivial amount of time refereeing team member conflicts. To ameliorate (but not totally quell) the discord, Levi-Strauss has resorted to giving employees training in group dynamics and methods of getting along (Mitchell 1994).

How, then, can managers best motivate workers through pay to contribute to team output? Four identifiable pay methods are worth considering:

1 The workers can simply share in the revenues generated by the team (or firm). We can call this reward system *revenue sharing*. The gain to each worker is the added revenue received minus the cost to the worker of the added effort expended. Under this method of reward, each worker has the maximum incentive to free ride, especially when the "team" is large.

2 The workers can be assigned target production or revenue levels and be given what are called *forcing contracts*, or a guarantee of one high wage level (significantly above their market wage) if the target is achieved and another, lower (penalty) wage if the target is not achieved. Under this system, each worker suffers a personal income loss from the failure of the team to work effectively to meet the target.

3 The workers can also be given an opportunity to share in the team or firm profits. *Profit sharing* (sometimes called "gain sharing") is, basically, another form of a forcing contract because the worker will get one income if the firm makes a profit (above some target level) and a lower income if the profit (above a target level) is zero.

4 The workers within different teams also can be rewarded according to how well they do relative to other teams. They can be asked to participate in *tournaments*, in which the members of the "winning team" are given higher incomes – and, very likely, higher hourly or monthly rates of pay – than the members of other teams. We say "very likely" because the winning team members may work harder, longer, and smarter in order to win the tournament "prize." Hence, the "winners'" pay per hour (or any other unit of time) could be lower than the "losers'."

All the pay systems just outlined may have a positive impact on worker input and, as a consequence, on worker output. For example, a number of studies show that profit sharing and worker stock ownership plans do seem to have a positive impact on worker productivity (Howard and Dietz 1969; Metzger 1975; FitzRoy and Kraft 1986; Wagner, Rubin, and Callahan 1988; Weisman and Kruse 1990; US Department of Labor 1993). One study of fifty-two firms in the engineering industry in the United Kingdom (40 percent of which had some form of profit-sharing plans and the rest did not) found that profit sharing could add between 3 and 8 percent to firm productivity (Cable and Wilson 1989). It has also been shown that the more "participatory" the decision-making process – the more information is shared, the more flexible the job assignment, and the greater the extent of profit sharing – the greater worker performance relative to more traditional organizational structures (Husled 1995; Ichniowski, Shaw, and Prennushi 1996).

To pay team members appropriately, managers must know how well teams are doing, not just in how many "widgets" the team produces, but also in terms of team contributions to firm profitability. CMC, a computer service company, assigns individual teams responsibility for individual major clients or for a collection of smaller clients and then develops profit-and-loss statements for each and every team. Higher managers recognize that team members have ground-level information on clients that managers can never know (except in screened forms). It wants to give teams the ability to respond to information received, but it also wants team members to know that their decisions will be monitored through their P&L statements' bottom line. Of course, higher managers can't rely totally on P&L statements of individual teams to maximize firm profits, simply because they often need teams to cooperate when the teams face the now-familiar Prisoner's Dilemmas.

Experimental evidence on the effectiveness of team pay

A question that has all too infrequently been addressed is which method of worker compensation is *more* effective in overcoming shirking and causing workers to apply themselves. One of the more interesting studies that addresses that question uses an experimental/laboratory approach to develop a tentative assessment of the absolute and relative value of the different pay methods on worker effort. Experimental economists Haig Nalbantian and Andrew Schotter (1997) used two groups of six university economics students in a highly stylized experiment in which the students' pay for their participation in the experiment would be determined by how "profitable" their respective teams were in achieving maximum "output."

The students did their "work" on computers that were isolated from one another. The students indicated how much "work" they would do in the twenty-five rounds of the experiment by selecting a number from 0 to 100. The higher the number selected the higher the cost to the student, just as rising effort tends to impose an escalating cost on workers. The students in each of the two teams always knew two pieces of important information: how much they "worked" (or the number they submitted) in each round and how much the "team" as a total "worked." They did not know the individual "effort levels" of the other students.[6]

---

[6] Granted, the experiment leaves much to be desired, which the authors fully concede. The experimental setting did not reflect the full complexity of the typical workplace: direct communication among workers, for example, can have an important impact on the effort levels of individual workers. The complexity of the workplace is why it is so difficult to determine how pay systems affect worker performance, especially relative to alternative compensation schemes.

Nonetheless, the researchers were able to draw conclusions that generally confirmed expectations from the theory at the heart of this textbook. They found that when the revenue-sharing method of pay was employed, the median "effort level" for each of the two teams started at a mere 30 (with a maximum effort level of 100), but because the students were then told how little effort other team members were expending in total, the students began to cut their own effort in each of the successive rounds. The median effort level in both teams trended downward until the twenty-fifth round, when the median effort level was under 13. That finding caused the researchers to assert: "Shirking happens" (Nalbantian and Schotter 1997, 315). They also were able to deduce that the *history of the team performance* matters: the higher the team performance at the start, the greater the team performance thereafter (although the effort level might be declining over the rounds, it would still be higher at identified rounds, the higher the starting effort level).

Nalbantian and Schotter (1997) found that forcing contracts and profit sharing could increase the initial level of effort to 40 or above, a third higher than the initial effort level under revenue sharing, but still the effort level under forcing contracts and profit sharing trended downward with succeeding rounds of the experiment. They also found that the tournaments that were tried, which forced the team members to think competitively, had median initial effort levels on a par with the initial effort levels observed under forcing contracts. However, the effort level tended to increase in the first few rounds and then held more or less constant through the rest of the twenty-five rounds. At the end of the twenty-five rounds, the teams had a median effort level of 40 to 50, or up to four times the final effort level under the revenue-sharing incentive system. Understandably, the authors concluded that "a little competition goes a very long, long way" (Nalbantian and Schotter 1997, 315).

Finally, the authors concluded that monitoring works, which is no surprise, but the extent to which monitoring hiked the effort level grabs attention. No monitoring system works perfectly, so the authors evaluated how the teams would perform with a competitive team pay system under two experimental conditions, one in which the probability of team members being caught shirking was 70 percent of the time and one in which team members being caught shirking was 30 percent of the time, with the penalty being stiff: loss of their "jobs." The median effort for one 70 percent team level started at about 75 (the predicted effort level from theory) and stayed there until the last round, at which point the effort level fell markedly (a result that should be even more understandable from our discussion of *opportunistic behavior* developed in Reading 7.1, The last-period problem). The median effort level for the other 70 percent team started at about 50, rose quickly to 70, and stayed there through the rest of the rounds (with one very large drop in effort in the middle of the rounds).

When the probability of being caught shirking dropped to 30 percent, the effort level of one team started at 70 and went up and down wildly between zero and 80 for the next twenty rounds, only to approach zero during the last five rounds. The effort level of the other team started close to zero and stayed very close to zero for most of the following rounds (reaching above 10 only twice).

Obviously, monitoring of team members can have a dramatic impact on team performance, but, as in all matters, the cost of the monitoring system can be high. The researchers have not yet been able to say, from the experimental evidence, whether the improvement in team performance is worth the cost of the monitoring system that is required. However, managers cannot wait for the experimental findings; they must find ways of minimizing the monitoring costs. One of the great cost-saving advantages of teams, which is not reflected in the way the experiments were run, is that teamwork tends to be self-monitoring, with team members monitoring one another. In the experiment, the team members could not monitor and penalize each other. If self-monitoring were imposed in a future experiment, we would not be surprised if the effort level increased.

Should all firms adopt the competitive team approach? The evidence suggests a strong "Yes." But we hasten to add a caveat that managers of some firms must keep in mind: greater effort to produce more output is desirable as long as it does not come with a sacrifice in "quality" (or some other important dimension of production). Competitive team production may be shunned in firms in industries such as pharmaceuticals and banking that can't tolerate concessions in their quality standards (because of the importance of reputation and also liability concerns, for example). The competition in the tournaments drives up "output" but can drive down "quality." Such firms would want to use reward systems that keep competition under control and quality standards up. They would also want to rely on close monitoring, despite the cost, because of the higher costs that they might suffer with defects. This leads to the obvious conclusion that the greater the cost of mistakes, the greater the cost that can be endured from relaxed competition and from monitoring.

Practical lessons for MBAs: considering marginal cost, ignoring sunk costs, and paying attention to incentive pay

Costs matter, and marginal costs matter especially. Those summary statements of lessons at the heart of this chapter need to be drilled home to MBA students mainly because of how much attention is given to total cost and average cost in worplace business discussions. Marginal cost (along with marginal revenue) – not total or average cost – is key to determining a firm's profit-maximizing output level, how much a product should be upgraded (or downgraded), and even how many different products a firm produces.

There is a very good reason for the scant attention to marginal cost: estimating a firm's marginal cost curve is not easy, especially for firms that produce several products. However, without a rough estimate of the structure of marginal cost, a firm can easily overproduce or underproduce – which means it can be charging too little or too much and making less maximum achievable profit. There is money to be made by incurring the cost of product development, a business maxim that MBA students widely appreciate. There is also money to be made by incurring the costs of estimating a firm's marginal cost function and then thinking about production decisions with the cost structures of this chapter in mind. At the very least, when managers are in discussions of whether to produce more, they should ask for an estimate of the marginal cost of producing more or less, with the figure derived stripped of any nonvariable costs.

A derivative lesson to be learned from the analytics in this chapter is that, in competitive markets, firms should produce in the short run in an output range in which marginal cost is on the rise. This means that the firm should produce in the output range in which the firm experiences diminishing returns. If a firm is experiencing increasing returns (and falling marginal costs) in the short run, it should at least consider the prospects that it is producing too little.

We noted that behavioral economic research reveals that many businesspeople allow costs incurred in the past, such as the historical costs of plant and equipment purchases, to affect their production decisions. Why? The historical costs are fully evident in readily available accounting statements. Managers sometimes feel a commitment to recovering costs incurred long ago, which means they make many pricing and production decisions with an eye toward recovering (or more than recovering) "costs" reported on accounting statements. An important admonition of this chapter is that costs incurred in the past, which cannot be recovered, are *sunk costs*. And sunk costs are simply not relevant costs for current production and product-development decisions. Sunk costs can be lamented but should be ignored for current decisions. There is absolutely nothing that can be done about them. The only relevant costs for today's production and product-development decisions are those costs that can be incurred or not incurred. Sunk costs are what their name suggests, sunk! This is why we stressed in this chapter that, in the short run, fixed costs should not affect production decisions. The only costs that are relevant to decisions on the production level in the short run and long run are those that vary with production decisions. Retail stores may stay open into the wee hours of the morning for one reason: most of the costs on the stores' accounting books are irrelevant to the decision of how long stores should stay open. The only relevant costs are the marginal costs, those costs that rise with the added hours. The relevant decision of when to close involves comparing the relevant marginal costs with the marginal gains (or added revenue) from adding hours.

Another practical lesson to be drawn from this chapter is that managers who see their firms operating under market conditions approaching perfectly competitive markets and recognize the cost advantages of potential economies of expanded scope should not stew over whether to expand their scale of operation. The only viable options are to expand or close. Competitors will expand their scales of operation, driving the market price of the good below the minimum production costs of those firms that hesitate to expand.

MBA students can take from this chapter (and much of the "organizational economics" sections of all chapters) the lesson that firms can obviously improve their bottom lines by creating and developing better products than those available on the market. They can negotiate with toughness, making sure that they pay no more for their resources (including labor) than other producers. But also embedded in this chapter's analysis is the suggestion that firms can improve their profitability by simply getting their incentives right (or, more realistically, improving their incentives) so that workers are motivated to work more cooperatively with the many teams that handle complex tasks within modern businesses. Managers need to look diligently for incentive systems that are having perverse effects, which they can have, and for incentive systems that can better overcome problems of "free riding," "shirking," and "Prisoner's Dilemmas" – all of which are concerned with the tough problem of getting people in large-group settings to seek cooperative solutions despite any natural inclination to do otherwise.

A final lesson to be taken from this chapter: watch out for market environments in which existing producers perceive themselves as price takers because of the lack of entry barriers. Making above-normal profits for long will be very difficult. If a firm must incur the costs of creating and developing a product that can be replicated by other firms at little or no costs, then the product will be replicated by many producers once the market is proved viable, wiping out all firms' profits in the process. In the 1990s, many entrepreneurs bought the "new economy" story that, at the cost of a personal computer, inexpensive software, and a homepage on the Internet, they could become sellers to the world. They did not recognize the central lesson of this chapter: if it doesn't cost very much to get into a market, covering product and market development costs will be difficult – and, accordingly, we had the dot.com boom and bust of the late 1990s.

Further reading online

Reading 9.1 Contestable markets

The bottom line

The key takeaways from chapter 9 are the following:

1   The demand curve facing a perfect competitor is horizontal (or perfectly elastic), meaning the firm is a price taker – that is, it cannot affect market price by any change in its output.

2   Marginal revenue for a perfect competitor is equal to market price.

3   A perfect competitor maximizes profits by producing where marginal cost equals marginal revenue, which equals market price.

4   If the price is below the perfect competitor's average total cost but above its average variable cost curve, the firm will not shut down in the long run. It is still more than covering its fixed costs and, therefore, is minimizing its losses (over what they would be if the firm ceased to operate). Such a firm will shut down once it is able to get out from under its fixed costs.

5   In perfectly competitive markets, any economic profits will be reduced to zero in the long run due to entry and the resulting increase in market supply and decrease in market price.

6   Perfect competition is an idealized market structure that can never be fully attained in the real world. Nonetheless, the model helps to illuminate the influence of competition in the marketplace, just as the idealized concepts of the physical sciences help to illustrate the workings of the natural world. Physicists, for example, deal with the concept of gravity by talking about the acceleration of a falling body in a vacuum. Vacuums do not exist naturally in the world, but they are useful as theoretical constructs to isolate and empha- size the directional power of gravitational pull. In a similar fashion, the theoretical con- struct of perfect competition helps to highlight the directional influence and consequences of competition.

7   The model of perfect competition also provides a benchmark for comparing the relative efficiency of real-world markets. The perfectly competitive model clarifies the rules of efficient production and suggests that free movement of resources is essential to achieving efficient production levels. Without a free flow of resources, new firms cannot move into profitable production lines, increase market supply, push prices down, and force other firms to minimize their production costs.

8   The prices firms pay for labor and other resources do not solely determine a firm's cost structures. Organizational structures have a large influence on costs of production.

Managers must pay attention to how they make use of teams as a means of tapping into workers' specialized knowledge and of increasing the incentives for workers to do what they are hired to do.

9 Cost-effective teamwork can be in the interest not only of principals/owners, but also of all team members, since teamwork can reduce shirking, lower the firm's cost structure, and increase the pay and job security of team members. The more competitive the product markets, the more important it is that managers organize teams and structure their pay in the most cost-effective way.

Review questions >>

1 Draw the short-run average and marginal cost curves, plus the demand curve, for a perfect competitor. Give the firm's demand, and identify the short-run production level for a profit-maximizing firm. Identify the profits.

2 On your graph for question 1, indicate with a P_m the minimum price the firm requires in order to continue short-run operations.

3 On your graph for question 1, darken the firm's marginal cost curve above its intersection with the average variable supply cost curve. Explain why that portion of the marginal cost curve is the firm's supply curve.

4 Why does a perfectly competitive firm seek to equate marginal cost with marginal revenue rather than to produce where average total cost is at a minimum?

5 If perfectly competitive firms are making a profit in the short run, what will happen to the industry's equilibrium price and quantity in the long run?

6 Suppose the market demand for a product rises. In the short run, how will a perfect competitor react to the higher market price? Draw a graph to illustrate your answer. What will happen to the market price in the long run? Why?

7 Suppose that you know absolutely nothing about price and cost in a particular competitive industry. How could you nevertheless determine whether the typical firm in the industry was making economic profits or losses?

8 Suppose a manager were to refuse to provide a fringe benefit that could lower the wages of their workers, but which on balance benefited workers. Why has this manager prevented the firm's average cost curves from being as low as possible?

9 When should a firm eliminate fringe benefits?

10   What points made in the discussion of teams in the chapter are applicable to your study teams? Does your university allow students to move among teams? Why or why not? How might the prospects of switching teams affect team performances? Should students be able to make monetary side-payments to students in other teams to switch teams?

11   In MBA study teams, in most programs, all team members are typically given the same grade for team projects. How does such a grading rule affect team member behavior? What would be the consequences of allowing teams to give different members different grades?

10

Monopoly power and firm pricing decisions

If monopoly persists, monopoly will always sit at the helm of government … its bigness is an unwholesome inflation created by privileges and exemptions which it ought not to enjoy. If there are men in this country big enough to own the government of the United States, they are going to own it.

Woodrow Wilson

That competition is a virtue, at least as far as enterprises are concerned, has been a basic article of faith in the American Tradition, and a vigorous antitrust policy has long been regarded as both beneficial and necessary, not only to extend competitive forces into new regions but also to preserve them where they may be flourishing at the moment.

G. Warren Nutter and Henry Alder Einhorn

At the bottom of almost all arguments against the free market is a deep-seated concern about the distorting (some would say corrupting) influence of monopolies. People who are suspicious of the free market fear that too many producers are unchecked by the forces of competition, but instead hold considerable monopoly power or control over market outcomes. Unless the government intervenes, these firms are likely to exploit their power for their own selfish benefit. This theme has been fundamental to the writings of economist John Kenneth Galbraith:

The initiative in deciding what is produced comes not from the sovereign consumer who, through the market, issues instructions that bend the productive mechanism to his or her ultimate will. Rather it comes from the great producing organization that reaches forward to control the markets that it is presumed to serve and, beyond, to bend the customers to its needs. (Galbraith 1967, 6)

This chapter is really a continuation of our earlier discussion of "market failures," for *monopoly* is often seen as one of the gravest of all forms of failure in markets. Accordingly, we examine the dynamics of monopoly power and attempt to place the consequences of those dynamics in proper perspective. We also consider the usefulness of antitrust laws in controlling monopoly and promoting competition. In chapter 11, we extend the model of monopoly developed here to two forms of partial monopoly market structures – monopolistic competition and oligopoly.

All market models that assume some degree of "monopoly power" (a phrase defined below) are especially relevant to MBA students because in these models firms can and must devise creative pricing strategies. A theme of this chapter and the next is that while firms can surely increase their profitability by producing "better mousetraps," they also have opportunities to increase their profitability through creative pricing, which does not necessarily carry the high product-development costs of "better mousetraps." However, in order to innovate through pricing strategies, the firm must be able to distinguish its "mousetrap" from all others. We submit also that while perfect competition has efficiency attributes for larger society, most MBA students will spend the bulk of their working hours trying to develop firms and products that offer monopoly pricing power.

In Part A we develop the theory of monopoly pricing that allows for creative pricing strategies. Part B lays out a variety of ways firms have been able to use the theory in the development of real-world pricing strategies that have a common feature, generating additional revenue through price discrimination among different groups of buyers.

Part A Theory and public policy applications

The origins of monopoly

We have defined the competitive market as the process by which market rivals, each pursuing his own private interests, strive to outdo one another. This competitive process has many benefits. It enables producers to obtain information about what consumers and other producers are willing to do. It promotes higher production levels, lower prices, and a greater variety of goods and services than would be achieved otherwise.

Monopoly power is the conceptual opposite of competition. Monopoly power is the ability of a firm to raise the market price of its good or service by reducing production and, hence, market supply. Whereas the demand curve of the competitive firm is horizontal (see chapter 9), a firm with monopoly power faces a downward sloping demand curve. To maximize its profits (or minimize its losses), such a firm need only search through the various price–quantity combinations on its demand curve. In very general terms, then, a firm with monopoly power is a *price searcher*. It can control the price it charges because other firms are to some extent unable or unwilling to compete. As a result, a monopolized market produces fewer benefits than perfect competition does. A monopoly's market power over its price is its control of its own production – and, therefore, market supply.

Businesses vary considerably in the extent of their monopoly power. The Postal Service and your local telephone company both had significant monopoly power, until the advent of overnight delivery, e-mail, cell phones, and Internet telephony. They confronted few competitors, as entry into their markets was barred by law. (E-mail, cell phone, and Internet telephony technology eventually rendered those legal barriers largely irrelevant.) IBM has had since the 1960s far less monopoly power in mainframe computing. Although IBM can expand or contract its sales to affect the price it charges for its computers (or business services), it is restrained by the possibility that other firms will enter its market. On a smaller scale, grocery stores face the same threat. They may have many competitors already, and they must be concerned about additional stores entering the market. Nevertheless, a grocery store still retains *some* power to restrict sales and raise its prices by virtue of its location, or other features that appeal to some consumers.

How does a monopoly arise? To answer that question clearly, we must reflect once again on the basis for competition. Competition occurs where rivals can enter markets in which profits exist and production technology allows many firms to produce at low costs (economies of scale are not significant for any firm). In the extreme case of perfect competition, there are no barriers to entry and competitors are numerous. Entrepreneurs are always on the lookout for any opportunity to enter such a market in pursuit of profit. Individual competitors cannot raise their prices – for, if they do, their rivals may move in, cut prices, and take away all their customers. If a wheat farmer, for example, asks more than the market price, customers can buy from others at the market price. For this reason, perfect competitors are called *price takers.* They have no real control over the price they charge.

The essential condition for competition is freedom of market entry. In perfect competition, entry is assumed to be completely free (meaning that it is costless). Conversely, the essential condition for monopoly is the presence of *barriers to entry.* Monopolists can manipulate price because such barriers protect them from being undercut by rivals.

Various economists have suggested that barriers to entry can arise from several standard sources:

- First, the monopolist may have sole (or dominant) ownership of a strategic resource, such as bauxite (from which aluminum is extracted).
- Second, the monopolist may have a patent or copyright on the product, which prevents other producers from duplicating it.

- Third, the monopolist may have an exclusive franchise to sell a given product in a specific geographical area. Consider the exclusive franchise that your local bus company has or the franchise that local electric utilities enjoyed everywhere in the country until very recently.
- Fourth, the monopolist may own the rights to a well-known brand name with a highly loyal group of customers. In that case, the barrier to entry is the costly process of trying to get customers to try a new product.
- Fifth, a firm might be able to develop a monopoly by keeping essential features of its product a "trade secret." Coca-Cola has been able to retain some monopoly control over Coke for more than a hundred years (well beyond the patent term) because its formula has remained a closely guarded company secret. Its monopoly power has been limited, however, because other firms (Pepsi Cola) have sought to imitate the taste of Coke.
- Sixth, as noted in chapter 6, firms can acquire monopoly power through network effects and the potential for "lock ins," or just high "switching costs" for consumers. Consumers are said to be "locked in" to a product when they are unable to move to other similar products. They are said to incur "switching costs" when they can move to other products but must incur out-of-pocket expenditures and opportunity costs to do so. (For example, the great majority of keyboards have the so-called QWERTY layout of keys, so named because those six letters are on the top row of letter keys. Keyboard manufacturers are reluctant to experiment with possibly more efficient layouts because keyboard users and firms are "locked in" to QWERTY, or keyboard users and manufacturers would incur high "switching costs" to move to another design. We cover the history of and debate over the relative efficiency of the QWERTY in online Perspective 10.)

Online
Perspective

- Finally, in a monopolized industry, production may be conducted on a very large scale, requiring huge plants and large amounts of equipment. The enormous financial resources needed to take advantage of large economies of scale can act as a barrier to entry because a new entrant operating on a small scale would have costs that were too high to compete effectively with the dominant firm.

All in all, these external barriers to entry can be thought of as costs that potential competitors must bear before they can compete. Such barriers may be "low," which means that a sole producer's monopoly power may be very limited, but such barriers could, theoretically, also be prohibitively high.

The limits of monopoly power

Even the pure monopolist's market power, however, is restricted in two important ways. First, without government assistance, the monopolist's control over the market for a product is never complete. Even if a producer has a true monopoly of a good, the consumer can still choose a *substitute good* whose production is not monopolized. For instance, until recently in most parts of the United States, only one firm has been permitted to provide a local telephone service. Yet people can always communicate in other ways. They can talk directly with one another; they can write letters or send telegrams; they can use their children as messengers. Obviously none of these alternatives are close substitutes for a telephone, but people can also choose to use less of their incomes on telephone services and more on rugs, bicycles, or any number of other things. The consumer's demand curves for all goods are downward sloping, reflecting the fact that not even a monopolist can force consumers to buy its product. As Friedrich Hayek has written:

If, for instance, I would very much like to be painted by a famous artist [one who has monopoly power] and if he refuses to paint me for less than a very high fee, it would clearly be absurd to say that I am coerced. The same is true of any other commodity or service that I can do without. So long as the services of a particular person are not crucial to my existence or the preservation of what I most value, the conditions he exacts for rendering these services cannot be called "coercion." (Hayek 1960, 136)

This is not to say that the effects of monopoly are not harmful. If monopoly means that one firm has few if any rivals providing the same product, then the monopoly is a force that reduces consumer choice.

But monopoly power can reflect beneficial considerations for consumers. A firm may gain monopoly power because it has built a better mousetrap or developed a good that was previously unavailable. In other words, a firm may be the only producer because it is the first producer, and no one has yet been able to figure out how to duplicate its product. In this instance, although monopolized, a new product results in an expansion of consumer choice. Furthermore, the monopoly may be only temporary, for other competitors are likely to break into the market eventually.

As Micklethwait and Wooldridge observed, when Henry Ford started his car company he

"was devoted to handcrafting toys for the super-rich," but it wasn't long before more than a million Americans were driving Model Ts. George Eastman bought his first (very difficult to use) camera in 1877 for $49.58 (which would be equal to about $500 in today's prices). By 1900, Eastman was selling Brownies for $1 under the slogan "You push the button and we do the rest." (Micklethwait and Wooldridge 2003, 77)

The point here is that innovation and competition resulted in large companies, which many would say had monopoly power, but those companies "improved the living standards of ordinary people, putting the luxuries of the rich within reach of the man in the street" (2003, 77).

Market conditions – the cost of production and the downward sloping demand curve for the good – also restrict the monopolist's market power. If the monopolistic firm raises its price, it must be prepared to sell less. How much less depends on what substitutes are available. The monopolist must also consider the costs of expanding production and of trying to prevent competitors from entering the market.

In an open market, monopoly power is typically dissolved in the long run. With time, competitors can discover weakly protected avenues through which to invade the monopolist's domain. The Reynolds International Pen Company had a patent monopoly on the first ballpoint pen that it introduced in 1945. Two years later other pen companies had found ways of circumventing the patent and producing a similar but not identical product. The price of ballpoint pens fell from an initial $12.50 (or about $125 in 2005 purchasing power) to the low prices of today. Many other products that are competitively produced today – calculators, video games, cell phones, and cellophane tape, to name a few – were first sold by companies that enjoyed temporary monopolies.

For years, Polaroid had a patent monopoly on the instant-photograph market. Now, digital photography has eclipsed any remaining monopoly Polaroid has had in instant pictures.

Kodak's Kodachrome 35 millimeter film, which was patented, has also been supplanted by digital pictures, with Kodak struggling to stay afloat at this writing in face of an onslaught of new digital camera entries.

When Apple introduced its highly succesful iPhone in the winter of 2007, it had that segment of the cell phone market to itself, and charged $600 (and even then could not meet market demand). Apple sold millions of iPhones by the month and made billions in profits. Its next generation iPhone was introduced in mid-2008 with upgrades in software features and performance with a one-third price reduction. By the start of 2009, Blackberry and Samsung released iPhone clones, with Apple responding by introducing a model that sold in Walmarts for $99. Thus the limits on monopoly power are crucial: in the long run, excessively high prices, restricted supply, and high profits give potential competitors the incentive to find ways to circumvent the monopolist's power and benefit consumers.

The most effective way for a monopoly to retain its market power is to enlist the coercive power of government to prevent competition. This strategy has been used effectively for decades in the electric utilities industry and the cable television market. The insurance industry and the medical profession, both of which are protected from competition through licensing procedures, are also good examples. However, even the power of the state may not be enough to shield an industry from competition forever. Consumer tastes and the technology of production and delivery can change dramatically over the very long run. The railroad industry's market, which enjoyed governmental protection from price competition for almost a

century, has been gradually eroded by the emergence of new competitors, principally airlines, buses, and trucks. Even the US Postal Service's monopoly on first-
class mail continues to be eroded by Federal Express and a host of other overnight
delivery firms, as well as by e-mail and fax machines (although fax machines now
represent a rapidly waning competitive threat to the mail or e-mail services).

Today, one of the best examples of government-protected monopoly power is in
the distribution of alcoholic beverages at the state level. A number of states require
that all out-of-state alcoholic beverages be distributed by in-state wholesale distributors. Moreover, the distributors must charge all retailers the same price. In Ohio,
beer wholesalers are guaranteed a markup of 25 percent, while wine distributors are
guaranteed a markup of 33 percent. The Spirits Wholesalers of America has supported such market restrictions on the grounds that "alcohol has to be treated as a
special product because when it is misused it causes devastating social consequences" (Hirsch 2005). However, because of the protected monopoly the distributors are
granted by the state, "Two-Buck Chuck" – the nickname given to Charles Shaw
wine, which sells for $1.99 at Trader Joe's grocery stores in California – sells for
$3.99 in Columbus, Ohio (Hirsch 2005).

Should government attempt to break up monopolies? Without state protection,
monopoly may eventually dissipate, so the relevant public policy questions are how
long the monopoly power is likely to persist if left alone and how costly it will be
while it lasts in terms of lost efficiency and unequal distribution of income. The
machinery of government needed to dissolve monopoly power is costly in itself.
Thus the decision whether to prosecute antitrust violations depends in part on
the costs and benefits of such an action and whether the benefits justify the costs.
As covered online in Reading 3.1, the first seller of hand calculators enjoyed a
temporary monopoly of the US market in 1969. Subsequently the industry developed very rapidly, however, and in retrospect it is clear that a long drawn out
antitrust action would have been inappropriate.

To give another example, in 1969 the Justice Department decided that an antitrust
suit was warranted against IBM, which enjoyed a monopoly of the domestic computer market, dominated by large mainframe computers. After more than a decade,
the Justice Department dropped the case in January 1982. The accumulated documentation from the proceedings filled a warehouse, and the Justice Department
and IBM devoted an untold number of lawyer-hours to the case. In the meantime,
new firms producing minicomputers and microcomputers seriously eroded IBM's
alleged monopoly, a trend that has continued (and accelerated) since 1982. Thus the
net benefits to society from the antitrust action against IBM were at best debatable,
and probably negative – that is, the costs most likely exceeded the benefits.

Similarly, the cost the US government has incurred to prosecute Microsoft for
antitrust violation (starting in 1998) may also, in the long run, outweigh the

achieved benefits. The courts did indeed rule that Microsoft is a "monopoly" in the operating system market, but the consumer benefits, in terms of lower prices and greater availability of products, that may result from Microsoft's monopoly are not yet obvious (see McKenzie 2000).

Equating marginal cost with marginal revenue

In deciding how often to play tennis, people weigh the estimated benefits of each game against its costs. Producers of goods follow a similar procedure, although the benefits of production are measured in terms of *revenue acquired* rather than personal utility. A producer will produce another unit of a good if the additional (or marginal) revenue it brings is greater than the additional cost of its production – in other words, if it increases the firm's profits. The firm will therefore expand production to the point where marginal cost equals marginal revenue ($MC = MR$). This is a fundamental rule that all profit-maximizing firms follow, and monopolies are no exception.

Suppose you are in the yo-yo business. You have a patent on edible yo-yos, which come in three flavors – vanilla, chocolate, and strawberry. (We will assume there is a demand for these products – you can work up quite an appetite yo-yoing!) The cost of producing the first yo-yo is $0.50, but you can sell it for $0.75. Your profit on that unit is therefore $0.25 ($0.75 minus $0.50). If the second unit costs you $0.60 to make (assuming increasing marginal cost) and you can sell it for $0.75, your profit for two yo-yos is $0.40 ($0.25 profit on the first plus $0.15 profit on the second). If you intend to maximize your profits, you – like the perfect competitor – will continue to expand production until the gap between the constant marginal revenue and the increasing marginal cost disappears. As a monopolist, however, you will find that your marginal revenue does not remain constant. Instead, it decreases over the range of production.

The monopolist's marginal revenue declines as output rises because its price must be reduced to entice consumers to buy more. Consider the price schedule in table 10.1. Price and quantity are inversely related, reflecting the assumption that a monopolist faces a downward sloping demand curve. As the price falls from $10 to $6 (column [2]), the number sold rises from one to five (column [1]). If the firm wishes to sell only one yo-yo, it can charge as much as $10. Total revenue at that level of production is then $10. To sell more – say, two yo-yos – the monopolist must reduce the price for each to $9. Total revenue then rises to $18 (column [3]).

By multiplying columns (1) and (2), we can fill in the rest of column (3). As the price is lowered and the quantity sold rises, total revenue rises from $10 for one unit to $30 for five units. With each unit increase in quantity sold, however, total revenue does not rise by an equal amount. Instead, it rises in declining amounts –

Table 10.1 **The monopolist's declining marginal revenue**

(1) Quantity of yo-yos sold	(2) Price of yo-yos ($)	(3) Total revenue (1 × [2]) ($)	(4) Marginal revenue (change in [3]) ($)
0	11	0	0
1	10	10	10
2	9	18	8
3	8	24	6
4	7	28	4
5	6	30	2

first by $10, then $8, $6, $4, and $2. These amounts are the marginal revenue from the sale of each unit (column [4]), which the monopolist must compare with the marginal cost of each unit.

At an output level of one yo-yo, marginal revenue equals price, but at every other output level marginal revenue is less than price. Because of the monopolist's downward sloping demand curve, the second yo-yo cannot be sold unless the price of both one and two units is reduced from $10 to $9. If we account for the $1 in revenue lost on the first yo-yo in order to sell the second, the net revenue from the second yo-yo is $8 (the selling price of $9 minus the $1 lost on the first yo-yo). For the third yo-yo to be sold, the price on the first two must be reduced by another dollar each. The loss in revenue on them is therefore $2. And the marginal revenue for the third yo-yo is its $8 selling price less the $2 loss on the first two units, or $6.

Thus the monopolist's marginal revenue curve (columns [1] and [4]) is derived directly from the market demand curve (columns [1] and [2]). Graphically, the marginal revenue curve lies below the demand curve, and its distance from the demand curve increases as the price falls (see figure 10.1).[1]

More details on the derivation of the marginal revenue curve can be found in online Reading 10.1 for this chapter.

Figure 10.2 adds the monopolist's marginal cost curve to the demand and marginal revenue curves from figure 10.1. Because the profit-maximizing monopolist will produce to the point where marginal cost equals marginal revenue, our yo-yo

[1] Prove this to yourself by plotting the figures in columns (1) and (2) versus the figures in columns (1) and (4) on a sheet of graph paper. (Another simple way of drawing the MR curve is to extend the demand curve until it intersects both the vertical and horizontal axes. Then draw the MR curve starting from the demand curve's point of intersection with the vertical axis to a point midway between the original and the intersection of the demand curve with the horizontal axis. This method can be used for any linear demand curve.)

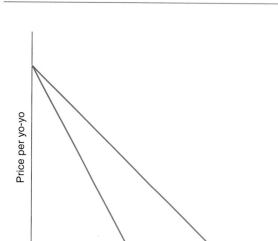

Figure 10.1 The monopolist's demand and marginal revenue curves
The demand curve facing a monopolist slopes downward, for it is the same as market demand. The monopolist's marginal revenue curve is constructed from the information contained in the demand curve (see table 10.1).

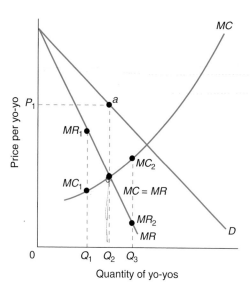

Figure 10.2 Equating marginal cost with marginal revenue
The monopolist will move toward production level Q_2, the level at which marginal cost equals marginal revenue. At production levels below Q_2, marginal revenue will exceed marginal cost; the monopolist will miss the chance to increase profits. At production levels greater than Q_2, marginal cost will exceed marginal revenue; the monopolist will lose money on the extra units.

maker will produce Q_2 units. At that quantity, the marginal cost and marginal revenue curves intersect. If the yo-yo maker produces fewer than Q_2 yo-yos – say, Q_1 – profits are lost unnecessarily. The marginal revenue acquired from selling the last yo-yo up to Q_1, MR_1, is greater than the marginal cost of producing it, MC_1. Furthermore, for all units between Q_1 and Q_2, marginal revenue exceeds marginal cost. In other words, by expanding production from Q_1 to Q_2, the monopolist can add more to total revenue than to total cost. Up to an output level of Q_2, the firm's profits will rise.

Why does the monopolist produce no more than Q_2? Because the marginal cost of all additional units beyond Q_2 is greater than the marginal revenue they bring.

Beyond Q_2 units, profits will fall. If it produces Q_3 yo-yos, for instance, the firm may still make a profit, but not the greatest profit possible. The marginal cost of the last yo-yo up to Q_3 (MC_2) is greater than the marginal revenue received from its sale (MR_2). By producing Q_3 units, the monopolist adds more to cost than to revenues. The result is lower profits.

After the monopolistic firm selects the output at which to produce, the market price of the good is determined. In figure 10.2, the price that can be charged for Q_2 yo-yos is P_1. (Remember, the demand curve indicates the price that can be charged for any quantity.) Of all the possible price–quantity combinations on the demand curve, therefore, the monopolist will choose combination a. More on monopoly profit and the potential for monopoly losses can be found in the appendix to this chapter. For long microeconomics courses, combine the monopolist's demand and marginal revenue curves developed in this chapter with the upward sloping marginal and the average cost curves developed in chapters 7 and 8.

[See online Video Module 10.1 Monopoly production]

The comparative inefficiency of monopoly

Chapter 9 concluded that in a perfectly competitive market, firms tend to produce at the intersection of the market supply and demand curves. That point (b in figure 10.3) is the most efficient production level, in the sense that the marginal benefit to the consumer of the last unit produced equals its marginal cost to the producer. All units whose marginal benefits exceed their marginal costs are produced. All possible net benefits to the consumer have been extracted from production.

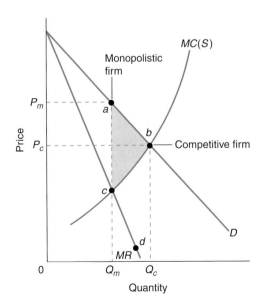

Figure 10.3 The comparative efficiency of monopoly and competition

Firms in a competitive market will tend to produce at point b, the intersection of the marginal cost and demand curves (with the price, or marginal benefit, given by the height of the demand curve). Monopolists will tend to produce at point c, the intersection of marginal cost and marginal revenue, and to charge the highest price the market will bear: P_m. In a competitive market, therefore, the price will tend to be lower (P_c) and the quantity produced greater (Q_c) than in a monopolistic market. The inefficiency of monopoly is shown by the shaded triangular area abc, the amount by which the benefits of producing $Q_c - Q_m$ units (shown by the demand curve) exceed their marginal cost of production.

For each unit between Q_m and Q_c, the marginal benefits to the consumer, as illustrated by the market demand curve, are greater than the marginal costs of production. These are net benefits that consumers would like to have, but that are not delivered by the monopolistic firm interested in maximizing profits rather than consumer welfare. The resources that are not used in the production of the monopoly good must either remain idle or be used in a less valuable line of production. (Remember, the cost of doing anything is the value of the next-best alternative forgone.) In this sense, economists say that resources are *misallocated by monopoly*. Too few resources are used in the monopolistic industry, and too many elsewhere.

On balance, then, the inefficiency of monopoly consists of the benefits lost minus the cost not incurred when output is restricted. When compared to the outcome under perfect competition, monopoly price is too high and output too low. In figure 10.3, the gross benefit to consumers of $Q_c - Q_m$ units is equal to the area under the demand curve, or $Q_m abQ_c$. The cost of those additional units is equal to the area under the marginal cost curve, or $Q_m cbQ_c$. Therefore, the net benefit of the units not produced is equal to the shaded triangular area abc. This area represents the inefficiency of monopoly, sometimes called the "dead-weight welfare loss" of monopoly. To put it another way, area abc represents the gain in consumer welfare that could be achieved by dissolving the monopoly and expanding production from Q_m to Q_c. This area helps explain why consumers prefer Q_c and producers prefer Q_m.

Figure 10.4(a) shows the additional benefits that consumers would receive from $Q_c - Q_m$ units, the area under the demand curve, $Q_m abQ_c$. The additional money that consumers must pay producers for $Q_c - Q_m$ units, shown by the area under the marginal revenue curve, is a much smaller amount: only $Q_m cdQ_c$. That is, the additional benefits of $Q_c - Q_m$ units exceed the cost to consumers by the area $abdc$. Consumers obviously gain from an increase in production.

Yet for virtually the same reason, the monopolistic firm is not interested in providing $Q_c - Q_m$ units. It must incur an additional cost equal to the area $Q_m cbQ_c$ (figure 10.4[b]), while it can expect to receive only $Q_m cdQ_c$ in additional revenues. The extra cost incurred by expanding production from Q_m to Q_c exceeds the additional revenue acquired by the shaded area cbd. Thus, an increase in production will reduce the monopolistic firm's profits (or increase its losses). Notice that consumers would gain more from an increase in production than the monopolist would lose. The shaded area in figure 10.4(a) is larger than the shaded area in figure 10.4(b). The difference is the triangular area abc. It is worth pointing out that if transactions costs were zero, or low enough, consumers would benefit by getting together and agreeing to "bribe" the monopolist to expand output to the competitive level. But the cost of this type of collective action is too high to make it an attractive option for consumers.

[See online Video Module 10.2 Inefficiency of monopolies]

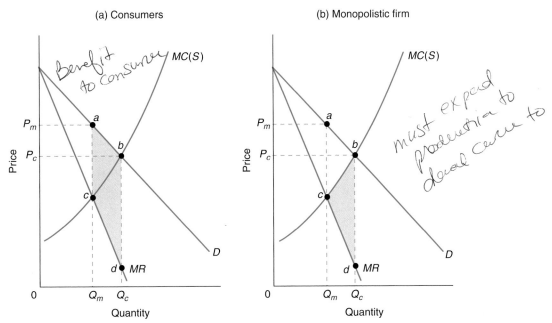

(a) Consumers (b) Monopolistic firm

[handwritten: Benefit to Consumer]

[handwritten: must exp'd production to demand curve to]

Figure 10.4 The costs and benefits of expanded production
If the monopolist expands production from Q_m to Q_c in panel (a), consumers will receive additional benefits equal to the area bounded by $Q_m abQ_c$. They will pay an additional amount equal to the area $Q_m cdQ_c$ for those benefits, leaving a net benefit equal to the shaded area *abdc*. To expand production, the monopoly must incur additional production costs equal to the area $Q_m cbQ_c$ in panel (b). It gains additional revenues equal to the area $Q_m cdQ_c$, leaving a net loss equal to the shaded area *cbd*. Thus, expanded production helps the consumer but hurts the monopolist.

Monopoly profits

A key concern of a monopoly is the maximization of its long-run economic profits (or profit above normal profits that, as noted in an earlier chapter, can be construed as a cost of doing business). In the short run, both perfectly competitive firms and monopoly firms can make economic profits, because of, say, a sudden rise in demand. In competitive markets, the economic profits will be eroded by new entrants that increase market supply and push the price down to where price equals the marginal cost and minimum average total cost of each firm. The monopolist, on the other hand, often can earn profits into the long run because barriers to entry protect its market position. Hence, the monopolist can constrict production and market supply into the long run, and it can keep its price above competitive levels and profits above normal profit levels into the future.

The persistence of monopoly profits into the long run is what makes monopoly ventures attractive for firms, but not for consumers who pay higher than

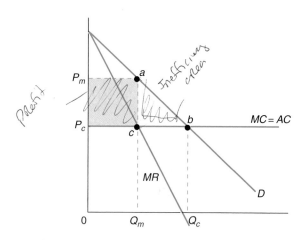

Figure 10.5 Monopoly profit maximization
Assuming constant marginal cost means that the long-run marginal costs and average cost curves are one and the same. A profit-maximizing monopolist will produce where $MC = MR$, or restrict production Q_m in order to charge a price of P_m, which will be above the competitive price P_c. The monopolist will make an economic profit equal to the shaded area, or P_cP_mac. The inefficiency of monopoly will equal the area bounded by abc, which is the difference between the area under the demand curve between Q_m and Q_c and the area under the marginal cost curve between Q_m and Q_c.

competitive prices. Accordingly, here we focus on monopolist long-run production decisions (and you will recall that in the long run all costs are variable, which means there is no need to distinguish between fixed and variable cost).

To show monopoly profits in the long run, we could simply include the bowed-down long-run average cost curve from chapter 8 in a graph with the monopolist's demand and marginal revenue curves. However, in the interest of simplifying and clarifying the monopoly analytics, we will assume that marginal cost is constant at all production levels, which means the marginal cost curve is horizontal. More important, the assumption of constant marginal cost means that the average cost of production always equals the marginal cost of production. If the long-run marginal cost of producing units of a good is always $5, then the long-run average cost of production is always $5. This means that the marginal cost and average cost of production curves are one and the same horizontal line in figure 10.5 labeled $MC = AC$. This graphical simplification will not affect the conclusions drawn, but will likely ease your understanding of the central points we intend to make.

As in previous discussion, the monopolist will produce where $MC = MR$, which means it will produce Q_m. The monopoly price will be P_m. (As a matter of reference, the competitive output and price levels will be Q_c and P_c, which means the inefficiency triangle abc in figure 10.5 corresponds to the inefficiency triangle abc in figure 10.3.) The monopoly revenues will be price times quantity, $P_m \times Q_m$, or the area bounded by OP_maQ_m. The total cost incurred to produce Q_m will be average cost times quantity, $AC \times Q_m$, or the area bounded by OP_ccQ_m. The monopoly (economic) profits will be total revenues minus total cost, or the shaded area bounded by P_cP_mac.

So long as the barriers to entry hold and demand stays where it is, the monopolist can expect to earn the identified monopoly profits. However, lots of things can happen in the long run, which can be long indeed. Demand can dissipate just because of a shift in consumer tastes. Microsoft might see itself having a monopoly in the operating system market, but its market demand can be undermined in the long run because people start using their MP3 players and cell phones for work that formerly could be done only with a personal computer. Technology is ever moving, and technological developments can be spurred by the monopoly price and profits identified in figure 10.5.

Price discrimination

Charging a fixed price for a good, for example P_m in figure 10.5, can be profitable, but surely there are more profitable pricing strategies since buyers are willing to pay higher prices for Q_m units than P_m. Businesses have become quite creative in developing means of charging different prices for different units sold.

A grocery store may advertise that it will sell one can of beans for $0.30, but two cans for $0.55. Is the store trying to give customers a break? Sometimes, this kind of pricing may simply mean that the cost of producing additional cans decreases as more are sold. At other times, it may indicate that customers' demand curves for beans are downward sloping and the store can make more profits by offering a volume discount than by selling beans at a constant price. In other words, the store may be exploiting its *limited monopoly power.*

Consider figure 10.6. Suppose the demand curve represents your demand for beans and the supply curve represents the store's marginal cost of producing and offering the beans for sale. If the store charges the same price for each can of beans, it will have to offer them at $0.25 each to induce you to buy two. Its total revenues will be $0.50. But, as figure 10.6 shows, you are actually willing to pay more for the first can – $0.30 – than for the second. If the store offers one can for $0.30 and two cans for $0.55, you will still buy two cans, but its revenues from the sale will be $0.55 instead of $0.50. Similarly, to entice you to buy three cans, the store need only offer to sell one for $0.30, two for $0.55, and three for $0.75, and its profits will rise further. The deal does not change the marginal cost of providing each can, which is below the selling price for the first two units and equal to the selling price for the third. The marginal cost of the first can is $0.09; the second, $0.14; and the third, $0.20. The total cost of the three cans to the store is $0.43, regardless of how the cans are priced.

A firm can discriminate in this way only as long as its customers do not resell what they buy for a higher price – and as long as other firms are unable to move into the market and challenge its monopoly power by lowering the price. In the case of canned beans, resale is not very practical. The person who buys three cans has little incentive to seek out someone who is willing to pay $0.25 instead of $0.20 for one can. The profit potential – $0.05 – is just not great enough to bother. But suppose a car dealer has two identical automobiles carrying a book price of $5,000 each. If the dealer

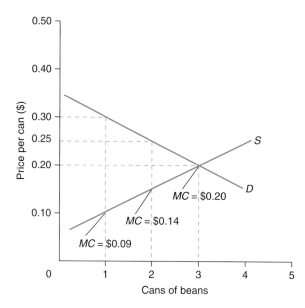

Figure 10.6 Price discrimination
By offering customers one can of beans for $0.30, two cans for $0.55, and three cans for $0.75, a grocery store collects more revenues than if it offers three cans for $0.20 each. In either case, the consumer buys three cans. But by making the special offer, the store earns $0.15 more in revenues per customer.

offered one car for $5,000 and two cars for $9,000, many people would be willing to buy the two cars selling for $9,000 and spend the time needed to find a buyer for one of them at $5,000. The $5,000 gain they stand to make would compensate them for their time and effort in searching out a resale. In Part B of this chapter, we will discuss creative ways in which firms can prevent consumers in the low-price market segment from reselling to consumers in the high-price market segment.

Thus, advertised **price discrimination** is much more frequently found in grocery stores than in car dealerships. But car dealers also discriminate with regard to price. The salesperson who in casual conversation asks a customer's age, income, place of work, and so forth is actually trying to figure out the customer's demand curve, so as to get as high a price as possible. Similarly, many doctors and lawyers quietly adjust their fees to fit their clients' incomes, using information they obtain from client questionnaires. Whether price discrimination is unadvertised and based on income, as in the case of doctors and car dealers, or advertised and based on volume sold, as in the case of utilities and long-distance phone companies, the important point is that the products or services involved are typically difficult, if not impossible, to resell.

Some monopolies' products are not difficult to resell, and so they cannot engage in price discrimination. For example, copyright law gives the publishers of economics textbooks some monopoly power, but textbooks are easily resold, both through a network of used-book dealers and among students. Thus, although

> **Price discrimination** is the practice of varying the price of a given good or service according to how much is bought and who buys it, supposing that marginal costs do not differ across buyers.

textbook publishers can alter their sales by changing the price, they infrequently engage in price discrimination. Nor do they encourage college bookstores to price-discriminate in their sales to students. The discounts that publishers give bookstores on large sales reflect the cost differences in handling large and small orders, not students' or professors' downward sloping demand curves for books. The same can be said about a host of other products protected by patents and copyrights.

The monopolist whose production level was shown in figure 10.3 is unable to discriminate among buyers or units bought by each buyer. A monopolist who is able to do so can produce at a higher output level than Q_m and earn greater profits. Just how much greater depends on how free, or "perfect," the monopolist's power to discriminate is.

Perfect price discrimination

The monopolist represented in figure 10.7 can charge a different price for each and every unit sold. Theoretically, this firm has the power of **perfect price discrimination** ("perfect" from the standpoint of the *producer*, not the consumer). Under perfect price discrimination, the seller's mar-

> **Perfect price discrimination** is the practice of selling each unit of a given good or service for the maximum possible price.

ginal revenue curve is identical to the seller's demand curve (because the marginal revenue of each unit sold equals the price). This is shown in figure 10.7, where the firm's marginal revenue curve is not separate and distinct from its demand curve, as in figure 10.4. Its demand curve is its marginal revenue curve. If the first unit can be sold for a price of, say, $20, the marginal revenue from that unit is equal to the price, $20. If the next unit can be sold for $19.95, the marginal revenue from that unit is again the same as the price, since selling the second unit doesn't require lowering the price on the first unit; and so on. In short, the seller extracts the *entire consumer surplus*.

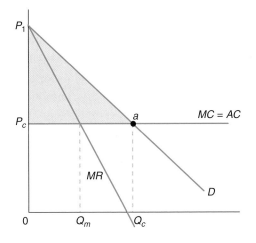

Figure 10.7 Perfect price discrimination
The perfect price discriminating monopolist will produce at the point where marginal cost and marginal revenue are equal (point a). Its output level, Q_c, is therefore the same as that achieved under perfect competition. But because the monopolist charges as much as the market will bear for each unit, its profits – the shaded area P_cP_1a – are higher than the competitive firm's. The inefficiency of monopoly is eliminated by perfect price discrimination, although the monopolist absorbs all of the consumer surplus.

As in figure 10.5, the perfect price discriminating monopolist in figure 10.7 equates marginal revenue with marginal cost. Equality occurs this time at point a, the intersection of the demand curve (now the monopolist's marginal revenue curve) with the marginal cost curve. Thus the perfect price discriminating monopolist achieves the same output level as that of the industry involved in perfect competition. In this sense the perfect price discriminating firm is an efficient producer. As before, profit is found by subtracting total cost from total revenue. Total revenue here is the area under the demand curve up to the monopolist's output level, or the area bounded by $0P_1aQ_c$. Total cost is the area bounded by $0P_caQ_c$ (found, you may recall, by multiplying average total cost times quantity). Profit is therefore the shaded area above the average total cost line and below the demand curve, bounded by ACP_1a.

Through price discrimination the monopolist increases profits (compare figure 10.5 with figure 10.7). Consumers also get more of what they want, although not necessarily at the price they want. In the strict economic sense, perfect price discrimination increases the efficiency of a monopolized industry. Consumers would be still better off if they could pay one constant price, P_c, for the quantity Q_c, as they would under perfect competition. This, however, is a choice the price discriminating monopolist does not allow.

[See online Video Module 10.3 Price discrimination part 1]

Discrimination by market segment

Charging a different price for each and every unit sold to each and every buyer is of course improbable, if not impossible. The best that most producers can do is to engage in imperfect price discrimination – that is, to charge a few different prices, as did the grocery store that sold beans at different rates. The practice is fairly common. Electric power and telephone companies engage in imperfect price discrimination when they charge different rates for different levels of use, measured in watts or minutes. Universities try to do the same when they charge more for the first course taken than for any additional course. Both practices are examples of multi-part price discrimination. Drugstores price discriminate when they give discounts to senior citizens and students, and theaters price discriminate by charging children less than adults (other than senior citizens). In those cases, discrimination is based on *market segment* – namely, age group. By treating different market segments as having distinctly different demand curves, the firm with monopoly power can charge different prices in each market. (More examples of creative price discrimination will be discussed in Part B of this chapter.)

> **Imperfect price discrimination** is the practice of charging a few different prices for different consumption levels or different market segments (based on location, age, income, or some other identifiable characteristic that is unrelated to cost differences).

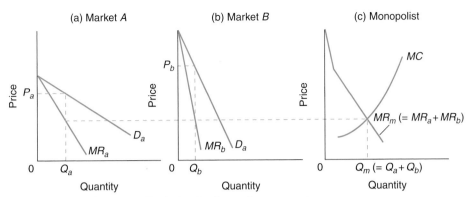

Figure 10.8 Imperfect price discrimination by market segments
The monopolist that cannot perfectly price discriminate may elect to charge a few different prices by segmenting its market. To do so, it divides its market by income, location, or some other factor and finds the demand and marginal revenue curves in each (panels [a] and [b]). Then it adds those marginal revenue curves horizontally to obtain its combined marginal revenue curve for all market segments, MR_m (panel [c]). By equating marginal revenue with marginal cost, it selects its output level, Q_m. Then it divides that quantity between the two market segments by equating the marginal cost of the last unit produced (panel [c]) with marginal revenue in each market (panels [a] and [b]). It sells Q_a in market A and Q_b in market B, and charges different prices in each segment. Generally, the price will be higher in the market segment with the lesser elastic demand (panel [b]).

Figure 10.8 shows how discrimination by market segment works. Two submarkets, each with its own demand curve, are represented in figure 10.8(a) and (b). Each also has its own marginal revenue curve. To price its product, the firm must first decide on its output level. To do so, it adds its two marginal revenue curves horizontally. The combined marginal revenue curve it obtains is shown in figure 10.8(c). The firm must then equate this aggregate marginal revenue curve with its marginal cost of production, which is accomplished at the output level Q_m in figure 10.8(c).

Finally, the firm must divide the resulting output, Q_m, between markets A and B. The division that maximizes the firm's profits is found by equating the marginal revenue in each market (shown in figure 10.8[a] and [b]) with the marginal cost of the last unit produced (figure 10.8[c]). That is, the firm equates the marginal cost of producing the last unit of Q_m (figure 10.8[c]) with the marginal revenue from the last unit sold in each market segment ($MC = MR_a + MR_b$). For maximum profits, then, output Q_m must be divided into Q_a for market A and Q_b for market B.

Why does selling where $MC = MR_a + MR_b$ result in maximum profit? Suppose that MR_a were greater than MR_b. Then, by selling one more unit in market A and one fewer unit in market B, the firm could increase its revenues. Thus the profit-maximizing firm can be expected to shift sales to market A from market B until the marginal revenue of the last unit sold in *A* exactly equals the marginal revenue of the last unit sold in *B*. And unless the common marginal revenue is equal to the marginal cost, the firm can increase its profit by adjusting output until it is.

Having established the output level for each market segment, the firm will charge whatever price each segment will bear. In market *A*, quantity Q_a will bring a price of P_a. In market *B*, quantity Q_b will bring a price of P_b. (Note that the price discriminating monopolist charges a higher price in a market with the less elastic demand – market *B*.) To find total profit, add the revenue collected in each market segment (figure 10.8[a] and [b]) and subtract the total variable cost of production (the area under the marginal cost curve in figure 10.8[c]) and the fixed cost.

[See online Video Module 10.4 Price discrimination part 2]

Applications of monopoly theory

Economics is a fascinating course of study because it often leads to counterintuitive conclusions. This is clearly the case with monopoly theory, as we can show by considering several policy issues.

Price controls under monopoly

Market theory suggests that price controls can cause monopolistic firms to increase their output. Figure 10.9 shows the pricing and production of a monopolistic electric utility that is not engaged in price discrimination. Without price controls, the utility will produce Q_m kilowatts and sell them at P_m. If the government declares that price to be too high, it can force the firm to sell at a lower price – for example, P_1. At that price, the firm can sell as many as Q_1 kilowatts. With the price controlled at P_1, the firm's marginal revenue curve for Q_1 units becomes horizontal at P_1a. Every time it sells an additional kilowatt, its total revenues rise since it doesn't have to lower the price on the previous kilowatts sold. If the price P_1 is set at the point where the demand curve and the *MC* curve intersect (as in figure 10.9) then the profit-maximizing monopolist will increase output to the efficient level – where the value consumers place on another unit of output equals the marginal cost of production.

Taxing monopoly profits

Some people claim that the economic profits of monopoly can be taxed with no loss in economic efficiency. By definition, economic profit represents a reward to the resources in a monopolized industry that is greater than is necessary to keep those resources employed where they are. It also represents *a transfer of income*, from consumers to the owners of the monopoly. Therefore, a tax extracted

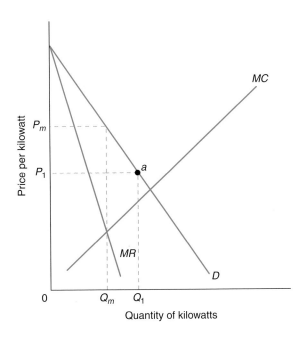

Figure 10.9 The effect of price controls on the monopolistic production decision
In an unregulated market, a monopolistic utility will produce Q_m kilowatts and sell them for P_m. If the firm's price is controlled at P_1, however, its marginal revenue curve will become horizontal at P_1. The firm will produce Q_1 – more than the amount it would normally produce.

solely from a monopoly's *economic* profits should not affect the distribution of resources and should fall exclusively on monopoly owners – or so the argument goes.

The reasoning behind this position is straightforward. When marginal cost is MC_1, this monopoly produces Q_{m2}, charges P_{m1}, in figure 10.10, and makes an economic profit equal to the shaded area $P_cP_{m1}ac$. Because marginal cost and marginal revenue are equal at Q_{m2}, the firm is earning its maximum possible profit. Expansion or contraction of production will not increase its profit. Even if the government were to take away 25, 50, or 90 percent of its economic profit, the firm would not change its production plans or its price (90 percent of the *maximum* profit is more than 90 percent of a smaller profit). Nor would it raise prices to pass the profits tax on to consumers. The monopolist price–quantity combination, P_{m1} and Q_{m2}, leaves the monopolist with the largest after-tax profit – regardless of the tax rate.

There is a practical problem with this, however. The economic profit shown in figure 10.10 is not the same as the firm's book (or accounting) profit. Book profit tends to exceed economic profit by the sum of the owners' opportunity cost and risk cost. For practical reasons, government must impose its tax on book profit, not economic profit. As a result, the tax falls partly on the legitimate costs of doing business, shifting the firm's marginal cost curve upward, from MC_1 to MC_2 in figure 10.10. The monopolist, in turn, will reduce the quantity produced from Q_{m2} to Q_{m1},

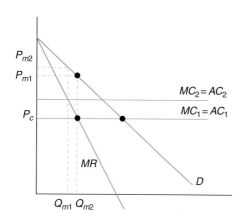

Figure 10.10 Taxing monopoly profits
Theoretically, a tax on the *economic* profit of monopoly will not be passed on to the consumer, but taxes are levied on book profit, not economic profit. As a result, a tax shifts the first marginal cost curve up, from MC_1 to MC_2, raising the price to the consumer and lowering the production level.

and raise the price from P_{m1} to P_{m2}. Thus, part of the government tax on profits is passed along to consumers as a price increase. Consumers are doubly penalized – first through the monopoly price, which exceeds the competitive price, and second through the surcharge, $P_{m2} - P_{m1}$, added by the profits tax.

 [See online Video Module 10.5 Monopoly profits and taxation]

Monopolies in "goods" and "bads"

Because monopolies restrict output, raise prices, and misallocate resources, students and policy makers tend to view them as market failures that should be corrected by antitrust action. If a monopolized product or service represents an economic good – something that gives consumers positive utility – restricted sales will necessarily mean a loss in welfare.

Large portions of the citizenry, however, may view some products and services as "bads." Drugs, prostitution, contract murder, and pornography may be goods to their buyers, but represent negative utility to others in the community. Thus monopolies in the production of such goods may be socially desirable. If a drug monopoly attempted to increase its profits by holding the supply of drugs below competitive levels, most citizens would probably consider themselves better off.

But the question is not quite that simple. A heroin monopoly may restrict the sale of heroin in a given market. Yet because the demand for heroin is highly inelastic (because of drug addiction), higher prices may only increase buyers' expenditures, raising the number of crimes they must commit to support their habit. Paradoxically, then, reducing heroin supplies (for example, because drug enforcement agents in Colombia wipe out a number of producers) could lead to addicts across the world committing more burglaries, muggings, and bank hold-ups.

Of course, drugs and other underground services are not normally subject to antitrust action; they are illegal. But the analogy may be applied to legal goods and services, such as liquor. Given the negative consequences of drinking, as well as religious prohibitions, many people might consider alcoholic beverages an economic "bad." In that case a state long-run liquor monopoly could provide a social service. By restricting liquor sales through monopoly pricing, government would reduce drunk driving, thus limiting the external costs associated with drinking. (Higher taxes also could accomplish the same objective – fewer liquor sales and less drunk driving.)

The total cost of monopoly

High prices and restricted production are not the only costs of monopoly. The total social cost of monopoly power is actually greater than is shown by the supply and demand model in figure 10.3.

The costs of entry barriers

Many firms erect barriers to entry in their markets to attempt to achieve the benefits of monopoly power. The resources invested in building barriers are diverted from the production of other goods, which could benefit consumers. The total social cost of monopoly also should include the time and effort that the Antitrust Division of the Department of Justice, the Federal Trade Commission (FTC), state attorneys-general, and various harmed private parties devote to thwarting attempts to gain monopoly power and to breaking it up when it is acquired.

The redistributional effects of monopoly

Another, more subtle, social cost of monopoly is its *redistributional effect.* Because of monopoly power, consumers pay higher prices than under perfect competition (P_m instead of P_c in figure 10.3). The real purchasing power of consumer incomes is thus decreased, while the incomes of monopoly owners go up. To the extent that monopoly increases the price of a good to consumers and the profits to producers, then, it may redistribute income from lower-income consumers to higher-income entrepreneurs. Many consider this redistributional effect a socially undesirable one.

In addition, when we measure the inefficiency of monopoly by the triangular area *abc* in figure 10.3, we are assuming that the redistribution of income from consumers to monopoly owners does not affect demand for the monopolized product and all other goods. This may be a reasonable assumption if the monopolist is a maker of musical toothpicks, but less reasonable for other monopolies, such as the postal, local telephone, and electric power services. Those firms, which are quite large in relation to the entire economy, can shift the demand for a large number of products, causing further misallocation of resources.

Monopoly effects on cost-saving incentives

Our analysis has assumed that a monopoly will seek to minimize its cost structure, just as perfect competitors do. That may not be a realistic assumption because the monopolist does not, by definition, face competitive pressure. In addition, principal–agent problems (and added costs) can begin to emerge when a market is moved from being divided among many producers to one totally controlled by one producer. This is because former principals (owners) in a small competitive firm can be moved to be agents (managers) in a large corporation, a change in function that can cause costs to rise. In the larger firm, as we saw in chapter 7, all agents can have less incentive to work diligently because monitoring can become more difficult. If a monopoly relaxes its attentiveness to costs, the result can be the inefficient employment of resources that is over and above the triangular dead-weight loss area.

Additional monopoly inefficiency from "rent seeking"

The actual economic inefficiency from monopoly can be greater than the *abc* triangles identified in previous figures, at least when we consider how monopolies can be created through entries provided by the political process. As long as there are monopoly profits – also called "rents" – to be garnered from market-entry restrictions or there is a payoff from government subsidies, political entrepreneurs representing special interest groups (various business trade associations, for example) can be expected to compete for the rents through lobbying (for example, providing political decision makers with lavish dinners and junkets to exotic locations for "working vacations"), campaign contributions, and outright bribes (see Tullock 1967; Krueger 1974; McChesney 1997). Rent seekers can be expected to assess their **rent-seeking** expenditures as investments, ensuring as best they can that the rates of return on such investments are no less than their investments on other business ventures.

> **Rent seeking** is the pursuit of monopoly profits through market restrictions and subsidies provided by the political process.

In the process of seeking rents through government protections and subsidies, the rent seekers can collectively devote more valuable resources to rent seeking than the expected rent is worth. In such case, the inefficiency of monopoly is greater than the inefficiency or dead-weight-loss triangle identified in figure 10.3. The net welfare loss from monopoly (or a subsidy) can, at the limit, include that dead-weight-loss triangle plus the profit rectangle (Tullock 1967). This is because all the people competing for the monopoly restrictions can at times collectively spend as much (or more) on lobbying than the total of the monopoly profits; such lobbying expenditures can soak up real resources, which can be realized in lost production of other goods.

Rent seeking is epitomized by the various individual companies and business trade associations in the capitals of the world, whose lobbyists are constantly knocking on the doors of key politicians. But rent seeking is not restricted to private businesses. When Congress began considering in 2008 various bailout and stimulus plans to rectify the financial-market meltdown, which precipitated a major economic down-turn, the National Conference of Mayors sent its lobbyists to Washington, DC (as did every other interest group) to lobby for the inclusion of more than 11,000 municipal projects in any orchestrated federal government relief programs. The list included a duck-pond park for one small California town and a senior citizen center for a small town in Texas (Poole 2008). Since the 1980s, universities in the United States have engaged in rent seeking, lobbying for so-called federal "legislative earmarks" or special appropriations for university projects (buildings and curriculum development) that are attached to (and buried in) budget bills.[2]

[See online Video Module 10.6 Public choice – rent seeking]

Durable goods monopoly

If prohibitive barriers to entry are in place, can a monopolist always charge the monopoly price indicated? Ronald Coase wrote a famous article in the 1970s in which he pointed out that even a monopolistic producer of a durable good would charge a competitive price for its product (Coase 1972).

Why? Because no sane person would buy all or any portion of the durable good at a price above the competitive level. Coase used the example of a monopoly owner of a plot of land. If the owner tried to sell the land all at one time, he would have to lower the price on each parcel until all the land was bought – where the downward sloping demand for land crossed the fixed vertical supply of land – which means that the owner would have to charge the competitive price (where the demand for the land and the supply of the land come together).

You might think that the sole/monopoly owner of land would be able to restrict sales and get more than the competitive price. However, buyers would reason that the monopoly owner would eventually want to sell the remaining land, but that land

---

[2] In fiscal year 2003, the *Chronicle of Higher Education* found that 716 US colleges and universities benefited from 1,964 "legislative earmarks" worth $2 billion (Krueger 2005). Economists from UCLA and the University of Toronto found that a $1 increase in lobbying expenditures can be expected to lead to a $1.56 increase in "earmarks." However, for those universities who have a member of Congress on either the House or Senate Appropriation Committee, a $1 increase in lobbying leads to a $4.50 increase in "earmarks." This means that universities' fortunes rise and fall with changes in the membership of the appropriation committees (Krueger 2005).

could be sold only at less than the price the owner is trying to charge for the first few parcels. Buyers would rationally wait to buy until the price came down, which means that the owner would sell nothing at the monopoly price, and would be able to sell the land only at the competitive price.

This analysis works out this way only because the land is *durable*. Monopolies can charge monopoly prices for nondurable goods because they have control over production. Thus, one way a monopoly can elevate its price above the competitive level is somehow to make the product less durable, or needing replacement. This may explain why many software producers are constantly bringing out new, updated, and upgraded versions of their programs – to make their programs less than durable in the minds of consumers.

Still, computer programs must remain "durable" to some degree and for some time, which ultimately imposes a competitive check on dominant software producers, for example Microsoft. The Justice Department seems to believe that Microsoft doesn't have competitors. Well, one of Microsoft's biggest competitors is none other than Microsoft itself. Any new version of, say, Windows, must compete head-to-head with the existing stock of old versions, which consumers can continue using at zero price. That very low price on old versions of Windows imposes a check on the prices that Microsoft can charge on any new version. Microsoft faced a major competitive challenge from Windows XP when the company introduced Windows Vista in late 2006 to highly critical reviews primarily for the new operating system's sluggishness, which encouraged both consumers and personal computer manufacturers to stay with Windows XP. Similarly, when Microsoft's Windows 7 appeared, it faced stiff competition from Windows Vista and, for that matter, all other versions of Windows installed on people's personal computers around the world. We cover the Microsoft monopoly and antitrust case in some depth in Reading 10.2 for this chapter, which is drawn from a book by one of the authors (McKenzie 2000).

Firms with monopoly power in a durable good face the problem of yielding to the temptation to attract more buyers. To overcome the desire (and impatience) to achieve market share a firm can negotiate contracts with buyers that include "most-favored-customer clauses." Such clauses would require the seller to extend to the buyer signing the contract any price concessions given in the future to other buyers. The customer signing the contract can reason that other customers will be less likely to get a cost advantage by waiting to buy. The most-favored-customer clause raises the cost of price concessions to the seller. Hence, buyers can be expected to be more willing to buy at the higher price the seller charges.

The monopoly seller also can rent (or lease) the good for short periods of time. If the rent is lowered to future customers, then the lower rent will shortly have to be extended to other customers renewing their rental contracts, increasing the cost of the price/rent concession and increasing buyers' confidence that the rent will not be lowered to others.

[See online Video Module 10.7 Durable goods monopoly]

Monopoly in government and inside firms

It is easy to think of monopolies in the private sector, but monopoly theory can also be used to explore the organization of governments and of departments within firms. Indeed, the monopoly model might be best applied to these entities because governments are often the sole-source suppliers of goods and services to the public and firm departments the sole-source suppliers to their firms. In the private sector, competition among producers keeps prices down and productivity up. A producer who is just one among many knows that any independent attempt to raise prices or lower quality will fail. Customers will switch to other products or buy from other producers, and sales will fall sharply. To avoid being undersold, therefore, the individual producer must strive continually to keep its production cost as low, or lower, than other producers striving to do the same. Only a producer who has no competition – that is, a monopolist – can hope to raise the price of a product without fear of losing profits.

Government monopolies

These points concerning the production and pricing decisions of monopolies apply to the public as well as the private sector. The framers of the Constitution, in fact, bore them in mind when they set up the federal government. Recognizing the benefits of competition, they established a system of competing state governments loosely joined in federation. As James Madison described in *The Federalist* papers, "In a single republic, all the power surrendered by the people is submitted to the administration of a single government: and the usurpations are guarded against by a division of the government into distinct and separate departments" (Hamilton, Jay, and Madison 1964).

Under the federal system, the power of local governments is checked not just by citizens' ability to vote but also by their ability to move somewhere else. If a city government raises its taxes or lowers the quality of its services, residents can go elsewhere, taking with them part of the city's tax base. Of course, many people are reluctant to move, and so government has a measure of market power, but competition among governments affords at least some protection against the abuses of that power. It doesn't take many people and businesses to move out of a political jurisdiction to send a strong signal to the political authorities that they have to be more competitive.

Local competition in government has its drawbacks. Just as in private industry, large governments can realize economies of scale in the production of services. Garbage, road, and sewage service can, up to a point, be provided at a lower cost on a larger scale. For this reason, it is frequently argued that local governments, especially in metropolitan areas, should consolidate. Moreover, many of the benefits that local governments offer spill over into surrounding areas. For example, people who live just outside San Francisco may benefit from its services without helping pay for them. One large metropolitan government, including both city and suburbs, could spread the tax burden over all those who benefit from city services.

Consolidation can be a mixed blessing, however, if it reduces competition among governments. When a government increases the geographical size of its jurisdiction, it restricts the number and variety of alternatives open to citizens and increases the cost of moving to another locale. Consolidation, in other words, can increase the government's monopoly power. As long as politicians and government employees pursue only the public interest, no harm may be done. But the people who run government have interests of their own. So the potential for achieving greater efficiency through consolidation could easily be lost in bureaucratic expansion and red tape. Studies of consolidation in government are inconclusive, but it seems clear that consolidation proposals should be examined carefully.

Departmental monopolies inside firms

When firms create departments to provide, say, their accounting or legal services and do not look outside the firm for alternative sources of supply, they have effectively created internal departmental monopolies, handing to the department sole-source monopoly status. Firms should at least consider the prospects that their own internal departments will act like monopolies. That is, internal departments will restrict their outputs in order to raise their prices for whatever services (or inputs) the departments provide their firms. The higher prices and profits can show up in departmental budgets that are greater than they need to be. Remember the principal–agent is potentially everywhere present. Departments can thus siphon off economic profits that would otherwise go to the firms' owners. The problem can be especially acute if higher managers do not compare the prospective costs of internal departments with those of obtaining the same services (or inputs) from outside suppliers. Consequently, to contain their costs, top managers are wise to let internal departments understand that their costs of delivery are regularly compared with those from outside suppliers. Of course, the competitive threat to internal suppliers (departments) is enhanced when top managers actually outsource, from time to time, a service or input. Internal departments may then seek to contain their costs for fear that they, too, can be replaced.

For a discussion of a controversial case of potential "lock in" (or high "switching costs), see online Perspective 10, The QWERTY keyboard – a case of lock in?

> **Online Perspective 10**
> The QWERTY keyboard –
> a case of lock in?

Part B   Organizational economics and management

Profits from creative pricing

For a monopoly firm to be successful, it has to choose the "right" price, given the demand (or specifics of the inverse relationship between price and quantity) for its products. But choosing the "right" price is easier said than done. For example, managers can never be completely sure what the demand for their company's product is. Moreover, a company's demand is not given from on high but is influenced by good management decisions, such as improving product quality, which may increase product credibility, and building a reputation for honesty and fair dealing. Other factors also affect demand, many of which are beyond managers' abilities to control or predict.

Managers, no matter how good they are, will always have to make guesses about the demands for their products – about how much they can sell of their products at different qualities and prices. There are statistical techniques for estimating product demand (a discussion of which goes beyond the purpose of this book) and, though these techniques are never perfect, they can help managers move from making *mere* guesses to making *educated* guesses.

In the real world, however, there is plenty of scope for creative pricing. And such creativity can be very profitable. We have discussed throughout this book how firms compete on many margins. Certainly better products at lower prices is a long-run consequence of firms struggling against each other for more consumer dollars. But in this chapter we concentrate on how managers can increase their firms' profitability through more creative pricing strategies. Managers can often do as much or more for their firms, and their careers, by coming up with better pricing approaches as by coming up with better products. Of course, as is true of everything else in business, managers must have the proper incentives to be creative in their pricing strategies.

Price discrimination in practice

Real-world managers are not limited to charging only one price for a product. As those businesspeople who fly frequently know, there are several different prices being charged for a coach seat (or a first-class seat) on most flights. For example, passengers who book their flights weeks in advance often pay less (often several hundred dollars less) than those who book just days before their departure. By charging different prices for the same product, firms are able to earn higher profits than are possible with only one price. Some creativity can be exercised by carefully announcing prices.

There is a joke based on the pricing creativity of optometrists. When a customer inquires about the price of a pair of glasses, the optometrist answers, "Seventy-five dollars," and then pays close attention to the customer's expression. If he doesn't cringe, the optometrist quickly adds, "for the lenses." If the customer still doesn't cringe, the optometrist adds, "for each one" (Friedman 1996, 134).

Beyond the humor, prices are often puzzles, and the kind of price discrimination theory described in Part A of this chapter can be used to unravel them.[3]

Hardback and paperback books

There are better – perhaps less devious – ways of charging different prices than the above joke may suggest. Book publishers cannot differentiate between every potential buyer of a book and charge each a different price. But they can separate the market into two broad categories of buyers – those who are most impatient to read the latest novel by, say, John Grisham, and those who want to read it but do not mind waiting a while. If publishers can separate (or *segment*) these groups, they can charge a different price to each group. But how can they do that? One method is to sell hardback and paperback editions of the same book. Hardback books are issued first and are sold at a significantly higher price than the paperback edition ("significantly" meaning higher than the cost difference in producing a hardback and a paperback edition) that will not be available until six months or more later. In this way, the seller charges those customers who are less sensitive to price (or who have an *inelastic* demand) a higher price than those who are sensitive to price (or who

---

[3] One of the authors has recently published extended explanations of an array of pricing puzzles in his book *Why Popcorn Costs So Much at the Movies, and Other Pricing Puzzles* (McKenzie 2008).

have an *elastic* demand). There is no problem with arbitrage in this case because those who pay the low price do so long after the high-price customers have made their purchases.

Price discrimination through time

Sellers don't always have to package their products differently, as publishers do, to distinguish between buyers who have inelastic demands and those who have elastic demands. Just after new electronic gadgets (USB disks, for example) are introduced, their prices can be quite high, only to fall later. Many chalk up their falling prices to reductions in production costs, which may very well be true. However, we suggest an additional explanation for why computer prices fall with the age of the models: The sellers are using *time* to segment their markets, charging those who are eager to get the new models a higher price and charging those who are less eager, as evidenced by their willingness to wait, a lower price.

After-Christmas sales

Department stores almost always have storewide sales after Christmas. Commonly, the explanation for after-Christmas sales is that stores want to get rid of excess inventories. There is a measure of truth to that explanation; stores cannot always judge correctly what will sell in December. However, it is also clear that shoppers have more inelastic demands before Christmas than they have after Christmas. Hence, the stores are often doing nothing more than segmenting their markets. They plan to hold after-Christmas sales and order accordingly. They are not making less money by the sales. They are, in truth, making more money because they can charge different prices in the two time periods, attracting customers they otherwise would have lost without lowering the price charged to the consumers who are less price sensitive.

Coupons

Grocery stores and the suppliers of the products that grocery stores sell also have found a way of getting customers to reveal how sensitive they are to price, which allows those who are less price sensitive to be charged more than those who are more price sensitive. In almost every daily newspaper you can find coupons (in the Sunday paper, pages of coupons) that, if you cut them out and take them to the designated store, allow you to save on a host of different products. No coupons, no savings.

Those who go to the trouble of cutting out these coupons and carrying them to the store are revealing themselves as being relatively price sensitive. So when you fail to present coupons as you go through the checkout line at your local supermarket, you are telling the cashier that you are not very sensitive to price, that your demand is relatively inelastic. The cashier responds by charging you more for the same products than he or she charged the coupon-laden customer ahead of you. The problem of arbitrage is handled by limiting the amount a customer can buy of a product. Moreover, not many people are tempted by the opportunity to buy one bottle of shampoo for 50 cents off and then resell it for 25 cents off to someone in the parking lot who doesn't have a shampoo coupon. The cost of creating the secondary market for something as cheap as shampoo is surely greater than the price differential, especially when few units can be bought at the favorable price and sold at a higher price.

Theater pricing

Sometimes a firm can profit by charging different prices to different customers without appearing to do so. This can be accomplished by putting the same price on two products that are consumed together by some customers but not by others. Consider the owner of a theater who realizes that some customers are willing to pay more to go to the movies than others are. Obviously, the owner would like to charge these customers more. But the owner has no way of determining who the price insensitive customers are when they are paying for their tickets. So how does the manager charge the price insensitive customers more without losing the remaining customers?

There is a way that we have all observed but probably didn't think of as an example of price discrimination. Assume that the theater owner believes that those customers who are willing to pay the most to watch a movie are generally (not always, but generally) the ones who most enjoy snacking while watching. If this assumption is correct (and we will argue in a moment that it probably is), the theater owner can take advantage of the inelastic demand of the enthusiastic movie watchers by charging a moderate price for the tickets to the movie and high prices for the snacks sold in the theater lobby. By keeping the ticket prices moderate, the customers with a high demand elasticity for the movie will still buy a ticket because they are not going to do much snacking anyway. Although the low-elasticity demanders will surely complain about the high prices on all the snacks they eat, they still consider the total cost of their movie experience acceptable because they were willing to pay more for their ticket than they were charged.

If it were not generally true that those who are willing to pay the most to watch a movie also enjoy snacking the most, then it is unlikely that we would observe such high prices for snacks at the movies.[4] For example, assume that the opposite were

---

[4] It should be noted that some economists have argued that the high price for snacks at movie theaters reflects the higher cost of supplying them in movie theaters than in food stores. As opposed to food stores, the snack shop in a movie theater is open for only a limited amount of time during the day. So, as the argument goes, the overhead cost is spread over less time and fewer sales (Lott and Roberts 1991). We do not quarrel with this reasoning, but we also believe that creative price discrimination provides at least part of the explanation for the high price of movie snacks.

true, that those who were not willing to pay much to watch a movie were the ones who enjoy snacking the most when watching the movie. If this were the case, the owner of the theater would find that charging moderate prices for the tickets and high prices for the snacks was not a very profitable strategy. Because the avid movie watchers are not snacking much, they would be willing to pay more than the moderate price to get into the theater. And because the other customers care more about snacking than seeing the movie, they would see little advantage in paying the moderate price for the movie when the snacks are so expensive. In this case, the most profitable pricing strategy would be high ticket prices and low snack prices. The enthusiastic movie watchers would still come despite the high ticket price. And the snackers would now be willing to pay the high ticket prices for the opportunity to eat lots of cheap snacks.[5] The fact that we do not see such pricing in theaters suggests that, at least for most consumers, our assumption is correct.

Prices and functionality

Any time a firm can identify consumers on the basis of their sensitivity to price, it is in a position to vary its price for different groups in ways that increase the consumers' incentive to purchase its product. The advantage of being able to separate customers willing to pay high prices (again, who have relatively inelastic demands) from those who are more price sensitive (who have relatively elastic demands) is so great in some cases that it explains why some firms will incur costs to reduce the quality of their products so that they can sell them for less.

For example, soon after Intel introduced the 486 microprocessor, it renamed it the 486DX and introduced a modified version, which it named the 486SX. The modification was done by disabling the internal math coprocessor in the original 486, a modification that was costly and reduced the performance of the 486SX. Intel then, in 1991, sold the 486SX for less – $333 as compared to $588 for the 486DX. Why would Intel spend money to damage a microprocessor and then sell it for less?[6] The answer is to separate out those customers who are willing to pay a lot for a microprocessor from

---

[5] Determining the exact combination of prices that maximizes profits depends on the relative differences in demand for the two types of customers. If, for example, the avid movie fans were willing to pay a tremendously high price to see the movie, and snackers couldn't care less about the movie but went into frenzies of delight at the mere thought of a Snickers bar, then the best pricing policy would be an extremely high ticket price with extremely low-priced (maybe free) snacks. In this case, the theater owner would probably stipulate that snack customers would have to eat the snacks in the theater to prevent them from filling large takeaway sacks with popcorn and candy bars. This would be no different than the policy of all-you-can-eat restaurants.

[6] It was cheaper to make the 486DX and then reduce its quality than it was to produce the lower-quality 486SX directly. This example, the following one, and several other cases of firms intentionally reducing the quality of their products are found in Deneckere and McAfee (1996).

those whose demand is more sensitive to price. Intel could sell the 486DX to the former at a price that would have driven the latter to competitive firms. Yet it managed to keep the business of the latter customers by lowering the price to them without worrying that this would drive the price down for the high-end customers. There was no way for the lower-price consumers to buy the lower-price product and sell it to the high-end consumers, because its performance had been reduced.

Similarly, with the emergence of the netbook computers (lightweight but cheap laptops with limited functionality), Microsoft faced a challenge to the dominance of its Windows operation system. Netbook manufacturers used the Linux operating system because it was free, which enabled manufacturers to hold the price of their netbooks to under $300. Microsoft initially responded by allowing manufacturers to install the then-dated Windows XP system (the version that predated Windows Vista) at a cut-rate price. With the advent of Windows 7 (the current version that corrected problems with Vista), Microsoft met the netbook/Linux challenge by introducing Windows 7-Starter, which is a strategically crippled version of the full Windows 7 operating system, designed for netbooks and other low-market personal computers. Starter, which is sold to computer manufacturers at cut-rate prices so they can price their machines competitively with systems using Linux, permits only three applications running at the same time. However, owners of netbooks with Starter are given the option of buying the full version of Windows 7 not by downloading the full version (it is already on their machines) but by buying a code that allows them to access the already installed full version – at a price, of course (Wingfield and Clark 2009).

Similarly, when IBM introduced its LaserPrinter E at the start of the 1990s, it set the price lower than the price for its earlier model, the LaserPrinter. The LaserPrinter E was almost exactly the same as the LaserPrinter except that the newer model printed at a rate of five pages per minute compared to the older model's rate of ten pages per minute. The LaserPrinter E was slower because IBM went to the expense of adding chips that had no purpose other than to cause the printer to pause. Why would IBM do that? Again, to separate its market between consumers with inelastic demand from those with elastic demand so that less could be charged to the latter without having to reduce the high price to the former.

Golf balls

One of the authors, Lee, enjoys playing golf. He buys brand-name golf balls that have been labeled with XXX to indicate they have some flaw and that are sold at a discount. Many good golfers are willing to pay the extra money for regular brand-name balls, which supposedly travel farther than the XXX balls. Lee, on the other hand, sees no advantage in hitting his balls farther into the woods. And anyway, he is not convinced that there really is any difference between the regular high-priced balls and the XXX balls, except that the manufacturer went to the extra expense of adding the XXXs. Although we have no documentation, we suspect that manufacturers simply put XXXs on a certain percentage of their balls so that they can separate their market between golfers like Lee, who are quite sensitive to price, and golfers who, because they have a reasonable idea where their balls are going, are not very sensitive to price.

Unadvertised prices

Another technique firms can use to separate price sensitive consumers from those who are less sensitive is to make unadvertised price discounts available, but only to those who search them out and ask for them. Obviously, those who go to the trouble to find out about a discount, and then ask for it, are more concerned over price than those who do not. AT&T used this approach to identifying customers for discounts on long-distance calls in the 1990s. According to an article in the *Wall Street Journal*, AT&T responded to Sprint Corporation's 10 cents a minute for calls during weekends and evening hours by offering a flat rate of 15 cents any time, a plan they called One Rate (Keller 1997). But AT&T really had two rates, one of which they did not advertise. The unadvertised rate, available only to those who asked for it, allowed AT&T customers to call around the clock for 10 cents a minute. As reported in the article, "AT&T customers can get dime-a-minute calling 24 hours a day, seven days a week – if they know to ask for it. That is the hardest part, for AT&T has been uncharacteristically quiet about the new offer. The company hasn't advertised the 10-cent rate; it hasn't sent out press releases heralding the latest effort to one-up the folks at Sprint" (Keller 1997, B1). The old adage about oiling only what squeaks certainly applies in this case. (We suspect that AT&T was not all that pleased with the *Wall Street Journal* simply because the publicity reduced AT&T's ability to segment its market by reducing the "search costs" that AT&T customers otherwise faced.)

The more competition and price rivalry in an industry, the smaller the gain a firm in that industry can realize from charging different customers different prices. Even relatively price insensitive customers will be bid away by rival firms when price competition is intense, if one firm tries to charge those customers much more than it does its more price sensitive customers. Nevertheless, the more the firms in an industry can segment their market so as to buffer the price competition among them, the greater the scope for creative pricing strategies that can increase profits, a point to which we can now turn.

Pricing cartels

Firms in an industry can simply get together and agree not to compete consumers away from each other through price reductions. This will allow them to keep prices, and their collective profits, higher than will be possible if all firms make a futile attempt to increase their market shares by charging lower prices. But there are two problems with this approach to reducing price competition. The first problem is that any agreement to restrict competition *can be* illegal, and firms and their managers who enter into such an agreement risk harsh antitrust penalties.

As discussed in Part A of this chapter, the second problem is that even if agreements to restrict price competition were not illegal, they would still be almost impossible to maintain. Members of industry cartels that have agreed to set prices above competitive levels are in another Prisoner's Dilemma. Although they are collectively better off when everyone abides by the agreement, each individual sees the advantage in reducing price below the agreed-upon amount. If other firms maintain the high price, then the firm that cheats on the agreement can capture lots of additional business with a relatively small decrease in its price. On the other hand, if the other firms are expected to cheat on the agreement, it would be foolish for a firm to continue with the high price because that firm would find most of its customers competed away. Only if all firms ignore Prisoner's Dilemma temptations, and take the risk of making the cooperative choice, can cartel price agreements be maintained. Not surprisingly, such agreements tend to break down.

Meet-the-competition pricing policy

Some pricing policies, however, can moderate price competition between rival firms without the need for a cooperative agreement. Ironically, these strategies reduce competition, when competition motivates most firms in an industry to implement them when the first firm does.

Consider a pricing policy that would seem to favor your customers with protection against high prices but which is a smart policy because it makes higher prices possible. The strategy is quite simple, involving an unqualified pledge: "We will meet or beat any competitor's price." A so-called "meet-the-competition" pricing policy tells your customers that if a competitor offers a lower price, you will match it, a policy commonly advertised as "guaranteed lowest prices." To implement such a policy, you inform your customers that if they can find a lower price on a product within thirty days of purchasing it from you, they will receive a rebate equal to the difference. Such price guarantees appear to benefit customers, but if they are offered by all or most competitors they allow all firms to charge higher prices. How can this be?

One straightforward explanation is that the price assurance gives customers some insurance and, because of that added attribute, increases their demand. The greater demand leads to higher prices.

But there is another explanation based on an equally simple proposition: if you want to charge higher prices, there is an obvious advantage in discouraging competitors from reducing their prices to compete your customers away. This is exactly what a meet-the-competition policy does. Your competitors are probably not all that anxious, in any event, to initiate a price-cutting campaign. Attempting to compete customers away from another firm through lower prices is always costly. If successful, the new business is likely to be worth less to the price-cutting firm than to the firm that loses it because the price is now lower. Also, existing customers will want to receive a lower price as well, which can eat deeper into any profits that otherwise might have been possible. Of course, if a price-cutting campaign aimed at capturing new customers fails to do so, the campaign is all cost and no benefit. So if your competitors know that you have a meet-the-competition agreement with your customers, they will have less, and likely nothing, to gain from cutting prices to try to attract those customers.

A meet-the-competition pricing policy can be good not only for your profits but also for your competitors. By allowing you to keep your prices higher than otherwise, your meet-the-competition policy gives your competitors more room to keep their prices high. This suggests that, as opposed to most competitive strategies that become less effective when mimicked by the competition, your meet-the-competition policy becomes more profitable when other firms in the industry implement the same policy. Just as your competitors are better off when you do not have to worry about the competitive consequences of keeping your prices high, so are you better off when your competitors are relieved of the same worry (Brandenburger and Nalebuff 1996, chapter 6).

Most-favored-customer pricing policy

A related pricing policy is to offer some of your customers the status of most-favored customer, which entitles them to the best price offered to anyone else. (Again, this policy must be checked with lawyers, given that some such policies in some circumstances might be construed as illegal.) If you lower your price to any customer under this policy you are obligated to lower it for all of your most-favored customers. As with the meet-the-competition policy, what at first glance appears to favor your customers can actually give the advantage to you. A most-favored-customer policy increases the cost of trying to compete customers away from rival firms by reducing price. And when one firm has such a policy, its reluctance to engage in price competition makes it easy for other firms to keep their prices high. So, as with meet-the-competition policy, the advantage that firms realize from a most-favored-customer policy is greater when all the firms in an industry have such a policy (Brandenburger and Nalebuff 1996).

If the idea that a policy of being quick to reduce prices for your customers can result in higher prices seems counterproductive, you are in good company. In their book *Co-opetition*, Brandenburger and Nalebuff (1996) relate how Congress, in an effort to control the cost of campaigning, required television broadcasters to make candidates for Congress most-favored customers. In the 1971 Federal Election Campaign Act, Congress made it against the law for television broadcasters to lower their rates for an ad to any commercial customer without also lowering their rates to candidates. The result was that television broadcasters found it extremely costly to reduce rates for anyone, and the networks made more money than ever before. Politicians had the satisfaction of knowing that they did not pay more for airtime than anyone else, but they likely ended up paying more (as commercial advertisers did also) than they would have without forcing the broadcasters to implement a most-favored-customer pricing policy.

Congress made a similar mistake in 1990, when it attempted to reduce government reimbursements for drugs by stipulating that Medicaid would pay only 88 percent of the average wholesale price for branded drugs – or, if lower, the lowest price granted anyone in the retail trade drug business. But instead of lowering prices, the law actually raised them. By making itself a most-favored customer, the federal government gave the drug companies a strong incentive to raise prices for everyone. And indeed that is exactly what happened, according to a study cited by Brandenburger and Nalebuff (1996, 104–5) that found that prices on branded drugs increased by 5 to 9 percent because of the 1990 rule changes. The advantage the government may have realized by keeping its price down to 88 percent of the average wholesale price was probably more than offset (it was often receiving a discount anyway) by the higher average prices. And certainly non-Medicare patients ended up paying higher drug prices.

Advantages of frequent-flyer programs

Another pricing strategy that allows the firms in an industry to reduce price competition has become increasingly common since the 1980s. This strategy involves a creative way of identifying those customers who are most likely to buy from your firm anyway and then lowering the price they pay. At first glance, such a strategy would appear counterproductive. Why would you lower the price for those who are likely to buy from you? The answer is that by making what appear to be price concessions to your most loyal customers, you can end up charging them higher prices.

A good way of explaining this seemingly paradoxical possibility is by considering the frequent-flyer programs that almost all airlines now have. These programs are commonly thought of as motivated by each airline's desire to compete business away from other airlines by effectively lowering ticket prices. No doubt this was the primary motivation when, in 1981, American Airlines introduced its AAdvantage program. The rapidity with which other airlines countered with their own frequent-flyer programs suggests intense competition between the airlines. But intended or not, the proliferation of these programs has had the effect of reducing the direct price competition between airlines and, as a result, may be allowing them to maintain higher prices than would otherwise have been possible. An airline's frequent-flyer program reduces the effective, if not the explicit, price it charges its most loyal customers, and reinforces their loyalty.[7] By increasing the motivation of an airline's frequent flyers to concentrate their flying on that airline, it decreases the payoff other airlines can expect from trying to compete those customers away with fare reductions. This allows the airline with the frequent-flyer program to keep its explicit fares higher than if other airlines were aggressively reducing theirs.[8] This decreased motivation to engage in price competition becomes mutually reinforcing as more airlines implement frequent-flyer programs.

From the perspective of each airline, it would be nice to be able to compete away customers from other airlines with lower fares, but collectively the airlines are better off by reducing this ability. And this is exactly what the spread of frequent-flyer programs has done, to some degree, by segmenting the airline market. There is now less competitive advantage in reducing airfares and less competitive disadvantage in raising them. The effect has been to *reduce the elasticity of demand* facing each airline, which allows all airlines to charge higher prices than would otherwise be sustainable.[9]

A pricing strategy similar to frequent-flyer programs has begun to spread in the automobile industry. In 1992, General Motors joined with MasterCard and issued the GM credit card. By using the GM card a consumer earns a credit equal to 5 percent of his charges that can be applied to the purchase or lease of any new GM vehicle (with a limit of $500 per year up to $3,500 for any one purchase). Although not all major automakers have followed the GM lead, several have. And the more automakers that join in, the better for the car industry in general. Just like

---

[7] Even when a person is a member of more than one frequent-flyer program, there is an advantage in concentrating patronage on one airline because the programs are designed to increase benefits more than proportionally with accumulated mileage.

[8] You may be thinking that keeping the explicit fares higher does not mean much if, because of the frequent-flyer programs, the actual fares to customers are lower because of the value of their mileage awards. But one of the big advantages of frequent-flyer programs is that they do not cost the airlines as much as they benefit the customer. Flights are seldom completely sold out, so most of the free flights awarded end up filling seats that are unsold. Of course, frequent flyers do use their mileage for flights they would have otherwise paid for, but by allowing frequent flyers to transfer their mileage awards to others, say a spouse or child, the airlines increase the probability that those who would not have otherwise bought a ticket will use those awards.

[9] Another way of seeing the advantage of segmenting the market is by recognizing that reducing the elasticity of demand facing each airline also reduces the marginal revenue of each airline and brings it more in line with the marginal revenue for the industry. The closer each firm's marginal revenue is to the industry's marginal revenue, the closer the independent pricing decisions of each firm in the industry will come to maximizing the firms' collective profits.

frequent-flyer programs, automobile credit cards allow a car company to focus implicit price reductions on its most loyal customers. An individual is not likely to be using a GM credit card unless she is planning to buy a GM car or truck. As the number of car companies that issue their own credit card increases, the more the auto market will become segmented and the less the advantage from price competition. Again, a pricing policy that allows a firm to target its more loyal customers and favor them with price cuts can have the effect of increasing the prices being charged.

The economics discussions of pricing strategies has mushroomed in recent years for two reasons. First, firms have found that they can make a lot of money by varying their prices. Because of the ongoing digital-communication revolution, firms now have the technology to change pricing with ease and at low cost. All firms have to do is send price changes through their servers to their linked cash registers. They can also adjust their prices in response to all the data they collect through scanners in checkout lines.

Second, any number of economists have adopted the research methodologies of psychologists and neuroscientists, which means they have conducted a large number of classroom and laboratory experiments on how people go about their shopping and how they react to prices. In online Reading 10.3, we cover the "endowment effect" as developed by "behavioral economists." Apparently, people will not pay as much to buy a given good when they do not have it than they will charge to sell the good when they have it. This is to say, a consumer who does not have good A might only pay a maximum of $100 for the good. But if a consumer has good A, she might not be willing to sell good A for anything less than $120 or even $150. Behavioralists argue that the buy and sell prices for a rational person should be the same (more or less).

Practical lesson for MBAs: monopoly power and barriers to entry from the firm's perspective

Much conventional analysis of pricing and production decisions under competitive and monopoly market structures is focused on their comparative *efficiency*. The central conclusion is that competitive markets are more *efficient* than monopoly markets. Although perfectly competitive markets maximize output, given cost and demand constraints, pure monopoly maximizes *inefficency* (or loss in welfare attributable to monopoly's reduction in output below the competitive output level). The policy implication is that a shift from monopoly to competitive markets makes for greater welfare, a conclusion that drives antitrust policy and enforcement in countries around the globe.

MBA students should understand such points, but many will surely draw another deduction: one of the last things a firm should do is get involved in any market that comes even close to perfectly competitive market conditions. In such markets, the best a firm can hope for is fleeting profits because profits will be eroded by intense price competition from among existing producers and new entrants entering the competitive fray at little to no cost. Under perfectly competitive market conditions, firms have no incentive to innovate in product and market development because the have little chance to recover the cost of innovations. This is the case because price competition from existing firms and new entrants will quickly erode any profits from innovations, and the market price will fall toward the non-innovating producers' marginal cost of production. The innovating firm will have little hope of recovering the firm's product and market developing costs.

Monopoly power may result in inefficiency from a societal perspective, but the analytics of this and the preceding chapters suggest that firms should seek monopoly power because it offers hope of making above-normal profits. With a monopoly, product and market development costs can be recouped, and maybe then some. The derivative lesson for MBA students is that in their roles as entrepreneurs (or "intrapreneurs," entrepreneurs within large firms), they should seek creative ways to develop their products and their markets, of course; however, they also should seek natural entry barriers or creative ways to develop artificial barriers. The development of products, markets, and entry barriers should go hand in hand, with perhaps as much or more attention given to the development of the latter. Entry barriers are crucial to making products pay. They are what enable firms to control market supply and, therefore, market price – and profits. Without entry barriers, all firm expenditures of product and market development can be for naught as new entrants reduce any newly created product to a "commodity," something everyone can produce and on which no one can recover development costs and make above-normal profits.

Conventional microeconomic analytics has branded (pun intended) branding, trade secrets, exclusive ownership of key resources, network effects, lock ins, switching costs, and patents and copyrights as efficiency-impairing entry barriers that give rise to monopoly power. MBAs should see them differently, as sources of above-normal profits. Their development also can be a means by which MBAs can put themselves on a career track to the executive suite. MBAs who devote firm resources to the development of products that can be easily and quickly replicated may see themselves in stalled careers, at best.

Further readings online

Reading 10.1 Marginal revenue curve – a graphical derivation

Reading 10.2 The Microsoft monopoly

Reading 10.3 The "endowment effect" and pricing

The bottom line

The key takeaways from chapter 10 are the following:

1 A monopolist maximizes its profits where its marginal cost equals its marginal revenue.

2 The monopolist faces a downward sloping demand curve, which means that its marginal revenue curve is also downward sloping but underneath its demand curve.

3 The consequences of monopoly are higher prices and lower production levels than are possible under perfect competition.

4 Monopoly power can also result in inefficiency in production, for the monopolistic firm does not produce to the point at which its marginal cost equals the consumer's marginal benefit – the product's price. Consumers might prefer that more resources be used in the production of a monopolized good and might be willing to pay a price that exceeds the cost of production for additional units of the good. However, the profit-maximizing monopolist stops short of that point.

5 In order for a monopolist to be able to garner monopoly profits, it must be protected, to one extent or another, with costly entry barriers.

6 The source of a monopolist's ability to charge an above-competitive price comes from its ability to materially change market supply through its own production decisions.

7 A monopolist's ability to hike its price and profits is restricted by the elasticity of its demand, which is influenced by the closeness of substitutes and the costs of entry facing other producers.

8 A monopolist can increase its profit and increase market efficiency through various and creative forms of price discrimination; however, its ability to price discriminate is constrained by the potential consumers have for reselling the good.

9 The new "network economy" often turns much economic analysis on its head. This is especially true when it comes to discussions of "monopoly power." A market for a network good might tend toward a single seller. At the same time, that single seller may have no, or very little, ability to profit from charging a high price, mainly because of the network effect.

10 A firm selling a network good will have to charge a very low (possibly a zero or negative price) initially to attract enough market share to achieve a critical level of network value. And once a firm producing a network good achieves a significant market share, it runs the risk of providing an opening for new firms if it attempts to profit by following the textbook monopoly practice of reducing output (which would reduce its network value) and charging a high price.

Review questions >>

1 Many magazines offer multi-year subscriptions at a lower rate than one-year subscriptions. Explain the logic of such a scheme. Why might it be considered evidence of monopoly power on the part of the magazines?

2 Explain why a monopolized industry will tend to produce less than a competitive industry.

3 "If a monopoly retains its market power over the long run, it must be protected by barriers to entry." Explain. List some restrictions on the mobility of resources that might help a firm retain monopoly power.

4 Why, from an economic point of view, should antitrust action not be taken against all monopolies?

5 Given the information in the table below, complete the monopolist's marginal cost and marginal revenue schedules. Graph the demand, marginal cost, and marginal revenue curves, and find the profit-maximizing point of production. Assuming that this monopolistic firm faces fixed costs of $10 and must charge the same price for all units sold, how much profit does it make?

Quantity produced and sold	Price ($)	Total variable cost ($)	Marginal cost ($)	Marginal revenue ($)
1	12	5		
2	11	9		
3	10	14		
4	9	20		
5	8	28		
6	7	38		

6   On the graph developed for question 5, identify the output and profits of a monopolist capable of perfect price discrimination.

7   Suppose a monopoly (not the one in question 5 – make up your own numbers) that is capable of imperfect price discrimination divides its market into two segments. Graph the demands for these two market segments ([a] and [b]). In a third graph (c), draw the monopolist's combined marginal revenue curve. Then, using the monopolist's marginal cost curve that you draw into (c), determine the monopolist's profit-maximizing output level. Indicate the quantity and price of the product sold in each market segment.

8   If buyers of the "network firm's" product fear that a "network firm" will become a true monopolist in the future, what does that fear do to the firm's current pricing policies?

9   How can antitrust enforcement in a market for a network good harm consumers?

10 Why does popcorn cost so much at the movies?

11 Why do many bars have "happy hours" (a couple of hours generally in late afternoon when drinks and appetizers are sold at discounts)?

12 Why are the prices of printer ink cartridges sometimes so high relative to the prices of printers?

13 Authors usually get a small fraction (say, 15 percent) of the gross revenue stream from any book they write, while the publisher gets what's left after royalty payments and all other costs. Assuming a positive marginal cost of book production, why might at times authors and publishers of books (with some monopoly power) be at odds over the pricing of books? Would the publisher or author(s) want the higher price? Indeed, graphically show the prices the authors and publisher of any given good would want. If the marginal cost of book production were constant and zero, would the author(s) and publisher then be in agreement over price?

14 Consider a good that is digital in nature. That is, the good is made totally of computer code, or 1s and 0s (or electrons) – software, for example. Suppose there are costs involved in the development of this good and in the making of a market for the good that must be incurred before the first copy of the digital good is sold. Assume also that there are very strong network effects associated with demand side of the good and that the short-run and long-run marginal cost of production of the good is zero and constant throughout the relevant range of production. Finally, assume that there is no way to prevent piracy. If asked by the CEO of the company producing this good how the good should be priced in the short run and long run, what strategy, or strategies, would you recommend? How would the potential for switching costs or lock in affect your recommendations?

Appendix: Short-run profits and losses

In the body of this chapter, we made a simplifying assumption that marginal cost is constant for all production levels in the long run, which means that the marginal cost and average cost curves are one and the same. Here, for those long microeconomic courses that allow for theoretical complications and refinements, we relax the constant marginal-cost assumption and employ again the assumption that marginal and average costs vary with output in the short run and long run. As will be seen, the conclusions drawn will be remarkably similar to the conclusions about monopoly production and pricing strategies developed in this chapter.

Short-run profits and losses

How much profit will a monopolist make by producing at the point where marginal cost equals marginal revenue and when producing under the types of costs curves developed in chapter 8? The answer can be found by adding the average total cost curve developed in chapter 8 to the monopolist's demand and marginal revenue curves discussed in this chapter (see figure A10.1). As we have shown, the monopolist will produce at the point where the marginal cost and revenue curves intersect, Q_1, and will charge what the market will bear for the quantity, P_1. We also know that profit equals total revenue minus total cost (*Profit = TR – TC*). Total revenue of P_1 times Q_1 is the rectangular area bounded by $0P_1aQ_1$. Total cost is the average total cost, ATC_1, times quantity, Q_1, or the rectangular area bounded by $0ATC_1bQ_1$. Subtracting total cost from total revenue, we find that the monopolist's profit is equal to the

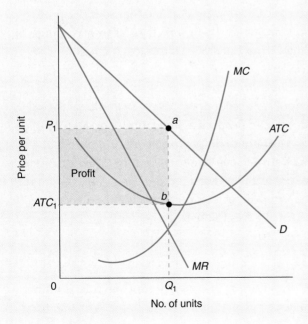

Figure A10.1 The monopolist's profits
The profit-maximizing monopoly will produce at the level defined by the intersection of the marginal cost and marginal revenue curves: Q_1. It will charge a price of P_1 – as high as market demand will bear – for that quantity. Because the average total cost of producing Q_1 units is ATC_1, the firm's profit is the shaded area ATC_1P_1ab.

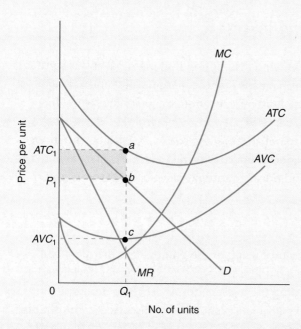

Price per unit

No. of units

Figure A10.2 The monopolist's short-run losses
Not all monopolists make a profit. With a demand curve that lies below its average total cost curve, this monopoly will minimize its short-run losses by continuing to produce at the point where marginal cost equals marginal revenue (Q_1 units). It will charge P_1, a price that covers its fixed costs, and will sustain short-run losses equal to the shaded area P_1ATC_1ab.

shaded rectangular area ATC_1P_1ab (mathematically, the expression $Profit = P_1Q_1 - ATC_1Q_1$ can be converted to the simpler form, $Profit = Q_1[P_1 - ATC_1]$).

As with perfectly competitive firms, monopolies are not guaranteed a profit. If market demand does not allow them to charge a price that covers the cost of production, they will lose money. Figure A10.2 depicts a monopoly that is losing money. Because losses are negative profits, the monopolist's losses are obtained in the same way as that of profits, by subtracting total cost from total revenue. The maximum price the monopolist can charge for its profit-maximizing (or, in this case, loss-minimizing) output level is P_1, which yields total revenues of P_1Q_1 or $0P_1bQ_1$. Total cost is higher: $0ATC_1aQ_1$. Thus the monopolist's loss is equal to the shaded rectangular area bounded by P_1ATC_1ab.

Of course, in the long run, when the monopoly firm is able to extricate itself from its fixed costs, it will shut down. Why does the monopolist not shut down? Because it follows the same rule as the perfect competitor. Both will continue to produce as long as price exceeds average variable cost – that is, as long as production will help to defray fixed costs. In figure A10.2, average fixed cost is equal to the difference between average total cost, ATC_1, and average variable cost, AVC_1 – or the vertical distance ac. Total fixed cost is therefore ac times Q_1, or the area bounded by $AVC_1 ATC_1ac$. Because the firm will suffer a greater loss if it shuts down (AVC_1ATC_1ac) than if it operates (P_1ATC_1ab), it chooses to operate and minimize its losses.

Production over the long run

In the long run the profitable monopolistic firm follows the same production rule as in the short run: It equates long-run revenue with long-run marginal cost. In figure A10.3(a), for

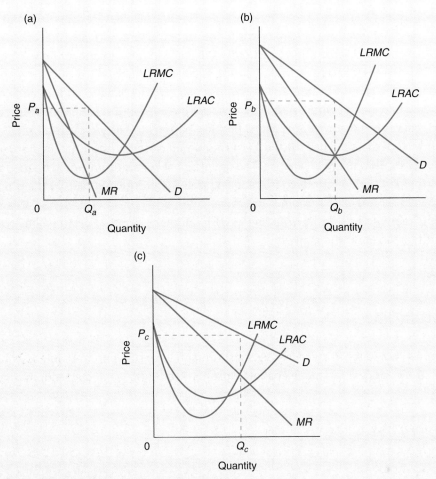

Figure A10.3 Monopolistic production over the long run
In the long run, the monopolist will produce at the intersection of the marginal revenue and long-run marginal cost curves (panel [a]). In contrast to the perfect competitor, the monopolist does not have to minimize long-run average cost by expanding its scale of operation. It can make more profit by restricting production to Q_a and charging price P_a. In panel (b), the monopolist produces at the low point of the long-run average cost curve only because that happens to be the point at which marginal cost and marginal revenue curves intersect. In panel (c), the monopolist produces on a scale beyond the low point of its long-run average cost curve because demand is high enough to justify the cost. In each case, the monopolist charges a price higher than its long-run marginal cost.

instance, the firm produces quantity Q_a and sells it for price P_a. (As always, profits are found by comparing the price with the long-run average cost. As an exercise, shade in the profit areas in figure A10.3.) Unlike the perfect competitor, the monopoly firm does not end up producing at the lowest point on the long-run average cost curve. With no competition, the monopolistic firm has no need to minimize average total cost. By restricting output, it can charge a higher price and earn greater profits than it can by taking full advantage of economies of scale.

Monopolists *may* produce at the low point of the long-run average cost curve, but only when the marginal revenue curve happens to intersect the long-run marginal and average cost curves at the exact same point (see figure A10.3[b]). In this case the monopolist produces quantity Q_b and sells it at a price of P_b, earning substantial monopoly profits in the process.

If the demand is great enough, the monopolist will actually produce in the range of diseconomies of scale (see figure A10.3[c]). How can the monopolist continue to exist when its price and costs of production are so high? Because barriers to entry protect it from competition. If barriers did not exist, other firms would certainly enter the market and force the monopolistic firm to lower its price. The net effect of competition would be to induce the monopolist to cut back on production, reducing average production costs in the process.

Monopolists cannot exist without barriers to market entry. If other firms had access to the market, the monopolist's profit would be its own undoing – for that profit will be competed away if others can enter the market.

The bottom line

A monopolist should set its price for the short run and long run with the same rule in mind: $MC = MR$. A monopolist can make economic profits, but it also can incur economic losses.

Review questions >>

1 Suppose a monopolist's demand curve increases. What will happen to the monopolist price and output level?
2 If a monopolist incurs economic losses, what will it do in the short run? In the long run?
3 Why would a monopolist ever produce when it is confronting diseconomies of scale?

11

Firm strategy under imperfectly competitive market conditions

Differences in tastes, desires, incomes and locations of buyers, and differences in the use which they wish to make of commodities all indicate the need for variety and the necessity of substituting for the concept of a "competitive ideal," an ideal involving both monopoly and competition.

Edward Chamberlin

We have so far considered two distinctly different market structures: *perfect competition* (characterized by producers that cannot influence price at all because of extreme competition) and *pure monopoly* (in which there is only one producer of a product with no close substitutes and whose market is protected by prohibitively high barriers to entry).

Needless to say, neither of those theoretical structures well describes most markets. Even in the short run, producers typically compete with several or many other producers of similar, but not identical, products. General Motors Corporation competes with Ford Motor Company and a number of foreign producers. McDonald's Corporation competes with Burger King Corporation, Carl's Jr., and any number of other burger franchises, as well as with Pizza Hut, Popeye's Fried Chicken, and Taco Bell.

In the long run, all these firms must compete with new companies that surmount the imperfect barriers to entry into their markets. In short, most companies competing in the imperfect markets can cause producers to be more efficient in their use of resources than under pure monopoly, although less efficient than in perfect competition. Part A of this chapter develops the theory of competition in obvious markets, those for products. Managers need to be mindful of competition in those markets, but they also must be able to operate efficiently in another competitive arena, the market for corporate control. Not only are entrepreneurs constantly on the lookout for new and better products to bolster their profits, but they also are scouting for underperforming firms they can buy at a low price, improve, and then sell for a higher price.

Markets that are less than perfectly competitive afford producers an opportunity to restrict output to raise their prices and profits, which can give rise to the type of market inefficiency discussed with reference to pure monopoly in chapter 10. Such market outcomes raise for many the specter of government regulation of markets with firms who have a great deal, or just some, monopoly power. Accordingly, toward the end of Part A we cover the dominant theories economists use to discuss government regulation, specifically, the "public-interest theory of regulation" and the "economic theory of regulation." We give special notice to the renewed case for regulation of the financial sector that has emerged from the worldwide financial meltdown of 2008, which, in turn, gave rise to the most serious recession since the Great Depression.

Whenever firms are able to make monopoly profits even in face of some competition in their product lines, there is the ever-present principal–agent problem, that managers will use their discretion over firm resources to pocket some of the profits in either pay or perks. Part B of this chapter is a study of an arena of competition – the market for corporate control – that can discipline managers who are tempted to take advantage of discretion. If managers misuse their firms' resources, then their firms' profits and stock prices will be depressed, opening the firms to takeovers by entrepreneurs who can buy the firms at depressed prices with the intent of correcting the misuse of firm resources and elevating the firms' stock prices. Part B will cover the ways firms can be taken over, as well as how managers can prevent such moves.

Part A Theory and public policy applications

On starting our study of so-called "real-world" market structures, one word of caution: Such a study can be frustrating. Although models may incorporate more or less realistic assumptions about the behavior of real-world firms, the theories developed from them are sometimes conjectural. Real-world markets are imperfect, complex phenomena that often do not lend themselves to hard-and-fast conclusions. This is because decision makers' decisions are so often *mutually interdependent*. That is, each decision maker's decisions depend on what other market participants do, or can be expected to do. Their behavior becomes something of a series of strategic games they play with one another, with each person's moves dependent upon how competitors can be expected to react.

Accordingly, the imperfect, real-world market structures of monopolistic competition and oligopoly developed in this chapter require that we view market movements often as a series of interdependent actions and reactions as is so often the case in games, in which outcomes are sometimes difficult to predict. Nevertheless, key insights can be developed, especially when considering how corporate takeover forces (which, as mentioned, will be considered in Part B) can make imperfect markets less imperfect, or more efficient.

Monopolistic competition

As we have noted in our study of demand, the greater the number and variety of substitutes for a good, the greater the elasticity of demand for that good – that is, the more consumers will respond to a change in price. By definition, a monopolistically competitive market such as the fast-food industry produces a number of different products, most of which can substitute for each other. If Burger Bippy raises its prices, consumers can move to another restaurant that offers similar food and service. But a price hike is unlikely to cost Burger Bippy all of its customers because of some combination of consumer ignorance, preference for Big Bippy burgers, and the power of habit. It has some *monopoly power*; therefore, it can charge slightly more than the ideal competitive price, determined by the intersection of the marginal cost and demand curves. Burger Bippy cannot raise its prices very much, however, without substantially reducing its sales.

The degree to which monopolistically competitive prices can stray from the competitive ideal depends on:

- the number of other competitors
- the ease with which existing competitors can expand their businesses to accommodate new customers (the cost of expansion)

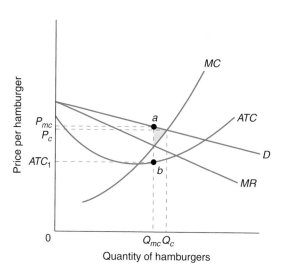

Figure 11.1 Monopolistic competition in the short run

As do all profit-maximizing firms, the monopolistic competitor will equate marginal revenue with marginal cost. It will produce Q_{mc} units and charge price P_{mc}, only slightly higher than the price under perfect competition. The monopolistic competitor makes a short-run economic profit equal to the area $ATC_1P_{mc}ab$. The inefficiency of its slightly restricted production level is represented by the shaded area.

- the ease with which new firms can enter the market (the cost of entry)
- the ability of firms to differentiate their products by location or by either real or imagined characteristics (the cost differentiation)
- public awareness of price differences (the cost of gaining information on price differences).

Given even limited competition, the firm should face a relatively elastic demand curve – certainly more elastic than the pure monopolist's.

Monopolistic competition in the short run

In the short run, a monopolistically competitive firm may deviate little from the price–quantity combination produced under perfect competition. The demand curve for fast-food hamburgers in figure 11.1 is highly, although not perfectly, elastic. Following the same rule as the perfect competitor and the pure monopolist, the monopolistically competitive burger maker produces where $MC = MR$. Because the firm's demand curve slopes downward, its marginal revenue curve slopes downward, too, like the pure monopolist's. The firm maximizes profits at Q_{mc} and charges P_{mc}, a price only slightly higher than the price that would be achieved under perfect competition (P_c).[1] The quantity sold with monopolistic competition is also only

---

[1] Remember, the perfect competitor faces a horizontal, or perfectly elastic, demand curve, which is also its price and marginal revenue curve. It produces at the intersection of the marginal cost and marginal revenue curves, which is where marginal cost equals price.

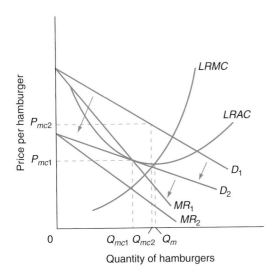

Figure 11.2 Monopolistic competition in the long run
In the long run, firms seeking profits will enter the monopolistically competitive market, shifting the monopolistic competitor's demand curve down from D_1 to D_2 and making it more elastic. Equilibrium will be achieved when the firm's demand curve becomes tangent to the downward sloping portion of the firm's long-run average cost curve Q_m. At that point, price (shown by the demand curve) no longer exceeds average total cost; the firm is making zero economic profit. Unlike the perfect competitor, this firm is not producing at the minimum of the long-run average total cost curve Q_m. In that sense, it is underproducing, by $Q_m - Q_{mc2}$ units. This underproduction is also reflected in the fact that the price is greater than the marginal revenue.

slightly below the quantity that would be sold under perfect competition, Q_c. Market inefficiency, indicated by the shaded area, is not excessive.

The firm's short-run profits may be slight or substantial, depending on demand for its product and the number of producers in the market. In our example, profit is the area bounded by $ATC_1P_{mc}ab$, found by subtracting total cost ($0ATC_1bQ_{mc}$) from total revenues ($0P_{mc}aQ_{mc}$), as with monopolies.

Monopolistic competition in the long run

Short-run profits will attract other producers into the market because surmounting the barriers to entry into monopolistic competition is not prohibitively costly. When the market is divided up among more competitors, the individual firm's demand curve will shift downward, reflecting each competitor's smaller market share. As a result, the marginal revenue curve will shift downward as well. The demand curve will also become more elastic, reflecting the greater number of potential substitutes in the market. (These changes are shown in figure 11.2.) The results of the increased competition are as follows:

- The quantity produced falls from Q_{mc2} to Q_{mc1}.
- The price falls from P_{mc2} to P_{mc1}.

Profits are eliminated when the price no longer exceeds the firm's average total cost. (As long as economic profit exists, new firms will continue to enter the market. Eventually the price will fall enough to eliminate economic profit.)[2]

Notice that the firm is not producing and pricing at the minimum of its long-run average cost curve, or quantity Q_m, as the perfect competitor would (nor did it in the short run).[3] In this sense, the firm is producing below capacity, by $Q_m - Q_{mc2}$ units.

In terms of price and quantity produced, monopolistic competition can never be as efficient as perfect competition. Perfectly competitive firms obtain their results partly because all producers are producing the same product. Consumers can choose from a great many suppliers, but they have no product options. In a monopolistically competitive market, on the other hand, consumers must buy from a limited number of producers, but they can choose from a variety of slightly different products. For example, the pen market offers consumers a choice between felt-tipped, fountain, and ballpoint pens of many different styles. This variety in goods comes at a price – the long-run price is above the minimum of the average total cost curve, as illustrated in figure 11.2.

Because of competition, however limited it is, firms must treat their customers with care. "Customer service" and hand-holding can be a part of a firm's product. Firms can compete by the extent of the care they offer, with some firms going so far as to live by the motto "customers are always right." But customer care can be expensive and subject to diminishing returns. Moreover customer treatment – or mistreatment – can exact a toll on a firm's employees, causing them to demand higher pay, which can hike the firm's cost structure. Considering these costs, might there be an optimum amount of customer care, which could vary among firms? In online Perspective 11 we develop further the economic way of thinking about customer care, and the lack thereof (emphasis on optimizing the "mistreatment" of customers).

 [See online Video Module 11.1 Monopolistic competition]

Oligopoly

In a market dominated by a few producers, into which entry is difficult – that is, in an oligopoly – the demand curve facing an individual competitor will be less elastic

---

[2] The monopolistic competitor will still have an incentive to stay in business, however. Economic profit, not book profit, falls to zero. Book profit will still be large enough to cover the opportunity cost of capital plus the risk cost of doing business.

[3] The perfect competitor produces at the minimum of the average total cost curve because its demand curve is horizontal; therefore, the demand curve's point of tangency with the average total cost curve is the low point of that curve.

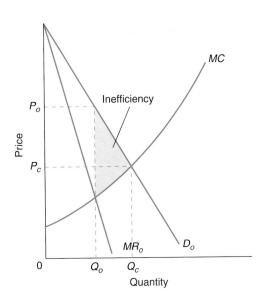

Figure 11.3 The oligopolist as monopolist
With fewer competitors than the monopolistic competitor, the oligopolist faces a less elastic demand curve, D_o. Each oligopolist can afford to produce significantly less (Q_o) and to charge significantly more (P_o) than the perfect competitor, who produces Q_c at a price of P_c. The shaded area representing inefficiency is larger than that of a monopolistic competitor.

than the monopolistic competitor's demand curve (see figure 11.3). If General Electric Company raises its price for light bulbs, consumers will have few alternative sources of supply. A price increase is less likely to drive away customers than it would under monopolistic competition, and the price–quantity combination achieved by the company will probably be further removed from the competitive ideal. In figure 11.3, the oligopolist produces only Q_o units for a relatively high price of P_o, compared with the perfect competitor's price–quantity combination of Q_cP_c. The shaded area representing inefficiency is fairly large.

Exactly how the oligopolist chooses a price is not completely clear. We will examine a few of the major theories proposed. Because each oligopolist is a major factor in the market, oligopolists' pricing decisions are *mutually interdependent*. The price one producer asks significantly affects the others' sales. Hence when one oligopolistic firm lowers its price, all the others can be expected to lower theirs, to prevent erosion of their market shares. The oligopolist may have to second-guess other producers' pricing policies – how they will react to a change in price, and what that might mean for its own policy. In fact, oligopolistic pricing decisions resemble moves in a chess game. The thinking may be so complicated that no one can predict what will happen. Thus, theories of oligopolistic price determination tend to be confined almost exclusively to the short run. (In the long run, virtually anything can happen.)

The oligopolist as monopolist
Given the complexity of the pricing problem, the oligopolistic firm – particularly if it is the dominant firm in the market – may simply decide to behave like a

monopolist (because it does have some monopoly power). As does a monopolist, Burger Bippy may simply equate marginal cost with marginal revenue (see figure 11.3) and produce Q_o units for price P_o. Here the oligopolist's price is significantly above the competitive price level, P_c, but not as high as the price charged by a pure monopolist. (If the oligopolist were a pure monopoly, it would not have to fear a loss of business to other producers because of a change in price.) Inefficiency in this market is slightly greater than in a monopolistically competitive market – see the shaded triangular area of figure 11.3.

The oligopolist as price leader

Alternatively, oligopolists may look to others for leadership in determining prices. One producer may assume price leadership because it has the lowest costs of production; the others will have to follow its lead or be underpriced and run out of the market. The producer that dominates industry sales may assume leadership. Figure 11.4 depicts a situation in which all the firms are relatively small and of equal size, except for one

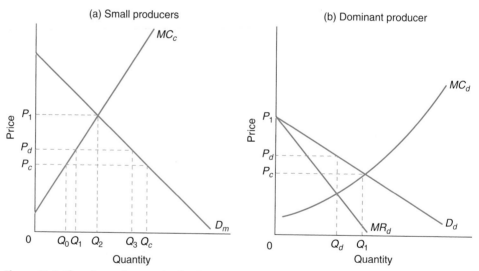

Figure 11.4 The oligopolist as price leader

The dominant producer who acts as a price leader will attempt to undercut the market price established by small producers (panel [a]). At price P_1 the small producers will supply the demand of the entire market, Q_2. At a lower price – P_d or P_c – the market will demand more than the small producers can supply. In panel (b), the dominant firm determines its demand curve by plotting the quantity it can sell at each price in panel (a). Then it determines its profit-maximizing output level, Q_d, by equating marginal cost with marginal revenue. It charges the highest price the market will bear for that quantity, P_d, forcing the market price down to P_d in panel (a). The dominant producer sells $Q_3 - Q_1$ units, and the smaller producers supply the rest.

large producer. The small firms' collective marginal cost curve (minus the large producer's) is shown in figure 11.4(a), along with the market demand curve, D_m. The dominant producer's marginal cost curve, MC_d, is shown in figure 11.4(b).

The dominant producer can see from figure 11.4(a) that, at a price of P_1, the smaller producers will supply the entire market for the product, say, steel. At P_1, the quantity demanded, Q_2, is exactly what the smaller producers are willing to offer. At P_1 or above, therefore, the dominant producer will sell nothing. At prices below P_1, however, the total quantity demanded exceeds the total quantity supplied by the smaller producers. For example, at a price of P_d, the total quantity demanded in figure 11.4(a) is Q_3, whereas the total quantity supplied is Q_1. The dominant producer will conclude that at price P_d, it can sell the difference, $Q_3 - Q_1$. For that matter, at every price below P_1, it can sell the difference between the quantity supplied by the smaller producers and the quantity demanded by the market.

As the price falls below P_1, the gap between supply and demand expands, so the dominant producer can sell larger and larger quantities. If these gaps between quantity demanded and supplied are plotted on another graph, they will form the dominant producer's demand curve, D_d (figure 11.4[b]). After it has devised its demand curve, the dominant producer can develop its accompanying marginal revenue curve, MR_d, also shown in figure 11.4(b). Using its marginal cost curve, MC_d, and its marginal revenue curve, it establishes its profit-maximizing output level and price, Q_d and P_d.

The dominant producer knows that it can charge price P_d for quantity Q_d, because that price–quantity combination (and all others on curve D_d) represents a shortage not supplied by small producers at a particular price in figure 11.4(a). Q_d, as noted earlier, is the difference between the quantity demanded and the quantity supplied at price P_d. So, the dominant producer picks its price, P_d, and the smaller producers must follow.[4] If they try to charge a higher price, they will not sell all they want to sell.

[See online Video Module 11.2 Price leadership]

The oligopolist in the long run

In an oligopolistic market, new competitors face significant barriers to entry; therefore, firms in oligopolistic industries can retain their short-run positions much longer than can monopolistically competitive firms.

---

[4] Consider market equilibrium with and without the dominant producer. In the absence of the dominant producer, the market price will be P_1, the equilibrium price for a market composed of only the smaller producers. The dominant producer adds quantity Q_d, which causes the price to fall, forcing the smaller producers to cut back production to Q_1 in figure 11.4(a).

Oligopoly is normally associated with such industries as the automobile, cigarette, and steel markets, which include some extremely large corporations. In those industries, the financial resources required to establish production on a competitive scale may comprise a formidable barrier to entry. One cannot conclude that all new competition is blocked in an oligopoly, however. Many of the best examples of oligopolies are found in local markets – for instance, drugstores, stereo shops, and lumber stores – in which one, two, or at most a few competitors exist, even though the financial barriers to entry can easily be overcome. Even in the national market, where the financial requirements for entry may be substantial, some large firms have the financial capacity to overcome barriers to entry. If firms in the electric light bulb market exploit their short-run profit opportunities by restricting production and raising prices, outside firms such as General Motors Corporation can move into the light bulb market and make a profit. In recent years, General Motors has in fact moved into the market for electronics and robotics.

While oligopoly power is a cause for concern, the basis for competition is the relative ability of firms to enter a market where profits can be made, not the absolute size of the firms in the industry. The small regional markets of a century ago, isolated by lack of transportation and communication, were perhaps less competitive than today's markets, even if today's firms are larger in an absolute sense. In the nineteenth century, the cost of moving into a faraway market effectively protected many local businesses from the threat of new competition.

Cartels: incentives to collude and to cheat

In either a monopolistically competitive market or an oligopolistic market, firms may attempt to improve their profits by restricting output and raising their market price. In other words, they may agree to behave as though they were a *unified monopoly*, an arrangement called a cartel. The principal purpose of these producers' anticompetitive efforts is to raise their prices and profits above competitive levels. In fact, however, a cartel is not a single, unified monopoly, and cartel members can find it very costly to behave as though they were. The size of monopoly profits provides a real incentive for competitors to collude – to conspire secretly to fix prices, production levels, and market shares. After they have reduced market supply and raised the price, however, each has an incentive to chisel on the agreement. The individual competitor will be tempted to cut prices in order to expand sales and profits. After all, if competitors are willing to collude for the purpose of improving their own welfare, they will probably also be willing to

> A **cartel** is an organization of independent producers intent on thwarting competition among themselves through the joint regulation of market shares, production levels, and prices.

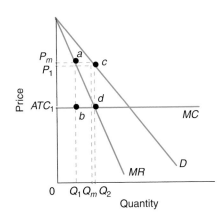

Figure 11.5 A duopoly (two-member cartel)
In an industry composed of two firms of equal size, firms may collude to restrict total output to Q_m and sell at a price of P_m. Having established that price–quantity combination, however, each has an incentive to chisel on the collusive agreement by lowering the price slightly. For example, if one firm charges P_1, it can take the entire market, increasing its sales from Q_1 to Q_2. If the other firm follows suit to protect its market share, each will get a lower price, and the cartel may collapse.

chisel on cartel rules to enhance their welfare further. The incentive to chisel can eventually cause the cartel to collapse. If a cartel works for long, it is usually because some form of external cost, such as the threat of violence, is imposed on chiselers.[5]

Although a small cartel is usually a more workable proposition than a large one is, even small groups may not be able to maintain an effective cartel. Consider an oligopoly of only two producers, called a duopoly. To keep the analysis simple, we assume here that each duopolist has the same cost structure and demand curve. We also assume a constant marginal cost, which means that marginal cost and average cost are equal and can be represented by one horizontal curve. Figure 11.5 shows the duopolists' combined marginal cost curve, MC, along with the market demand curve for the good, D. The two producers can maximize monopoly profits if they restrict the total quantity they produce to Q_m and sell it for price P_m. Dividing the total quantity sold between them, each will sell Q_1 at the monopoly price $(2 \times Q_1 = Q_m)$. Each will receive an economic profit equal to the area bounded by $ATC_1 P_m ab$, which is equal to total revenues $(P_m \times Q_1)$ minus total cost $(ATC_1 \times Q_1)$.

A duopoly is an oligopolistic market shared by only two firms.

Once each firm has curbed production, each firm may reason that by reducing the price slightly – to, say, P_1 – and perhaps disguising the price cut through customer rebates or more attractive credit terms, it can capture the entire market and even raise production to Q_2. Each firm may imagine that its own profits can grow from the

[5] A cartel may provide members with some private benefit that can be denied nonmembers. For example, local medical associations can deny nonmembers the right to practice in local hospitals. In that case, the cost of chiseling is exclusion from membership in the group.

area bounded by ATC_1P_mab to the much larger area bounded by ATC_1P_1cd. This tempting scenario presumes, of course, that the other firm does not follow suit and lower its price. Each firm must also worry that if it doesn't cheat, the other will be cutting price and capturing most of the market share.

Thus each duopolist has two incentives to chisel on the cartel. The first is offensive, to garner a larger share of the market and more profits. The second is defensive, to avoid a loss of its market share and profits. Generally, firms that seek higher profits by forming a cartel will also have difficulty holding the cartel together because of these dual incentives. As each firm responds to the incentives to chisel, the two firms undercut each other and the price falls back toward (but not necessarily to) the competitive equilibrium price, at the intersection of the marginal cost and demand curves. Just how far the price will decline depends on the firms' ability to impose penalties on each other for chiseling.

The strength and viability of a cartel depend on the number of firms in an industry and the freedom with which other firms can enter. The larger the number of actual or potential competitors, the greater the cost of operating the cartel, detecting chiselers, and enforcing the rules. If firms differ in their production capabilities, the task of establishing each firm's share of the market is more difficult. If a cartel member believes it is receiving a smaller market share than it could achieve on its own, it has a greater incentive to chisel. Because of the built-in incentives first to collude and then to chisel, the history of cartels tends to be cyclical. Periods in which output and prices are successfully controlled are followed by periods of chiseling, which lead eventually to the cartel's destruction.

 [See online Video Module 11.3 Cartels]

Game theory: cartels and the Nash equilibrium

The temptation to cheat on a cartel agreement can be usefully illustrated with a simple Prisoner's Dilemma payoff matrix, which allows us to introduce the so-called "Nash equilibrium," an economic/game-theoretic construct popularized by *A Beautiful Mind*, a book about the life of mathematician John Nash by Sylvia Nasar (1998) that became a movie in 2001. Assume that we are dealing with two firms (a duopoly), Firm *A* and Firm *B*, each providing jungle cruises in a remote tourist resort. The profits that each firm can earn depend on (1) the price each charges and (2) the price the other firm charges. We restrict each firm's pricing to two possibilities, a high (monopoly) price and a low (competitive) price, with the four possible pricing combinations shown in the four cells of the payoff matrix in table 11.1. In each cell, the profits of *A* are shown on the left and the profits of *B* are shown on the right. The two firms maximize their joint profits when each charges the high price for jungle cruises, which yields $1,000 for each one. In negotiations,

Table 11.1 **Game theory: cartel incentives and the Nash equilibrium**

| | | Firm B | |
		High price ($)	Low price ($)
Firm A	High price	1,000/1,000	400/1,200
	Low price	1,200/400	500/500

the only price strategy that both firms could agree on is for both to charge the high price. But notice that if Firm A charges the high price, Firm B will be able to earn $1,200 by charging the low price. And if Firm A charges the low price, Firm B will make $400 charging the high price, but $500 charging the low price. So no matter which price B thinks A will charge, it pays B to charge the low price. Exactly the same situation holds for A. The temptation then is for both of them to cheat on the agreement to charge the high price. The dilemma is, of course, that while cheating is the best pricing strategy for both, it leads to the worse possible collective outcome for the two firms – total profits of $1,000 as opposed to total profits of $2,000.

The outcome in which both firms charge the low price is referred to as a *Nash equilibrium*, after John Nash, whose work economists have followed since the 1950s and who won the Nobel Prize in Economics in 1994 for his contributions to game theory. Game theory is the study of how people make decisions when the payoff they receive depends not only on their own choices, but also on the decisions of others. The Prisoner's Dilemma is just one of many possible games that game theory analyzes (as we have seen at various points in this book).

A Nash equilibrium occurs when each decision maker has made the best decision for herself given the decisions that others have made – any unilateral change by a decision maker would make her worse off. For example, in the above Prisoner's Dilemma, when each firm is charging the low price, if either one of the firms shifted to a high price its profits would fall by $100. So, as indicated, the low-price/low-price outcome is a Nash equilibrium. The low-price decision is also what game theorists have called a "dominant strategy," meaning the one that yields the largest payoff to a decision maker regardless of what other decisions others make. Not every Nash equilibrium is the result of a dominant strategy; the Battle of the Sexes is an example of a game that is not. Even when everyone is doing the best they can do, given what others are doing, if someone changed their decision, it would pay others to change theirs as well.

As good as the movie *A Beautiful Mind* is, it misrepresents the Nash equilibrium and the implications of game theory for economics in a key scene, one of the most interesting in the movie and where Nash supposedly gets the idea for the Nash equilibrium. The scene finds Nash in a bar with some male friends. Three good-looking women come in, but Nash and his friends all agree that the blonde is the best looking of the three. In discussing the best strategy for meeting these women, and possibly getting dates, the friends decide that if they all make a play for the blonde none of them will likely be successful, so their best chance would be to concentrate their attention on the other two. While that may have been the best strategy, it wasn't one that would lead to a Nash equilibrium. With Nash and his friends ignoring the blonde, the chance of getting a date with her goes up, and so the best payoff for each of them is now to switch strategies and make a play for the blonde.[6]

Government-supported cartels

Government can either encourage or discourage a cartel. Through regulatory agencies that fix prices, determine market shares, and enforce cartel rules, government can keep competitors or cartel members from doing what comes naturally – chiseling. In doing so, government may be providing an important service to the industry. Perhaps that is why, in most states, insurance companies oppose deregulation of their rate structures. In seeking or welcoming regulation, an industry may calculate that it is easier to control one regulatory agency than a whole group of firms plus potential competitors.

In 1975, the airline industry opposed President Ford's proposal that Congress curtail the power of the Civil Aeronautics Board to set rates and determine airline routes. As the *Wall Street Journal* reported when Congress was debating airline deregulation:

The administration bill quickly drew a sharp blast from the Air Transport Association, which was speaking for the airline industry. The proposed legislation "would tear apart a national transportation system recognized as the finest in the world," the trade group said, urging

---

[6] In another scene from the movie, Nash is talking to his professor about his paper on game theory and his then newly formulated Nash equilibrium, and his professor tells him that his theory discredits almost 200 years of economic theory. This comment is also in Nasar's book, in which she explains that the Nash equilibrium in a Prisoner's Dilemma "contradicts Adam Smith's metaphor of the Invisible Hand in economics" (Nasar 1998, 119). The suggestion here is that Smith was wrong in arguing that when each person pursues his (or her) own interest, he/she is also serving the collective interest of others in the game. Exactly the opposite is true in a Prisoner's Dilemma, where the result of each person trying to do as well as possible is the minimization of the collective welfare. But Smith was careful to point out that the Invisible Hand worked only under certain conditions – those in which private property rights were enforced, markets were contestable, people were free to buy from and sell to those who made them the best offer, and public goods such as national defense and certain types of infrastructure are provided collectively.

Congress to reject it because it would cause "a major reduction or elimination of scheduled air service to many communities and would lead inevitably to increased costs to consumers." (*Wall Street Journal* 1975)

The real reason the airlines opposed deregulation became clear in the early 1980s, when several airlines filed for bankruptcy. Partial deregulation, begun in 1979, had increased competition, depressing fares and profits. Fares began to rise again in 1980, mainly because of rapidly escalating fuel costs. Real fares have nonetheless fallen significantly since deregulation and the big airlines are being forced to operate more efficiently in response to the competitive pressures coming from small innovative airlines that are capturing a larger share of the airline market with lower costs and prices (*The Economist* 2004b).

Government can suppress competition in many other ways that have nothing to do with price. Prohibiting the sale of hard liquor on Sunday, for example, can benefit liquor dealers, who might otherwise be forced to stay open on Sundays. In Florida, a state representative who managed to get a law through the legislature permitting Sunday liquor sales was denounced by liquor dealers. Domestic and global competitive pressures have weakened restrictions on liquor sales and on how long retailers can stay open in countries where those restrictions have been most severe (*The Economist* 2004a).

Cartels with lagged demand

Our analysis of cartels has been based on the presumption of a "standard good," one not subject to the forces of network effects and lagged demand introduced in chapter 6. Under market conditions of network effects and lagged demand, the pricing strategies of a cartel are potentially different. You might remember that the value of a network good to individual consumers goes up as more consumers buy the good. The demand for a lagged-demand good can also rise as use of the product is extended and more learn about the good and its value. When the market is split among two or more producers, each firm can understand that if it lowers its price, more goods will be sold currently, but even more goods will be sold in the future, when the benefits of the network effects and lagged demand (and "rational addiction" also considered in chapter 6) kick in. However, each firm can reason that the additional future sales generated by its current price reduction could be picked up by one of the other producers. The benefits are, in other words, external to the firm making the current sacrifice of a lower price. So each producer can reason that it should not incur the current costs of a lower price for the benefit of others. Each producer individually has an impaired incentive to lower the price.

On the other hand, each producer can also see that all the producers have a collective incentive to lower the price currently. Why? To stimulate future demand

and to raise their future price and profits. A cartel under such circumstances would be organized to do what all the producers have an interest in doing: lower the price (not raise the price, as in conventional markets). The problem is that the incentive to go its own way or to chisel on the cartel remains strong for each firm, as is true in the conventional type of cartel, which suggests that consumers may not get the lower current price because of cartel cheating (Lee and Kreutzer 1982).

 ## The case of the natural monopoly

So far, our discussion of monopoly power has assumed rising marginal costs. One argument for regulation, however, is based on the opposite assumption. Some believe that industries such as electric utilities are **natural monopolies**, meaning that the marginal cost of producing additional units actually decreases over the long run. That is, within the relevant range of the market demand, the long-run marginal cost curve in figure 11.6 slopes downward. Natural monopolies are seen as prime candidates for regulation because their dominance in the market allows them to exert considerable monopoly power, provided that entry is restricted.

> A **natural monopoly** is a market structure characterized by a decline in long-run average cost of production within the range of the market demand, which means that the market will be served most cost-effectively with only one producer.

Figure 11.7 illustrates the relationship between the long-run average and marginal cost curves and the demand and marginal revenue curves for electric power generation (which is widely thought to be a prime example of a natural monopoly for a wide territory). According to traditional theory, a firm with such decreasing costs will tend to expand production and lower its costs until it becomes large enough for its production decisions to influence price – that is, until it achieves monopoly power. Then it will choose to produce at the point at which all monopolists produce: where marginal cost equals marginal revenue. Thus, the

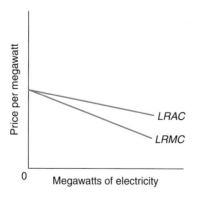

Figure 11.6 Long-run marginal and average costs in a natural monopoly
In a natural monopoly, long-run marginal cost and average costs decline continuously over the relevant range of production because of economies of scale. Although the long-run marginal and average cost curves may eventually turn upward because of diseconomies of scale, the firm's market is not large enough to support production in that cost range.

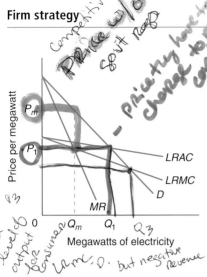

(handwritten annotations:) Competitive / Price w/o govt regB / price they have to maintain / charge to control. / Govt regulated price. / doesn't change traditional monopoly prices / as that would encourage competition. they / get govt. subsidy to survive. / ideal level of output for consumer. / LRMC:0. but negative revenue

Figure 11.7 Creation of a natural monopoly
Even with declining marginal costs, the firm with monopoly power will produce at the point where marginal cost equals marginal revenue, making Q_m units and charging a price of P_m. Unless barriers to entry exist, other firms may enter the market, causing the price to fall toward P_1 and the quantity produced to rise toward Q_1. At that price–quantity combination, only one firm can survive – but without barriers to entry, that firm cannot afford to charge monopoly prices. At a price of P_1, its total revenues just cover its total costs. Economic profit is zero.

monopolistic firm in figure 11.7 will sell Q_m megawatts at an average price of P_m, generating monopoly profits in the process. In other words, firms in decreasing-cost industries tend naturally toward only one producer remaining viable in the market.

Although a firm with decreasing costs can expand until it is the major if not only producer, it will not necessarily be able to price like a monopoly. Suppose a "natural monopoly" flexes its market muscle and charges P_m for Q_m units. Another firm, seeing the first firm's economic profits, may enter the industry, expand production, and charge a lower price, luring away customers. To protect its interests, the firm that has been behaving like a monopoly will have to cut its price and expand production to lower its costs. It is difficult to say how far the price will fall and output will rise, but only one firm is likely to survive such a battle, selling to the entire market at a price that competitors cannot undercut. That price will be approximately P_1 in figure 11.7.

If the price does fall to P_1 and only one firm survives, its total revenue will be its price times the quantity produced, Q_1 (or $P_1 \times Q_1$). Notice that at that level, the firm's average cost is equal to P_1; therefore, the total cost of production (the average cost times the quantity sold) is equal to the firm's revenue. The firm is just covering its cost of production, including the owners' risk cost. Now alone in the market, the firm may think it can restrict output, raise its price, and reap an economic profit. Still, it faces the ever-present threat of some other company entering the market and underpricing its product.

[See online Video Module 11.4 Natural monopolies]

The economics and politics of business regulation

Name an industry that has not, in some way, been under the authority of a government regulatory agency at some time. At the start of the twentieth century such a task would have been relatively simple. Today, with government extending its activities in all directions, it is not. Almost every economic activity either is, or has been at some time in the past, subject to some type of regulation at one stage or another. The list of federal regulatory agencies virtually spans the alphabet – FAA, FDA, FEA, FPC, FRS, FTC, ICC, NTHSA, OSHA, SEC – to say nothing of the various state utilities commissions, licensing boards, health departments, and consumer protection agencies. As a result, it is much easier to list regulated industries than to name an unregulated one. Air transport, telephone service, trucking, natural gas, electricity, water and sewage systems, stock brokering, health care, taxi services, massage parlors, pharmacies, postal services, television and radio broadcasting, toy manufacturing, beauty shops, ocean transport, legal advice, slaughtering, medicine, embalming and funeral services, optometry, oyster fishing, banking, and insurance – all are regulated. In the 1960s and 1970s especially, regulation was one of the nation's largest growth industries (although there was something of a "recession" in regulations in the 1980s). Why have people been willing to substitute the visible foot of government for the invisible hand of competition?

Explaining regulation – why and how it happens – is a major challenge to economists. Although several insightful theories have been proposed, statistical tests of those theories are incomplete and are at times based on crude data. Some instances of regulation or changes in regulatory policy cannot be explained by current theories. At best, we can only review the two major lines of explanation for the existence of so much regulation – the public interest theory and the economic theory of regulation.

The public interest theory of monopoly regulation

Regulation of monopoly has often been justified on the grounds that it is in the public interest, meaning that it helps to achieve commonly acknowledged national goals. Economists' theories of regulation designed to promote the public interest tend to be based on the goal of increasing market efficiency.

Figure 11.8 shows a cartelized industry producing at an output level of Q_m and selling at a price of P_m. That output level is inefficient because the marginal benefit of the last unit produced (equal to its price) is greater than its marginal cost. Although consumers are willing to pay more than the cost of producing additional units, they are not given the chance to buy those units. The cartel's price–quantity combination not only creates economic profit for the owners, which may be considered inequitable or unjust, but also results in the loss of net benefits, or dead-weight welfare loss, equal to the shaded triangular area abc.

Regulation can force firms to sell at lower prices and to produce and sell larger quantities. Ideally, firms can be made to produce Q_c units and to sell them at price P_c, which is the same price–quantity combination that could be achieved under highly competitive conditions. At that output level, the marginal benefit of the last unit produced is equal to its marginal cost.

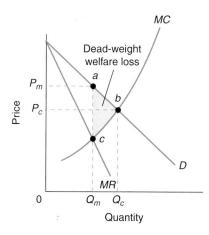

Figure 11.8 The effect of regulation on a cartelized industry

The profit-maximizing cartel will equilibrate at point *a* and produce only Q_m units and sell at a price of P_m. In the sense that consumers want Q_c units and are willing to pay more than the marginal cost of production for them, Q_m is an inefficient production level. Under pure competition, the industry will produce at point *b*. Regulation can raise output and lower the price, ideally to P_c, thereby eliminating the dead-weight welfare loss that is equal to the shaded triangle *abc* and which results from monopolistic behavior.

Government regulators need not demand that a company produce Q_c units. All they have to do is require a company to charge no more than P_c. After that order has been given, the portion of the demand curve above P_c, along with the accompanying segment of the marginal revenue curve, becomes irrelevant. The firm simply is not allowed to choose a price–quantity combination above point *b* on the demand curve. Then the profit-maximizing producer will choose to sell at P_c, the maximum legal price. With marginal revenue guaranteed at P_c, the firm will equate marginal revenue with marginal cost and produce at Q_c, the efficient output level.

Ideal results cannot be expected from the regulatory process, however. The cost of determining the ideal price–quantity combination can be extraordinarily high, if not prohibitive. Because regulators do not work for regulated industries, they will not know the details of a company's marginal cost or demand elasticity. The problem is particularly acute for regulators of monopolies because there are no competitors from which alternative cost estimates can be obtained. Furthermore, if prices are adjusted upward to allow for a company's higher costs, a regulated firm may lose its incentive to control costs. The regulated price could conceivably end up being the monopoly price, with what-would-have-been monopoly profits converted into added costs (for example, higher pay and perks for managers of the regulated firm).

The cost of the regulatory process must be emphasized. If regulation is truly to serve the public interest, it must increase the efficiency of the entire social system. That is, its benefits must exceed its costs. Too often, regulation protects large and politically influential firms and industries against competition of small firms by imposing regulations that raise small firms' costs more than large firms'. Though most people assume that businesses are against regulation, the truth is that many of the most politically influential of the businesses subject to regulation favor them. As discussed earlier in this chapter, the major airlines fought against the elimination of regulation in the 1970s. According to one study, businesses spend hundreds of billions of dollars a year resisting changes in regulation (both reductions and increases in regulation) because they benefited from the existing regulations (Crain and Hopkins 2001).

The special case for regulating natural monopolies

Natural monopolies are often singled out as deserving special regulatory attention because, as we saw earlier, only a single producer will emerge in such a market.

From a purely theoretical perspective, the existence of a natural monopoly is insufficient justification for regulation. Unless there are significant barriers to entry into an industry and an inelastic market demand, natural monopolies should not be able to charge monopoly prices. In reply to this argument, proponents of regulation hold that some industries, such as electric utilities, require such huge amounts of capital that no competitor could be expected to enter the market to challenge the natural monopoly. That argument presumes, however, that electric power generation must take place on an extremely large scale. Such is not necessarily the case (as solar panels show). Furthermore, if economic profits exist, many large corporations can raise the capital needed to produce electricity on a profitable scale.

Proponents of the regulation of natural monopolies point also to insufficient output and revenues. Even if an unregulated industry produces Q_1 units and prices that output at P_1 (see figure 11.9), it has not reached the efficient output level. That would be the level at which marginal cost equals marginal benefit – the point at which the marginal cost curve intersects the demand curve, Q_2, in figure 11.9. Why does output fall short?

Given the market demand curve, the firm could sell an output of Q_2 for only P_2, earning total revenues of P_2 times Q_2. Because the average cost of producing at that output level – AC_1 on the vertical axis – would be greater than the price, total costs, at $AC_1 \times Q_2$, would be greater than total revenues. The loss to a firm that tried to

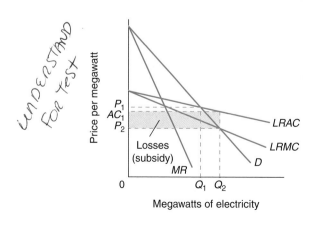

Figure 11.9 Underproduction by a natural monopoly

A natural monopolist that cannot price discriminate will produce only Q_1 megawatts – less than Q_2, the efficient output level – and will charge a price of P_1. If the firm tries to produce Q_2, it will make losses equal to the shaded area, for its price (P_2) will not cover its average cost (AC_1).

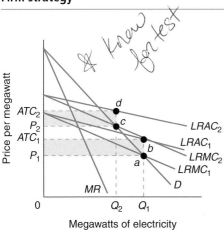

Figure 11.10 **Regulation and increasing costs**
If a natural monopoly is compensated for the losses it incurs in operating at the efficient output level (the shaded area P_1ATC_1ba), it may monitor its costs less carefully. Its cost curves may shift up, from $LRMC_1$ to $LRMC_2$ and from $LRAC_1$ to $LRAC_2$. Regulators will then have to raise the price from P_1 to P_2, and production will fall from Q_1 to Q_2. The firm will still have to be subsidized (by an amount equal to the shaded area P_2ATC_2dc), and the consumer will be paying more for less.

produce at the efficient output level is shown by the shaded area on the graph. To produce at the efficient output level, a company would require a subsidy to offset that loss (which creates inefficiencies of its own because of the economic distortions created by the tax necessary to raise the revenue for the subsidy), or it would have to be able to price discriminate, charging progressively lower prices for additional units sold.

After a firm is given a subsidy, its pricing and production decision must be closely monitored, for its incentive to control costs will be weakened. If the firm allows its cost curves to drift upward, the price it can charge will also rise. In figure 11.10, the firm's long-run marginal and average cost curves shift up from $LRMC_1$ and $LRAC_1$ to $LRMC_2$ and $LRAC_2$. Following the rule that price should be set at the intersection of the long-run marginal cost and demand curves, regulators permit the price to rise from P_1 to P_2. The firm's subsidized losses shrink from the shaded area P_1ATC_1ba to P_1ATC_2dc, but the quantity produced drops also, from Q_1 to Q_2. Consumers are now getting fewer units at a higher price.

Thus, production may be just as inefficient with regulation as without it. Critics point to the US Postal Service as an example of an industry that is closely regulated and subsidized, yet highly inefficient. If the postal industry were truly a natural monopoly, it would be a low-cost producer and would not need protection from competition. Proponents of regulation see the inefficiencies we have just demonstrated as an argument for even more careful scrutiny of a regulated firm's cost – or for government control of production costs through nationalization.

Not all natural monopolies need subsidies to operate at an efficient output level. For all megawatts up to Q_1 in figure 11.9, the unregulated firm can charge up to P_1, a price that just covers its costs on those units. If its product cannot be easily resold, the firm can price discriminate, charging slightly lower prices for the additional units beyond Q_1. As long as its marginal prices are on or below the demand curve and above the marginal cost curve, the firm will cover its costs while moving toward the efficient output level – and it can do so without giving other firms an incentive to move into its market. If its product can be resold, however, some people will buy at the lower marginal prices and resell to those who are paying P_1, cutting off the firm's profits.

A special case for regulating the country's financial industry became fully evident with the emergence of the so-called "Great Panic" in the fall of 2007 and the resulting so-called "Great Recession" that followed. We take up the special case for regulating banking and for extending bank regulations to "non-bank" financial institutions in online Reading 11.1.

The economic theory of regulation

Beginning in the 1960s, many economists began to see regulation as a product of the supply of and demand for politically provided benefits (Stigler 1971; Breyer 1982). Government is seen as a supplier of regulatory services to industry. Such services can include price fixing, restrictions on market entry, subsidies, and even suppression of substitute goods (or promotion of complementary goods). For example, regulation enabled commercial television stations to get the Federal Communication Commission (FCC) to delay the introduction of cable television.

These regulatory services are not free; they are offered to industries willing to pay for them. In the political world, the price of regulatory services may be campaign contributions or lucrative consulting jobs, or votes and volunteer work for political campaigns. Regulators and politicians allocate the benefits among all the various private interest groups so as to equate political support and opposition at the margin.

Firms demand regulation that serves their private interest. As we have seen, forming a cartel in a free market can be difficult, both because new firms may enter the market and because colluders tend to cheat on cartel agreements. The cost of reaching and enforcing a collusive agreement can be so high that government regulation is attractive by comparison.

The view that certain forms of regulation emerge from the interaction of government suppliers and industry demanders seems to square with much historical evidence. As Richard Posner has observed:

The railroads supported the enactment of the first Interstate Commerce Act, which was designed to prevent railroads from price discrimination because discrimination was undermining the railroad's cartels. American Telephone and Telegraph pressed for state regulation of telephone service because it wanted to end competition among telephone companies. Truckers and airlines supported extension of common carrier regulation to their industries because they considered unregulated competition excessive. (Posner 1974, 337)

Barbers, beauticians, lawyers, and other specialists all have sought government licensing, which is a form of regulation. Farmers have backed moves to regulate the supply of the commodities they produce. Whenever deregulation is proposed, the industry in question almost always opposes the proposal. Gasoline retailers in North Carolina (and a dozen other states) got a state statute passed that restricts gas stations from selling gasoline below their "wholesale price" (except for ten days during the grand opening of a new station). Through the threat and actuality of lawsuits by mom-and-pop gas stations, the law obviously places a lower bound on price competition and restrains the creative efforts of convenience stores from using gasoline pricing as a means of bringing in customers who buy higher-margin non-gasoline products on their refueling stops (Associated Press 2005a).

To the extent that regulation benefits all regulated firms, whether or not they have contributed to the cost of procuring it, industries may consider regulation a public good. This creates a free-rider problem, which occurs when people can enjoy the benefits of a scarce good or service without paying directly for it by pretending not to want it. Some firms will try to free ride on others' efforts to secure regulation. If all firms free ride, however, the collective benefits of regulation will be lost.

The free-rider phenomenon is particularly noticeable in large groups, whose cost of organizing for collective action can be substantial. Someone must bear the initial cost of organization. Yet because the benefits of organization are spread more or less evenly over the group, the party that initiates the organization may incur costs greater than the benefits it receives. Thus collective action may not be taken. Free riding may explain why some large groups, such as secretaries, have not yet secured government protection. Everyone may be waiting for everyone else to act. Small groups may have much greater success because of their proportionally smaller organizational costs and larger individual benefits. Perhaps it was because only a few railroad companies existed in the 1880s that they were able to lobby success-fully for the formation of the ICC.

There are some exceptions to this rule. Several reasonably large groups, including truckers and farmers, have secured a high degree of government regulation, whereas many highly concentrated groups, such as the electrical appliance industry, have not. In highly concentrated industries, it may be less costly to develop private cartels than to organize to secure government regulation. In industries composed of many firms, on the other hand, any one firm's share of the cost of securing regulation may be smaller than its share of the costs of establishing and enforcing a private cartel. Large groups also control more sizable voting blocks than do small groups. Large groups may have the advantage of established trade associations, whose help can be enlisted in pushing for protective legislation (Olson 1971, chapters 1, 2).

In broad terms, the economic theory of regulation explains much about govern-ment policy – but that is one of its weaknesses. The theory is so broad that its usefulness as a predictor is limited. It does not enable economists to forecast which industries are likely to seek or achieve government regulation. Nor does it explain the political movement to deregulate the trucking and banking industries, or to regulate the environment. Neither of these trends appears to meet directly the demand of any particular business interest group. In general, any self-interested group will be better represented the larger its interest in the outcome, the smaller its size, the more homogeneous its position and objectives, and the more certain the outcome.

For a contrarian take on how firms should treat their customers, see online Perspective 11, The value of "mistreating" customers.

Online Perspective 11
The value of "mistreating" customers

Part B Organizational economics and management

The first part of this chapter was concerned with competition among firms with pricing power in final product markets. Managers are pressed to operate efficiently in such competitive markets, or face a loss of market share and, perhaps, their jobs. But competition hardly stops with the final product markets. Whole firms can be bought and sold, and entrepreneurs will be in search of firms to buy, most prominently underperforming firms, because they are the firms where resources can possibly be redeployed with the potential for greater profits. This section of the chapter is about managing with an eye toward the market for corporate control.

"Hostile" takeover as a check on managerial monopolies

It may appear that our discussion of monopolies applies only to "markets" and has little or nothing to do with the management of firms. Indeed, the theory of monopolies is directly applicable to management problems because firms often rely exclusively on internal departments (and their employees) to provide a variety of services, such as legal, advertising, and accounting, as well as for production of parts that are assembled into the firm's final goods sold to consumers. In such cases, the internal departments can begin to act like little monopolies, cutting back on what they could produce and demanding a higher price (through their firm's budgetary processes) for what they do than is required. Outsourcing some of a firm's needed services is one way to avoid the inefficiencies of internal monopolies.

Outsourcing can improve a firm's profitability in two ways. First, it offers firms the opportunity to get some of their services cheaper from competitive outside bids. Second, it can make the remaining internal departments work more efficiently as they become aware of the threat of being replaced by more competitive outside suppliers. For example, in 2004, Western Michigan University took bids to provide its needed custodial care from the union of its sixty custodial workers and from five outside private custodial firms. The university replaced its in-house custodial workers with workers employed by Commercial Sanitation Management Services because that company's bid reduced the university's maintenance cost by $1.5 million a year (Davis 2005).

Still, managers can become complacent and allow their departments to act monopolistically – and inefficiently. They may become lax for other reasons as well, spending more on office perks than necessary, expanding the size of the firm beyond its core competencies, and generally being too lavish with shareholder profits. Top management may be tempted to take advantage of the Prisoner's Dilemma in which each shareholder finds herself. Each shareholder may shirk on monitoring the behavior of the managers of the firms. Corporate takeovers, which threaten the jobs of management teams who disregard shareholders' interests, represent an important check on management discretion. Of course, when confronted with a "hostile" takeover attempt, managers have found an array of legal means of defeating the takeover. These defenses are covered in online Reading 11.2.

Reasons for takeovers

Corporate takeovers occur for many reasons and in different ways. There may be complementarities in the production and distribution of the products of two firms that can be best realized by one firm. Two firms may find that they can realize economies of scale by combining their operations. Or one firm may be supplying another firm with the use of highly specific capital, and a merger between the two reduces the threat of opportunistic behavior that can be costly to both (a subject covered in chapter 7).

Most takeovers are what are referred to as "friendly," that is, the managements of the two firms work out a mutually agreeable arrangement. Disney's takeover of ABC was a friendly one. Indeed, takeovers occur for the same reason that all market transactions occur: generally speaking, efficiencies are expected, meaning that both parties can be made better off. So it should not be surprising that most takeovers are friendly.

But there are takeovers that are opposed by the management of the firms being taken over, as was the case, at least initially, in Oracle's takeover of PeopleSoft in late 2004. These takeovers are referred to as "hostile" and are commonly seen as undesirable and inefficient. "Hostile" takeovers are depicted as the work of corporate "raiders" who are interested only in turning a quick profit and who disrupt productivity by forcing the targeted firms to take expensive and distracting defensive action.

If managers of target corporations always acted in the interest of their shareholders (the real owners of the corporation), then a strong case could be made for regarding so-called hostile takeovers as inefficient. Managers of the target corporation would then oppose a takeover only if it could not be made in a way that benefited their shareholders, as well as those of the acquiring corporation. But if managers could always be depended upon to act in the interest of their shareholders, then there would be no need for many of the corporate arrangements that have been discussed in this book.

The market for corporate control

The strongest argument in favor of "hostile" takeovers is that they bring the interests of managers more in line with those of shareholders than would otherwise be the case. There is a so-called "market for corporate control" that allows people who believe that they can do a better job of managing a company and maximizing shareholder return to oust the existing management by outbidding them for the corporate stock. Although such takeover attempts are infrequent and not always successful, just the threat of a "hostile" takeover provides a strong disincentive for managers to pursue personal advantages at the expense of their shareholders. This disincentive suggests that the possibility of "hostile" takeovers provides an efficiency advantage, an advantage related to the primary concern of this section, which is why "hostile" takeovers are less hostile than they are commonly depicted.

A takeover is often considered hostile for the very reason that it promotes efficiency. A management team that is doing a good job of managing a firm efficiently has little to fear from a rival management team taking over. The stock price of a well-managed firm will generally reflect that fact, and a corporate raider will not be able to profit from buying the firm's stock in the hope of increasing its price through improved management. A takeover is likely only when the existing managers are not running the firm efficiently because of incompetence, the inability to abandon old ways in response to changing conditions, or intentionally benefiting personally at the expense of shareholders. But under these circumstances, a takeover that promises to increase efficiency will not be popular with existing managers because it threatens to put them out of work. Not surprisingly, managers whose jobs are threatened by a takeover will see it as "hostile."

The fact that pejorative terms such as "hostile takeover" and "corporate raiders" are so widely used testifies to the advantage existing managers have over shareholders at promoting their interests through public debate. The costs from a "hostile" takeover are concentrated on a relatively small number of people, primarily the management team that loses its pay, perks, and privileges. Each member of this team will lose a great deal if the team is replaced and so has a strong motivation to oppose a takeover. And even a grossly inefficient management team can be organized well enough to respond in unison to a takeover threat. That unified voice will usually characterize a takeover as hostile to the interests of the corporation, the shareholders, the community, and the nation, and we might expect managers to be more vociferous the more inefficient the management.

But if a takeover is actually efficient, what about the voice of those who benefit? Why is the media discussion of takeovers dominated by the managers who lose rather than by the shareholders who win? And there is plenty of evidence that the shareholders of the target company in a hostile takeover do win. For example, during the takeover wave in the 1980s, it was estimated that stock prices of targeted firms increased about 50 percent because of hostile takeovers, which suggests that the managers of the targeted firms may have destroyed a considerable amount of their corporations' value before being targeted for takeover (Jensen 1988).

As will be discussed later in this section, this increase in stock values does not necessarily *prove* that a takeover is efficient. The takeover could depress the stock prices of the firm that is taking over the target firm, for example.[7] But even if the takeover is not efficient, the shareholders of the target firm should favor it and counter the negative portrayal that company managers put forth. But this seldom happens because there are typically a large number of shareholders, few of whom may have more than a relatively small number of shares. Most shareholders have a diversified portfolio and are only marginally affected by changes in the price of any particular corporation's stock. The probability that the actions of a typical individual stockholder will have an impact is very low, approaching zero. So even if the gain to shareholders far exceeds the loss to management, the large number of shareholders and their diverse interests make it extraordinarily difficult for them to speak in unison. As indicated earlier, shareholders are disadvantaged because they are in a Prisoner's Dilemma with respect to influencing the terms of the debate on behalf of their collective benefit.

---

[7] However, Michael Jensen minces few words on what the data imply: "[T]he fact that takeover and LBO premiums [or added prices] average 50% above market price illustrates how much value public-company managers can destroy before they face a serious threat of disturbance. Takeovers and buyouts both create value and unlock value destroyed by management through misguided policies. I estimate that transactions associated with the market for corporate control unlocked shareholder gains (in target companies alone) of more than $500 billion between 1977 and 1988 – more than 50% of the cash dividends paid by the entire corporate sector over this same period" (Jensen 1989, 64–5).

If shareholders and management were on equal footing at influencing the public perception of takeovers, almost no takeovers would be reported as hostile. Consider a hypothetical situation that is similar to what is commonly seen as a hostile takeover.

Assume that you are the owner of a beautiful house on a high bluff overlooking the Pacific Ocean near Carmel, California. You are extremely busy as a global entrepreneur and unable to spend much time at this house. As the house and grounds require full-time professional attention, you have hired a caretaker to manage the property. Assume that you pay the caretaker extremely well (mainly because you want him to bear a cost from being fired for shirking and engaging in opportunism), and give him access to many of the amenities of the property. He's very happy with the job, and you are pleased enough with his performance.

But one day a wealthy CEO who is planning to retire in the Carmel area makes you an offer on the house of $15 million, about 50 percent more than you thought you could sell it for. Although you were not interested in selling at $10 million, you find the $15 million offer very attractive. For whatever reason, the house is worth more to the retiring CEO than to you. It could be that the CEO values the property more than you simply because she will have more time to spend living in and enjoying the house. Or it could be because the CEO believes that a profit can be made on the house by bringing in a caretaker who will do a far better job managing the property, thus increasing its value to above $15 million. But it really makes little difference to you why the CEO values the house more than you do, and you are quite happy to sell at the price offered.

Imagine how surprised you would be if, as the sale of your house was being negotiated, the news media reported that your property was the target of a hostile takeover by a "house raider" interested only in personal advantage. What's so hostile about being offered a higher price for your property than you thought it was worth? And are you somehow worse off because the buyer also sees private benefit in the exchange?

But the media wasn't interested in your opinion. Instead, reporters had been talking to your caretaker, who knew he would lose his job if the sale went through. So the caretaker reported that the sale of the property was the result of a hostile move by an unsavory character. Obviously this is silly, and the media is not likely to report this, or any similar sale of a house, as a hostile takeover. But is this situation any sillier than reporting a corporate takeover as hostile when the owners of the corporation (the shareholders) are being offered a 50 or 100 percent premium to sell their shares?

The two situations are not exactly the same, but they are similar enough to call into question the "hostility" of most hostile takeovers. One important difference between the two situations is that if such a report did start to circulate about the sale of your house, and somehow threatened that sale, you would have the motivation and ability to clearly communicate that it was your house, you found the offer attractive, and there was nothing at all hostile about the sale. This difference explains why our example should not be taken as a criticism of the press. When there is one owner (or a few), as in the case of a house, the press can easily understand and report that owner's perspective. But when there are thousands of owners, as in the case of corporations, it is much easier for reporters to obtain information about a corporation from its top managers.

The fact that there are a multitude of owners in the case of corporations is the basis for other differences between the sale of a house and the sale of a corporation. Just as reporters find that it is easier to rely on top management for information on a corporation, so do the owners of a corporation find it easier to rely on management to make most corporate decisions, even major decisions such as those that affect the sale of the corporation. Obviously, the reason for granting a management team the power to act somewhat independently of shareholders is that shareholders are so large in number, so dispersed in location, and so diverse in interests that they cannot make the type of decisions needed to manage a corporation, or much else, for that matter. But as we have discussed in detail throughout this text, there are risks associated with letting agents (managers) act on behalf of principals (owners/share-holders). As the owner of the house outside Carmel, would you want your caretaker to negotiate the sale for you? Only if the caretaker were subject to a set of incentives that go a long way in aligning his interests in the sale with yours.

The efficiency of takeovers

Are hostile takeovers efficient? Not everyone believes they are. Hostile takeovers are commonly seen as ways to increase the wealth of people who are already rich at the expense of the corporation's average workers (not just its managers), the corporation's long-run prospects, and the competitiveness of the general economy. For example, responding to a hostile takeover bid for Chrysler Corporation in the mid-1990s by Kirk Kerkorian, a major newspaper ran an editorial: "[W]hen Kerkorian was complaining about insufficient return to stockholders, the value of [his] investment in Chrysler had more than tripled, to $1.1 billion. That's not good enough? To satisfy his greed, Kerkorian seems prepared to endanger the jobs of thousands of Americans and the health of a major corporation so important to the economy" (*Atlanta Journal – Constitution* 1995).

This editorial comment ignores the efficiency effects of a corporate takeover. But at the same time, the effect of a hostile takeover on economic efficiency is more complicated than has been suggested in this chapter so far. The stockholders of the corporation being taken over do gain (see Grinblatt and Titman 2002, for a review of the extensive literature on this topic). But what about the common stockholders (whose earnings can vary with the success of their companies since they are residual claimants) and bondholders (whose earnings are set by fixed interest rates) of the takeover corporation? Don't they lose as their firm runs up lots of debt to pay high prices for the stock of the acquired firm? Also, doesn't the threat of a hostile takeover motivate managers to make decisions that boost profits in the short run but which harm the corporation's long-run profitability? And what about the fact that important parts of an acquired firm are often spun off after a hostile takeover, leaving a much smaller firm and many of its workers laid off? Shouldn't these losses be set against any gains that the shareholders of acquired firms receive, and isn't it possible that the losses are larger than the gains?

The evidence from the 1980s, when hostile takeovers were at their peak, suggests that the magnitude of the gains to the shareholders of a corporation that is targeted for a takeover is quite large.[8]

Winner's curse

Those who own something that others are bidding for should be expected to see their wealth increase. So it is not really surprising that takeover bids increase the wealth of the corporation's stockholders, although the magnitude of the gains is impressive. But that is not necessarily true for the stockholders of a corporation mounting a takeover bid. In a competitive bidding process it is possible to bid too much, and some believe that this is particularly true of the corporation making the winning bid. The winning bid is typically made by the bidder who is most optimistic about the value of the object of the bidding (see Thaler 1992). This is no problem when bidding for something the bidder wants for its subjective value (say, an antique piece of furniture) because the object probably is worth more to the winning bidder than to others. But when bidding for a productive asset (such as an offshore oil field) that is

---

[8] A study by the Office of the Chief Economist of the Securities and Exchange Commission (SEC) looked at 225 successful takeovers from 1981 to 1984 and found that the average premium to shareholders was 53.2 percent. In a follow-up study for 1985 and 1986, the premium was found to have dropped to an average of 37 and 33.6 percent, respectively. These averages probably understate the gains because they compare the stock price one month before the announcement of a takeover bid with the takeover price, and often the price begins increasing in response to rumors long before a formal offer is tendered (Jarrell, Brickley, and Netter 1988). These percentages represent huge gains in total dollars, amounting to $346 billion over the period 1977–86 (in 1986 dollars), according to one study (Jensen 1988, 21). We should point out that this estimate applied to all mergers and acquisitions (M&As), not just "hostile" takeovers. But "hostile" or not, takeovers consistently increase the value of the acquired firm's stock, and probably increase it more when the takeover is opposed by management than otherwise, because offering a higher price is a way around a reluctant management.

valued for its ability to generate a financial return, the value of the object is less dependent on who owns it.[9] Therefore, if the average bid is the best estimate of the value of the object, then there is a good chance that the winning bid is too high.

Economists have referred to this possible tendency to overbid as the "winner's curse." But for two very good reasons, the winner's curse may not be all that prevalent. First, people who are prone to fall victim to this curse are not likely to acquire (or retain) the control over the wealth necessary to keep bidding on valuable property, certainly not property as valuable as a corporation. Second, in many bidding situations, each bidder often receives information on how much others are willing to pay as the bidding process takes place and then adjusts his evaluation of the property accordingly. This is the case in corporate takeovers when offers to pay a certain price for a corporation's stock are made publicly.

So, we should expect that the winning bid for the stock of a corporation targeted for a takeover will fairly accurately reflect the value of that corporation to the winner and therefore will not greatly affect the wealth of the acquiring corporation's stockholders; we should also expect that the more competitive the bidding process, the closer the bid price to the actual stock value. And that is exactly what the evidence suggests.[10]

Bondholders

What about the possibility that the additional value that shareholders of a target corporation realize is paid for by losses to bondholders? For example, a takeover could increase the risk that either the acquiring or the acquired firm will suffer financial failure, while also increasing the possibility that one or both will experience very high profits. Shareholders stand to benefit from the high profits if they occur, and so they can find the expected value of their stock increasing because of the increased risk. The additional risk cannot generate a similar advantage for bondholders because the return to bondholders is fixed. They lose if the corporation

---

[9] In general, of course, the value of the asset will depend to some degree on who owns it. The highest bidder will likely have good reason to believe that she is better able to utilize the asset to create value. In the case of an oil field, the possibilities for one owner to obtain more wealth than another are probably quite limited. In the case of a corporation, the importance of management no doubt provides more opportunity for some owners to run the business more profitably than others.

[10] According to a 1987 study by economists Gregg Jarrell and Annette Paulsen, stockholders of acquiring corporations realized an average gain of between 1 and 2 percent on 663 successful bids from 1962 to 1985. Interestingly, and not surprisingly, as takeover activity increased, the return to acquiring firms decreased, with the average percentage return being 4.95 in the 1960s, 2.21 in the 1970s, and –0.04 (but statistically insignificant) in the 1980s (Jarrell and Paulsen 1989).

goes bankrupt, but they don't share in any increased profits if the corporation does extremely well. According to several studies of takeovers from the 1960s–1980s, however, takeovers do not impose losses on bondholders (Dennis and McConnell 1986; Lehn and Paulsen 1987). No doubt some bondholders suffer small losses while others realize small gains, but the best conclusion is that, even in the worst case, any losses to bondholders do not come anywhere close to offsetting the gains to stockholders.

Takeover mistakes

So far, we have been discussing the average wealth effect on shareholders and bondholders from takeovers. Just because the average wealth effect of a hostile takeover is positive does not mean that all such takeovers create wealth. People make mistakes in the market for corporate takeovers, just as they do in other markets and in all aspects of life. The question is not whether people make mistakes, but whether they are subjected to *self-correcting forces* when they do. The bidders subject to the winner's curse should themselves be the target of a takeover. The evidence suggests that in the case of hostile takeovers, they are. Economists Mark Mitchell and Kenneth Lehn asked, "Do bad bidders become good targets?" (Mitchell and Lehn 1990). Looking at takeovers between January 1980 and July 1988, they found that those firms resulting from takeovers that were wealth-reducing (according to the response of stock prices) were more likely to be challenged with a subsequent takeover than were firms whose takeovers had proven to be wealth-increasing. The market for corporate control does not prevent mistakes from being made, but it creates the information and motivation vital for correcting them when they occur (Mitchell and Lehn 1990).

Short-run versus long-run profits

If you are a corporate manager, you may be thinking that the threat of a takeover could motivate you to act in ways that increase the value of the corporate stock in the short run, but which are harmful to the profitability of the corporation in the long run. Is it true that managers are less likely to be ousted in a hostile takeover if they concentrate on short-run profits at the expense of long-run profits?

The answer might be "Yes" if the prices of corporate stock reacted only to short-run profits, but should we expect only short-run performance reports to control stock prices? If they did, then there would be money to be made by investors who took the long view. If a stock's price were inflated by short-run gains that were not likely to continue into the future, then investors could sell the stock in anticipation that future performance wouldn't likely match current performance, which means that investors could buy the stock back when its price declined with dampening future gains, pocketing capital gains between the difference in the current sell price and the future buy-back price. If the stock were depressed because of the impact of current poor earnings that were not expected to continue into the future, then investors could buy the stock currently at the depressed price and sell the stock when its price reflected higher earnings in the future. The buying and selling of the stock would mean that the company's long-term prospects would necessarily be taken into account in the market price of the stock (perhaps not perfectly, but only because of the costs of information on what will happen in the future and because of ever-present uncertainties about what the future will bring).

How should managers of the company be expected to make their decisions relating to short-run and long-term market forces? Consider a decision facing you as a manager on whether to commit to an expensive research and development project that will reduce profits over the near term but is expected to more than offset this loss with higher profits in the future. Should you be fearful that investing in this project will, because of the reduction in current profits, drive the price of your stock down, making your corporation more vulnerable to a hostile takeover? The answer is probably "No," if your estimate of the long-run profitability of the project is correct. A takeover is unlikely for two good reasons. First, the obvious fact that price–earnings ratios vary widely between different stocks provides compelling evidence that stock prices reflect more than current profits. Second, studies indicate that a corporation's stock price generally increases when the corporation announces increased spending on investment, and generally decreases when a reduction in investment spending is announced (McConnell and Muscarella 1985). A study by Bronwyn Hall found that, over the period 1976–85, the firms taken over by other firms did not have a higher ratio of research and development to sales than did firms in the same industry that were not taken over.[11] There is no reason for managers to become short-sighted because of the threat of a hostile takeover. Indeed, the best protection against a takeover, hostile or otherwise, is to make decisions that increase the long-run profitability of the corporation, even if those decisions temporarily reduce profits.

Break-ups

What about the fact that after a corporation is taken over it is sometimes broken up as the acquiring firm sells off divisions, often ones that have been profitable? Isn't this disruptive and inefficient? There is no doubt that takeovers are disruptive, particularly when they result in parts of the acquired firm being spun off. But disruption is not necessarily inefficient. Indeed, any economy has to motivate a rapid response to changing circumstances if it is to be efficient, and such a response is necessarily disruptive. Making the best use of resources in a world of advancing

---

[11] Hall's study is discussed by Jensen (1988).

technologies, improved opportunities, and global competition requires continuous disruption. The alternative is stagnation and relative decline.

Many of the mergers that took place in the 1960s and 1970s created large conglomerate structures that, even if efficient at the time, soon ceased to be efficient. Increased global competition began rewarding smaller firms with quicker response times to changing market conditions. Technology reduced the synergies that might have existed at one point by having different products produced within the same firms. It became less costly for firms to buy inputs and components from other firms, thus increasing the ability to specialize in their core competencies (in the vernacular of earlier chapters, transaction costs fell).

In many cases, these changes made the divisions of the corporation worth more as separate firms than as parts of the whole. Many managers, however, prefer to be in charge of a large firm rather than a small one and are reluctant to divest divisions that are worth more by themselves or as part of another organizational structure. This managerial reluctance of the 1960s and 1970s, and into the 1980s was partly responsible for depressed stock prices. Corporate raiders were able to take advantage of the depressed prices by buying a controlling interest in conglomerates and then increasing their total value through spinning off some of their divisions.[12]

Laid-off workers

Another complaint about the spinning off of divisions and downsizing that often accompanies takeovers is that workers are laid off. The claim is made that although stockholders may come out ahead, they do so at the expense of workers who lose their jobs. But the questions we need to consider are:

- Is this a valid criticism of takeovers?
- Which workers are most likely to be laid off and how big is the cost to the workers when compared to the gain to shareholders?

The fact that workers are laid off after hostile takeovers is consistent with the view that these takeovers promote *efficiency*. The most natural thing in the world for managers to do when sheltered against the full rigors of competition is to let the workforce grow larger than efficiency requires.[13]

---

[12] Others have explained the advantages of moving toward smaller and more focused firms with the existence of improved, more efficient capital markets that have made it attractive for firms to substitute reliance on external capital markets for internal capital markets, which favor multidivision firms (see Bhide 1990).

[13] This is most evident in what are often referred to as "bloated government bureaucracies," a fact that is partially attributable to the absence of the takeover option.

Economic progress occurs most rapidly when there are strong pressures to produce the same output with less effort – that is, to lay off workers when they are no longer needed. Taking this measure often causes dislocations in the short run, but in the long run it increases the availability of the most valuable resource (human effort and brainpower) to expand output elsewhere in the economy. So, a strong argument can be made that one of the advantages of the market for corporate control is the increased pressure on managers to control the size of their workforce.

Some of the efficiencies derived from hostile takeovers (and therefore some of the benefits to corporate shareholders) are the result of workers losing their jobs, but the evidence suggests that the workers most likely to lose their jobs are executives and managers, not line workers.[14] Moreover, even if many line workers are harmed in the case of losing their jobs from a hostile (and friendly) takeover, it does not mean that most of the workers harmed are necessarily made worse off by a *system* that encourages (or doesn't discourage) takeovers. Workers harmed in the case of their firm's takeover can receive offsetting benefits from the efficiency improvements they, the workers, realize through the lower price of the goods they buy. The lower prices can result because a multitude of other firms are taken over (or feel the threat of a takeover), the result of which is that their costs are more tightly controlled than would otherwise be the case.

---

[14] In one study, sixty-two hostile takeover attempts (fifty of which were successful) from 1984 to 1986 were examined (Bhagat, Shleifer, and Vishny 1990). According to this study, layoffs were common, but seldom exceeded 10 percent of the workforce and were typically far less than that. Also, it was estimated that the probability of being laid off was 70 percent higher for white-collar workers than for blue-collar workers. The jobs of managers, not those of workers on the line, were most at risk. In addition, layoffs at targeted firms that were not taken over were greater (as a percentage of the workforce) than those in firms that were taken over. This latter fact suggests that the threat of a takeover provides a strong incentive for efficiencies even when no takeover actually occurs.

Practical lessons for MBAs: collusion delusions and takeover threats

Two key lessons emerge from the economic way of thinking developed in this chapter. The first key lesson is that the prospects of overcoming competitive pricing pressures through collusion among producers should most often be set aside for what collusion really is, a snare and delusion. *If* all firms get together and agree to restrict production and *if* they do just that, then all producers can charge a higher price and make greater profits. That is the snare.

But the prospect of successful collusion is largely a delusion for most producers in most markets because the motivation behind the snare for the collusion is greater profits. Producers who are snared by the prospects of greater profits from collusive restrictions on industry output will naturally be snared again by the prospects of their expanding their productions when all producers have agreed to cut back on market supply. Cartels emerge and collapse under the same force, greed!

Managers who devote their own time and firm resources to the development of industry cartels can wreck their careers because price fixing and other forms of collusion are illegal under the United States' and world's antitrust laws (see the review of antitrust laws in online Readings 11.3 for this chapter), and because the resources used on forming cartels will most often be a waste for two reasons. First, rampant cheating on cartel rules can be expected among cartel members. Second, to the extent cartel members hold to their agreement, the higher price and profits will attract new entrants who can be expected to take up much of the production slack.

The second key lesson from this chapter comes from a myopic view of the force of market competition. MBA students naturally think of their firms' most serious competitive threat being other producers of the same or similar products (or other buyers of the same or similar resources). The threat of losing market share to competitors is understandably a pressing concern; however, MBA students should be ever mindful of the threat from takeover entrepreneurs who are forever scanning the business landscape for opportunities. Firms operating with something close to maximum efficiency have little to fear as the high buyout prices for efficiently operated firms should protect them from takeover entrepreneurs.

Rather, takeover entrepreneurs are most interested in firms that are being mismanaged, and sometimes the greater the extent of mismanagement the better (assuming the corrective policies for the mismanagement are transparent). Mismanaged firms harbor the potential for capital gains through replacing management teams, changing incentives, and adjusting the organizational and financial structures. Takeover entrepreneurs' operating rule is as common as it is simple in profitable businesses: buy low and sell high! The size of mismanaged firms should be of little consequence to many takeover entrepreneurs. Large mismanaged firms may require massive takeover funding, but such funding levels should be easily raised if there are massive profits to be made from correcting mismanagement on a large scale.

The rules are clear: Well-managed firms don't allow for much of a spread between the buying and selling prices. Poorly managed firms do. And as they pursue their trade, takeover entrepreneurs (much abused by management teams that are displaced in takeovers) tend to do the world an economic favor: They redeploy the world's scarce resources more efficiently. MBA students who attest that they work for grossly mismanaged firms should consider a career switch, to become a takeover entrepreneur (after first learning how to amass takeover capital and to correct mismanagement).

Of course, there are stock traders who never seek to buy out mismanaged firms. They simply short the stocks. This means they effectively borrow shares of mismanaged firms with the intent of repaying the shares they have shorted at a later date with shares that are bought at prices depressed by mismanagement revelations. The current shorting of the stocks of mismanaged firms can be depressed by the short trades.

Further readings online

R

Reading 11.1 The special case for regulating banking

Reading 11.2 Hostile takeover defenses

Reading 11.3 Antitrust laws in the United States

The bottom line

The key takeaways from chapter 11 are the following:

1 Firms in monopolistically competitive and oligopoly markets will follow the same production rule for profit maximization that perfect competitors and pure monopolies follow: they will produce where marginal cost and marginal revenue are equal.

2 Monopolistic competitors may earn zero economic profits in the long run, but they will not produce at the minimum of their long-run average cost curve.

3 The downward sloping demand faced by a dominant producer in a market can be derived from the gaps between the quantity demanded and supplied at various prices by all other smaller producers.

4 The profit incentive firms have to form cartels in their markets is a cause for the cartels' failures as members cheat on cartel production and pricing agreements.

5 At times, producers demand government regulation because such regulation can enable the producers to restrict their aggregate production and charge above-competitive prices.

6 Asset bubbles do happen, as they have happened. Economists have explained asset bubbles with theories founded in both rational and irrational decision making.

7   Although the analysis of imperfect competition tells us something about the working of real-world markets, it does not answer all the questions economists have asked. The theories presented here have by no means done a perfect job of predicting the consequences of imperfect competition. Thus our conclusions regarding the pricing and production behavior of firms in monopolistically competitive and oligopolistic markets are tentative at best.

8   Economists seeking to make solid, empirically verifiable predictions about market behavior rely almost exclusively on supply and demand and monopoly models. Although predictions based on those models may sometimes be wrong, they tend to be easier to use and may be more reliable than predictions based on models of imperfect competition. Predictions aside, it is important to remember that most markets are imperfect.

9   The competitiveness of the capital market – including the market for entire firms – will act as a discipline on managers who might believe that they can take advantage of their discretionary authority. Capital markets also induce managers to find the most cost-effective methods of production.

Review questions >>

1   Under what circumstances could a monopolistic competitor earn an economic profit in the long run?

2   To achieve the efficiency of perfect competition, must a market consist of numerous producers? If not, what other conditions are required?

3   How does the number of producers in a market affect the chances of forming a workable cartel?

4   How do the costs of entering a market affect the chances of forming a workable cartel?

5   Must a monopolist employer share the monopoly profits with the managers and workers? If not, why not? If so, what does "profit sharing" do to the monopolist's output level? Prices?

6   Should antitrust laws attempt to eliminate all forms of imperfect competition? Why or why not?

7   "In an economy in which resources can move among industries with relative ease, a cartel attempting to maximize short-term profits will sow the seeds of its own destruction." Explain.

8   How would a cartel in a market for a network good collude on price? Explain.

9   Suppose that the managers of a firm allowed their internal departments to act as little monopolies or suppose that the managers paid their workers more than the labor market would bear. What would happen in capital markets? To the firm?

10 Why would you expect the market for corporate control not to work very well when there is a stock-market bubble of the type experienced in the late 1990s and into 2000? Can you explain some of the unethical management behavior and deceptive accounting practices that came to light in the early 2000s as the result, at least partially, of a breakdown in the market for corporate control?

11 Would you expect government-run organizations to be more or less efficient than privately owned firms? Explain your answer with reference to capital markets.

12 As noted in chapter 8, Federal Judge Richard Posner has argued that one of the "failures of capitalism" has come in the form of executive pay schemes that encouraged excessive risk taking in financial markets. The judge has called for higher marginal tax rates on very high income earning executives (especially in financial firms) on the grounds that such rates will depress their take-home pay and discourage risk taking. How do you evaluate his argument?

13 Consider two compensation schemes for financial executives. (1) Executives are granted bonuses based on annual profits. (2) Excutives are granted shares of their companies' stock based on annual profits but the shares cannot be sold for a specified number of years. Which pay scheme will result in the greater risk taking on the part of the executives? What is your reasoning?

12

Competitive and monopsonistic labor markets

Labour, like all other things which are purchased and sold, and which may be increased or diminished in quantity, has its ... market price.

David Ricardo

Professional football players earn more than ministers or nurses. Social workers with college degrees generally earn less than truck drivers, who may not have completed high school. Even the best history professor and researcher probably earns less than a mediocre professor of accounting on most campuses.

Why do different occupations offer different salaries? Obviously not because of their relative worth to us as individuals. Just as there is a market for final goods and services – calculators, automobiles, dry cleaning – there is a market for labor as a resource in the production process. In competitive labor markets, the forces of supply and demand determine the wage rate workers receive.

By concentrating on the economic determinants of employment – those that relate most directly to production and promotion of a product – we do not mean to suggest that other factors are unimportant. Many noneconomic forces – such as social status, appearance, sex, race, and personal acquaintances – influence who is employed at what wage. Our purpose is simply to show how economic forces affect the wages paid and the number of employees hired. Such a model can show not only how labor markets work but also how attempts to legislate wages, such as minimum-wage laws, affect the labor market.

As noted in chapter 3, the general principles that govern product markets govern labor markets, and the general principles that govern labor markets also apply to the markets for other resources, principally land and capital. The use of land and capital has a price, called *rent* or *interest*, which is determined by supply and demand. Furthermore, land, capital, and labor are all subject to the law of diminishing marginal returns. Beyond a certain point and given a fixed quantity of at least one resource, more land, labor, or capital will produce less and less additional output.

But because workers have minds of their own, with their own interests which are not the same as those who hire them, there are important differences in the market for labor and the market for, say, turbines or asphalt, that warrant a separate consideration of labor markets. In this chapter we discuss some of those considerations as we examine how the way workers are paid, as well as how much, can motivate improved performance. This chapter refines and extends the analysis of competitive labor markets introduced in chapter 3, and then discusses labor markets in which the employment and wage levels are controlled by a single employer (or are dominated by a few employers, or employers that have some control over the wage rates they pay by their individual demand for workers).

In Part A, we develop the theory of wage determination under competitive and monopsonistic (or noncompetitive) labor market conditions. In chapter 4, we explained how a government-imposed minimum wage undermines employment opportunities for covered workers in competitive labor markets. In closing Part A, we explore how a minimum wage can actually increase employment in monopsonistic labor markets (but only if set appropriately).

In Part B, we extend our earlier discussion of the benefits and pitfalls of tying worker pay to performance. In online Perspective 12 we take up an issue that often perplexes many people, especially businesspeople, why professors have tenure and businesspeople (generally) do not.

Online
Perspective

Part A   Theory and public policy applications

The demand for and supply of labor

As noted in chapter 3, labor is a special kind of commodity, one in which people have a personal stake. The employer buys this commodity at a price: the *wage rate* the laborer receives in exchange for his or her efforts. In a competitive market, the interaction of supply and demand determines the price or wage rate of labor, as it does other prices. To understand why people earn what they do, we must first consider the determinants of the demand and supply of labor.

The demand for labor

As with a demand curve for a product, the demand curve for labor generally slopes downward. At higher wage rates, employers will hire fewer workers than at lower wage rates.

> The **demand for labor** is the inverse relationship between the real wage rate and the quantity of labor employed during a given period, everything else held constant.

The demand for labor is derived partly from the demand for the product produced. If there were no demand for mousetraps, there would be no need – no demand – for mousetrap makers. This general principle applies to all kinds of labor in an open market. Plumbers, textile workers, and writers can earn a living because there is a demand for the products and services they offer. The greater the demand for the products and for the labor needed to produce it, the higher the wage rate, everything else held equal.

> **Labor productivity** is how much a worker can produce per unit of time (per hour, week, month).

Labor productivity – that is, the quantity of output a laborer can produce in a given unit of time – is another critically important determinant of the demand for labor. The price of the final product puts a value on a laborer's output, but her productivity determines how much she can produce. Together, labor productivity and the market price of what is produced determine the market value of labor to employers, and ultimately the employers' demand for labor.

We can predict that the demand for labor will rise and fall with increases and decreases in both productivity and product price. Suppose, for example, that mousetraps are sold in a competitive market, in which their price is set by the interaction of supply and demand. Mousetrap production is likely subject to diminishing marginal returns. As more and more units of labor are added to a fixed quantity of plant and equipment, output expands by smaller and smaller increments.

You may recall from our review of firms' cost structures in chapters 7 and 8 that while there may be increasing marginal returns initially when a variable resource is added to a fixed quantity of another resource, the additional returns to additional units of the variable resource must, eventually, reverse course. This is a technological fact of life, not a matter of economic logic. We showed in chapter 9 that in competitive markets firms would produce in the range where their marginal cost curves are upward sloping. That is, they will produce where they encounter diminishing returns. This outcome is a matter of economic logic, and leads to the conclusion that firms will produce in an output range in which they confront diminishing returns. That is, within the relevant range of production in competitive markets, firms will find the marginal product of labor diminishing when more workers are hired, which is a good reason firms must see their wage rate fall before hiring additional workers. Additional workers simply can't add as much to output as prior workers, not because the additional workers are inherently less skilled or diligent, but rather because they simply are additional workers who must work with a fixed plant and equipment.

Column (2) of table 12.1 illustrates diminishing marginal returns. The first laborer contributes a marginal product – or additional output – of six mousetraps per hour. From that point on, the marginal product of each additional laborer diminishes. It drops from five mousetraps to four to three, and so on, until an extra laborer adds only one mousetrap to total hourly production.

The employer's problem, after production has reached the range of marginal diminishing returns, is to determine how many laborers to employ. She does so by considering the value of the marginal product of labor. Column (3) shows the market price of each mousetrap, which we assume here remains constant at $2. By multiplying that dollar price by the marginal product of each laborer (column [2]) the employer arrives at the value of each laborer's marginal product (column [4]). This is

Table 12.1 Computing the marginal value of labor

(1) Units of labor	(2) Marginal product of each laborer (per hour)	(3) Price of mousetraps in product market ($)	(4) Value of each laborer to employer (value of the marginal product) ([2] × [3]) ($)
First laborer	6	2	12
Second laborer	5	2	10
Third laborer	4	2	8
Fourth laborer	3	2	6
Fifth laborer	2	2	4
Sixth laborer	1	2	2

the highest amount that she will pay each laborer. She is willing to pay less (and thereby gain profit), but she will not pay more.

If the wage rate is slightly below $12 an hour, the employer will hire only one worker. She cannot justify hiring the second worker if she has to pay him $12 for an hour's work and receives only $10 worth of product in return. If the wage rate is slightly lower than $10, the employer can justify hiring two laborers. If the wage rate is lower still – say, slightly below $4 – the employer can hire as many as five workers.

Following this line of reasoning, we can conclude that the demand curve for mousetrap makers slopes, as do the demand curves for other goods, downward. That is, the lower the wage rate, everything else held constant, the greater the quantity of labor demanded. Theoretically, what is true of one employer must be true of all. That is, the market demand curve for a given type of labor must also slope downward (see figure 12.1).[1] Thus, profit-maximizing employers will not employ workers if they have to pay them more in wages and fringe benefits than they are worth. What they are worth depends on their *productivity* and the *market value* of what they produce.

If the price of the product, mousetraps in this example, increases, the employer's demand for mousetrap makers will shift – say, from D_1 to D_2 in figure 12.1. Because the market value of the laborers' marginal product has risen, producers now want to sell more mousetraps and will hire more workers to produce them. Look again at table 12.1. If the price of mousetraps rises from $2 to $4, the value of each worker's marginal product doubles. At a wage rate of $10 an hour, an employer can now hire as many as four workers. (Similarly, if the price of the final product falls below $2, the demand for workers will also fall – with the demand curve shifting from D_1 to D_3 in figure 12.1.)

When technological change improves worker productivity, the demand for workers may increase. If workers produce more, the value of their marginal product may rise, and employers may then be able to hire more of them. Such is not always the case, however. Sometimes an increase in worker productivity decreases the demand for labor. For instance, if worker productivity increases throughout the industry,

---

[1] The reader may get the impression that the market demand curve for labor is derived by horizontally summing the value of marginal product curves of individual firms, which are derived directly from tables such as table 12.1. Strictly speaking, that is not necessarily the case, mainly because the total number of workers hired by all firms can affect the supply of the final product (mousetraps), which can cause the market price of the final product to fall. The fall in the price of the final product can undercut the value of additional workers (since their value equals their marginal products multiplied by market price). This means that the true market demand curve can be more inelastic than the sum of all individual employers' demand curves. However, these are refinements of theory that are considered in other, more advanced textbooks and courses.

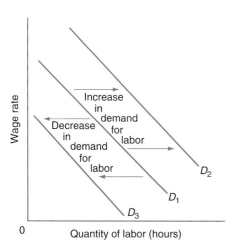

Figure 12.1 Shift in demand for labor
The demand for labor, as with all other demand curves, slopes downward. An increase in the demand for labor will cause a rightward shift in the demand curve, from D_1 to D_2. A decrease will cause the leftward shift, to D_3.

rather than in just one or two firms, more mousetraps may be offered on the market, depressing the equilibrium price. The drop in price reduces the value of the workers' marginal product and may outweigh the favorable effect of the increase in productivity. In such cases the demand for labor will fall. Consumers will pay less, but employees in the mousetrap industry will have fewer employment opportunities and earn less.

The supply of labor

The supply curve for labor generally slopes upward. As explained briefly in chapter 3, at higher wage rates, more workers will be willing to work longer hours than at lower wage rates (see figure 12.2). If you survey your MBA classmates, for example, you will probably find that more of them would be willing to work at a job that pays $50 an hour than would work for $20 an hour. (At $500 an hour, most would be willing to work without hesitation, aside from a few lawyers, surgeons, and consultants whose opportunity cost exceeds $500 an hour!)

The supply of labor depends on the opportunity cost of a worker's time. Workers can do many different things with their time. They can use it to construct mousetraps, to do other jobs, to go fishing, and so on. Weighing the opportunity cost of each activity, the worker will allocate her time so that the

> The **supply of labor** is the assumed positive relationship between the real wage rate and the number of workers (or work hours) offered for employment during a given period, everything else held constant.

marginal benefit of an hour spent doing one thing will equal the marginal benefit of time that could be used elsewhere. Because some kinds of work are unpleasant, workers will require a wage to make up for the time lost from leisure activities such as fishing. To earn a given wage, a rational worker will give up the activities she

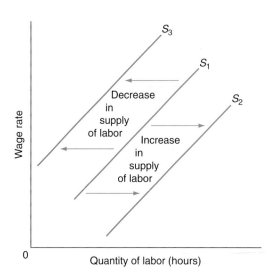

Figure 12.2 Shift in the supply of labor
The supply curve for labor slopes
upward. An increase in the supply of
labor will cause a rightward shift in the
supply curve from S_1 to S_2. A decrease
in the supply of labor will cause a
leftward shift in the supply curve, from
S_1 to S_3.

values least. To allocate even more time to a job (and give up more valuable leisure-time activities), a worker will require a higher wage.

Given this cost–benefit trade-off, employers who want to increase production have two options. They can hire additional workers or ask the same workers to work longer hours. Those who are currently working for $20 an hour must value time spent elsewhere at less than $20 an hour. To attract other workers (people who value their time spent elsewhere at more than $20 an hour) employers will have to raise the wage rate, perhaps to $22 an hour. To convince current workers to put in longer hours – to give up more attractive alternative activities – employers will also have to raise wage rates. In either case, the labor supply curve slopes upward. More labor is supplied at higher wages.[2]

The supply curve for labor will shift if the value of employees' alternatives changes. For example, if the wage that mousetrap makers can earn in toy production goes up, the value of their time will increase. The supply of labor to the mousetrap industry should then decrease, shifting upward and to the left from S_1 to S_3 in figure 12.2. This shift in the labor supply curve means that less labor will be offered at any given wage rate, in a particular labor market. To hire the same quantity of labor – to keep mousetrap makers from going over to the toy industry – the employer must increase the wage rate.

---

[2] We note in passing that it is possible for the labor supply curve to bend backwards beyond some high wage rate. That is, beyond some wage rate, workers will choose to use some of their higher incomes to "buy" additional leisure, which means they will provide a lower quantity of labor on the market. While such a backward bending supply curve of labor is possible, we focus our attention on the upward sloping curve because that is the usual case.

The same general effect will occur if workers' valuation of their leisure time changes. Because most people attach a high value to time spent with their families on holidays, employers who want to maintain operations on holidays generally have to pay a premium for workers' time. The supply curve for labor on holidays lies above and to the left of the regular supply curve. Conversely, if for any reason the value of workers' alternatives decreases, the supply curve for labor will shift down to the right. If wages in the toy industry fall, for instance, more workers will want to move into the mousetrap business, increasing the labor supply in the mousetrap market.

Equilibrium in the labor market

A competitive market is one in which neither the individual employer nor the individual employee has the power to influence the wage rate. Such a market is shown in figure 12.3. Given the supply curve S and the demand curve D, the wage rate will settle at W_1, and the quantity of labor employed will be Q_2. At that combination, defined by the intersection of the supply and demand curves, those who are willing to work for wage W_1 can find jobs.

The equilibrium wage rate is determined much the same way as the prices of goods and services are established. At a wage rate of W_2, the quantity of labor employers will hire is Q_1, whereas the quantity of workers willing to work is Q_3. In other words, at that wage rate a *surplus* of labor exists. Note that all the workers in this surplus group except the last one are willing to work for less than W_2. That is, up to Q_3, the supply curve lies below W_2. The opportunity cost of these workers' time is less than W_2. They can be expected to accept a lower wage, and over time they will begin to offer to work for less than W_2. Other unemployed and employed workers must then compete by accepting still lower wages. In this manner, the wage rate will

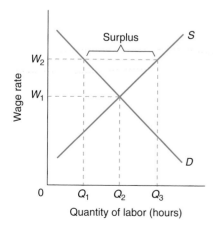

Figure 12.3 Equilibrium in the labor market
Given the supply and demand curves for labor S and D, the equilibrium wage will be W_1 and the equilibrium quantity of labor hired Q_2. If the wage rate rises to W_2, a surplus of labor will develop, equal to the difference between Q_3 and Q_1.

fall toward W_1. In the process, the quantity of labor that employers want to hire will expand from Q_1 toward Q_2.

Meanwhile, the falling wage rate will convince some workers to take another opportunity, such as going fishing or getting another job. As they withdraw from this market, the quantity of labor supplied will decline from Q_3 toward Q_2. The quantity supplied will meet the quantity demanded – meaning no labor surplus – at a wage rate of W_1.

In practice, the money wage rate – the number of dollars earned per hour – may not fall. Instead, the general price level may increase while the money wage rate remains constant. But the real wage rate – that is, what the money wage rate will buy – still falls, producing the same general effects: fewer laborers willing to work, and more workers demanded by employers. When economists talk about wage increases or decreases, they mean changes in the real wage rate, or in the purchasing power of a worker's paycheck.

Conversely, if the wage rate falls below W_1, the quantity of labor demanded by employers will exceed the quantity supplied, creating a *shortage*. Employers, eager to hire more workers at the new cheap wage, will compete for the scarce labor by offering slightly higher wages. The quantity of labor offered on the market will increase, but at the same time these slightly higher wages will cause some employers to cut back on their hiring. In short, in a competitive market, the wage rate will rise toward W_1, the equilibrium wage rate.

[See online Video Module 12.1 Competitive labor markets]

Why wage rates differ

In a world of identical workers doing equivalent jobs under conditions of perfect competition, everyone would earn the same wage. In the real world, of course, workers differ, jobs differ, and various institutional factors reduce the competitiveness of labor markets. Some workers therefore earn higher wages than others. Indeed, the differences in wages can be inordinately large. (Compare the hourly earnings of actor Tom Hanks to those of elementary school teachers.) Wages differ for many reasons, including differences in the nonmonetary benefits (or costs) of different jobs. Conditions in different labor markets may differ in such a way as to cause wages to differ. Differences in the inherent abilities and acquired skills of workers can generate substantial differences in wages. Finally, discrimination against various groups often lowers the wages of people in those groups.

Differences in nonmonetary benefits

So far, we have been speaking as though the wage rate were the key determinant of employment. What about job satisfaction and the way employers treat their employees – are these issues not important? Some people accept lower wages in order to live in the Appalachians or the Rockies. College professors forgo more lucrative work to be able to teach, write, and set their own work schedules. The congeniality of colleagues is another significant nonmonetary benefit that influences where and how much people work. Power, status, and public attention also figure in career decisions.

The trade-offs between the monetary and nonmonetary rewards of work will affect the wage rates for specific jobs. The more value people place on the nonmonetary benefits of a given job, the greater the labor supply. Added to wages, nonmonetary benefits could shift the labor supply curve from S_1 to S_2 in figure 12.4, lowering the wage rate from W_2 to W_1. Even though the money wage rate is lower, however, workers are better off according to their own values. At a wage rate of W_1, their nonmonetary benefits equal the vertical distance between points a and b, making their full wage equal to W_3. The *full wage rate* is the sum of the money wage rate and the monetary equivalent of the nonmonetary benefits of a job.

Workers who complain that they are paid less than workers in other occupations often fail to consider their full wages (money wage plus nonmonetary benefits). The worker with a lower monetary wage may be receiving more nonmonetary rewards, including comfortable surroundings, freedom from intense pressure, and so on. The worker with the higher money wage may actually be earning a lower full wage than the worker with nonmonetary income. Certainly many executives must wonder whether their high salaries compensate them for their lost home life and leisure time, and teachers who envy the higher salaries of coaches should recognize that a somewhat higher wage rate is necessary to offset the increased risk of being fired that goes with coaching.

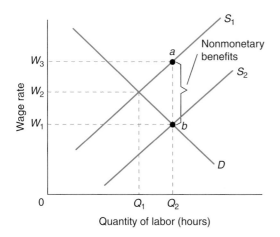

Figure 12.4 The effect of nonmonetary rewards on wage rates
The supply of labor is greater for jobs offering nonmonetary benefits – S_2 rather than S_1. Given a constant demand for labor, the wage rate will be W_2 for workers who do not receive nonmonetary benefits and W_1 for workers who do. Even though wages are lower when nonmonetary benefits are offered, workers are still better off; they earn a total wage equal, according to their own values, to W_3.

Employers can benefit from providing employees with nonwage benefits. A favorable working climate attracts more workers at lower wages. Although providing benefits can be costly, doing so is worthwhile as long as providing the benefit serves to lower wages more than raise other labor costs. Some nonwage benefits, such as air conditioning and low noise levels, also raise worker productivity. Needless to say, an employer cannot justify unlimited nonwage benefits. Employers will not pay more in wages – monetary or nonmonetary – than a worker is worth. In a competitive labor market they will tend to pay all employees a wage rate equal to the value added by the marginal employee – the last one hired.

Lax work demands as a fringe benefit

We also should note a widely used, but often unrecognized, fringe benefit that varies across workplaces: lax work demands. It is easy to assume that the only way employers can remain competitive in pricing their final products is for employers to impose heavy work demands on their workers, which can lead to higher productivity (and a higher demand for workers). Lax work demands can do the opposite, which is why they should be avoided – or so it might be thought, without considering the effect of lax work demands on the supply of labor. The lax work demands can certainly reduce the demand for labor, but they can increase the supply of labor even more.

Why? Workers may just prefer to work under such relaxed conditions. The resulting lower wage rate can more than compensate employers for their lost productivity. That is, employers might lose $1 an hour by lowering their work demands, but their wage rate can fall by even more, say, by $1.50 an hour because of the increased labor supply. Workers can also be better off, on balance. Workers may lose $1.50 an hour in pay but gain $2 an hour in value from not having to work as hard. By relaxing work demands under such labor market conditions, employers can actually be more competitive in their final product markets because their overall labor costs are not as high as those of employers with more pressing work demands. Just as firms may have to compete on wages and fringe benefits, employers also may have to compete on the production demands they place on their workers. We have talked about "shirking" throughout this text in, admittedly, somewhat derogatory terms. This is only because we have always implicitly assumed that "shirking" amounts to workers (and all agents) not working up to the demands placed on them and not meeting their contractual obligations to justify their wages. Employers must be ever-mindful that the division between laxed work demands and shirking can be as thin as a knife's edge. That is, some shirking (that is, relaxed work demands) is not shirking at all, but rather a fringe benefit that can enhance firm profitability. Keep this qualification in mind as you read our discussions of shirking in the rest of the chapter.

Differences among markets

Differences in nonmonetary benefits explain only part of the observed differences in wage rates. Supply and demand conditions may differ between labor markets. As figure 12.5(a) shows, given a constant supply of labor, S, a greater demand for labor will mean a higher wage rate. Conversely (figure 12.5(b)), given a constant demand for labor, a greater supply of labor will mean a lower wage rate. Depending on the relative conditions in different markets, wages may – or may not – differ significantly.

People in different lines of work may also earn different wages because consumers value the products they produce differently. Automobile workers may earn more than textile workers because people are willing to pay more for automobiles than for clothing. Consumer preferences contribute to differences in the value of the marginal product of labor and ultimately in the demand for labor.

By themselves, relative product values cannot explain long-run differences in wages. Unless textile work offers compensating nonmonetary benefits, laborers in that industry will be attracted to higher wages elsewhere, perhaps in the automobile industry. The supply of labor in the automobile industry will rise and the wage rate will fall. In the long run, the wage differential will decrease or even disappear.

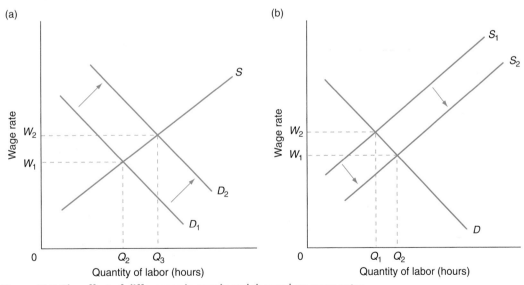

Figure 12.5 The effect of differences in supply and demand on wage rates

In competitive labor markets, higher demand for labor (D_2 in panel [a]) will bring a higher wage rate. A higher supply of labor (S_2 in panel [b]) will bring a lower wage rate.

Certain factors may perpetuate the money wage differential in spite of competitive market pressures. Textile workers who enjoy living in North or South Carolina may resist moving to Detroit, Michigan, where automobiles are manufactured. In that case, the nonmonetary benefits associated with textile work offset the difference in money wages. In addition, the cost of acquiring the skills needed for automobile work may act as a barrier to movement between industries – a problem we shall address shortly.

Differences among workers

Differences in labor markets do not explain wage differences among people in the same line of work. *Differences among workers* must be responsible for that disparity. Some people are more attractive to employers. Employers must pay such workers more because their services are eagerly sought after, but they can afford to pay them more because their marginal product is greater.

Professional basketball star forward Kobe Bryant earns an extremely high salary. The Los Angeles Lakers are willing to pay him well both because of his popularity among fans – Bryant's presence in the lineup attracts bigger crowds – and because he is successful. Because a winning team generally attracts more support than a losing one, Bryant's presence indirectly boosts the team's earnings. In other words, Bryant is in a labor submarket like that shown by curve D_2 in figure 12.5(a). Other players are in submarket D_1.

Differences in skill may also account for differences in wages. Most wages are paid not just for a worker's effort but also for the use of what economists call **human capital**.

Human capital is the acquired skills and productive capacity of workers.

We usually think of capital as plant and equipment – for instance, a factory building and the machines it contains. A capital good is most fundamentally defined, however, as something produced or developed for use in the production of something else. In this sense, capital goods include the education or skill a person acquires for use in the production process. The educated worker, whether a top-notch mechanic or a registered nurse, holds within herself capital assets that earn a specific rate of return. In pursuing professional skills, the worker, in much the same way as the business entrepreneur, takes the risk that the acquired assets will become outmoded before they are fully used. Students who have majored in history expecting to teach have all too often found that their investment in human capital did not pay off. Many were unable to get teaching jobs in their chosen field. Some have ended up as bartenders and cab drivers.

Finally, wage differences can result from *social discrimination* – whether sexual, racial, religious, ethnic, or political. Potential employees are easily grouped according to identifiable characteristics, such as sex or skin color. If employment decisions are made primarily on the basis of the group to which the individual belongs, rather than on individual merit, a form of discrimination (called "statistical discrimination") has occurred. Thus a qualified woman may not be considered for an executive job because women as a group are excluded. To the extent that employers prefer to work with certain groups, such as whites or men, the labor market will be segmented. Employees in different submarkets, with different demand curves and wage differentials, will be unable to move easily from one market to another. The barriers to the free movement of workers allow wage differences that have little to do with productivity to persist.

Competition among producers in the market for final goods can weaken (but not necessarily eliminate) discriminatory practices. Suppose that employers harbor a deep-seated prejudice against women, which depresses the market demand and wage rates for female workers. If women are just as productive as men, an enterprising producer can hire women, pay them less, undersell the other suppliers, and take away part of their markets. Under competitive pressure, employers will start to hire women in order to keep their market shares. As a result, the demand for women workers will rise whereas the demand for men will fall. Such competition may not eliminate the wage differential between men and women, but it can reduce it. In industries in which employers face little competition, employment discrimination is more likely, according to a substantial number of econometric studies.[3]

Monopsonistic labor markets

Competition is bad for those who have to compete. Not only as producers but as employers, firms would rather control competitive forces than be controlled by them. They would like to pay employees less than the market wage – but competition does not give them that choice.

Similarly, workers find that competition for jobs prevents them from earning more than the market wage. Thus doctors, truck drivers, and barbers have an interest in restricting competition in their labor markets. Acting as a group, they can acquire some control over their employment opportunities and wages.

Such power is difficult to maintain without the support of the law or the threat of violence, whether real or imagined. It comes at the expense of the consumer, who will have fewer goods and services to choose from at higher prices. As always, one group's exercise of power leads not only to market inefficiencies but also to other groups' attempts to counteract it. The end result can be a reduction in the general welfare of the community.

This section examines both employer and employee power in the labor market; the conditions that allow it to persist; its influence on the allocation of resources; and its effects on the real incomes of workers, consumers, and entrepreneurs.

---

[3] For reviews of the economic literature on labor market discrimination, see Alexis 1974; Marshall 1974; Cain 1986; and Gunderson 1989.

The monopsonistic employer

Power is never complete; the limitations of knowledge and the forces of law, custom and the market always circumscribe it. Within limits, employers can hire and fire and can decide what products to produce and what type of labor to employ. But certain laws restrict the conditions of employment (working hours, working environment), as well as employers' ability to discriminate among employees on the basis of sex, race, age, or religious affiliation. Competition imposes additional constraints. In a highly competitive labor market, an employer who offers very low wages will be outbid by others who want to hire workers. Competition for labor pushes wages up to a certain level, forcing some employers to withdraw from the market but permitting others to hire at the going wage rate.[4]

A **pure monopsony** is the sole buyer of a good, service, or resource protected by barriers to entry by other employers or barriers to exit by employees.

For the individual employer, then, the freedom of the competitive market is a highly constrained freedom. Not so, however, for those lucky employers who enjoy the power of a monopsony. (Monopsony should not be confused with *monopoly*, the single seller of a good and service.) The term is most frequently used to indicate the sole or dominant employer of labor in a given market. A good example of a monopsony is a large coal-mining company in a small town with no other industry. A firm that is not a sole employer but that dominates the market for a certain type of labor is said to have monopsony power. By reducing the demand for workers' services, monopsony power allows employers to suppress the wage rate.

Monopsony power is the ability of a producer to alter the price of a resource by changing the quantity employed.

The cost of labor

Monopsony power reduces the costs of competitive hiring. Assume that the downward sloping demand curve D in figure 12.6 shows the market demand for workers, and the upward sloping supply curve S shows the number of workers willing to work at various wage rates. If all firms act independently – that is, if they compete with one another – the market wage rate will settle at W_2, and the number of workers hired will be Q_2. At lower wage rates, such as W_1, shortages will develop. As the market demand curve indicates, employers will be willing to pay more than W_1. If a shortage exists, the market wage will be bid up to W_2.

An increase in the wage rate will encourage more workers to seek jobs. As long as there is a shortage, however, the competitive bidding imposes costs on employers.

---

[4] Competitors who do not hire influence the wage rate just as much as those who do; their presence on the sidelines keeps the price from falling. If a firm lowers its wages, other employers may move into the market and hire away part of the workforce.

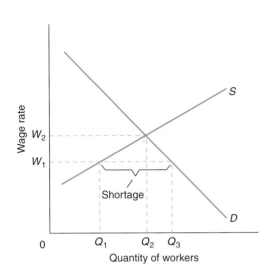

Figure 12.6 The competitive labor market
In a competitive market, the equilibrium wage rate will be W_2. Lower wage rates, such as W_1, would create a labor shortage, and employers would offer a higher wage to compete for the available workers. In pushing up the wage rate to the equilibrium level, employers impose costs on one another. They must pay higher wages not only to new employees but also to all current employees, in order to keep them.

The firm that offers a wage higher than W_1 forces other firms to offer a comparable wage to retain their current employees. If those firms want to acquire additional workers, they may have to offer an even higher wage. As they bid the wage up, firms impose reciprocal costs on one another, as at an auction.

Because any increase in wages paid to one worker must be extended to all, the total cost to all employers of hiring even one worker at a higher wage can be substantial when the employment level is already large. If the wage rises from W_1 to W_2 in figure 12.6, the total wage bill for the first Q_1 workers rises by the wage increase W_2 minus W_1 times Q_1 workers. Table 12.2 shows how the effect of a wage increase is multiplied when it must be extended to other workers. Columns (1) and (2) reflect the assumption that as the wage rate rises, more workers will accept jobs. If only one worker is demanded, he can be hired for $20,000. The firm's total wage bill will also be $20,000 (column [3]). If two workers are demanded, and the second worker will not work for less than $22,000, the salary of the first worker must also be raised to $22,000. The cost of the second worker is therefore $24,000 (column [4]): $22,000 for his services plus the $2,000 rise that must be given to the first worker.

The cost of additional workers can be similarly derived. When the sixth worker is added, she must be offered $30,000 and the other five workers must each be given a $2,000 rise. The cost of adding this new worker, called the marginal cost of labor, has risen to $40,000.

The **marginal cost of labor** is the additional cost to the firm of expanding employment by one additional worker.

Table 12.2 **Market demand for workers**

(1) No. of workers willing to work	(2) Annual wage of each worker ($)	(3) Total wage bill ([1] × [2]) ($)	(4) Marginal cost of additional worker (change in [3]) ($)
1	20,000	20,000	20,000
2	22,000	44,000	24,000
3	24,000	72,000	28,000
4	26,000	104,000	32,000
5	28,000	140,000	36,000
6	30,000	180,000	40,000

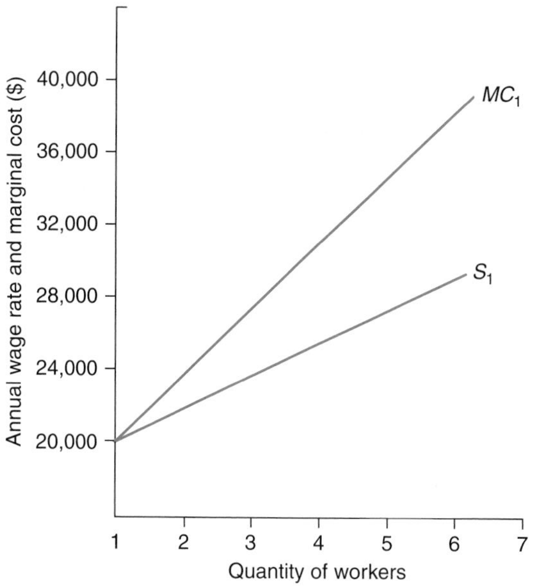

Figure 12.7 The marginal cost of labor

The marginal cost of hiring additional workers is greater than the wages that must be paid to the new workers; therefore, the marginal cost of labor curve lies above the labor supply curve.

Figure 12.7, based on columns (1) and (4) of table 12.2, shows the marginal cost of labor graphically. The marginal cost curve lies above the supply curve because the cost of each new worker hired (beyond the first worker) is greater than the worker's salary.

The monopsonistic hiring decision

The monopsonistic employer does not get caught in the competitive bind. By definition, it is the only or dominant employer. Like a monopolist, the monopsonist can search through the various wage–quantity combinations on the labor

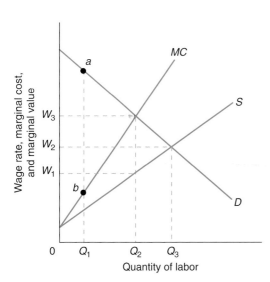

Figure 12.8 The monopsonist
The monopsonist will hire up to the point at which the marginal value of the last worker, shown by the demand curve for labor, equals his marginal cost. For this monopsonistic employer, the optimum number of workers is Q_2. The monopsonist must pay only W_1 for that number of workers – less than the competitive wage level, W_2.

supply curve for the one that maximizes profits. The monopsonist will keep hiring more workers as long as their contribution to revenues is greater than their additional cost, as the marginal cost of labor curve MC in figure 12.8 shows. To maximize profits, in other words, the monopsonist will hire until the marginal cost of the last worker hired (MC) equals his marginal value, as shown by demand curve for labor. Given the demand for labor, D, the monopsonist's optimal employment level will be Q_2, where the marginal cost and demand for labor curves intersect. Note that that level is lower than the competitive employment level, Q_3.

Why hire where marginal cost equals marginal value? Suppose the monopsonist employed fewer workers – say, Q_1. The marginal value of worker Q_1 would be high (point a), while her marginal cost would be low (point b). The monopsonist would be forgoing profits by hiring only Q_1 workers. Beyond Q_2 workers, the reverse would be true. The marginal cost of each new worker would be greater than her marginal value. Hiring more than Q_2 workers would reduce profits.

After the monopsonist has chosen the employment level Q_2, it pays workers no more than is required by the labor supply curve, S. In figure 12.8, the monopsonist must pay only W_1 – much less than the wage that would be paid in a competitive labor market, W_2. In other words, the monopsonist hires fewer workers and pays them less than does an employer in a competitive labor market.

It is the monopsonistic firm's power to reduce the number of workers hired that enables it to hold wages below the competitive level. In a competitive labor market, if one firm attempts to cut employment and reduce wages, it will not be able to keep its business going, for workers will depart to other employers willing to pay the going market wage. The individual firm is not large enough in relation to the entire labor market to exercise monopsony power; therefore, it must reluctantly accept the market wage, W_2, as a given.

[See online Video Module 12.2 Monopsony labor markets]

Employer cartels: monopsony power through collusion

Envying the power of the monopsonist, competitive employers may attempt to organize a cartel. An *employer cartel* is any organization of employers that seeks to restrict the number of workers hired in order to lower wages and increase profits.

The usual way of lowering employment is to establish restrictive employment rules that limit the movement of workers from one job to another. Such rules tend to reduce the demand for labor. In figure 12.9, demand falls from D_1 to D_2. As a result, the wage rate drops, from W_2 to W_1, and employment falls, from Q_3 to Q_2. Although the method of limiting employment is different from that used in monopsony, the effect is the same. Whether the monopsonistic firm equates marginal cost with marginal value (shown by curve D_1) or the employer cartel reduces the demand for labor (to D_2), employment still drops to Q_2. In both cases, workers earn a wage rate of W_1 – less than the competitive wage.

One industry in which employers have tried to cartelize the labor market is professional sports. Owners of teams have developed complex rules governing the hiring of athletes. In the National Football League (NFL), for example, teams acquire rights to negotiate with promising college players through an annual draft. After one team has drafted a player, no other team in the league can negotiate with him (unless he remains unsigned until the next year's draft). Teams can buy and sell draft rights as

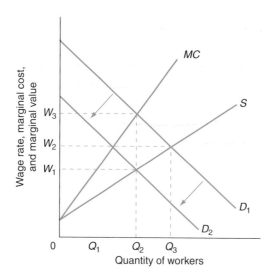

Figure 12.9 The employer cartel
To achieve the same results as a monopsonist, the employer cartel will devise restrictive employment rules that artificially reduce market demand to D_2. The reduced demand allows cartel members to hire only Q_2 workers at wage W_1 – significantly less than the competitive wage, W_2.

well as rights to players already drafted, but within leagues they are prohibited from competing directly with one another for players' services. Violations of these rules carry stiff penalties, including revocation of a team's franchise.

Monopsony and the minimum wage

In chapter 4, we discussed at length the impact of the imposition of a federal minimum wage on competitive labor markets. We noted how a minimum wage would curb employment and cause employers to try to offset the added labor costs associated with a minimum wage with reductions in fringe benefits and hikes in work demands. The analysis of a minimum wage under monopsony market conditions is much more straightforward; however, the employment consequence may be surprising.

Consider again figure 12.9, used in our analysis of an employer cartel. Suppose that the monopsony (or the employer cartel) restricts labor market demand and pays a wage of W_1 and hires Q_2 workers because its marginal cost of labor is the MC curve. Now, suppose that the government imposes a minimum wage equal to the competitive wage rate, W_2. W_2 then becomes the monopsonist's marginal cost of labor curve up to where W_2 intersects D_1.

If the monopsony weights off its marginal cost of labor, now W_2, it can increase its profits by hiring labor up to Q_3, the competitive equilibrium employment level. Note that, perhaps surprisingly, the imposition of the minimum wage under monopoly causes employment to rise from Q_2 to Q_3. The monopsonist expands employment beyond Q_2 because by doing so it can make additional profits (over and above what they would otherwise have been, not over and above what they would have been had the monopsonist remained unconstrained in the wage rate now paid by the minimum wage). Moreover, there are no adjustments in fringe benefits or work demands that the monopsonist can make to mute the impact of the minimum wage. You may recall that, in chapter 4, competitive employers adjusted their fringe benefits and work demands in response to the minimum wage, but that was only because the minimum wage set up an initial disequilibrium in the labor market in the form of a shortage. In the case of the monopsonist, the monopsonist does not end up in a disequilibrium: the quantity of labor demands at W_2 is exactly equal to the quantity of labor supplied at W_2.

Does this mean that the minimum wage does not undercut the employment opportunities for the covered workers? No, not necessarily. First, the minimum wage could be set so high – say, above W_3 in figure 12.9 – that even monopsonies would curb their employment when faced with a minimum wage. Second, monopsonies could control a minor portion of all labor markets, meaning that the negative employment effects in competitive labor markets more than offset any possible positive employment effects in the more limited monopsony-controlled labor markets. The presence of some monopsonized markets could help explain why. As mentioned in chapter 4, the measured negative employment effects of minimum-wage increases have generally been small.[5]

For a discussion of the economics of academic tenure, see online Perspective 12, Why professors have tenure and businesspeople don't.

Online Perspective 12
Why professors have tenure
and businesspeople don't

Part B   Organizational economics and management

Paying for performance

Up to this point in the chapter, our discussion has focused on how labor "markets" work, and our interest has been on how the wage rate and other benefits are determined by the broad forces of supply and demand. However, markets must ultimately work with the interests of workers in mind. The problem most firms must solve is how to get workers to do what they are supposed to do, which is to work effectively and efficiently together for the creation of firm profits. This is an extraordinarily difficult task. There is a lot of trial and error in business, especially as it relates to how workers are paid. At the same time, thinking conceptually about the payment/incentive problem can help firms moderate the extent of errors in business.

One of the most fundamental rules of economics, and the *raison d'être* for the discussions in the "organizational economics and management" sections, is that if you offer people a greater reward, then they will do more of whatever is being rewarded, everything else being equal. Many people find this proposition to be objectionable because it implies that people can, to one degree or another, be "bought." Admittedly, incentives may not matter in all forms of behavior. Some

---

[5] See online Reading 4.1 for references to the econometric studies on the employment effects of the minimum wage.

people will sacrifice their lives rather than forsake a strongly held principle. However, the proposition that incentives matter applies to a sufficiently wide range of behaviors to be considered a "rule" that managers are well advised to keep in mind: pay someone a higher wage – such as time and a half – and they will work longer days. Pay them double time, and they will even work holidays. There is some rate of pay at which a lot of people will work almost any time of the day or night on any day of the year.

This rule for incentives is not applicable only to the workplace. Parents know that one of the best ways to get their children to take out the garbage is to tie their allowance to that chore. According to research, if mentally ill, institutionalized patients are paid for the simple tasks they are assigned (for example, sweeping a room or picking up trash), they will perform them with greater regularity.[6]

Even pigeons, well known for having the lowest form of bird brain, respond to incentives. Granted, pigeons may never be able to grasp the concept of monetary rewards (offering them a dollar won't enlist much of a response), but pigeons apparently know how to respond to food rewards (offer a nut in the palm of your outstretched hand and a whole flock will descend and maybe leave their mark on your shoulder). From research, we also know that pigeons are willing to work – measured by how many times they peck colored levers in their cages – to get food pellets, and they will work harder if the reward for pecking is raised. Researchers have also been able to get pigeons to loaf on the job, just as humans do. How? Simply lower their rate of "pay."[7]

The "right" pay

The rules of incentives appear to encourage managers everywhere to link workers' pay to some measure of performance. Clearly, as noted earlier in this book, the lone worker in a single proprietorship has the "right" incentive. His or her reward is the same as the reward for the whole firm. The full cost of any shirking is borne by the worker/owner. However, such a congruence between the rewards of the owners and workers is duplicated nowhere else. Opportunities to shirk abound in large organizations.[8]

---

[6] For a review of the experimental literature on the connection between pay and performance of institutionalized patients, see McKenzie and Tullock 1994, chapter 4.

[7] For a review of the relevant literature, again see McKenzie and Tullock 1994, chapter 4.

[8] There are always "gaps" between the goals of the owners and the workers, and the greater the number of workers, typically, the greater the gap in incentives. In very large firms, workers have greatly impaired incentives to pursue the goals of the owners. Layers of bureaucracy separate workers from the owners, communications about the firm's goals are often imperfect, and each worker at the bottom of the firm's pyramid can reason that her contributions to the

How can managers improve incentives, reduce shirking, and increase worker productivity? The well-known management guru Frederick Taylor (1895) strongly recommended piece-rate pay as a means of partially solving what he termed the "labor problem," but both management and labor largely ignored him in his own time and for the good reasons discussed in this chapter. As the story referenced above, paying workers on a piece rate doesn't guarantee diligent performance.

There is a multitude of ways of getting workers to perform that don't involve money pay, and many of them are studied in various disciplines, one being organizational behavior, which draws on the principles of psychology. Managers do need to think about patting workers on the back once in a while, clearly defining corporate goals, communicating goals in a clear and forceful manner, and exerting leadership.

Southwest Airlines, one of the more aggressive, cost-conscious, and profitable airlines, motivates its workers by creating what one analyst called a "community . . . resembling a 17th century New England town more than a 20th century corporation." The airline *bonds* its workers with such shared values as integrity, trust, and altruism (Lee 1994). But a company with a productive corporate culture is almost surely a company with strong incentives in place to reward productivity. Without taking anything away from the corporate culture at Southwest Airlines, it should be pointed out that one reason that it has the lowest cost in the business is that its pilots and flight attendants are paid by the trip. This, along with a strong corporate culture, explains why Southwest's pilots and flight attendants hustle when the planes are on the ground. Indeed, Southwest has the shortest turn-around time in the industry. It pays for the crews to do what they can to get their planes back in the air quickly (Banks 1994, 107).

Motorola organizes its workers into teams and allows them to hire and fire their cohorts, determine training procedures, and set schedules. Federal Express' corporate culture includes giving workers the right to evaluate their bosses and to appeal their own evaluations all the way to the chairman. It's understandable why Federal Express delivery people move at least twice as fast as US

firm's revenues and goals, or the lack of them, can easily go undetected. A recurring theme of this book is that when monitoring is difficult, one can expect many workers to exploit opportunities to improve their own wellbeing at the expense of the firm and its owners. And the opportunities taken can result in substantial losses in worker output. Management specialist Edward Lawler reported that during a strike at a manufacturing firm, a secretary was asked to take over a factory job and was paid on a piece-rate basis. Despite no previous experience, within days she was turning out 375 percent more output than the normal worker who had spent ten years on the job and was constantly complaining that the work standards were too demanding (Lawler 1990, 58). Obviously, the striking worker had been doing something other than working on the job.

postal workers: FedEx workers have incentives to do so, whereas postal workers do not.[9]

We don't want to criticize the traditional, nonincentive methods for getting things done in business. Indeed, we have discussed the issue of "teams" much earlier in the book, and the importance of virtues such as "trust" are raised before we conclude this chapter. At the same time, we wish to stress a fairly general and straightforward rule for organizing much production: *Give workers a direct, detectable stake in firm revenues or profits in order to raise revenues and profits. Pay for performance.* One means of doing that is to make workers' pay conditional on their output: the greater the output from each worker, the greater the individual worker's pay.

Ideally, we should dispense with salaries, which are paid by the week or year, and always pay by the "piece" – or "piece rate." Many firms – for example, hosiery mills – do pay piece rates: they pay by the number of socks completed. Piece rates can be expected to raise the wages of covered workers for two reasons: First, the incentives can be expected to induce workers to work harder for more minutes of each hour and for more hours during the workday. Second, the piece-rate workers will be asked to assume some of the risk of production, which is influenced by factors beyond the workers' control. For example, how much each worker produces will be determined by what the employer does to provide workers with a productive work environment and what other workers are willing to do. So, piece-rate workers can be expected to demand, and receive, a *risk premium* in their paychecks. One study has, in fact, shown that a significant majority of workers covered under "output-related contracts" in the nonferrous foundries industry earn between 5 percent and 12 percent more, depending on the occupation, than their counterparts who are paid strictly by their time at work. Of that pay differential, about a fifth has been attributable to workers' risk bearing, which means that a substantial share of the pay advantage for incentive workers is attributable to the greater effort that covered workers expend (Petersen 1991).

However, such a rule – paying by the piece – is hardly universally adopted. Indeed, piece-rate workers make up a fairly small portion of the total workforce (though we have not been able to determine precisely how prevalent piece-pay systems are). Many automobile salespeople, of course, are paid by the number of cars sold. Many lawyers are paid by the number of hours billed (and presumably services provided). Musicians are often paid by the number of concerts played.

---

[9] FedEx actually tracks its delivery people on their routes, and the workers understand that their pay is tied to how cost-effective they are in their deliveries. Postal workers understand that they are not being so carefully monitored, mainly because there are no stockholders who can claim the profits from getting more work done.

But there are relatively few workers in manufacturing and service industries whose pay is directly tied to each item or service produced. Professors are not paid by the number of students they teach. Office workers are not paid by the number of forms processed or memos sent. Fast-food workers are not paid by the number of burgers flipped. Most people's pay is directly and explicitly tied to time on the job: they are generally paid by the hour or month or year.

Admittedly, the pay of most workers has some indirect and implicit connection to production. Many workers know that if they don't eventually add more to the revenues of their companies than they take home in pay, their jobs will be in considerable jeopardy. The question we find interesting is why a "piece rate" – or direct "pay for performance" – is not a more widely employed pay system, given the positive incentives it potentially provides.

Many explanations for the absence of a piece-rate pay system are obvious and widely recognized.[10] The output of many workers cannot be reduced to "pieces." In such cases, no one should expect pay to be tied to that which cannot be measured with tolerable objectivity. Our work as university professors is hard to define and measure. In fact, observers might find it hard to determine when we are working, given that, while at work, we may be doing nothing more than staring at a computer screen or talking with colleagues in the hallway. Measuring the "pieces" of what secretaries and executives complete is equally, if not more, difficult. We noted early in this book that Lincoln Electric, which has had considerable success with its pay-for-performance (as explained below), once tried to pay its typists by the keystroke, but the company quickly terminated the typists' "piece-rate pay" when one typist was caught constantly hitting a single key while she ate her sandwich on her lunch break (Roberts 2004, 42).

If a measure of "output" is defined when the assigned tasks are complex, the measure will not likely be all-inclusive. Some dimensions of the assigned tasks will not be measured, which means that workers' incentives may be grossly distorted. They may work only to do those things that are defined and measured – and related to pay – at the expense of other parts of their assignments. If workers are paid by the number of parts produced, with the quality of individual parts not considered, some workers could be expected to sacrifice quality in order to increase their production count. If professors were paid by the number of students in their classes, you can bet they would spend less time at research and in committee meetings (which would not

[10] For a review of arguments offered by psychologists against incentive pay plans, see Kohn 1993a, 1993b. Kohn sums up his argument as follows: "Do rewards motivate people? Absolutely. They motivate people to get rewards" (Kohn 1993b, 62), suggesting that the goals of the firm might not be achieved in the process, given the complexity of the production process and the margins workers can exploit.

be all bad). If middle managers were paid solely by units produced, they would produce a lot of units with little attention to costs. There is an old story from the days before the fall of communism in the former Soviet Union. According to the story, the managers of a shoe factory were given production quotas for the number of shoes they had to make, and they were paid according to how much they exceeded their quota. What did they do? They produced lots of shoes, *but only left ones*!

Much work is the product of "teams," or groups of workers, extending at times to the entire plant or office. Pay is often not related to output because it may be difficult to determine which individuals are responsible for the "pieces" that are produced. Because we took up the problems of forming and paying teams in chapter 9, here we remind readers only that team production creates special incentive problems. Having "small" teams, which make each team member's contributions, or lack thereof, visible to others on the team, is one way to enhance incentives.

[See online Video Module 12.3 Labor economics]

Piece-rate pay and worker risk

When workers are paid by salary, they are given some assurance that their incomes will not vary with firm output, which can go up and down for many reasons that are not under the workers' control. For example, how many collars a worker can stitch to the bodies of shirts is dependent upon the flow of shirts through the plant, over which the workers doing the stitching may have no control. When workers are paid by the piece, they are, in effect, asked to assume a greater risk, that shows up in the variability of the income they take home. This means that piece-rate workers have to be paid a higher *average* income than if they were offered a predictable wage. Without the higher average income for those working at a piece rate, workers would choose to work for employers paying a predictable wage, and those paying a piece rate would either be unable to hire anyone, or have to hire poorly skilled workers. So in order for the piece-rate system to work – and be profitable for the firm – the increase in expected worker productivity has to exceed the *risk premium* that risk averse workers would demand. This means that a piece rate (or any other form of incentive compensation) is often not employed in many firms simply because the risk premium workers demand is greater than their expected increase in productivity. This is often the case because workers tend to be risk averse (or reluctant to take chances, or assume the costs associated with an uncertain and variable income stream).

Even if workers are not more risk adverse than employers, piece-rate pay systems may also be avoided because employers are likely to be in a better position to assume the risk of production variability than their employees are. This is because much of the variability in the output of *individual* workers will be "smoothed out" within a whole *group* of employees. When one worker's output is down, then another worker's output will be up. Workers will, in effect, be able to buy themselves out of the risk. If each of the workers sees the risk cost of the piece-rate system at $500 and the employer sees the risk cost at $100, then each worker can agree to give up, say, $110 in pay for the rights to a constant income. The worker gains, on balance, $390 in nonmoney income ($500 in risk cost reduction minus the $110 reduction in money wages). The employer gives up the piece-rate system simply because it can make a profit – $10 in this example – off each worker ($110 reduction in worker money wages minus the $100 increase in risk cost). One would therefore expect, other things being equal, piece-rate pay schemes to be more prevalent in "large" firms than in "small" ones. Large employers are more likely to be able to smooth out the variability.

If paid by the work done, workers would also have to worry about how changes in the general economy would affect their workloads and production levels. A downturn in the economy, due to forces that are global in scope, can undermine worker pay when pay is tied to output. When DuPont introduced its incentive compensation scheme for its fibers division in the late 1980s – under which a portion of the workers' incomes could be lost if profit goals were not achieved, but would be multiplied if profit goals were exceeded – the managers and employees expected, or were told to expect, substantial income gains (Hayes 1988). However, when the economy turned sour in 1990, employee morale suffered as profits fell and workers were threatened with reduced incomes. The incentive program was canceled before the announced three-year trial period was up (Koening 1990). DuPont obviously concluded that it could buy back worker morale and production by not subjecting pay to factors that were beyond worker control. Each individual employee could reason that there was absolutely nothing she could do about the national economy or, for that matter, about the work effort of the 20,000 other DuPont workers who were covered by the incentive program. They could rightfully fear that the free riding of all other workers put their incomes at risk.

Piece-rate (and other forms of incentive) pay schemes also are more likely to be used in situations where the risk to workers is low relative to the benefits of the improved incentives. This means that they will tend to be used where production is not highly variable and where, in the absence of piece-rate pay, workers can easily exploit opportunities to shirk – where workers cannot be easily monitored. For example, salespeople who are always on the road (which necessarily means that no one at the home office knows much about what they do on a daily basis) will tend to be paid, at least in part, by the "piece," in some form or another, say, by the sale.

Piece-rate pay systems also can be used only when and where employers can make credible commitments to their workers to abide by the pay system that they establish and not to cut the *rate* in the *piece rate* when the desired results are achieved. Unfortunately, managers are all too often unable to make the credible commitment for the same reason that they might find, in theory, the piece-rate system to be an attractive way (in terms of worker productivity and firm profits) to pay workers. The basic problem is that both workers *and* managers have incentives to engage in opportunistic behavior to the detriment of the other group.

Managers understand that many workers have a natural inclination to shirk their responsibilities, to loaf on the job, and to misuse and abuse company resources for personal gain. Managers also know that if they tie their workers' pay to output, then output may be expected to expand: fewer workers will exploit their positions and loaf on the job. At the same time, the workers can reason that incentives also matter to managers. As is true of workers, managers are not always angels and can be expected, to one degree or another, to exploit their positions, achieving greater personal and firm gain at the expense of their workers.

Hence, workers can reason that if they respond to the incentives built into the piece-rate system and produce more for more pay, then managers can change the deal. The managers can simply raise the number of pieces that the workers must produce in order to get the previously established pay, or managers can simply dump what will then be excess workers. Recall our earlier example (in note 8) of the secretary who, when asked during a strike to take over a job that had been done by a piece-rate worker with ten years' experience, quickly began producing 375 percent more than the experienced worker had. Workers in that firm were obviously shirking despite the piece-rate pay because they were afraid that the employer would reduce the per piece rate if they produced as much per hour as they could.

To clarify this point, suppose a worker is initially paid $500 a week, and during the course of the typical week she produces 100 pieces – for an average pay of $5 per piece. Management figures that the worker is spending some time goofing off on the job and that her output can be raised if she is paid $5 for each piece produced. If the worker responds by increasing her output to 150 pieces, management can simply lower the rate to $3.50 per piece, which would give the worker $525 a week and would mean that the firm would take the overwhelming share of the gains from the worker's – not management's – greater efforts. The worker would, in effect, be working harder and more diligently with little to show for what she has done. By heeding the piece-rate incentive, the worker could be inadvertently establishing a higher production standard.

These threats are real. In the 1970s, managers at a General Motors panel stamping plant in Flint, Michigan, announced that the company would allow workers to leave after they had satisfied daily production targets. Workers were soon leaving by noon. In response, management increased production targets. The result was a bitter workforce (Klein, Crawford, and Alchian 1978).

So, one reason that piece-rate systems aren't more widely used is that managers can abuse the systems, which means that workers will not buy into them at reasonable rates of pay. Indeed, the piece-rate system can have the exact opposite of the intended effect. We have noted that workers can reason that their managers will increase the output demands if they produce more for any given rate. However, the implied relationship between output and production demands should also be expected to run the other way: that is, the workers can reason that if managers will raise the production requirements when they produce more in response to any established rate, then managers should be willing to lower the production requirements when the workers lower their production after the piece-rate system is established. Hence, the establishment of the piece-rate system can lead to a reduction in output as workers cut back on production.

The lesson of this discussion is not that piece-rate pay incentives can't work. Rather, the lesson is that getting the piece-rate pay system right can be tricky. Managers must convincingly *commit* themselves to holding to the established piece rate and not exploiting the workers. The best way for managers to be believable is to create a history of living up to their commitments. They must create a valuable reputation with their workers, which is all the more important when performance targets are imprecise (Baker, Gibbon, and Murphy 1994).

Lincoln Electric's pay system

Recall the case of Lincoln Electric described briefly in chapter 1. Lincoln Electric, a major producer of arc-welding equipment in Cleveland, makes heavy use of piece-rate pay. As Roberts (2004) and Miller (1992) have stressed, the Lincoln Electric pay system continues to contribute to worker productivity for several reasons:

- First, the company has a target rate of return for shareholders, with deviations from that target either adding to or subtracting from their workers' year-end bonuses, with the bonus often amounting to 100 percent of workers' base pay.
- Second, employees largely own the firm, a fact that reduces the likelihood that piece rates will be changed.
- Third, management understands the need for credible commitments. According to one manager, "When we set a piecework price, that price cannot be changed just because, in management's opinion, the worker is making too much money ... Piecework prices can only be changed when management has made a change in the method of doing that particular job and under no other conditions. If this is not carried out 100 percent, piecework cannot work" (Miller 1992, 117).
- Fourth, Lincoln pursues a permanent employment policy. Permanent employees are guaranteed only 75 percent of normal hours, and management can move workers into different jobs in response to demand changes. Also, workers have agreed to mandatory overtime when demand is high (meaning that the firm doesn't have to hire workers in peak demand periods). In other words, workers and management have agreed to share some of the risk.

- Fifth, to combat quality problems, each unit produced is stenciled with the initials of the workers who produced it. If a unit fails after delivery because of flaws in production, the responsible workers can lose as much as 10 percent of their annual bonus.
- Sixth, large inventories are maintained to smooth out differences in the production rates of different workers.
- Finally, with its reward system heavily weighted to performance pay, Lincoln has attracted workers motivated by monetary rewards and willing to work hard. Workers who aren't so motivated don't apply to Lincoln or, if they try working at Lincoln and find that they aren't willing to keep up with the pace of the coworkers, tend to resign and work elsewhere.

The importance of the self-selection of workers in the Cleveland plant became clear to Lincoln management when the company bought plants in other countries and instituted its piece-rate pay system, only to learn that the workers at the foreign plants had not self-selected to respond to Lincoln's pay system. The result was that the company's acquisitions were failures simply because its piece-rate system did not inspire the effort response experienced in the Cleveland plant (Bartlett and O'Connell 1998).

When managers can change the rate of piece-rate pay

Does this mean that managers can never raise the production standard for any given pay rate? Of course not. Workers should be concerned only if the standard is changed because of something *they* – the workers – did. If management in some way increases the productivity of workers (for example, introduces computerized equipment or rearranges the flow of the materials through the plant), independent of workers' effort, then the piece-rate pay standard can be raised. Workers should not object. They are still getting their value for their effort and are not worse off. What managers must avoid doing is changing the foundations of the work and then taking more in terms of a lower *pay rate* than they are due, which effectively means violating the contract or commitment with their workers.

There is a powerful lesson in what the manager at Lincoln Electric said: "Piecework prices can only be changed when management has made a change in the method of doing that particular job and under no other conditions" (Miller 1992, 117). Otherwise, piece-rate pay can have the exact opposite effect of the one intended.

Two-part pay systems

There are innumerable ways of paying people to encourage performance. The two-part pay contract – *salary plus commission* – is obviously a compromise between straight salary and straight commission pay structures. For example, a worker for a job placement service can be paid a salary of $4,000 a month, plus 10 percent of the fees received for any placement. If the recruiter can be expected to place two workers a month and the placement fee is $15,000, the worker's expected monthly income is $7,000 ($4,000 plus 10 percent of $30,000).

This form of payment can be mutually attractive to the placement firm and its recruiters because it accomplishes a couple of important objectives. First, the system can be a way by which workers and their employers can share the risks to reflect the way the actual placements depend on both the workers' and the employers' actions. Whereas each worker understands that her placements are greatly affected by how hard and smart she personally works, each also knows that often, to a nontrivial degree, the placements are related to what all other workers and the employer do. Worker income is dependent on, for example, how much the employer advertises, seeks to maintain a good image for the firm, and develops the right incentives for *all* workers to apply themselves.

Workers have an interest in everyone in the firm working as a team, and working productively, just as the employer does. Productive work by all can increase firm output, worker pay, and job security. As a consequence, although each worker may, in one sense, "prefer" all income in the form of a guaranteed fixed monthly check, the worker also has an interest in commission pay – *if everyone else is paid commission and if perverse incentives are avoided.* Hence, a pay system that is based, to a degree, on commission can raise the incomes of all workers. Put another way, to the extent that one worker's income is dependent upon other workers' efforts, we should expect workers to favor a pay system that incorporates strong production incentives for all workers.

With the two-part pay system, workers are given some security in that they can count on, for some undetermined amount of time, a minimum income level – $4,000 per month in our example. The workers shift some of their risk to their employer, but the risk the employer assumes need not equal the sum of the risk that the workers avoid. This is because, as noted earlier, the employer usually hires a number of people, and the variability of the income of the employer is, therefore, not likely to be as great as the variability of the individual workers' income.

[See online Video Module 12.4 Two-part pay packages]

Why incentive pay equals higher pay

Of course, firms can expect that incentive schemes that enhance firm profits do not come free of charge. According to one early study, some 200 punch-press operators in Chicago who were paid piece rate earned, on average, 7 percent more than workers who did much the same jobs but who were paid a straight salary (so much per unit of time – for example, hour, week, or month) (Pencavel 1977). According to another study involving more than 100,000 workers in 500 manufacturing firms within two industries, the incomes of the footwear workers on some form of piece-rate or salary-plus-commission pay averaged slightly over 14 percent more than the workers on salaries (with the differential ranging up to 31 percent for certain types of jobs). The workers in the men's coats and suits industry on piece rate averaged between 15 and 16 percent more than the salaried workers (Seiler 1984). And the best evidence available suggests that the more workers' incomes are based on incentive pay, the greater the income differential between those who earn piece-rate pay (or any other form of incentive pay) and those who don't.

Of course, it may be that the income differential between incentive-paid and salaried workers is a matter of the difference in the demands of the jobs incentive-paid workers and salaried workers take. Incentive-paid jobs may pay more because they are the jobs the most competent workers are most eager to take. However, the studies cited have attempted either to look at incentive-paid and salaried workers in comparable jobs or to have adjusted (by statistical, econometric means) the pay gaps for differences in the "quality" of the different jobs.[11]

One of the more obvious explanations for why incentive-paid workers earn more than salaried workers is that the incentive-paid workers accept more risk. After all, the incomes of the incentive-paid workers can vary not only with the workers' effort, but also with the promotional efforts of their firms and general economic conditions in the market, among a host of other factors. A firm's ad campaigns can complement a worker's efforts to sell a product or service. A downturn in the national economy can make selling more difficult, effectively dropping the workers' rates of pay per hour (albeit for a long or short period of time). The incentive-paid workers' greater average pay amounts to a risk premium intended to account for the prospects that income may not always match expectations.

The business lesson is simple: to get workers to accept incentive pay, employers have to raise the pay. If both incentive-paid and salaried jobs were paid the same, workers would crowd into the salaried jobs, increasing the number of workers available to work for salaries and reducing the number of workers available to work on commission. The incomes of the salaried workers, everything else being equal, would tend to fall, whereas the incomes of the incentive-paid workers would tend to rise. If there were no considerations other than risk under the different pay schemes, the wage differential would continue to widen until the income difference

---

[11] The study by Pencavel (1977) adjusts data for differences in education, experience, race, and union status. The second study by Seiler (1984) adjusts for differences in union status, gender, location of employment, occupation, type of product, and method of production, among other variables.

was about equal to the difference in the added "risk cost" the incentive-paid workers suffered. That is to say, if the risk cost (or premium) were deducted from the pay of incentive-paid workers, the resulting net pay of the incentive-paid workers would be about the same as the pay of salaried workers.

But risk doesn't explain the entire differential. One of the studies mentioned at the start of this discussion found that the "risk premium" accounted for only a little more than 3 percentage points of the pay differential in the footwear industry and only 6 percentage points of the difference in men's clothing (with a great deal of variance reported across occupational categories) (Seiler 1984). A simple dictum (one that is central to all the "organizational economics and management" sections of this book) explains the differential: incentives matter! Incentive-paid workers simply gain more from extra work than do their salaried counterparts. A salaried worker is no doubt required to apply a given, minimal level of effort on the job. Salaried workers can choose to work more and produce more for the company. Their extra work might have some reward – a future raise or promotion – but such prospects are never certain. Many workers believe, with justification, that their raises are more directly tied to the number of years they survive at their firms than to how much extra they work and produce.

By way of contrast, the rewards of incentive-paid workers are much more immediate, direct, and contractual. Incentive-paid workers know that if they produce or sell more for their firms, their incomes will rise immediately and by a known amount. Accordingly, they have a greater incentive to apply themselves. One study in the early 1960s found that incentive pay improved worker productivity by as much as 40 percent, not all of which, as will be argued, is necessarily due to extra effort (Mangum 1962).

Incentive pay does more than just motivate greater effort. Different methods of pay are likely to attract different workers (Lazear 2000). Workers who are relatively unproductive, or who just don't want to compete aggressively, are likely to opt out of incentive-paid work, preferring salaried jobs. In short, workers who tend to be more productive than average can be expected to self-select into jobs with incentive pay. We should expect some firms to use incentive pay elements in many jobs simply to cull the unproductive workers. Job applicants who know that they are willing to work hard will convincingly communicate this willingness to prospective employers through their acceptance of the the challenge of incentive pay.

If business becomes more uncertain, less predictable – as many seem to think it has since the 1980s with the growing complexity and globalization of business – we would expect the income gap between incentive-paid and salaried workers to widen. Employers will want to increase their competitive positions by giving their workers a greater incentive to work harder and smarter. Employers will want to shift a share of the growing business risk to their workers, at a price, of course, through greater reliance on commissions. At the same time, relatively speaking, more workers might seek to move to salaried jobs to avoid greater risk. However, their efforts will simply hold salaries down, widening the gap between incentive-paid and salaried jobs.

Honest dealing with workers

Crucial to managers' performance is the problem of getting workers to deal honestly when their pay is at stake. For example, consider the manager whose salesforce works out in the "field," far removed from headquarters. The salespeople are hard to monitor and they know a great deal more about the sales potential in their territories than the managers at headquarters. How do the managers get the salespeople to reveal the sales potential of their districts when they know that the information will affect their sales performance criteria and the combination of the salary and commission components of their compensation package? If the manager at headquarters simply asks the salespeople how much they can sell in their areas, there is a good chance the salespeople will understate the sales potential. After all, some understatement harbors the potential of raising the salary and commission rate.

One solution is to offer the sales personnel a menu of combinations of salary and commission rates. Consider the set of three salary–commission rate combinations illustrated in figure 12.10, which has salary on the vertical axis and sales on the horizontal axis. One pay package has a high salary, S_1, and a low commission rate, which is described by the low slope of the straight, upward sloping compensation line that emerges from S_1 on the vertical axis. Another pay package has a lower salary component, S_2, and a higher commission rate, and yet a third has an even lower salary, S_3, and an even higher commission rate.

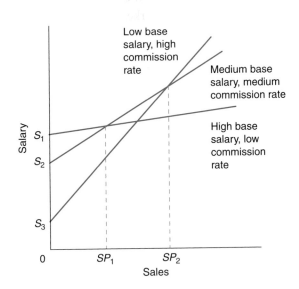

Figure 12.10 Menu of two-part pay packages
By varying the base salary and the commission rate, employers can get salespeople to reveal more accurately the sales potential of their districts. A salesperson who believes that the sales potential of his district is great will take the income path that starts at a base salary of S_3. The salesperson who doesn't think the sales potential of his district is very good will choose the income path that starts at S_1.

What's a salesperson to do? Lying about the sales potential of his or her territory won't help. Indeed, the salesperson isn't even asked to lie. All she must do is choose from among the compensation packages in a way that she, not the manager, believes will maximize total pay. The salesperson who sees little prospect for sales will choose the package with the salary of S_1. The salesperson will be compensated for the limited sales potential by a high salary. The salesperson who believes that the sales potential will be greater than SP_1 (on the horizontal axis) but less than SP_2 will choose the package with a salary of S_2. The salesperson who believes that the "sky is the limit" (meaning a sales potential greater than SP_2) will choose the package with the low salary of S_3. This is the approach for establishing salary–commission rate pay contracts at IBM (Milgrom and Roberts, 1992, 400–2). It's not a sure-fire way of making salespeople totally honest, but it can improve the managerial decision, and that's all that real-world managers can hope to achieve.

Our focus in this chapter has been exclusively on labor, but labor is hardly the only resource. Firms need plant and equipment, which they can buy or lease. We explain in online Reading 12.1 how the Irvine Company, a major real estate company in Southern California, structures its contracts for rental property in shopping malls to maximize both its own and its tenants' profitability.

Practical lessons for MBAs: avoid becoming a monopsony

Monopsony analytics can easily be misleading. Taken uncritically, it can suggest to MBA students that being a monopsony employer of labor (or any other resource) can yield a competitive advantage. After all, as the monopsony graphical analytics suggest, a monopsony can pay workers a wage rate lower than would be paid if the market were fully competitive. Such can indeed be the case, but only when the monopsony is somehow assumed into existence or somehow is magically imposed on a local labor market with all other employers magically removed.

Firms that become large employers are *not* magically imposed on local labor markets. They generally grow within their labor markets as they expand the reach of their sales through attractive product development and pricing. As they grow in sales, firms usually increase their demands for labor within their local markets and increase the overall demand for labor. Their growth causes them to push the wage rate that they and other firms pay up and above the competitive levels that would have prevailed absent the growth in the dominant firms in the local labor market. The upward press of their wage rates paid can make for a competitive cost disadvantage for the growing firms. Hence, to keep their labor costs under control and their product prices competitive, would-be monopsonists should avoid dominating their local labor markets by expanding production in other markets within the country or across the globe where wage rates are relatively low and where expanding firms can have minimal upward influence on the prevailing wage rates.

There are two very good reasons large firms have plants in various locations. First, the spread of production facilities enables them to spread their production risks. For example, the spread of production facilities reduces the chance that a natural disaster in a given locale will wipe out firms' ability to continue in business even for a short time. Second, the spread of production across various locales can reduce the firms' labor costs by their studiously avoiding becoming demand-elevating monopsonies in given labor markets.

Further reading online

Reading 12.1 Incentives in the Irvine Company rental contracts

The bottom line

The key takeaways from chapter 12 are the following:

1 The demand for labor is influenced by the laborer's productivity and the price of the laborer's product. The supply of labor is influenced by workers' opportunity costs.

2 In a competitive labor market, wage rates are determined by the interaction of willing suppliers of labor (employees) and demanders of labor (employers).

3 Suppliers of labor (workers) are influenced significantly by the nonmonetary benefits of employment, as well as by the value they place on their next-best alternative to employment. Differences in money wage rates may not reflect true differences in full wage rates.

4 In competitive labor markets, wage rates above the intersection of supply and demand give rise to market surpluses, which can cause the wage rate to fall toward equilibrium. Wage rates below the intersection of supply and demand give rise to market shortages, which can cause the wage rate to rise.

5 Monopsonists will maximize profits by hiring workers up to the point that the marginal cost of the last worker equals her marginal value. Monopsonists can pay less than the competitive wage rate because it can restrict the market demand for labor.

6 A minimum wage imposed on monopsony labor markets can cause an increase in the number of workers hired.

7   Workers who are paid for performance incur a risk cost, which can explain why they often earn more than workers who are paid a straight salary. In addition, workers who are paid for performance are also induced to produce more, which enables them to earn more.

8   In order for piece-rate pay systems to result in an increase in worker production, employers must be able to credibly commit to refuse to lower the rate of pay when workers increase their output.

9   Although paying for performance has a nice ring to it, providing the "right" pay for the "right" performance is a serious, not always easily resolved problem for managers. Accordingly, there are profits to be made from getting incentives right as surely as there are profits to be made from getting product designs right.

10 One reason for employers paying workers in two parts – salary plus some form of commission (or tie-in to performance) – is that both employer and employee can gain. The employer can accept the risk associated with having to meet a regular, contracted salary payment, and the employee can want the salary because it reduces her risk and, at the same time, gives the employer an incentive to work hard at keeping the work going (in order that the salary can be met with relative ease).

[See online Video Module 12.5 Ten major lessons, which, as suggested by the title, draws out the ten overarching lessons that can be drawn from this textbook.]

Review questions >>

1   The government requires employers to pay time and a half for labor in excess of forty hours a week. How should managers be expected to react to that law? What effect should such a law have on the quantity of labor demanded? Why?

2   Does union support of laws outlawing child labor square with the private interests of union members? How could the minimum wage rate and migrant housing standards affect the wages of union members? How can they be expected to affect the prices of consumer goods? Explain, using supply and demand graphs.

3   Suppose the government requires employers to pay a minimum wage of $10 per hour to workers over twenty-two years of age. What effect should such a law have on the employment opportunities and wage rates of persons under twenty-two?

4   How can government mandates requiring that employers provide their workers with particular fringe benefits make workers worse off? How do such mandates affect the supply and demand curves for labor? What happens to the market wage and employment level?

5 When would employers relax their work demands on their employees? Develop a supply-and-demand-for-labor graph that shows how relaxed work demands can be profitable to employers. When would employers stop relaxing their work demands?

6 What is the difference between "lax work demands" and "shirking"?

7 Are there reasons for believing that it is unlikely that minimum-wage laws would benefit workers even in the case of some monopsony power by the employer?

8 Workers paid on a piece-rate basis often use the term "rate buster" for someone who responds to the piece rate by turning out lots of output. Is "rate buster" a term of endearment here? How does a reputation by management for honesty and credibility help eliminate the problem reflected by the term "rate buster"?

9 Is it possible that piece-rate pay can make firms less profitable even when piece-rate pay decreases worker shirking and increases worker productivity? Explore with a supply-and-demand-for-labor graph.

References

Abowd, John M., 1990. Does performance-based managerial compensation affect corporate performance? *Industrial and Labor Relations Review* 43: 52S–53S

Adam, Scott, 1995. Manager's journal: the Dilbert principle, *Wall Street Journal*, May 22: A14

Akerlof, George A., 1970. The market for lemons: qualitative uncertainty and the market mechanism, *Quarterly Journal of Economics* 84: 488–500

Alchian, Armen A. and Harold Demsetz, 1973. The property rights paradigm, *Journal of Economic History* 33: 17

Alexis, M., 1974. The political economy of labor market discrimination: synthesis and exploration, in A. Horowitz and G. von Furstenberg (eds.), *Patterns of Discrimination*, Lexington, MA: D. C. Heath/Lexington Books

Alonzo-Zaldivar, Ricardo, 2005. Insurance option has workers pay more, *Los Angeles Times*, May 23: A1.

Alpert, William T., 1986. *The Minimum Wage in the Restaurant Industry*, New York: Praeger

Amihud, Y. and B. Lev, 1981. Risk aversion as a managerial motive for conglomerate mergers, *Bell Journal of Economics* 12: 605–17

Anderson, Terry L. and Peter Jenson Hill, 2004. *The Not So Wild, Wild West: Property Rights on the Frontier*, Stanford, CA: Stanford University Press

Ariely, Dan, 2008. *Predictably Irrational: The Hidden Forces that Shape Our Decisions*, New York: HarperCollins Publishers

Aristotle, *Ethics*, vol. 8, no. 9

Armentano, Dominick T., 1990. *Antitrust and Monopoly: Anatomy of a Policy Failure*, Oakland, CA: Independent Institute

Arrow, Kenneth, 1963. *Social Choice and Individual Values*, New York: Wiley

Arthur, W. B., 1996. Increasing returns and the new world of business, *Harvard Business Review* 74(4): 100–9

Associated Press, 2005a. Store says two others selling gas too cheap, *Winston-Salem Journal*, May 5: B5

2005b. North Carolina fails to make cut for U.S. airbus factory, *Winston-Salem Journal*, May 6, available on May 9, 2005 at www.journalnow.com/servlet/Satellite?pagename=WSJ/ MG Article/WSJ_BasicArticle&tc=MGArticle&cid=1031782569685

2005c. Senate looks at raising minimum wage, *Wall Street Journal*, March 6: A17

Atlanta Journal – Constitution, 1995. Long-term risk (editorial), April 15: A10

Axelrod, Robert and W. D. Hamilton, 1987. The evolution of cooperation, *Science* 211: 1390–6

Bacevich, Andrew, 2008. *The Limits of Power: The End of American Exceptionalism*, New York: Metropolitan Books

Baker, George, 2000. The use of performance in incentive contracting, *American Economic Review* 90(2): 415–20

Baker, George, Robert Gibbon, and Kevin Murphy, 1994. Subjective performance measures in optimal incentive contracts, *Quarterly Journal of Economics* 109: 1125–56

Balaker, Ted and Adrian T. Moore, 2005. *Offshoring and Public Fear: Assessing the Real Threat to Jobs*, Santa Monica, CA: Reason Foundation, Policy Study 33, available on May 19, 2005 at www.rppi.org/ps333.pdf

Banks, Howard, 1994. A sixties industry in a nineties economy, *Forbes*, May 9: 107–12

Barham, Catherine and Nasima Begum, 2005. Sickness absence from work in the UK, in *Labour Market Trends*, London: Office for National Statistics, Labour Market Division, April

Barker, Colin, 2009. Dell's Ireland plant to shed 1,900 jobs, *CNET News*, January 8, accessed February 5, 2009 from http://news.cnet.com/8301-1001_3-10136439-92.html

Barkham, Patrick, 1999. The banana wars explained, *Guardian*, March 5, accessed on March 9, 2009 from www.guardian.co.uk/world/1999/mar/05/eu.wto3

Bartlett, C. A. and J. O'Connell, 1998. Lincoln Electric: venturing abroad, Boston: Harvard University Graduate School of Business, Case 3–398–095

Bastiat, Frédéric, 1996. *Economic Sophisms*, Irvington-on-Hudson, NY: The Foundation for Economic Education, Inc., trans. and ed. Arthur Goddard, Library of Economics and Liberty, available on January 4, 2004 at www.econlib.org/library/Bastiat/basSoph3. html>

Baumol, William J., 1982. Contestable markets: an uprising in the theory of industry structure, *American Economic Review* 72: 1–15

Becker, Gary S. 1971. *Economic Theory*, New York: Alfred A. Knopf
     1976. *The Economic Approach to Human Behavior*, Chicago: University of Chicago Press

Becker, Gary S. and Kevin M. Murphy, 1988. A theory of rational addiction, *Journal of Political Economy* 96(4): 675–700

Becker, W., J. Ronen, and G. H. Sorter, 1974. Opportunity costs – an experimental approach, *Journal of Accounting Research*, Autumn: 317–29

Bendavid, Naftali, Elizabeth Williamson, and Sudeep Reddy, 2009. Stimulus package unveiled, *Wall Street Journal*, January 16: A1

Bennett, James T. and Manuel H. Johnson, 1983. *Better Government at Half the Price*, Ottawa, IL: Carolina House

Bentley, Arthur, 1967. *The Process of Government*, Cambridge, MA: Belknap Press, Harvard University Press

Berlau, John, 2007. The subprime FHA, *Wall Street Journal*, October 15, accessed January 14, 2009 from http://online.wsj.com/article/SB119241016826258768.html

Bernanke, Ben, 2009. Comments before the Federal Open Market Committee, December 9, 2003, as reprinted in Ben Bernanke vs. the journal on inflation, *Wall Street Journal*, June 23: A15

Bethel, Tom, 1998. *The Noblest Triumph: Property and Prosperity through the Ages*, New York: St. Martin's Press

Beverage Digest, 2008. Elasticity: big price increases cause Coke volume to plummet, November 21: 3–4

Bhagat, Sanjai, Andrei Shleifer, and Robert W. Vishny, 1990. Hostile takeovers in the 1980s: the return to corporate specialization, in Martin N. Bailey and Clifford Winston (eds.), *Brookings Papers on Economic Activity*, Washington, DC: Brookings Institution

Bhide, Amar, 1990. Reversing corporate diversification, *Journal of Applied Corporate Finance* 3: 70–81

Black, William K., Kitty Calavita, and Henry N. Pontell, 1995. The savings and loan debacle of the 1980s: white-collar crime or risky business? *Law & Policy* 17(1): 23–55

Blalock, Garrick, Vrinda Kadiyali, and Daniel H. Simon, 2005a. The impact of post 9/11 airport security measures on the demand for air travel, Ithaca, NY: Economics Department, Cornell University, Working Paper, February 23 version

    2005b. The impact of 9/11 on road fatalities: the other lives lost to terrorism, Ithaca, NY: Economics Department, Cornell University, Working Paper, February 2 version

Blinder, Alan, 1987. *Hard Heads, Soft Hearts*, Reading, MA: Addison-Wesley

Boehm, Christopher, 1993. Egalitarian behavior and reverse dominance hierarchy, *Current Anthropology* 14: 227–54

Boulding, Kenneth E., 1970. *Economics as a Science*, New York: McGraw-Hill

Bowles, Samuel and Herbert Gintis, 2001. The evolution of strong reciprocity, Amherst, MA, Department of Economics, University of Massachusetts, Working Paper

Brandenburger, Adam M. and Barry J. Nalebuff, 1996. *Co-Opetition*, New York: Currency/ Doubleday

Breit, William and Kenneth G. Elzinga, 1985. Private antitrust enforcement: the new learning, *Journal of Law and Economics* 28(2): 405–43

Breyer, Stephen, 1982. *Regulation and Its Reform*, Cambridge, MA: Harvard University Press

Brickley, James A., Sanjai Bhagat, and Ronald C. Lease, 1985. The impact of long-range managerial compensation plans on shareholder wealth, *Journal of Accounting and Economics* 7: 115–29

Brickley, James A. and Frederick H. Dark, 1987. The choice of organizational forms: the case of franchising, *Journal of Financial Economics* 18: 401–20

Brody, Jane E. 2005. As Americans get bigger, the world does, too, *New York Times*, April 19: D1

Brown, Charles, Curtis Gilroy, and Andrew Kohen, 1982. The effect of the minimum wage on employment and unemployment, *Journal of Economic Literature* 20: 487–528

Brownell, Kelly D. and Thomas R. Frieden, 2009. Ounces of prevention – the public policy case for taxes on sugared beverages, *New England Journal of Medicine* 360 (18, April 30): 1805–8

Browning, Edgar, 1974. Why the social insurance budget is too large in a democracy, *Economic Inquiry* 13: 373–88

Buchanan, James M. and Yong J. Yoon, 2000. Symmetric tragedies: commons and anti-commons, *Journal of Law and Economics* 43(1): 1–13

Bulow, Jeremy and Lawrence Summers, 1986. A theory of dual labor markets with applications to industrial policy, discrimination and Keynesian unemployment, *Journal of Labor Economics* 4(3): 376–414

Bureau of Labor Statistics, 2004. *The Effect of Outsourcing and Offshoring on BLS Productivity Measures*, March 26, available on August 20, 2004 at www.bls.gov/lpc/lproffshoring.pdf

Burgelman, Robert, 2002. *Strategy Is Destiny: How Strategy-Making Shapes a Company's Future*, New York: Free Press

Bush, Winston C., 1972. Individual welfare in anarchy, in Gordon Tullock (ed.), *Explorations in the Theory of Anarchy*, Blacksburg, VA: University Publications, Inc.

Buurma, Christine, 2009. Energy consumption by the numbers, *Wall Street Journal*, January 9: R2

Byrne, John A., 1996. Has outsourcing gone too far? *Business Week*, April 1: 27

Cable, John and Nicolas Wilson, 1989. Profit-sharing and productivity: an analysis of UK engineering firms, *Economic Journal* 99: 366–75

Cain, G. G., 1986. The economic analysis of labor market discrimination: a survey, in O. Aschenfelter and R. Layard (eds.), *Handbook of Labor Economics*, London: Elsevier Science Publishers

Cannon, Michael F., 2003. Three avenues to patient power, *Brief Analysis*, Dallas, TX: National Center for Policy Analysis, 430, January 30, available on August 17, 2004 at www.ncpa.org/iss/hea/2003/pd013003a.html

Card, David and Alan B. Krueger, 1995. *Myth and Measurement: The New Economics of the Minimum Wage*, Princeton, NJ: Princeton University Press

Carmichael, H. L., 1988. Incentives in academics: why is there tenure? *Journal of Political Economy* 96(2): 453–72

Cartwright, Dorwin, 1968. The nature of group cohesiveness, in Dorwin Cartwright and Alvin Zander (eds.), *Group Dynamics: Research and Theory*, 3rd edn, New York: Harper and Row

Chernova, Yuliya and Sari Krieger, 2009. How to go green in hard times, *Wall Street Journal*, January 9: R1

Cherrie, Victoria, 2005. Dell requests rezoning for new access road in agricultural area, *Winston-Salem Journal*, April 30: B1

Christensen, Clayton M., 1997. *The Innovator's Dilemma: When New Technologies Cause Great Firms to Fail*, Cambridge, MA: Harvard Business School Press

Chung, Juliet, 2009. Looming tariffs whet appetite for delicacies, *Wall Street Journal*, March 31: A3.

Coase, Ronald H., 1937. The nature of the firm, *Economica* 4(16): 386–405
    1972. Durability and monopoly, *Journal of Law and Economics* 15: 143–9
    1988. *The Firm, the Market, and the Law*, Chicago: University of Chicago Press: 33–55 (reprinted from Ronald H. Coase, The nature of the firm, *Economica* 4 (1937): 386–405)

Cobb, William E., 1973. Theft and the two hypotheses, in Simon Rottenberg (ed.), *The Economics of Crime and Punishment*, Washington, DC: American Enterprise Institute for Public Policy Research

Coleman, Major D., Michael Lacour-Little, and Kerry D. Vandell, 2008. Subprime lending and the housing bubble: tail wags the dog? Social Science Research Network, September 2, accessed January 14, 2009 from http://papers.ssrn.com/sol3/papers.cfm?abstract_id=1262365

Congressional Budget Office, 2009. *The Estimated Costs to Households from the Cap-and-Trade Provisions of H.R. 2454*, June 19, as accessed on June 25, 2009 from http://cbo.gov/ftpdocs/103xx/doc10327/06-19-CapTradeCosts.htm

Cooter, Robert and Thomas Ulen, 1988. *Law and Economics*, Glenview, IL: Scott Foresman

Cosmides, Leda and John Tooby, 1992. Cognitive adaptation for social exchange, in Jerome H. Barkow, Leda Cosmides, and John Tooby (eds.), *The Adapted Mind*, New York: Oxford University Press

Craig, Lynn, 2003. The time cost of children: a cross-national comparison of the interaction between time use and fertility rate, University of New South Wales, Sydney, paper presented at the IATUR Conference on Time Use Research, September 15–17, available on August 17, 2004 at www.sprc.unsw.edu.au/people/Craig/Time%20Cost%20of%20Children%20Time%20use%20and%20Fertility.pdf

Crain, W. Mark and Thomas D. Hopkins, 2001. *The Impact of Regulatory Costs on Small Firms: A Report for the Office of Advocacy*, Washington, DC: U.S. Small Business Administration, RFP No. SBAHW-00-R-0027, available on March 31, 2005 at www.sba.gov/advo/research/rs207.pdf

Crandall, Robert, 1985. Assessing the impact of the automobile export restraints upon U.S. automobile prices, Brookings Institution, December, mimeo

Crucini, Mario J. and James Kahn, 1996. Tariffs and aggregate economic activity: lessons from the Great Depression, *Journal of Monetary Economics* 38(3): 427–67

Dahl, Jonathan, 1994. Many bypass the new rules of the road, *Wall Street Journal*, September 29: B1

Daniels, Mitch, 2009. Indiana says "no thanks" to cap and trade, *Wall Street Journal*, May 15: A11

David, Paul A., 1985. Clio and the economics of QWERTY, *American Economic Review* 75(2): 332–7

Davidow, William and Michael Malone, 1992. *The Virtual Corporation*, New York: HarperCollins

Davis, Bob, 2009. World economies plummet, *Wall Street Journal*, May 21: A1

Davis, Laura J., 2005. Privatization brings big savings to Michigan's state universities, Chicago: Heartland Institute, April, available on May 13, 2005 at www.heartland.org/Article.cfm?artId=16769

Dawkins, Richard, 1976. *The Selfish Gene*, Oxford: Oxford University Press

Demick, Barbara, 2009. China links birth defects to pollution, *Los Angeles Times*, February 2: A6

Demsetz, Harold, 1967. Toward a theory of property rights, *American Economic Review* 57: 347–59

Deneckere, Raymond J. and R. Preston McAfee, 1996. Damaged goods, *Journal of Economics and Management Strategy* 5(2): 149–74

Dennen, Rodgers Taylor, 1975. From common to private property: the enclosure of the open range, PhD dissertation, Economics Department, University of Washington

Dennis, Debra K. and John J. McConnell, 1986. Corporate mergers and security returns, *Journal of Financial Economics* 16: 143–87

DeLorenzo, Thomas J., 1985. The origins of antitrust: an interest group perspective, *International Review of Law and Economics* 5: 73–90

Dore, Ronald P., 1987. *Taking Japan Seriously*, Stanford, CA: Stanford University Press

Dornbush, Rudiger and Paul Krugman, 1976. Flexible exchange rates in the short run, *Brookings Papers on Economic Activity*, March: 537–75

Drucker, Peter, 2001. *Management Challenges for the 21st Century*, New York: HarperBusiness

Dunbar, Robin, 1998. The social brain hypothesis, *Evolutionary Anthropology* 6: 178–90

Dunlap, Al and Bob Andelman, 1996. *Mean Business: How I Save Bad Companies and Make Good Companies Great*, New York: Times Books

Dunn, L. F., 1985. Nonpecuniary job preferences and welfare losses among migrant agriculture workers, *American Journal of Agricultural Economics* 67(2): 257–65

Dyer, Geoff and Tom Braithwaite, 2009. U.S. tyre duties spark China clash, *FT.com*, accessed on September 15, 2009 from www.ft.com/cms/s/0/f67c6fe6-a024-11de-b9ef-00144feabdc0.html

Earley, P. Christopher, 1989. Social loafing and collectivism: a comparison of the United States and the People's Republic of China, *Administrative Science Quarterly* 34(4): 565–82

The Economist, 1999. Lessons from Microsoft, March 6: 21

2004a. Dead firms walking, September 23, available on June 21, 2005 at www.economist.com/business/displayStory.cfm?story_id=3219857

2004b. Low-cost airlines, July 8, available on June 21, 2005 at www.economist.com/displaystory.cfm?story_id=S%27%298L%25Q%21%2F%21%20P%23L%0A

2004c. Turbulent skies, July 8, available on August 21, 2005 at www.economist.com/business/displaystory.cfm?story_id=2897525

Editors. *Wall Street Journal*, 2009. Obama's global tax raid, May 6: A14

Eichengreen, Barry, 1989. The political economy of the Smoot-Hawley tariff, *Research in Economic History* 12: 1–43

Energy Information Administration, 2007. *Emissions of Greenhouse Gases in the United States, 2006*, tables 5–9 (November), as accessed on May 24, 2009 from http://usasearch.gov/search?affiliate=eia.doe.gov&v%3Aproject=firstgov&query=emissions+GDP and www.eia.doe.gov/oiaf/1605/archive/gg02rpt/gasfig1.html

Esty, Daniel C. and Andrew Winston, 2009. *Green to Gold: How Smart Companies Use Environmental Strategy to Innovate, Create Value, and Build Competitive Advantage*, New York: Wiley

Evans, David S., Albert Nichols, and Bernard Reddy, 1999. *The Rise and Fall of Leaders in Personal Computer Software*, Cambridge, MA: National Economic Research Associates, January 7

Farrell, J. and P. Klemperer, 2007. Coordination and lock-in: competition with switching costs and network effects, in M. Armstrong and R. H. Porter (eds.), *Handbook of Industrial Organization*, Amsterdam: Elsevier

Fast, N. and N. Berg, 1971. The Lincoln Electric Company, *Harvard Business School Case*, Cambridge, MA: Harvard Business School Press

Feenstra, Robert C., 1992. How costly is protectionism? *Journal of Economic Perspective* 6(3): 159–78

Fehr, Ernst and Klaus M. Schmidt, 2002. Theories of fairness and reciprocity – evidence and economic application, in M. Dewatripont, L. Hansen, and S. J. Turnovsky (eds.), *Advances in Economics and Econometrics*, 8th World Congress, Cambridge: Cambridge University Press

Feldstein, Martin, 2009. Tax increases could kill the recovery, *Wall Street Journal*, May 13, 2009: A19

Ferrell, Greg, 2000. Online time at office soars, *USA Today*, February 18: 1A

Fishback, Price V., 1992. *Soft Coal, Hard Choices: The Economic Welfare of Bituminous Coal Miners, 1890–1930*, New York: Oxford University Press

Fisher, Franklin M., 1998. Direct testimony, *U.S. v. Microsoft Corporation*, Civil Action No. 98–1233 (TPJ), filed October 14, available on August 16, 2004 at www.usdoj.gov/atr/cases/f2000/2057.pdf

Fisher, Richard W., 2005. Protect us from protectionists, *Wall Street Journal*, April 25: A14

FitzRoy, Felix R. and Kornelius Kraft, 1986. Profitability and profit-sharing, *Journal of Industrial Economics* 35(2): 113–30

  1987. Cooperation, productivity and profit sharing, *Quarterly Journal of Economics* 103: 23–36

Fleisher, Belton M., 1981. *Minimum Wage Regulation in Retail Trade*, Washington, DC: American Enterprise Institute

Flint, Joe, 2005. Blockbuster faces state suit over no late fees, *Wall Street Journal*, February 22: D2

Forelle, Charles and Nick Wingfield, 2009. EU hits Microsoft with new antitrust charges, *Wall Street Journal*, January 17–18: B5

Frank, Robert H., 1988. *Passions within Reason: The Strategic of the Emotions*, New York: W. W. Norton

Frank, Robert H., Thomas Gilgorich, and Dennis T. Regan, 1996. Do economists make bad citizens? *Journal of Economic Perspectives* 10 GJ: 187–92

Frank, Steven A. 2009. Evolutionary foundations of cooperation and group cohesion, in Simon A. Levin. (ed.), *Games, Groups, and the Global Good*, Heidelberg: Springer

Frauenheim, Ed, 2005. Getting tough with China? *CNET News.com: Tech News First*, May 20, available on May 23, 2005 at http://news.com.com/Getting+tough+with+China/2100-1022-5714390.html?part=dtx&tag=ntop&tag=nl.e703

Fresh Plaza, 2008. EU, Latin America look to WTO talks for banana deal, December 8, accessed March 9, 2009 from www.freshplaza.com/news_detail.asp?id=34605

Friedman, David, 1996. *Hidden Order: The Economics of Everyday Life*, New York: HarperBusiness

Friedman, Milton, 1962. *Capitalism and Freedom*, Chicago: University of Chicago Press, 40th anniversary edition, republished in 2002

Friedman, Milton and Rose Friedman, 1998. *Two Lucky People*, Chicago: University of Chicago Press

Friedman, Milton and L. J. Savage, 1948. The utility analysis of choices involving risk, *Journal of Political Economy* 56: 279–304

Furnham, A., 1993. Wasting time in the board room, *Financial Times*, March 10: 11

Galbraith, John Kenneth, 1967. *The New Industrial State*, Boston: Houghton Mifflin

Gelbach, Jonah B., Jonathan Klick, and Tyhomas Stratmann, 2007. Cheap donuts and expensive broccoli: the effect of relative prices on obesity, Tallahassee, FL: College of Law, Florida State University, Research Law Paper no. 261, March 21, accessed August 27, 2009 from the Social Science Research Network, http://papers.ssrn.com/sol3/papers.cfm?abstract_id=976484

Ghosn, Carlos, 2005. *Shift: Inside Nissan's Historic Revival*, New York: Doubleday, U.S. edn

Gibbons, Robert and Kevin J. Murphy, 1992. Optimal incentive contracts in the presence of career concerns: theory and evidence, *Journal of Political Economy* 100(3): 468–506

Gilder, George, 1989. *Microcosm: The Quantum Revolution in Economics and Technology*, New York: Simon and Schuster

Gintis, Herbert, 2000a. *Game Theory Evolving*, Princeton, NJ: Princeton University Press
    2000b. Strong reciprocity and human sociality, *Journal of Theoretical Biology* 211: 169–79

Girion, Lisa, 2005. Obesity is costly to state, report says, *Los Angeles Times*, April 6: C1

Gladwell, Malcolm, 2000. *The Tipping Point: How Little Things Can Make a Big Difference*, Boston: Little, Brown & Co.

Gneezy, Uri and Aldo Rustichini, 2000. A fine is a price, *Journal of Legal Studies* 29(1): 1–17

Goldberg, Jonah, 2003. Bah Humbug: blame uninformed voters, Townhall.com, December 26, as available on October 5, 2004 at www.townhall.com/opinion/columns/jonahgoldberg/2003/12/26.1606/html

Goodman, John C. and Gerald L. Musgrave, 1992. *Patient Power: Solving America's Health Care Crisis*, Washington, DC: Cato Institute

Goodman, John C., Gerald L. Musgrave, and Devon M. Herrick, 2004. *Lives at Risk: Single-Payer Health Insurance around the World*, Dallas: National Center for Policy Analysis, July

Gordon, H. Scott, 1954. The economic theory of a common property resource: the fishery, *Journal of Political Economy* 62(2): 124–42

Greenhouse, Steven, 2005. Can't retail behemoth pay more? *New York Times*, May 4: C1

Greenspan, Alan. 2007. *The Age of Turbulence: Adventures in a New World*, New York: Penguin.

Greenville, Jared W. and T. G. MacAulay, 2004. Tariffs and steel: the U.S. safeguard actions, Sydney: Agricultural and Resource Economics, University of Sydney, paper presented at the Annual Conference of the Australian Agricultural and Resource Economics Society, Melbourne, February

Grinblatt, S. J. and S. Titman, 2002. *Financial Markets and Corporate Strategy*, Boston, MA: McGraw-Hill/Irwin

Gunderson, Morley, 1989. Male–female wage differentials and policy responses, *Journal of Economic Literature* 27(1): 46–72

Gurbaxani, Vijay and Seungjin Whang, 1991. The impact of information systems on organizations and markets, *Communication of the ACM* 34(1): 59–73

Halberstam, David, 1986. *The Reckoning*, New York: Avon Books

Hamilton, Alexander, John Jay and James Madison, 1964. *The Federalist: A Commentary on the Constitution of the United States*, no. 51, New York: Random House, Modern Library edn

Hanke, Steve H. 2008. Testimony on rising food prices: budget challenges, before the Committee on the Budget, U.S. Congress, House of Representatives, July 30, as accessed on January 14, 2008, from http://web.jhu.edu/gcpa/government/federal/images/pdfs/Hanke_30-07-2008.pdf

Hansell, Saul, 2005. Wal-Mart ends online video rentals and promotes netflix, *New York Times*, May 20: C3

Hardin, Garrett, 1968. The tragedy of the commons, *Science* 62: 1243–54

Hare, A. Paul, 1952. A study of interaction and consensus in different-sized groups, *American Sociological Review* 17: 261–8

Hashimoto, Masanori, 1982. Minimum wage effects on training to the job, *American Economic Review* 70: 1070–87

Hayek, F. A., 1944. *The Road to Serfdom*, Chicago: University of Chicago Press
    1945. The use of knowledge in society, *American Economic Review* 35(3): 519–30
    1948. The meaning of competition, in F. Hayek, *Individualism and Economic Order*, Chicago: University of Chicago Press
    1960. *The Constitution of Liberty*, Chicago: University of Chicago Press

Hayes, L., 1988. All eyes on DuPont's incentive program, *Wall Street Journal*, December 5: B1

Heller, Michael A., 1998. The tragedy of the anticommons: property in transition, *Harvard Law Review* 111: 621–88

Henderson, David R. 2009. A Nobel for practical economics, *Wall Street Journal*, October 13: A19

Henrich, Joseph, Robert Boyd, Samuel Bowles, Colin Camerer, Ernst Fehr, Herbert Gintis, and Richard McElreath, 2001. In search of homo economicus: behavioral experiments in 15 small-scale societies, *American Economic Review: Papers and Proceedings* 91: 73–8

Herszenhorn, David M. 2009. Senate releases second portion of the bailout fund, *New York Times*, January 16: A1

Hesson, Robert, 1979. *In Defense of the Corporation*, Stanford, CA: Hoover Institution Press

Hewitt, Michael, 2004. Commissioners pass Dell plant incentives, *Winston-Salem Journal*, December 14, available on April 25, 2005 at www.journalnow.com/servlet/Satellite?pagename=WSJ%2FMGArticle%2FWSJ_BasicArticle&c=MGArticle&cid=1031779670184

Heyne, Paul, 1994. *The Economic Way of Thinking*, New York: Macmillan

Hirsch, Jerry, 2005. Is wholesale change in alcohol pricing on tap? *Los Angeles Times*, April 11: C1

Hirshleifer, Jack, 1999. There are many pathways to cooperation, *Journal of Bioeconomics* 1: 73–93

Hobbes, Thomas, 1968. *Leviathan*, ed. C. B. Macpherson, Baltimore, MD: Penguin (first published in 1651)

Hoffman, Elizabeth, Kevin A. McCabe, and Vernon L. Smith, 1998. Behavioral foundations of reciprocity: experimental economics and evolutionary psychology, *Economic Inquiry* 36: 335–52

Holmstrom, Bengt, 1979. Moral hazard and observability, *Bell Journal of Economics* 10: 74–91

Holmstrom, Bengt and Stephen Kaplan, 2001. Corporate governance and merger activity in the United States: making sense of the 1980s and 1990s, *Journal of Economic Perspectives* 15(2): 121–44

Homans, George C., 1950. *The Human Group*, New York: Harcourt, Brace, Inc.

Horngren, C. T., 1999. *Cost Accounting: A Managerial Emphasis*, Englewood Cliffs, NJ: Prentice Hall

Howard, Bion B. and Peter O. Dietz, 1969. *A Study of the Financial Significance of Profit Sharing*, Chicago: Council of Profit Sharing Industries

Hufbauer, Gary Clyde and Paul L. E. Grieco, 2005. The payoff from globalization, Washington, DC: Institute for International Economics, May, available on June 2, 2005 at www.iie.com/publications/papers/hufbauer0505.htm

Hufbauer, Gary Clyde *et al.*, 1986. *Trade Protection in the United States: 31 Case Studies*, Washington, DC: Institute for International Economics

Husled, Mark, 1995. The impact of human resource management practices on turnover, productivity and corporate financial performance, *Academy of Management Journal* 38(2): 635–72

Ichniowski, Casey, Kathryn Shaw, and Giovanna Prennushi, 1996. The effects of human resource practices on productivity, Cambridge, MA: National Bureau of Economic Research, Working Paper 5333

Ingrassia, Paul, 2005. Junk cars, *Wall Street Journal*, May 17: A12

James, John, 1951. A preliminary study of the size determinants in small-group interaction, *American Sociological Review* 16: 444–74

Jarrell, Gregg A., James A. Brickley, and Jeffrey M. Netter, 1988. The market for corporate control: the empirical evidence since 1980, *Journal of Economic Perspectives* 2: 49–68

Jarrell, Gregg A. and Annette B. Paulsen, 1989. The returns to acquiring firms in tender offers: evidence from three decades, *Financial Management* 18: 12–19

Jensen, Michael, 1988. Takeovers: their causes and consequences, *Journal of Economic Perspectives* 2(1): 21–48

1989. Eclipse of the public corporation, *Harvard Business Review* 67(5): 61–74

Jensen, Michael and William H. Meckling, 1976. Theory of the firm: managerial behavior, agency costs and ownership structure, *Journal of Financial Economics* 3: 325–8

1979. Property rights and production functions: an application of labor-managed firms and codetermination, *Journal of Business* 52: 469–506

Jensen, Michael and Richard S. Ruback, 1983. The market for corporate control: the scientific evidence, *Journal of Financial Economics* 11(5): 5–50

Johnson, David L., 1974. An analysis of the costs and benefits for criminals in theft, St. Cloud, MN: Economics Department, St. Cloud State College, mimeo

Joskow, Paul, 1985. Vertical integration and long-term contracts: the case of coal-burning electric generating plants, *Journal of Law, Economics, and Organization* 1: 33–80

Kahneman, Daniel, Richard H. Thaler, and J. Knetsch, 1990. Experimental tests of the Endowment and the Coase Theorem, *Journal of Political Economy* 98(6): 1325–48

Kalita, Mitra, 2009. Americans see 18% of their wealth vanish, *Wall Street Journal*, March 13: A1

Kant, Immauel, 1999 [1781]. *Critique of Pure Reason*, Cambridge: Cambridge University Press

Kanter, Rosebeth M., 1973. *Commitment and Community: Communes and Utopias in Sociological Perspective*, Cambridge, MA: Harvard University Press

Kaplan, Karen, 2009. Calls to tax junk food gain ground. *Los Angeles Times*, August 23, accessed on September 15, 2009 from www.latimes.com/news/nationworld/nation/la-sci-junk-food-tax23-2009aug23,0,5244082.story

Karstensson, Lewis, 2003. The merchant and Mr. Reagan, *American Journal of Economics and Sociology* 62(3): 568–82

Keeling, R. F., S. C. Piper, A. F. Bollenbacher, and J. S. Walker, 2009. Atmospheric carbon dioxide record from Mauna Loa, La Jolla, CA: Carbon Dioxide Research Group, Scripps Institution of Oceanography, University of California, accessed February 9, 2009, from http://cdiac.ornl.gov/trends/co2/sio-mlo.html

Keller, John J., 1997. Best phone discounts go to hardest bargainers, *Wall Street Journal*, February 13: B1, B12

Kelly, Kevin, 1998. *New Rules for the New Economy*, New York: Viking/Penguin

Keynes, John Maynard, 1936. *The General Theory of Employment, Interest and Money*, New York: Harcourt Brace, republished in 1991

Kirzner, Israel, 1973. *Competition and Entrepreneurship*, Chicago: University of Chicago Press

Klein, Benjamin, Robert Crawford, and Armen Alchian, 1978. Vertical integration, appropriable rents, and the competitive contracting process, *Journal of Law and Economics* 21: 297–326

Klein, Benjamin and Keith B. Leffler, 1981. The role of market forces in assuring contractual performance, *Journal of Law and Economics* 89(4): 615–41

Klein, Benjamin and Lester F. Saft, 1985. The law and economics of franchise tying contracts, *Journal of Law and Economics* 28: 345–61

Klein, Joel I. *et. al.*, 1998. Complaint, *United States of America v. Microsoft Corporation*, May 20, available on August 20, 2004 at www.usdoj.gov/atr/cases3/micros/1763.htm

Klein, Richard G., 2000. Archaeology and the evolution of human behavior, *Evolutionary Anthropology* 32: 391–428

Knauft, Bruce, 1991. Violence and and sociality in human evolution, *Current Anthropology* 32: 391–428

Knight, Frank H., 1921. *Risk, Uncertainty, and Profit*, Chicago: University of Chicago Press, republished in 1971

Koening, R., 1990. DuPont plan linking pay to fibers profit unravels, *Wall Street Journal*, October 25: B1

Kohn, Alfie, 1993a. *Punished by Rewards*, Boston, MA: Houghton Mifflin
1993b. Why incentive plans cannot work, *Harvard Business Review*, September–October: 54–63

Kosters, Marvin and Finis Welch, 1972. The effects of minimum wages on the distribution of changes in aggregate employment, *American Economic Review* 62: 323–31

Krueger, Alan B., 2005. Economic scene: the farm-subsidy model of financing academia, *New York Times*, May 26: C2

Krueger, Ann O., 1974. The political economy of the rent-seeking society, *American Economic Review* 64: 291–303

Krugman, Paul, 2008. *The Return of Depression Economics and the Crisis of 2008*, New York: W. W. Norton

2009. Out of the shadows, *New York Times*, June 19: A21

Laband, David N. and Bernard F. Lentz, 1990. Entrepreneurial success and occupational inheritance among proprietors, *Canadian Journal of Economics* 23(3): 101–17

1990. *Strategic Pay: Aligning Organizational Strategies and Pay Systems*, San Francisco: Jossey-Bass

Labaton, Stephen, 2009. Tough enough: senior lawmakers have doubts on spreading the regulatory reach, *New York Times*, June 18: B1

Lawler, Edward E., 1968. Effects of hourly overpayment on productivity and work quality, *Journal of Personality and Social Psychology* 10: 306–14

1990. *Strategic Pay: Aligning Organizational Strategies and Pay Systems*, San Francisco: Jossey-Bass

Lazear, Edward, 1979. Why is there mandatory retirement? *Journal of Political Economy* 87: 1261–84

2000. Performance pay and productivity, *American Economic Review* 90: 1346–61

Lazear, Edward and S. Rosen, 1981. Rank-order tournaments as optimum labor contract, *Journal of Political Economy* 89(3): 841–64

Lean, Geoffrey, 2007. Global warming "is three times faster than worst predictions," *The Independent*, June 3, accessed on February 5, 2009 from www.independent.co.uk/environment/climate-change/global-warming-is-three-times-faster-than-worst-predictions-451529.html

Ledyard, John O., 1995. Public goods: a survey of experimental research, in John H. Kager and Alvin E. Roth (eds.), *Handbook of Experimental Economics*, Princeton, NJ: Princeton University Press

Lee, Dwight R., 1990. Why it pays to have tough profs, *The Margin*, September–October: 28–9

Lee, Dwight R. and David Kreutzer, 1982. Lagged demand and a perverse response to threatened property rights, *Economic Inquiry* 20: 579–88

Lee, Dwight R. and Richard B. McKenzie, 1998. How the client effect moderates price competition, *Southern Economic Journal* 64(3): 741–52

Lee, Louis, 1996. Without a receipt you may get stuck with that ugly scarf, *Wall Street Journal*, November 18: A1

Lee, William G., 1994. The new corporate republics, *Wall Street Journal*, September 26: A12

Lehn, Kenneth and Annette B. Paulsen, 1987. Sources of value in leveraged buyouts, in Murray Weidenbaum (ed.), *Public Policy towards Corporate Takeovers*, New Brunswick, NJ: Transaction

Leighton, Linda and Jacob Mincer, 1981. Effects of minimum wages on human capital formation, in Simon Rothenberg (ed.), *The Economics of Legal Minimum Wages*, Washington, DC: American Enterprise Institute

Lessig, Lawrence, 2001. *The Future of Ideas: The Fate of the Commons in a Connected World*, New York: Random House

Levitt, Stephen D. and Stephen J. Dubner, 2005. *Freakonomics: A Rogue Economist Explores the Hidden Side of Everything*, New York: William Morrow, revised edition 2006

Lichter, Robert, Linda Lichter, and Stanley Rothman, 1990. *Watching America*, New York: Prentice Hall

Liebowitz, Stan J. and Stephen E. Margolis, 1995. Path dependence, lock-in and history, *Journal of Law, Economics, and Organization* 11(1): 205–26

  1999. *Winners, Losers, and Microsoft: How Technology Markets Choose Products*, Oakland, CA: Independent Institute (reprinted from Stan J. Liebowitz and Stephen E. Margolis, The fable of the keys, *Journal of Law and Economics* 33 (1990): 1–25)

Lisser, Eleena de, 1999. Windows shopping – one-click commerce: what people do now to goof off at work, *Wall Street Journal*, September 24: A1

Locke, John, 1690. *The Second Treatise of Civil Government*, as found on August 10, 2004 at http://oregonstate.edu/instruct/phl302/texts/locke/locke2/2nd-contents.html

Los Angeles Times Wire Service, 2005. More goods from China face limits, *Los Angeles Times*, May 19: C3

Lott, Jr., John R. and Russell D. Roberts, 1991. A guide to the pitfalls of identifying price discrimination, *Economic Inquiry* 29(1): 14–23

Ludwig, D. S., K. E. Peterson, and S. L. Gortmaker, 2001. Relation between consumption of sugar-sweetened drinks and childhood obesity: a prospective, observational analysis, *Lancet* 357: 505–8

Luna, Nancy, 2005. Lack of late fee empties shelves, *Orange County (CA) Register*, February 18: business 1

Malatesta, Paul H. and Ralph A. Walkling, 1988. Poison pill securities: stockholder wealth, profitability, and ownership structure, *Journal of Financial Economics* 20(1): 347–76

Mandelson, Peter, 2009. We need greater global governance, *Wall Street Journal*, June 19: A13

Mangum, G. L., 1962. Are wage incentives becoming obsolete? *Industrial Relations* 2: 73–96

Manne, Henry G., 1963. Mergers and the market for corporate control, *Journal of Political Economy* 73: 110–20

Marks, Mindy, 2004. Minimum wages and fringe benefits, Economics Department, St. Louis: Washington University, Working Paper

Marshall, Ray, 1974. Economics of racial discrimination, *Journal of Economic Literature* 12: 849–71

Marwell, Gerald and Ruth Ames, 1981. Economists free ride, does anyone else? *Journal of Public Economics* 15: 295–310

Maslow, A. H., 1954. *Motivation and Personality*, New York: Harper and Row

Mathewson, G. Frank and Ralph A. Winter, 1985. The economics of franchise contracts, *Journal of Law and Economics* 28: 503–26

McCabe, K. and V. L. Smith, 1999. A comparison of naive and sophisticated subject behavior with game theoretic predictions, *Proceedings of the National Academy of Sciences of the USA* 97: 3777–81

McChesney, Fred S., 1997. *Money for Nothing: Politicians, Rent Extraction and Political Extortion*, Cambridge, MA: Harvard University Press

McConnell, John J. and Chris J. Muscarella, 1985. Capital expenditure decisions and market value of the firm, *Journal of Financial Economics* 14: 399–422

McCormack, Richard, 2008. U.S. container exports still dominated by junk – scrap paper, scrap metal and bulk commodities, *Manufacturing and Technology News*, July 31, 15(14), as accessed March 25, 2009 from www.manufacturingnews.com/news/08/0731/PIERS.html

McKenzie, Richard B., 1977. Political ignorance: an empirical assessment of educational remedies, in Gordon Tullock (ed.), *Frontiers of Economics*, Blacksburg, VA: University Publications

1987. The loss of textile and apparel jobs: the relative importance of imports and productivity, *Cato Journal*, winter: 731–46

1994. *Times Change: The Minimum Wage and the New York Times*, San Francisco: Pacific Research Institute

1996. In defense of academic tenure, *Journal of Institutional and Theoretical Economics* 152(2): 325–41

1997. *The Paradox of Progress*, New York: Oxford University Press

2000. *Trust on Trial: How the Microsoft Case Is Transforming the Rules of Competition*, Boston, MA: Perseus

2008. *Why Popcorn Costs So Much at the Movies, and Other Pricing Puzzles*, Heidelberg: Springer/Copernicus

2010. *Predictably Rational? In Search of Defenses of Rational Behavior in Economics*, Heidelberg: Springer

McKenzie, Richard B. and Roman Galar, 2004. The importance of deviance in intellectual development, *American Journal of Economics and Sociology* 63(1): 19–49

McKenzie, Richard B. and Dwight R. Lee, 1991. *Quicksilver Capital: How the Rapid Movement of Wealth Has Changed the World*, New York: Free Press

1992. A reexamination of the relative efficiency of the draft and the all-volunteer army, *Southern Economic Journal* 58 (January): 644–54

2008. *In Defense of Monopoly: How Market Power Fosters Creative Production*, Ann Arbor, MI: University of Michigan Press

McKenzie, Richard B. and Thomas Sullivan, 1987. The NCAA as a cartel: an economic and legal reinterpretation, *Antitrust Bulletin* 3: 373–99

McKenzie, Richard B. and Gordon Tullock, 1994. *The New World of Economics*, New York: McGraw-Hill

McMillan, John, 2002. *Reinventing the Bazaar: The Natural History of Markets*, New York: W. W. Norton

Metzger, Bertram L., 1975. *Profit Sharing in 38 Large Companies, I & II*, Evanston, IL: Profit Sharing Research Foundation

Meyer, Stephen, 1981. *The Five-Dollar Day: Labor, Management, and Social Control in the Ford Motor Company, 1908–1921*, Albany, NY: State University of New York Press

Micklethwait, John and Adrian Wooldridge, 2003. *The Company: A Short History of a Revolutionary Idea*, New York: The Modern Library

Mikkelson, Wayne H. and Richard S. Ruback, 1985. An empirical analysis of the interfirm equity investment process, *Journal of Financial Economics* 14: 523–53

Milgrom, Paul and John Roberts, 1992. *Economics, Organization and Management*, Englewood Cliffs, NJ: Prentice Hall

Miller, Gary J., 1992. *Managerial Dilemmas: The Political Economy of Hierarchy*, New York: Cambridge University Press

Miller, Scott, 2005. WTO urges caution on textile limits, *Wall Street Journal*, April 25: A2

Mises, Ludwig von, 1962. *The Ultimate Foundations of Economic Science: An Essay on Method*, Princeton, NJ: D. Van Nostrand

Mitchell, Mark L. and Kenneth Lehn, 1990. Do bad bidders become good targets? *Journal of Political Economy* 98(2): 372–98

Mitchell, R., 1994. Managing by values, *Business Week*, August 1

Moore, Gordon E., 1994. The accidental entrepreneur, *Engineering & Science* 62(4): 23–30

Muñoz, Lorenza, 2005. Blockbuster settles state probes into late-fee ads, *Los Angeles Times*, March 30: C1

Murphy, Robert P., 2009. The economics of climate change, *The Library of Liberty*, July 6, 2009, as accessed July 6, 2009 from www.econlib.org/library/Columns/y2009/Murphyclimate.html#note_1

Nalbantian, Haig R. and Andrew Schotter, 1997. Productivity under group incentives: an experimental study, *American Economic Review* 87(3): 314–41

Nasar, Sylvia, 1998. *A Beautiful Mind*, New York: Simon and Schuster

National Center for Health Statistics, 2009. *Health, United States, 2008, with Chart Cook on Trends in the Health of Americans*, Hyattsville, MD: U.S. Government Printing Office, accessed August 6, 2009 from www.cdc.gov/nchs/data/hus/hus08.pdf

National Center for Policy Analysis, 1994. Answering the critics of medical savings accounts, *Brief Analysis*, Dallas, TX: National Center for Policy Analysis, September 16

National Heart, Lung, and Blood Institute, 1998. *Clinical Guidelines on the Identification, Evaluation, and Treatment of Overweight and Obesity in Adults: The Evidence Report.* Bethesda, MD: National Heart, Lung, and Blood Institute

Navarro, Peter, 2008. *The Coming China Wars: Where They Will Be Fought and How They Can Be Won, Revised and Expanded Edition*, rev. edn, Upper Saddle River, NJ: FT Press

Neumann, W. R., 1986. *The Paradox of Mass Politics*, Cambridge, MA: Harvard University Press

Neumark, David and William L. Wascher, 2008. *Minimum Wages*, Cambridge, MA: MIT Press

New York Times, 2005. Lenovo of China completes purchase of IBM's PC unit, May 5: C5

Nishiguchi, Toshihiro, 1994. *Strategic Industrial Sourcing: The Japanese Advantage*, New York: Oxford University Press

Nishiguchi, Toshihiro and Ikeda Masayoshi, 1996. Suppliers' process innovation: understated aspects of Japanese industrial sourcing, in Toshihiro Nishiguchi (ed.), *Managing Product Development*, New York: Oxford University Press

Norberg, Johan, 2009. *Financial Fiasco: How America's Infatuation with Home Ownership and Easy Money Created the Economic Crisis*, Washington, DC: Cato Institute

Obama, Barack, 2009. Barack Obama: 21st century regulatory reform, *FT.com*, as accessed on June 18, 2009 at www.ft.com/cms/s/0/12b0b48a-5b54-11de-be3f-00144feabdc0.html

Olson, Mancur, 1971. *The Logic of Collective Action: Public Goods and the Theory of Groups*, Cambridge, MA: Harvard University Press

Ostrom, Elinor, 1990. *Governing the Commons: The Evolution of Institutions for Collective Action*, Cambridge: Cambridge University Press

2000. Collective action and the evolution of social norms, *Journal of Economic Perspectives* 14: 137–58

Oyer, Paul, 1998. Fiscal year ends and nonlinear incentive contracts: the effect on business seasonality, *Quarterly Journal of Economics* 113: 149–85

Paletta, Damian, 2009. Historic overhaul of finance rules, *Wall Street Journal*, June 18: A1

Parsky, Gerald (commission chair), 2009. *Commission on the 21st Century [California] Economy*, Sacramento, CA: Governor's Office, State of California, September, accessed on September 30, 2009 from www.cotce.ca.gov/documents/reports/documents/Commission_on_the_21st_Century_Economy-Final_Report.pdf

Pearce, Jone L., 1987. Why merit pay doesn't work: implications for organization theory, in D. B. Balkin and L. R. Gomez-Mejia (eds.), *New Perspectives in Compensation*, Englewood Cliffs, NJ: Prentice Hall

Peers, Martin, 2005. At Blockbuster, new strategies raise tensions over board seats, *The Weekly Review* (*Wall Street Journal*), April 18, as found on April 22, 2005 at http://online.wsj.com/article_print/0, SB111378718174309203,00.html

Peers, Martin and Ann Zimmerman, 2005. Dissident Icahn wins board seats at Blockbuster, *Wall Street Journal*, May 12: A1

Pencavel, J. H., 1977. Work effort, on the job screening, and alternative methods of remuneration, *Research in Labor Economics*, 225–59

Peters, Mark, 2009. U.S. plays catch-up in efficiency credits, *Wall Street Journal*, April 13: C4

Peters, Thomas J., 1994. *Tom Peters Seminar: Crazy Times Call for Crazy Organizations*, New York: Vintage Books

Petersen, Tron, 1991. Reward systems and the distribution of wages, *Journal of Law, Economics, and Organizations* 7 (special issue): 130–58

Peterson, John M. and Charles T. Stewart, 1969. *Employment Effects of Minimum Wage Rates*, Washington, DC: American Enterprise Institute for Public Policy Research

Pew Research Center Survey, 2004. Roper Center, Accession no. 0448774, February 4–16

Poole, Robert, 2008. Stimulus shouldn't be an excuse for pork, *Wall Street Journal*, December 10: A18

Porter, Lyman W. and E. E. Lawyer, 1965. Properties of organization structure in relation to job attitudes and job behavior, *Psychological Bulletin* 77: 23–51

Posner, Richard A., 1974. Theories of economic regulation, *Bell Journal of Economics and Management Science* 5(2): 335–58

2009a. Capitalism in crisis, *Wall Street Journal*, May 7: A17

2009b. *A Failure of Capitalism: The Crisis of '08 and the Descent into Depression*, Cambridge, MA: Harvard University Press

Prestowitz, Jr., Clyde V., 1988. *Trading Places: How We Allowed Japan to Take the Lead*, New York: Basic Books

Price, Daniel M., 2009. Free trade, green trade, *Wall Street Journal*, May 6: A23

Princeton Survey Research Associates, 2004. Roper Center, Accession no. 0454615, April 15

Radford, R. A., 1945. The economic organization of a POW camp, *Economica* 12: 189–201

Radia, Ryan, 2009. European officials target Microsoft over Internet Explorer, Press Release, Washington, DC: Competitive Enterprise Institute, as accessed January 20, 2009 at http://cei.org/node/21524

Ragan, James F., 1977. Minimum wages and the youth labor market, *Review of Economics and Statistics* 59: 129–36

Raupach, Michael R., Marland Gregg, Philippe Ciais, Corinne Le Quéré, Josep G. Canadell, Gernot Klepper, and Christopher B. Field, 2007. Global and regional drivers of accelerating CO_2 emissions, *Proceedings of the National Academy of Sciences*, accessed on February 5, 2009 from www.pnas.org/content/104/24/10288

Read, Leonard E., 1983. I, pencil, *The Freeman*, November (originally published in *The Freeman* in 1958), available on July 19, 2004 at www.fee.org/vnews.php?nid=1321

Reuters, 2009. Barack Obama, Greta Garbo and China's trade surplus, January 19, 2009, accessed on January 28, 2009, at www.reuters.com/article/reutersEdge/idUSTRE50I12020090119

Richman, Sheldon, 1981. The rape of Poletown, *Inquiry*, August 3: 24

Rivoli, Pietra, 2006. *The Travels of a T-Shirt in the Global Economy: An Economist Examines the Markets, Power, and Politics of World Trade*, New York: Wiley

Roberts, John, 2004. *The Modern Firm: Organizational Design for Performance and Growth*, New York: Oxford University Press

Robins, James A., 1996. Why and when does agency theory matter? A critical approach to the role of agency theory in the analysis of organizational control, Irvine, CA: Graduate School of Management, University of California, Irvine, Working Paper

Rogers, John, 2008. Despite home upgrades, Gore still "hypocrite" on energy use, group says, *The City (Nashville) Paper*, June 18, accessed on February 6, 2009 from www.nashvillecitypaper.com/news.php?viewStory=60895

Rosenthal, Mathew, 2009. India rejects U.S. proposal of carbon limits, *Wall Street Journal*, July 20: A7

Rothbard, Murray, 1977. *America's Great Depression*. Auburn, AL: Ludwig von Mises Institute

Rubin, Paul H., 1978. The theory of the firm and the structure of the franchise contract, *Journal of Law and Economics* 21(1): 223–33

   1990. *Managing Business Transactions: Controlling the Costs of Coordination, Communication, and Decision Making*, New York: Free Press

   2002. *Darwinian Politics: The Evolutionary Origin of Freedom*, New Brunswick, NJ: Rutgers University Press

Rush, Rebecca, 2005. Chiquita's threat to the Caribbean Islands: the new banana wars, *CounterPunch*, March 26, accessed on March 9, 2009 from www.counterpunch.org/rush05262005.html

Ryngaert, Michael and Jeffry Netter, 1988. Shareholder wealth effects of the Ohio antitakeover law, *Journal of Law, Economics, and Organization* 4: 373–83

2008 *The Subprime Solution: How Today's Global Financial Crisis Happened and What to Do about It*, Princeton, NJ: Princeton University Press

Scott, Anthony, 1955. The fishery: the objective of sole ownership, *Journal of Political Economy* 63: 116–24

Seiler, Eric, 1984. Piece-rate vs. time-rate: the effect of incentives on earnings, *Review of Economics and Statistics* 66(3): 363–75

Sethi, Rajiv and E. Somanathan, 1996. The evolution of social norms in common property resource use, *American Economic Review* 86: 766–88

Shapiro, Carl and Joseph Stiglitz, 1984. Equilibrium unemployment as a worker discipline device, *American Economic Review* 74(3): 433–44

Shavell, Steven, 1979. Risk sharing and incentives in the principal and agent relationship, *Bell Journal of Economics* 10(1): 55–73

Shepherd, William G., 1984. Contestability vs. competition, *American Economic Review* 74: 572–87

Shiller, Robert J., 2005. *Irrational Exuberance*, 2nd edn, Princeton, NJ: Princeton University Press

Simon, Herbert, 1951. A formal theory of employment relationship, *Econometrica* 19: 293–305

Simon, Stephanie, 2009. More states considering tax breaks to woo jobs, *Wall Street Journal*, February 2: A1

Smith, Adam, 1937. *An Inquiry into the Nature and Causes of the Wealth of Nations*, New York: Modern Library

Smith, C. and R. Watts, 1982. Incentive and tax effects of executive compensation plans, *Australian Journal of Management* 7: 139–57

Smith, Vernon L., 1962. An experimental study of competitive market behavior, *Journal of Political Economy* 70: 111–37

Soloman, Deborah and Damian Paletta, 2009. U.S. seeks rest of the bailout cash, *Wall Street Journal*, January 13: A1.

Solomon, Susan, Gian-Kasper Plattner, Reto Knutti, and Pierre Friedlingstein, 2009. Irreversible climate change due to carbon dioxide emissions, *Proceedings of the National Academy of Sciences* 106 (6, February 10): 1704–9, accessed February 5, 2009 from www.pnas.org/content/early/2009/01/28/0812721106.full.pdf+html

Somin, Ilya, 2003. Voter knowledge and constitutional change: the new deal experience, *William and Mary Law Review* 45: 595–615

Sowell, Thomas, 2009. *The Housing Boom and Bust*, New York: Basic Books

Spencer, Herbert, 1896. *Principles of Sociology*, London: Williams and Norgate

Stecklow, Steve, 1994. Evangelical schools reinvent themselves by stressing academics, *Wall Street Journal*, May 12: A1

Steiner, Mary C., Natalie D. Munro, Todd A. Surovell, Eitan Tchernov, and Ofer Bar-Yosef, 1998. Paleolithic population growth pulses evidenced by small animal exploitation, *Science*, September 25, available at www.science mag.org, accessed December 19, 2004

Stephenson, Frederick J. and Richard J. Fox, 1992. Corporate strategies for frequent-flier programs, *Transportation Journal* 32(1): 38–50

Stigler, George J., 1971. The theory of economic regulation, *Bell Journal of Economics* 2(1): 3–21

Stiglitz, Joseph E., 2009. Obama's ersatz capitalism, *New York Times*, April 1: A25

Stokes, Donald E. and Warren E. Miller, 1962. Party government and the saliency of congress, *Public Opinion Quarterly* 26: 531–46

Stout, David, 2009. Senators skeptical of plan on financial regulation, *New York Times*, June 19: B1

Talley, Ian and Thomas Bartley, 2009. Energy chief says U.S. open to carbon tariff, *Wall Street Journal*, March 18, accessed July 20, 2009 from http://online.wsj.com/article/SB123733297926563315.html

Taylor, Frederick W., 1895. A piece rate system, *American Society of Mechanical Engineers Transactions* 16: 856–93

Tellis, Gerald and Peter Golder, 2002. *Will and Vision: How Late Comers Grow To Dominate Markets*, New York: McGraw-Hill

Thaler, Richard H., 1992. *The Winner's Curse: Paradoxes and Anomalies of Economic Life*, New York: Free Press

    2000. Toward a Positive Theory of Consumer Choice, as reprinted in *Quasi Rational Economics*, New York: Russell Sage Foundation: 3–24

Thaler, Richard H. and Cass R. Sunstein, 2008. *Nudge: Improving Decisions about Health, Wealth, and Happiness*, New Haven, CT: Yale University Press.

Thomas, Paulette, 1996. Work week: teams rule, *Wall Street Journal*, May 28: A1

Thompson, Donald N., 1971. *Franchise Operations and Antitrust*, Lexington, MA: D. C. Heath

Tichy, Noel M. and Stratford Sherman, 1993. Jack Welch's lessons for success, *Fortune*, January 25: 86–93

Trivers, Robert L., 1971. The evolution of reciprocal altruism, *Quarterly Review of Biology* 46: 35–57

Tucker, William, 1997. How rent control drives out affordable housing, *Policy Analysis* 274 (May 21), Washington, DC: Cato Institute, available on August 17, 2004 at www.cato.org/pubs/pas/pa-274es.html

Tullock, Gordon, 1967. The welfare costs of tariffs, monopolies, and theft, *Western Economic Journal* 5: 224–32

    1972. *Toward a Mathematics of Politics*, Ann Arbor, MI: University of Michigan Press

Uchitelle, Louis and Edmund L. Andrews, 2009. Economy slides at fastest rate since late 1950s, *New York Times*, April 30: A1

US Department of Labor, 1993. *High Performance Work Practices and Firm Performance*, Washington, DC: Bureau of National Affairs

US Department of State, 2002. Projected Greenhouse Gases, Washington, DC: May, as accessed May 24, 2009 from www.eia.doe.gov/oiaf/1605/archive/gg02rpt/gasfig1.html

Veblen, Thorstein, 1902. *The Theory of the Leisure Class: An Economic Study of Institutions*, New York: Macmillan

Wagner, John L., Paul A. Rubin, and Thomas J. Callahan, 1988. Incentive payment and non-managerial productivity: an interrupted time series analysis of magnitude and trend, *Organizational Behavior and Human Decision Processes* 42(1): 47–74

Walker, Marcus, 2009. Record GDP drop sharpens pain across euro zone, *Wall Street Journal*, May 16: A5

Wall Street Journal, 1975. Less regulation of airline sector is urged by Ford, October 9: A3
    2009. A California quake (editorial), September 30: A22

Wallison, Peter J., 2009. Too big to fail, or succeed, *Wall Street Journal*, June 18: A17

Warren-Bolton, Frederick R., n.d. Direct testimony, State of New York *ex rel.* Attorney-General Dennis C. Vacco, *et al. v.* Microsoft Corporation, Civil Action No. 98–1233 (TPJ), p. 21, available on August 20, 2004 at www.usdoj.gov/atr/cases/f2000/2079.htm

Washington Post, 2005. U.S. can consider textile-import limit, April 28: E2

Wauzzinski, Robert A., 2003. *The Transforming Story of Dwelling House Savings and Loan: A Pittsburgh Bank's Fight against Urban Poverty*, Lewiston, NY: Edwin Mellen

Weisman, Martin L. and Douglas L. Kruse, 1990. Profit sharing and productivity, in Alan S. Blinder (ed.), *Paying for Productivity: A Look at the Evidence*, Washington, DC: Brookings Institution: 95–140

Wessels, Walter J., 1987. Minimum wages: are workers really better off? Paper prepared for presentation at a conference on minimum wages, Washington, DC, National Chamber Foundation, July 29

White, Erin, 2005. To keep employees, Domino's decides it's not all about pay, *Wall Street Journal*, February 17: A1

White, Harrison C., 1991. Agency as control, in John W. Pratt and Richard J. Zeckhauser (eds.), *Principals and Agents: The Structure of Business*, Boston, MA: Harvard Business School Press: 187–212

White, Lawrence J., 2002. International trade in services: more than meets the eye, New York: Stern School of Business, Working Paper, February 28, available on May 10, 2005 at www.stern.nyu.edu/eco/wkpapers/workingpapers02/02-13 White.pdf
    2008. *How Did We Get into This Financial Mess?* Washington, DC: Cato Institute, no. 110, November 18, as accessed January 14, 2009 from www.cato.org/pubs/bp/bp110.pdf

Whitehouse, Mark, 2009. Imbalance in nation's savings clouds forecasts of recovery, *Wall Street Journal*, March 23: A2

Williams, Nicole, 2007. Al Gore's personal energy use is his own "Inconvenient Truth": Gore's home uses more than 20 times the national average, Nashville, TN: Tennessee Center for Policy Research, accessed February 6, 2009 from www.tennesseepolicy.org/main/article.php?article_id=367

Williams, Walter, 2005. Minimum wage, maximum folly, *Capitalism Magazine*, March 23, as available on August 20, 2005 at www.capmag.com/article.asp? id4173

Williamson, Oliver E., 1967. Hierarchical control and optimum size firms, *Journal of Political Economy* 75(2): 123–38
    1990. *Economic Organization*, New York: New York University Press
    1998. *The Economic Institutions of Capitalism*, New York: Free Press

Wilson, James Q., 1993. *The Moral Sense*, New York: Free Press

Wingfield, Nick and Don Clarke, 2009. Microsoft gambles on Windows 7 "Starter," *Wall Street Journal*, April 20: B1

Wirthman, Lisa, 1997. Superior snooping: new software can catch workers goofing off, but some say such surveillance goes too far, *Orange County (Calif.) Register*, July 20: 1, 10

Withers, Lanita, 2008. Officials break ground for FedEx hub, *Greensboro News and Record*, November 21, accessed February 5 from www.news-record.com/content/2008/11/21/article/officials_break_ground_for_fedex_hub

WorldNetDaly.com, 2007. Gore's "carbon offsets" paid to firm he owns: critics say justification for energy-rich lifestyle serves as way for former VP to profit, accessed February 6, 2009, from www.worldnetdaily.com/news/article.asp?ARTICLE_ID=54528

Wortham, Jenna, 2009. Doing good with unused gift cards, *New York Times*, August 24: B7

Wriston, Walter B., 1989. On track with the deficit, *Wall Street Journal*, January 6: A1

Young, Wesley, Laura Graff, and James Romoser, 2009. The price of Dell, *Winston-Salem Journal*, March 13: A1

Index